Development through Adulthood

Development through Adulthood

An Integrative Sourcebook

Oliver Robinson

palgrave
macmillan

First published 2013 by
PALGRAVE MACMILLAN

Palgrave Macmillan in the UK is an imprint of Macmillan Publishers Limited, registered in England, company number 785998, of Houndmills, Basingstoke, Hampshire RG21 6XS.

Palgrave Macmillan in the US is a division of St Martin's Press LLC, 175 Fifth Avenue, New York, NY 10010.

Palgrave Macmillan is the global academic imprint of the above companies and has companies and representatives throughout the world.

Palgrave® and Macmillan® are registered trademarks in the United States, the United Kingdom, Europe and other countries.

ISBN 978–0–230–29799–9

This book is printed on paper suitable for recycling and made from fully managed and sustained forest sources. Logging, pulping and manufacturing processes are expected to conform to the environmental regulations of the country of origin.

A catalogue record for this book is available from the British Library.

A catalog record for this book is available from the Library of Congress.

10 9 8 7 6 5 4 3 2 1
22 21 20 19 18 17 16 15 14 13

Printed and bound in Great Britain by
CPI Antony Rowe, Chippenham and Eastbourne

Contents

Tables

Figures

Boxes

Preface

No man ever steps in the same river twice, for it's not the same river and he's not the same man.

Heraclitus

Heraclitus, who lived around 500 BC, was one of many wise men to have noticed that change is the only true constant in life. Developmental psychologists have spent the last century or so trying to find scientific order to the changes that occur across the course of human life, and have increasingly focused their research on adults. The research shows that adults, despite the folksy notion of being 'grown-ups', are in fact on a white-knuckle ride of lifelong change and development. And that is what this book is all about – the many and varied changes and transitions of adult life.

Children receive systematic guidance, nurturing and support to help with the challenges of their growth and development. In contrast, adults are given little if any advice on how best to develop, and to manage the peaks and troughs of life. There seems to be an implicit assumption that adults should just know how to cope with the ageing process, how to become wiser and how to act more maturely. In reality, most of us make it up as we go along, muddling through as best we can and dealing with what life sends our way. But adulthood doesn't need to be that haphazard, for there is now a wealth of research and theory that adds up to a provisional map of how the journey unfolds.

Adult development and ageing are broad fields, and the kinds of research questions that an adult development researcher might address are varied. Here is a selection of such questions to give you a sense of their diversity:

- How do life-goals and values typically change as we get older?
- Does being emotionally mature mean being emotionally complex or being happy?
- In what ways do young adults typically change cognitively while at university?
- How can wisdom be cultivated?

- What are the long-term effects of physical exercise on cognitive ability in old age?
- What are the major life-stages that define the chapters of adulthood?
- What are the determinants of a positive and fulfilling retirement?
- Does having children make people happier?
- What is the nature of a 'quarterlife crisis'?
- What are the key challenges that parents experience when having a second child?
- During which period of adult life are people most prone to mental health difficulties?
- Do early attachments shape adult intimate relationships?
- How do people cope with the bereavement of a spouse?

The structure of the book

Given the diversity of these topics, providing a comprehensive sourcebook on adult development is a tough task. The literature is spread across disciplines including developmental psychology, gerontology, social psychology, sociology, health psychology, psychiatric epidemiology, neuroscience, thanatology, occupational psychology, transpersonal psychology and nursing. Given this spread, it's important to lay firm foundations, and Chapter 1 helps to provide this by clarifying the basic concepts that underpin the book and outlining the tenets of the biopsychosocial approach that acts as a guiding framework.

A further challenge to creating an integrative sourcebook on adult development is that there is both quantitative and qualitative research on the subject, which lack integration due to an institutionalised schism between them in psychology. Correspondingly, previous adult development textbooks have typically focused solely on quantitative methods (for example, Cavanaugh & Blanchard-Fields, 2006; Lemme, 2005; Schaie & Willis, 2002). This book aims to move beyond this methodological divide; therefore Chapter 2 reviews both quantitative and qualitative methods in lifespan and adult development research, along with ideas for their creative combination.

All of the chapters in the book overlap in focus to some degree, as the topics are inter-related and interdependent. Chapters 3 to 5 focus on the development of three particular mental faculties – cognition, emotion and motivation. Each chapter emphasises one of these three, but pulling at any one brings the other two with it, as they are not actually separable in a neat way. What we think (cognition) affects how we feel (emotion) and how we behave (motivation), and vice versa – how we feel affects how we think and behave, and how we behave affects our thoughts and feelings in return (Magnusson, 1995; Piaget, 1981; Stevens-Long & Michaud, 2002). One can conceive of cognition, emotion, and action as three corners of a triangle that is forever changing shape – not separate but distinct nonetheless, and when one moves, the others move too, in a reciprocal dance.

Chapters 6, 7, 8, 9 and 10 all cover 'whole-person' features of adult development, including transitions, psychosocial life stages, personality, morality, spirituality and wisdom. These topics all features elements of cognition, emotion and motivation combined. In Chapter 11 mental disorder is discussed in relation to the adult lifespan, and Chapters 12 and 13 cover social and occupational development. The book finishes in Chapter 14 with a review of research on death and dying.

Box features

There are four kinds of box features in the book: *Individual voices, Alternative perspectives, Cross-cultural perspectives* and *Real-world applications*.

The *Individual voices* box features include excerpts from participants in qualitative studies that provide a personal and experiential account of the phenomenon being discussed. This will help to remind the reader of the real-world relevance of the abstract ideas contained in the book, and will counteract the general tendency in academic psychology towards abstraction and group aggregation (Laslett, 1989; Maslow, 1966). Furthermore, each chapter begins with an individual story from participants who have been involved in my own research into life transitions and development, and several other people whose stories are personally known to me. Names and place names have been changed in these short accounts, to protect confidentiality.

The *Real-world applications* box features either describe an intervention that has been shown to help people, or give recommendations based on research on how to cultivate desirable development or maximise opportunities at a particular stage of life.

The *Alternative perspectives* box features present unconventional or controversial views on a particular issue, which may run counter to, or criticise, the dominant approach that is taken in a particular field.

Cross-cultural perspectives box features provide a focus on research done in cultures beyond the English-speaking world, and beyond Western Europe. The book is mainly based on research and theory from North America and Britain. To counteract this cultural specificity, the *Cross-cultural perspectives* features describe selected studies and data from other non-English-speaking cultures.

Now it's time to get started. I hope you enjoy the book, whether you are a student, academic, therapist or someone who is simply interested in the ups and downs of adult life. Although textbooks are typically dipped into sporadically, and some chapters are read while others are omitted, if you do have time to read the chapters in chronological order, the integrative picture of adult development that the book endeavours to portray will be more strongly and effectively conveyed.

Acknowledgements

I would like to extend my thanks to those who helped with the preparation of this manuscript, including Alex Stell, Gordon Wright and the three anonymous reviewers for their insightful comments and feedback on the first draft, and to Lyn and Philip Robinson for their punctilious proofreading of the second draft. I am grateful to Jenny Hindley and Paul Stevens at Palgrave Macmillan for their editorial guidance, and to Mritunjai Sahai for typesetting the book so well. Thanks also to Gordon Wright for helping to source the many journal articles needed for the book and for helping produce the index, and to Monisha Juttla, Sanna Rasmussen, Ross Friday, Alaa Khaddour and John Greer for helping to produce and format the citations and bibliography of the book. And finally thanks to my wife Faez for her unwavering support, and for putting up with me for 15 long months of working evenings and weekends.

Publisher's Acknowledgements

The publisher and author would like to thank the organizations and people listed next for permission to reproduce material from their publications:

Wiley-Blackwell for Figure 1.6, which is taken from Sameroff (2010, p. 18) and for Figure 12.5, which is taken from Rollins and Feldman (1970, pp. 25–6).

Wolters Kluwer Health and Association of American Medical Colleges for Figure 4.6, which is taken from Hojat et al. (2009, p. 1188).

Elsevier for Figure 5.2, which is taken from Heckhausen (2000, p. 215, Figure 1); for Figure 11.4, which is taken from *Neurobiology of Aging*, 22, Ruitenberg et al. (2001, p. 578); for Figure 11.6, which is taken from de Lau and Breteler (2006, p. 526); and for Figure 12.3 which is taken from Kalmijn (2003, p. 242).

Taylor and Francis for Figure 8.1, which is taken from Armon and Dawson (1997, p. 441), reprinted by permission of Taylor & Francis Ltd, http://www.tandfonline.com on behalf of Journal of Moral Education Ltd.

Oxford University Press for Figure 11.2, which is taken from Häfner et al. (1998, p. 103).

Alzheimer's Disease Research for Figure 11.3, which is taken from Alzheimer's Disease Research, a programme of the American Health Assistance Foundation. Copyright © 2011, http://www.ahaf.org/alzheimers.

Chris Fraley for permission to use the data in Figure 12.1, which is taken from Experience in Close Relationship Scale norms, http://internal.psychology.illinois.edu/~rcfraley/measures/ecrr.htm.

Material is individually acknowledged throughout.

Every effort has been made to trace all copyright holders but, if any have been inadvertently overlooked, the publisher will be pleased to make the necessary arrangements at the first opportunity.

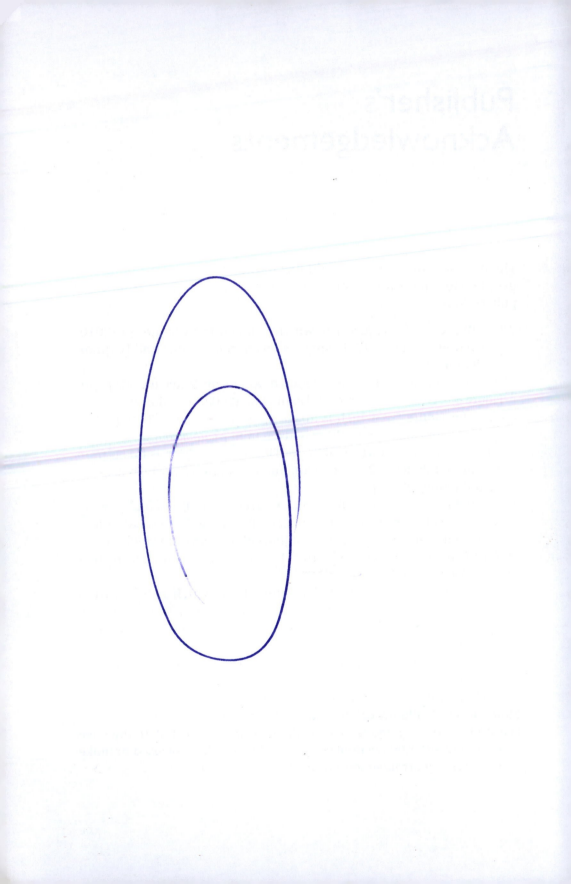

1

Adulthood, Development and the Biopsychosocial Paradigm

Life is like riding a bicycle – to keep your balance, you must keep moving.

Albert Einstein

During a research interview I asked Joe, aged 68, whether he thought he had developed since he had become an adult. He responded that in his early thirties, he recalled becoming more mature and responsible than he was as a younger man, particularly after the birth of his first child. He then said that his career seniority and income peaked in his fifties, a time when he was most recognised by others as being a 'success' and a 'man of influence'. He felt that his memory had declined slightly over the past few years, but he reckoned he was quicker at solving crosswords than he had ever been. Finally, he reflected that now, in his late sixties, he was much more happy and at peace with the world than he was earlier in life. Retirement from full-time work had helped this, as his job as a managing director had involved a lot of pressure and reputation-management. Joe reflected that he thought all of those changes were important developments that had occurred in his adult life.

Adulthood and *development* are two words that appear at first glance to be simple enough to define. In actuality, both are surprisingly difficult to pin down. Given that this whole book hangs on their meanings, we start with a reconnaissance and critical evaluation of their varying definitions. This is followed by an overview of the biopsychosocial approach to studying development, which characterises the theoretical ethos of the book. Once all that is covered, we will have the basic foundations in place, and so can move onto research methods used in adult development – the topic of Chapter 2.

Ways of defining adulthood

The legal definition of adulthood

Being an adult has a defined legal meaning. The law views an adult as a person who, by the fact of reaching a certain age, is able to make informed, autonomous decisions about what they do or refrain from doing, and is therefore *legally accountable* for those actions. The 'age of majority' is the official term for the age at which a person legally enters adulthood. Those who are below this age are correspondingly referred to as 'minors'. In the majority of the world's nations, the age of majority is 18.[1] When a young person has reached the age of majority, parents are no longer legally responsible for them or held accountable for their actions.

The age of majority does not necessarily correspond to the legal age at which a person may engage in *specific* activities that are prohibited to children and permitted to adults, such as marriage, having sexual intercourse, purchasing and consuming alcohol, gambling and driving a car. The ages at which these activities are permitted tend to cluster within a few years of the age of majority, as they are all considered to be dependent on adult responsibility. Table 1.1 shows age limits for the UK and USA on a variety of child-prohibited activities. As you can see, all occur within the age range of 16 to 21, a period that is often referred to as the *transition to adulthood* (Levinson, 1986).

In the eyes of the law, children are considered to lack the capacity to imagine the future implications of their actions for themselves and others, and therefore to know if their actions may or may not lead to harm. An adult, by contrast, is considered capable of understanding the *outcomes* and *implications* of their actions and therefore able to make informed decisions about which course of action to pursue. This means that they can avoid actions that might lead to harming themselves or others in the future. Correspondingly, activities that are restricted to minors but permitted to adults include those that have the potential for harm – for example, smoking, sex, gambling, debt, driving, drinking and dangerous jobs. Contractually binding obligations such as marriage and full-time employment are also restricted to adults, as entering such contracts in an informed way entails an ability to foresee long-term outcomes, and

---

[1] Source: http://www.interpol.int/Public/Children/Default.asp.

Table 1.1 Minimum legal ages for sexual consent, cigarette purchase, alcohol purchase, driving a car, joining the army, marrying without parental consent, casino entry and voting

Adult-limited activity	UK age limit	USA age limit
Having sex	16	16–18 (varies by state)
Purchasing cigarettes	18	18
Purchasing alcohol	18	21
Gaining a driving licence	17	16
Joining the army	18	17 (with parental consent) 18 (no parental consent)
Marriage with parental consent	16	15–16 (varies by state)
Marriage without parental consent	18 (except Scotland – 16)	18 (except Nebraska – 19 & Mississippi – 21)
Entering a casino	18	18–21 (varies by state)
Voting in elections	18	18

this foresight is considered to be an adult capacity. Voting in political elections is also legally restricted to adults, due to the assumption that children are not well placed to select between voting alternatives in a free and informed manner. The only conditions under which adult rights are revoked are if a person has (a) been found guilty of committing a crime or (b) been sectioned under the Mental Health Act.

In summary, the legal definition of an adult is an autonomous citizen who has reached the age of majority and can therefore make informed decisions for themselves; be held responsible for those decisions, and participate in the contractual obligations of society.

Personal and social definitions of adulthood

A person is legally an adult when they reach the age of majority, but they may not actually view themselves as an adult, and others may not either. Research has found that when young people between the ages of 18 and 25 are asked if they consider themselves to be an adult, the most common answer is 'in some respects yes and in some respects no'(Arnett, 1998).This finding alludes to the fact that adults in modern countries go through a stage of life during which they are legally considered to be an adult, but are not in adult roles. Arnett (2000) refers to this in-between phase as *emerging adulthood* – it spans the period of life from the end of adolescence into the mid-twenties. It is like adolescence, insofar as it is an exploratory, non-committal period for many, but it is different because the young person has more independence from parents and has adult rights.

When asked about what it means to be an adult, individuals in the emerging adulthood phase mention various things that they have not yet acquired (Arnett, 2000; Lanz & Tagliabue, 2007; Lopez et al., 2005). These include: the achievement of financial independence from parents; leaving education and gaining stable employment; a strong sense of personal responsibility; moving out of the parental home; marriage and parenthood. These markers of adulthood are rarely reached by the legal adult transition, and are typically achieved after the age of 25 (Arnett, 1998; 2006). For a selection of individual quotes from emerging adults on what it means to be an adult, see Box 1.1.

Box 1.1   Individual voices

Personal meanings of being an adult

Lopez et al., (2005) interviewed 18 young people between the ages of 18 and 25 about their views on what it means to be an adult, and what signifies entry to adulthood, and collated their responses into common themes. Example quotes from the young people they spoke to are given next.

Responsibility

> I guess the biggest word that I relate with adulthood is responsibility ... I think being an adult means that, that you've learned your lessons and you're able to take care of yourself. (p. 17)

Independence from parents

> I'm at a point in my life where I'm tired of them [parents] helping me because I wanta be independent and I think that's another part of being an adult, being independent. Not to say you're gonna carry the weight of the world on your shoulders, but, you know, you're more prone as a child to ask your parents for something than you are as an adult. (p. 18)

Entry into workforce and career stability

> I feel like my career is the most important right now just because that's gonna probably lead the direction that my life is gonna go

> **Box 1.1 Continued**
>
> in. So I wanta make sure that I have a good career choice and that,
> you know, I'm happy with what I'm doing. If I'm not happy with my
> future job, then I probably won't be too happy with other aspects
> of my life. (p. 16)
>
> **Having and taking care of a family**
>
> When I got married, that was one, and then when both my kids were
> born, that's when it really set in, where I can't do anything ... nothing
> I do is for myself anymore. You gotta think about others. You can't
> just go off and do what you wanta do, like I used to. (p. 17)

Personal definitions of adulthood such as those in Box 1.1 are shaped
by social norms, and these differ by ethnic group. For example, one
study found that Latino parents of Los Angeles college students defined
adulthood by event-related markers including marriage and getting a job,
while white parents defined adulthood more by financial and personal
independence (Saetermoe, Beneli & Busch, 1999). Arnett & Galambos
(2003) report that being in a committed long-term relationship is a
signifier of adulthood for some ethnicities and nationalities more than
others; 71 per cent of Argentines, 55 per cent of Israelis, 28 per cent of
African Americans and 14 per cent of White Americans see it as a mark
of entry into adulthood. In some cultures that are defined by conflict,
the transition to adulthood may involve rites of passage that relate to
participation in the conflict. For example, Peteet (1994) has researched
perceptions of rites of passage into adulthood among Palestinian men,
and these are described in Box 1.2.

Does 'adulthood' really exist?

The label 'adulthood' places a single word on a very large part of the
lifespan – it suggests that 20-year-olds, 50-year-olds and 80-year-olds
are all in some key sense the same. The word 'adult' comes from the
Latin *adultus* meaning 'grown up' or 'mature', and therefore implies
that after the age of 18 a person exists on a plateau of developmental stability. This reflects a widely held social belief that childhood =
growth, and adult = no growth. If this book says one thing, it is that
this belief is wrong – adulthood is in fact a bumpy ride of growth,
decline, peaks, troughs and developmental dramas. Some theorists

---

Box 1.2   Cross-cultural perspectives

Markers of adulthood and rites of passages into adulthood for Palestinian men

Peteet's account of the transition to adulthood in Palestine is a reminder of how important gender is to the adult transition in many countries, and also how rites of passage can be forged from adverse circumstances (Peteet, 1994). In Palestine, for a boy to make the transition to manhood, he must first learn to portray the appropriate traits of *adult masculinity*. These include overt expressions of fearlessness and assertiveness, such as through the defence of honour, reputation, kin and community from external aggression. Beatings or detentions from the Israeli military act as an overt demonstration of manhood, and may actively be sought as proof of masculinity. 'Real men' gain respect and obedience when resisting submitting to the control of others. Importantly, manhood can be lost if one is not vigilant about displaying and protecting it.

There are two further marks of adult development that Peteet mentions. First, personal control through sacrifice of one's own needs for others is a key demonstration of adulthood. Second, is a quality referred to as 'aql', which is a combination of social common sense, rationality, judiciousness, prudence and wisdom. Males are typically assumed to begin acquiring 'aql' at 20 and to attain it fully around the age of 40. As a quality it bears many similarities to the qualities that young people are expected to attain at the age of majority in Western countries (Peteet, 1994).

---

suggest that we should refer to at least three different phases of adulthood – productive adult life, retired adult life and dependent old age (Laslett, 1989). So the book you are reading is in many ways about the fact that there is no such thing as adulthood, which is no small irony seeing as the word is in the title. The other word in the title is *development*, which is just as complex to define as adulthood, perhaps even more so.

Defining adult development

'Development' is a surprisingly difficult concept to define. According to one definition, development refers to *all enduring changes* that occur during human life, both those that lead to gain and those that lead to loss (Baltes, Reese & Lipsitt, 1980; Magnusson, 1995; Uttal & Perlmutter, 1989).The term is used in the title of this book in this sense as a signifier for the totality of enduring changes in adulthood, both positive and negative.

Another definition of development uses the word to specifically refer to enduring changes that are considered positive or optimal – that is, changes that lead to a better status quo than previously achieved (Bronfenbrenner, 1979; Commons, 2002; Valsiner, 2000). This positive definition is often used in contrast to the term *ageing*, which refers to age-related declines that occur in adulthood. What criteria should be used to judge whether a person is changing in a way that is positive? This is an easier question to answer in relation to child development, for the optimal direction is towards becoming more like an adult, but it is a harder question to answer for adults. Here, five possible positive directions for adult development are described; orthogenetic, evolutionary, veridical, eudaimonic and virtuous. Each one specifies a trajectory of positive change through adulthood, and each has something to contribute to an overall conception of what it means for adults to develop optimally. Figure 1.1 provides a visual illustration of these five directions and their corresponding ideals.

Five directions for positive adult development

1. *The orthogenetic direction*

   Orthogenetic development is change that brings about higher levels of integrated complexity (Werner, 1940).This occurs by way of three interacting processes: (1) *differentiation* of internal forms within an organism, (2) *articulation* of these forms into definable and related parts, and (3) *integration* of those parts into systems. Think of an embryo growing; it develops into more and more different cells (differentiation), and these cells are then combined into organs (articulation), and all of these organs are co-ordinated together into systems such as the circulation and digestion systems (integration). The embryo becomes more and more complex as orthogenesis proceeds, leading to the development of the foetus and then a human infant. Orthogenesis can also be seen in child development, as children become more physically complex and develop increasingly complex cognitive understandings of the world (Werner, 1940). It has also been suggested that orthogenesis defines psychological development in adulthood, through enhanced cognitive-affective and behavioural complexity and hierarchical integration (Erikson, 1968a; Kegan & Lahey, 2009; Valsiner, 2000).

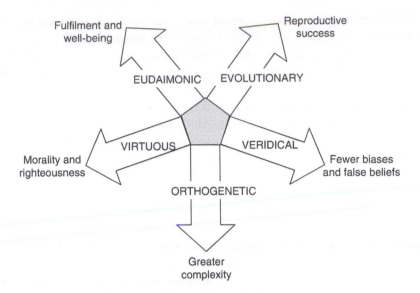

Figure 1.1   Five directions of positive adult development

The benefit of an orthogenetic view of positive development is that complexity is measurable and does not require an interpretative value judgement. It also creates a thread of theoretical continuity between development in embryos, babies, children and adults. If increased complexity defines development at all stages of life, which is a parsimonious solution to the question of what it means to develop in a positive and optimal way (Valsiner, 2000). The problem with orthogenesis as an ideal for adulthood, however, is that there may exist ways of changing in a valued or productive direction that may involve a change towards simplicity rather than complexity, or show no increase or decrease in complexity. Furthermore, some theorists even suggest that systems have an optimal level of complexity and can become *too* complex (May, Sugihara & Levin, 2008). If a system becomes too complex, then it can become more prone to failure, as more complexity means more hierarchical co-ordination and integration, and more mediating layers between levels. So, if there is a maximum level of complexity for adaptive functioning in human beings, more of it may not always be a good thing. This suggests we may need to balance an orthogenetic view of the direction of development with other complementary directions.

2. *The evolutionary direction*
   Evolution through natural selection is all about competition – those organisms that survive and reproduce in greater numbers are the

winners, while those that do not, die out. Evolutionary psychologists suggest that passing on our genes is programmed into us as *the* fundamental goal of living and development (for example, Belsky, 1995). When viewed from an evolutionary perspective, this means that developmental progress in adulthood is manifest in the improved capacity to survive to reproductive age, acquire a mate, retain a mate, have children and engage in effective parenting (Kenrick et al., 2010). People who have more children and provide a safe and nurturing environment for their children are more highly developed from this evolutionary viewpoint (Kenrick et al., 2010).

What makes a person more likely to reproduce? The motivational developmental theory of Heckhausen, Wrosch and Schulz (2010), which is discussed in Chapter 5, takes an evolutionary perspective. It states that developmental success is indexed by how much a person can control their environment, and thus change it to meet their needs or to eliminate threats, and thus ensure their own survival and reproduction.

A problem with maintaining a purely evolutionary/adaptive view of the direction of adult development is that optimal functioning is indexed solely by a person's reproductive success. If a person acts in a way that benefits himself and his genetic legacy, but is harmful to the environment or other people, or in a way that is based on duplicity and lies, from the evolutionary perspective it is still a sign of evolutionarily developed behaviour. To prevent the conclusion that quantity of offspring is the sole and ultimate benchmark of human development, it helps to counterbalance the idea of evolutionary success with other enduring ideals that humans aim for beyond the act of reproduction – these can be termed the 'higher needs' of development (Maslow, 1968).

3. *The veridical direction*

The capacity to view oneself and the world in an unbiased and undistorted way has long been seen to be an indicator of maturity (Basseches, 2003; Maslow, 1998). Typically, children have more positive biases in their self-concept than adults do, due to self-serving biases that boost positive self-regard during this period of life when such regard is fragile (Mezulis et al., 2004). The gradual relinquishing of these biases is widely considered to be a positive development in adults (Taylor, 1989). A lack of false opinions about other people is also considered to be an important development of a mature adult mind, and conversely biased attitudes towards particular ethnic or socio-economic groups based on simplistic, prejudicial or stereotypical evaluations are a sign of immaturity (Allport, 1979). The veridical direction to adult development involves replacing false beliefs about self or others with more accurate ones, irrespective of whether the more accurate beliefs are more or less complex than the previously-held false ones, or whether or not they make you feel happy.

Veridical development not only means observing oneself and the world in a more accurate way, it also involves a greater tendency to be *truthful*. Chapter 7 discusses *authenticity* as an ideal for personality development, which is a person's capacity to know themself and express their thoughts and feelings *truthfully*, rather than hiding thoughts and feeling, prevaricating and pretending to be somebody else by putting on an act. This can also be seen as a form of veridical development.

A distorted or false view of oneself and the world is not only considered immature, but in extreme cases is considered to be indicative of mental illness. For example, false or distorted beliefs about self or world (delusions), and/or sensory perceptions that do not relate to the physical world (hallucinations) are considered to be symptoms of psychosis, while grossly exaggerated positive self-concepts are indicative of narcissistic personality disorder (APA, 2000).

The difficulty with ascertaining the veridical direction to development is that some people disagree on what is and what is not true or false. For example, in Chapter 10 we cover spiritual development, which is a controversial area because for some, spiritual knowledge and values are truthful, while for others they are false and thus are evidence of developmental regress or cognitive deficiency (Dawkins, 2007). Another difficulty with the veridical direction is that there is evidence that truth or accurate perception may not be conducive to wellbeing – for example the depressive realism hypothesis states that depressed people have been shown, on average, to have a more realistic view of their own importance, reputation and abilities than non-depressed people (Dobson & Franche, 1989). So developing an accurate and veridical concept of reality may not make you happy. It might, in fact, make you miserable. To counteract this view, the next direction suggests that positive adult development is all about an enhanced sense of wellbeing.

4. *The eudaimonic direction*

Eudaimonia is a word that can be traced to Aristotle – it means the pursuit of fulfilment and wellbeing. Aristotle suggested that it describes an ideal for all humans to aim towards in development, and psychologists have found that humans are indeed motivated towards happiness, personal growth, purpose and wellbeing

(Ryff, 1995; Seligman, 2011). Giving eudaimonia the status of a developmental direction suggests that we can judge how developed adults are by how fulfilled they are and their level of wellbeing. Charlotte Bühler (1964), whose theory we encounter later in Chapter 5, took this view, suggesting that *fulfilment was the ultimate direction and benchmark of adult development*:

> By development, we mean a succession of events which follows a certain order, forms a definite pattern, has direction and represents a whole. In the person's subjective experience, this *direction* is towards certain *results* ... We suggest the concept of *fulfilment* as one which would cover any result to which a person might aspire. (Bühler, 1964, p. 1)

In Chapter 4, we focus more intensively on the lifelong eudaimonic search for wellbeing in terms of its emotional aspects – the pursuit of happiness. Ryff (1995) suggests that beyond mere happiness, eudaimonic wellbeing has six dimensions, all of which need to be pursued if optimal development is to be established. They are purpose in life, self-acceptance, environmental mastery, positive relationships, autonomy and personal growth. Of these, personal growth is rated most highly in young and middle-aged adults, but less so by older adults (Ryff, 1989b). The relative balance of the six dimensions changes with age, therefore eudaimonic development should be evaluated relative to a person's age and stage of life, as well as to any fixed definitions of fulfilment or happiness (Ryff, 1995).

The difficulty of defining development as eudaimonic fulfilment is that one person may be fulfilled despite having done or achieved little, or despite lacking orthogenetic complexity, while another person may be less fulfilled but be highly developed in an evolutionary, virtuous or veridical sense. A quote that springs to mind here is from Thomas Edison, the inventor of the light bulb and much more. Edison said: 'Discontent is the first necessity of progress. Show me a thoroughly satisfied man, and I'll show you a failure' (Edison, 1968, p. 110). Clearly Edison was not enamoured with placing fulfilment and satisfaction aloft as life's goal. He was more interested in a kind of restless progress, typified by his own life of endless inventions and achievements.

5. *The virtuous direction*
Virtue is defined by being a good or righteous person, and as a developmental ideal for adults it has thousands of years of heritage. For example, over 2500 years ago, the Buddha said, 'Just as treasures are uncovered from the earth, so virtue appears from good deeds,

and wisdom appears from a pure and peaceful mind. To walk safely through the maze of human life, one needs the light of wisdom and the guidance of virtue.' For an adult to develop in a virtuous direction, they may become more concerned for others, more able to take into account the wellbeing of a greater number of people and living things. A finding of direct relevance to this developmental direction is that virtue is central to lay definitions of maturity and optimal functioning. When a sample of adults were asked open-ended interview questions about (a) what constitutes maturity/immaturity, and (b) what defines an ideal person, the most frequent responses to these two questions emphasised virtue. The number one indicator of maturity was being *orientated towards others*, and immaturity was defined primarily as being *self-centred*, while the number one indicator of being an ideal person was being *caring* (Ryff, 1989a).

Theories of moral development and wisdom are covered in Chapters 8 and 9, and these cover how and when virtuous thoughts and behaviours develop. The virtuous direction of development can also be found to some degree in other parts of the book – for example, ideas such as 'self-actualisation' (discussed in Chapters 5 and 7), and 'generativity' (discussed in Chapter 7) emphasise aspects of virtue.

The difficulty with stating that optimal adult development tends in the direction of virtue is that conceptions of the common good and ethics differ across cultures, so that one person's virtue may be another person's vice. For example, in some cultures music is virtuous and can be used to help, heal and promote development; but in other traditions music is a vice that corrupts and must be avoided. The difficulty in deciding what is developmentally virtuous and what is not is discussed in Chapters 8 and 9.

Three kinds of change in development

No matter which of these five developmental directions one is referring to, changes over time can be thought of as being one of three kinds (Lerner & Kauffman, 1985; Lerner, 2001b; Magnusson, 1995).

1. *Quantitative continuous change* involves steady increments in a measurable variable over time, for example a gradual slowing of reaction time with age. This kind of pattern may involve a gradual increase, decrease, or curvilinear change.
2. *Quantitative discontinuous change* involves a sudden shift in amount or extent of a variable, for example a sudden increase in visual ability following an operation on cataracts.

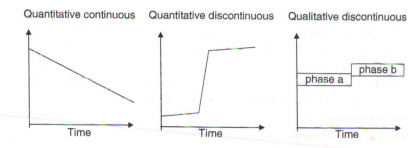

Figure 1.2   Three kinds of change in development

3. *Qualitative discontinuous change* involves a change to a new state that is *different in kind* from what came before, for example a change from being employed to unemployed, or from being single to being married, or from being able to have children to being post-menopausal.

The three kinds of change are illustrated in Figure 1.2. Both quantitative continuous and quantitative discontinuous can be illustrated using a line graph, but qualitative discontinuous change requires the illustration of a discrete break between two separate phases.

Stability would at first glance appear to be the opposite of these kinds of change, but that is not always the case. Surface stability may hide change at a deeper level. For example, very elderly adults tend to decline in certain cognitive capacities; so the natural trajectory for variables such as memory and reaction time is downwards in later life. If an elderly person manages to maintain *stability* despite the biological tendency for decline, then this may be due to developing new strategies to compensate for their biological loss of capacity (Baltes, 1997; Salthouse, 1984). Stabilisation in the face of decline is a form of development, but it will not show up on a graph as growth – it will show up as a flat line. Therefore it is important to remember that manifest stability may hide latent change.

The biopsychosocial paradigm of development

The biopsychosocial paradigm states that in order to fully understand human development, biological, psychological and social levels of analysis must be included. There are many models of development that take a biopsychosocial approach (for example, Baltes et al., 1980; Chapman, Nakamura & Flores, 1999; Elder, 1994; Erikson, 1968a; Feldman & Fowler, 1997; Lerner & Kauffman, 1985; Magnusson, 1995; Neugarten & Datan,

1996; Wapner & Demick, 2002), all of which entail a commitment to the following four premises:

1. Human development happens concurrently at biological, psychological and social levels throughout life, and a full descriptive account of development must include all three levels.
2. Development at each of these three levels reciprocally influences the other two levels; therefore nature (biology) and nurture (social environment) are in constant complex interaction, when considering how and why psychological development occurs.
3. Biological, psychological and social descriptions and explanations are all as valid as each other, and no level has causal primacy over the other two.
4. Any aspect of human development is best described and explained in relation to the whole person and their social context, as well as to their biological and cognitive-affective parts. This can be called a holistic or contextualist viewpoint, and can be contrasted with the reductionist approach to development, which tends to focus solely on biological or mechanistic explanations (Lerner, 2001a).

Erik Erikson referred to this three-way focus on biology, psychology and social context as 'triple book-keeping', and considered it essential to understanding development (Stevens, 2008). The remainder of the chapter provides an introduction to each of the three components; first, I provide an overview of what is known about how the developing adult brain and genes shape, and are in return shaped by development. Then I outline a framework for conceiving what the 'psych' bit of biopsychosocial means, and then the chapter concludes with a model of social influences to individual development. The ensuing section assumes some knowledge of the brain, but in case you need a reminder, Figure 1.3 shows all parts of the brain that are mentioned subsequently.

The ever-changing brain: Adult neurogenesis and angionesis

The scientific understanding of the adult brain has been overturned over the past two decades, and the news is good. Until 1990, it was widely accepted by scientists that neuron loss was inevitable, and that no new neurons were formed in adulthood. This is now known to have been a mistaken view. In the 1990s, new ways of measuring neuron number called 'stereological' techniques showed that neuron death in the hippocampus or the cerebral cortex is *not* a normal part of ageing after all. There is no reduction in neurons in the hippocampus with age and only a 10 per cent average reduction in cortical neuron across the age

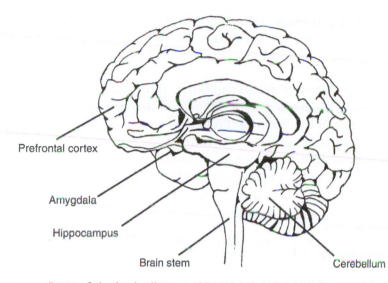

Prefrontal cortex

Amygdala

Hippocampus

Brain stem

Cerebellum

Figure 1.3   Parts of the brain discussed in this section shown in lateral section: prefrontal cortex, amygdala, hippocampus, brain stem, cerebellum

spectrum. Many other variables, including sex, are stronger predictors of neuron number than age (Morrison & Hof, 1997).

Furthermore, a revolutionary recent finding in neuroscience is that new neurons are constantly formed from stem cells in parts of the adult brain, a process called **adult neurogenesis** (Eriksson et al., 1998; Lledo, Alonso & Grubb, 2006). The area of the brain that is most active in neurogenesis is the hippocampus, which is involved in learning and memory. Research shows that thousands of new neurons are produced in the hippocampus every day (Lledo, Alonso & Grubb, 2006).

Studies with rats have provided important clues as to what promotes or inhibits adult neurogenesis. Providing rodents with an enriched environment (that is, a cage with more learning opportunities, more social interaction and more space to live in) is correlated with more neurogenesis in the hippocampus (Fowler et al., 2002). Also, exercise helps; rats that have a running wheel in their cage have twice as many new hippocampal neurons as those that do not (Van Praag, Kempermann & Gage, 1999). Other studies have shown that stress leads to decreased neurogenesis in the hippocampus (Zhao, Deng & Gage 2008).

Neurogenesis has been implicated as a possible source of recovery from strokes. A stroke occurs when the blood supply to the brain is disturbed, leading to neurological damage and cell death. Within two–four weeks of the damage, neurogenesis of new cells is apparent within the site of the damage, particularly around blood vessels (Jin et al., 2006; Ohab et al., 2006). There is in fact a migration of 'neuroblasts' (infant neurons) from areas where neurogenesis is known to occur, such as the hippocampus, towards the site of the damage, travelling up to 4 mm (a long way for a neuroblast – the equivalent of a person walking 1.5 miles through syrup) (Ohab et al., 2006).

The brain's system of blood capillaries that feed it with oxygen and nutrients can also develop in adulthood; *angiogenesis* is the growth of new capillaries in the brain. Initially it was believed that angiogenesis, like neuronal development, was limited to childhood, but it is now known that angiogenesis occurs during adulthood and can be induced by exposure to a complex physical and social environment (Black, Zelazny & Greenough, 1991), as well as by exercise (Black et al., 1990).

Brain plasticity – How the brain is affected by experience, behaviour and social environment

We know that the brain is causal implicated in behaviour and conscious experience because if the brain is damaged, then mental and behavioural activity is correspondingly impaired, and drugs that operate on the brain change behaviour and conscious experience. What is less well grasped, however, is that behaviour and experience cause changes in the brain in return. This tendency of the brain to change its structure and function in response to experiences and the environment is called *brain plasticity*, or *neuroplasticity*. An understanding of brain plasticity is central to a biopsychosocial approach to development, because it provides evidence that the brain is not a unilateral cause of all things psychological, for it is itself shaped and sculpted by experience, behaviour and relationships (Perry & Szalavitz, 2006). Factors that affect the structure of the brain include diet, exercise, alcohol/drug consumption, stress and relationships.

Diet and the brain. What you eat and how much you eat changes your brain. Evidence suggests that a low-calorie diet is associated with reduced risk of developing Alzheimer's disease and Parkinson's disease (Logroscino et al., 1996; Luchsinger, Tang, Shea & Mayeux, 2002), while excessive calorie intake is a major risk factor for stroke (Bronner, Kanter & Manson, 1995). Research on rats has shown that a high-fat, high-sugar diet reduces synaptic functioning in the hippocampus (Molteni et al., 2002).

The body contains antioxidant systems to remove unwanted oxygenated molecules or prevent them from being formed. Vitamin E is an antioxidant that can protect learning and memory functioning and can slow the progression of Alzheimer's disease (Mattson, Chan & Duan, 2002). Dietary supplements of fruit and vegetables high in Vitamin C, which is also an antioxidant, can reverse neuronal ageing (Galli et al., 2002; Joseph et al., 1999). Essential fatty acids (Omega-3 and Omega-6) are also essential for brain functioning (Haag, 2003). If these fatty acids are removed from the diet of rats, cognitive impairment and developmental disorder is observed (Wainwright, 1992).

Exercise and the brain. Exercise is good for the brain in all sorts of ways. It improves synaptic plasticity, enhances adult neurogenesis and boosts angiogenesis (van Praag, Kempermann & Gage, 1999). It can also reverse the effects of an unhealthy diet (Molteni, 2004). In elderly adults (60–79 years old), engaging in a programme of aerobic exercise is associated with increases in brain volume, in both grey and white matter regions, showing that brain growth is possible even in old age (Colcombe et al., 2006).

Social environment and the brain. Social environments in infancy and childhood come to be encoded in the structure of the brain. Findings from research with rats and mice show that disruptions in the mother–infant relationship result in neuroendocrine, neurochemical and behavioural changes in the adult rat (Cirulli, Berry & Alleva, 2003). Social isolation in rats also reduces neurogenesis (Fowler et al., 2002), and delays the positive effects of exercise on neurogenesis (Stranahan, Khalil & Gould, 2006). Mice that are reared in a communal nest (a natural social environment for rodents) have higher levels of nerve growth factor in the brain (an important protein for neuronal health and growth) than those reared in standard laboratory conditions (Branchi et al., 2006).

The effect of stress on the brain. Stress and trauma can change the brain in a variety of ways. Mild and short-term stress can be good for the brain (McEwen, 1999), but prolonged exposure to stressors leads to sustained production of stress hormones in the kidneys, and some of these, called glutocorticoids, are damaging to the brain if produced for too long (Sapolsky, 1999). The most well-known glutocorticoid is *cortisol*. It is essential for a variety of important bodily functions, but it inhibits glucose uptake by cells, and if it is produced in excessive amounts it can cause neural degeneration, disruption of synaptic plasticity, atrophy of dendrites, and even neuron death (Sapolsky, 1999; Uno et al., 1989).

The hippocampus is one area of the brain that is particularly prone to stress-related damage and atrophy. Lupien et al. (1998) found that humans with prolonged elevated cortisol levels have a reduced hippocampal volume and showed deficits in memory tasks, while chronic stress causes shortening and de-branching of dendrites in the hippocampus and suppresses neurogenesis (Bremner, 1999; McEwen, 2000). Sufferers of Post-Traumatic Stress Disorder have been found to have chronically raised cortisol levels, and brain scans have shown that they have deficits on measures of hippocampal function and reduced hippocampal volume, relative to normal adults (Bremner, 1999).

Effect of drugs and alcohol on the brain. The plasticity of the brain is bad news if a person engages in the excessive consumption of neurotoxic substances. Alcoholism increases the shrinkage of the cerebral cortex, the limbic system, the hypothalamus and the cerebellum (Lishman, 1990; Sullivan et al., 2000). The frontal lobes are particularly vulnerable to alcohol-induced atrophy (Pfefferbaum et al., 1997). Other drugs are less well researched in relation to brain function, but a recent study showed that methamphetamine abusers show severe atrophy in the hippocampus (Thompson et al., 2004).

Box 1.3   Alternative perspectives

A story of extreme brain plasticity: The woman with half a brain

The psychiatrist Normand Doidge has collated case studies that illustrate the power of neuroplasticity in his book *The Brain that Changes Itself* (2008). Among these is the case of Michelle Mack. Michelle was born with no left hemisphere in her brain, due to an unknown problem encountered by her mother during pregnancy. In the first few years of her life, she was subject to numerous tests to ascertain what was wrong with her, as she showed a variety of cognitive deficits and difficulties controlling the right side of her body. However, she survived and by the time she reached adulthood, her development had proceeded astonishingly well. In her mid-thirties, when Doidge interviewed her, she was living a relatively normal life – she had a part-time job, she could hold normal conversations, laugh at jokes and be an engaged member of her local church. This provides powerful evidence of the ability of the brain to adapt to extreme environmental trauma – in this case, the absence of an entire cerebral hemisphere could be managed due to the plasticity of the brain.

Genetic plasticity: The effects of behaviour and environment on gene expression

Genes are not separate from biopsychosocial influences – what we do and the environments we are in change how our genes are expressed. The processes by which experience and environments affect genes are referred to as *developmental epigenetic* mechanisms (Gluckman et al., 2009). Epigenetic mechanisms can also refer to processes by which environmental events or behaviours lead to changes in genetic expression that are inherited by offspring; for more on this, read Pembrey et al. (2006).

In order to understand genetic plasticity and developmental epigenetics, a few words are necessary on the basics of cellular genetics. In every cell in your body is an identical DNA genome, wound tightly into 23 chromosomes. In order for DNA to instruct physical development, it must be unwound and turned into proteins, which in turn become the physical structures of the body. To achieve this process, DNA from a cell nucleus is unwound and *transcribed* into a molecule called mRNA, which is then *transported* out of the nucleus into the cell body, where it is *translated* into proteins by small structures called ribosomes. These three processes of transcription, transportation and translation are influenced by a host of factors, including those that have their origin in behaviour and environment. One process that turns genes on and off, and thus alters the transcription process, is the 'methylation' of DNA, which involves adding a molecule called a methyl group to a DNA sequence in such a way that the DNA is turned off or on.

There is evidence to support the effects of environment on genetic expression from research on a variety of species. In turtles and other reptiles, the temperature at which an egg is incubated (an environment factor) influences which sex the animal becomes, showing that somehow temperature has turned some genes on, and others off, to develop male or female sexual characteristics (Wibbels, Bull & Crews, 1991). In hamsters, day length and testosterone levels influence DNA expression in the brain (Bittman et al., 1999). In rats and cats, various forms of environmental stimulation and stress influence how DNA is synthesised into proteins in the nervous system (Gottlieb, 1998), while in humans, examination stress affects DNA expression in immune cells (Glaser et al., 1990).

Gilbert Gottlieb (1991; 1998) developed a theoretical model of epigenetic influences on development, termed **probabilistic epigenesis**. In this model, there is regulation of genetic expression by neural, behavioural, physical environment and social environment factors. Because environments are not perfectly predictable, this process is not predetermined but is *probabilistic*, and therefore

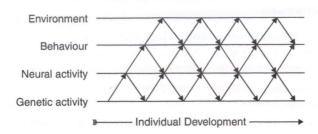

Figure 1.4 Gottlieb's simplified scheme showing four mutually interacting levels of development, between which there are reciprocal influences (also called co-actions)

Source: Gottlieb (1991, p. 6). Copyright © American Psychological Association. Reprinted with permission.

we can never talk with complete certainty about how a person's development will progress in the future, as there are always unknowns in the equation. In the model, four levels of development are viewed as being reciprocally linked, by way of two-way influences, as illustrated in Figure 1.4. Each pair of up-down arrows in the diagram is termed a *co-action*. A co-action is what occurs when two things reciprocally influence each other, without one being the cause and the other being the effect. To illustrate a co-action, imagine two people shaking hands – which person is the cause and which person is the effect? It actually makes no sense to say, for both are influencing each other in a co-action. Co-actions are at the heart of biopsychosocial theorising, for they help to account for how genes shape brains and environments, and how environments and brains then shape genetic expression in return.

In summary, it is now well supported by research that genes lead to different phenotypes depending on information coming from outside the cell, and even from outside the organism. According to Gottlieb (1998), this means that nothing in development is hardwired; development emerges from a combination of reciprocal influences at the genetic, organismic and environmental levels. This has empowering implications, for it says that how your genes express themselves in the structures of your body is, to a degree, under your control.

Where does the 'psych' part fit in to the biopsychosocial paradigm? A 4-Quadrant Model

To understand the biopsychosocial paradigm, a clear sense of how the psychological level relates to biological and social levels is essential. Ken Wilber's 4-Quadrant model of development provides one

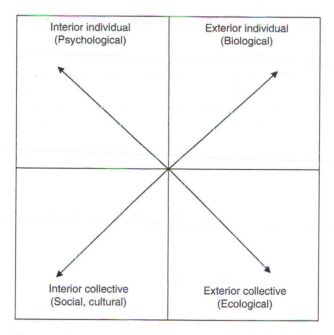

Figure 1.5   A four-quadrant model of development
Source: Based on Wilber (2000a).

effective way of construing their relation. In the model, the developing human being (or any other developing organism) can be viewed
through four quadrants, as illustrated in Figure 1.5. These quadrants
are formed by crossing two categorical variables: exterior/interior and
individual/collective.

The top right quadrant is the **biological** perspective – from here the
person is seen as an object composed of physical organs and organic
matter. The top left quadrant is the **psychological** perspective, which
views the individual person as a conscious agent with intentions,
behaviours, feelings and thoughts. The bottom left quadrant is the **social**
perspective, which views a person as *part of a social group or social
context*, while the bottom right quadrant is the **ecological** perspective,
which views the human being as part of the physical world and as part of
surrounding ecosystems. This helps us to see how the psychological perspective fits in – it views the human being as a conscious individual with
an inner life and intentions, who is simultaneously a biological being
and part of social and ecological systems. Psychology should therefore
constantly interact with biology, sociology and ecology to glean insights
from the disciplines that specialise in the other three quadrants, while
maintaining its distinguishable features. Wilber suggests that maintaining

a focus on all four quadrants marks an *integral* perspective (Wilber, 1997; 2000a; 2000b).

Healthy development, according to Wilber's theory, requires change in the four quadrants to progress in harmony. As a simple example, if a person aims to have children, they need to develop a particular intention and commitment (top left), there are particular biological requirements (top right), necessary social and cultural supports (bottom left) and an appropriate physical environment (bottom right). If all these developments harmonise, then there is more chance that the transition to parenthood will be made successfully than if one aspect is pursued irrespective of the others (see Chapter 6 for more on the transition to parenthood). This is true of any other developmental transition or change process.

Social systems and human development

Uri Bronfenbrenner (1979; 1994) proposed a biopsychosocial theory of how different social environments shape and sustain human development. To use Wilber's terminology, it relates to the 'lower left quadrant' of development. The theory describes how social systems fit within each other like a set of Russian dolls; large social systems such as a nation state are composed of smaller communities, which in turn are composed of social groups, organisations and families. Bronfenbrenner's aim was to create a theory that distinguished between these different levels of social system, to provide an alternative to referring to 'the environment' as a singular entity. The model proposes that social systems influencing the developing human being can be arranged by their size, from largest to smallest:

1. *The Microsystem* – the pattern of activities, roles, and interpersonal relations experienced by the developing person on a day-to-day basis.
2. *The Mesosystem* – all the settings in which the developing person actively participates and all the people they interact with.
3. *Exosystems* – the various systems that the person does not participate in, but affects them and their development, such as a partner's workplace or an elderly parent's care home.
4. *The Macrosystem* – the cultural system of common rituals, laws, conventions and customs and in which a person develops.

An example of the macrosystem shaping development is the phenomenon of 'age-grading timetables'. Bernice Neugarten, whose work spanned both psychology and sociology, found that cultures have expectations for how and when adult development milestones should be reached (Neugarten, 1996). Relative to these culturally created age-grading systems, individuals can self-appraise whether they are 'early', 'on-time' or 'late' in their work-life, home achievements and transitions relative to social expectations:

> Every society has a system of social expectations regarding age-appropriate behaviour, and these expectations are internalized as the individual grows up and grows old, and as he moves from one age stratum to the next. There is a time when he is expected to go to work, to marry, a time to raise children, a time to retire, even a time to grow sick and to die. (Neugarten & Datan, 1996, p. 102)

Timing through such key life milestones in line with a culture or subculture's norms is a macrosystemic influence on the course of adult life (Neugarten, 1996; Neugarten & Datan, 1996). Mesosystem and microsystem phenomena include romantic relationships, marriage, family, children and friendships. These are covered in Chapter 11 on social relationships.

Adulthood is a time of never-ending psychological and behavioural change, partially because of the major alterations that occur in social environment over its course (Bronfenbrenner, 1994). The formative role of environments on human development gave Bronfenbrenner cause for optimism, for it means that there are higher, wiser levels of human development that have as yet been unrealised, which may be unlocked by improvements in technology, education and community (Bronfenbrenner, 1979).

More recently, an integrative model of human development has been proposed by Sameroff (2010), based on the original Bronfenbrenner model of nested systems but also referring to the biological and psychological twin nature of the individual at the centre of the various social systems. Figure 1.6 represents the key structures of the theory. At the centre is the person, who is conceived as a *biopsychological self-regulating system*, composed of biological and psychological parts. This self-regulating person is embedded in, and influenced by, social systems including parents, family, peers, community and geopolitical environment. The overall complex of developmental systems is termed the *biopsychosocial ecological system*.

Part of a biopsychosocial approach is accepting that historical events affect the course of individual lives. Bronfenbrenner referred to this as the 'chronosystem' of development (Sameroff, 2010). Baltes, Reese and

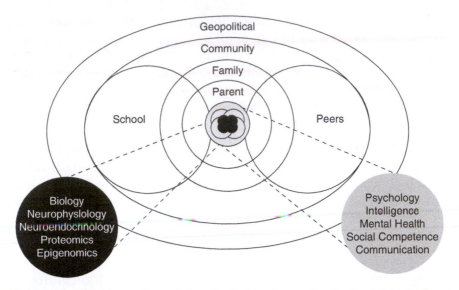

Figure 1.6 The biopsychosocial ecological system – developing biological and psychological systems embedded in multiple social systems

Source: Sameroff (2010, p. 18). Copyright © John Wiley & Sons. Reproduced with permission.

Lipsitt (1980) referred to it as *history-graded influences*. Box 1.4 describes Glen Elder's research on the effects of the historic Great Depression of the 1930s on childhood and adulthood.

Box 1.4　Alternative perspectives

The influence of the Great Depression on individual development

A well-known example of the influence of history on human development is sociologist Glen Elder's research on the effects of the Great Depression in the 1930s (Elder Jr., 1994; 1998). He looked at data from several longitudinal studies that commenced before the Great Depression and found that as this historical event unfolded, there was a cascade of effects down to the individual level. The loss of jobs and income that this event caused led to individual and marital stress, and increased irritability and anger in fathers. This in turn reduced the effectiveness of parenting, leading to difficulties with child adjustment. Correspondingly, young children during the 1930s

> **Box 1.4   Continued**
>
> were more adversely affected in the long-term than adolescents (Elder Jr., 1998).
>
> The research raises some key questions about the science of adult development. It suggests that unlike in the natural sciences where natural laws do not change appreciably over time, in psychological development what is true at one time may not be true half a century later. Adult development theory must therefore be continually revisited, and research findings repeatedly tested, to establish if they still hold. We will come across other examples of history shaping development at various points later in the book, for example in the historical changes to the nature of retirement (Chapter 13) and changes in the experience of bereavement over the past century (Chapter 14).

Concluding comments

So now you have the basic foundations for the remainder of the book. You have hopefully grasped that being an adult has not only a legal meaning, but also has personal and social meanings too; a person may be legally an adult at 18, but it may be another ten years before they *feel* like an adult. Furthermore, development in adulthood can happen in all kinds of positive and negative ways, and the positive ways (such as becoming happier, more virtuous, more adaptive, more complex and more knowledgeable) may conflict with each other. This means that change in adult life requires compromise and balance.

Development is something that occurs on biological, psychological and social levels, and these three levels are bound together interdependently; what happens on one level leads to change in the other two, and vice versa, due to reciprocal influences. I encourage you to keep this issue of reciprocal influence between levels in mind when reading the rest of the book – it is easy to forget when reading research papers, because traditional psychological research methods such as experiments are aimed at establishing linear causality, when in fact, development is much more like a tug of war than a chain reaction.

Questions for you to reflect on

- Have a look at the list of activities in Table 1.1. What do you think these activities have in common that make them prohibited to children?

- It seems that human beings are taking longer and longer to grow up. Why do you think this is so?
- What does being an adult mean to you? Ask your friends and see if they agree.
- In what ways would you *ideally* like to change as you grow older? Whatever your answer is – this is what positive development means to you.
- Think of a major transition in adult life such as (a) becoming a parent, (b) going through menopause or (c) moving into a nursing home in old age, and try and think of the *biological, psychological* and *social* challenges that are involved in it.

Summary points

- Legal adulthood commences when a person reaches the 'age of majority' – at which point they are considered autonomous and responsible citizens who can control their actions and consider the implications of them. Within a few years of the legal onset of adulthood, a person is allowed to smoke, drink, gamble, have sexual intercourse, get married, vote and get a mortgage. All of these activities are precluded to children because adult capacities of forethought and impulse control are necessary for their safe use.
- Personal definitions of adulthood typically include common criteria such as financial independence, moving out of the parental home, having a responsible attitude, desisting from adolescent risk behaviours and becoming a parent. Emerging adulthood is a period of life during which individuals often consider themselves part-adult and part-adolescent.
- Development can be defined neutrally or progressively. The neutral definition is any enduring change that leads to loss or gain. The progressive definition is any change that leads to an improvement in functioning over time, according to some criterion that defines what 'improvement' means.
- Progressive development can be called positive development or optimal development. It involves change in a direction towards an ideal. Various ideals for adult functioning can be conceived, of which five of the most important are: the orthogenetic direction (increased complexity), the eudaimonic direction (towards increased wellbeing), the veridical direction (towards increased truth and knowledge), the virtuous direction (towards improved moral character) and the evolutionary direction (towards improved probability of survival and reproduction).
- Developmental change can be quantitative continuous (a gradual change in a measurable variable), quantitative discontinuous (a sudden leap in a measurable variable) and qualitative discontinuous (a change from one state to a different state that is not different in amount, but in kind). All three of these forms of change can be assessed in developmental research.
- The biopsychosocial paradigm views development as occurring concurrently at biological, psychological and social levels throughout life, and that development at each of these three levels reciprocally influences the other two levels, by way of 'co-actions'.
- Biological, psychological and social descriptions and explanations are all as valid as each other, and no level has causal primacy over the other two.

- The brain shapes behaviour, but is also shaped by behaviour. The capacity of the brain to adapt to behaviour and the environment is called *neuroplasticity*. Diet, stress, social environments and toxins can all change the structure and functional localisation of the brain.
- Genetic expression is altered by behaviour and environments. A model that describes how this occurs is the model of *probabilistic epigenesis*, which states that genes, brain, behaviour and environment shape one another reciprocally.
- The psychological level of analysis is that which takes into account individual internal experiences – that is, intentions and subjectivity. Wilber's four quadrant model provides a framework for conceiving how that relates to biological, social and ecological levels of analysis.
- Bronfenbrenner's model of social influences on development conceives of multiple levels of social systems in which a developing person is embedded: *the microsystem* – the daily pattern of social activities; the *mesosystem* – key social settings, for example, home and work environments; *exosystems* – the various influencing social systems that the person does not actively participate in, and the *macrosystem* – the cultural milieu that a person lives in.
- Development is shaped by historical changes, as illustrated by Elder's research on the effects of the Great Depression on children and adults.

Recommended reading

Arnett, J. J. (1998). Learning to stand alone: The contemporary American transition to adulthood in cultural and historical context. *Human Development*, 41, 295–315.

Baltes, P. B., Reese, H. W. & Lipsitt, L. P. (1980). Life-span developmental psychology. *Annual Review of Psychology*, 31, 65–110.

Bronfenbrenner, U. (1979). *The Ecology of Human Development*. Boston, MA: Harvard University Press.

Gottlieb, G. (1998). Normally occurring environmental and behavioral influences on gene activity: From central dogma to probabilistic epigenesis. *Psychological Review*, 105, 792–802.

Lerner, R. M. (2001). *Concepts and Theories of Human Development*, 3rd edn. London: Psychology Press.

Lledo, P-M., Alonso, M. & Grubb, M. S. (2006). Adult neurogenesis and functional plasticity in neuronal circuits. *Nature Reviews Neuroscience*, 7, 179–193.

Morrison, J. H. & Hof, P. R. (1997). Life and death of neurons in the aging brain. *Science*, 278, 412–419.

Neugarten, B. L. (1996). Continuities and discontinuities of psychological issues into adult life. In D. A. Neugarten (ed.) *The Meanings of Age: Selected Papers of Neugarten, B. L.* (pp. 88–95). London: University of Chicago Press.

Sameroff, A. (2010). A unified theory of development: A dialectic integration of nature and nurture. *Child development*, 81, 6–22.

2

Research Methods in Adult Development

The pursuit of truth is like picking raspberries. You miss a lot if you approach it from only one angle.

Randal Marlin

Martin was born in London in the second week of April 1970, which meant he was automatically entered into the British Cohort Study (BCS). The BCS is an on-going longitudinal study that has tracked the lives of all who were born in that week in 1970 in England, Scotland and Wales. Over the years, the BCS has collected data using questionnaires, tests, interviews and medical examinations. At the age of five, Martin remembers thinking that he was the only one being studied, and that he must therefore be special in some way, so was surprised to learn a few years later that he was one of 17,000 in the study. He doesn't remember much about the 1980 and 1986 assessments. In 1996, 2000 and most recently 2004 he became aware of how the study had expanded into a variety of new topics. At that last phase of data collection, about 60 per cent of all the babies in the original cohort were still involved with the study. Longitudinal studies such as these provide an important empirical lens on how people change across the lifespan.

Description, understanding, explanation and prediction

A comprehensive science of adult development should aim to *describe*, *understand* and *explain* the changes, transitions and turning points that occur during adulthood, and correspondingly be able to *predict* their occurrence to some degree. But what exactly do these words – describe, understand, explain, predict – mean? A brief reconnaissance of their meanings is provided here as a prelude to presenting the research designs and methods used in the study of adult development.

Description. The aim of descriptive research in adult development is to establish what a developmental phenomenon, life event or transition actually is, what kinds of experience it brings with it, and what kind of change occurs. To describe a phenomenon scientifically requires accurately and systematically representing its defining features (and its context if necessary), by way of numbers, words or both. Given that psychologists often discuss things that can't be directly observed (for example, wellbeing, love or vocation), this process of careful and systematic definition is essential, otherwise it's quite possible that people are referring to different things by the same word.

Understanding. To *understand* a developmental phenomenon means to know how it meaningfully relates to a broader context or system. The developmental psychologist Blasi (1976) gives a mathematical example to illustrate this. A young child may learn the sum '3 × 6 = 18' without understanding it. In order to understand it, she must learn that it relates to a system of mathematical rules more generally, and thus is equivalent to 3 + 3 + 3 + 3 + 3 + 3 = 18, or 6 × 3 = 18, and that it also implies 18 / 3 = 6 (Blasi, 1976). The parallel of this in adult development is to understand how different developmental facts fit together into a meaningful and systematic pattern. Let's say, for example, that a man has a tendency to be aggressive in adult romantic relationships. If it is established that he grew up in a care home where he used aggression as a way of preventing being bullied, then his adult aggression might be *understood* better, for it is no longer an isolated fact but is meaningfully related to a bigger picture. This is not explanation, for explanation requires an attempt at answering *why* something occurs.

Explanation. To explain an occurrence or phenomenon entails providing some kind of answer to the perennial question of 'why?' Following the philosophy of Aristotle, Killeen (2001) describes four different kinds of explanation of behaviour, which are based on four causes: *efficient, material, formal and final* (Baltes & Willis, 1977; Killeen, 2001). These all contribute to a science of adult development, as described in Table 2.1.

Prediction. Description, understanding and explanation all work together to facilitate prediction. If descriptive research establishes that development proceeds in a particular direction at a certain age, from this a *descriptive prediction* about that age group can be made. Alternatively, all four kinds of explanation – final, formal, efficient and causal – permit *explanatory predictions.* To illustrate the difference between descriptive and explanatory prediction, we can think of predicting a full moon. Simply by

Table 2.1 Efficient, material, formal and final explanations of behaviour and development

Explanation	Description
Efficient cause explanation	Explanation through establishing what *leads* to an event or change, or makes it *more likely* to occur. It can refer to *distal causes*, which occurred at an earlier time point, or *proximal causes*, which occur directly prior to an effect. For example, research shows that child abuse makes depression more likely in adulthood – this is therefore a *distal* risk factor (Spataro et al., 2004), while other research shows that stressful life events in adulthood tend to trigger the onset of depression – this is a *proximal* cause (Brown, Harris & Hepworth, 1998).
Material cause explanation	Establishing a physical substrate of a psychological or behavioural development, such as a pattern of neural activity, a particular brain system or other biological factor such as hormone level or blood pressure. For example, in Chapter 3 on cognitive development, research will be discussed that explains decline in reaction time in old age by way of deterioration in the brain's white matter – this is a material cause explanation (Madden et al., 2004).
Formal cause explanation	Explaining a phenomenon by recourse to a model, theory or law. In natural science, a formal explanation of why apples fall to the ground is by recourse to the law of gravity. Such an explanation would be as follows: objects that have mass are attracted to one another, and both the apple and the earth have mass, therefore the object of lesser mass (the apple) is drawn towards the object of greater mass (the earth). In adult development, a similar kind of explanation is invoked when a theory or model is employed to explain why a developmental change or event occurs. For example, if it was found that a person was more emotionally positive in old age than when they were younger, that could be explained by recourse to the positivity effect or socio-emotional selectivity theory (Carstensen & Mikels, 2005). See Chapter 4 for more on these theories.
Final cause explanation	An explanation for behaviour provided by way of describing its function, goal or purpose. In everyday life, final cause explanations are the standard approach to explaining behaviour. Some simple examples are: *Q: Why are you on a diet? A: To get fit and lose weight.* *Q: Why are you leaving your job and going back to study at university? A: To change my career and become a doctor.* *Q: Why are all those people congregating in the street together with placards? A: To protest against changes to pension policy.* Final cause explanation is directly relevant to adult development, because developmental changes are often initiated intentionally to achieve a goal, and thus have a motive, function or purpose (Bühler, 1967). For example, a researcher may ask: 'why do people voluntarily retire from full-time work?' The answer to this question may be framed in terms of final cause explanations, that is, the function and purpose of retiring. Research on this question has established a variety of different motives for voluntary retirement, described in Chapter 13.

observing its movements and shape every day, a robust prediction could be about when the moon will next be full. However, that prediction would be purely descriptive. An explanatory prediction would also state *why* the moon would be full on a particular date, by recourse to planetary movements, the operation of gravity, the elliptical orbit of the moon, and so on.

Developmental research designs

To meet the tasks of description, understanding, explanation and prediction in the study of adult development, researchers employ a variety of research designs. These can be broadly split into *synchronic* and *longitudinal* designs (Ruspini, 2002). Synchronic designs gather data at one specific point in time, and can be *cross-sectional, life-event focused* or *biographical*, while longitudinal studies can be either *dynamic or predictive* designs.

Cross-sectional studies

A cross-sectional study gathers data at a single time-point from people of varying ages, in order to gather a representative cross-section of the population and examine age differences. For example, political orientation in older and younger adults could be compared to see if the propensity for conservatism is different across age groups. Age differences that are found in the data may be attributable to an age effect, cohort effect or sampling error. An *age effect* occurs when an age difference is attributable to a reliable and generalisable ageing/maturation process, and therefore replicable across demographic groups and time periods. A *cohort effect* is a difference between age groups that reflects the fact that the age groups have grown up at different times and thus been exposed to different socio-historical environments. The possibility of cohort effects undermines the capacity of cross-sectional data to inform developmental models. For example, if it was found in a cross-sectional study that older adults performed less well in an IQ test than younger adults, this would not necessarily warrant the conclusion that IQ decreases in old age. It may instead be that the older age group grew up in a time of less exposure to IQ-type tests, and that a cohort effect may be why they performed worse, not because they have declined with age (Flynn, 1999). *Sampling error* occurs if an age difference is due to the fact that the older and younger groups differ in other ways. For example, if a study compared intelligence in younger and older adults, but 80 per cent of the younger adults had a college education, and only 10 per cent of the older adults did, then any differences between the groups may be due to this difference between the samples, rather than age or cohort.

Time-sequential cross-sectional designs: In a time-sequential design, two or more cross-sectional studies are conducted a number of years apart and the findings from each cross-sectional phase are compared to look for change in the age-difference data over time (Schaie, 1965). Using a time-sequential design, a research programme can investigate whether a cross-sectional pattern holds or changes over time. If it holds, then this adds to the likelihood of it being an age effect, and not a cohort effect.

Life-event studies

Life-event studies focus on gaining knowledge about a particular event within adulthood that has developmental implications. Examples mentioned in this book include, among others, the transition to parenthood, divorce, career change, menopause and retirement. Life-event research can focus on different aspects of a developmental life event, such as what predicts it, what defines it, how it is experienced and what outcomes it has for development. Individual differences in life events can also be studies, for example the different experiences of retirement (for example, Robinson, Demetre & Corney, 2011). Life-event studies thus help to describe, explain, predict and understand the particular developmental vicissitudes of adult life.

Biographical studies

Biographical studies involve collecting data on adult development by way of written or spoken accounts of a person's adult life given in retrospect. They have been used in adult development since the 1950s, starting with the work of Bühler (1951; 1959). Biographical research assumes that a person's written or spoken story about their past can illuminate the ups and downs of development and the life cycle (Lieberman & Falk, 1971), despite being reliant on memories that are imperfectly and selectively recalled (Kotre, 1995). Biographical research can be used in the following ways:

1. To develop and test theory about how life and development is experienced as a whole (Levinson, 1986).
2. To study the process of autobiographical memory itself, and how it changes with age (Kotre, 1995; Schroots & van Dijkum, 2004).
3. To study how people create and develop a storied narrative of identity over the adult life course (Mcadams, 2001; Wilt, Cox & McAdams, 2010).
4. To reconstruct the structure and function of life stories, and to establish what kind of life stories are related to positive outcomes in adulthood (McAdams, 1993).

5. To explore how childhood experiences are related to outcomes in adulthood, for example the self-perceived links between childhood experiences and adult psychopathology (Roff & Ricks, 1970).
6. To give participants a chance to tell their own life story, and benefit from the cognitive and emotional benefits that this process has been shown to bring (de Vries, Birren & Deutchman, 1990).

Longitudinal designs

Longitudinal studies follow a sample of individuals over a period of time, and collect data from them at multiple times, at agreed intervals. Such studies can be divided into predictive and dynamic types (Neugarten, 1996). In the *predictive longitudinal* type, data are gathered at two points in the lifespan to establish whether variable A, measured at time 1, predicts variable B, measured at time 2. For example, predictive longitudinal research has been used to help establish that smoking predicts cancer in later life (Speizer et al., 1999). In the *dynamic design* type of longitudinal study, the aim is to track the trajectory of quantitative change over time. The Seattle Longitudinal Study (discussed in Chapter 3) is one study that has employed a dynamic longitudinal design and has tracked longitudinal changes in cognitive ability in American adults over many decades (Schaie, 1996).

Longitudinal research can be conducted over any duration, but for a study to be of relevance to development, it needs ideally to last a matter of years, rather than months or days. The principal benefit of a longitudinal study is that it is immune to cohort effects, and is actually looking at real change over time, rather than inferring change from static data (Baltes & Nesselroade, 1979). However there are challenges and difficulties associated with longitudinal research that should be taken into account when considering such a research design, four of which are described in Table 2.2.

Sequential longitudinal designs: A sequential longitudinal design is comprised of two longitudinal studies conducted several years or more apart (Schaie and Baltes, 1975). This kind of design gets around the time-of-measurement problem, for if the same changes over time are observed in both samples, then it is less likely that the results are due to temporarily environmental change, and more likely that they are due to a generalisable age effect. Sequential longitudinal studies require a lot of time and resources to conduct, and are beyond the scope of many researchers. A more manageable alternative to a sequential longitudinal design is undertaking a replication of a previous longitudinal study, or encouraging replications of one's own longitudinal study. This way, sequential longitudinal studies can be achieved as a co-operative effort

Table 2.2 Four difficulties associated with longitudinal research

1 – The selective nature of longitudinal samples	Longitudinal research designs require a long-term commitment from participants that may last years, and therefore those who choose to participate may be particularly conscientious or interested in psychology, and so not necessarily representative of the general population (Schaie, 1988).
2 – Attrition effects	There will be attrition of the longitudinal sample over time, as some participants will drop out or loose contact with the research team. If attrition of participants is systematically from a particular kind of participant, then differences between later and earlier findings can potentially be caused by this attrition. In longitudinal studies of cognitive ability it has been found that attrition tends to be from lower-ability participants, which would systematically increase mean levels in later assessments (Schaie, 1988).
3 – Funding difficulties	Finding funding for a longitudinal study that lasts decades can be a difficult prospect. Research funding bodies tend to want results within a year or two, rather than in a decade or two, therefore combining cross-sectional with longitudinal data is a way of having immediate results as well as a more long-term product.
4 – Time-of-measurement effects	Any change found by a longitudinal study can be attributed to a 'time-of-measurement' effect (Schaie, 1965). This is when a temporary environmental event or change, such as a natural disaster or recession, affects the sample in a way that is not generalisable to other cohorts or time periods. For example, a time of high unemployment may increase the prevalence of depression, so if a recession hits when a sample group are around the age of 40, and unemployment correspondingly increases, mean-level depression symptoms may increase across the sample. This finding would be strongly affected by the time-of-measurement effect of the recession, and it would be unwise to infer a general tendency to depression around the age of 40.

between researchers, and the historical stability of longitudinal effects can be assessed accordingly.

Accelerated longitudinal designs

An accelerated longitudinal design is an approach to studying change that is quicker than a standard longitudinal design. In such a study the total age range under study is split into smaller age groups, each of which is followed for a period of time (Lerner, Schwartz & Phelps, 2009). As a hypothetical example, a study could be conducted on longitudinal changes in aggression in men between the ages of 20 and 60. To achieve this, participants could be recruited who are aged 20, 25, 30, 35, 40, 45, 50 and 55, and are then assessed every six months for five years. The change shown by each group across the five-year period could be then be combined into a composite growth curve to illustrate longitudinal change from 20 to 60.

Accelerated longitudinal studies are popular alternatives to standard longitudinal research, and will be encountered at a number of points in later chapters (for example, Carstensen et al., 2011). An advantage of accelerated longitudinal designs over standard longitudinal designs is that they are less time-consuming and thus more achievable within a research funding deadline. They are also less likely to be subject to problematic sample attrition (that is, participants getting bored with the study, and so dropping out) (Farrington, 1991). However, the design does mean that cohort effects can still influence findings, as different age groups are involved, and these groups may still change in ways that relate to their cohort rather than to their age (Loeber & Farrington, 1994).

Quantitative methods in adult development

Having chosen a research design, a developmental researcher must decide whether to use quantitative or qualitative data, and whether to use a quantitative or qualitative analysis. Quantitative methods turn human behaviour, cognition, emotion and personality into numbers, by way of calculating the frequency, strength, typicality or prevalence of the phenomenon under study. Various quantitative data collection strategies can be used to study developmental change, events and transitions in adult development, a short list of which is given further.

Data collection strategies

Cognitive ability tests – Cognitive ability tests quantify an individual's capacity to solve a particular set of problems, the most famous of which are IQ tests. A difficulty with using such tests in a longitudinal study is that individuals can get better at the test with practice and familiarity, leading to artificially elevated levels of performance at later points in the study (Schaie, 1988).

Psychometric questionnaires – Psychometric questionnaires are structured quantitative questionnaires, which use rating scales or forced-choice response forms to elicit numerical self-reports of personality traits, values, self-perceptions or attitudes. Data from such questionnaires can be used to compare age groups or track changes over time.

Observation and rating – In this data collection method, a researcher observes behaviour or a video recording, and to quantify it either: (a) notes down frequencies of a particular behaviour, or (b) gives ratings to observed behaviour on quantitative scales. This data can be used to see how behaviour changes with age, for example one observational study looked at the extent to which older and younger show different eye movements in response to arousing emotional scenes (Rösler et al., 2005).

Experience sampling – In this approach, participants are given a hand-held computer or smartphone which is programmed to beep at certain moments during the day. When a beep sounds, the participant rates some aspect of their current experience, for example to rate their current level of happiness on a scale of 1–5 (Conner et al., 2009).

Archival records – Any source of quantitative information gathered in the past for non-academic purposes can potentially be co-opted as data. For example, the *Office of National Statistics* collects census data and nationally representative quantitative data for the UK on topics such as marriage, divorce, employment patterns and mental/physical health. This can provide useful information on age-related phenomena in adults, for example it is used in Chapters 6 to provide data on life expectancy, and in Chapter 12 for data on marriage and divorce rates by age.

Physiological measures – A variety of physiological variables can be measured as part of developmental psychology research, in order to search for material explanations of psychological changes. Popular physiological measures include brain scans, hormone tests (for example, done through a saliva sample), heart rate, skin conductance or physical health measures.

Quantitative analysis in developmental research: The dilemma of the aggregate

Having collected quantitative data from longitudinal or cross-sectional research, a researcher must choose how to analyse and present the numerical data. A common choice is to illustrate quantitative age differences or change in a graph with age on the x-axis, the target variable on the y-axis and a single line that represents either the mean or 'best fit' line for the whole sample. Such a graph can represent age differences from cross-sectional data or age-related change in longitudinal data. It is a popular approach to data presentation, but there are limitations in focusing on mean-level graphs or regression best-fit lines. In longitudinal research, the dilemma is that change in the average does not necessarily reflect individual-level change (Lerner et al., 1996; Singer & Willett, 2003). For example Figure 2.1 shows two hypothetical samples of four people who have had their wellbeing measured over time. The black line represents the sample mean. In both samples, the mean level shows no change over time. However in graph A, the mean accurately reflects individual-level stability, but in graph B the same mean line misrepresents a combination of individual declines and inclines. In order to

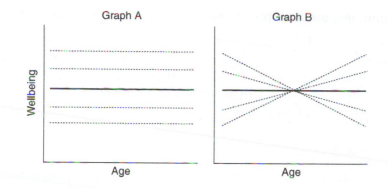

Figure 2.1   Hypothetical graphs showing (A) mean-level stability reflecting individual-level stability over time, (B) mean-level stability reflecting individuals who both increase and decline with age

Note: Solid line = mean score, dashed lines = individual scores

provide additional information that counteracts the potentially distorting effects of the mean or growth curve, lines for individual participants can be included in the graph. We will see this strategy used for real in Chapters 3 and 4.

Another problem in using a regression best-fit line or mean-level line is that the *variance* of the sample's scores at each age is not shown. If the variance of the scores is large, then the changes in mean-level signify less than if the variance is small, because when variance is greater the overlap between age points is greater. In order to provide some indication of the spread/variance of scores at each time point, standard error or confidence interval bars can be included on the graph, or an indication can be given of the total range of scores at different age groups (for example, Schaie & Willis, 2002). Alternatively, *latent growth curve analysis* can be used, which is a more complex analysis process that includes estimates how well the growth curve line fits the sample as a whole (more on this later).

A more radical alternative to group-level aggregation is analysing and presenting data at the level of one individual at a time. One such approach, termed 'intra-individual analysis', employs a form of statistics that is not familiar to most psychologists, so requires specialist training. For those interested in learning more about this approach, see Molenaar et al. (2009) or Nesselroade and Ram (2004). The other approach is referred as single-case experimental design, and is relatively easy to understand. It involves examining a series of graphs, each of which shows change over time for a *single* person. A visual comparison of the trends in these individual person graphs is used to elicit generalised conclusions (see Barlow & Hersen, 1984).

Longitudinal analysis techniques

There are a number of analysis tools that are designed for processing longitudinal data. These are referred to using a bewildering array of names, which can be confusing for the novice. Here I shall briefly mention two of the most well-known; latent growth-curve analysis and multi-level (also called hierarchical) modelling.

Latent growth-curve analysis (using structural equation modelling)

This technique analyses longitudinal data that have been gathered at 3 time points or more, in order to establish a 'latent change profile', which is a change line of best fit for the sample. A latent growth curve is a growth curve that is not directly observed, but is inferred from aggregating longitudinal change profiles across multiple participants. The technique establishes both a latent change profile (the general change tendency in the sample as a whole), and also calculates the extent to which the change profile reflects individual cases in the sample. The outcome of a latent growth-curve analysis is a box-and-arrow structural equation model that summarises correlational relationships between measured and latent variables. The following two *latent variables* are always represented in the diagram:

- *The intercept* – The point at which a line showing change meets the vertical axis of the graph – that is, its starting value. This value is also called the *constant*, as it acts as a constant or baseline against which later change can be measured.
- *The slope* – If change occurs, there will be a slope to the graph. If the change is an increase, this is referred to as a positive slope, while if negative change occurs, this is called a negative slope. The slope is indexed using a number that conveys how much positive / negative change occurs over a defined time period (for example, if you were measuring happiness and age, the slope would show how much change in happiness per year has occurred).

The latent growth-curve model gives data on how much the intercept and the slope vary across individuals – this demonstrates the model's *goodness of fit.* Models can also be used to check whether change in one variable predicts change in another variable. This is done by running a regression with the predictor variable as the Independent Variable (IV) and the outcome variable as the Dependent Variable (DV). Common packages for Latent Growth Curve Analysis include *Mx* (Neale et al., 2006), and *Mplus* (Muthén & Muthén, 1998). The advantage of these complex models is their ability to convey aggregate-level change and variance concisely, and to break samples into meaningful subgroups. The disadvantage of using this kind of analysis is that their specialist annotation systems can make research less accessible to a wide audience of academics, students or laypersons.

Multi-level modelling (also called hierarchical modelling or hierarchical linear modelling)

This statistical tool is a way of modelling different levels of influence on developmental change. Influences on the process of change in development can be viewed as a *nested hierarchy* of systems, as was discussed from a theoretical perspective in the previous chapter. Let's take the development of reading ability in childhood as an example; a child's efforts and abilities will affect reading ability development, as will the teacher, class, school, school district, region and national culture, all of which are nested within each other.

Multilevel modelling is a way of modelling lots of levels of influence simultaneously at the level of the whole sample (Bryk & Raudenbush, 1987). The resulting output takes the format of a regression model with each level of influence being shown as an IV. The independent contribution of each hierarchical level to the DV is specified and given a weighting. In order to carry out such analysis in SPSS, *multi-level mixed effects models* are appropriate (part of the advanced statistics add-on in SPSS v.18). STATA and SAS are both capable of multi-level modelling, and specialist packages such as MLwin and HLM are also available.

Qualitative methods in adult development

When the term qualitative is used in research methods, it can mean three things – a particular kind of *data*, an approach to *analysis*, and a methodological *paradigm*. These can be defined as follows:

- *Qualitative data* is open-ended text that is gained by way of interviews, focus groups, written texts such as essays or diaries, archival documents or field notes. It is a requirement for conducting biographical research studies, but can also be used in any of the other research designs too. For example, qualitative longitudinal research tracks changes over time using a diary or a series of interviews.
- *Qualitative analysis* is the process of extracting order from qualitative data in a way that does not involve translation of the words into numbers. There are many forms of qualitative analysis, and

these will be described below, but all involve the extrapolation of general categories, themes or patterns, from written or spoken text.

- The **qualitative paradigm** is more than just qualitative data and analysis combined. It is a research *movement*, with special interest groups, specialist journals and a history that is defined in opposition to the quantitative emphasis of orthodox psychology. The qualitative paradigm combines the deployment of qualitative data and analysis with philosophies that emphasise the *interpretive* role of the researcher and the *socially embedded* nature of scientific knowledge (Howitt, 2010). It is correspondingly critical of quantitative research that is based on the philosophy of positivism, which states that psychological phenomena can be measured objectively and laws of behaviour can be inferred in the same way that physical laws can be (Wiggins, 2011). The qualitative paradigm has developed standards for establishing research validity and credibility that are in some respects distinct from evaluative criteria for quantitative research. For a summary of these criteria, read Yardley (2000), or Elliott, Fischer and Rennie (1999).

Qualitative data collection techniques

The think-aloud method (and write-down method)

The *think-aloud* method (also called talk-aloud method or verbal protocol method) elicits spoken data in real-time about a problem, puzzle or issue. In this method, a participant voices aloud their reasoning when engaged in solving a task or answer questions. This method of data collection is central to research into post-formal cognitive development, described in Chapter 3 (for example, Sinnott & Johnson, 1997). A similar real-time reasoning method asks adults to *write down* their reasoning when engaged in solving a problem. Commons, Richards and Kuhn (1982) employed this method to study adult cognitive development. They gave participants four stories that described making a complex choice between multiple alternatives, and instructed them to write down their reasoning and solution. These written reasoning protocols served as the data used for analysis.

Structured interview methods

While think-aloud methods involve no interaction between participant and researcher during data collection, interviews necessarily involve a verbal interaction between researcher and participant. *Structured interviews* involve a pre-given sequence of questions that are said in the same manner and order to each participant, in order to standardise the interview as much as possible. A number of these interview-based methods are reviewed in later chapters, including the *Moral Judgment Interview* (Chapter 8), the *Ethic of Care Interview* (Chapter 8), the *Berlin Wisdom Interview* (Chapter 9), the *Faith Development Interview* (Chapter 10) and the *Subject–Object Interview* (Chapter 7). The aim of all of these structured interview methods is to reliably assess a person's developmental level on a particular scheme. Analysis of the data from structured interview methods is typically quantitative – researchers will read the interview transcript and rate its contents on a scale that corresponds to a predefined developmental coding scheme.

Retrospective interview methods

Interviews about a person's past can be used to study a variety of developmental phenomena. This can be achieved through the *semi-structured interview*, which involves covering a series of topics over the course of a fairly long interview, with a series of questions that can be asked in any order and adapted to the flow of each interview. Two classic longitudinal studies that employed semi-structured interviews were the *Lives through Time* study by Block (1971), and the *Harvard Grant Study*, a 40-year long study of male adult lives (Vaillant, 1977). Both of these major studies tended towards quantitative analysis of the qualitative data gained from the semi-structured interviews.

Certain specialist interview-based techniques are designed to elicit a complete life story, such as the *Life Story Interview*, an intensive interview-based process for eliciting a person's life story. The process takes two–three hours and covers perceived life chapters, peak experiences, nadir experiences, turning points, early memories, adolescent memories, adult memories, significant others in development, social contexts, personal ideology, conceptions of the future and sources of stress (McAdams, 1993).

The *Lifeline Interview Method* (LIM) aims to discuss a person's life story, while using a visual stimulus – a 'lifeline' – to focus the discussion (Assink & Schroots, 2010). To create the lifeline, an empty graph (the 'LIM grid'), is presented to the participant, with time on the x-axis and quality of life (positive = high, negative = low) on the y-axis. The interviewer asks the participant to draw a 'lifeline' representing change in quality of life from birth to present age. Once the line has been drawn in, peaks and troughs are labelled with the life events that they correspond to.

Guided autobiography groups gather life-story data using a group-based format (Birren & Cochran, 2001). Participants attend ten group sessions of two hours each. They write a two-page life story prior to each group session in response to the week's theme, and then read that out to the rest of the group, who respond with feedback. Themes that are addressed during the ten session series include: major branching points in life, family history, role of money, experience with death, the history of aspirations and goals. This method can be used as a source of empirical data or as a therapeutic technique.

Qualitative analysis

Qualitative data, once collected, can be analysed in a variety of ways. Quantification of the data is one option, and this proceeds either through counting the frequency of themes, words or concepts in a text. For a thorough review of how to quantify qualitative data using this process, read Gottschalk and Gleser (1979). Alternatively a researcher can allocate numerical ratings to the text on defined criteria – for example, as done in the Berlin Wisdom Interview (Baltes & Staudinger, 2000).

If qualitative data are submitted to a qualitative analysis, then four fundamental objectives can be pursued, which provide a useful taxonomy of basic analysis types – *theoretical analysis, content analysis, phenomenological analysis* and *narrative analysis*.

Theoretical analysis

The objective of a theoretical analysis of qualitative data is to develop or test a theory or model. The most well-known form of theoretical analysis is Grounded Theory (Strauss & Corbin, 1998). Others include Protocol Analysis (Ericsson & Simon, 1993); the Interactive Model (Miles & Huberman, 1994) and Flexible Structural Analysis (Valsiner, 2005). The aim for all of these analytical processes is to develop a box-and-arrow scheme that summarises a process or structure. If the set of concepts that results from such an analysis is purely descriptive, it is referred to as a *model*, while if it also includes antecedents, context and/or consequences, it can validly be called a theory (Strauss & Corbin, 1998). A challenge in this analytical process can be in meaningfully combining concepts or themes into a structure or system. To aid this process, techniques for exploring relations between themes can be used, such as Relational Analysis (Robinson, 2011a).

Content analysis

The objective of content analysis is to summarise and simplify complex qualitative data into a set of categories (Hsieh & Shannon, 2005). Categories for a content analysis can be established from existing theory before the research has been conducted, or can be derived during the process of analysis based on the researcher's interaction with the data. Data that has been submitted to a content analysis can be used to develop a descriptive typology, or to test a hypothesis about changes over times or differences between people (for example, Malamuth & Spinner, 1980). For example, in a hypothetical study on how 'being in love' is variously described across adulthood, content analysis could assign categories to individual responses to the question 'what does it mean to be in love' and then compare category frequencies across age groups.

Phenomenological analysis

The basic objective of a phenomenological analysis is to represent the lived experience of individuals in a systematic and empathic way. This involves endeavouring to gain a personal connection with participants whose accounts are being analysed, and committing to avoid imposing theory on to these experiences, but rather to letting them speak for themselves (Smith, Flowers & Larkin, 2009). Phenomenological techniques such as IPA (Interpretative Phenomenological Analysis) prefer to use small, homogenous samples from a particular group or social environment, so that each person is given a clear voice in the analysis and findings relate to a definable context.

Narrative analysis

Spoken information that a person provides about their own life is typically relayed in a *narrative* form, that is, it will be told as a story, with continuity effects, contrast effects, dramatic moments, episodes and a definable plot (Kotre, 1995; McAdams, 1993). The objective of narrative analysis is to explore how these narrative forms are used to portray human life and experience, and in adult development it also involves exploring how the *changes* of life are represented. The emphasis of this method is on language and the story-construction process, and this is what differentiates it from the other aforementioned analytical methods (Howitt, 2010).

The complementary roles of qualitative and quantitative methods in adult development research

As mentioned at the beginning of the chapter, the science of adult development should aim to comprehensively *describe*, *understand* and *explain* the changes, transitions and turning points of adulthood, and be able to *predict* their occurrence to some degree. Qualitative and quantitative research can contribute to these objectives in complementary ways.

The complementarity of quantitative and qualitative methods is being recognised and accepted more in psychology, and research studies are now being published that use both methods within one research initiative to enhance one another (Creswell & Plano Clark, 2007).

In relation to the aim of description, both quantitative and qualitative methods have much to offer. Quantitative data can describe when, for whom, for how long and at what intensity a developmental change occurred. It can help to describe whether a quantitative change is continuous or discontinuous (see Chapter 1 for more on these varieties of change). Meanwhile, qualitative data can provide a rich description and conceptual map of the structures, systems or experiences that define a developmental event or transition. By having both words and numbers together, a description is more likely to be full and accurate than either one alone.

In terms of explanation, quantitative methods are adept at establishing what makes an outcome more likely in terms of the presence or absence of various factors – this is a kind of efficient causal explanation. They are also uniquely placed to explore the physical and neurological correlates of developmental change. On the other hand, qualitative methods are adept at generating formal theory, and so can provide formal explanations, and can also explore final cause explanations for phenomena by exploring *intent* – that is, what goal or outcome a transition or developmental activity aims to achieve.

This brings us, finally, to the question of prediction. Qualitative and quantitative methods both have something to bring to the table here as well. Let's take the example of divorce – a major adult life event and time of change. Quantitative prediction, based on normative quantitative findings, can establish the likelihood of change in a given variable after a divorce – for example, how likely it is that a person will experience a decline in mental health. On the other hand, a qualitative model of divorce may describe a set of discrete phases for how divorce is coped with and how the post-divorce state is experienced. Both of these – quantitative predictions of changes in amount and qualitative predictions of changes in kind – can help with prediction in applied contexts. In summary, the ways in which quantitative and qualitative methods can contribute to the goals of developmental research are shown in Table 2.3.

Concluding comments

Research methods used in adult development and ageing are designed to elicit knowledge about change and developmental events, and there are lots of options to choose from. You are not limited to selecting from

Table 2.3   The contributions of qualitative and quantitative methods to adult development

	Description of developmental change or event	Explanation or understanding of developmental change or event	Prediction of developmental change or event
Quantitative Methods	Describe quantitative change – magnitude, duration, continuity vs. discontinuity. Describe timing, intensity, frequency of developmental events.	Efficient cause-effect relations: Establishing distal and proximal antecedents. Material correlates and causal relations, by way of relating development to physiological measures.	Quantitative prediction: Hypothesising the likely change trajectory of a group or individual on a defined variable.
Qualitative Methods	Describe qualitative change – represent discrete phases of a process. Describe the experience and meaning of developmental events and changes.	Final cause explanation: goals and motives of making changes to life. Formal cause explanation: Explanation by recourse to a grounded theory or model. Understanding: Viewing a development in the context of the whole person and their social environment.	Qualitative prediction: Hypothesising what new goal, ability, concern or behaviour will emerge next in the course of an adult's life.

the options described in this chapter – you can be creative and think up new ways of designing studies, collecting data and analysing it. Many of the pioneering researchers in adult development that you will read about in later chapters have innovated their own methods to address research problems, so why not you?

Questions for you to reflect on

- Could you design a research project to study what children, adolescents and young adults think 'being an adult' means, and whether that differs or changes by age? Try and think of a way of doing it that no-one else will have thought of before.
- Can you describe the difference between an age effect, a cohort effect, a time-of-measurement effect and a sampling effect?

- If you are a researcher whose aim is to see how people change in their political attitudes as they grow older, but you haven't got the time and money for a full longitudinal study, what are your options?
- What are the problems in analysing age differences or age-related change by only focusing on the average of a sample? How can a researcher provide evidence that an average represents individuals in the sample?
- Do you think quantitative research and qualitative research entail different skills? If so, what and why?

Summary points

- The field of adult development aims to describe, understand, explain and predict changes, transitions and turning points across the course of adulthood.
- Four kinds of explanation of development are possible: efficient (what leads to it?), material (what happens in the brain and body that makes it happen?), formal (what regular form does it normally take?) and final (what is its function and purpose?)
- Developmental research designs can be either synchronic (data collected at one point in time) or longitudinal (data collected over an extended period of time).
- Synchronic designs include cross-sectional, life-event focused and bio-graphical studies. Cross-sectional designs compare age groups at one point in time, life-event studies focus on a particular part of the adult life course and biographic studies use retrospective accounts of the past to reconstruct change.
- Cross-sectional designs are prone to cohort effects – that is, age differences that are due to historical differences rather than age-related differences.
- Longitudinal designs include dynamic and prospective types. Dynamic longitudinal research aims to study the trajectory of change, while pro-spective research aims to establish a predictive relation across time.
- Accelerated longitudinal designs are ways of studying longitudinal change in multiple age ranges and then combining those changes together into a composite change profile for adulthood.
- Quantitative data are often presented at the level of the sample, as mean-level change. The problem with these graphs is that means may or may not represent individual change, as described in Figure 2.1.
- There are specialist techniques for analysing longitudinal data, including latent growth-curve analysis and multi-level modelling, that provide a variety of parameters to describe change and what predicts change.
- Qualitative data is in the form of words, gained from interviews, focus groups, diaries, think-aloud exercises or any other source of text. Data can be analysed to derive or test theory, to describe experiences, to develop content categories and to explore the use of narrative and story-telling in adult development.
- Quantitative methods and qualitative methods have complementary roles in the study of adult development, as they both contribute to com-plementary aspects of description, explanation and prediction.

Recommended reading

Baltes, P. B. & Nesselroade, J. R. (1979). History and rationale of longitudinal research. In J. R. Nesselroade & P. B. Baltes (eds) *Longitudinal Research in the Study of Behavior and Development* (pp. 1–39). New York: Academic Press.

Bryk, A. S. & Raudenbush, S. W. (1987). Application of hierarchical linear models to assessing change. *Psychological Bulletin*, 101, 147–158.

Howitt, D. (2010). *Introduction to Qualitative Methods in Psychology*. London: Prentice Hall.

Killeen, P. R. (2001). The four causes of behaviour. *Current Directions in Psychological Science*, 10, 136–140.

Lerner, R. M., Schwartz, S. J. & Phelps, E. (2009). Problematics of time and timing in the longitudinal study of human development: Theoretical and methodological issues. *Human Development*, 52, 44–68.

McAdams, D. P. (2001). The psychology of life stories. *Review of General Psychology*, 5, 100–122.

Nesselroade, J. & Ram, N. (2004). Studying intraindividual variability: What we have learned that will help us understand lives in context. *Research in Human Development*, 1, 9–29.

Ruspini, E. (2002). *Introduction to Longitudinal Research*. New York: Routledge.

Schaie, K. W. (1965). A general model for the study of developmental problems. *Psychological Bulletin*, 64, 92–107.

Schaie, K. W. & Baltes, P. B. (1975). On sequential strategies in developmental research. *Human Development*, 18, 384–390.

Recommended website

The following webpage provides a detailed description of life story interviewing, guided autobiography and other scales and methods: http://www.sesp. northwestern.edu/foley/instruments/

3

Cognitive Development

The man who views the world at 50 the same as he did at 20 has wasted 30 years of his life.

Muhammad Ali

Melissa had two children when she was in her late twenties. She decided to give up her full-time career to focus on being a mother, at least until the children were of school age. Over the ensuing five years, her cognitive abilities changed noticeably. She described being more forgetful than she was prior to having the children, which she attributed to the ongoing tiredness that comes with disrupted sleep and the constant care that young children require. She also noticed that her knowledge of current affairs significantly declined, as she found less time to read the newspaper and keep in touch with global events. On the flipside, she said that her ability to 'multi-task' had improve markedly – she was better able at managing competing priorities on her time and to combine doing a task while keeping her attention on the children. She envisaged a time after the children had got older when she would maybe enrol in an adult educational course that would help her re-engage the analytical cognitive abilities that she had excelled in during her twenties, but which she thought had declined since she had become a mother.

Research on cognitive development in adulthood is presented in this chapter in two parts. The first part presents the 'Neo-Piagetian' paradigm, which studies the emergence of new ways of thinking and solving problems over time. The second half presents the psychometric paradigm to studying cognitive ageing, which studies quantitative change in cognitive ability over adulthood, by way of scores on IQ tests, reaction time tests and memory tests.

The Neo-Piagetian paradigm

Based on six decades of research with children, Jean Piaget developed a stage theory of child cognitive development, which states that as they grow up, children develop new capacities for problem-solving and knowledge that permit a more complex and accurate view of the real world. Piaget (1994) viewed cognitive development as a process that heads in a particular direction – towards integrated complexity. This occurs by way of two interacting processes, termed 'assimilation' and 'accommodation'. When a child learns or perceives new things that fit their existing cognitive assumptions and ideas, *assimilation* occurs, whereas when new facts upset a child's cognitive order, *accommodation* of these facts must occur by re-arranging cognitive schemas. For a comprehensive review of Piaget's child development theory, read Flavell (1963), or for a briefer summary, read Wadsworth (1996). To provide a brief context for discussing the Piagetian approach to adult development, it is important to understand Piaget's final stage of child development – the stage of *formal operational thinking* – for it is the springboard for adult thinking.

This form of thinking emerges around the beginning of the teenage years, and is the result of the emergence of a number of new mental capacities. One new ability that appears at this stage is *internalised problem-solving*, which occurs through the combined use of internal reasoning, logic, imagination and planning strategies (Inhelder & Piaget, 1958). Thanks to this internalised thinking, a formal-operational child can for the first time employ highly abstract operations, such as formulae, algebra, metaphor, and can start to think in terms of causality, theories and systems of ideas (Piaget, 1994).

Another key formal-operational ability is the capacity to have hypotheses about actions before acting; to consider what is *possible* and *likely* prior to testing out that prediction through trial-and-error. This permits the teenager to, for the first time, accurately predict whether a course of action will lead to harm to self or others, and can therefore be avoided (Inhelder & Piaget, 1958). This ability to foresee the possible harmful consequences of actions is fundamental to the legal definition of adulthood described in Chapter 1. Along with this greater capacity to imagine, predict and idealise, adolescents also develop the capacity to reflect on the past, themselves and their own thinking – this is termed 'metacognition' (Flavell, 1996).

People are always learning or perceiving new things that challenge their understanding of the world and themselves, so in principle, development never stops (Flavell, 1963). Yet Piaget did not theorise about what emerges after formal operational thinking. He did however explicitly say that there may exist further stages beyond formal operational stage in adults (Piaget, 1972). Subsequently, a number of Neo-Piagetian researchers took up his challenge of studying adults using Piagetian methods, to explore the nature of post-formal cognition. For cognitive development to qualify as a post-formal stage, it must include new abilities and must be an advance along both the orthogenetic (that is, more complex) and veridical (that is, more accurate and truthful) directions of development (see Chapter 1 for more on the directions of adult development). Post-formal theories can be grouped into those that describe adult shifts in *epistemic cognition*, *systematic cognition* and *real-world complex problem solving*.

Epistemic cognition – Adult development models

Perry's model of intellectual development in the college years

Epistemic cognition involves thinking about knowledge itself – about what is real, what is true, what is right and what is certain. One of the first studies of epistemic cognitive development in adulthood was conducted by William Perry (1970). He conducted a four-year longitudinal study with a cohort of 84 college students, interviewing them every year for four years. Students were asked about their experience of studying, their views on knowledge and truth, and their moral values. The data were submitted to a qualitative theoretical analysis, and from this a model was developed that specified how students typically develop in terms of epistemic cognition over their time at university.

The developmental trajectory that Perry described is shown in Table 3.1. It starts with *dualistic* thinking, then moves on to *multiplistic* thinking, then to *relativistic* thinking, then finally to acceptance of pragmatic *commitments* within a relativistic worldview. Individual examples of these stages are given in Box 3.1. While most students showed progression forwards through these stages, Perry also observed a minority of individuals who changed back to earlier stages, showing that progression is not inevitable.

Perry's model was based on the accounts of Harvard students in the late 1960s, and has been replicated in other samples and at different times since the original study (Gilligan & Murphy, 1979; Dawson, 2004). A potential criticism of the theory is that it was based on a sample comprised mostly of social science students, and relativistic thinking is a hallmark of much theory in the social sciences. In a sample comprised of science students or mathematics students, it may be that relativistic thinking would emerge over the course of university less frequently.

Table 3.1   Perry's stages of epistemic cognitive development during the college years

1	Dualistic thinking	Knowledge is true or false, and actions are right or wrong. Right answers for everything exist, and authorities hold correct views on this knowledge.
2	Multiplistic thinking	Diversity of opinion is perceived as legitimate, more uncertainty is found in knowledge, differences in 'good expression' perceived, people have a right to their own opinion.
3	Relativistic thinking	All knowledge and values are perceived as contextual and relativistic. Dualistic right / wrong thinking is relegated to structured problem-solving such as maths, but is also viewed as resting on assumptions.
4	Committed thinking	Personal commitments to values, theories and goals are taken, despite understanding that they are not absolute or perfect.

Box 3.1   Individual voices

Example responses from the four developmental levels within Perry's scheme (Perry, 1970)

Dualistic thinking

Well, in high school we took a course like that, a history course. In that course the teacher would be telling you exact facts and here it's altogether different. I don't know. I like it better when they ... give you something concrete, exactly what happened – not go off on a tangent on some phase that appears on the surface not to have anything to do with the subject. I don't particularly care for that. So that's the way with almost all the courses that I've come in contact with ... They know more than me, so who am I to argue? (p. 76)

Multiplistic thinking

Another thing I've noticed ... if you try to use the approach the course outlines, then you find yourself thinking in complex terms: weighing more than one factor in trying to develop your own opinion. Somehow, for me, just doing that has become extended beyond the courses ... Somehow what I think about things now seems to be more – ah, it's hard to say right or wrong – but it seems (pause) more sensible. (p. 100)

Box 3.1   Continued

Relativistic thinking

You see I've got myself into the position that any relativist gets into ... if you don't have an absolute truth, what is truth? And I don't know. (Laughs) And if you don't ... have some sort of a standard outside of yourself, what is going to be your standard? And so I don't really have one, and admittedly I'm in a lot of difficult problems ... the only thing that I can even argue on is the value of emotional responses. That is where my, my relativism has taken me. (p. 130)

Committed thinking

There are so many values you can't possibly line up all of them ... you pick out something that you kind of like after a while, rather than trying to do what you see is being liked. I mean, you come here, and you get a total view of everything, and you see a whole lot of values ... Every one of them is a good thing in its own way and so you instinctively want to be at least a little bit aware and take part in all of them. But you can't ... You kind of focus on the type of career you want and when you think about that ... it means you have to drop certain things and focus more on others. (p. 156)

Dialectical thinking: Embracing paradox

A defining feature of the later stages of development in Perry's scheme is the importance of embracing the paradoxes and contradictions in values and knowledge. Other theorists have suggested that this involves a process called *dialectical thinking* (Basseches, 1980; Kramer, Kahlbaugh & Goldston, 1992; Riegel, 1973). Dialectical thinking involves cognitively considering *dualisms* or *opposites* (for example, particular-general, true-false, good-bad, cause-effect, better-worse, independent-dependent, certainty-uncertainty). It approaches truth and knowledge on the assumption that mentally constructed opposites mean paradoxes and contradictions are inevitable. It seeks to transcend them through the process of creative synthesis and 'both-and' solutions. A dialectical solution is found when a higher-level synthesis between opposing concepts can be found that meaningfully embraces *both* of them (Kramer, Kahlbaugh & Goldston, 1992; Riegel, 1973).

An example from contemporary physics helps to illustrate dialectical thinking (Riegel, 1973). The current view of electrons and photons is that they exist as *both* a wave *and* a particle, even though waves and particles act differently and have different physical effects. Mysteriously, these tiny subatomic entities behave as a particle when they are observed or measured, but as a wave otherwise. This is referred to as the *wave/particle paradox*. It illustrates a principle that is observable at all scales of reality – that some dualisms are unsolvable, so need to be embraced rather than reduced to one side or the other (Riegel, 1973; Sameroff, 2010).

The reflective judgement model

King and Kitchener furthered research into epistemic cognition using a similar interview-based procedure to Perry (Kitchener & King, 1981; Kitchener et al., 1989). They carried out longitudinal and cross-sectional research with their technique, termed the *Reflective Judgment Interview (RJI)*. In this interview, the following four problems representing science, social science, religion and history are presented to participants:

1. Most historians claim that the pyramids were built as tombs for kings by the ancient Egyptians, using human labour, and aided by ropes, pulleys, and rollers. Others have suggested that the Egyptians could not have built such huge structures by themselves, for they had neither the mathematical knowledge, the necessary tools, nor an adequate source of power.
2. Many religions of the world have creation stories. These stories suggest that a divine being created the earth and its people. Scientists claim, however, that people evolved from lower animal forms (some of which are similar to apes) into the human forms known today.
3. There have been frequent reports about the relationship between chemicals that are added to foods and the safety of these foods. Some studies indicate that such chemicals can cause cancer, making these foods unsafe to eat. Other studies, however, show that chemical additives are not harmful, and actually make the foods containing them safer to eat.
4. The safety of nuclear energy is currently being debated by scientists in many fields. Some scientists believe that nuclear energy is safe and that nuclear energy can alleviate our dependence on non-renewable resources. Others argue that nuclear energy is

unsafe and that nuclear energy plants will lead to widespread and long-term environmental pollution.

Responses to these problems are probed by the following series of standardised questions that aim to access epistemic cognitions:

1. What do you think about this?
2. How did you come to hold that point of view?
3. On what do you base that point of view?
4. Can you ever know for sure that your position on this issue is correct?
5. When two people differ about matters such as this, is it the case that one opinion is right and one is wrong? If yes, what do you mean by 'right'? If no, can you say that one opinion is in some way better than the other?
6. What do you mean by 'better'?
7. How is it possible that people have such different views about this subject?
8. How is it possible that experts in the field disagree about this subject?

Using this methodology, seven epistemic cognitive stages were established in longitudinal data and cross-sectional samples across adolescent and young adult students (King & Kitchener, 2002). These stages can be categorised into three periods, as described next.

Pre-reflective Reasoning

- *Stage 1* is defined by absolutist assumptions about the nature of knowledge: There is a single, concrete system of knowledge and belief, both of which are determined, without uncertainty. Knowledge can be gained with certainty by way of observation.
- *Stage 2* modifies this with the assumption that knowledge is incomplete because not everyone has access to it.
- *Stage 3* then adds to this that even legitimate authorities may not know things with certainty.

Quasi-reflective Reasoning

- *Stage 4* sees that knowledge is inherently uncertain, because we always have incomplete information.
- *Stage 5* is the same as Perry's relativism stage: objective knowledge does not exist and we can only know within a context through subjective interpretation of data. Beliefs are justified within a context by the rules of inquiry for that context.

Reflective Reasoning

- *Stage 6* views some judgements as better than others, despite the contextual nature of inquiry. Some viewpoints are seen as more rational, reasonable, evidenced or well-founded than others in a way that is not entirely contextually specific.
- *Stage 7* considers that an *evolving truth* is possible by way of critical thinking, comparing and contrasting existing views and aiming for constant justification of one's own position.

This stage model supports the basic trajectory of Perry's model, in that it describes moving from absolutist views of knowledge to a more multiplistic view, then to a relativistic position, and finally to a position in which the absolute and the relative can be balanced (Perry, 1970). The model has more stages than Perry's model, which may relate to the broader age range of the sample, which included high-school students and graduate students. In a review of studies that used the RJI, it was found that high-school students consistently emphasised pre-reflective thinking, undergraduate students were normally in Stages 3 and 4, while graduate students typically showed Stage 5 and upwards (King & Kitchener, 1994).

The Social Paradigm Belief Inventory (SPBI)

Research into epistemic cognition has mainly used interviews and think-aloud protocols as the method of investigation, but questionnaires have also been developed. *The Social Paradigm Belief Inventory* (SPBI) is a psychometric assessment of paradigms of thinking, including absolutist, relativistic and dialectical thinking (Kramer, Kahlbaugh & Goldston, 1992). Participants are asked to rate their agreement with items such as: 'There can be a perfect society. This is because there is a right order to things; however it is our task to discover what this order is and put it into action' (absolute thinking); and 'There can never be a perfect society. This is because everyone has a different conception of what such a society would be like, and there can never be enough consensus on what to work toward' (dialectical thinking).

Cross-sectional research using the SPBI has found that relativistic thinking is at its peak during college years, and then declines with age thereafter. Dialectical thinking increases in prevalence between college age and young adulthood, and then remains at the same level into old age (Kramer, Kahlbaugh & Goldston, 1992). However research is lacking to suggest whether or not this change occurs in non-college attenders. High scores on the SPBI have been shown to predict various useful traits and capacities such as greater creativity (Yang, Wan & Chiou, 2010), more effective conflict resolution (Kramer, 1989) and lower levels of cognitive bias (Follett & Hess, 2002).

The Model of Hierarchical Complexity

An influential theory of postformal thinking has been developed by Michael Lamport Commons and colleagues, termed the *Model of Hierarchical Complexity* (Commons, 2008). It shares the assumption of the epistemic cognition models that more complex cognitive stages emerge in adulthood, but is based on a mathematical model of what complexity means. The model postulates four cognitive stages that are progressively more hierarchically complex than formal operations: these are *systematic, metasystematic, paradigmatic* and *cross-paradigmatic* (Commons & Ross, 2008). Table 3.2 gives a brief description of these four postformal stages.

Based on this stage model, cognitive tasks can also be rated for complexity. More complex tasks require co-ordination of more sub-tasks and sub-goals before the overall goal of completion or solution can be accomplished, so the more complex a task, the more cognitively

Table 3.2   The four adult stages of Commons' Model of Hierarchical Complexity

1	*Systemic Stage*	At this stage a person can solve problems that have multiple causes and/or multiple solutions. It is more complex than formal operational thinking, which tends towards conceiving single causes and solutions. It has echoes of the relativistic thinking described by Perry and Kramer.
2	*Metasystematic Stage*	Those who reach this stage can compare and contrast different problems and tasks, by comparing multiple similarities and differences, in order to establish commonalities and universalities. This level brings a consideration of the relationship between different systems of thought, or worldviews.
3	*Paradigmatic Stage*	At this stage, people develop the capacity to view the fundamental assumptions underlying a particular 'metasystem' or universal principle, and so develop the capacity to 'reframe' problems in new ways or show that an existing way of understanding a problem is incomplete. This facilitates high-level thinking that can lead to major innovations.
4	*Cross-paradigmatic Stage*	After paradigmatic thinking has been mastered, an individual may go on to develop the capacity to compare, contrast and transform entire paradigms, and in so doing view an academic field, or problem type, in an entirely new way.

developed a person needs to be to complete it (Fischer & Yan, 2002). This means that successful completion of a particular task complexity can be used as an indicator of cognitive development.

Another method employed to test this model employs qualitative data with quantitative analysis. Participants are given a complex problem to solve, and are asked to write down their reasoning or speak their reasoning aloud. The transcript of this verbal reasoning is then subject to an analysis that endeavours to elicit the complexity of the argument (Dawson, 2004). A technique for achieving this task is the *Lexical Abstraction Assessment System* (LAAS) (Dawson, 2004). It analyses textual data by labelling elements within it according to eight increasingly abstract levels:

1. Sensori-motor systems (SS)
2. Single representations (SR)
3. Representational mappings (RM)
4. Representational systems (RS)
5. Single abstractions (SA)
6. Abstract mappings (corresponds to formal operations) (AM)
7. Abstract systems (corresponds to systematic operations) (AS)
8. Single principles (corresponds to metasystematic operations) (SP)

Increased complexity

Based on the presence of these elements in the text, a score is awarded to a participant's response that indicates the level of conceptual complexity in it. In a cross-sectional sample of 406 participants who were interviewed about ethical problems, an analysis using the LAAS showed a pattern of age-graded increases in complexity from childhood up to early adulthood (Dawson-Tunik et al., 2005). Those at the representational mappings level ranged between ages five and 13, those at the single abstractions level between seven and 18, those at the abstract mappings level between ten and 21, those at the abstract systems level between 17 and 23 and at the single principles level the range was 22–3. The pattern is suggestive of the emergence of higher levels of cognitive complexity in early adulthood.

Complex real-world problem-solving

The capacity to handle the complexities of real-world problems has also been proposed to be a postformal shift in adult cognitive development.

To study how adults reason through real-world tasks, Sinnott & Johnson (1997) presented a variety of problems to university research administrators, including the following problem:

> You are administering a $2 million project with funding from a pharmaceutical company and a government funding body. The grant has a 2-year timetable and there are just 2 months left before a final report must be submitted. One graduate student on the team has been convicted of possession of cocaine in the last few weeks. Another graduate student has left for another job and taken much of the data with him. The original data is necessary to file a complete report. What do you do? What do you say to the funders?

Real-world problems such as this one contain features that differentiate them from standard cognitive ability tasks. While standard cognitive ability problems, such as those found in an IQ test, have pre-defined correct solutions, real-world problems are open-ended, unstructured, or 'ill-defined'. Defining the nature of the problem itself is therefore central to solving ill-structured problems, for until that happens it is often not apparent what needs to be solved. Instead of a single solution, a real-world problem will have a number of possible solutions that have pros and cons for different people involved. Based on her research into real-world problem-solving in adolescents and adults, Jan Sinnott (1998) concluded that real-world postformal thinking involves using a number of strategic abilities. These include the following:

1. The capacity to shift between different views of a situation.
2. The ability to adopt multiple theories about the causes, nature and solution of a problem.
3. The willingness to engage in *process-product shifts*, which means being able to switch between seeing things in the process of change, and seeing things statically as structures.
4. The capacity to create and utilise multiple goals, multiple solutions and multiple methods to move through the situation or problem.
5. The ability to work with paradox, for in real-world problems, contradictions and tensions are inevitable.

Harnessing these skills improves communication and relationships with others, creativity and mental flexibility, and promotes tolerance of alternative perspectives (Sinnott, 1998). These skills can be trained – Box 3.2 presents a story that is used as part of an education programme to get young people to think about real-world situations in post-formal ways (Sinnott, 1998).

Additional challenges of real-world problems are their socially-embedded and emotionally charged nature (Sinnott, 1991). Typically, a complex real-world problem will involve multiple persons, all of whom have concerns, agendas and feelings to consider. Linear logic is not of much use in this instance – such problems require social intuitions and interpersonal judgements about whose feelings are more important than others and where the greater good lies. Furthermore, real-world problems have emotion-inducing implications and consequences, and a major challenge is that one must try to retain clarity of thought and decision-making despite the emotional pressures of real life (Sinnott, 1991; Blanchard-Fields, Jahnke & Camp, 1995).

Box 3.2   Alternative perspectives

The farmer's horse story

Sinnott (1998) suggests that the following story can be used to help train postformal thinking. What features of the story do you think reflect postformal thinking and why?

A farmer's horse has disappeared. The farmer's neighbour comes to commiserate, saying 'I pity you! What terrible luck!'

'You never can tell,' replies the farmer.

Soon the horse returns, leading another wild horse! 'What good fortune!' says the neighbour, 'You now have _two_ horses!'

'You never can tell,' replies the farmer.

Soon the farmer's firstborn decides to break the wild horse and is immediately thrown from the ground, breaking his leg badly. 'How awful, what terrible luck you've had! And you're so poor already!' laments the concerned friend, who knows quite well that farms need every worker, and more.

'You never call tell,' replies the farmer, who is beginning to acquire a reputation for being a man of few words.

The very next day, the Cossacks ride into the village and conscript every able-bodied soldier they can find. Young people with broken legs are not selected! The farmer smiles, but not as broadly as the neighbour does. 'What amazing luck, how fortunate you were to be able to save your child when so many were taken!'

Of course, the farmer replies 'You never can tell.'

What do these post-formal theories have in common?

The epistemic, systematic and real-world problem-solving theories of adult cognition presented earlier are all based on the idea that adults develop new ways of understanding and knowing that make them qualitatively different from adolescent cognition. While the theories are clearly different in detail, Kallio (2011) has proposed that the common denominator underpinning them is a shift towards *integrative ability*. In epistemic cognition, integrative ability is manifest in successively higher-level co-ordination of ideas within a person's worldview and personal philosophy. In the hierarchical complexity of task performance, it is shown in an adult's developing ability to co-ordinate small-scale tasks into higher-order tasks and to draw together concepts into systems and paradigms; while in real-world problem-solving, integrative ability is shown in the capacity to combine logical thinking with emotional regulation, empathic abilities, practical judgements and social cognition. Therefore the different post-formal stage theories may in fact be different phenotypic manifestations of the same journey towards integration and wholeness that is characteristic of the 'orthogenetic' direction of adult development, described in Chapter 1.

The psychometric paradigm of cognitive ageing

The psychometric paradigm of cognitive ageing investigates how performance on IQ tests changes over the course of adult life. It also studies the effects of interventions aimed at boosting aspects of IQ in different age groups. IQ tests focus on logical reasoning, general knowledge, memory and perceptual skills, using puzzles and questions that are easy to administer and easy to score. They don't include tests of creativity, movement-based ability (for example, dance or sport) or interpersonal/emotional intelligence, for these other abilities are more problematic and time-consuming to test and are traditionally considered to be forms of talent, not intelligence.

There is currently a consensus that psychometric intelligence involves a combination of general and specific abilities. Both Carroll (1993) and McGrew (1997) suggest a three-level hierarchical model, at the top of which sits general intelligence or 'g', which is required to varying degrees in most cognitive tasks. At the level below g, the following abilities are located:

1. Crystallised intelligence (breadth and depth of acquired knowledge)
2. Fluid intelligence (reasoning and solving unfamiliar problems)
3. Short-term memory
4. Long-term memory
5. Processing speed
6. Quantitative/numerical ability
7. Linguistic ability (reading / writing)

Below these seven generic abilities, Carroll's model locates a third tier of task-specific abilities (Carroll, 1993; McGrew, 1997). It is the level of the seven broad abilities listed previously that has been the main focus of research on cognitive ageing in adulthood. Next I summarise cross-sectional and longitudinal findings on how such abilities vary across the adult years, and discuss various theories that attempt to explain why age-related changes occur. Finally, the effects of physical and cognitive interventions to improve cognitive performance in adulthood are discussed.

The Seattle Longitudinal Study (SLS)

Led by K. Warner Schaie and Sherry Willis, the Seattle Longitudinal Study (SLS) has been investigating changes in cognitive abilities across the adult lifespan and across generational cohorts for over half a century. Since 1956, every seven years the study has assessed cognitive abilities in a cross-section of adults between the ages of 25 and 88. Each cohort has then been followed up longitudinally every seven years for repeated assessments (Schaie, 1996).

For each cognitive ability assessment, participants in the SLS complete the *Primary Mental Abilities Test* (PMA), which measures *inductive reasoning, spatial orientation, number skills, verbal ability (meaning & fluency), perceptual speed* and *memory* (Thurstone, 1943). These are similar to the second tier abilities in the Carroll three-tier model (Carroll, 1993). The tests are typical of IQ assessments; they involve being shown words, numbers or abstract shapes, and being asked to memorise them or find a solution to a problem.

The SLS website, the address for which is given at the end of this chapter, gives a comprehensive list of all the publications based on the SLS data. Here, the most widely publicised findings are discussed – the cross-sectional and longitudinal age differences in the primary cognitive abilities. Cross-sectional data from the 1991 study are shown in Figure 3.1A – these are typical of cross-sectional findings from all phases of the SLS. The graph shows that means for reasoning, perceptual speed, spatial orientation and memory are significantly lower in older adults than in younger adults. Verbal ability and numeric ability means are highest in the middle adulthood group and show less age-related decline (Schaie, 1994).

The longitudinal data, however, tell a different story. Graph B in Figure 3.1 shows an 'accelerated longitudinal' analysis (see Chapter 2 for more on accelerated longitudinal designs). To create the lines in this graph, seven-year changes from different age groups were all aggregated together into a single line. So, for each seven-year gap (shown on x-axis), the incline between two ages represents the *average change* for all participants over that seven-year period. Each seven-year mean change is then added on to the previous one. For example if the change between 25 and 32 was on average +5 points, and the change between 32 and 39 was also +5 points, then the graph would place these one after the other to show an average ten-point increase over the 14-year spread. This 'tip-to-toe' approach leads to a smooth growth curve, based on eight seven-year longitudinal change calculations. The accelerated longitudinal findings show a more positive picture in relation to ageing than the cross-sectional findings; perceptual speed peaks in early adulthood, but the remaining abilities peak in late midlife. No other cognitive ability declines significantly before the age of 60 (Schaie, 1996).

The data in Figure 3.1 show that cross-sectional and longitudinal data do not always agree (Schaie, 1965). The cross-sectional data show a more pronounced decline than the longitudinal data due to a *cohort effect* – individuals born earlier in the twentieth century do worse on intelligence tests than those born more recently. This cohort effect has been labelled the Flynn effect after the philosopher James Flynn who has studied it intensively. It partly explains why age differences in the cross-sectional data are more pronounced – the younger group do better not solely because of their age but because of this historical improvement in IQ performance (Flynn, 1999).

The longitudinal data show less decline over adulthood than the cross-sectional findings, however there are questions over the validity of the longitudinal results, due to the possibility of practice effects. Individuals in the longitudinal study took the cognitive tests every seven years in identical form across their adult life, so it is likely that they became practiced at completing them and may have even remembered questions from previous assessments. This would mean that later test scores were artificially enhanced through practice, which may account for the less pronounced age-related decline.

The mean-level differences that are shown in Figures 3.1 are the most well-known of the SLS findings, and are frequently shown in textbooks on cognitive development. However, Schaie (1996) warns against exclusive focus on mean-level change statistics. He points out that mean-level graphs are average patterns that do not reflect any particular person, and that in the SLS data, almost every possible age-related permutation was observed at the level of the individual (Schaie, 1996). Furthermore, a mean may not even reflect the majority of the sample, for example Schaie and Willis (2002) found in the SLS data that despite the mean-level longitudinal decline between the ages of 74 and 81, 60 per cent of the sample maintain their intellectual functioning between these ages and do not decline. The changes in the mean are in fact due to the *minority* of the sample who are declining, while the rest remain stable.

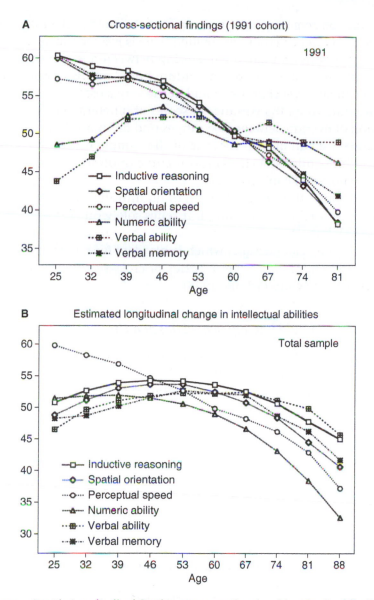

Figure 3.1 Seattle Longitudinal Study – cross-sectional and longitudinal findings
Source: Schaie (1994, p. 306). Copyright © American Psychological Association. Reprinted with permission.

Schaie and Willis (2002) suggest considering an additional statistic to complement the mean-level change data – the *degree of ability overlap* between age ranges. In the SLS, this overlap is considerable; for example, when comparing those aged 81 with those aged 25 year, there is a 75 per cent overlap in verbal meaning scores, a 99 per cent overlap in numeracy scores and a 93 per cent overlap in word fluency scores. This degree of overlap suggests that many 80-year-olds will perform better than

25-year-olds on cognitive tasks. It shows that chronological age by itself is *not* a basis for inferring cognitive ability; there is just too much variability within age groups and too much overlap between age groups to make any useful assertion about an individual based on his/her age alone. Therefore, mean-level changes should at the very least by complemented with information on the variance of scores at different ages, or with an indication of overlap between age ranges and an indication of how representative a mean growth curve is of the sample as a whole. Recent statistical innovations, such as growth curve analysis and hierarchical modelling now make this possible.

The SLS shows that in the domain of quantitative cognitive ageing, research may well be misleading if it relies solely on cross-sectional *or* longitudinal data. Designs that combine both are preferable – for instance Schaie's 'most efficient design', which is his ideal for robust quantitative ageing research. This involves a series of cross-sectional studies and longitudinal follow-ups (Schaie, 1965).

Crystallised and fluid intelligence – Lifespan changes

Crystallised and fluid intelligence are two forms of cognitive ability that were originally proposed by Cattell (1971) to be the most general dimensions of intelligence, and are included as two of the second-tier abilities within Carroll's hierarchical model (McGrew, 1997; 2009). They can be defined as follows:

- **Fluid intelligence** (Gf) pertains to the capacity to solve novel problems and to employ forms of inductive/deductive reasoning. Quiz shows on TV that get people to solve unusual problems, such as 'The Krypton Factor', 'The Cube' or 'The Crystal Maze' are tests of fluid intelligence.
- **Crystallised intelligence** (Gc) is the store of information that has been acquired through education and experience. It is typically assessed by psychologists using vocabulary tests. Quiz shows such as 'Mastermind', 'Jeopardy' and 'The Weakest Link', which require people to recall information, are tests of this kind of intelligence.

The relation of these two abilities to adult age is different. Horn and Cattell (1967) studied a cross-section of adults between adolescence and old age and found that fluid intelligence was higher in younger adults than older adults, while crystallised intelligence was higher in older adults. More recent research has replicated this (Baltes & Lindenberger, 1997; Ronnlund and Nilsson, 2006). An explanation proposed for this finding is that fluid intelligence is more dependent on biological hardware, and therefore declines with age-related physical decline, while crystallised intelligence is more influenced by environmental factors and experience, and therefore continues to accumulate across adulthood and is less susceptible to age-related decline (McArdle et al., 2002).

McArdle et al. (2002) employed an accelerated longitudinal design to assess change in fluid and crystallised ability across the whole lifespan. 1193 participants between the ages of two and 95 years completed the *Woodcock–Johnson Psycho-Educational Battery–Revised*, as part of the process of developing norms for the test, and were tested a second time between one and ten years later. Fluid reasoning was measured by way of two tests; the first was a concept formation task in which a rule must be derived that links elements together and the second was a task in which the missing components of a pattern must be inferred. Crystallised intelligence was assessed by way of two kinds of vocabulary test.

The two graphs from McCardle et al.'s study are reproduced in Figure 3.2. Each graph shows a smoothed age curve for fluid ability (Gf) and crystallised ability (Gc), with lines above and beneath representing 95 per cent confidence intervals. All individual change trajectories are shown as well – this provides an immediate sense of the individual level variability that underpins the group-level line. The graphs show that during childhood, upward trajectories are rapid and universal for both abilities, but once in adulthood, upward and downward individual trajectories can occur at all age ranges. Overall, fluid intelligence has a slower initial growth rate, an earlier peak and a faster decline, while crystallised ability shows continued growth up to the age of 30 and then a flatter profile through adulthood. This fits with previous findings, and also shows how individual-level change is often not accurately represented at the mean level.

Perceptual speed and processing speed

The speed of any system, whether it is a computer, a supply chain, a postal system or a nervous system, affects how well it functions. The processing speed theory of cognitive ageing proposes that as adults grow older, the speed at which their nervous system operates slows, and that this slowing affects a wide array of abilities and tasks (Birren & Fisher, 1995; Fozard et al., 1994; Salthouse, 1996; Madden, 2001). It has therefore been suggested that age-related declines in task speed may be an indirect measure of age-related declines in the efficiency of the nervous system (Vercruyssen, 1993). Certain tasks are considered to be particularly good measures of speed, as the key challenge in completing them is speed

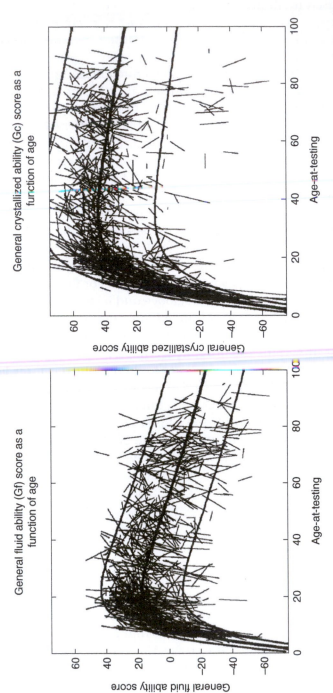

Figure 3.2 A comparison of multilevel age curves for fluid and crystallised intelligence, based on longitudinal intervals one–ten years long

Source: McCardle et al. (2002, p. 133). Copyright © American Psychological Association. Reprinted with permission.

of perception and response (Deary, Johnson & Starr, 2010; Der & Deary, 2006; Salthouse, 1996). These include:

- *Simple reaction time* – The task is to press a button as quickly as possible after a visual or auditory stimulus is presented.
- *Choice reaction time* – The task is to press one of a selection of buttons as quickly as possible after a light has flashed from a matched array – for example, lights labelled 1–4 and buttons labelled 1–4.
- *Inspection time* – The task is to discriminate between the lengths of two lines that are flashed up on a screen, by pressing one of two buttons to indicate the longest line. The lines are presented at ever-decreasing durations, and there is no timing of the actual response. The speed is in the perception, not the response.
- *The Digit Symbol Substitution* Test – Rows of double boxes are presented across a page with a digit in the top box and nothing in the bottom box. A code table specifies a symbol to match each digit. The task is to insert the matching symbols as quickly as possible.

Choice reaction time requires monitoring and selection of alternatives, while simple reaction time does not, therefore the former is a more complex task than the latter. Der and Deary (2006) analysed cross-sectional data on these two kinds of reaction time from 7216 individuals aged 18 to 82. The means for two-year age groups across that age span are shown in Figure 3.3.

The graph shows that simple reaction time does not show any mean-level decline until the age of 60, and after the age of 70 there is an exponential slowing, which is more pronounced in women. Choice reaction time declines in a linear and constant fashion across adulthood in this cross-sectional dataset. This suggests that simple reaction time, which is a more pure measure of speed, is more resilient to ageing than choice reaction time. The study also found that the intra-individual standard deviation for response time increased with age too, for both kinds of reaction time, suggesting that the older people get, the more erratic their responding gets. These cross-sectional age-related findings were given further support by findings from an 8-year longitudinal study (Deary & Der, 2005).

The processing speed theory of ageing

The processing speed theory of cognitive ageing suggests that the slowing of information processing capacity with age is a basic and causative factor behind many other cognitive ageing phenomena (Birren & Fisher,

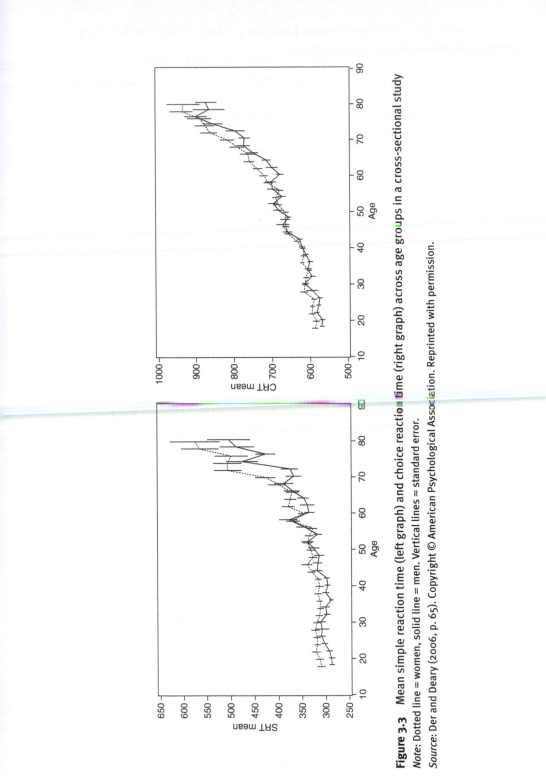

Figure 3.3 Mean simple reaction time (left graph) and choice reaction time (right graph) across age groups in a cross-sectional study

Note: Dotted line = women, solid line = men. Vertical lines = standard error.

Source: Der and Deary (2006, p. 65). Copyright © American Psychological Association. Reprinted with permission.

1995; Salthouse, 1996). Salthouse (1996) proposes two mechanisms by which slowing affects intellectual functioning more generally:

1. The *limited time* mechanism: As a result of cognitive operations occurring more slowly, the final product of intellectual processes is impaired. Salthouse gives the analogy of a car assembly line, in which if a single operation is not finished in time, this creates difficulties further down the line and in the finished car.
2. The *simultaneity* mechanism: In complex problem-solving, a large amount of information is worked on simultaneously. If that information is processed more slowly, that can lead to a bottleneck that reduces the quality of higher level thinking, leading to a higher rate of errors or repetitions. Salthouse's analogy for this process is juggling, a task for which there are no deadlines or time limits, but which requires quick perceptions and quick responses because there is a lot going on at once.

Processing speed theory is supported by neurological evidence (Dennis & Cabeza, 2008). The evidence stems from analysis of *white matter* in the brain. White matter appears white because it is composed primarily of axons covered by fatty myelin sheaths. Myelin enhances the speed and efficiency of transmission of impulses down the axons, and any deterioration in the myelin sheaths slows axon conduction. There are ways of assessing the integrity of white matter, for example a form of imaging termed *diffusion tensor imaging* (DTI). Research has found that deterioration of white matter occurs with age, and that it correlates with response times, suggesting that age-related slowing may be due to gradual decline in the quality of white matter with age (Madden et al., 2004). More recently, research has suggested that it is specifically in the anterior brain areas, such as the frontal lobes, that white-matter decline is associated with perceptual slowing (Kennedy & Raz, 2009).

Other cognitive theories of age-related decline

The processing speed theory of cognitive ageing is just one of a number of cognitive theories put forward to explain decreases in abilities in old age. Three other theories are the *sensory deficit theory*, the *attentional deficit theory* and the *inhibition deficit theory*. For a comprehensive review of these theories, see Dennis and Cabeza (2008).

Sensory deficit theory states that age-induced decline in vision and hearing leads to cognitive decline. Evidence for the sensory deficit theory is mainly based on research showing strong correlations between sensory and cognitive abilities (Baltes & Lindenberger, 1997). Neurological evidence also supports this theory, as there is an age-related decrease in activity in sensory areas of the brain with age (Cabeza et al., 2004).

Attentional deficit theory (also called resources deficit theory) postulates that ageing is associated with a reduction in the amount of attentional capacity, which results from reduction in frontal lobe efficiency (Craik, 1986). A corollary of this is the *environmental support hypothesis*, which states that age-related differences are smaller when there is an environment that is structured to reduce distractions and attentional demands (Craik, 1986). See McDowd & Shaw (2000) for a review of this theory.

Inhibition deficit theory locates the source of cognitive decline in working memory, specifically the failure to inhibit irrelevant information from being processed (Hasher & Zacks, 1988). When there is an inhibitory deficit, too much information enters working memory, and leads to mental clutter that clogs up the system. Research that supports this hypothesis shows that older adults do make more indirect associations, and remember more irrelevant information than younger adults (for a review, see Zacks, Hasher & Li, 2000).

In summary, there are all kinds of ways that cognitive decline may manifest in old age. However some real-world abilities seem to be remarkably age-resilient, and it is to these that we turn next.

Real-world age-resilient abilities

Crosswords and typing

Declines shown in cognitive test ability do not necessarily correspond to declines in real-world abilities and activities, because factors such as motivation, persistence and personality also influence real-world functioning and performance (Salthouse, 2004). Crossword puzzles are an example of a task that, even when done in a timed setting, shows no evidence of age-related decline. Salthouse (2004) gained cross-sectional adult data from four studies on timed crossword performance. Crossword enthusiasts were given 15 minutes to answer as many crossword questions from the New York Times as possible. Across the studies, the peak performing age groups were 50–9, 60–9 and 70–9, showing that this ability is one that peaks late.

In another series of studies, Salthouse (1984) studied age-related differences in typing ability. 74 skilled touch-typists between the ages of 19 and 72 participated. They were given a typing task as well as a non-typing choice reaction time task. It was found that older typists were slower in choice reaction time but not in speed of typing, because they were more able to read ahead and process letters in advance than younger typists. Figure 3.4 shows the age-related difference patterns in

choice reaction time and typing speed in the second of Salthouse's studies reported in his 1984 paper. Salthouse concluded that older typists had
compensated for slower perceptual speed by the use of a different, less
speed-dependent process. Based on this he suggested that the creative
use of compensatory cognitive mechanisms by older adults can offset or
prevent decline in task performance.

Work performance

Many of the cognitive abilities measured using psychometric tests peak
in early adulthood (Salthouse, 2012). However those in the most senior
positions in companies tend to be in their fifties and sixties and work performance in a CEO role tends to peak around the age of 60 (Salthouse,
2012). Furthermore, in a meta-analysis of age and job performance
across multiple professions, the correlation between them was 0.06,

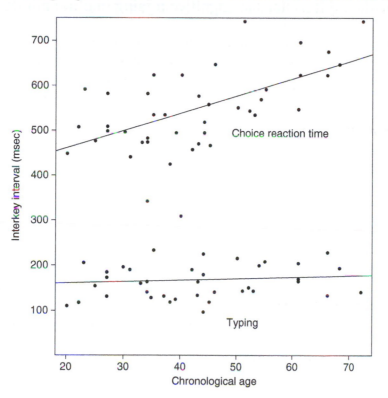

Figure 3.4   Choice reaction times and typing speed (interkey interval in milliseconds)
by age in a cross-sectional sample

Note: Each point represents a single person, and the solid lines illustrate regression
equations.

Source: Salthouse (1984, p . 355). Copyright © American Psychological Association. Reprinted
with permission.

suggesting almost no systematic relation (McEvoy & Cascio, 1989). What might account for this age-related disparity between cognitive ability scores and work performance? Salthouse (2012) puts forward a number of explanations. Firstly, he states it may be due to the influence of factors such as personality, motivation and emotional intelligence that influence work performance but are not assessed in psychometric intelligence tests. Secondly, it may be that the kinds of novel 'mental gymnastics' required by cognitive ability tests are not actually required in work settings, where individuals can rely more on their acquired knowledge. Finally, it may be that individuals find ways of compensating for age-related cognitive losses in a work environment. In Chapter 5, this issue is revisited in the discussion of Selection, Optimisation and Compensation (SOC) theory, which suggests strategies for maintaining performance in older age.

Individual differences in cognitive ageing in older adults

It is now generally accepted that despite reliable mean-level changes with age in cognitive abilities, there are all kinds of different ageing patterns at the individual level (Tucker Drob & Salthouse, 2011). Several studies have specifically focused on individual differences in cognitive change in older adults. Wilson et al. (2002a) studied cognitive changes in 694 older Catholic clergy members over a period of six years, and found that while average decline occurred in all six abilities measured (story retention, word retention, word generation, work knowledge, working memory, perceptual speed), there were individual differences that included clear cognitive improvements well into old age. Figure 3.5 shows *individual* trajectories on the six abilities for a randomly selected 25 per cent of the sample. The graphs show that individual change profiles include declines, neutral gradients and increases.

In another study, Christensen et al. (1999) tested memory, spatial ability, speed and crystallised intelligence in 426 adults over the age of 70. Participants were tested twice, with 3.5 years between assessments, and longitudinal change trajectories were computed for all individual participants. Individual diversity was clearly apparent, with some significant individual improvements occurring in all abilities up to and over the age of 90!

Who improves, who maintains, who declines in cognitive ability?

Given the fact that individuals can decline, maintain or improve their cognitive ability at all ages, the question can then be posed – what leads to improvement or decline? When the Seattle Longitudinal Study findings were analysed to search for predictors of positive cognitive ageing, the data showed both physical and psychosocial correlates. These included an absence of disease, an above-average education, occupational pursuits with high complexity and low routine, high satisfaction with life, a stable family life, reading, travel, continuing education, and participation in clubs/associations (Schaie, 1996). However, correlations do not mean causes, and these associations could be explained in number of ways – for example they could all be outcomes of socio-economic advantage. More recent research has focused on the importance of education and diet for cognitive ageing, and has taken a more experimental approach.

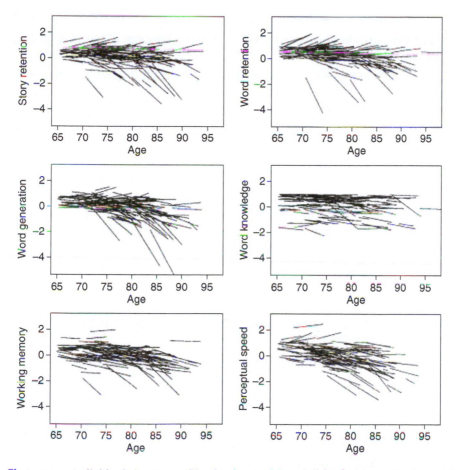

Figure 3.5   Individual change profiles in six cognitive abilities between the ages of 65 and 95

Source: Wilson et al. (2002a, p. 188). Copyright © American Psychological Association. Reprinted with permission.

Education and the cognitive reserve hypothesis

The number of years in education is one of the most reliable predictors of positive cognitive ageing. A proposed mechanism for how education influences cognitive change in adulthood is the *cognitive reserve hypothesis*. This suggests that those who have more enriched socioeconomic environments during childhood and early adulthood have more resilient cognitive and/or neurobiological architectures that protect against age-related cognitive deficits later in adulthood (Stern, 2009). However, not all studies have found this age-protective effect of education, so there is a question mark of the validity of this hypothesis (Tucker Drob & Salthouse, 2011).

Diet and cognitive ageing

A number of studies have investigated the link between diet and cognitive functioning in adults. Specific foods and dietary supplements have been studied for their capacity to protect against cognitive ageing in adulthood. In a comprehensive review of the literature, Solfrizzi, Panza and Capurso (2003) conclude that diets based on complex carbohydrates, fibre, cereals, red wine, fresh fruit and vegetables, and non-animal fat, protect against cognitive decline. Olive oil, as a source of mono-unsaturated fatty acids, was found to reduce the risk of cognitive decline. The reason that fatty acids prevent cognitive decline may be due to their structural role in neuronal membranes and neuronal transmission. Vegetables also seem to help – in a recent longitudinal study with a sample of older women, it was found that consumption of green vegetables was associated with lower levels of cognitive decline, but no association was found between fruit intake and cognitive change (Kang & Ascherio, 2005).

Ways of enhancing cognitive ability in older adults

The plasticity of adult cognitive ability has been demonstrated by a variety of intervention studies that show how cognitive and physical training can significantly improve intellectual functioning.

Cognitive training interventions

In 1983, 229 persons over the age of 64 were selected from the Seattle Longitudinal Study for participation in a training programme. This group were trained in inductive reasoning and spatial orientation – two abilities that had shown a high level of decline in older adults. Of the intervention sample, 54 per cent had already declined on at least one of these abilities, while 22 per cent of this group had declined on both measures. After evaluating the programme, it was that found that half of the training group showed improvement in their performance after the programme (Schaie, 1996).

Taking a lead from this intervention study, a major training programme was initiated across multiple locations in the USA, entitled ACTIVE (Advanced Cognitive Training for Independent and Vital Elderly) (Willis et al., 2006). 2832 older age participants participated in this programme, all of whom were over 65. Participants were randomly allocated to either a no-training control group or one of the following three intervention groups:

1. *Memory Training* – training mnemonic strategies for remembering word lists, sequences of items, text material and details of stories, over ten hours of sessions.
2. *Reasoning Training* – training strategies for reasoning tasks and everyday reasoning tasks, over ten hours of sessions.
3. *Speed of Processing Training* – training visual search skills and strategies for locating visual information quickly, over ten hours of sessions.

Self-reported and performance-based measures of cognitive ability and daily function were assessed before training, directly after training, and then one year, two years, three years and five years after the training. Relative to controls, participants increased performance in the ability targeted by the training programme, and differences were still detectable after 5 years. The reasoning training was also related to a significant increase in self-reported ability to handle activities of daily living relative to non-trained group, but performance measures of basic problem-solving did not show this improvement. Tucker Drob & Salthouse (2011) state that the intervention was of limited success due to this lack of transference of the training to performance of other daily tasks, and that the self-report data suggests that participants may have thought they were performing better in normal life but were not actually doing so.

Physical activity interventions TP

Aerobic fitness training has long been known to promote physical health in older adults (Hopkins et al., 1990). There is also now convincing evidence that this kind of training has a positive effect on cognitive functioning too (Erickson & Kramer, 2009). Colcombe and Kramer (2003) meta-analysed studies that looked at effect of physical training interventions (including aerobic exercise training or aerobic + strength training) on cognitive ability in adults over the age of 55. They grouped cognitive ability tasks into four categories – speed, visuospatial, controlled and executive processes.

The meta-analysis found that fitness training interventions increased cognitive performance in older adults on average by half a standard deviation, across all cognitive tasks (particularly those involving executive control skills such as planning, attentional control and scheduling). Training regimens that included both strength and aerobic exercises showed a stronger effect than programmes based on just aerobic exercises (Colcombe & Kramer, 2003).

Research done with mice suggests possible neurological mechanisms through which exercise exerts a positive effect on cognitive ability, including increased neurogenesis in the hippocampus and improved cellular growth more generally (Cotman, Berchtold & Christie, 2007). Brain-scan research on humans provides further support for the beneficial effects of fitness training in older adults. Colcombe et al. (2006) studied 40 individuals between 60 and 79 over the course of an aerobic exercise trial. Grey and white matter volume was computed by MRI before and after the trial. Those who participated in the aerobic fitness training showed significant increases in grey and white matter, but the control group did not. This suggests that under certain conditions, the brain can continue to grow in old age.

Concluding comments

Two influential paradigms to studying cognitive development have been presented in this chapter – the Neo-Piagetian and psychometric paradigms. These two schools have existed in parallel for many decades but rarely acknowledge each other's existence or contribution. The Neo-Piagetian paradigm has only been around since the 1970s, compared with the 1930s for psychometric research on cognitive ageing. Correspondingly, it is lacking a corpus of long-term longitudinal research across adulthood to support its claims for change, particularly studies done with middle-aged and older adults, but such studies will hopefully be forthcoming in the next decade.

Despite a lack of integration in the literature, there is a strong case for proposing that the two paradigms are complementary: the Neo-Piagetian approach looks at *qualitative* change, while the psychometric approach models *quantitative* change. Qualitative change occurs when a new ability or cognitive structure emerges that was not previously present – such a change can be found using the open-ended modes of data collection used in Neo-Piagetian research but psychometric intelligence tests are blind to such changes – they can only measure increases or decreases in pre-existing abilities. On the flipside, psychometric tests can illuminate incremental ability change that the more interpretative methods of the Neo-Piagetian paradigm cannot. Given these complementary contributions, the presence of both paradigms would seem to be ideal for an integrative lifespan developmental psychology.

Questions for you to reflect on

- Has your worldview changed since you were a teenager? In what ways? Do you think that this relates to any of the post-formal cognition models described in Part 1 of the chapter?
- Have you ever tested your reaction time? There are a number of websites that will allow you test it for free. You could experiment on yourself and see if it becomes slower as you get older.
- What kinds of cognitive ability do intelligence tests not measure? Which of these other abilities do you think would be useful in real life and why?

Summary points

- Jean Piaget stated that a phase of cognitive development termed the formal operational period is achieved in adolescence. Researchers have used variants of Piaget's approach to explore 'post-formal' developments in adulthood.
- Epistemic cognition is thinking about knowledge itself. The ability to consider alternative points of view, and so deal with 'dialectical' problems, or consider 'relativistic' points of view develops during early adulthood.
- The model of hierarchical complexity suggests that four levels of emergent cognitive complexity are possible in adulthood: systematic, metasystematic, paradigmatic and cross-paradigmatic. All of these levels entail greater ability to manage complex sets of ideas and rules.
- Real-world complex problem solving entails the ability to work with 'ill-defined' problems that involve balancing the viewpoints of others with complex possible solutions and outcomes.
- The Seattle Longitudinal Study is one of the longest ever longitudinal studies conducted on a psychological topic. For over half a century, it has accumulated data on cross-sectional age differences, longitudinal change and differences between cohorts. The overall picture from the study is that different cognitive abilities age at different rates.
- Fluid intelligence is the capacity to solve novel problems. This ability tends to decline with age in adulthood. Crystallised intelligence is general knowledge – this ability declines little with age.
- Reaction time slows with age, and the processing speed theory of cognitive ageing suggests that the slowing process underlies other age-related cognitive deficits.

- Individuals vary substantially in their cognitive ability age profile, and there are measures that can be taken to improve cognitive performance in old age, such as a diet with lots of fatty acids and green vegetables, and taking regular aerobic exercise.

Recommended reading

Birren, J. E. & Fisher, L. M. (1995). Aging and speed of behavior: Possible consequences for psychological functioning. *Annual Review of Psychology*, 46, 329–353.

Colcombe, S. J., Erickson, K. I., Scalf, P. E., Kim, J. S., Prakash, R., McAuley, E. Elavsky, S., Marquez, D. X., Hu, L., Kramer, A. F. (2006). Aerobic exercise training increases brain volume in aging humans. *The Journals of Gerontology Series A: Biological Sciences and Medical Sciences*, 61, 1166–1170.

Dawson, T. (2004). Assessing intellectual development: Three approaches, one sequence. *Journal of Adult Development*, 11, 71–85.

Der, G. & Deary, I. J. (2006). Age and sex differences in reaction time in adulthood: Results from the United Kingdom health and lifestyle survey. *Psychology and Aging*, 21, 62–73.

Kitchener, K. S., King, P. M., Wood, P. K. & Davison, M. L. (1989). Sequentiality and consistency in the development of reflective judgment: A six-year longitudinal study. *Journal of Applied Developmental Psychology*, 10, 73–95.

McArdle, J. J., Ferrer-Caja, E., Hamagami, F. & Woodcock, R. W. (2002). Comparative longitudinal structural analyses of the growth and decline of multiple intellectual abilities over the life span. *Developmental Psychology*, 38, 115–142.

Salthouse, T. A. (1984). Effects of age and skill in typing. *Journal of Experimental Psychology: General*, 113, 345–371.

Schaie, K. W. (1994). The course of adult intellectual development. *American Psychologist*, 49, 304–313.

Sinnott, J. D. (1998). *The Development of Logic in Adulthood: Postformal Thought and its Applications*. New York: Springer Publishing Co.

Tucker Drob, E. & Salthouse, T. A. (2011). Individual differences in cognitive aging. In T. S. Chamorro-Premuzic, V. Stumm & A. Furnham (eds) *The Wiley-Blackwell Handbook of Individual Differences* (pp. 242–267). London: Wiley-Blackwell.

Recommended websites

Website on the Reflective Judgment Model and Reflective Judgment Interview: http://www.umich.edu/~refjudg/index.html

Website for the Seattle Longitudinal Study: http://www.uwpsychiatry.org/sls/

Lynn Hasher's research and publications: http://psych.utoronto.ca/users/hasherlab/

Dare Association, Inc. – includes publications on Model of Hierarchical Complexity and instruments for assessing post-formal reasoning: http://dareassociation.org/instruments.php

4

Emotional Development

Conquer your passions and you conquer the world.

Hindu proverb

Vivien entered therapy in her late thirties. Over the course of the sessions, she told the therapist that she had domineering parents who had pressured her into marriage in her early twenties, and since then she had been dissatisfied with her life and had felt trapped. For much of her life she had successfully bottled up the emotions she was feeling towards her parents and husband, and had learnt not to express them openly. She said that she had been suppressing her emotions for so long that she had become 'numb' to them, and felt guilty about them. She had avoided public emotional expression for so long because she was scared of what would happen if she let her feelings of anger and frustration out. Over the course of her time in therapy, Vivien explored how to safely express these long-hidden feelings and this substantially improved her assertiveness, her self-belief and her sense of wellbeing.

Since the age of 18, have you noticed any changes in the kinds of emotions you regularly experience? Have you become more aware of your emotions, or more able to control them? If your answer is yes to any of these, you have personally experienced emotional development during adulthood. This chapter considers research and theory on these kinds of emotional changes in adulthood and it also reviews research on how emotions relate to particular adult contexts and events, including higher education, marriage, miscarriage and motherhood. Before getting started on this, a brief introduction to the functionalist approach to emotions will help to provide some theoretical context. A point of terminology clarification is necessary first; the words *affect* and *emotion* are often used interchangeably in the psychological literature, but in this chapter they refer to concepts at different levels of abstraction, following Izard (1993). Affect *includes* emotions, such as happiness, joy, sadness and fear, but also includes drives and impulses such as hunger, thirst, sex drive and aggression. It is therefore a more general concept than emotion.

The functionalist theory of emotions

The nature and function of emotions has been the subject of heated debate for thousands of years. In ancient Greek philosophy, the school of Stoicism promoted the virtue of subduing emotions through rational thought and restrained behaviour, and said that wise, mature men should not experience emotions at all (Sihvola & Engberg-Pederson, 1998). Aristotle, on the other hand, thought that emotions are functional and healthy if felt to a moderate degree, but unhealthy and dangerous when extreme (Sihvola & Engberg-Pederson, 1998). He analysed the social and personal *functions* of emotions in terms of their relation to action, and so was the first person to promote a functionalist view of emotion.

Like Aristotle, modern functionalist theory views emotions as useful and adaptive sources of information, if and when they are experienced within a normal range of intensity (Bretherton et al., 1986; Izard, 1993; 2009). Emotion and cognition are conceived as different but inseparable faculties of mental life; there is never an emotion without some kind of thought, and vice versa (Izard, 2009; Piaget, 1981). Research on emotions shows that they serve a variety of important intrapersonal and interpersonal functions, a short list of which is shown in Table 4.1 (Izard, 2009).

There are *dimensional* and *discrete* approaches to theorising about emotion from a functionalist perspective. Dimensional theories conceive all emotions as placed on generic scales, such as pleasure–displeasure or activation–deactivation (Reisenzein, 1994). Particular emotions are understood by their place on such scales, for example anger is *unpleasant* and *activating*, while sadness is *unpleasant* but *deactivating*. Discrete theories, on the other hand, view emotions as separate and qualitatively different. For example, Izard's theory contains six basic emotions, two of which are positive (joy, interest), and four of which are negative (sadness, fear, anger, disgust). Each of these is defined by different brain systems, conscious feelings, action tendencies, facial expressions, vocal expressions and hormonal changes. Each basic emotion is considered to have evolved to support a particular adaptive function – for example the function of sadness is to slow the cognitive and motor systems when energy needs to be conserved,

Table 4.1 The intrapersonal and interpersonal functions of emotion

The intrapersonal functions of emotions	The interpersonal functions of emotions
Motivation: Providing subjective motivation for, and guidance for, behaviour and decision-making	*Motivation*: Working out how to behave in an unfamiliar situation by observing the emotional reactions of others
Goal monitoring: An indicator of perceived progress towards valued goals (for example, happy if achieve goal), or perceived maintenance of standards (for example, guilty if transgress standard)	*Manipulation*: Influencing the emotions of others to achieve certain ends – for example, in emotion-inducing advertising or media
Purveyor of meaning: Encapsulating the significance, value or personal meaning of an event or memory	*Social cognition*: Providing a working model of what another person will, or will not do, based on their emotional signals
Attention focusing: Shaping the contents and focus of conscious attention (for example, focusing on fear-inducing stimuli)	*Attention*: Social referencing (where an inexperienced person or child relies on a more experienced person's affective interpretation of a situation)
	Empathy: Inferring a person's subjective from their behaviour and facial expression

the function of happiness/joy is to maintain focus on the same goal or behaviour, while the function of anger is to mobilise energy and muscles under conditions of interpersonal threat (Izard & Ackerman, 2000).

Emotions have bodily, neurological, experiential and social aspects, meaning that there are many different ways of assessing emotion in research studies (Coan & Allen, 2007; Izard, 1993). Self-report measures assess the experiential aspect; observational assessments can assess the bodily and social aspects, while physiological measures such as heart rate or skin conductance can pick up on internal bodily changes that indicate particular emotions. EEG measures or brain scans can assess neural activity that is indicative of particular emotional patterns. Studies on emotional developments in adulthood have been studied and will be discussed, but first here is a very brief review of emotional developments in childhood.

Emotional developments in childhood: A very brief review

Emotional development in the young infant is characterised by the predictable emergence of new emotions over time (Sroufe, 1997). Classic observational research by Bridges (1932) suggested that distress, excitement and delight develop in the first three months, and then fear, disgust and anger at six months. Izard (1978) added that at eight months, infants will cringe in fear as their arm is being prepared for an injection, and show anger at the nurse by refusing to interact with her afterwards. Elation and affection can be observed by approximately 12 months, while jealousy appears at 18 months, and joy appears at approximately 24 months (Bridges, 1932). Emotional *language* begins around 18–20 months on average. There is then a rapid increase of emotional terms after the age of two. Emotion words produced by an average 28-month-old include: happy, fun, love, proud, surprised, good, bad, sad, scared, mad, angry (Bretherton & Beeghly, 1982). Of these, love is the most prevalently used emotional word (87 per cent of infants), while surprise and anger are the least frequently used (13 per cent and 17 per cent of children respectively).

The recognition of emotions in *others* develops in a more-or-less reliable sequence throughout infancy and childhood. Negative facial expressions elicit frowning and crying by six–nine months, and a more complex understanding of the meaning of facial expressions is gained soon after – if a mother frowns at a ten-month-old as she approaches a toy, the infant is less likely to pick it up (Charlesworth & Kreutzer, 1973). At the end of the first year, infants show evidence of understanding that other people are emotionally affected by objects and events (Bretherton et al., 1986).

Over the course of childhood, children are able to verbally reflect on their own emotions and emotions in others with increasing complexity, clarity and accuracy. Selman (1981) found that at the age of three, children do not distinguish between inner emotion and outer emotional expression, so there is no understanding of 'hiding' an emotion. By the age of six, children can distinguish between an inner emotion and its outer expression, and understand inner as being 'true'. In response to a short film showing emotional individuals, children can make attributions concerning the cause of a protagonist's happiness, sadness, anger or fear (Strayer, 1993). These attributions of emotions change with age: for five-year-olds, the explanation of an emotion is based on an *event* that occurred, for seven- and eight-year-olds, explanations are focused on the *persons* in the scenario; and for 13-year-olds, explanations were more focused on the protagonists' *inner states* and interpretations of situations (Roberts & Strayer, 1996). Adolescence is the time when the idea of unconscious emotions and determinants of emotion are first apparent (Selman, 1981). This provides for a more complex schematic conception of internal determinants of emotional state, and paves the way for adult conceptions of emotion (Izard, 1993).

Adult emotional development

As with all forms of development, emotional changes in adulthood are more varied and multidirectional than developmental changes in childhood (Baltes, 1987). In this chapter, research and theory on five kinds of emotional change through adulthood will be reviewed. These five areas are:

1. Changes in emotional complexity and the capacity to express emotional experiences in words across adulthood.
2. Changes in happiness, wellbeing and life satisfaction across adulthood, and individual/group differences in the happiness-age relation.
3. Change in the tendency to focus on and remember positive or negative emotional information.
4. Changes across adulthood in levels of emotional intelligence and emotional regulation.
5. Changes in emotional experience that result from specific adult life events or changes in role.

Developments in emotional complexity and emotional integration

The orthogenetic developmental principle was described in Chapter 1. It conceives of healthy human development as a progression towards higher levels of integrated complexity. Corresponding to this, research clearly documents the increasing complexity of children's emotions, in terms of cause, experience, description and consequence (Sroufe, 1997). An important question however is whether this increasing emotional complexity is also evident in the adult years. In a cross-sectional study on complexity levels in emotional statements across the lifespan, Labouvie-Vief, DeVoe and Bulka (1989) interviewed 100 individuals from ages ten to 77 about personal experiences of anger, fear, sadness and happiness within the last month. They were asked to talk about the causes, context, course and consequence of these feelings. The findings suggested four levels of emotional complexity in the responses, labelled presystemic, intrasystemic, intersystemic and integrated. These are briefly described in Table 4.2. Emotional complexity level showed a strong correlation with age ($r = .48$), and a positive upward trajectory was found into middle adulthood, with slight declines shown in the over-60 age group. Means of the emotional complexity level across age groups are shown in Figure 4.1.

With increasing complexity comes increased consciousness of both negative and positive emotions. This means that advancing emotional complexity does not necessarily bring about wellbeing or increased happiness. Dynamic Integration Theory suggests that 'positive emotionality' and 'emotional complexity' are both valid emotional developmental directions, which do not necessarily correspond, so need to be balanced.

Table 4.2 The four stages of emotional complexity development

Emotional Complexity Level	Emotional state description	Emotional regulation description
Presystemic	External, action-based, simple, undifferentiated	Impulsive, unable to tolerate tension, oriented towards personal comfort
Intrasystemic	Generalised, conventional, technical	Control based on ideal abstract state, mental control of emotions
Intersystemic	Vivid, felt sense, dynamic metaphors, bodily sensations, complex and dynamic comparisons	Distancing oneself from the situation, thinking of alternatives, inner tendencies acknowledged, greater understanding of others' feelings and thoughts
Integrated	Tension of physical/mental, integration of convention and subjective experience	Emotions seen as opportunities for action or new inner perspective-taking, subjectivity within broad social concerns and context

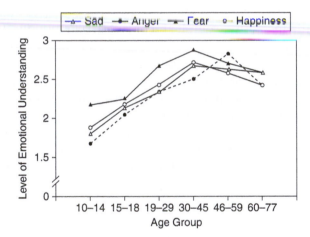
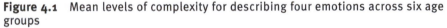

Figure 4.1 Mean levels of complexity for describing four emotions across six age groups

Source: Labouvie-Vief, DeVoe and Bulka (1989, p. 432). Copyright © 1989 The American Psychological Association (APA). Reproduced with permission.

The terms used in the theory to refer to these twin emotional challenges are: *Affect optimisation* (becoming more prone to positive emotions and less prone to negative emotions over time) and *affect complexity* (becoming able to handle and process more complex emotional information,

and being more self-aware of one's own emotional complexity)
(Labouvie-Vief, Grühn & Studer, 2010). Four emotional styles can be
established by crossing the variables of affect complexity and affect
optimisation, as follows:

1. Dysregulated: low complexity and low optimisation
2. Complex: high complexity but low optimisation
3. Self-protective: low complexity but high optimisation
4. Integrated: high complexity and high optimisation

In the theory, the integrated type is considered ideal in terms of emotional maturity. When age differences in the four types are compared
in early, young, middle and older adults, the proportion of integrated
individuals is 30 per cent for early adults, and 40–1 per cent for the
young, middle and older adult groups, suggesting a relatively constant
prevalence through adulthood. However, the proportion of dysregulated persons is significantly less in older adults than all younger groups
(Labouvie-Vief & Medler, 2002).

Changes in happiness and subjective wellbeing with age

Research has investigated how happiness and subjective wellbeing tend
to change across the lifespan, based on the assumption that increases
over time are desirable (see eudaimonic direction of development in
Chapter 1). Subjective wellbeing is composed of three variables: positive
affect, life satisfaction and absence of negative affect (Diener et al., 1999),
while happiness can be measured using self-report questionnaires that
ask questions such as 'Some people are generally very happy. They enjoy
life regardless of what is going on, getting the most out of everything.
To what extent does this characterization describe you?' (Lyubomirsky,
2008). Other methods used to track change in happiness are the *experience
sampling method*, which requires people to rate how happy they currently
are on an electronic recording device, and *text analysis*, which counts the
number of happy words in a written or spoken text.

The findings on wellbeing and age are good news for elderly adults.
Recent reviews have concluded that as adults age, negative emotions
become more infrequent, positive emotions become more frequent and
life satisfaction gets higher, when average levels are compared (Charles
& Carstensen, 2010; Charles, Reynolds & Gatz, 2001; Mroczek & Kolarz,
1998). Evidence supporting this 'positivity effect' comes from cross-
sectional and longitudinal research, conducted with questionnaires, text
analysis and experience sampling assessment tools.

Cross-sectional questionnaire-based findings

Cross-sectional studies of the relation between age and happiness/subjective wellbeing are mixed in their findings – some have shown stable wellbeing across age groups (Campbell, Converse & Rodgers, 1976; Diener & Suh, 1997; Herzog, Rogers & Woodworth, 1982; Larson, 1978), while others have shown declining happiness with age (Doyle & Forehand, 1984; Wilson, 1967). Other studies have looked at age-related change in particular emotions, and have found that anger and shame are higher in young adults than older adults (Phillips et al., 2006; Schieman, 1999).

A particularly large recent study by Arthur Stone and colleagues (2010) collated cross-sectional data from a Gallup survey of 340,000 American adults, on wellbeing, enjoyment, happiness, stress, worry, anger and sadness. The results, reproduced in Figure 4.2, show different age profiles for all of these six emotions. Enjoyment and happiness remain relatively stable, with a slight dip in midlife followed by a rise back to early adult levels or slightly higher in the over sixties. Stress is disproportionately higher in young adults relative to other age groups, and there is a particularly pronounced decline in stress after the age of 50. Worry remains relatively constant and then also declines over the age of 50. Anger has a linear negative relationship with age – there is a constant but gradual decline across all age groups, so those over 70 have the lowest mean. Sadness shows a slight incline in midlife relative to other age groups, with a peak around the age of 50. The age profiles are almost identical in all six emotions for men and women, with women reporting consistently higher levels of stress, worry and sadness than men (Stone et al., 2010). This is an important study both in terms of its sample size and the range of emotions assessed, but as with all cross-sectional studies, the age differences may be an effect of cohort as well as age. For example, are the young adults more stressed because they are young, or because they have grown up in a more stressful time?

Cross-cultural studies have found some cultural differences in the happiness–age relation. Butt and Beiser (1987) looked at happiness data from 13 nations (Australia, Brazil, Canada, France, India, Italy, Japan, Korea, Philippines, Singapore, UK, USA and Germany) from the *World Values Survey*, and found that over-fifties were generally the happiest in all countries except Brazil, where everyone was fairly happy. Robinson (2012) analysed data from the European Social Survey across 30 European nations, and found that happiness levels increased with age in wealthier European nations such as Norway and Switzerland, but decreased with age in less wealthy European nations such as Romania and Ukraine.

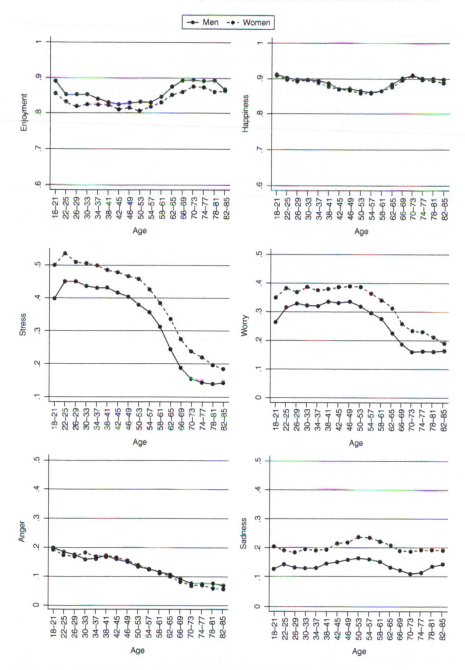

Figure 4.2 Six emotions – four-year age group means in a US adult sample

Source: Stone et al. (2010, p. 9989). Copyright © PNAS (Proceedings of National Academy of Sciences) Reproduced with permission.

Longitudinal questionnaire-based findings

Research on emotional change over adulthood that has used a longitudinal design is less prevalent than cross-sectional research. One such study was conducted by Charles, Reynolds and Gatz (2001). A mixed-age sample, from 15 to 102 were assessed for positive and negative affect in 1971 (N = 2044), 1985 (N = 1333), 1988 (N = 1482), 1991 (N = 1482) and 1994 (N = 1734). Negative affect decreased over time across *all* time points, supporting the view that with ages comes a generalised lower tendency towards negativity. Positive affect remained stable across adulthood to the age of 50, at which point it showed a decline. Variance in affect ratings was also analysed, to compare the spread of scores at different ages. The variance in negative affect is highest around the ages 35–40, suggesting that this age group shows the greatest variety in negative emotional tendencies. However, variance in positive affect is highest in the oldest age groups, suggesting that the greatest variety of positive emotional expression is in older adults.

What variables promote positive wellbeing change over time? Mroczek and Kolarz (1998) employed a questionnaire data collection strategy and found that marriage moderates the age-wellbeing relationship. Married men get less negative with age, but non-married men do not. Other domestic variables have been empirically related to emotion include size of household; Schieman (1999) found that anger decreases with age, but that this relationship is far less pronounced when household composition, time pressure and financial circumstances are controlled for; larger households, less time and less money are all related to more anger. Physical health is also an important predictor of happiness, particularly in older age groups (Kunzmann, Little & Smith, 2000).

Text-analysis research

Pennebaker and Stone (2003) employed a different data collection approach in their study of positive and negative emotionality in different age groups. They analysed written texts and interviews from 3000 participants across three countries (US, UK and New Zealand). The texts were submitted to a word-frequency analysis using *Linguistic Inquiry and Word Count (LIWC)* software. They found a small but significant change in frequency of positive and negative words used with age – an increase in positive words and a decrease in negative words across age groups. Figure 4.3 shows the mean-level differences. It should be pointed out that the over-seventies group was small in number (just 46 participants compared with almost 2000 young adults in the sample), and therefore the mean of this group is less reliable.

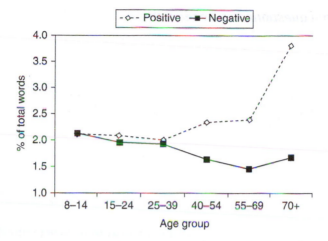

Figure 4.3   Positive and negative emotion words as per cent of total words in autobiographical accounts, by age group

Source: Pennebaker and Stone (2003, p. 296). Copyright © American Psychological Association. Reproduced with permission.

Experience sampling studies

Carstensen et al. (2000) used an experience sampling methodology to study the relation between emotion and age. Over the course of one week, participants (N=184, aged 18–94) were required to rate their experience of 19 emotions at random intervals when a beeper sounded (anger, guilt, pride, sadness, happiness, fear, accomplishment, shame, amusement, anxiety/worry, joy, contentment, irritation, frustration, disgust, interest, embarrassment, boredom, and excitement). Given the small cross-sectional sample, they aggregated the sample into three adult age groups (18–34, 35–64 and 65–94). Negative affect was highest in the 18–34 age group, and slightly higher in the 65–94 age group than the 35–64 age group. The tendency to report experiencing *both* positive and negative emotions at any particular moment increased with age, suggesting a more complex emotional make-up in the older adults. While this study was an innovation in terms of data collection, it was limited by a traditional cross-sectional design, and thus was prone to cohort effects.

Following on from this, Carstensen et al. (2011) produced an 'accelerated longitudinal analysis' of experience sampling data (see Chapter 2 for a description of accelerated longitudinal designs) using the same 184 individuals who participated in the aforementioned cross-sectional study (Tsai, Levenson & Carstensen, 2000). The participants were measured again five years later, and then again after another five years, using the experience sampling method. Attrition levels were high – 40 per cent of the original sample did not take part in phase 2, and 45 per cent of

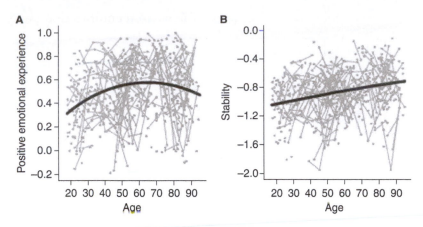

Figure 4.4   Growth curves (black) and individual-level change (grey) showing longitudinal positive emotional experience and emotional stability trajectories

Source: Carstensen et al. (2011, p. 28). Copyright © American Psychological Association. Reprinted with permission.

phase 2 did not take part in phase 3. To make up the shortfall, additional individuals were recruited to take the place of those who opted out, meaning that some of the developmental trajectories were five years in duration, some were ten years in duration, and some were single phase data points without a trajectory. Growth curves for the whole sample are shown in Figure 4.4 – there is a linear increase in emotional stability, and a curvilinear relation of positive emotionality and age.

The two graphs also include trajectories for individual participants in grey – they show the high level of individual variability that the generic growth curves hide. At all ages there are steep individual increases and decreases over time as well as more moderate gradients. The benefit of providing individual level data in this way is that the graph provides a very clear sense of how representative a growth curve is of the sample as a whole. In this instance, it shows that the curve does not reflect many of the individual participants– it tells us about the group as a whole, but not necessarily about anyone within it. Therein lies a profound limitation of group-level findings – they often have limited applicability to understanding the individual person, which makes their application in an applied context problematic.

The positivity effect in older adults

The tendency in older adults to remain happy despite the losses associated with old age has been termed the 'positivity effect' (Carstensen & Mikels, 2005; Mather & Carstensen, 2005). It has been hypothesised that this is due to older adults dwelling on positive memories and perceptions more than younger adults (despite the general human tendency to focus more on negative stimuli – Rozin & Royzman, 2001). The positivity effect has been linked to neurological age-related differences, for example a consistent finding across studies is that older adults show an alteration in the activity of the amygdala, and greater usage of the frontal cortex. This neurological age-related difference has been termed the *Fronto-amygdalar Age-related Differences in Emotion* (FADE) effect (St. Jacques, Bessette-Symons & Cabeza, 2009), and has been proposed as a possible material cause explanation of the positivity effect (see Chapter 2 for more on material causes).

Socio-Emotional Selectivity Theory: Another theory that has been put forward to explain the positivity effect is Socio-Emotional Selectivity Theory. This theory suggests that a person's perception of their future influences their emotional state and their social behaviours. If time is perceived as limited or constrained, for example an ending is perceived as approaching, a person focuses more on cultivating positive feelings and emotions, and less on knowledge acquisition or achievement (Carstensen, Isaacowitz & Charles, 1999; Strough, Berg and Sansone, 1996). Older adults, being closer to the end of the life, are hypothesised to have a short 'time horizon' and correspondingly show a bias towards positive stimuli and positive memories. The predictions of the theory have been tested and have been supported in older adults, in young people who have a terminal illness, and adults who are anticipating moving to a new region (Fredrickson & Carstensen, 1990).

Cognitive sources of the positivity effect: Evidence to support a cognitive basis for the positivity effect has been found in experimental studies that have compared young and old adults in (a) responses to emotional stimuli and (b) recall of emotional memories (Mather & Carstensen, 2005). In one study, older adults responded more quickly to positive faces that were flashed up on the screen than negative faces, suggesting a subconscious preference for positivity, but this was not shown by younger adults (Mather & Carstensen, 2003). Another study used eye-tracking software and found that older adults spend less time than younger adults looking at negative images, again suggesting a positivity preference in the older group (Rösler et al., 2005). Furthermore, younger adults have been found to perceive problematic situations as more severe and stressful than older adults, which supports the hypothesis that older people see the world in a more positive light relative to their younger counterparts (Charles & Almeida, 2007).

Other research on the positivity effect has focused on emotional memories. Research shows that younger adults remember more negative than positive information, while older adults remember more positive than negative information. For example in one study, images were shown with positive, negative or neutral content to young adults, middle-aged adults and older adults. The participants were tested for recognition and recall of the images. The amount of positive and negative information recalled was the same in younger and middle-aged adults, but older adults remembered a higher proportion of positive images (Charles, Mather & Carstensen, 2003).

Autobiographical memory is what a person remembers about his/her own life. Age differences in the positive and negative bias in auto-biographical information were explored in a study of 300 women (all nuns) between the ages of 47 and 102 (Kennedy, Mather & Carstensen, 2004). The women completed a series of questionnaires about physical and mental health in 1987, and 14 years later were asked to recall the information that they provided. It was found that older women recalled the information they gave about their health 14 years previously more positively than it was actually given, while the younger women recalled it more negatively than it was given, suggesting a switch from a neg-ativity bias to a positivity bias in autobiographical memory with age (McConatha & Huba, 1999). It seems young adults tend to think they were worse than they actually were in past, while older adults think they were better than they actually were!

This experimental research on the positivity effect is an important body of research, however all the studies are based on cross-sectional designs, and thus may be highlighting a cohort effect rather than an ageing effect; it may be that older people are more positive because of the era that they grew up in, rather than their age per se. Furthermore, there is the possibility of sampling error in such studies – if younger and older adults are sampled from different populations (for example, university students and older adults from the community), then differences between them may be due to a demographic or socio-economic difference, rather than an age difference.

Changes in emotional intelligence and emotional regulation across adulthood

This chapter has so far discussed changes in how adults *describe* and *experience* emotion as they age. Now we move on to changes and develop-ments in how adults *manage* and *regulate* their emotions. People vary in the extent to which they can accurately recognise and effectively regulate emotions in themselves and others (Diamond & Aspinwall, 2003; Mayer, Salovey & Caruso, 2004). This varying capacity to manage and perceive feelings is termed 'emotional intelligence' (EI). Emotional intelligence theory fits well with the functionalist perspective on emotions that was discussed earlier, for in both theories, emotions are considered to be useful information that can be stored, retrieved and processed to help goal-directed activity. Mayer, Caruso and Salovey (2000) propose four 'branches' of emotional intelligence, as follows:

Branch 1. The ability to perceive emotions
Branch 2. The ability to generate and use emotions in communication or cognition
Branch 3. The ability to understand emotions and emotional meanings
Branch 4. The ability to manage, modulate and control emotions

Research suggests that these abilities are all correlated, and that there is a single 'emotional intelligence' factor that influences them all (Palmer et al., 2005).

Cross-sectional research has studied age differences in emotional intelligence, and has reliably found a positive effect of age on EI (Bar-On, 1997; Extremera, Fernández-Berrocal & Salovey, 2006). Mayer, Caruso and Salovey (2000) compared an adolescent sample (ages 12–16) with an adult sample (ages 17–70), to test the hypothesis that adults would fare better on the test. It was found that adults did do better, but only on tests of emotional understanding and processing emotions. There was no difference in the ability to identify emotions. In another diverse professional adult sample, Wong, Wong and Law (2005) found a correlation of .30 between EI and age, while in more age-restricted student sample, a correlation of .23 was found between EI and age (Wong et al., 2007). Other studies have also found a small but significant positive correlation between self-reported EI and age (Van Rooy, Alonso & Viswesvaran, 2005).

Further cross-sectional self-report research has found age-differences in specific aspects of emotional intelligence. Branch 4, the ability to control and moderate emotions, is one area that has been found to be higher in later stages of adulthood. Lawton et al. (1992) found that older adults were higher in their self-reported capacity to control and moderate emotions than young adults. Gross et al. (1997) similarly found a higher capacity in older adults to control anger, anxiety and unhappiness, when compared with younger adults, both in American and Norwegian samples.

Experimental findings support these survey-based findings on emotional control and age. Tsai, Levenson and Carstensen (2000) assessed emotional arousal in relation to watching sad and amusing films, and found older adults showed less physiological reaction to both kinds of films, suggesting less emotional reactivity and more control. In another study, Charles and Carstensen (2008) found that older adults described less anger and more detachment in response to spoken criticism. Furthermore, it has been found that older adults can predict their own emotional response to situations better than younger adults (Nielsen, Knutson & Carstensen, 2008).

While the capacity to regulate emotions may increase in the over sixties, the capacity to perceive emotions (Branch 1 of EI) may not. When presented with images of eyes and full faces in various states of emotional expression, younger adults (18–32 years) were superior to older adults (60–87 years) in perceiving negative emotions, but there was no difference for positive emotions (Sullivan, Ruffman & Hutton, 2007).

Empathy in adulthood

Empathy is the capacity to perceive emotions in others, to simulate that emotion in oneself, and the ability to respond to such emotions with care and sensitivity (Batson, 2009). Cognitive processes in empathy include the inference of another person's emotional experience from their facial expressions, postures, speech and actions, while emotional processes are involved in activating an equivalent emotional experience in oneself (Baron-Cohen & Wheelwright, 2004; Preston & de Waal, 2002). Empathy can be triggered by positive or negative emotions in others, whereas sympathy is by definition triggered by witnessing or hearing about *distressing emotions* in another person, leading to a desire to alleviate that distress in some way. Empathy for someone may be delayed – it may be that a person is only able to empathise with another person's perspective in

---

Box 4.1   Individual voices

Gunther (2008) has studied the phenomenon of 'deferred empathy' – a capacity that is developed during adulthood. Deferred empathy involves a retrospective evaluation of an interpersonal encounter in the past, at which point an understanding of another person's perspective and feelings is gained. This deferment may be due to personal emotions that were being felt that prevented a clear empathic connection with the other person's feelings at the time. Example quotes from an individual's account of deferred empathy, and the ensuing sense of forgiveness, are given next.

> When I went to the counsellor, what she did was, put me in a chair in front of an empty chair, and that was my mother. And so, I got to

Box 4.1   Continued

talk to my mom about this secret. And I also got to get up from my seat, and sit in her seat, and feel what she might have been feeling, and that was probably the strongest moment of empathy I think I've ever felt ... all of a sudden I got this *huge* epiphany. (p. 1034)

I just wanted to tell her that I forgave her. I just forgive you and I understand. It was the biggest moment of empathy and the irony of that was I just felt tenderness toward her. She wasn't minimized in my mind, she was greater in my mind because she did want something that must have been difficult for her, but she found a way through my sister to tell me what I needed to know. I thought she was pretty amazing. (p. 1036)

I think my moment of empathy with my mom definitely helped at that point in my life to release a lot [of stress], you know, to get to become whole again. Somehow that empathy took me to a place where I could release my anger; I could release forgiveness ... and the rest of the stuff could be handled. (p.1037)

retrospect – a phenomenon referred to as deferred empathy. See Box 4.1 for a personal account of deferred empathy.

Empathy is central to effective interpersonal interaction and to emotional intelligence (Davis, 1983; Mayer, DiPaolo & Salovey, 1990). An absence of empathy is related to aggression and antisocial behaviours (Miller & Eisenberg, 1988), and also is a characteristic of autism (Baron-Cohen & Wheelwright, 2004). On the other hand, excessive empathy can also be dysfunctional, for example it can lead to 'compassion fatigue' in those professions that involve regularly encountering people who are distressed (Abendroth & Flannery, 2006).

People vary in their ability to empathise in a productive manner, and studies have attempted to establish whether these differences are systematically related to age. Cross-sectional studies have mostly not found any significant age differences in empathy (Eysenck et al., 1985; Diehl, Coyle & Labouvie-Vief, 1996). Longitudinal research similarly finds that age is not a strong predictor of empathy. Grühn et al. (2008) reported a longitudinal study of self-reported empathy conducted in the USA, which started with 400 participants. They measured empathy four times across a 12-year period, administering the empathy scale of the *California Personality Inventory* in 1992, 1994, 1998 and 2004. The outcome of the study was that no reliable mean-level age-graded change was found, however change

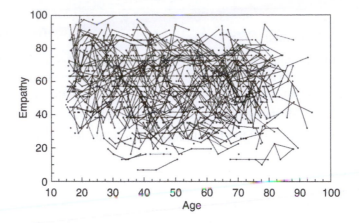

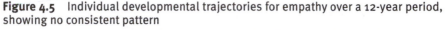

Figure 4.5   Individual developmental trajectories for empathy over a 12-year period, showing no consistent pattern

Source: Grühn et al., (2008, p. 760). Copyright © American Psychological Association. Reprinted with permission.

was apparent at the individual level. All individual developmental trajectories in empathy from the study are shown in Figure 4.5.

Individual-level empathy change is clearly apparent in Figure 4.5, but these changes are all in different directions so there is no general trend across the sample as a whole. So what *did* predict empathy increase or decrease in these individuals? Increases in empathy were more likely in individuals who reported high levels of positive emotion, while those who decreased in empathy were lower in positive emotion and had more depressive symptoms. So it may be that being happy is good for empathy – perhaps one is more likely to take the perspective of another if troubling emotions do not cloud one's own mind, or conversely it may mean that the act of empathy, and the corresponding sense of social connection it brings, is conducive to happiness.

What Figure 4.5 strongly suggests is that empathy is a capacity that can increase or decrease during adult life. Given this possibility of change, a variety of adult training programmes have been devised to promote its development. Evaluation of these programmes has shown them to be generally effective (Angera & Long, 2006; Crabb, Moracco & Bender, 1983; Erera, 1997; Long et al., 1999; Stepien & Baernstein, 2006). Box 4.2 gives an example exercise for promoting empathy in romantic relationships.

Emotions within specific contexts in adulthood

The chapter has so far focused on emotional development without considering the particular life contexts that elicit different emotions. A number of studies have taken an alternative, more contextualised approach,

---

Box 4.2 Real-world applications

Training empathy

Long et al. (1999) describe a set of exercises for developing empathy in romantic relationships, including the following:

The speaker/listener technique + empathy checking exercise

The speaker-listener technique involves one person adopting the role of the speaker, and describing their opinions and experience of a particular topic. The other person is the listener – their job is to listen then periodically summarise what the speaker has said and the speaker's feelings about the topic. The speaker is then asked how well the listener accurately represented and understood what had been said and felt, and to rate it on a scale of 1 to 10. If the listener has described the message in such a way that the speaker felt clearly understood, this shows empathic connection. If a complete empathic understanding was not achieved during the first attempt, then the speaker communicates the message again and the process continues. Have a go yourself with a friend and see how good your sense of empathic communication is.

---

such as studying emotions within a particular role (for example, being a mother, spouse or carer), or in relation to a particular life event (for example, medical training, miscarriage, seeing grown-up children, bereavement or job loss).

Empathy at medical school

A vocational context in which longitudinal change in empathy has been studied is medical training. A finding that has been replicated across cross-sectional and longitudinal studies is that in general, empathy towards patients decreases during medical training, particularly during the second or third year (D. Chen et al.; Hojat et al., 2004; Sherman & Cramer, 2005). Hojat et al. (2009) conducted a study with students at Jefferson Medical College, during which empathy was measured five times; at the beginning of the training and then at the end of each year for four academic years. One hundred and twenty-one students gave data on all five of those occasions. Longitudinal changes are shown in Figure 4.6; for both men and women there is clear dip in empathy

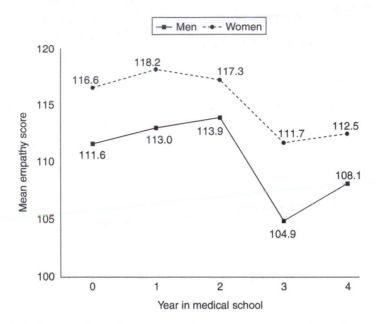

Figure 4.6   Longitudinal changes in mean empathy scores across four years of medical school for 56 men and 65 women at Jefferson Medical College, Philadelphia, Pennsylvania, 2002–8

Source: Hojat et al. (2009, p. 1188) Copyright © 2009 Association of American Medical Colleges. Reprinted with permission.

in the third year of training. The authors of the research speculate that this may be a result of the way that medical training promotes emotional detachment, distance and neutrality. Yet empathy is central to the person-focused nature of medical care, and it correlates with clinical competence, therefore the authors express concern that this decrease occurs and suggest that it could have negative consequences for patient care (Hojat et al., 2002).

Despite this mean-level decrease in year three of medical training, 27 per cent of medical students do *not* show an empathy decline. The authors state that more research is needed on what differentiates these 'empathy-protected' students from the others. In summary, this vocational research area suggests that empathy is heavily modifiable by context in adulthood.

Emotional responses to miscarriage

A number of qualitative studies have studied emotional responses to miscarriage. Some of these have focused on accounts of miscarriage from a medical or clinical care perspective (for example, Wong et al., 2003; Smith et al., 2006), while others have focused more on the personal experience of miscarriage (Manca & Bass, 1991; Simmons et al., 2006). The qualitative research on the personal experience of women after miscarriage convey the powerful and complex emotional reactions that negative life events can bring about. Emotions reported by the women include fear, shock, sadness, discouragement, yearning, frustration and anger. This cocktail of negativity in response to a major life event reflects the fact that, in real life, emotions occur in messy combination, and not in neat isolation as the graphs in Figure 4.2 might have us believe.

'Forbidden emotions' in mothers with young children

Motherhood is an adult role with profound emotional implications, some of which are not considered socially acceptable. Rotkirch and Janhunen (2009) asked Finnish mothers of young children to write down emotions that they experienced as a mother which they perceived as 'forbidden' and guilt-inducing. The 63 accounts they received ranged in length from one line to three pages. A content analysis showed the most frequent 'forbidden' maternal emotions were fatigue, anger, aggression, rage and guilt. Guilt about their own behaviour as mothers was described by *all* participants. The sources of this sense of guilt and shame included the following:

- Aggression towards the child (either actual or imagined)
- Self-destructive or suicidal thoughts
- Thoughts of leaving child
- Wishing child had not been born
- Physical absence from child due to work commitments
- Not corresponding to one's own idea of being a 'good mother'
- Favouring one child over another

Extracts from individual accounts of maternal guilt and shame are shown in Box 4.3.

Box 4.3   Individual voices

Personal descriptions of maternal guilt and shame (Rotkirch & Janhunen, 2009):

The one-year-old sometimes wants to be in my arms all evening. My husband is home from work and I finally try to get for instance

---

Box 4.3   Continued

some housework done. Then I get irritated over having to carry the child all the time. A few times I have picked up the baby in my arms and cursed at the same time, my grip has probably also been inappropriately tight (not that it hurt, though). After a few minutes I feel shame and self-loathing. (p. 97)

'I WANT MY LIFE BACK!' The scream ends up coming out as a sigh. I think of all the things I could do without my children ... These thoughts make me feel guilty. If these wishes would come true, my children would be dead. The thought makes me cry. I want my life back, to be something else than a mother and at the same time I want to be a mother – the best of mothers. The equation seems impossible. (pp. 98–9)

You easily snap at your children if things aren't alright with your spouse. This is followed by enormous guilt, but that's just how it is. Although I try all I can, I can't be sufficiently present for my children, if my mind is occupied by our couple relations. (p. 99)

I really thought that I would die, because I had slept so little ... I felt boundless desperation, shame, loneliness and disappointment at myself. I can't get my child to sleep, I'm a bad mother. I also felt guilty for having these feelings. I was supposed to become such a good and happy mother ... I never discussed these issues at the child-welfare clinic, I always said everything was fine. The clinic nurse was certainly the kind of person I could have talked to, but I could not reveal such things there, or say them aloud. (p. 101)

I feel guilt and shame because I yell at my children and most of all because I haven't formed a proper emotional bond with my youngest ... One can't talk about these issues with one's own face and emotions. If you mention that you find your child irritating, you are seen as mentally ill or plain crazy, you are a bad mother who should never have had children since you can't take care of them or love them. (p. 101)

Emotional climate in long-term marriage

A study into the emotional experience of marriage compared middle-aged couples who had been married for 15 years or more, with older couples who had been married for 35 years or more (Carstensen,

Gottman & Levenson, 1995). The 156 couples who participated were observed in a laboratory while discussing three topics for 15 minutes each; (a) the events of that day, (b) a problem area in their marriage, and (c) an agreed pleasant topic. They also completed a questionnaire on relationship problems. Videos of the exchanges were then coded for the presence of emotions. It was found that elderly couples displayed more affection than middle-age couples when dealing with a conflict, while middle-age couples displayed higher levels of anger, disgust, belligerence, and whining than older couples. This is one of the few observational studies in the literature on emotion in adults, and it suggests that older adults manage the emotional challenges of marriage to a superior extent than younger couples. However an open question is whether the effects observed were due to age, or length of marriage, or both.

Women in their early sixties: Emotions when interacting with grown-up children

In Chapter 2, it was mentioned that life-event-specific research can contribute to an understanding of adult development, by throwing light on the dynamics of a particular transition or life phase. A recent example of life-event-specific research in relation to emotion was a study by Impett, English and John (2010). Using a sample of college-educated women in their early sixties who had grown-up children, they asked participants to complete a structured diary form every day for seven days before bedtime, including open-ended questions and rating scales. They also measured attachment security using the Experiences in Close Relationship Scale (see Chapter 12). In each diary entry, participants were asked to recount a positive event and a negative event of the day – the high point and low point. Questions for each event were: What happened? When and where? Who else was involved? What were your thoughts and feelings? Participants also rated six emotions on a seven-point scale for each event: joy, pride, love, sadness, anger, and fear.

The data was analysed to explore the effect on emotions of interacting with grown-up children. It was found that on average, women experienced more joy, pride and love when children were present, both in relation to negative and positive events, particularly if they had a secure non-avoidant attachment style. However, if negative events involved children, the events evoked more sadness than in the negative events that did not include children. The study shows that the bond between mothers and grown-up children is still very much present – it induces love, pride and joy when there are positive interactions and sadness if there is a problem that relates to the child. Diary studies such as this are rare in the

Box 4.4   Alternative perspectives

Alternatives to self-report measures of emotion

The majority of research reviewed in this chapter has looked at emotion by way of self-report, either through questionnaires, experience sampling or interviews. But what about studying emotions that people are unaware of or unwilling to admit to? This can be researched using ratings of emotion by spouses or friends. Research from the field of health psychology suggests that reports by spouses of negative emotions are in fact more predictive of health-related outcomes than self-reports. Several studies have found that spouse reports of anger and anxiety are related to indicators of coronary heart disease, while self-reports were not (Kneip et al., 1993; Smith et al., 2008), and that men particularly tend to under-report negative emotionality (Ketterer et al., 2004). These studies suggest that gaining data on emotional state from friends and partner is an essential future direction for research on emotional development in adulthood.

Another technique that helps to move beyond the current over-reliance on self-reports is observation. Researchers can be trained to rate the presence of emotions in others based on their words, facial expression and body language (for example, Carstensen, Gottman & Levenson, 1995). Observation is rarely employed in adult development studies, but is used a lot in child development. We adult development psychologists need to learn from our child development counterparts how to do it, for otherwise we are limited to researching what adults or their partners and friends will admit to and can express in words. The body often betrays emotion that words do not, and this fact should be reflected in the corpus of research on emotional development.

literature, but have the potential to provide important quantitative and qualitative longitudinal data that can be related directly to particular relationships, activities and life events.

Concluding comments

Here ends the chapter on emotional development, but we are far from done with the topic of emotion. In all the ensuing chapters, emotion and empathy come back again and again, in relation to life stages, transitions, morality, wisdom, relationships, mental illness, career and bereavement. I mentioned back in the preface of the book that emotion is not really separable from action and cognition, and that bigger issues like career and family are products of these three faculties interacting in social settings, so although the structure of the textbook forces me to separate topics out into different chapters, try and remember that such separation does not really exist in human beings. It is just necessary for the purposes of constructing a textbook. It is your job as the reader to join the dots and connect it back into the bigger picture.

Questions for you to reflect on

- What kind of activities make you feel happy? Do you think your answer to that question will be the same in 20 years' time? If not, why not?
- There are a number of theories that try and explain why adults tend to become more positive and less negative as they get older. Some of these are biological, some are cognitive, and some are social. Can you think of criticisms of these different theories?
- What do you think is better – being emotionally complex or emotionally positive? If you had to choose one, which would you choose?
- Do you know anyone who you think is particularly emotionally intelligent? What kind of qualities do they possess? Do those qualities fit with the theory of emotional intelligence described in this chapter?

Summary points

- The functionalist theory of emotions states that emotions have evolved to serve adaptive intrapersonal and interpersonal functions – they motivate us, help us to understand the motives of others and help us to prioritise between goals.
- Emotions develop in childhood in a predictable sequence, which leads to increasing complexity in a child's capacity to express emotions and understand emotions in others. The capacity for understanding what brings about emotions is still increasing in adolescence.
- Dynamic Integration Theory states that, across the lifespan, individuals are challenged to balance increases in 'affect complexity' with 'affect optimisation', which means that development is served both by being more complex and happier. These two do not necessarily correspond, so a balance must be struck.
- Cross-sectional and longitudinal research suggests that with age comes a decreased tendency to feel negative emotions and a maintained tendency to feel happiness and enjoyment. However, in less wealthy countries where pension provision, health services and other services for elderly people are more problematic, happiness tends to decline in later life.

- Older adults tend to focus on and remember positive emotional information more than younger adults.
- Emotional intelligence (EI) correlates positively with age, but there is currently no longitudinal research that has traced the development of EI over the course of adulthood.
- Empathy does not systematically increase with age, but change in adulthood in empathy does seem to relate to how happy a person is, and it can be improved by way of empathy training programmes.
- Research carried out on emotions experienced within particular life contexts provides an important complementary perspective to more generic approaches of measuring emotional developments in adulthood.

Recommended reading

Carstensen, L. L., Isaacowitz, D. M. & Charles, S. T. (1999). Taking time seriously. A theory of socioemotional selectivity. *The American Psychologist*, 54, 165–181.

Carstensen, L. L., Turan, B., Scheibe, S., Ram, N., Ersner-Hershfield, H., Samanez-Larkin, G. R., Brooks, K. P. & Nesselroade, J. R. (2011). Emotional experience improves with age: Evidence based on over 10 years of experience sampling. *Psychology and Aging*, 26, 21–33.

Charles, S. T. & Carstensen, L. L. (2010). Social and emotional aging. *Annual Review of Psychology*, 61, 383–409.

Diamond, L. M. & Aspinwall, L. G. (2003). Emotion regulation across the life span: An integrative perspective emphasizing self-regulation, positive affect, and dyadic processes. *Motivation and Emotion*, 27, 125–156.

Grühn, D., Rebucal, K., Diehl, M., Lumley, M. & Labouvie-Vief, G. (2008). Empathy across the adult lifespan: Longitudinal and experience-sampling findings. *Emotion*, 8, 753–765.

Labouvie-Vief, G. & Medler, M. (2002). Affect optimization and affect complexity: Modes and styles of regulation in adulthood. *Psychology and Aging*, 17, 571–588.

St. Jacques, P. L., Bessette-Symons, B. & Cabeza, R. (2009). Functional neuroimaging studies of aging and emotion: Fronto-amygdalar differences during emotional perception and episodic memory. *Journal of the International Neuropsychological Society*, 15, 819–825.

5

Motivational Development

Strong lives are motivated by dynamic purposes.
                                                Kenneth Hildebrand

Julia grew up in a small village in Italy, where there was a strong social expectation that she should stay in the village to look after her mother, who was a widower. However, she had a different goal – to go to university and to travel. She decided not to pursue this goal for many years, so instead got a job at the hairdresser in the village and followed the demands of her mother and the culture around her. But her goal to study and explore the world never went away, and she would often daydream about it while she was cutting hair. In her mid-twenties, she decided to start putting together a plan to realise her goal, and at the time met a man who shared her aspirations. The two of them decided to move to London. Despite intense pressure from her mother, relatives and neighbours not to go, she left, found a flat in London and started intensive studies in English. She then pursued her goal by enrolling on a degree course – a part-time philosophy BA. When I interviewed here, she was in the third year of her degree and already thinking about what her next goal would be.

What really motivates you? What makes you want to get up in the morning? What do you want to accomplish in life? What or who do you most desire? Your answers to these questions bring you into the domain of motivational development. The Latin root of the word 'motivation' means movement, and the scientific study of motivation is the study of bodily movement that is motivated by a drive, emotion or thought, and is aimed at helping to realise a goal. If there is no goal towards which movement is orientated, any outcomes that result from it are considered *unmotivated* or *unintentional* (Lewis, 1990). This chapter will first discuss the 'push and the pull' of motivation – drives, needs and goals, in relation to the changes of adult life. We first summarise the research that shows how primary drives typically change with age, and then introduce theories and research into how goals and motivated pursuits develop and change across adulthood.

The primary drives across adulthood

Primary drives are internal stimuli such as hunger, thirst, libido and the urge to sleep. They indicate that a biological need is not being met and provide a motivating force to resolve the situation. What makes these drives 'primary' is that they are instinctual and unlearnt, and exist as motivating forces in all cultures and in all historical epochs (Hull, 1943). The intensity and frequency of these drives alter over the course of adulthood, and this helps to explain changes in adult behaviour over time.

Sex drive

For young adults, sexual thoughts and urges occupy a considerable amount of waking consciousness. Recent research with a sample of 283 American university students found that young men think of sex on average 19 times a day, and young women think of it on average ten times a day (Fischer, Moore & Pittenger, 2012). Around those averages there is considerable individual variability – the maximum sexual thoughts that was recorded in one day was 140 for a woman and 388 for a man!

This preoccupation with sex wanes with age: research using cross-sectional samples has found that older adults think of sex less frequently than younger adults. One study asked 4420 persons of varying ages what they were thinking about in the previous five minutes (Cameron & Biber, 1973). They found that the prevalence of sexual thoughts increases from pre-adolescence to adolescence, and then declines progressively through older age groups. Table 5.1 summarises this data for males and females.

Box 5.1　Cross cultural perspectives

Sex and age in Germany

A recent study from Germany examined the intensity of sexual *desire* and frequency of sexual *activity* across a large, nationally representative

Box 5.1 Continued

cross-sectional sample of 2341 adults (Beutel, Stöbel-Richter & Brähler, 2007). Participants firstly rated the intensity of their sexual desire over the past four weeks, and the percentage of men and women who responded either 'high' or 'very high' to the question about their intensity of sexual desire was found to decline as a function of age, as illustrated in Figure 5.1.

Frequency of sexual desire (rated in relation to the past four weeks) also showed a similar negative relation with age. While the majority of young adults report frequent or very frequent sexual desire (72 per cent of men, 55 per cent of women), this proportion gets smaller across age groups, and correspondingly, in over 70 age group, 47 per cent of men and 78 per cent of women report not having any sexual desire at all in the past four weeks.

In terms of sexual activity, up to the age of 50 over 95 per cent of women and men in relationships are sexually active, and then this percentage declines across successively older age groups, so that in the over 70 age group, 31 per cent of women and 54 per cent of men in a relationship reported being sexually active in the previous 12 months. For those not in a relationship, men and women show comparable sexual activity under the age of 40, but for the over-forties, single women are less sexually active than single men.

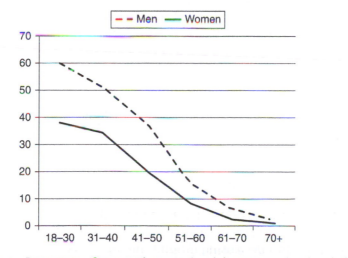

Figure 5.1 Percentage of men and women in adult age groups rating their intensity of sexual desire as 'high' or 'very high'

Source: Based on data from Beutel, Stöbel-Richter and Brähler (2007).

Table 5.1   Percentages of males and females of varying age groups responding 'yes' to if in the last five minutes they had a thought about sex

Ages	Males – %	Females – %
8–11	25	27
12–17	53	41
18–25	48	33
26–39	33	19
40–55	20	9
56–64	19	12
65+	9	6

Table 5.2   Potential interactive causes of appetite loss and reduced food intake in the elderly

Biological factors	• Declines in the senses of taste and smell with ageing, resulting from physiological changes in taste buds and olfactory structures. • Decreased and/or less frequent sensations of hunger, potentially due to slower emptying of the stomach. • Changes with age in hormones that regulate hunger, such as increased levels of glucagon. • Tooth loss (also called edentulism). • Common use of drugs in the elderly that have appetite-suppressant side-effects. • Physical disabilities that limit shopping and cooking.
Psychosocial factors	• Depression (which is associated with weight gain in younger adults, but weight loss in older adults). • Bereavement, which may lead to depression, or to loss of partner who does the cooking, or to social isolation at mealtimes. • Poverty, due to low income in the elderly. • Fatigue. • Cognitive decline due to dementia making cooking and/or remembering mealtimes more problematic.

Source: Based on Hays and Roberts (2006).

Hunger and the 'anorexia of ageing'

Hunger is another drive that tends to typically decline in old age. Body weight typically increases through adulthood, particularly in midlife, and then tends to start decreasing around the age of 65–75 (Hays & Roberts, 2006). This decline in appetite and food intake in the elderly that results in weight loss has been called the 'anorexia of ageing' (Hays & Roberts, 2006; Morley, 1997). A review of research on the anorexia of ageing, by nutrition scientists Hays and Roberts (2006), concluded that problematic food intake reduction in the elderly is a phenomenon that stems from both physiological and psychosocial mechanisms. These are summarised in Table 5.2.

Hays and Roberts (2006) suggest that insufficient food intake in the elderly is a potential health problem, and they propose interventions that can help maintain a satisfactory food intake in the elderly, such as promoting variety in food consumption, help with food preparation, and enhancing flavours in foods, particularly salt and sugar, and the use of specially devised nutritional supplements.

Thirst

Thirst goes the same way as hunger with age. There is a greater tendency in older adults to not drink enough fluids when dehydrated, which can lead to dangerous dehydration (Rolls & Phillips, 1990). This reduced fluid intake seems to be due to a decrease in the thirst drive that occurs in older adults (Farrell et al., 2008; Kenney & Chiu, 2001), which may in turn result from changes in physiological control systems associated with thirst, both in the brain (Farrell et al., 2008), and in the kidneys (Kenny & Chiu, 2001).

Sleep

The final drive-based behaviour that also declines with age is sleep. Individuals typically need an hour less sleep in their seventies than they did in their twenties (Harbison, 2002). A recent study compared three adult age groups in how much sleep they gained over eight hours in a sleep laboratory (Dijk et al., 2010). They found that young adults slept for 7.2 hours, middle-aged adults slept for 6.8 hours, and older adults for 6.5 hours. All mean differences between these age groups were significant. The lower sleep time in the older age group was primarily due to an increase in the number of times that participants woke up during the sleep period, which suggests declining 'sleep efficiency' with age (Dijk et al., 2010).

The overall picture from the aforementioned research on primary drives is a general age-related decline in the intensity of biological urges. Although this appetitive decline in later life is often characterised in pathological terms – for example, as the 'anorexia of ageing' or 'reduced sleep efficiency' – perhaps also it is a liberation for the ageing adult to be partially freed from the push of these basic biological drives, thus leaving more time to be motivated towards meeting higher needs or helping others.

Box 5.2   Alternative perspectives

Development of goal-directed behaviour in children: A brief review

The capacity to orient behaviour intentionally towards goals emerges according to a predictable sequence in early childhood. Several theoretical models of this process have been developed (Kopp, 1982; Lewis; 1990). Michael Lewis postulated five developmental levels of intentionality that emerge in developmental sequence. The first of these is *reflex-based necessity*, in which automatic action occurs that serves an internal need, such as crying or breathing. Level two is *environment-induced action*, which refers to action that is initiated in response to an environmental stimulus, such as an infant seeing a rattle and hitting it. At this level there is no internal representation of a goal, meaning that the stimulus itself is interacted with directly.

Level three is *goal-directed intent*, which is the first level at which goals appear. The child develops the capacity for establishing a goal that they want to achieve, and holding it in working memory for a period of time while behaviour is repeatedly directed towards it, often using a trial-and-error strategy. Kopp (1982) refers to this new stage as the emergence of *control*, and with it comes the ability to delay goal-directed action on request, or inhibit an action if necessary – for example, toilet training. Around the age of three a child will add to their goal-directed behaviour repertoire by monitoring their own behaviour relative to their goals.

Level four is the stage of *diverse intent*, which is characterised by the capacity to balance and prioritise multiple goals, by establishing which alternative goal is more favourable and more achievable. The final level of intentionality is *conscious intent*. At this stage, a child is aware of their own goals, of their actions, and the implications that these have on self and others. The capacity for conscious intent continues to develop through adolescence and provides the basis for being a responsible, autonomous adult (see the legal definition of adulthood in Chapter 1).

Classic lifespan goal theories

The Life Goal Theory of Charlotte Bühler

Charlotte Bühler was a pioneering theorist who worked at the Vienna Institute in the 1920s and 1930s, and then at the University of Southern

California from the 1940s to the 1960s. Over the course of her career she devised a theory of lifespan development, which was based on *life goals* (Bühler, 1935; 1967). A life goal is a long-term aim which specifies a path towards fulfilment and personal growth. In the theory, such goals emerge from four 'basic tendencies': *need satisfaction* (for example, eating), *upholding internal order* (for example, having defined values and beliefs), *creative expansion* (for example, striving for newness and growth) and *self-limiting adaptation* (for example, actions designed to fit in with social mores). The first two of these promote stability, the latter two promote change, and they often conflict, leading to tension between contradictory goals. Bühler described five developmental phases during which life goals emerge and mature, with approximate beginning and end ages:

Phase 1. Birth to age of 15: life goals are not present.
Phase 2. Tentatively trying different life goals, and exploring their consequences.
Phase 3. The major period of setting life goals, involving establishing clear, committed and autonomous goals that define career, social life and home life.
Phase 4. 45–65: Goals are reviewed and a re-orientation to new or modified goals is considered.
Phase 5. 65+: Progress towards life goals is reviewed as a totality, and a sense of fulfilment, resignation or failure is experienced depending on the outcome of this review.

At all stages of adult life, there is a need to combine goals that promote *comfort* (stability-focused goals) with goals that promote *accomplishment* (change-focused goals) (Bühler, 1964). Bühler suggested that accomplishment goals are dominant in the early and middle periods of adulthood, while comfort goals become dominant in the later stages of life. This reflects the tenets of Socio-Emotional Selectivity Theory, discussed in Chapter 4.

Maslow's Developmental Theory of Needs

Abraham Maslow developed a theory of lifespan development that drew directly on Bühler's theory of life goals (Maslow, 1968; 1971; 1987). Both Maslow and Bühler were pioneers in the field of humanistic psychology, which emphasised goals and personal growth as central to a healthy life (De Robertis, 2006). Maslow's theory further proposed a hierarchy of *needs*, which occur sequentially in development. Basic biological needs (primary drives) have first priority and occur first in the developmental sequence – these include needs such as warmth, food, water, shelter and safety. If any one of these is lacking, *or* there is the imminent prospect of such a lack, goal-directed behaviour is initiated towards rectifying the lack or anticipated lack. If a person lives in an environment where food, water, shelter or safety is scarce or lacking, the majority of goal-directed action will be focused on meeting these needs.

If biological needs are satisfied, then psychological needs become the focus of attention. In Maslow's theory these occur in the following order: *belongingness, love, esteem* and *knowledge*. More recent theories of psychological needs emphasise the need for a sense of *autonomy* and *competence* too (Ryan & Deci, 2000). When a person's psychological needs are met, then a person can address the highest need, which is termed *self-actualisation*. The process of self-actualisation is the conscious goal of trying to fulfil one's potential by way of committing to a meaningful cause beyond oneself:

> Self-actualizing people are, without one single exception, involved in a cause outside their own skin, in something outside of themselves. They are devoted, working at something, something which is very precious to them ... One devotes his life to the law, another to justice, another to beauty or truth. (Maslow, 1971, p. 42)

Maslow wrote extensively about individuals who were in the self-actualisation stage of development, using examples such as Abraham Lincoln and Aldous Huxley (Maslow, 1950). His descriptions of the self-actualising personality are discussed in Chapter 7.

There is a key tension in motivational development that both Bühler and Maslow point to. Humans are not motivated solely to make life easy and comfortable, but also they are motivated to grow and to stretch themselves, even though such growth means a certain amount of stress and tension. They conclude that a motivational mix of growth *and* stability is essential for health, for growth without stability leads to chaotic change, while stability without growth leads to boring sameness (Bühler, 1968; Maslow, 1968). This elusive search for balance between change and stability is also at the heart of more recent motivational theories discussed further.

Contemporary lifespan goal theories

The Motivational Theory of Lifespan Development

A recent theory that builds on the work of Bühler is the *Motivational Theory of Lifespan Development* (Heckhausen, Wrosch & Schulz, 2010). It describes effective goal pursuit across the lifespan, and like Bühler's theory it focuses on long-term goals, which take many years to achieve. The model specifies *action opportunity periods* during which particular goals are best pursued. Figure 5.2 presents a visualisation of these; as the

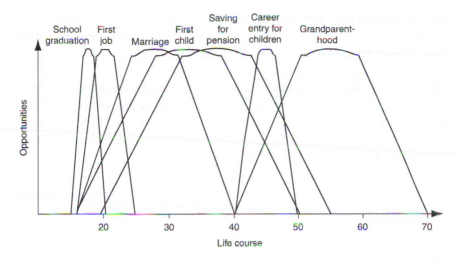

Figure 5.2   Age-graded sequence of opportunities to realise developmental goals

Source: Heckhausen (2000, p. 215, Figure 1). Copyright © 2000 Heckhausen, J. Reproduced with permission.

figure shows, some action opportunity periods are longer than others, but all have a definable age-linked peak (Heckhausen, Wrosch & Schultz, 2010). Some action opportunities have *developmental deadlines* past which action and goal-setting is fruitless. For example, a 40-year-old cannot realistically set a goal to train as a professional footballer, and a woman after the menopause is not able to get pregnant (Heckhausen, 2000).

This developmental action timetable is a result of both social and biological constraints. One social constraint is the set of age-based legal limitations on access to certain resources and activities: for example, sex, voting, marriage or drawing a state pension. Another constraint is the set of normative social *expectations* about when certain activities should be undertaken in the life course (Neugarten, Moore & Lowe, 1968). Biological constraints on goal-setting include the gain and loss of fertility, disability, illness and death.

In order to best adapt to new life challenges, an adult must be aware of these opportunities for action, and must select appropriate development goals from those that are available. If a chosen goal brings growth, fulfilment, challenge and esteem, while not interrupting the pursuit of other important goals, then development is enhanced, but if there is conflict between goals or a goal brings about anxiety or boredom, then development is impeded (Heckhausen, Wrosch & Schultz, 2010). Having a diversity of goals prevents too much dependence on one goal for personal evaluations of success. If failure to reach one goal does occur, the presence of other goals will buffer its negative effects (Heckhausen, 2000).

The notion of *control* is central to this theory. It is defined as the capacity to manage the discrepancy between one's actual state and one's goal state in an effective way (Schulz & Heckhausen, 1996). *Primary* control involves taking actions that attempt to move closer to a goal by taking actions. *Secondary* control involves dropping, switching or changing the meaning of goals. Research has found that secondary control (goal flexibility) increases in prevalence in older age, while primary control (goal pursuit) gradually decreases, as an adaptive response to the fact that older individuals experience more age-related changes to their health and appearance that are beyond their control than younger adults (Thompson et al., 1998).

Jochen Brandstädter and colleagues have researched the balance of primary of secondary control in different age groups, and refer to them as follows (Brandtstädter & Renner, 1990; Brandtstädter & Rothermund, 2002):

1. Tenacious goal pursuit – a process of maintaining focus on the goal and finding a way around the problem to keep moving in the same direction.
2. Flexible goal adjustment – a process of modifying, changing, re-interpreting or getting rid of the goal so that the problem no longer exists.

Goal pursuit entails top-down convergent thinking (that is, this is my goal, how will I get there?), while flexible goal adjustment requires holistic bottom-up thinking (that is, which goals should I modify, change, prioritise, given everything that is going on right now?). For successful living, you need to be tenacious enough to pursue your goals, but flexible enough to know when to change focus and adjust. This is the 'stability-flexibility dilemma' (Brandstädter & Rothermund, 2002). If you are not flexible enough, you get trapped in existing commitments, but if you are too flexible then you never see anything through to its conclusion or persevere in the face of obstacles.

The *Tenacious Goal Pursuit Scale* and the *Flexible Goal Adjustment Scale* assess these two processes (Brandstädter & Renner, 1990). Example items from the goal pursuit scale are 'Even if everything seems hopeless, I still look for a way to master the situation,' and 'If I run into a problem, I usually double my efforts.' Example items from the goal adjustment scale are 'I can adapt quite easily to changes in a situation,' and 'In general, I am not upset very long about an opportunity passed up.'

A number of studies have investigated how goal pursuit and goal adjustment relate to wellbeing and age. In a cross-sectional study of adults between the ages of 30 and 60, it was established that these two processes are almost entirely independent of one another; the correlation between the two scales was just $r = 0.06$. This shows that being good at one does not mean being good at the other. Both processes correlated positively with life satisfaction (tenacity: $r = .29$, flexibility: $r = .37$) and negatively with depression (tenacity: $r = -.33$, flexibility: $r = -.32$) (Brandstädter & Renner, 1990). They are also associated with success in achieving life goals, and it is interesting that flexibility was more associated with goal progress then tenacity, suggesting that it is more important to know when to quit than to keep committed. Age groups were compared on the two scales in the same study, and the age-related findings are shown in Figure 5.3; it was found that tenacity drops with age, and flexibility is highest in the over fifties.

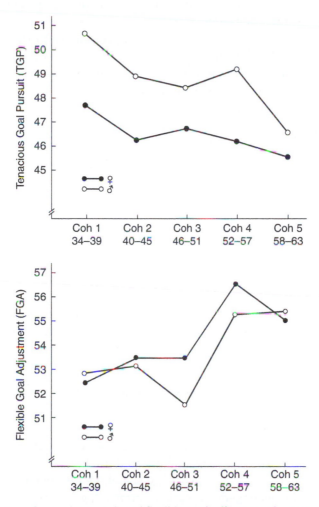

Figure 5.3   Tenacious goal pursuit and flexible goal adjustment by age and sex

Note: Solid circles = female, open circles = male. N = 890.

Source: Brandstädter and Renner (1990, p. 63). Copyright © American Psychological Association. Reprinted with permission.

Selection, Optimisation and Compensation (SOC) Theory

Selection, Optimisation and Compensation theory is a motivational approach to understanding how people manage the effects of ageing. It was originated by Paul Baltes (1997) as part of a biopsychosocial paradigm of lifespan development (Baltes, Reese & Lipsitt, 1980). In the theory, goal-directed behaviour has three possible functions; growth, maintenance and the prevention of loss. The relative prevalence of gain and loss changes over the lifespan, as ageing induces greater losses, while gains become less likely. This changing balance is illustrated in Figure 5.4.

In this theory, three interacting strategic processes, termed *selection, optimisation* and *compensation*, aim to facilitate development by *maximising gains* and *minimising losses*. Table 5.3 provides definitions of these three processes, along with example strategies and example questionnaire items for them. The questionnaire items in the table are taken from a 12-item self-report measure of the SOC model (Freund & Baltes, 1998). For each item, two alternatives are presented from which participants must select the one that they consider to be most like themselves. A composite index of SOC based on this questionnaire has been found to correlate with positive emotions, life satisfaction and an absence of loneliness in older adults (Freund & Baltes, 1998).

Box 5.3   Individual voices

Arthur Rubinstein – SOC strategies for maintaining piano performance in old age

A real-life example of the interacting processes of selection, optimisation and compensation is provided by Baltes (1997), when describing the behaviour of an eminent 80-year old pianist:

> When the concert pianist Arthur Rubinstein, as an 80-year-old, was asked in a television interview how he managed to maintain such a high level of expert piano playing, he hinted at the coordination of three strategies. First, Rubinstein said that he played fewer pieces (selection); second, he indicated that he now practiced these pieces more often (optimisation); and third, he suggested that to counteract his loss in mechanical speed, he now used a kind of impression management, such as introducing slower play before fast segments, so to make the latter appear faster (compensation). (Baltes, 1997, p. 371)

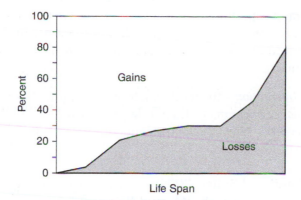

Figure 5.4   Changing ratio of gains to losses postulated to occur across the human lifespan

Source: Baltes (1997, p. 370). Copyright © American Psychological Association. Reproduced with permission.

Table 5.3   Definitions, example strategies and example questionnaire items for the three SOC model processes

Process	Definition	Example Motivational Strategies	Example Forced-choice Item from SOC Questionnaire
Selection	Selection of specific goals into which attention and action should be invested, from a pool of alternatives	Elective selection: choosing and committing to specific developmental goals Loss-based selection: searching for new goals in the face of loss	I always focus on the one most important goal at a given time vs. I am always working on several things at once
Optimisation	Intentional allocation of personal resources to achieving highest possible level of functioning in chosen domain	Practice of skills. Allocating extra time. Persisting at a task.	I make every effort to achieve a given goal vs. I prefer to wait for a while and see if things will work out by themselves
Compensation	Substitution of processes and strategies with alternatives if a loss or decline occurs in the previously used domain	Finding new means to achieve a desired end. Getting help from others.	When things don't go as well as they used to, I keep trying other ways of doing it until I can achieve the same result I used to. vs. When things don't go as they used to, I accept it.

An additional aspect of the SOC model is *goal orientations*. Given that development has three functions: growth, maintenance and prevention of loss, three trait-like goal-orientations are proposed as general motivational tendencies:

1. *Growth orientation* – the tendency to strive for growth and change
2. *Maintenance orientation* – the tendency to strive for stability
3. *Loss-prevention orientation* – the tendency to strive to avoid negative change or loss

Ebner, Freund and Baltes (2006) compared these three orientations in younger adults (ages 18–26), middle-age adults (ages 40–59) and older adults (ages 65–84). All participants were asked to generate a list of the six most important goals in their life, then rate each goal on the extent to which it was aimed at growth, maintenance or prevention of loss. Results showed that in younger adults and middle-aged adults, a growth orientation was dominant, while in older adults a maintenance orientation was stronger than a growth orientation. Prevention of loss was significantly higher in middle-aged adults and older adults than in younger adults. The same study showed that goal orientation varies in relation to wellbeing across the three age groups, as shown in Figure 5.5. In young and middle adulthood, growth orientation had a modest positive correlation with wellbeing, while in the older age group it had a negative correlation with wellbeing. The opposite

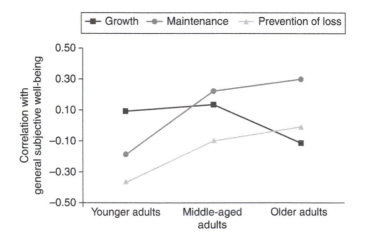

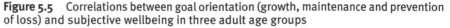

Figure 5.5   Correlations between goal orientation (growth, maintenance and prevention of loss) and subjective wellbeing in three adult age groups

Source: Ebner, Freund and Baltes (2006, p. 669). Copyright © American Psychological Association. Reprinted with permission.

pattern was true of the maintenance orientation; in younger adults it had a negative correlation with wellbeing, while in middle aged and older adults the relation with wellbeing was positive. Loss prevention orientation had a negative relation with subjective wellbeing in all age groups, suggesting that it relates to a general negativity, however this negative association is strongest in the young adult group (Ebner, Freund & Baltes, 2006).

In summary, if a goal orientation is appropriate to age, it is conducive to wellbeing, but if it is predominant at the wrong age, it is maladaptive and related to low wellbeing. A growth orientation fits best between young adulthood and a maintenance orientation fits better with old age (Rapkin & Fischer, 1992).

Self-efficacy in adulthood

For goal-directed behaviour to develop through adulthood, a person's self-belief in their ability to achieve goals must also develop. Such a belief is based on positive *self-efficacy* evaluations. A positive self-efficacy appraisal says *yes I can,* when wondering about whether one can reach a goal, while a negative appraisal is *no I can't.* Such an appraisal stems from monitoring performance in similar tasks, from observing others do the task and from what others have said by way of encouragement or discouragement (Bandura, 1977). Self-efficacy develops by way of creating a self-fulfilling prophecy – if you estimate that you *can* do a task, then you are more likely to have a go, so you get more practice at doing it, which means you are likely to get better at it, which in turn makes you feel more capable, and thus your initial sense of self-efficacy leads to higher self-efficacy in the long-term (Gecas, 1989). If a person constantly appraises *I can't* in relation to their goals, they may experience a chronic sense of incapacity to do anything successfully, and this can lead to inactivity. This process is termed *learned helplessness* (Schunk, 1991).

Cross-sectional research suggests that self-efficacy has a curvilinear relationship with age, with an increase from childhood into early adulthood, a peak in middle age and decline after the age of 60 (Gurin & Brim, 1984; Woodward & Wallston, 1987). However, another large cross-sectional study found no evidence of decline in self-efficacy in later life – it was found that self-efficacy decreases in early middle age, stabilises for the remainder of midlife, and then increases in the early sixties (Lachman, 1986). These cross-sectional findings may be influenced by cohort effects, so future longitudinal research in this area is required.

Motivational maturity: The importance of intrinsically motivated and integrated goals

What makes for mature goal-directed behaviour? Answering this question requires a clear description of a developmental ideal for motivated behaviour (Emmons, 1999). Sheldon and Kasser (2001) attempted to answer it based on theory and research. They stated that intra-personal and inter-personal *integration* is the ideal for goals (this reflects the orthogenetic direction to development, described in Chapter 1). To best serve integration, they suggest that mature goals have the following two features:

a) They are chosen as fully self-endorsed, are inherently satisfying to pursue and are coherent with personal values and sense of self (and therefore lend themselves to intra-personal integration).
b) They support basic needs, such as personal growth, connecting with others and contributing to the community (and therefore promote inter-personal integration).

Deci and Ryan (1985) refer to goals that support these two criteria as *intrinsically motivated goals*. On the other hand, *extrinsically motivated goals* are those that are undertaken for later gain and reward, and may not be intrinsically satisfying or need-satisfying. Ryan and Deci (2000) classify extrinsically motivated goals into four kinds:

- *Externally regulated goals*: These are forced by someone else or by the pressure of the environment, with no experience of personal influence or choice – they are what we *must* do ('I am doing it because the situation demands it').
- *Introjected goals*: These emerge from internalised societal or parental standards, and are adhered to out of fear of guilt or shame, rather than desire or want. They are what we feel we *should* do ('I am doing it because I am forcing myself to').
- *Identified goals*: Those goals that one feels one ought to strive for *and* which one also wants to do ('I am doing it because I feel I ought to, I feel it's valuable').
- *Integrated goals*: Extrinsic goals that emerge from an autonomous choice, and are experienced as in line with one's own preferences, interests and attributes ('I am doing it because the outcome will be rewarding').

Integrated extrinsic goals and intrinsically motivated goals are considered to be most conducive to mental health and therefore the most mature. In a cross-sectional study of adults aged 17 to 82, Sheldon and

Kasser (2001) found that mature goals are more common in older adults. They asked participants to write down ten personal goals, and then rate these goals according to four motivational states, based on Ryan and Deci's typology. It was found that age was positively associated with the intrinsic and identified states, and negatively associated with external and introjected motivation. Goal content was also assessed for maturity. Goals that were focused on community contribution, self-acceptance and emotional intimacy were more prevalent in older age adults, while goals focused on financial success, fame and recognition decreased with age. The findings suggested that the relationship of wellbeing and age is mediated by goals.

In a later study, Sheldon, Houser-Marko and Kasser (2006) compared goals in 175 college students and their parents. Participants wrote down six current personal goals. In addition, parents were asked to write down goals when they were the same age as their child. They were then asked to rate the goals on the same four motivations as the aforesaid – external, introjected, identified and intrinsic. Age was found to be associated with increased autonomy and intrinsic motivation, both when students were compared with parents, and when current parental goals were compared with goals they recalled from early adulthood.

In a large cross-sectional study, Morgan and Robinson (2012) compared the intrinsic and extrinsic goals of 2557 adults, using a psychometric measure called the *Aspirations Index*. It was found that the strength of intrinsic goals relative to extrinsic goals was significantly higher in midlife adults than young adults, and higher in older adults than midlife adults. This positive relation with intrinsic focus and age was found when aspirations were rated for their cognitive importance, *and* for the extent of behavioural striving directed towards them.

Like Sheldon and Kasser, Emmons (1999) also specifies *integration* as key to positive goal-directed action. A key aspect of integration is the challenge in having both long-term and short-term goals, and getting these two to integrate. If day-to-day goals link to life goals, then integration is greater than if they do not. His research finds that lack of goal integration is predictive of distress, supporting the idea that adaptive goal pursuit should be integrative. Emmons indicates that the solution to the challenge of long-term and short-term goals is not to remove one and focus on the other, but rather to have concrete, manageable goals to direct specific actions, along with higher-level goals that give a sense of meaning and purpose.

The importance of intrinsic motivation for goals is apparent in older adults too. Van Hiel and Vansteenkiste (2009) studied two samples of grandparents with an average age of 68 and 75 respectively. They assessed intrinsic goal attainment by compounding goal attainment in the following subscales: *self-acceptance, affiliation* and *community contribution*. They assessed extrinsic goal attainment by way of *appearance, achievements* and *prestige* subscales. They found that intrinsic goal attainment in older adults was associated with subjective wellbeing, ego integrity, lower death anxiety and greater acceptance of death. Extrinsic goal attainment, in contrast, was unrelated to wellbeing in Study one and associated with stronger feelings of despair and disappointment in Study two.

Purpose and meaning in adulthood: The search for ultimate goals

The empirical study of meaning in life was strongly influenced by the work of Victor Frankl. In his book *Man's Search for Meaning* (1984), Frankl reflects on his time in a concentration camp and suggests that the search for meaning is the primary motivation in adult life. This, he said, is evidenced by the simple fact that humans will die for meaningful ideals and values, and if they have a cause or goal to which they are passionately committed they will be able to withstand much suffering on the road to achieving it. Meaning is such a dynamic construct that it may only be fully realised towards the end of life, even in one's dying moments. Frankl wrote:

> Consider a movie; it consists of thousands upon thousands of individual pictures, and each of them makes sense and carries a meaning, yet the meaning of the whole film cannot be seen before its last sequence is shown. However, we cannot understand the whole film without having first understood each of its components, each of the individual pictures. Isn't it the same with life? Doesn't the final meaning of life, too, reveal itself, if at all, only at its end, on the verge of death? (Frankl, 1984, p. 168)

For Frankl, mental health is imparted through the *struggle* involved in pursuing a worthwhile life goal and a life of purpose. Goal pursuit brings about inevitable strain, as there is a tension between current state and ideal state which seeks resolution. The lack of such tension may temporarily bring a sense of relaxation, but in the long-term it creates an 'existential vacuum' in which there is nothing to strive for.

A number of researchers have endeavoured to quantify Frankl's theory and measure the meaning that he described as a primary life motive

(Morgan & Robinson, 2012; Reker, 2005). Reker, Peacock and Wong (1987) developed the *Life Attitude Profile* to assess various dimensions of Frankl's conception of meaning in life. The subscales of the resulting questionnaire are: Will to Meaning, Life Purpose, Existential Vacuum, Life Control, Death Acceptance, Goal Seeking and Future Meaning. A cross-sectional study of 300 adults was conducted, with 60 adults in each of the following age groups: 16–29, 30–49, 50–64, 65–74 and 75+. The study found that the Will to Meaning scale does *not* change with age. Other aspects of the scale were age-linked. Goal Seeking decreases with age, as does the importance of Future Meaning. On the other hand, Death Acceptance and Life Purpose both show higher means in older age groups than in young adults. Existential Vacuum mean scores are highest in middle age, suggesting a midlife dip in meaning and sense of purpose. The presence of a life purpose and the absence of an existential vacuum were found at all ages to be related to wellbeing, as Frankl would have predicted.

Adult motivation in context: The motive to volunteer

The chapter so far has focused on goals and motivation at a general level, rather than at the level of real-life contexts. There are additional areas of literature, some of which are not within psychology, that look at motivation within a particular occupational, leisure or relationship context. One such domain is the area of volunteering.

Volunteering is the activity of engaging in helping roles that are not aimed directly at material gain or mandated or coerced by others, and are perceived as beneficial to others (Cnaan, Handy & Wadsworth, 1996). Research has been conducted on the motivations for engaging in volunteering activity using both quantitative and qualitative methods, and the overall picture is one of a complex set of motivations that differ according to age and life stage. Motives involve a combination of altruistic (other-oriented) and egoistic (self-oriented) goals (Blanchard, 2006). The Volunteer Functions Inventory (VFI) is an assessment tool for quantitatively assessing motives for volunteering (Clary et al., 1998). It originally located six basic motives for volunteering, but a seventh has been added more recently (Okun & Schultz, 2003). The seven motive domains are:

1. Career: developing and enhancing one's career
2. Enhancement: enhancing and enriching personal development and sense of worth

3. Social: conforming to the norms of significant others
4. Protective: escaping from negative feelings
5. Learning and skill practice: learning new skills and practicing underutilised abilities
6. Value: Expressing personal altruistic values
7. Making friends: using volunteer activities to meet like-minded peers

The presence of these motives has been verified in a study with older adults (Okun, Barr & Herzog, 1998). The typology was employed in a study that looked at the relationship between volunteer motivation and age (Okun & Schultz, 2003). Four motives were significantly negatively related to age: career ($r = -.48$), learning ($r = -.18$), enhancement ($r = -.12$) and protective ($r = -.22$) motives. Making friends, social and values motives were not significantly related to age, however a curvilinear relationship between the making friends motive and age was found; younger adults and adults in their sixties showed this motive to a greater degree than middle aged adults or adults in their seventies or eighties. The authors speculate that the friend motive in elderly adults may reflect a desire to replenish social networks after retirement from full-time work.

Qualitative studies support this distinction in volunteering motivations in younger and older adults. Rehberg (2005) collected data from 118 telephone interviews with young adults (average age of 24) from Switzerland who volunteer for international charities. Motivations mentioned by respondents included descriptions of altruistic helping motives, motives surrounding the gaining of new and stimulating experiences, as well as instrumental motives of seeking to further a career in the non-profit sector. Example quotes from this study are shown in Box 5.4.

Box 5.4   Individual voices

Motives for international volunteering in young adults (Rehberg, 2005)

Achieving something positive for others

> Yes, my main motivation is knowing that you can have an effect and that you can be of help, that I can do something, where I can see a result maybe. Well, maybe I see . . . yes, I've constructed that well or something like that. Simply the motivation, knowing that those people are better off after such a stay. Interview 36

Box 5.4   Continued

Quest for the new

Culture is very important for me, and getting to know other cultures. I've realised that many problems stem from misunderstandings between cultures. It's my wish to develop a greater tolerance between peoples. I also want to refine my understanding for people. I've also realised that the way somebody acts only makes sense if I know his or her culture better. Interview 12

Quest for oneself

Right now I'm somewhat disoriented in my job, what I want to do in the future, where I'm heading professionally, and maybe such a program can clarify or open perspectives. Interview 53

Motives in combination

My motivation is that you can do something which is of help to somebody, that you can achieve something. In such a voluntary program one really gets to know the people, the culture and the living conditions, and that shows you how well off we are in Switzerland. The culture is also very interesting, of course, as is the group of volunteers. You get to know new people, you also learn something about yourself and to value yourself more, because it certainly can be very stressful. Interview 84

Brown et al. (2011) conducted a qualitative study into volunteer motivations in adults between the age of 57 and 88. All respondents had volunteered for *Habitat for Humanity*, a scheme in which a house is built in one week for a person in need. The volunteering motives they found lacked the instrumental quality of the motives described by the young adults in Rehberg's study and by the quantitative findings of Okun and Schultz (2003). Their thematic scheme encompassed a variety of helping motives: giving time, giving self, giving money, doing things for others and active involvement. Circumstantial conditions were other key aspects of the motive to volunteer, including being financially able, having partner support, having availability of time, feeling good and being retired. The absence of potentially hindering conditions was noted too, such as the absence of health problems.

Concluding comments

Current theories and research literature on motivational development in adulthood help to provide answers to a number of questions about why humans behave as they do. Changes in drives explain why older adults eat, drink and have sex less than younger adults. Theories of goal pursuit account for why different goals are relevant only to particular portions of the lifespan, while SOC theory provides an account of how older people maintain performance in goal-directed activity. Issues of motivation will crop up again in later chapters on morality, personality and spirituality, so bear these ideas in mind for a while longer.

Questions for you to reflect on

- Why do older adults and younger adults typically have different goals? What do the different theories in this chapter say to help answer this question?
- Are you better at goal pursuit or goal adjustment? Can you think of a recent project where you had to adjust your goal so that you could keep pursuing it?
- Do you know any adults over the age of 65 who are still working? How do they use the strategies of selection, optimisation and compensation to maintain performance in their job? Perhaps you could ask them if they've had to change their approach to work as they've got older.

Summary points

- The primary drives are unlearnt internal urges to meet biological needs, such as sex drive, hunger, thirst and sleep. Research suggests that the intensity and frequency of these drives decreases with age, thus changing motivational dynamics in human beings as they move through adulthood.
- Charlotte Bühler and Abraham Maslow both developed influential theories of how motivation changes with development. Bühler's theory focused on how *life goals* develop and change with age, while Maslow focused on how *needs* change as a person develops. Maslow's highest need is self-actualisation.
- The motivational theory of lifespan development states that action opportunities are shaped by the lifespan, and that such opportunities come and go and a person ages, due to both social norms and biological constraints.
- The balance between goal pursuit (primary control) and goal flexibility (secondary control) is essential for adaptive development. The balance changes as a person ages, so that less pursuit and more flexibility

is emphasised in elderly persons, relative to younger persons. Also, as people age, they generally become more focused on behaviours that maintain the status quo rather than on behaviours that lead to growth and change.

- SOC theory specifies three motivational processes that are employed to minimise losses in life: selection, optimisation and compensation. These are used to make the most of out of a person's resources if they experience any loss of a particular ability.
- The kinds of goals a person focuses on relate to their position in the life course. Adolescents tend to aim at improvement, young adults tend to have goals relating to their profession and health, while midlife adults are focused on goals relating to the health.
- Purpose and meaning is imparted by a high-level goal that integrates day-to-day goals into a long-term sense of direction and contribution.
- There are many kinds of goals, and not all are equally healthy or mature. Goals that are mature are enjoyable, coherent with one's own sense of self, and support personal growth while connecting with other people and the community.
- Volunteering is an area in which an understanding of motivation is important. Motives for volunteering differ by age group and are complex. The research demonstrates that one activity can serve lots of different goals, as volunteering serves career goals, self-development goals, social goals and self-protective goals.

Recommended reading

Baltes, P. B. (1997). On the incomplete architecture of human ontogeny. Selection, optimization, and compensation as foundation of developmental theory. *The American Psychologist*, 52, 366–380.

Brandtstädter, J. & Rothermund, K. (2002). The life-course dynamics of goal pursuit and goal adjustment: A two-process framework. *Developmental Review*, 22, 117–150.

Bühler, C. (1967). Human life goals in the humanistic perspective. *Journal of Humanistic Psychology*, 7, 36–52.

Ebner, N. C., Freund, A. M. & Baltes, P. B. (2006). Developmental changes in personal goal orientation from young to late adulthood: From striving for gains to maintenance and prevention of losses. *Psychology and Aging*, 21, 664–678.

Heckhausen, J., Wrosch, C. & Schulz, R. (2010). A motivational theory of life-span development. *Psychological Review*, 117, 32–60.

Reker, G. T., Peacock, E. J. & Wong, P. T. P. (1987). Meaning and purpose in life and well-being: A life-span perspective. *Journal of Gerontology*, 42, 44–49.

Sheldon, K. M. & Kasser, T. (2001). Getting older, getting better? Personal strivings and psychological maturity across the life span. *Developmental Psychology*, 37, 491–501.

6

Psychosocial Life Stages, Transitions and Crises

In youth you find out what you care to do and who you care to be...In young adulthood you learn whom you care to be with ... In adulthood, however, you learn what and whom you can take care of.

Erik Erikson

Guy was approaching 40, was working 11 hours a day, and was just too busy with work to notice that both his wife and son felt neglected. For years, his life has revolved around his work, and the pressure of his lifestyle had led to a growing tendency in him towards aggression and irritability. One day his wife told him she was filing for divorce, which led to a period of emotional turmoil in Guy's life and a total rethink of his priorities and aspirations. He reflected that he went through an all-consuming crisis for several years. After his wife had moved out, he changed job, and then tried a new career as a self-employed consultant. He started to spend more time with his son, and found satisfaction in being a parent – a role that he previously had given little attention to. He picked up new hobbies such as dancing, and found renewed interest in reading science books – an interest that he had when he was younger but that had disappeared under the weight of his career. Guy reflected that following this period of crisis, he changed in many positive ways, including becoming a more loving parent to his son.

The previous three chapters focused on the development of a particular mental modality – either cognition, emotion or motivation. In this chapter, the focus is on the whole person in their social context, and the all-consuming phases and transitions that define adulthood as a totality. This *holistic* approach to adult life stages and transitions has enduring popular appeal, due to the ease of translating it into literature that is accessible to non-specialists. In this chapter, we will first refer to theoretical ideas from Erik Erikson and Daniel Levinson, before discussing holistic life stages and transitions, including emerging adulthood, early adulthood, early adult crisis, the transition to parenthood, midlife, menopause, the Third Age and the Fourth Age.

Erik Erikson's model of the life-cycle

The holistic approach to studying life stages and life transitions began with the work of Erik Erikson. Erikson was born in Germany in 1902, and in the late 1920s became an art teacher in Vienna. There he met Sigmund Freud's daughter Anna, who introduced him to Vienna's Freudian community and to psychoanalytic ideas. In response to the rise of Nazism in the 1930s, Erikson moved to the USA with his family and set up as a child analyst in Boston. There he made connections with researchers at Harvard. Despite not having a degree, he went on to have an illustrious career in academia, including professorships at Yale, the University of California and Harvard University. He died in 1994.

Erikson referred to his integrative approach to studying development as 'triple book-keeping' – by this he meant that in order to understand human development, *biological*, *psychological* and *social* factors should be studied interdependently (Erikson, 1950). The relationship between individual and society, according to him, in the theory is defined by *mutuality* – this means that a person shapes their social context while the social context in turn shapes them and their development (Stevens, 2008). The notion of 'ego' is central to Erikson's scheme of individual development. The ego ties human thought, affect and behaviour together into a singular whole that develops over time. Its function is to integrate drives, thoughts, emotions, fantasies, personality, moral standards and social relations into an *identity* – a sense of being a unique, integrated and authentic person (Erikson, 1968a; 1980). Life is a never-ending search for wholeness, according to Erikson. This sense of wholeness is never fully achieved by the ego, and therefore the search for it continues across the whole lifespan.

Erikson proposed an eight-stage model of the life-cycle, which is summarised in Table 6.1. In Chapter 3, the idea of dialectical thinking was introduced as part of the discussion on post-formal cognition. Here we encounter the idea again, as Erikson used dialectics to characterise his theory. A dialectic is a pair of opposites that conflict (that is, more of one means less of the other) and yet cannot exist in isolation from one another. Erikson used a different dialectic to define each stage of his model. The aim at each stage is to find a balance between the pairs of opposites, until it's time to move onto the next stage and the next challenge. When you look at the dialectics in Table 6.1 you might think that one of each pair of terms is desirable, and the other is not; for example in the *self-esteem vs. inferiority* dialectic, surely self-esteem is better? Erikson was in fact of the view that *both* extremes are problematic. For example if self-esteem becomes excessive, it turns into narcissism and arrogance, while too much inferiority can turn into depression and self-loathing. A healthy balance is in fact found in a sense of self worth balanced with a sense of humility (Erikson, 1968; 1980).

Table 6.1   Erikson's eight stages of the life-cycle

Stage	Approximate Age Range	Developmental task of that stage	Dialectic	Significant others	Virtue arising from successful passage
1	0–1.5 years	Attachment to primary caregiver	Trust vs. mistrust	Mother	Hope
2	1.5–3 years	Gaining some basic control over self and environment	Autonomy vs. shame and doubt	Parents	Will
3	3–6 years	Becoming purposeful and directive	Initiative vs. guilt	Family	Purpose
4	6 years–puberty	Developing social, physical and school skills	Self-esteem vs. inferiority	School	Competence
5	Adolescence	Experimentation and exploration of ideals and social contexts	Identity vs. role confusion	Peer groups, role models	Authenticity
6	Early adulthood	Establishing intimate bonds of love and friendship	Intimacy vs. isolation	Partner / spouse, friends	Love
7	Middle adulthood	Fulfilling life goals that involve concern for future generations	Generativity vs. stagnation	Children, younger generation	Caring
8	Late adulthood	Looking back over life and accepting its meaning	Integrity vs. despair	Mankind	Wisdom

According to Erikson, if an imbalance in a developmental dialectic becomes sufficiently extreme, it leads to a crisis. A *crisis* is a transition point between stable periods of adult life that results in heightened vulnerability and stress. Each crisis is a turning point and a chance to make changes that will bring balance to an imbalanced life structure.

You might think from reading a summary of Erikson's theory such as Table 6.1 that a person would be located in one particular developmental stage, depending on their age. In fact Erikson was of the view that people oscillate between at least two of these developmental dialectics. The stage at which a particular dialectic is highlighted is not the only time it exists as a developmental challenge; it is just the time that it is usually dominant. The adolescent and adult phases of this model will be returned to later in this chapter. Erikson's scheme can be best thought of as a tool to think with and as a simplified map of life, rather than a prescriptive set of invariant stages (Stevens, 2008). His holistic approach provided a starting point for researchers and theorists who have since emulated his focus on the whole person's journey through definable life stages, crises and formative transitions. In the late 1960s and mid-1970s, there was a rush of neo-Eriksonian research and theory. Marcia's research into identity statuses in adolescence, which will be described shortly, was one of the first and most influential of these approaches, and was the first to quantify Eriksonian concepts (Marcia, 1966). Other neo-Eriksonian research employed qualitative methods, but given that most journals at the time were not open to reporting qualitative research, these studies were mostly published in book form (Gould, 1978; Levinson, 1978; Lidz, 1976; Loevinger, 1976; Sheehy, 1976; Vaillant, 1977; White, 1975).

Levinson and the life structure

Daniel Levinson was one of the most influential of the neo-Eriksonian crowd. He introduced the *life structure*, as a concept that linked inner and outer sides of adult development. External aspects of the life structure include work roles, family commitments, leisure pursuits and social networks, while internal aspects include identity, personal values, goals and interests. The developmental challenge is to get, and keep, these two sides in balance. Levinson states that wholeness and balance is found in their creative and harmonious integration (Levinson, 1978). If this is a achieved, a person has a life structure, and if not, they are probably trying to build one.

If inner and outer are at any time out of balance, this may provoke a transitional time during which a better life structure is sought. For example, if a person inwardly values and desires sport, but has no time in his/her life structure devoted to sport, then inner and outer are out of balance. Such an imbalance can be addressed by altering one's lifestyle or one's values and goals. The timing of major life structure transitions is influenced by predictable social and biological changes such as the transition to parenthood or retirement. This predictability is the basis of Levinson's stage model of adult development (Levinson, 1978; 1996). We return to the model several times in this chapter – firstly in relation to early adulthood, and secondly in relation to midlife crisis.

Transition and crisis

Transitions and crises are unstable episodes in a person's life during which important aspects of his/her ways of thinking, feeling, behaving, identifying and relating to others undergo wholesale change (Schlossberg, 1981; Caplan, 1964). There is typically a triggering event for a crisis, for example a career crisis may be occasioned by being fired, or a personal crisis may be brought about by illness or bereavement (Clausen, 1995; Hopson & Adams, 1976). The triggering event is then followed by changes in behaviour, goals, identity, relationships, work and/or family roles that are aimed at bringing balance back to life and reducing stress (Clausen, 1995; Robinson & Smith, 2010b). Crisis is a particularly intense and urgent form of transition, characterised by serious emotional difficulties and challenges to sense of self and world, which if not resolved may lead to severe dysfunction or breakdown (Slaikeu, 1990).

Crises and transitions can lead to growth and development, but can also lead to decline (Parry, 1990). A number of variables can affect whether the outcome of a transition is positive or negative, including health, financial resources and social support (Schlossberg, 1981). For example, successful resolution of an adult crisis often entails a moratorium from major commitments (Waterman, 1993), which in turn requires financial and social resources to take time out, for example from work or childrearing. Retraining is often an essential part of a career transition but this also requires money, time and social resources. Despite all this, crisis and transition provides an opportunity for growth and development for the following reasons:

- Habit, routine and fear of uncertainty mean that people often avoid change even when the status quo is distressing, dissatisfying or stagnating. A transition or crisis may provide a stimulus for change that overcomes the inertia to remain the same and avoid disruption (O'Connor & Wolfe, 1987)
- Coping with crisis can increase a person's sense of autonomy, strength, empowerment and confidence, as it provides direct evidence

of one's ability to manage in difficult situations (Robinson, 2008; Robinson & Smith, 2010a; Wethington, Kessler & Pixley, 2004)

- Transition and crisis involve an enhanced focus on, and exploration of, the self and identity, which can in turn lead to enhanced self-understanding and self-knowledge (Levinson, 1978; Horton, 2002)
- Transition can precede higher orthogenetic integration, as existing schemas are consciously questioned and reassessed, and a more coherent and encompassing worldview sought (Erikson, 1980; Parry, 1990)
- Transition and crisis often entail a re-consideration of values, priorities and goals. This can lead to an increased sense of life's meaningfulness, and an invigorated sense of purpose (Denne & Thompson, 1991)
- Transition and crisis can lead to the removal of a life structure within which a person feels passive and helpless, and replacing it with a life structure that is more empowering and conducive to self-determination (Levinson, 1978; Hopson & Adams, 1976)
- The confrontation with a major crisis can lead to an enhanced appreciation for everyday existence and an increased enjoyment of life (Tedeschi & Calhoun, 1995)

As we will see throughout this chapter, transitions and crises are shaped by biological age and by life stage. There is evidence that they are not dispersed evenly through adult life, and cluster around certain age groups (Clausen, 1995). According to one study, midlife is the main time of transition for men, while the early thirties is a more frequent time for transitions for women (Wethington, Kessler & Pixley, 2004).

Box 6.1   Alternative perspectives

Adolescence and identity crisis: A modern phenomenon?

At a biological level, the beginning of adolescence is defined by the onset of puberty and the all-consuming physical changes that come with the start of menstruation for women and the start of sexual function in men. At earlier points in history, this was taken to mean that parenthood was a good idea from the early teenage years; however the modern view is that adolescents should generally not be burdened with the pressures of adult commitments such as parenthood, but instead should be able to explore and to keep learning (Fasick, 1994). Erikson

Box 6.1   Continued

(1950) termed adolescence a *psychosocial moratorium*, by which he meant that its defining feature is a chance to explore and experiment without the pressure to commit to any particular role or institution.

The main developmental challenge that Erikson equated with adolescence is the quest for *identity*. Marcia developed the theory of identity statuses, to further clarify the nature of identity formation in adolescence that Erikson described (Marcia, 1966; 1993). By combining the effects of two processes, *identity exploration* and *commitment*, Marcia conceived of four possible identity statuses in adolescence:

1. *Identity Diffusion (ID)* – No commitments made, and no identity exploration attempted.
2. *Foreclosure (F)* – Identity is set according to a prearranged cultural template, without any active identity exploration.
3. *Moratorium (M)* – An adolescent is engaged in active exploration of alternative aspects of themselves, but is yet to commit to a clear identity.
4. *Identity Achievement (IA)* – Exploration has been successfully engaged in and an autonomous identity adopted.

Research has found that the status of *Identity Achievement* is related to better interpersonal relationships, more balanced thinking and more effective decision-making (Schwartz, 2001). Central to the search for identity in adolescence is time for *exploration*. In past centuries, exploratory trial-and-error in adolescence was rarely available, as children were often in work from the age of 14 and married by 18. So adolescence is arguably a modern phenomenon – an extension of childhood to allow young people to develop their own identities (Bakan, 1971).

Emerging adulthood

Between adolescence and adulthood, there is arguably a distinct and definable life stage that runs between approximately the ages of 18 and 25 and is characterised by features that distinguish it qualitatively from what comes before and after. Levinson (1986) refers to this phase as the *Leaving the Family* phase, and also as the *Early Adult Transition* (Levinson 1978). Jeffrey Arnett (2000) has labelled this phase *Emerging Adulthood,* and has gathered a wide-ranging body of evidence to support its existence as a definable life stage. The theory of emerging adulthood has also met with criticism from various quarters (for example, Hendry & Kloep, 2007), and this will be mentioned as part of a general critique of holistic stage theories at the end of the chapter.

Emerging adulthood is an in-between stage during which a person is part-adolescent and part-adult. Arnett has found that the majority of young people, when asked if they feel if they have reached adulthood yet, respond 'yes and no' (see Figure 6.1). Key differences between adolescence and emerging adulthood include (a) the fact that adolescence is defined for the majority by living with parents, whereas emerging adults typically have moved out of the family home, (b) that after the age of 18 people are given adult rights such as driving, drinking, voting and marriage and (c) that due to increased independence from family, the scope for experimentation and risk-taking is greater than in adolescence.

Key differences between emerging adulthood and later adulthood include (a) presence of continuing education for many, (b) a non-committal approach to relationships and career, (c) a lack of financial independence from parents, (d) frequent changes in residence and work, (e) and a tendency to question one's own worldview and experiment with alternatives (Arnett, 2000; 2007a). As emerging adulthood comes to an end, the diversity and exploratory attitude that is characteristic of

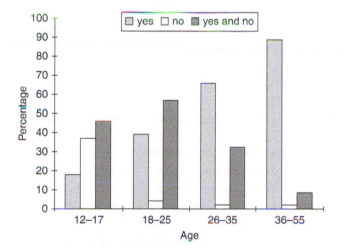

Figure 6.1   Frequencies of response to the question 'Do you feel that you have reached adulthood yet?' categorised by four age groups

Note: N = 519.

Source: Arnett (2000, p. 472). Copyright © American Psychological Association. Reproduced with permission.
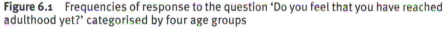

emerging adulthood becomes less prevalent, while long-term commitments in work and home-life become the norm.

The stage of emerging adulthood is a culturally-specific and historically-recent phenomenon. Arnett (2000) pins its emergence to the 1960s in Western industrialised cultures and to social changes that have permitted continued identity and role exploration after adolescence. This is firstly because increased per-capita affluence has allowed those between the ages of 18 and 25 to defer full-time entry to the workforce, in favour of study and higher education. Secondly, changes in social norms since the 1960s now mean that young people do not need to be in a marriage to experience sex, and that marriage, partnership and parenthood can be deferred to the late twenties or early thirties (Arnett, 2000; 2001).

In a variety of cultures and environments, emerging adulthood is still not the norm. For example, in cultures where marriage and parenthood still typically begin in the late teenage years or early twenties, emerging adulthood is not a definable life stage for most. Also, in environments where young people must work from a young age or remain living in the parental household, emerging adulthood will be marked by its absence (see Box 6.2).

Box 6.2   Cross-cultural perspectives

Submerging adulthood? Children of unauthorised immigrants in the USA during the transition to adulthood

Emerging adulthood is the time during which a young person engages in further exploration after the end of adolescence, thus deferring adult commitments for a number of years. For young immigrants whose parents have entered a Western country illegally, opportunities for post-adolescent exploration may not exist (Suarez-Orozco et al., 2011). A study of the children of unauthorised immigrants in the USA found that these individuals reach adulthood only to find that they are unable to gain work, social security or a driving licence legally and that work opportunities are typically limited to physical labour or cleaning jobs, even if they have managed to get a good public education. Furthermore, they typically contribute a substantial proportion of their earnings to their parents, meaning they have insufficient funds to live independently. The authors of the study conclude that 'for unauthorized young adults, this phase can be characterized as a time of not emerging but, rather, of *submerging* adulthood. They must now adapt to living below the surface of legality' (Suarez-Orozco et al., 2011, p. 455).

Early adulthood

Early adulthood is the period that runs between emerging adulthood and midlife. It starts in one's mid-twenties and concludes around the age of 40. In Erikson's map of the life course, early adulthood is allocated a specific task, and that is to develop a sense of *intimacy* by way of becoming *socially embedded* (Stevens, 2008). Intimacy is defined here as the ability to be close to others, whether as a lover, a friend, a colleague or a participant of society more generally. It requires the courage to enter into social commitments and roles, without the fear of being engulfed or trapped by those bonds. This challenge of developing intimacy contrasts with the tasks of adolescence and emerging adulthood, which are principally focused on becoming *separate* and *free* from constraint. Intimacy, on the other hand, requires an acceptance of limitation and attachment in order to be embedded in relationship, family and work (Lidz, 1976). Hard-won adolescent freedoms must be renounced to move into adult roles.

Partnership, career and parenthood are all expressions of intimacy, under Erikson's definition. If these kinds of intimacy are not achieved, a person will experience isolation, or even exclusion from the social world. This is a difficult situation to be in, for the adult may become detached from the world around them, leading to depression, resentment or anger. On the flipside, excessive intimacy can lead to feelings of *engulfment* and a loss of individuality (Erikson, 1968b; Laing, 1969). As with all of Erikson's life stages, positive development is found in a balance between the extremes; not too embedded and not to detached. If a balance is achieved, early adulthood brings a sense of healthy mutuality – a capacity to be both 'me' and 'we'. This challenge of individuality and togetherness is particularly salient in the transition to parenthood, which is discussed later in the chapter.

Levinson built on Erikson's ideas of early adulthood, by emphasising its contradictions; it is the peak period of biological functioning and physical prowess, but is also a vulnerable time as a person endeavours to build a sustainable life structure for the first time and to find financial security (Clausen, 1995; Levinson, 1978; 1996). It is also a time of heightened risk for being diagnosed with a variety of mental illnesses, a point that will be returned to in Chapter 11.

Levinson breaks up early adulthood into three substages; *Entering the Adult World*, the *Age Thirty Transition* and *Settling Down*. *Entering the Adult World* runs approximately between 22 and 28, the principle task of which is to fashion a life structure that links self and society. This fits with Erikson's challenge of intimacy. Here, a young person must balance *transience* with *stability*. Transience refers to the avoidance of finalised commitments and keeping options open, while stability is formed by long-term roles at home and at work. The *Age Thirty Transition* is an opportunity to work on the flaws and limitations of the life structure that defined one's twenties and update it for the challenges of the following decade of life.

The stage of *Settling Down* (approximately ages 33–40) is one step further into adulthood. Here a person makes further social investment, by developing stronger ties with family, work and community, while continuing to pursue personal aspirations. The two tasks of this phase are termed (a) *establishing a niche in society*, and (b) *trying to make it*. Pulkkinen, Nurmi and Kokko (2002) studied goals in this age group using interview data from 283 Finnish participants. Unsurprisingly, *family* and *profession* emerged as the two most valued domains for goal-directed behaviour at this age.

The *Settling Down* period is defined by advancement within a stable life structure for around half, while for the remainder it is a time of decline, breaking out, change or instability. Half of the unstable group in Levinson's study described temporary transitional experiences in this age range similar to the Age Thirty Transition or the Midlife Transition (which we will move on to shortly), while others describe more constant problems. In a nutshell, the *Settling Down* period is a time of life during which a person either gets ahead or falls behind in ways that are increasingly hard to remedy in midlife.

Early adult crisis ('quarterlife' crisis)

The term 'quarterlife crisis' was coined in 2001 with the publication of a popular book on the topic by Robbins and Wilner's (2001), followed by a self-help book by Barr (2004). The authors of these books were journalists who presented an anecdotal and selective picture of crisis in early adulthood. More recently, a programme of research has been conducted on crisis in early adulthood, based on in-depth interviews with individuals about crises between the ages of 25 and 35 (Robinson, 2008; 2011b; Robinson & Smith, 2010a; 2010b). Fifty participants of varying backgrounds and ethnicities recounted crisis episodes from their late twenties or early thirties in semi-structured interviews (Robinson, Smith & Wright, 2012). Analysis of the accounts showed that such crises revolve around emotionally painful separations from a long-term relationship, or separation from a job, or both. A four-phase process was found to be common to cases of early adult crisis, each phase of which is defined by (a) a particular life situation, (b) a particular sense of identity, (c) a central motivation and d) a dominant affect. This 'multi-level phase model' of early adult crisis is summarised in Table 6.2. In Phase 1 of a crisis, the person has a set of specific and enduring roles and commitments, and thus is 'out' of emerging adulthood

Table 6.2 The multi-level phase model of early adult ('quarterlife') crisis

	Life situation	Affect	Identity	Motivation
Phase 1: Locked-In	Commitments at home and at work	Constriction, entrapment, frustration	Identified with role, focused on impression	Extrinsic motivation
Phase 2a: Separation	Termination of problematic commitment(s)	Emotional upheaval and distress	Uncertain and confused	Avoidance – focus on change and escape
Phase 2b: Time Out	Moratorium, avoidance of committed roles	Declining emotional distress and guilt	Fluid, open, exploratory, unsure	Motivation to recover and reflect
Phase 3: Exploration	Tentative steps towards new commitments	Anxiety and excitement	More achieved and empowered	Search motivation
Phase 4: Rebuilding	Re-commitment to a new relationship or job	Passion and enjoyment	Closer fit between self and life structure	Intrinsic motivation

(Arnett, 2000). However, these adult roles prove to be unsupportive of identity, aspirations and values, and are separated from in Phase 2a. Following separation, a temporary moratorium and identity-exploration occurs in Phase 2a and 3, and the process of constructing adulthood begins again in Phase 4.

For simplicity's sake, the four phases are presented in a linear sequence in Table 6.2 (see overleaf), but in individual cases non-linear movement between phases was evident. For example, a person may separate from a job (Phase 2), and then when faced with the anxiety of change in Phase 3 may temporarily head back into the job or career that was the source of the problem. Another example is that a person may start to rebuild a new life structure (Phase 4) by retraining, and then change their mind about the direction they are heading in, leading to another separation (Phase 2) followed by a new period of exploring for alternatives.

In summary, quarterlife crisis can be interpreted as an emotionally fraught breakdown in early adulthood life structure and identity, followed by attempts to build a more balanced life structure and more coherent adult identity.

The transition to parenthood

The transition to being a parent is traditionally considered to be a key marker on the road to adult maturity (Nelson, 2003; Palkovitz, 2007).

For 92 per cent of first-time parents, this transition occurs within the life stage of early adulthood (20–40). According to the Office for National Statistics, in 2010 the average age of a woman at first childbirth was 27 for non-married mothers and 30 for married mothers (www.ons.gov.uk), and for 45 per cent this occurs in unmarried couples.

The commencement of parenthood is a biopsychosocial transition in a complete sense, as it involves physical, psychological and social changes in the lives of the parents. For the woman the opening phase of the transition to parenthood is pregnancy, personal experiences of which are described in Box 6.3. At this point, women typically seek information from a number of sources about pregnancy, labour and motherhood, to gain some kind of control of the process. Research shows that advice is most often taken from books, followed by friends, specialist classes and one's mother (Deutsch et al., 1988).

Box 6.3   Individual voices

Issues of control during pregnancy

Realisations of not being in control, and of accepting this, described by women who are pregnant for the first time:

Schneider (2002) explored women's experiences of pregnancy, and found frequent descriptions of a sense of losing control, and having to come to terms with that:

> I was remembering saying to my mother that it's the first time in my life that I haven't felt in control. I'm not in control any more and it's made me aware of – I've never thought about it before – of almost what a control person I am in a way, and that's not necessarily a good thing, but I've always thought I support myself and basically I'm in control of myself. Now it's just all happening to me and I really don't have any control. Beth
>
> I feel a bit like a vessel, it's all just happening to me. Grace
> I feel more grounded but that doesn't mean I'm in control. I've relinquished control to a degree. I can't control the changes – I think I've accepted that. Maureen
>
> It was just amazing! Before I had the ultrasound I thought, 'Am I really pregnant?' But then I saw the arms and legs and I knew there was something there. It was just so hard to comprehend. Maria

Following the birth of the first child, there are dramatic changes in daily routines, activities and sleep patterns for parents (Nelson, 2003). The extent of this change in daily living is difficult to grasp in advance, thus a recommended antenatal exercise is to imagine a day in one's life after the baby is born (see Box 6.4).

Box 6.4   Real-world applications

Antenatal exercise for parents – Changes in one's 24-hour routine

This exercise is aimed at helping expectant first-time parents grasp the enormity of the change to their daily routines that will occur after their baby is born (Ockenden, 2002). Each parent is given a sheet with 10 24-hour clock faces, as illustrated next, and asked to fill one in for now, and one for when the baby is six weeks old, describing daily activities. Both parents are reminded that a baby of six weeks might sleep on average 10–12 hours in 24, feed approximately eight times and that each feed might occupy up to an hour. The two parents then discuss what they have written down and gain advice from an expert or experienced mother on the reality of the daily routine at six weeks post-birth.

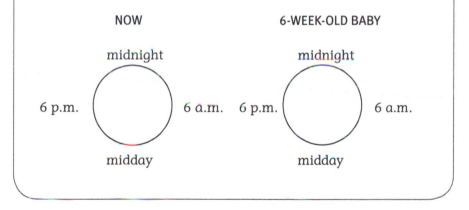

Parents will experience changes in their mood in the months following birth. Tiredness, sleep deprivation and physical weakness, combined with the challenges of adapting to a new and demanding lifestyle, can lead to emotional instability, mood swings and hypersensitivity (Belsky & Kelly, 1994; Winson, 2009). The mother also has to handle the change in body shape that often comes with pregnancy and the post-natal state, which may require adjustment in body expectations (Winson, 2009). Emotions may also relate to reflections on their own experience of being parented as a child (Nelson, 2003), potentially leading to an experience of delayed empathy (see Chapter 4), as the challenges of parenting provide a new perspective on what one's own parents experienced at this stage of life.

For both parents, the transition to parenthood requires taking on a new label and role; the man becomes a father and the woman a mother. This can take months or years (Rubin, 1984).

The mother may experience a sense of being removed from the social world while she takes time off work to care for her newborn, prior to re-emerging into society with an altered status (van Gennep, 1960). At around the age of eight months, an infant will typically become more demanding emotionally and clingy, while being more physically mobile and so more demanding of constant attention. This often occurs when mothers are looking to re-establish their sense of independence and personal identity away from the child, and so can be a challenging time (Mercer, 2004). For men, the growth and sense of reward that comes with fathering may be at the expense of career advancement, particularly in the case of single fathers (Palkovitz, 2007). One 32-year-old single father said: 'I'd be way beyond this as far as career was concerned. As personal growth is concerned, I couldn't touch it without the children. I've grown personally more than I could ever expect to have grown with the children than without. But career-wise, I could have excelled way beyond where I'm at now' (Palkovitz, Christiansen & Dunn, 1998).

In a synthesis of qualitative research on the transition to motherhood, Nelson (2003) reports that mothers typically describe becoming more patient, more capable of love and empathy, and more endowed with a strong sense of purpose and meaning. On the flipside, the transition brings with it a deep sense of loss that should be consciously acknowledged, even though it may be considered taboo to discuss it. Mothers must grieve the loss of the independent person they were before motherhood commenced and 'let go' of their previous identity (Rubin, 1984), if they are to make the transition successfully. The changes can be emotionally overwhelming; around one in five mothers and one in seven fathers describe some distress or evidence of mental health problems (Morse, Buist & Durkin, 2000). Post-natal depression is a clinical condition that a minority of mothers develop after the birth of a child, which is described in Chapter 11.

Midlife: The afternoon of life

Midlife is a phase of life during which a person typically describes feeling both young and old simultaneously, for at this age they are enjoying the gains of earlier adult development while encountering age-related declines for the first time, such as menopause and the loss of physical strength or figure (Lachman, 2004). For research purposes, midlife is defined as ages 40 to 60, and some researchers distinguish between early midlife (approximately

40–50) and late midlife (approximately 50–60) (Kim & Moen, 2001), a distinction which is becoming increasingly salient in a social world where organisations for the 'over-fifties' abound, such as SAGA in the UK.

Those in lower socio-economic groups tend to report an earlier entry into midlife, as well as an earlier exit, corresponding to their tendency to marry earlier, have children earlier and become grandparents earlier (Kuper & Marmot, 2003). The age of 60–5 is the generally agreed timeframe for shifting out of middle adulthood into late adulthood; however, this does not necessarily reflect real-life experience; those over 65 still commonly view themselves as middle-aged (Lachman, 2004).

Midlife is appraised by all adult age groups as a predominantly positive period of life (Freund & Ritter, 2009). *The Baby Boomers at Midlife* survey (cited in Lachman, 2004) reported that 64 per cent of adults in midlife said they felt hopeful about the next five years and 80 per cent were satisfied with their life. However, at the individual level, the trajectory of personal wellbeing through midlife changes in various ways including positively, negatively, neutrally and in a u-shaped dip that decreases and then recovers (Lachman et al., 1994). For those in the workforce, midlife is typically the peak period of accomplishment, respect and responsibility at work (unless career is based on physical or sporting prowess, in which case the peak is likely to occur in early adulthood). On the flipside, the prosperity of midlife comes with strings attached: As a person enters their forties and fifties, obesity becomes more likely, as do other lifestyle diseases, and a loss of physical stamina and sexual potency may well occur (Vermeulen, 1993). Individuals in midlife have to therefore come to terms with being 'over the hill' and closer to the end of life than its beginning. Age-related anxieties become more prevalent, including anxieties about disease, dependence, loss of attractiveness, loss of mobility, and future loss of status and loss of earning power (Laslett, 1989).

Life stage theorists have focused on what characterises midlife in terms of a central task or concern. For Erikson (1980) the concern that defines midlife as a life stage is generativity, which can be defined as the motivation to give care, attention and resources to younger people and to leave a positive legacy for future generations (see Chapter 7 for more on generativity). Erikson's theory is all about balance, and either too much or too little generativity at midlife is problematic. Too much generativity leads to a person overextending themselves in the service of others, which may lead to stress, burnout and the loss in capacity to contribute. Too little generativity leads to *stagnation*, and if stagnation takes a hold a person in midlife may become caught up in self-absorption, productivity for productivity's sake, and a lack of attachments or relationships with younger people.

While Erikson focused on generativity vs. stagnation as the key polarity in midlife, Jung (1966) focused on the gender identity in midlife. In Jungian theory, the male part of identity is called the *animus*, and the female part is the *anima*. In midlife, an exploration of one's opposite-gender identity is a key part of finding wholeness and maturity. A man should open to his anima and so get in touch with his caring and nurturing side, while a woman should explore the masculine side of her personality. Levinson found support for Jung's theory, as gender-related identity issues are a predominant conscious concern in midlife men and women (Levinson, 1978; 1996). Hollis (1993) suggests that in early adulthood, adults may typically adopt a stereotypical gender identity because they are aiming to 'fit in' with the adult world and its gender norms. Midlife requires an early adult rigid or socially appropriate persona to be replaced by a more authentic identity in which there is a greater expression of inner convictions in everyday behaviour. Authenticity as a mature mode of functioning is discussed in more detail in Chapter 7. The switch to more authentic living may take a crisis, and that brings us to the discussion of midlife crisis.

Midlife transition and crisis

Crisis is the thing that is most strongly associated with midlife in the popular imagination (Freund & Ritter, 2009). But is there an empirical basis for the existence of a midlife crisis? Levinson (1978) found in his professional sample that most adults around the age of 40–5 undergo a life transition, which is characterised by a juxtaposition of feeling both young and old. Levinson refers to the typical images and ideas associated with *young* and *old* as archetypes. The *young* archetype is associated with birth, growth, future possibility, immortality, initiation, visions of things to come and heroism, but also fragility, impulsiveness, lacking in experience and lack of solidity. Archetypal 'young' images are infants, dawn, spring, seeds, blossoms and the New Year. In contrast, the *old* archetype is associated with completion, maturity, wisdom, stability, structure, completion, accomplishment, termination, senility, impotence, death and mortality, while images of oldness include Father Time, the Wise Old Man, the Grim Reaper, winter and night.

O'Connor and Wolfe (1987) interviewed 64 individuals about their experience of midlife crisis, and found a five phase process that has clear parallels with the structure of quarterlife crisis shown in Table 6.2, suggesting that quarterlife and midlife crises proceed in a similar manner. The five phases of O'Connor and Wolfe's model are:

1. *Stability* – Living in established, stable roles and relationships
2. *Rising Discontent* – A critical voice emerges, dissatisfaction with the status quo, energy for change and growth

3. *Crisis* – Emotional turmoil experienced, major changes initiated, questioning of core beliefs, values, self-worth, self-concept, fundamental ways of behaving
4. *Redirection and Adaptation* – Active pursuit of new directions and create tentative experiments to adapt to the changing conditions of self and circumstance
5. *Re-stabilizing* – A new direction taken based on what has been found in the crisis and redirection phases, and an assertion of new identity and purpose. A greater sense of autonomy and authenticity is described in this new set of commitments relative to those that defined life pre-crisis

Prevalence data suggests that midlife crisis is only experienced by the minority of persons. Brim (1992) found that just 10 per cent of adult males experience a midlife crisis. Wethington (2000) conducted interviews with 724 adults and found that among respondents aged over 50, 34 per cent reported that they had experienced a midlife crisis, with a peak age in the late forties and early fifties. Midlife crisis was also defined by a growing awareness of age and oldness, leading to a re-evaluation of life's priorities, and encounters with difficult transitional life events such as divorce, job loss, bereavement or illness. Although midlife crisis may be an event that only a minority of adults experience, this does not make it any less important – psychologists need to understand both majorities and minorities.

Menopause

During midlife, the menopause (also called the climacteric) is a key transition for women. Menopause typically occurs at some point between the ages of 46 and 58, with an approximate mean age of 51–2, and involves the termination of the menstrual cycle and the end of reproductive potential (Vermeulen, 1993). A 'premenopausal period' occurs over a number of years prior to menopause, during which time the menstrual cycle lengthens (Vermeulen, 1993). During menopause itself, approximately 80 per cent of women in Western countries experience symptoms such as sweating and hot flushes, but this seems to be less prevalent in East Asian countries, suggesting that the biological features of this transition relate to social environment (Greendale, Lee & Arriola, 1999). Hormone Replacement Therapy (HRT) is a popular treatment for those who are experiencing menopausal symptoms, but the popularity of HRT has declined in the last ten years due to studies that show a possible link with cardiac problems and cancer (Rossouw et al., 2002).

Alongside its biological features, menopause is characterised by concurrent psychological and social changes that are typical of late midlife, such as children leaving home and a conscious concern with physical ageing (Amore et al., 2004; Hall et al., 2007; Lindh-Astrand et al., 2007). A variety of qualitative studies have found that menopause is characterised by a combination of negative and positive experiences (Berterö, 2003; Cifcili et al., 2009; Hvas, 2001; Lindh-Astrand et al., 2007; Stotland, 2002). These are summarised as follows:

Positive experiences:

- Relief at removal of the risk of pregnancy, bringing a sense of liberation
- Happiness about cessation of periods and associated menstrual symptoms
- Seeing menopause as an opportunity and trigger to change life in positive ways
- The sense of a beginning of a new life, characterised by increased freedom and maturity
- Improved sex life
- Enhanced respect from men, in certain cultures

Negative experiences:

- Grief about the sense of loss of youth and fertility
- Uncomfortable menopausal symptoms, including hot flushes, headaches, sore breasts
- Social difficulties associated with hot flushes and sweating
- Fear of becoming old and physical signs of ageing
- Increased irritability, mood swings and sensitivity
- Loss of sexual interest

Some theorists suggest that men experience an equivalent of menopause in midlife, termed the 'andropause' or male menopause, which results from the lowering of testosterone and other biological changes such as lower sex drive and energy levels (Vermeulen, 1993; 2000). Claasen (2004) interviewed men about this, and a sample of interview extracts from his study is shown in Box 6.5.

Box 6.5　Individual voices

Experiences of male menopause in men at midlife

The following are extracts from interviews with five South African men between the ages 45 and 55, from Claasen (2004), on the topic of a 'male menopause' in midlife.

Box 6.5   Continued

I think the reality that one cannot deny is your body getting older. There are many other options that you might have had when you were younger which you just don't have anymore. We used to go hiking regularly when I was younger over weekends and that is just not an option and it is much more difficult for me to say yes, in the last two years. I've just said no, we cannot do that. (p. 66)

Physically there have been changes, I walk around the block now and I am out of breath while in the past I could walk around ten times. (p. 67)

I do get tired in the afternoons and it makes me irritable. I combat that by using multi-vitamins and sleep more often. (p. 67)

To an extent it also feels as if my self-confidence is declining in this phase. You feel unsure about a lot of things and it eats away at your self-confidence. (p. 70)

Yes, one of the difficult ones to talk about is what happens on a sexual dimension: of course, my sexual appetite has diminished quite a lot and I think that has brought a new dimension in my relationship with (wife's name) in the sense that we are not now primarily sexual partners but maybe more friends. And I can remember in the first 20 years of our marriage how much that drove my behaviour, the sexual side of the relationship. (p. 74)

The Third Age

The phrase 'Third Age' can be traced to the 1970s, when *Les Universités du Troisieme Age* was founded in France and the *Universities of the Third Age* was subsequently set up in England. These organisations aimed to provide education to the over-sixties, and they led to the term 'Third Age' being in common use by the 1990s. It was transferred into the academic literature by the publication of *A Fresh Map of Life: The Emergence of the Third Age* by Laslett (1989). Laslett postulated four basic eras of the human life-cycle: the First Age (childhood and full-time education), the Second Age (reproductive and productive adulthood), the Third Age (fulfilment of personal interests) and the Fourth Age (dependency and decline).

The onset of the Third Age, according to Laslett's theory, is initiated by leaving the full-time workforce and children moving out of the family home. These are both forms of *retirement from major life roles*, and together bring about the Third Age. The age of onset is variable but typically clusters around 60–5, which is the current retirement age range in most Western countries, but can be earlier or later (Laslett, 1989). Aspects of this life stage are discussed in more detail in Chapters 12 and 13, in terms of the literature on retirement, children leaving home and grandparenting.

The presence of the Third Age as a normative life stage is a historically recent phenomenon; it is a product of social developments across the early twentieth century that led to improved income for adults over working age, the lowering of the age of retirement from 70 to 65 (or lower in some industries), and an increase in life expectancy from under 50 at the turn of the twentieth century to over 80 by the year 2000 (as illustrated in Figure 6.2). These developments have given rise to the Third Age; a period in which a person can enjoy life after full-time work and their childrearing endeavours without the burdens of elderly frailty and disability (Laslett, 1989). However, the same modern world that gave birth to the Third Age might also get rid of it – the UK government has a plan to change retirement age to 68 by 2046, and this may be the first step towards a long-term drift towards a compression of Third Age, in order to offset the financial challenges of providing pensions and subsidised services to this ever-growing sector.

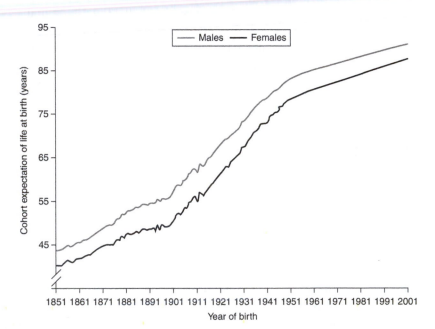

Figure 6.2 Average life expectancy – change between 1851 and 2001 for males and females in England and Wales

Source: Report, Decennial Life Tables (2000–2), Office for National Statistics licensed under the Open Government Licence v.1.0. Reprinted with permission.

The Fourth Age

It is common to hear older adults referred to as one group – perhaps as 'pensioners' or 'the elderly'. However, at least two stages of older adult life should be distinguished, as the developmental challenges and opportunities contained in them are completely different. These two stages can be referred to as the Third Age and the Fourth Age (Laslett, 1989). While the onset of the Third Age is primarily a socially induced transition, brought about by retirement and the empty nest, the transition to the Fourth Age is primarily a biologically induced transition – it is initiated by the dependency and loss of autonomy that advanced old age brings (Baltes, 2003). While the Third Age sees many abilities remaining at a high level relative to younger adults, the Fourth Age is characterised by decline in physical and cognitive capacities.

Box 6.6   Individual voices

Adjusting to the Fourth Age

Strategies for adjusting to old age were explored by Agren (1998) in a longitudinal qualitative study. Interviews were conducted with 129 persons at the age of 85, and then later at the age of 92. Adjustment strategies with individual examples are given next.

Balancing – Balancing positive experiences against negative ones.

> Of course it gets lonely in the dark but I think I'm doing quite well still so I'm quite content. Of course some days are more tiring and sad but it doesn't matter so much. I know that I have nothing to expect but I have to take time as it comes and I can manage quite well ... I could do a lot before but not any longer but I have to accept that so I ... I mean on the whole I feel quite satisfied. (p. 113)

One day at a time – Taking one day at a time to gain control and focus on the present.

> You have to be glad for every day that passes – that one is able to stand up. Yes, you have to take the day as it comes. (p. 113)

Substitution – focusing on an activity that one is still able to perform instead of one that one can no longer do. Before I could

Box 6.5   Continued

read a book and then time passes quickly you know. I cannot keep on cleaning all the time. That is impossible, you know. But I am happy as long as I can hear what they say on the phone. I can hear that very well. (p. 114)

Losing Interest – In order to cope with the loss of an activity, an adaptive strategy is to find a reason to lose interest in doing it.

I turn the pages and read the paper and I think that it's quite a lot that I do not understand but I do not try very hard to understand it, but I say to myself – it was sad. I guess it is because it doesn't interest me, for example – it doesn't concern me, I do not have to get into this, I don't have to do that or something like that. (p. 114)

For research purposes, over 85s are usually classified as Fourth Age (Baltes & Smith, 2003), however at an individual level there is great variability in the onset of the Fourth Age. At the time of writing, both Queen Elizabeth and the Pope are both in their mid-eighties and still managing a workload and schedule that would challenge an ordinary person in the prime of life! Clearly, individuals can still be high functioning in their late eighties and nineties, but the probability of dependency becomes considerably greater after the age of 85. *The Berlin Aging Study* has shown that relative to those between the ages of 70 and 85, those over 85 have lower wellbeing, lower functioning and higher levels of illness and disability (Baltes & Smith, 2003).

A peculiar feature of the Fourth Age relative to other age groups is the gender imbalance. Members of the Fourth Age are predominantly female; there are twice as many women alive than men over the age of 85. There is also an increase over the age of 85 in the number of adults who live alone due to the bereavement of their spouse or partner. Smith (2002) suggests that for those who reach it, this final stage of life provides the ultimate test of a person's psychological resilience and mental health, as any weaknesses that exist from earlier adult stages will surface when a person is being confronted by their own irreversible frailty and loss of independence. Some examples of adjustment strategies employed by individuals in the Fourth Age are shown in Box 6.6.

A range of subsidised assistance and services exists for elderly adults; the government-funded and charitable organisations that provide these can be considered the Fourth Age industry. For older adults who continue to live at home and who have difficulties with cooking, meals-on-wheels services provide home-delivered freshly cooked food for a small fee (typically about £3 for a two-course meal in the UK). Various local authorities also provide care assistants to help elderly adults with household tasks such as shopping, cleaning or laundry. Some local authorities also provide an alarm service for a fee, which involves installing a button at an elderly person's home that is linked to a rapid response service, and can be used if he/she needs emergency assistance. In order to qualify for these services, elderly adults must first be assessed to be classified as either 'critical risk to independence', 'substantial risk to independence', 'moderate risk to independence' or 'low risk to independence'.

If living at home is no longer considered safe or appropriate, a variety of supported residential options can be considered for elderly adults. Choosing the kind of care environment is an important decision that many adults must make at some point for their elderly relatives or for themselves. If and when a transition into supported housing occurs, there are five main types of supported residence currently available in the UK that can be considered:

1. *Retirement housing developments* (also called sheltered housing or retirement villages) are groups of flats or bungalows for older people. Most developments provide self-contained homes with their own front doors, with some common facilities for all residents such as a lounge, a restaurant, a garden and a laundry.
2. *Extra care housing* (also called very sheltered housing or assisting living) is like retirement housing but for older people who are frail and less able to do things for themselves. They consist of flats with bathrooms and access suitable for less mobile people and wheelchair users.
3. *Close care developments* consist of independent flats or bungalows built adjacent to a care home. Residents have some services such as cleaning included in their service charge and other services can be purchased from the care home when necessary.
4. *Care homes* are residential settings where a number of older people live, usually in single or double rooms, with access to on-site care services. Care homes provide help with washing, dressing and giving medication.
5. *Nursing homes* (also called homes registered for nursing) provide personal care (help with washing, dressing and giving medication), and have a qualified nurse on duty 24 hours a day. Some nursing homes are registered to meet a specific care need, for example dementia

or terminal illness. An increasingly popular approach to nursing homes and care homes is the *Eden Alternative* approach (see Box 6.7).

Box 6.7   Alternative perspectives

The Eden Alternative

The Eden Alternative was founded in the USA in 1991 by Dr. William Thomas, with the aim of transforming the quality of care in long-term care homes for the elderly and tackling loneliness in old age. Since its inception, hundreds of homes across the world have joined the Eden initiative and thousands of individuals who work with elderly persons have been training in the Eden ethos.

Eden homes are based on the philosophy that a care environment should provide elderly individuals with meaning, variety, fun and continuous contact with plants, animals and children. Residents in Eden Alternative homes are referred to as Elders. Typically an Eden home will have a variety of live-in pets, arrangements with local schools for children to visit regularly and more activities such as gardening for residents to get involved in. Research has shown that implementing the Eden approach improves quality of life, lessens depression and reduces dependency on drugs in long-term care (Thomas, 1992; 1996). However the introduction of animals and spontaneity into a care home is not without its challenges, thus training in the Eden Alternative is essential (Sampsell, 2003). The Eden Alternative movement is now also developing ways of helping and educating those who care for elderly relatives at home. For more about the Eden Alternative, visit the websites listed at the end of the chapter.

The number of adults in the Fourth Age is predicted to increase dramatically in the decades to come, as life expectancy continues to rise. This will present a major challenge to researchers, politicians and the care system, and Baltes (2003) cautions against excessive optimism in relation to what can be done for this age group. The limitations of human longevity will be found at some point, for it is biologically unlikely that the increase in human life expectancy (see Figure 6.2) that defined the twentieth century can continue to increase indefinitely. At some point, we will find the biological cap for a human lifetime. But by then, who knows, a Fifth Age?

Concluding comments: A critique of psychosocial stage and transition theories

This chapter has presented theories that view adult life as a series of qualitatively different holistic life stages and all-consuming transitions or crises. These theories are premised on the idea that age and life events provide a basis for delineating universal life stages and transitions. Leo Hendry and Marion Kloep (2007), in a concise critique of the theory of emerging adulthood, make a series of points that are relevant to the neo-Eriksonian holistic stage theory tradition more generally, and Arnett's responses to their points are also more generally relevant (Arnett, 2007b). Have a read through them, and decide for yourself which position is more convincing.

Hendry and Kloep's first point is that development is often domain-specific, that is, a person may develop faster in one area than another, yet life stage theories assume global patterns of development – they do not provide room for domain-specific differences within persons. Arnett's response to this point is that domain-specific and generic models of development can coexist happily, as they are formed at different levels of abstraction.

Hendry and Kloep's second point is that development is reversible, due to the possibility of regression to an earlier developmental stage at any point, therefore forward progress through life stages is not inevitable, and there may also be movement in the opposite direction. This clarification of the nonlinear nature of development requires holistic theories to retain caveats that progress is not inevitable, but actually fits within the Eriksonian framework, for Erikson considered regression possible and often inevitable.

Another point that Hendry and Kloep make is that emerging adulthood is only a reality for the affluent middle classes in Western societies who can afford longer periods of education and exploration prior to taking on adult commitments, and they consider that this ethnocentric specificity is a drawback in the theory. The same could be said of many of the theories presented here that are also based on middle-class Western samples, including Levinson's stage theories based on American middle-class individuals, and the theory of quarterlife crisis, which was based on a predominantly middle class British sample. All of these theories are based on data gathered at a particular point in history, in affluent Western countries.

Arnett replied to this criticism by saying that he thinks that the historically situated nature of a theory is not a problem, it is simply a reflection of taking a biopsychosocial perspective. All theories mentioned in this chapter are biopsychosocial in nature – that is, they recognise that stages and transitions occur as a result of interacting combinations of biological, psychological *and* social factors. Correspondingly, as historical social conditions change, existing stages and transitions change, new ones may appear and others may disappear. For example, the Third Age has only been around as a recognisable life stage for half a century (see Chapter 13), and the Fourth Age is a product of increased life expectancy leading to greater numbers living to an age where they are no longer independent. These psychosocial stage transitions are clearly products of recent history and the ever-changing shape of the human life. The question of whether the theories and stages apply across all demographics and socio-economic groups within Western cultures, or whether some of them are middle-class phenomena, is a question that can only be answered by continuing research.

A final point that Hendry and Kloep make is that using age as the basis of categorising general developmental stages and transitions is problematic (for example, placing the typical age of entry into midlife at 40), for individuals increasingly live in ways that do not accord with age-graded norms. Given this very valid criticism, it should be emphasised that ages given for the stages and transitions discussed in this chapter are very approximate indications, mainly used for research sampling purposes. All stages and transitions encountered in this chapter are actually induced by a combination of biological, psychological and social conditions. However, Neugarten, Moore and Lowe (1968) described a growing tendency in Western society for non-normative adult life course patterns, and more recent authors have also found that developments in adulthood are increasingly pluralistic in nature, and that universal life stages are being over-ridden in favour of individualized choices and stages (Côté, 2000; Heinz, 2002). The more this individualisation of development occurs, the more stage theories must adapt to accommodate adulthood's increasing flexibility, or become outdated.

Questions for you to reflect on

- Why do you think that the phase of Emerging Adulthood didn't exist earlier in history?
- What key events and/or changes precipitate the following five transitions?
  - the transition from adolescence to emerging adulthood
  - the transition from emerging adulthood to early adulthood
  - the transition from early adulthood to midlife
  - the transition from midlife to the third age
  - and the transition from the third age to the fourth age
- When a person enters the Third Age, they no longer have the stress of work and childcare. However research shows that some people find this transition difficult. Why do you think that might be?

Summary points

- Erik Erikson was the founder of the holistic psychosocial approach to studying and theorising about the life-course, and since him a variety of neo-Eriksonian theorists have presented theories using a similar framework.
- Erikson broke down the lifespan into eight stages, each of which is characterised by a dominant developmental challenge. Each challenge is defined by a pair of opposites, and for the three stages of adulthood these are: *intimacy vs. isolation* (early adulthood), *generativity vs. stagnation* (middle adulthood) and *integrity vs. despair* (late adulthood).
- Daniel Levinson devised the concept of the *life structure*. A life structure is a combination of internal and external features of adult life that must be kept in balance if a person is to remain healthy and if development is to be optimised.
- Transitions are unstable times in adult life that involve substantive change. A crisis is a transition that has a greater urgency and emotional salience than most.
- Crises can be opportunities for growth, due to the fact they bring scope for change, provide evidence of personal strength and coping capacity, lead to attention being focused at the self, goals and problematic schemas, and can help bring about a lifestyle that is more conducive to wellbeing and satisfaction.
- Adolescence is a time during which identity is explored and the ego develops into a singular entity. Identity statuses relate to the presence of identity exploration and commitment. Ideally, if a person has explored and found an autonomous identity, they are located at the 'identity achievement' stage.
- Emerging adulthood is a period of life that runs approximately between 18 and 25, which intersperses adolescence and fully-fledged adulthood. It is typified by a substantial amount of exploratory and experimental behaviour, and by a variety of adult capacities allied to a lack of financial and residential independence. Emerging adulthood is ideally an opportunity to explore adult roles without the requirement to make lifelong commitments.
- A quarterlife crisis occurs if a long-term commitment is made, an identity formed around that commitment, which is found to be unsustainable so is terminated. The crisis involves the experience of emotional upheaval followed by renewed exploration of alternatives for adulthood.
- Midlife is a time during which a person is both young and old, and the gains and losses of life are juxtaposed. If a person's awareness of advancing age leads to a fundamental reappraisal of their life structure, they may experience a midlife crisis.
- Both males and females experience a menopausal transition in midlife. For women, menopause involves the cessation of menstruation and the ending of the reproductive phase of life, while for men it involves a series of major hormonal changes that require adjustment.
- The Third Age of life is induced by the arrival of retirement from full-time work and children moving out of home. It is a time during which a

person is less defined by productivity, and more by fulfilment. It can only be engaged in if there is a pension, or other source of income that can sustain a life beyond full-time work.

- The Fourth Age of life is induced by the growing dependency and disability of advanced age, and is typically encountered at age 85 or over.
- Many older persons enter sheltered accommodation, a retirement village or a nursing home in later life due to the requirement for more constant care than can be provided in a home setting, and/or a desire for more social interaction.

Recommended reading

Arnett, J. J. (2000). Emerging adulthood: A theory of development from the late teens through the twenties. *American Psychologist, 55,* 469–480.

Baltes, P. B. (2003). Extending longevity: Dignity gain – or dignity drain? *Aging Research, 3,* 15–19.

Erikson, E. H. (1980). *Identity and the Life Cycle.* London: W. W. Norton & Co.

Hendry, L. B. & Kloep, M. (2007). Conceptualizing emerging adulthood: Inspecting the emperor's new clothes? *Child Development Perspectives, 1,* 74–79.

Lachman, M. E. (2004). Development in midlife. *Annual Review of Psychology, 55,* 305–331.

Laslett, P. (1989). *A Fresh Map of Life: The Emergence of the Third Age.* London: George Weidenfeld & Nicolson Limited.

Levinson, D. J. (1986). A conception of adult development. *American Psychologist, 41,* 3–13.

Marcia, J. E. (1966). Development and validation of ego identity status. *Journal of Personality and Social Psychology, 3,* 551–558.

O'Connor, D. J. & Wolfe, D. M. (1987). On managing midlife transitions in career and family. *Human Relations, 40,* 799–816.

Robinson, O. C. & Smith, J. A. (2010). Investigating the form and dynamics of crisis episodes in early adulthood: The application of a composite qualitative method. *Qualitative Research in Psychology, 7,* 170–191.

Wethington, E. (2000). Expecting stress: Americans and the 'midlife crisis'. *Motivation and Emotion, 24,* 85–103.

Recommended websites

Jeffrey Arnett – Emerging Adulthood information: www.jeffreyarnett.com

Website for pregnancy and parenthood: www.mumsnet.com

The University of the Third Age: www.u3a.org.uk

Information about the Eden Alternative: www.edenalt.org (USA) or www.eden-alternative.co.uk (UK)

UK online register of meals-on-wheels services: www.direct.gov.uk/en/HomeAndCommunity/InYourHome

Information on decisions about care homes for the elderly: www.ageuk.org.uk/home-and-care/care-homes/care-homes-6-things-to-think-about/

7

Personality Development

Treat people as if they were what they ought to be, and you help them to become what they are capable of being.
Johann Wolfgang von Goethe

Looking back on his teenage years, Robert recalled that he was nervous, shy and worried about what other people thought of him. After leaving school and moving into higher education, he started to develop more self-belief, but was still hesitant to voice his mind – he felt it was easier to not say anything controversial and avoid being noticed. By the time he hit 30, he had been through a number of relationships and challenging experiences, which together had given him confidence that he need not hide his own opinions so much. He had in fact lost his earlier shyness and become quite outspoken. By his mid-thirties he was, he said, different in many ways from his earlier adolescent self – more able to express his own mind without feeling threatened by whether others would like it or not. He had, he said, 'become his own man'.

Every human being has a habitual and unique way of thinking, feeling and behaving, which can be referred to as their personality. Research now shows that over the course of adulthood, people's personalities change and mature, and that this happens in predictable ways. This chapter covers personality change and stability across adulthood from various theoretical perspectives, including *trait theory*, which assesses personality using quantitative ratings on questionnaires; *ego-development theory*, which uses sentence-completion data to infer stages of optimal personality development, and *life story theory*, which uses autobiographical narratives to assess personality development. First, we turn to trait theory, which is currently the most widespread approach to studying personality.

Trait theory

In the 1930s, a psychologist called Gordon Allport turned to the English dictionary as a starting point for developing a model of personality traits (Allport & Odbert, 1936). From this he collated 18,000 personality adjectives, which must have been a time-consuming business! He grouped the words into categories, and later Raymond Cattell continued this processing by employing the statistical technique of factor analysis to cluster personality adjectives together (Cattell, 1943; 1945). Cattell's analyses led to a model of 16 basic personality traits, and the first ever pencil-and-paper personality test. Since then, other researchers have developed more simplified models, the most widely researched of which is the Five Factor Model (also known as the Big Five), first developed by Norman (1963). The five traits that comprise it, which are claimed as the fundamental dimensions of human personality (Goldberg, 1993), are:

1. **Openness to Experience** – outgoing/energetic vs. solitary/reserved
2. **Conscientiousness** – sensitive/nervous vs. secure/confident
3. **Extraversion** – inventive/curious vs. consistent/cautious
4. **Agreeableness** – efficient/organised vs. easy-going/careless
5. **Neuroticism** (also referred to as its opposite 'Emotional Stability') – friendly/compassionate vs. cold/unkind[1]

There are a number of other competing trait models, including the HEXACO model, which adds a sixth factor onto the Five Factor Model, termed *Honesty–Humility* (Lee & Ashton, 2008). However, given space limitations, research presented in this chapter on the relation between traits and age will focus on the Big Five. The Big Five questionnaires have been administered to hundreds of thousands of individuals over recent decades, resulting in major cross-sectional and longitudinal studies and meta-analyses. It is to the cross-sectional studies we turn first.

Cross-sectional adult age differences in the Big Five traits

In 1997, Sam Gosling and Jeff Potter commenced *The Gosling–Potter Internet Personality Project*, for which they placed a Big Five personality

---

[1] The first letters of the Big Five spell out the acronym 'OCEAN', which is a convenient way of memorising them.

questionnaire on the Internet for members of the public to access and complete. Over the years, it was completed by hundreds of thousands of respondents, and in 2003 a cross-sectional analysis was conducted with the 132,000 participants from the USA and Canada, in order to explore the relation between the Big Five personality traits and age (Srivastava et al., 2003).

The study found adult age differences on three of the Big Five traits. Conscientiousness increased in a linear manner with age, with greatest differences being within early adulthood. Agreeableness increased between the ages of 30 and 50. Openness to Experience declined gradually with age, while age did not relate to Extraversion. Neuroticism declined linearly with age for women, but stayed constant for men – this was the only trait for which men and women had different age profiles.

A limitation of this Internet-based study is that recruiting on the Internet may not provide data that are representative of the population more generally. In the late 1990s, when the data were being collected, far more young adults were on the Internet than older adults, and so the older adults who answered the survey may have been a particularly technology-savvy and proactive group, rather than a genuine cross-section of the elderly population, which potentially would lead to an artificially elevated mean conscientiousness score in the older age groups.

More recently, cross-sectional studies have been conducted using nationally representative samples in the UK, Germany and Australia. Donnellan and Lucas (2008) analysed data from the British Household Panel Study (N ≥ 14,039) and the German Socio-Economic Panel Study (N ≥ 20,852). The mean-level age difference findings from both studies are shown in Figure 7.1. Both British and German surveys show identical age profiles on four of the five traits: Extraversion decreased with age; Agreeableness increased with age; Openness to Experience decreased after the age of 60, while Conscientiousness showed a u-shaped relation with age, with highest levels in middle age. Neuroticism showed a different relation to age in the UK and Germany – Neuroticism declined across age groups in the UK sample, but increased across age groups in Germany. This suggests that British people tend to calm down with age, but German people tend to get more unstable! The British pattern was replicated in a nationally representative Australian sample (Lucas & Donnellan, 2009), which may show that national profiles have a cultural basis, for Australian culture is markedly similar to British culture in a variety of ways, due to its status as an ex-British colony and current Commonwealth member.

When these European findings are compared with the Internet-based study of Srivastava et al. (2003), it is evident that both studies

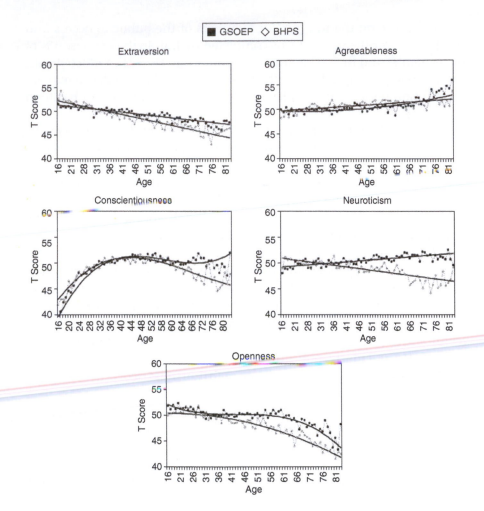

Figure 7.1   Adult age differences in the Big Five in two nationally representative studies from Britain (BHPS) and Germany (GSOEP)

Source: Donnellan & Lucas (2008, p. 560). Copyright © American Psychological Association. Reprinted with permission.

show Agreeableness and Conscientiousness increasing with age, while Openness to Experience decreases. Extraversion decreases more in the European sample than in the American sample, and the Neuroticism-age relation seems to vary by country. As with all cross-sectional research, age differences found in the aforementioned studies may be partly a product of cohort effects, that is, the different historical context in which different age groups have lived. Only longitudinal analyses avoid cohort effects, so it is to these that we turn now.

Box 7.1   Cross-cultural perspectives

Personality age differences in Germany, Italy, Portugal, Croatia and South Korea

In 1999, Robert McCrae and colleagues collected Big Five trait data using the NEO-PI-R questionnaire from adult samples in five countries: Germany, Italy, Portugal, Croatia and South Korea. The researchers hypothesised that they would find the same cross-sectional age differences as had been found in American data, based on an assumption that personality changes stem from intrapersonal maturational factors that exist independent of culture or context. The hypothesis was supported for four of five traits. It was found that in all cultures, Extraversion and Openness to Experience were significantly higher in young adults when compared with older adults, while Conscientiousness and Agreeableness were consistently lower in young adults, particularly the 18–21 age group. Age effects on Neuroticism were less pronounced, and in Croatia and Portugal there were no consistent linear age effects for this trait. The lack of consistent cross-cultural age difference in Neuroticism is also shown in the comparison of the UK and Germany in Figure 7.1. This may suggest a stronger role for culture in influencing emotional stability than in other traits.

Four kinds of longitudinal change in traits

Longitudinal research can elicit four different kinds of change calculation in personality traits; *mean-level change, rank-order change, ipsative change* and *individual change* (Caspi, Roberts & Shiner, 2005; Donnellan, Conger & Burzette, 2007; Roberts & DelVecchio, 2000). It is important to have a basic understanding of these before progressing further, so here is a brief description of all four:

- **Mean-level change**: Change over time in the average level of a trait across a whole sample. If mean-level change is found, this indicates that individuals within the sample have generally changed on a trait in the same way. If everyone changes but in different directions, mean-level change will not show up.

- **Rank-order change**: The degree to which the rank ordering of individuals within a sample is maintained over time. The main way of assessing rank-order change is the 'test-retest correlation', which involves correlating scores at time point one with scores from the same sample at time point two. The higher the correlation, the higher the rank-order stability.

- **Ipsative change**: Change that occurs in a person's profile across multiple traits. This is the only change measure that looks at the configuration of *multiple* traits and assesses the extent to which that configuration is maintained over time. Figure 7.2 shows a hypothetical example of a person whose ipsative profile has been maintained, and a person whose ipsative profile has changed.

- **Individual-level change**: (also referred to as intra-individual stability): A way of calculating individual-level change is by taking a person's score at Time 1 and subtracting it from a score at Time 2, then dividing that by the standard error of the two scores to standardise it (Donnellan, Conger & Burzette, 2007). This is called the *reliable change index (RCI)*, and it provides an indicator of change between two time points. An RCI score of 1.96 or more is considered to be a significant positive change, and a score of -1.96 or less a significant negative change.

Figure 7.3 contains three illustrations of a hypothetical sample of four participants who have had Extraversion levels assessed on two occasions.

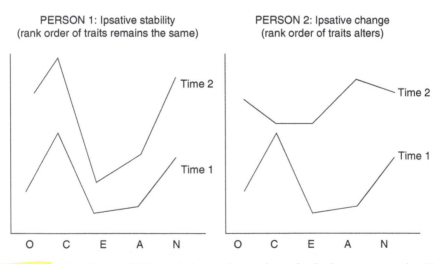

Figure 7.2   Ipsative stability and change in two hypothetical persons on the Big Five t raits

Key: O = Openness to Experience, C = Conscientiousness, E = Extraversion, A = Agreeableness and N = Neuroticism.

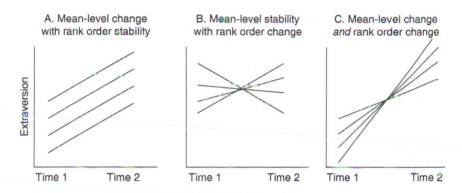

Figure 7.3 Mean-level change and rank-order change illustrations in a hypothetical sample of four persons and two longitudinal assessment occasions

In Graph A there is mean-level change but no rank-order change, in Graph B the reverse is true, while Graph C shows change in both rank-order and mean-level. The three graphs illustrate that these two kinds of change can occur concurrently or independently.

Longitudinal research on personality trait change

Mean-level change

In 2006, Brent Roberts, Kate Walton and Wolfgang Viechtbauer published a meta-analysis of longitudinal studies of mean-level personality trait change across the lifespan. Having located 92 longitudinal studies with a combined sample of 50,120, they re-categorised the traits in the studies into Five Factor Model traits, to provide a basis for synthesising the findings. However, they made one change to the standard Big Five model – they split Extraversion into two parts – Social Vitality (general sociability and gregariousness) and Social Dominance (confidence, autonomy, dominance). This split was done due to findings from previous longitudinal research that had found these two aspects of Extraversion to change differently with age (Helson, Jones & Kwan, 2002).

The results from the meta-analysis are shown in Figure 7.4. Agreeableness, Conscientiousness, Social Dominance and Emotional Stability means increase throughout life, which may reflect the fact that higher scores on these traits reflect personality maturity in adults (Caspi, Roberts & Shiner, 2005). Social Vitality decreases marginally through adulthood, while Openness to Experience increases during adolescence, and then stabilises through most of adult life followed by a slight decrease

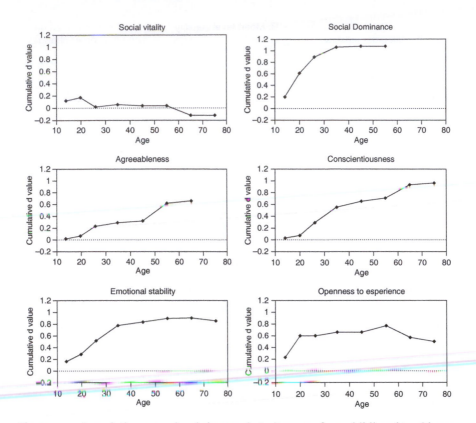

Figure 7.4   Cumulative mean-level changes in trait scores from childhood to old age

Source: Based on the meta-analysis of Roberts, Walton and Viechtbauer (2006, p. 15). Copyright © American Psychological Association. Reprinted with permission.

in adults over the age of 60. The meta-analysis found no significant sex differences in patterns of mean-level change and continuity, which suggests that the normative course of trait change is the same for both sexes. The aforementioned cross-sectional findings of Srivistava et al. (2003) also support the view that age affects the personality traits of both men and women in similar ways.

To ascertain the age group that sees the most personality change, the meta-analysis computed the total change across *all* traits for each age group. It was found that the majority of normative personality trait change occurs in young adulthood, that is, between the ages of 18 and 40. This may relate to the number of formative life events and role changes in this period, such as getting married, becoming a parent and starting a career (Roberts & Mroczek, 2008).

Roberts, Walton and Viechtbauer's (2006) meta-analysis is an important synthesis of research on mean-level personality trait change, but it is important to re-emphasise that the analysis is focused on *mean-level change*, which represents change that occurs in the same way and at the same age in most people. If people change in lots of different directions, this will not show up as mean-level change, but it *will* show up as rank-order change, for when some people go up and others go down on a trait, their rank-order moves around (as illustrated in Graphs B and C of Figure 7.2). This brings us to the next kind of longitudinal trait change.

Rank-order trait change

Rank-order change in personality was subject to a meta-analysis by Brent Roberts and Wendy DelVecchio (2000), in which 152 studies were collated that provided information on the rank-order change (that is, test–retest correlations) for different age groups. Their findings are shown in Figure 7.5 – each bar shows the average test-retest correlation across all traits for ten age groups. Rank-order stability increases from $r = 0.35$ in infancy (0 to 2.9), to $r = 0.51$ in the college years (18 to 21.9), followed by an almost linear increase up to the age group 50 to 59, who show a test-retest correlation of $r = 0.75$, followed by $r = 0.72$ in the 60 to 73 age group. Clearly, rank-order stability increases across childhood and adulthood, but even in the age group 60 to 73, the coefficient of $r = 0.72$ shows there is still considerable rank-order change. It seems that despite the tendency towards increasing stability, there is room for rank-order change throughout adult life.

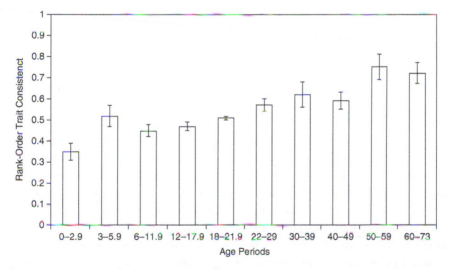

Figure 7.5 Meta-analysis calculations of rank-order consistency in ten age categories, with 95 per cent confidence interval

Source: Roberts and DelVecchio (2000, p. 15). Copyright © American Psychological Association. Reprinted with permission.

Ipsative trait change

Ipsative change occurs when an individual's profile across multiple traits alters over time. Jack Block conducted a pioneering longitudinal study on ipsative personality change between the school years and midlife (Block, 1971). He identified various subgroups of ipsative change patterns, such as a group of men who became more extraverted and rebellious relative to other traits, as they moved from adolescence into young adulthood. More recent studies have found that ipsative change can move in all kinds of directions in adulthood. In a sample of young adults, Roberts, Caspi and Moffitt (2001) found that 50 per cent of individuals had highly consistent profiles over time (correlations between .6 and .87), while 7 per cent showed ipsative correlations of .3 or under, and 1.1 per cent of the sample showed negative correlations. The average level of ipsative stability was $r = .70$, but at the individual level this varied from $r = -.74$ (showing change to an almost opposite profile) to $r = 1$ (showing no change at all). Another study found that ipsative stability can be found across a 45-year time interval (average of $r = .29$) showing that personality profiles retain some ipsative similarity over many decades (Soldz & Vaillant, 1999).

Individual-level change

When studying longitudinal change in personality, it is possible to explore differences in individual change profiles by employing the *reliable change index*, which gives an indication of the positive, neutral or negative change profile for *each person*. An example study by Allemand, Gomez and Jackson (2010) assessed personality change over ten years in a middle-aged sample of 892 adults, and found no significant mean-level change in the Big Five traits. *However*, individual-level change measures showed a minority of the sample *were* changing substantially. For example on Agreeableness, 11 per cent of the sample declined significantly and 9 per cent increased, while on Neuroticism, 9 per cent decreased and 2 per cent increased. Although this did not affect the mean-level findings, it shows that a substantial minority do undergo change. In support of this, a longitudinal study on young adults found that 10 to 30 per cent of participants increased or decreased on various traits over the eight years of the study, while the majority remained stable (Roberts, Caspi & Moffitt, 2001). But who comprises this 'fluid minority'? Although they may buck the general trend, it is important to know who they are, for unusual examples of personality phenomena can unearth some important personality phenomena that are less evident in the average (for example, Querstret & Robinson, in press). Perhaps they have had unusual life experiences? It is the link between such experiences and personality change that we turn next.

Genes and environment in adult trait change

Behavioural genetics is the application of twin studies and adoption studies to tease apart the influence of genes and environment on psychological traits and abilities. Such methods can be used to assess how much personality change is influenced by genes and environment. The general conclusion is that personality change in *childhood* is principally influenced by genes, while personality change in *adulthood* is principally environmentally influenced, with genes accounting for at most 30 per cent of adult change (Plomin & Nesselroade, 1990; McGue, Bacon & Lykken, 1993). If environment is the primary driver of adult personality change, what kinds of events or experiences can lead to a shift in personality? In line with the biopsychosocial framework outlined in Chapter 1, these can be broadly grouped into biological, psychological and socially induced events, as illustrated by the following examples.

Biologically induced events. A recent study has shown that adult personality traits can be changed by pharmacological means. In an experimental study, 52 participants were given a dose of psilocybin, a psychedelic substance which is the active ingredient in magic mushrooms. Following the session, participants showed increased levels of Openness to Experience, and in those participants who reported a mystical experience when taking psilocybin, this remained raised at a follow-up assessment a year after the event (MacLean, Johnson & Griffiths, 2011).

Psychologically stressful events. Research has looked as the impact of stressful events on personality change. A longitudinal study by Lockenhoff et al. (2009) gained data from a mixed-age sample of adults on personality traits at two time points separated by eight years, and assessed the occurrence of 'extremely adverse events' (defined as horrifying or frightening) in between. Approximately one quarter of the sample reported that they had experienced an extremely adverse event in the study period (these reported events included witnessing an accident or crime, bereavements, life-threatening illness or severe conflicts). Those who had such an experience showed an increase in Neuroticism and a decrease in Openness to Experience over time, which suggests that traits can be altered by life events in different ways.

Socially induced events. Roberts, Walton and Viechtbauer (2006) state that change in social roles is one of the primary sources of personality change. In a group of women who were studied between the ages of 20 and 43, those who were stay-at-home mothers demonstrated less change in assertiveness and sense of personal control than women who were in part-time or full-time employment (Roberts, 1997; Helson & Picano, 1990). It has also been found that women who work in midlife are rated by observers as more assertive and independent but less warm than women who do not (Vandewater & Stewart, 1998).

Box 7.2   Alternative perspectives

Criticisms of trait theory

Trait theory provides the basis for much contemporary research on personality development, and has undoubted advantages in its capacity to chart quantitative change over time, to compare age groups and to relate trait change to particular life events or biological factors. However the approach is not without its critics. Over the past two decades, a number of critiques of trait theory have been published, and key points from them are synthesised here into six points.

1. Trait-theory research is principally focused on the group level of analysis, when personality is in fact an individual-level phenomenon (Bannister & Fransella, 1986). Furthermore, trait-theory questionnaires gain personality profiles that are not unique but are shared with others, so individuality is omitted from the outset (Bannister & Fransella, 1986).
2. Trait-theory research is mainly conducted using self-report questionnaires, and this means that it can only include aspects of personality that participants are consciously aware of and are happy to outwardly and honestly disclose. Trait data can alternatively be gathered from third-party sources (for example, spouse ratings – Smith et al., 2008), but this data is also dependent on conscious awareness and concerns about disclosure.
3. In trait-theory, personality traits are viewed as fixed attributes that a person possesses, which cause a person to behave in a particular way. However, personality has been found to change systematically according to social context (Robinson, 2009) and according to the social roles and groups that a person is within (Reicher & Haslam, 2006).
4. Trait-theory omits a consideration of long-term goals as important components of personality (Allport, 1961). Goals are

Box 7.2   Continued

qualitatively different rather than quantitatively different from each other, that is, the goal to be a surgeon is different in kind from the goal to set up a new IT business, and as such the difference between them cannot be measured quantitatively using rating scales. Furthermore, changes in long-term goals are qualitative changes, for example changing from a goal to a new job towards a new goal to travel the world.

5. Trait-theory gains superficial data about personality due to its reliance on global numerical ratings, and as such can be characterised as a 'psychology of the stranger' (McAdams, 1992). This approach can be contrasted with the more in-depth data gathered using the life-story method, which is described later in the chapter.

6. Trait scores provide an indication of a person's principle behavioural characteristics, but omit an analysis of the different motives that may underlie the same trait. For example, a person may appear extravert because (a) they enjoy stimulation and being with other people, (b) because they fear social rejection and think that extraversion is the most likely way of achieving popularity, or (c) because they think that such behaviour is required in the role that they occupy (Querstret & Robinson, in press).

The mature personality: Five conceptions

Personality change in adulthood is supported by research using trait questionnaires, and it appears that people tend to change in a normative direction as they get older. But is that a good direction? Is personality improving with age, like a good wine, or gradually deteriorating with time, like a loaf of bread? To answer the vintage wine vs. stale bread question, we need a model of what constitutes the ideal personality and what traits or characteristics are indicative of mature adulthood. There have been a number of theories of the mature adult personality, five of which are discussed here; the *authentic* personality, the *socially effective* personality, the *generative* personality, the personality built around *mature defence mechanisms*, and the *self-actualised* personality.

Maturity #1: The authentic personality

'To thine own self be true' wrote Shakespeare in *Hamlet*, while St. Augustine in his *Confessions* wrote 'Seek for yourself, O man;

search for your true self'. These are literary descriptions of the ideal of authenticity – of having a personality that is honest, open and true, rather than duplicitous and concealing. Authenticity is based on incorporating the virtues of honesty and truth into personality, and therefore aligns with the 'veridical' direction of development (see Chapter 1).

An early description of authenticity was given in Carl Jung's theory of human development. Jung stated that all healthy adult human beings strive towards *individuation* – a combination of personal autonomy, originality and a commitment to expressing outwardly how one thinks and feels inwardly. In Jung's scheme, an obstacle to the process of individuation is the 'persona', which is a public façade designed to meet the expectations of family and society, and to conceal parts of one's personality that are perceived as undesirable (Jung, 1966). In adolescence, the requirement to adopt or conceal behaviours becomes a pressing concern due to the growing role of the peer group in shaping identity. An adolescent in a social group may risk being ostracised or rejected from that group if they do not adopt the right dress code, language and habits. This can lead to a preponderance of 'false-self behaviour' in adolescence, which is a precursor of adult inauthenticity (Harter, Waters & Whitesell, 1997).

A persona or false self can be a major hindrance to healthy adult development if it becomes used too much, and if the authentic self is appraised as *generally* inappropriate or undesirable (Jung, 1966). A mature adult must at some point come to the realisation that they can act in ways that are an honest reflection of their interests, aspirations and hopes, without fear of social rejection or disapproval, otherwise they will end up locked in behind a façade of conformity. Carl Rogers (1961) considered that a fundamental outcome of successful therapy was effective release from living behind such a façade.

The humanistic psychologist Sidney Jourard studied authenticity and self-disclosure in adults, and concluded that the capacity to disclose things candidly about oneself and one's past to at least *one* other person is a requirement for psychological health. His research suggested that children and their parents rarely disclose fully and authentically to one another, while partners and spouses are the most likely sources and recipients of authentic self-disclosure (Jourard, 1971).

More recent research on self-reported authenticity has found that it is a related to a host of positive outcomes, including self-esteem (Kernis & Goldman, 2006); wellbeing and life satisfaction (Wood et al., 2008); meaning in life (Schlegel et al., 2009); happiness and positive affect (Wood et al., 2008) and emotional intelligence (Gillath et al., 2010). Conversely a number of markers of mental and physical ill-health show a strong relationship with inauthentic functioning. These include stress and stressful events (Wood et al., 2008), attachment insecurity (Lopez & Rice, 2006), depression, anxiety and physical illness symptoms (Ryan, Laguardia & Rawsthorne, 2005). This body of evidence suggests that authenticity is a healthy and mature personality development. However, there are cultural environments in which authenticity is not so adaptive, as discussed in Box 7.3.

Box 7.3   Cross-cultural perspectives

The dangers of authenticity when living in an oppressive regime

Authenticity is a healthy way of functioning, but in some contexts it can also be dangerous. Authentic self-expression, and the rejection of conformity that often comes with it, is problematic in a society that is intolerant of personal opinion and criticism. In a totalitarian or repressive society that punishes open or frank self-expression, if a person holds political views that might lead to arrest or detention, a false public front is an adaptive necessity. *Child 44* by Tom Rob Smith (2009) is a story about life under Stalin in the Soviet Union, and is a potent depiction of the importance of falsity and inauthenticity in such a regime. It is a reminder that ideals for adult functioning are shaped by society and culture, and that human beings are more able to develop in a healthy direction *If* they live in a healthy society.

Maturity #2: The socially effective personality

In 2000, Bob Hogan and Brent Roberts put forth a theory of personality maturity termed the *Socioanalytic Model of Maturity*. The term 'socioanalytic' stems from the authors' synthesis of two ideas – the 'socio' bit is from the sociologist G. H. Mead, who suggested that individuality is shaped by community, while the 'analytic' bit comes from Sigmund Freud, who described maturity as the 'capacity to love and to work'. The combination of these led Hogan and Roberts to a view of maturity as the capacity to love, work *and* be an effective part of a social community. This is based on the notion of the *ideal citizen* – a person who develops their skills and seeks excellence, but always bears in mind what is good for the community as a whole.

Hogan and Roberts translate this model into three of the Big Five traits, so that maturity is equated to being more *agreeable*, more *emotionally stable* and more *conscientious*. This fits with the research on mean-level trait change over adulthood, as people do indeed on average become more agreeable, conscientious, and emotionally stable over the course of their lives (Roberts, Walton & Viechtbauer, 2006). Research also shows that those who possess these three traits to a higher degree are more effective in love, work and health (Caspi, Roberts & Shiner, 2005). A meta-analysis by DeNeve and Cooper (1998) also found that Emotional Stability and Conscientiousness predict life satisfaction, while happiness and positive affect are predicted by Emotional Stability and Agreeableness. So it appears that the traits that are conducive to wellbeing.

Hogan and Robert criticise individualistic notions of maturity that define ideal human functioning without reference to society more broadly, such as the model of authenticity described before. They suggest that a personality, if it is to bring adaptive benefits, must impart admiration and respect within a community. Characteristics that promote this include the following: a tendency to praise, support and encourage others; the maintenance of a positive, steady mood; a sense of self-esteem allied to self-deprecation; consistency and reliability in the honouring of commitments; playing by the rules of society; and a contribution to the community by way of helping others. If this contribution is balanced with the pursuit of self-interest, then a person will be integrated into society while having a strong sense of individuality.

Maturity #3: The generative personality

Generativity is an ongoing tendency to offer help, time and resources to others, particularly to the younger generation. It is the desire to 'make a difference' in positive ways. It is likely that a person will become more generative as they move from early adulthood to midlife, and generativity can therefore be seen as an indicator of maturity. Generativity as a personality ideal is aligned with the virtuous direction of development mentioned in Chapter 1, as it brings benefits to the personality and to the community, while facilitating the transmission of knowledge, guidance and resources from the older, established generation, to the younger, emerging generations (McAdams, Hart & Maruna, 1998).

Erik Erikson (discussed in Chapter 6) theorised that generativity defines middle adulthood as a life stage. This has been borne out by research, to a degree. The *Loyola Generative Scale* measures the trait of generative concern, and scores on this measure peak in midlife (McAdams, Hart & Maruna, 1998). Another generativity measure requires participants to list ten goals that they are currently working on. Goals are then coded for generative content, such as: (a) involvement with the next generation; (b) providing care, help or guidance to another person; and (c) making a creative contribution to society. Research using this instrument has shown that generative goals are equally prevalent in midlife and older age, but lower in young adulthood (McAdams, Hart & Maruna, 1998). Another assessment instrument is the Generative Behaviour Checklist (GBC), which measures the frequency of 50 kinds of generative acts over the last two months. It elicits higher frequencies in midlife than in younger or older adulthood (McAdams, Hart & Maruna, 1998).

Keyes and Ryff (1998) found that generativity is higher in adults who have more education. Given that a higher level of education is correlated with income, this may signify that generative giving is dependent on having sufficient resources to not have to focus on meeting one's own basic needs all the time. Gender is also a factor in generativity; women score higher on generativity measures than men. However age cancels the gender difference out – older men and women show the same level of generativity (Keyes & Ryff, 1998). Generativity is also related to certain traits of the Five Factor Model; higher scores on Extraversion, Openness, Emotional Stability, and Agreeableness are correlated with generativity (Aubin & McAdams, 1995).

Maturity #4: The self-actualised personality

Abraham Maslow's theory of development was introduced in Chapter 5 – it views human development as passing through a hierarchical sequence of motivational needs. At the bottom of this hierarchy are physiological needs such as food and safety; as long as these are lacking, action will be focused on trying to meet them. At the next level up, action is focused on meeting the psychological needs of belongingness, esteem and love. Once a person has met those needs, he/she moves up to a point at which there is no longer a perceived lack or deficiency motivating life, and so 'self-actualisation' emerges, which is the desire to fulfil one's potential in the service of a self-transcending cause. The 'self-actualised' personality defines a person who consistently resides at the top of the hierarchy of needs, and who is therefore the embodiment of mature development (Maslow, 1968; 1974).

Table 7.1 lists the key characteristics of the self-actualised personality. These were derived from a qualitative research study that analysed characteristics of high-functioning individuals; people who showed high levels of ability, psychological health and wisdom. This list of exemplars included Abraham Lincoln, Thomas Jefferson, Albert Einstein, Eleanor Roosevelt, Jane Addams, Aldous Huxley, William James and Albert Schweitzer (Maslow, 1950). Biographic materials of these persons were

Table 7.1   The key characteristics of the self-actualised personality

Characteristic	Description
1. Clarity of thought and perception	The ability to see situations without bias or prejudice, to understand the view of others, and to accurately predict future events and outcomes.
2. Humility and empathy	A capacity to listen to others and to put their needs on a par with one's own, allied to a realisation of the limits of one's own understanding.
3. Simplicity of personality	Spontaneous expression, and a lack of effortful self-presentation and impression-management.
4. Authenticity	A commitment to outwardly expressing one's innermost convictions and values.
5. Vocation	A dedicated pursuit of a long-term goal in career or voluntary work that has a strong ethical component, and is considered to be a personal calling.
6. Peak experiences	A tendency to experience peak experiences that take a person beyond normal waking consciousness, and a realisation that science and rational thought are limited by their use of language, while there may be truths beyond words.
7. Creativity	Flexibility of thought, originality of ideas, a willingness to make mistakes in the pursuit of new ideas that improve on what has come before.
8. Emotional Security	A lack of inhibiting anxieties, a warm disposition and a low degree of internal conflict.
9. Autonomy and attachment	Independent, valuing privacy, yet engaged in fruitful and committed relationships with selected others.

Source: According to Maslow (1974; 1998).

qualitatively analysed to search for common denominators (Goble, 1970). The results of this analysis are the characteristics shown in Table 7.1. Maslow later simplified and distilled this list of characteristics down to just two core elements: (1) Authenticity: the acceptance and expression of a person's inner nature and core self; and (2) Excellent psychological health: the minimal presence of psychological stress, distress, bias and delusion (Maslow, 1998).

The self-actualised personality may be a model of maturity, but it also has a child-like quality, because for such a person, work is deeply enjoyable and thus becomes more like play. Furthermore, there is less of an abrupt division between self and world than at earlier points in adult development, due to fewer defence mechanisms (Maslow, 1998). This idea of there being a childlike aspect to the high levels of development conflicts with theories that state development is a progressive movement *away* from the simplicity of childhood. Yet for Maslow, the peak of maturity entails not just a movement beyond earlier stages, but also a cyclical return to the source and recapturing one's 'core nature' that can be lost in the process of socialisation. A person's core nature is their basic, unlearnt personality traits and inclinations, which is expressed spontaneously when acting authentically (Maslow, 1974).

A criticism of Maslow's self-actualised personality model is that it is based on an analysis of persons that *he* chose to be exemplars of maturity, which were generally all liberal, spiritual, humanistic thinkers and politicians. Those of a more conservative disposition may construe the endpoint of development in a way that is closer to the socio-analytic model of maturity, and based more on tangible indices of social recognition such as income and influence (Hogan & Roberts, 2004). Despite the criticisms, the self-actualised personality remains one of the few models of maturity that is empirically based on the examination of persons who have reached high levels of performance, social recognition and integrity. Psychologists tend to focus on what is true of normal populations, but Maslow (1950) realised that in order to understand the higher reaches of development, you had to focus on those who are abnormally excellent. Self-actualisation is an ideal that can be intentionally pursued and is a popular concept for self-help books. Box 7.4 summarises some behaviours that are considered to promote it.

Box 7.4   Real-world applications

Behaviours that promote a self-actualised personality

1. Do things that mean that you continually keep learning throughout adulthood; try new things and make sure not to stay in your comfort zone too much.
2. Develop ways of become aware of your own feelings, such as the mindfulness meditation exercises mentioned in Chapter 10, as your gut feelings are often the voice of your 'core self'.
3. Avoid playing up to the expectation of others – be prepared to stand up for what you value and believe in, even if it makes you unpopular.
4. Try to focus on expressing what you genuinely think and feel, rather than trying to impress people with what you think they want to hear. People are good at picking up on dishonesty, and so your attempts to impress will usually backfire in the end.

Box 7.4 Continued

5. Take responsibility for the decisions you make and don't try and control what is out of your control.
6. Follow through on what you say to people you'll do, or say no before you start.
7. Don't be afraid to ask for help or go into therapy – in Maslow's view, therapy is just part of the adult growth process, it doesn't need to be orientated towards fixing something.

Maturity #5: Mature defence mechanisms

The longest longitudinal study of adult life ever conducted is *The Harvard Grant Study of Adult Development*. The study has followed two groups of participants for 70 years, both of whom were born in the late 1930s, and has charted their development in personality, mental health, relationships and adjustment. George Vaillant, who led the study, was influenced by Erikson's conception of adult development and ageing, and like Erikson he imported concepts from psychoanalytic thinking to illuminate the development of personality maturity over time (Vaillant, 1976; 1977; 2002). The concepts he employed were *defence mechanisms*, which are psychological strategies used to handle and cope with the presence of distress, conflict and threat.

Over the course of the many decades of the study, Vaillant noticed a clear shift in how adults employ defence mechanisms to manage stress, away from immature defences, towards an increasing reliance on mature defences (Vaillant, 2002). Immature personalities are formed around the habitual use of *projection, dissociation, fantasy* and *acting out. Projection* is the tendency to deny unwanted feelings and attribute them to others instead. This leads to a personality that tends to blame others and reject the possibility of emotional weaknesses in oneself. *Dissociation* is the tendency to put on an act to maintain self-image, even if that is dissociated from one's own core sense of self. This leads to a personality that is split into inner and outer. *Fantasy* is the tendency to distort relationships and activities into imaginary or unrealistic versions, which leads to a personality that is detached from the real world. *Acting out* involves expressing anger and impulses without restraint, which can lead to antisocial personality tendencies.

For the majority of participants in the study, immature coping declined in frequency over the course of adult life. In their place, adaptive defence strategies emerged; *suppression, humour, altruism* and *sublimation*.

Suppression involves control of, or delay of, gratification of aggressive or sexual impulses. It is the very essence of adult responsibility, according to Vaillant, and thus correlates strongly with adult adjustment. *Humour* helps turn painful or difficult emotions into manageable emotion, and is therefore central to mature personality functioning. *Altruism* involves the satisfaction of giving to others, which helps maintain healthy relationships. *Sublimation* involves turning strong impulses into creative or productive energy – the process of 'turning lust into lust for life'. A creative or productive personality is typically structured around successful sublimation.

The data from the Harvard Grant study showed a significant increase in the use of suppression between adolescence and midlife, and then between 50 and 75, altruism and humour increased significantly. Very few individuals regressed in their defence mechanisms over time – between the ages of 50 and 75, only four people decreased in the maturity of their defences, and two were alcoholics, one was seriously ill and the other had Alzheimer's disease. The study suggests that the gradual evolution of coping strategies over adulthood into more adaptive and virtuous forms is a normative process of growing maturity.

Theories of ego development

Loevinger's theory of ego development

In the 1930s, a graduate student by the name of Jane Loevinger came to work with Erik Erikson Erikson at the University of California. She proceeded to create her own neo-Eriksonian view of development, which by the 1970s had developed into the *theory of ego development*. Ego development is a lifelong endeavour to find unity and coherence in one's personality. This model contains nine stages of personality maturation, which successively *integrate* the personality over time, bringing about consistency, complexity, meaning and wholeness. This is achieved through the systematic and harmonious integration of a person's impulses, temperament, cognitions, traits, goals and roles (Loevinger, 1976).

Loevinger developed her theory based on research with a particular assessment tool – the Washington Sentence Completion Test (SCT) (Loevinger, 1998). This was initially developed for use with women, and then was adapted for men. It comprises 36 incomplete sentences that the respondent has to complete. Example sentence-completion items are:

1. My main problem is …
2. Being with other people …
3. The thing I like about myself is …

This form of assessment provides open-ended data that must be categorised. Each response to the sentence completion questionnaire is classified as *impulsive, self-protective, conformist, self-aware, conscientious, individualistic,* or *integrative,* and a total rating is given. Although this coding is a somewhat subjective process that leaves the gate open for researcher bias, inter-rater agreement between trained coders is good, ranging from $r = .89$ to $r = .96$ (Holaday, Smith & Sherry, 2000).

As with Kohlberg's stage theory of development (see Chapter 7) and postformal models of cognitive development (see Chapter 3), Loevinger's theory is based on Piaget's view of developmental stages; each one is a step up an irreversible, invariant process of developing a more complex ego-structure. Each new stage is qualitatively different from the previous one, and is characterised by a new ego structure. These stages are briefly described in Table 7.2.

Changes through the nine ego development stages are progressions towards being a more mature, integrated, and secure human being. Moving up the scale brings new freedoms; firstly, freedom from impulses (the self-protective stage), then freedom from convention (the self-aware stage), and then freedom from conflict (the autonomous stage). Therefore, it can be viewed as the incorporation of wider freedoms in human functioning.

Ego development theory makes bold and broad claims for the interrelation of a whole host of developmental changes, including cognition, affect, motivation, personality, social relationships and more. Some think the theory makes excessive claims, and that its key terms are unclear (Caprara & Cervone, 2000). For example, sometimes the ego is defined as a process, sometimes as a force and other times as a structure, while it is also said to mean the same as the self (Loevinger & Knoll, 1983).[2]

The aspect of the theory that is most open to question is the invariant order of the ego development stages – do people really pass through the stages in the exact sequence postulated, or do they skip or reverse stages? There is little evidence to settle this question either way, as most longitudinal research on the model looks at average change over time across a population, rather than stage-by-stage advance in individuals (for example, Manners, Durkin & Nesdale, 2004). Furthermore, there is a question mark over whether the stages are really stages with qualitative transitions between them or whether ego development is in fact more of a continuum (Hauser, 1976; 1993).

A final criticism that has been raised by Loevinger herself is that the theory may be biased in the direction of women, who generally

---

[2] Equating the term 'ego' with self does not clarify things because the term 'self' can mean many thing in psychology too (Harré, 1998).

Table 7.2   Loevinger's nine stages of ego development

Stage number and name	Typical age	Description of stage
1. Presocial	Baby	The self is not fully differentiated from the world or the caregiver.
2. Impulsive	Toddler	Bodily impulses are a predominant preoccupation, and control is provided by restraints, rewards and punishments.
3. Self-Protective	Young child	Self-control of impulses emerges, leading to a sense of volition, opportunism and manipulation, allied to a tendency to externalise blame.
4. Conformist	Older child and adolescent	Identity is shaped by the rules of the group, if there is trust in the group. Personality is still self-centred, as the dominant aim is maximising a sense of belonging.
5. Self-Aware	Young adulthood	An increase in reflective self-awareness and self-criticism, allied to a greater interest in interpersonal relations.
6. Conscientious	Middle adulthood	Life becomes based on values of responsibility and the pursuit of high ideals and long-term goals. There is more self-criticism and evaluation of one's own personal standards, and how they relate to behaviour.
7. Individualistic	Adulthood – Rare	There is a stronger sense of individuality and self-understanding, an acceptance that autonomy conflicts with connection and intimacy, and a recognition of internal conflicts, without resolution.
8. Autonomous	Adulthood – Very rare	At this stage, the realisation of autonomy is premised on the importance of collectives and social groups. This dialectical interplay of free person and norm-driven society is accepted as an expression of tensions inherent in the nature of human existence.
9. Integrated	Adulthood – Exceptionally rare	At this stage a person has an identity in which all aspects of the self are integrated and co-ordinated. With this comes exceptional wisdom, emotional balance and psychological health.

score higher than men (Loevinger, 1985; Loevinger & Knoll, 1983). The *Sentence Completion Test* was initially developed for women only, and it may be that the theory itself reflects women's development more than men's development. At the heart of the model is the increasing realisation of *autonomy*. While this would have been the pressing developmental challenge for women in the 1950s and 1960s, who were the principal subjects for developing the theory, it is questionable whether autonomy is the marker of psychological maturity for men. For example, Carol Gilligan (1982) has stated that men's primary challenge in development is with attachment not with autonomy. Therefore ego development theory may not be as relevant to men as it is to women.

Kegan's theory of the evolving self

Loevinger has not been the only theorist to apply Piagetian stage-theory ideas to personality. Robert Kegan, a Harvard professor, has also proposed a stage theory of the developing ego in which qualitatively new, more complex, stages of selfhood emerge over time (Kegan, 1982). The developmental sequence in his theory is similar to Loevinger's. It starts with the *incorporative self*, which corresponds to Loevinger's presocial stage. Next emerges *the impulsive self*, which is oriented towards the mother-baby dyad and is prior to any assertion of independence, which corresponds to Loevinger's impulsive stage. Once impulses are controlled, through toilet training and verbalised thought, and the first moves towards independent action are taken, the *imperial self* is reached, which corresponds to Loevinger's self-protective level. Following that, the *interpersonal self* emerges at approximately the beginning of the teenage years – this is a parallel of the conformist stage. It brings a new push for inclusion and popularity with adolescent peers. This is then surmounted by the *institutional self*, which replaces the malleable interpersonal self with a more solid and autonomous identity that is defined by roles that link the person to stable institutions – it is the first ego-stage of adulthood and resembles the conscientious stage of the Loevinger's model. The *interindividual self* is the following stage, which is realised when mutual interdependence between individuals is achieved as a locus for identity. This resembles the autonomous stage in Loevinger's model.

Kegan has developed an interview-based assessment tool for his model termed the *Subject–Object Interview* (Kegan, 1994). In the interview, a researcher asks a series of questions to determine how the participant experiences and makes sense of real-life situations that have emotional, cognitive and interpersonal elements. An example question from the interview is 'Can you tell me of a recent experience of being angry about something?' Interviews are scored by two raters to indicate which level of the model is dominant in the person's descriptions. A longitudinal study with 22 adults was conducted using the Subject–Object Interview. Participants were measured four times over four years, and the majority showed gradual increases in complexity over the course of the four years of the study (Kegan, 1994).

In summary, models of ego development describe stages that a person journeys through on his or her way to a more *complex and integrated personality, each of which is a temporary balance on that path*. Ego development theorists such as Kegan and Loevinger emphasise increased complexity as the vehicle of progress and benchmark of maturity. But this is questionable as a comprehensive schema for personality maturity, given that there are other directions to adult development, as described in Chapter 1, such as the ethical direction and veridical direction. We might ask ourselves: is developing a simpler but more honest or ethical way of functioning sometimes a step towards maturity? If so, then there is more to personality maturation than models of ego development imply. One other way that a person may mature over time is in how they construct a story of their life, and it is to that topic that we now turn.

The life story approach to personality development

Many psychologists now take the view that the study of personality should go beyond trait models and questionnaires to include personality assessments that provide more detail, richness and subtlety. Dan McAdams is one such theorist; he divides the study of personality into three levels: (1) traits, (2) characteristic adaptations (that is, personal projects, habits and hobbies and other enduring patterns of behaviour), and (3) the life story (Hooker & McAdams, 2003).

The life story has direct relevance to the study of adult development, for it provides a retrospective view on how a person's life and identity has changed and developed over time (McAdams, 2001). In his book *The Stories We Live By* (1993), McAdams presents a method for eliciting a person's life story in a comprehensive and standardised way, which was briefly described in Chapter 2. The process covers topics such as perceived life chapters, peak experiences, nadir experiences, turning points, early memories, adolescent memories, adult memories, significant others, social environments, personal ideology, conceptions of the future and sources of stress (McAdams, 1993). The life story that is elicited using this method typically includes much of what you expect in any story; scenes, chapters, plots, high points, low points, turning points, and a central character (the self).

Continuity effects attempt to emphasise sameness in the life story, and thus to create a bond between the present and the past (Kotre, 1995). This helps to strengthen a core sense of self at the heart of a life story and to emphasise permanence in the face of inevitable change. Kotre (1995) points to the frequent use of the words 'always' and 'never' in autobiographical narrative as sources of continuity and stability – for example, 'I have always had a difficult relationship with my father' or 'I have never had much luck in love.'

Contrast effects, on the other hand, emphasise the *difference* between the past and the present, in order to create a separation between a past event or life phase and a new one. A typical contrast effect is the assertion that 'I am a new person – I am not the same person as I was then.' Contrast effects are shown when retrospective data is compared with longitudinal data on personality change – people's retrospective accounts typically imply greater change than concurrent longitudinal measures, suggesting that their memory inserts a contrast effect to imply a greater sense of maturity now than in the past (Kotre, 1995).

The life story is a selective series of 'nuclear episodes' that are bound together into a narrative (McAdams, 1993). What kinds of episodes are typically incorporated into the life story? Priority tends to be given to the *first* and *last* occurrence of particular activities, roles, events, and experiences. **Primacy events** such as the first day a work, the first experience of sexual intercourse, the first romantic relationship, moving into one's first house, have an emphasised role in the life story, as do **final endings** such as experiences of divorce, bereavement, children moving out of home or retirement. There is a disproportionate tendency to focus on events in late adolescence and early adulthood, which is called the 'reminiscence bump' (Mackavey, Malley & Stewart, 1991). This may relate to the greater number of primacy events and major decisions that occur in that period relative to later in adult life (Kotre, 1995).

A life story has a private and a public version. The private version is stored within a *life story schema* – a cognitive representation of life's major episodes and the links between them (Habermas & Bluck, 2000). The public version is a presentational device, told within the context of conversations with others about one's own life (Pasupathi, 2001), that is recounted to others in selective, and sometimes dramatised, form (McAdams, 2001).

Monica Pasupathi (2001) has found that life stories are told differently depending on who is listening – this is called **co-construction**. The more a particular version is told, the more that account becomes reified as the correct version in the mind of the person telling it. Furthermore, people are motivated to maintaining consistency in the telling of the life story, and this is an important source of personality stability over time (Pasupathi, 2001).

Development of the life story during adolescence and adulthood

While personality traits can be assessed in young children (see John et al., 1994), the life story cannot, for it has not yet been constructed in childhood.

Life stories appear in rudimentary form in adolescence (Habermas & Bluck, 2000), and by the end of adolescence, various abilities emerge that combine to facilitate the construction an adult life story. These include:

- *Biographical coherence* – the ability to meaningfully relate a single event to the rest of one's life.
- *Causal coherence* – the ability to infer how an event from earlier life is causally related to later events and outcomes.
- *Thematic coherence* – the capacity to describe an overarching theme or principle that integrates many episodes from their life.

It is during emerging adulthood that a person first begins the work of integrating his or life story into a meaningful pattern (McAdams, 2001). At this life stage, stories are typically focused on values, beliefs and ideology, and are focused on the future. In middle age the life story tends towards an increasing focus on loss and mortality, on 'generative' motifs (those focused on a personal legacy and benefit to others), and on endings (McAdams, 2001). Then in later life, narratives of retirement from full-time work show themes of renewed freedom and/or the loss of status and identity (Robinson, Demetre & Corney, 2011).

Some particular features of life stories relate to personality maturity; for example, life stories that include 'redemptive episodes' predict various positive outcomes. Redemptive episodes describe difficult times during which suffering and stress were turned around into a positive outcome. This narrative knack of finding the 'silver lining' in hard times is related to enhanced generativity and wellbeing (Affleck & Tennen, 1996; Bauer, McAdams & Sakaeda, 2005; King & Hicks, 2007; McAdams, 2006).

Ego development level is one way of measuring personality maturity, and it has been found to relate to how a life story is told. McAdams (1985) found that in comparison with adults low in ego development, adults high in ego development include more kinds of plot in their life story, and show greater narrative complexity. Ego development is related to the capacity to elaborate alternative conceptions of how life might have turned out had different choices been made, a conscious struggle with life's challenges and a mixture of confidence and humility (King, 2001; King & Hicks, 2006).

Consolidating the life story in old age: The life review

In 1963, a psychiatrist called Robert Butler wrote an influential article on a phenomenon that is characteristic of old age, which he termed the 'life review'. The life review, he stated, is a universal process engaged in by elderly adults during which they intensively reminisce about past events in their life. Butler (1963) suggested that the life review is particularly prominent in those for whom advanced age had brought about a loss of independence (that is, they are in the Fourth Age of life – see Chapter 6); a person at this point of life is aware of approaching death and thus particularly motivated to resolve past conflicts and find closure on the past before life ends. Also, this reminiscence on the past can be an important source of happiness and self-esteem in old age, particularly if age-related deteriorations make the present arduous (Coleman & O'Hanlon, 2004).

Undergoing a process of life review in the final years of life is not without risks, for it involves dragging skeletons out of cupboards that have been shut for a very long time and re-living experiences that may be emotionally painful (Kotre, 1995). In order to differentiate between positive and negative reminiscence in old age, Wong and Watt (1991) devised a typology of six forms of reminiscence, which are summarised in Table 7.3, and examples from which are shown in Box 7.5. They investigated whether some of these types were more associated with well-being than others by interviewing 171 elderly adults, half of whom were living in institutions (mean age 82), and half of whom were living in the community (mean age 74). All participants were classified as high or low wellbeing, based on the sum of multiple ratings given by a panel of experts; a psychologist, a psychiatrist, a geriatric nurse and a gerontological recreational worker. The study found that subjects who were ageing successfully and had high wellbeing engaged in *integrative* and *instrumental* reminiscence more than those who were ageing unsuccessfully, and also engaged in less *obsessive* reminiscence. This suggests that reminiscence can occur in a variety of ways in adulthood, some of which are healthy, and some not.

Butler (1963) proposed that the life review is engaged by all who reach advanced old age, but research has shown that this is not the case; the extent of reminiscence that an elderly person engages in depends on their environment, personality and past experiences (Cappeliez & O'Rourke, 2002; Coleman, 1974; Wink & Schiff, 2002). It seems that it is particularly functional when there are unresolved painful memories (Coleman, 1974). *If* the life review proceeds successfully, disparate events and experiences of the past are brought together into a coherent and meaningful story, and any burdens of guilt, resentment, anxiety or anger surrounding past memories are resolved. This brings with it a sense of wholeness and peace in the final years of life.

Butler (1980) suggested that therapists who work with elderly adults should aim to facilitate a constructive resolution to the life review process. Since then, an industry of reminiscence and life review therapy has been created, including group-based interventions such as Guided

Box 7.5   Individual voices

Types of reminiscence in elderly adults

Individual examples of integrative, instrumental and obsessive reminiscence extracts are shown next, taken from Wong and Watt (1991, p. 276).

Integrative

> When I was a teenager, my parents broke up and both remarried. I was very resentful because they did not seem to care about my feelings or needs. But as I grow older and look back, I understand that they were really not compatible with each other. They had suffered for many years before their divorce. Now, I'm on good terms with both sets of parents.

Instrumental

> During the Great Depression, life was very hard. There were very few jobs, and money was difficult to come by. But we learned to survive by budgeting and making do without many things. The lessons I learned in those years have really helped me in trying to live on my old-age pension.

Obsessive

> My husband died when I was away for two days visiting my friends in the West. He fell in the bathtub and eventually died because there was no one there to help him. It has been years now, but I still cannot forgive myself for leaving him home alone for two days.

Autobiography (Birren & Cochran, 2001) and Life-Review Process Therapy (Haight, 1988), suggesting that Butler's words were somewhat prophetic. A recent meta-analysis of 20 outcome studies of life review or reminiscence interventions found that there was a consistent positive effect on reducing symptoms of depression in the elderly (Bohlmeijer, Smit & Cuijpers, 2003).

Concluding comments

'Personality' is a term that can mean many things to psychologists, and this chapter has portrayed the field's diversity. Trait theory sees

Table 7.3 Six types of reminiscence shown in elderly adults

Reminiscence type	Description
1. Narrative	The provision of routine biographical information, or the telling of past anecdotes that may be of interest to the listener.
2. Integrative	This is the kind of reminiscence that comprises the life review. It aims to integrate events and memories in order create a sense of coherence, identity and reconciliation with regard to one's past, and is indicated by statements implying acceptance of past experiences (see example in Box 7.5).
3. Transmissive	This is reminiscence aimed at passing on one's own experiences and heritage to others by way of past experiences. It involves references to the culture, wisdom and practices of a past era, and lessons that can be learned from the past.
4. Instrumental	Reminiscence aimed at drawing on the past to solve present problems, by way of recalling past plans, strategies and attempts at overcoming difficulties (see example in Box 7.5).
5. Obsessive	Reminiscence characterised by repeated thinking about past events that induce a sense of guilt, bitterness, anxiety or despair (see example in Box 7.5).
6. Escapist	A tendency to glorify the past and deprecate the present, also referred to as *defensive reminiscence*. Boasts of past achievements and exaggerations of past enjoyments are indicative of this reminiscence type.

Source: Wong and Watt (1991).

personality through the lens of psychometric questionnaires, and its principle research focus is with variables and measurement at the group level rather than with individual people (Eysenck, 1952). The trait approach has made strides in showing convincing quantitative longitudinal change and cross-sectional differences across adulthood at the level of the sample average. However as we discussed in Chapter 1, the sample average is potentially misleading as it may not reflect individuals in the sample. This limitation of focusing on the mean is being addressed by new analytical methods that trait theorists are using to look at subgroups of individuals and single cases, as discussed earlier in the chapter.

The life story approach gains detailed data about how a person experiences their life as an unfolding narrative, and this provides a holistic complement to the more abstract and genetic trait assessments. Assessment is time-consuming, and is interpersonally challenging as a participant will only disclose sensitive aspects of their life story to a person that they trust. Both trait and life story approaches are essentially descriptive and value-neutral. In contrast, *prescriptive* models of ideal personality functioning are based on notions of personality maturity. Such models include self-actualisation, social effectiveness, ego development, authenticity and mature defence mechanisms. Which is correct? There's no easy answer to that, but it's quite likely that each has something to contribute.

Questions for you to reflect on

- What are some of the limitations of only assessing change in personality traits when studying personality development in adulthood?
- If you were going to tell your life story, which key events or episodes would you be sure to include and why? In what ways have those events influenced your personality?
- Would you like your personality to change in the future in any way? If yes, list the changes you would like and then look back over the chapter to see if they fit with one or more of the models of personality maturity or ego development.

Summary points

- Cross-sectional age differences in the Five Factor Model personality traits show that Agreeableness and Conscientiousness increase with age, while Extraversion and Openness decline.
- Longitudinal mean-level change shows that Conscientiousness, Social Dominance, Agreeableness and Emotional Stability increase with age, while Openness to Experience and Social Vitality remain fairly constant.
- Longitudinal rank-order change shows that test-retest correlations get progressively stronger through adulthood, with the highest levels being in the over-fifties and over-sixties.
- Other forms of longitudinal change parameter include Ipsative change (change in score profile across multiple traits) and individual change (an index of reliable change over time for each person).
- Genes and environment influence personality development, and in adulthood environmental events such as drug-taking, changing social roles and being under stress can affect personality trait development in a variety of ways.
- The life story is a central part of personal identity, and involves the creation of an autobiographical narrative of who 'I' am. It emerges developmentally in adolescence and continues to develop throughout the whole of life.

- The capacity to find the redemptive message in adverse life experiences, that is, to view how it has helped rather than hindered development, is related to wellbeing and integrity.
- There are multiple models of the mature personality, including the following: the socio-analytic model (maturity = being a pillar of society), the authenticity model (maturity = being true to oneself and honest with others), the generativity model (maturity = transcending self-interest), the self-actualisation model (maturity = fulfilling one's potential and reaching for one's goals), the defence-mechanism model (maturity = use of healthy ways of dealing with conflict) and the ego-development model (maturity = integrated, complex ego).
- Loevinger's ego development theory is a stage theory of optimal personality development, which stipulates that the person develops through a series of predictable stages of growth, each of which is more complex and integrated than the last. The stages that apply to adulthood are *conformist, self-aware, conscientious, individualistic, autonomous* and *integrated*.
- Many older adults engage in is a process of *life review* – a lengthy reflection on one's personal life story in order to deal with past regrets, confusions or secrets, and to find coherence and meaning in life's disparate episodes (Staudinger, 2001). When successful, a life review can bring a sense of integrity, coherence and completion. However, there are also dangers inherent in the life review as it may open up past wounds that have been concealed for so long that it is difficult to heal them at such a late point in life (Kotre, 1995). Therapeutic intervention can help steer the life review towards a positive outcome.

Recommended reading

Caspi, A., Roberts, B. W. & Shiner, R. L. (2005). Personality development: Stability and change. *Annual Review of Psychology*, 56, 453–484.

Habermas, T. & Bluck, S. (2000). Getting a life: The emergence of the life story in adolescence. *Psychological Bulletin*, 126, 748–769.

Hogan, R. & Roberts, B. W. (2004). A socioanalytic model of maturity. *Journal of Career Assessment*, 12, 207–217.

Loevinger, J. & Knoll, E. (1983). Personality: Stages, traits and the self. *Annual Review of Psychology*, 34, 199–222.

Maslow, A. H. (1950). Self-actualizing people: A study of psychological health. *Personality*, 1, 11–34.

McAdams, D. P. (1993). *The Stories We Live By: Personal Myths and The Making of the Self.* New York: Guilford Press.

Pasupathi, M. (2001). The social construction of the personal past and its implications for adult development. *Psychological Bulletin*, 127, 651–672.

Roberts, B. W. & DelVecchio, W. F. (2000). The rank-order consistency of personality traits from childhood to old age: A quantitative review of longitudinal studies. *Psychological Bulletin*, 126, 3–25.

Roberts, B. W., Walton, K. E. & Viechtbauer, W. (2006). Patterns of mean-level change in personality traits across the life course: A meta-analysis of longitudinal studies. *Psychological Bulletin*, 132, 1–25.

Useful websites

Complete a Big Five personality questionnaire online: www.outofservice.com/bigfive

Website on life story interviewing: www.sesp.northwestern.edu/foley/instruments/interview/

The Harvard Study of Adult Development: http://adultdev.bwh.harvard.edu/research-SAD.html

Website on life story interviewing: www.sesp.northwestern.edu/foley/instruments/interview/

The Harvard Study of Adult Development: http://adultdev.bwh.harvard.edu/research-SAD.html

8

Moral Development

We have, in fact, two kinds of morality side by side: one which we preach but do not practice, and another which we practice but seldom preach.

Bertrand Russell (1928)

In her late thirties, Laura had an affair with a work colleague. When I interviewed her she was in her mid-forties, and it was clear that she still felt deeply conflicted about the affair and found it difficult to discuss. She felt guilty that she had resorted to deceit for so long, and had not managed to live up to own high moral standards. She said that at the time she thought up complex moral justifications for her actions and wrote them down in her diary. For example, she convinced herself temporarily that the affair was warranted on the basis that her husband (20 years her senior) was offering her little in the way of intimacy and passion. As the affair became more serious, she had to think up even greater lies to explain her absence to her husband, while her sense of guilt and anxiety about the situation grew. Her husband eventually discovered the affair and left her. Soon after that, the man she was having an affair with abruptly ceased contact with her. Finding herself alone and confused, she spent the next few years in therapy, trying to come to terms with how she had got herself into such a moral dilemma.

What does it mean to be a good person? And importantly for adult development – what does it mean to become a *better* person? We have already discussed a number of theorists who view adult development as having an ethical dimension, such as Abraham Maslow, who viewed mature persons as committed to a socially beneficial cause (Chapter 4), and Erik Erikson, who suggested that an indicator of mature adulthood is generativity – the desire and capacity to give to others (Chapter 6). These and other theorists agree that positive development in adulthood heads in the direction of greater virtue. This chapter deals with theories about the changing nature of morality over the course of adulthood.

Lawrence Kohlberg: A pioneer in moral development

Lawrence Kohlberg was born in New York in 1927. As a young man he was a sailor during World War II, before returning to American to study psychology. During his doctoral studies at the University of Chicago in the late 1950s, he encountered Jean Piaget's developmental theory (see Chapter 3) and applied it to the topic of moral development. Over the course of his career he became one of the foremost exponents of the Piagetian approach to lifespan development (Crain, 2005), as well as one of the most cited names in Psychology as a whole (Haggbloom et al., 2002). He spent his career teaching at the University of Chicago and Harvard University.

Box 8.1   Alternative perspectives

John Rawls's veil of ignorance: A moral thought experiment

John Rawls was writing on ethical philosophy at the same time as Kohlberg was writing about moral development, and Kohlberg was influenced by Rawls' ideas. One of Rawls' most popular concepts is the 'veil of ignorance', which is a thought experiment to get people to think about what it means to be socially just (Rawls, 1971). The thought experiment goes like this:

> You get to create a brand new society, and have to decide how goods are distributed, how people are rewarded and who gets extra help and benefits. **But** where you then end up in the resulting society is a lottery – you might end up in the advantaged elite, a child of unemployed alcoholics, or profoundly disabled. You have no idea of your eventual position, not even of your ethnicity, your gender or whether you'll have a sound body or not.

What would *you* do, given a veil of ignorance on your own position in society?

Kohlberg borrowed from moral philosophy to help form his theory of moral development. He was influenced by the ancient Greek philosopher Plato, who said that morality is based on a pursuing a perfect ideal of goodness (Kohlberg, 1970). Following Plato, Kohlberg said that it is possible to become morally *better* over time precisely because one can more closely approximately the ideal of goodness. Kohlberg was also very influenced by a moral philosopher who was writing at the same time as him, called John Rawls. Rawls' view was that morality is based on impartiality and the principles of fairness and social justice. One of Rawls's most famous ideas, which exemplifies his emphasis on impartiality, was the thought experiment called 'the veil of ignorance' (Rawls, 1971), described in Box 8.1. In 1971 Kohlberg contracted a tropical disease that left him chronically in pain, and this is said to be the main reason why, in 1987, he drowned himself in Boston Harbour. Even his demise was a moral controversy – no slight irony for a specialist in the subject.

Kohlberg's method: The Moral Judgment Interview

Kohlberg devised a method for investigating moral reasoning titled the *Moral Judgment Interview*. In this method, three hypothetical moral dilemmas are presented to the participant, and after each one the researcher asks a series of standardised questions. Responses to the questions are taped and transcribed, and the transcription of the interview is then analysed. Here is an example of one Kohlberg's problems and the standardised questions that follow it:

> In Korea, a company of Marines was greatly outnumbered and was retreating before the enemy. The company had crossed a bridge over a river, but the enemy were mostly still on the other side. If someone went back to the bridge and blew it up, with the head start the rest of the men in the company would have, they could probably then escape. But the man who stayed back to blow up the bridge would probably not be able to escape alive; there would be about a 4:1 chance he would be killed. The captain himself is the man who knows best how to lead the retreat. He asks for volunteers, but no one will volunteer. If he goes himself, the men will probably not get back safely and he is the only one who knows how to lead the retreat.
>
> 1. Should the captain order a man to go on this very dangerous mission or should he go himself? Why?
> 2. What is the best justification for saying it is right to send someone besides himself?

a. Why or how do you say it is right to save more lives in this case, when it means ordering someone to his death?

3. What is the best, or most important reason for saying it is wrong to send someone else, when ordering someone else will save more lives?

4. Does the captain have the right or the authority to order a man if he thinks it best to? Why?

5. Would a man have the right to refuse such an order? Why?

6. The captain has a family, the men do not. Should that enter into his decision? How?

   a. If he is going to pick someone to go, how should he pick someone? Why?

7. There is some conflict between fairness and survival here. Which is more important, or how can he deal with both here? What does fairness mean anyhow, and why is it important?

Colby et al. (1983, pp. 82–3)

Responses to each dilemma are scored according to set criteria: *issues*, *norms* and *elements*. The *issue* is the overall view that a participant takes in a dilemma, that is, which course of action to take. Moral *norms* constitute the standards that they profess are important, such as: preservation of life, right to property, truth, importance of affiliation, erotic love, authority, law, contract, civil rights, religion, conscience and punishment. *Elements* constitute the specific ways in which norms are applied, such as consulting others, retribution, seeking reward, serving social ideal, reciprocity etc. For a full description of the scoring system, which is rather complex, see Colby et al. (1983).

Kohlberg's six-stage model

Using findings from the Moral Judgment Interview, Kohlberg's model of moral development was developed and tested over the course of several decades (Crain, 2010). The model consists of six sequential stages, grouped into three higher-order levels. When being assessed, a person could be assigned to a particular stage or be scored as in-between two stages, if they showed evidence of both.

Pre-conventional Level

Stage 1 – Heteronomous morality

Stage 1 is typical of young children. At this stage, they assume that morality is determined by a fixed set of rules handed down by authorities, whose opinion is unquestioned. Moral behaviour means obedience to authority and the avoidance of breaking rules, and correspondingly avoiding punishment and maximising reward. At this stage, it is the *consequences* of an action, but not the intention behind an action, that defines morality, thus an accidental act from which harm results is perceived to be equivalent to an intentional act of harm.

Stage 2 – Instrumental purpose and exchange

At stage 2, an individualistic perspective is taken to morality. Everybody has their own interests to pursue, and the moral thing to do is to pursue one's own interest while trying to avoid harming others. The right thing to do is to follow the rules if it is in *your* immediate interest, while letting others do the same. *Exchange* is the defining feature of moral behaviour at this stage, so what is deemed to be right is a good deal or a fair exchange between two individuals.

Conventional Level

Stage 3 – Mutual interpersonal expectations and conformity

At stage 3, maintaining good relationships becomes the focus of moral concern. The feelings, agreements and expectations of relationships start to take primacy over individual interests. The right thing to do is to live up to what is expected of you and to maintain relationships through trust, loyalty, respect and gratitude. The reasons for doing right include the need to be a good person in your own eyes and the eyes of others, maintain agreed rules, and the belief in the Golden Rule – to 'do unto others as you would have them do unto you'.

Stage 4 – Social system and conscience

At stage 4, a person takes into account the whole social system and culture that they are in, and considers the moral correctness of actions in terms of their effects on that system. The right thing to do is to fulfil the duties of a citizen, contribute to society effectively, and uphold laws unless they conflict with other social duties. Keeping society balanced and effective and avoiding its possible breakdown is the key reason for acting morally.

Post-conventional Level

Stage 5 – Social contract and individual rights

At stage 5, a person starts to consider both moral and legal points of view, and to recognise that moral norms can conflict. The morally right thing to do is to be aware that people and society hold a variety of values and opinions, some of which may be culturally specific. Some non-relative values, such as life and liberty, should be upheld in any society and regardless of majority opinion. At this stage of development, the morally correct action emerges out of the tension of (a) a sense of obligation to law because of one's acceptance of the social contract to abide by laws; (b) a volitional commitment to family, friendship, trust, and work obligations; and (c) a concern for whether laws and duties are based on enhancing the greatest good for the greatest number. At the previous stage, the goal is to keep society functioning and abide by the general consensus. But not all societies are good ones, and consensus is not always right. At stage 5, the idea of going *beyond* moral norms becomes acceptable.

Stage 6 – Universal ethical principles

In stage 6, behaviour becomes entirely principled. Morality is based on following ethical principles that apply universally, such as equality of human rights and respect for the dignity of all persons. Laws are considered valid only if they seem to rest on such principles. The reason for doing the right thing is a belief in the reality and existence of universal moral principles and an unwavering commitment to them. This stage fits with the morality of figures such as Gandhi, who claimed that everyone must be treated equally and impartially, whether they are your parent or a stranger. At this level, family members do not warrant special treatment for all are equal. Stage 6 was never actually found by Kohlberg in *any* of his participants, so he removed it from his scoring scheme and referred to it as a purely 'theoretical stage'. So the question of whether people can act purely from principle, without moral conflict, was never quite solved by Kohlberg.

Longitudinal studies with adults using Kohlberg's method

A number of longitudinal studies on Kohlberg's model have been conducted that have followed individuals into adulthood. Kohlberg conducted a 20-year longitudinal study starting in 1955, using male participants who were aged ten, 13 or 16 when first interviewed, and then assessed at three–four year intervals for 20 years (Colby et al., 1983). Moral dilemmas were administered in the same format at each assessment, and at the end of the study an analysis was conducted on all 58 participants who were interviewed twice or more over the 20-year duration.

The findings showed that the typical stage for ten-year-olds was stage 2, for 13–14 year olds it was 2/3, for 16–18 year olds it was 3/4. No one under the age of 20 gained a 4 or 5 on *any* of the dilemmas presented to them. Between the ages of 20 and 36, an increasing number scored at level 4 and 4/5. Just four individuals out of 58 scored a 4/5 overall, all of whom were adults, and not a single person qualified as an overall Level 5 at any time point. This shows how rare post-conventional morality is in Kohlberg's model. The longitudinal findings support of the idea of a stage model, by showing that in children and young adults moral reasoning progressed towards a higher moral level over time, and no participant developed in such a way that a stage in the sequence was missed out (for example, no one moved directly from stage 2 to stage 4).

Holstein (1976) carried out a three-year longitudinal study using Kohlberg's method with a sample of adolescents and middle-aged adults and found general support for the model. However this study also found evidence of *regression* to lower stages in middle-aged adults. In 22 per cent of individuals who reached Stage 4 or higher, later assessment showed a reversion to an earlier stage. This suggests that movement up through the stages is not inevitable, and that as individuals age they may re-connect with the importance of conventional morality, after being more post-conventionally idealistic as a young adult.

Another longitudinal analysis using Kohlberg's method was conducted by Armon & Dawson (1997). 44 participants including children, adolescents, adults and older adults were interviewed four times at four-year time intervals. Development through Kohlberg's stages was found to be linear, sequential and rapid during childhood and adolescence, but slower and less predictable in adult age groups. Figure 8.1 shows the developmental trajectories for all participants in the sample; the scores on the y-axis translate as 100 = stage 1, 200 = stage 2, 300 = stage 3, 400 = stage 4 and 500 = stage 5. The trajectories show that over the age of 40, change in moral reasoning stage becomes less pronounced and involves both progressive and regressive trajectories, and only three participants scored at a pure post-conventional level (that is, a score of 500 – Stage 5).

There are some inherent problems in conducting longitudinal research using Kohlberg's methods. Such a study requires participants to engage many times with the same moral dilemmas. This may act as a form of moral education, thereby improving moral reasoning over time relative to a norm group. Advance may therefore be greater than the normal population in these samples. Secondly, participants may well become aware of Kohlberg's theory during the process and this may encourage them to self-present in a positive light by producing more complex, post-conventional responses. Finally, there is a lack of longitudinal research with adults over the age of 60 using Kohlberg's methods, so the question of what happens to moral reasoning stage in old age is unclear.

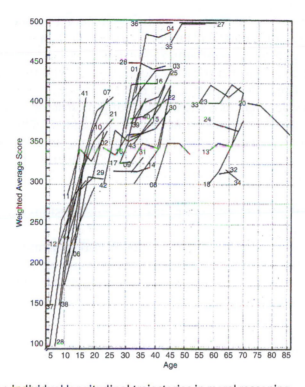

Figure 8.1   44 individual longitudinal trajectories in moral reasoning

Source: Armon & Dawson (1997, p. 441). Copyright © Journal of Moral Education Ltd. Reprinted by permission of (Taylor & Francis Ltd, http://www.tandfonline.com) on behalf of Journal of Moral Education Ltd.

The Minnesota 'Neo-Kohlbergian' approach

Kohlberg's interview and scoring method has not been widely used by other researchers, perhaps due to its time-consuming and complex nature. In order to make Kohlberg's theory more accessible to researchers, James Rest and colleagues developed a pencil-and-paper assessment based on Kohlberg's model – the *Defining Issues Test* (Rest et al., 1974; Rest et al., 1999). The test, and the neo-Kohlbergian theory that underpins it, is referred to as the Minnesota approach to moral development (Thoma, 2002).

When completing the Defining Issues Test (DIT), a person must read through a series of moral dilemmas, some of which are identical to Kohlberg's dilemmas. After reading each dilemma, they must rate 12-sentence long extracts of reasoning on a five-point scale to indicate how much they agree with it. Over 40,000 people have completed the DIT, which attests to its popularity as an assessment tool (Rest et al., 1999). People generally do better on the DIT than on Kohlberg's method, arguably as they don't have to articulate their own reasoning (Rest et al., 1999).

The neo-Kohlbergian theory that the DIT is based on does not refer to moral stages, but instead calls them *moral schemas*. Moral schemas are cognitive structures for evaluating moral concerns, which change as a person develops. So rather than the stage concept, with its implication of a rigid staircase of development, this neo-Kohlbergian approach considers moral development as a series of overlapping schemas, each of which is defined by the dominance of one central moral idea. Individuals can be scored as having a dominant schema ('consolidated morality'), or having a mixture of schemas ('transitional morality'). The three moral schemas in the Minnesota model are as follows:

1. *Personal interests schema*: In this schema, decisions are considered moral if they have good effects on oneself and one's close relations and friends. This maps on to Kohlberg's stages 2 and 3.
2. *Maintaining norms schema*: In this schema, morality is based on the importance of upholding social rules and roles, maintaining established social practices, and the application of existing laws. The ultimate good is safety and predictability within society. This maps on to Kohlberg's stage 4.
3. *Post-conventional (also called principled) schema*: In this schema, morality is based on conscious moral ideals, which are open to debate and tests of logical coherence. A moral ideal should permit a fair distribution of rights and responsibilities within society and within any given situation. *Any* explicit, rational moral philosophy qualifies as post-conventional in this sense (Rest et al., 2000). This schema matches on to Kohlberg's stages 5 and 6.

King and Mayhew (2002) reviewed the evidence for sequential development through these schemas, based on longitudinal research with the DIT on college students. They conclude that being at university promotes moral development, with students showing a decrease in the maintaining norms schema and an increase in the post-conventional schema. The authors of the review conclude that higher education plays an important role in moral development.

After developing the DIT, the Minnesota group developed a broader theory of what determines moral behaviours, which moves beyond moral schemas and moral cognition. Their 'Four Component Model', derived in the late 1980s, conceptualises moral functioning as the outcome of the following four processes: (1) ethical sensitivity – the ability to attend to and identify moral issues, (2) moral judgement – the ability to reason and justify moral courses of action, (3) moral motivation – prioritising morally correct choices against other drives and goals, (4) moral character – focusing on moral and prosocial concerns in an enduring and habitual manner (Bebeau, 2002). For a comprehensive set of review articles on the DIT and the Four Component Model, the reader is referred to volume 30, issue 3 of the *Journal of Moral Education* (2002).

The moral cognition – moral action question

Ever since Kohlberg's theory was devised, critics have asked to what degree moral reasoning actually causes moral behaviour and prevents antisocial behaviour. Research done with children and students on moral reasoning and moral behaviour suggests a tenuous relation. Bear & Richards (1981) found that when sex, verbal ability and social class were controlled for, moral reasoning contributed just 8 per cent of the variance in conduct ratings of pupils and students. Other research with children has continued to find ambiguous results (Miller et al., 1996).

An influential review paper on the moral reasoning/moral action question in adults was produced by Blasi (1980). Studies included in the review looked at the Kohlbergian moral reasoning in relation to delinquency, honesty, altruism and conformity. Results in all of these areas have been mixed. Out of the studies on delinquency, ten out of 15 showed statistically significant difference in moral reasoning between delinquents and matched groups of non-delinquents. Of the 17 studies that examined honesty, seven found a positive relation, seven a negative relation, and three found mixed relations with moral development. 11 out of 19 studies on moral reasoning and altruistic behaviour show a positive relation, while eight did not.

One of the most interest areas covered in Blasi's review was the relation between moral reasoning and performance in Milgram's electric shock experiment (which tests for the tendency to obey authority even when told to act immorally). In Milgram's infamous procedure, a lab-coated professor asks participants to administer electric shocks to another person in a neighbouring room, as part of a word-learning experiment. However the experiment is in fact a deception to investigate how much pain a person would inflict if they perceive themselves to be under orders from an authority figure. In actuality, no one is receiving real electric shocks, and the person in the neighbouring room is an actor. In studies that assessed *both* moral reasoning and how far participants will go in the Milgram experiment, astonishingly there was *no* relation between moral reasoning level and the tendency to quit giving electric shocks (Blasi, 1980). This suggests that moral reasoning is not sufficient as a basis for moral action in a pressured situation such as Milgram's experimental set-up.

Has the DIT fared better than Kohlberg's methods in its relation to moral action? Research on students using the DIT and moral behaviour measures have also produced mixed results. In a study with 53 college males, a strong negative relationship ($r = -.48$) was found between performance on the DIT and cheating behaviour (Malinowski & Smith, 1985). But in a study with 145 teacher education students, a weak relation of $r = -.20$ was found between moral reasoning and academic misconduct (Cummings et al., 2001). Based on this research, the following conclusion seems warranted – there is much more to morality than is assessed in Kohlberg's model or in the neo-Kohlbergian schema model. But what is missing? There have been a host of answers to that question, and we shall turn to some of them now, starting with a famous critique of Kohlberg's model by Carol Gilligan.

Carol Gilligan and the ethic of care

In the late 1970s, Carol Gilligan encountered the work of Lawrence Kohlberg and suspected a bias in his research and theory towards a masculine view of morality. The case against Kohlberg was damning – the sample that he used to develop his theory was all male, and the sample for his major longitudinal study was all male too. She observed that male participants were more likely to be higher up Kohlberg's scale than female participants, but men in the real world were clearly no more moral than women, indeed the opposite could be argued given the greater male propensity for criminal behaviour (see Figure 8.2). In

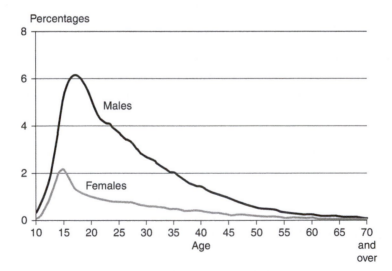

Figure 8.2 Offenders as a percentage of the population: by age and gender, 2006, England and Wales

Source: Office for National Statistics licensed under the Open Government Licence v.1.0. Reprinted with permission. http://www.statistics.gov.uk/cci/nugget.asp?id=1661

a pioneering series of qualitative studies Gilligan interviewed over 200 adolescents and adults about moral decision-making, and these findings were brought together in her book *In a Different Voice* (Gilligan, 1982). The book is still in print today.

The moral dilemmas that Gilligan used in her research included hypothetical ones like Kohlberg's method, and also real dilemmas from the individual's own life. She found that the hypothetical moral dilemmas were superior at assessing principles of justice and moral logic, while real-life dilemmas were better ways of assessing prosocial or antisocial tendencies (Gilligan, 1982; Gilligan & Murphy, 1979).

Gilligan's findings pointed towards a normative difference in how male and female participants reasoned through moral problems. Men, she found, were more concerned with the unbiased and impartial application of rules and rights – this was termed the *ethics of justice*. Women, on the other hand, base their morality on the importance of relationships, responsibilities and the duty of looking after those in need – this was termed the *ethic of care*. The ethic of care develops firstly as a desire to care for and be good to others. This then evolves to a more embracing notion of care, in which caring activities are orientated towards enhancing the wellbeing and development of others *and* oneself. See Box 8.2 for example female and male extracts from Gilligan's book.

Box 8.2   Individual voices

Gilligan (1982) provides the following quotes as exemplars of male and female views of morality. The male exemplar emphasises rights and justice:

Interview: *What does morality mean to you?*

Nobody in the world knows the answer. I think it is recognizing the right of the individual, the rights of other individuals, not interfering with those rights. Act as fairly as you would have them treat you. I think it is basically to preserve the human being's right to existence. I think that is the most important. Secondly, the human being's right to do as he pleases, again without interfering with somebody else's rights. Young adult male from Gilligan (1982, p. 19)

The female account emphasis *personal* responsibility and care:

Some sense of trying to uncover a right path in which to live, and always in my mind is that the world if full of real and recognizable trouble, and it is heading for some sort of doom, and is it right to bring

Box 8.2   Continued

children into this world when we currently have an overpopulation problem, and is it right to spend money on a pair of shoes when I have a pair of shoes and other people are shoeless? It is part of a self-critical view, part of saying, 'How am I spending my time and in what sense am I working?' I think I have a real drive, a real maternal drive, to take care of someone – to take care of my mother, to take care of children, to take care of other people's children, to take care of my own children, to take care of the world. Young adult female from Gilligan (1982, p. 99)

The female mode of moral reasoning is likely to be scored as a 'conventional' morality within Kohlberg's scheme, because post-conventional levels are by definition based on the application of abstract moral principles, rather than relationships, caring and compassion. Gilligan, in contrast, postulates that the ethics of justice and the ethics of care are *both* central to human development, and that the detached, impartial rationality upon which Kohlberg laid so much emphasis is not enough.

According to Gilligan, when male and female notions of moral goodness come together, moral maturity is more closely approximated; men gain a stronger sense of compassion and empathy, even if that means compromising on impartiality, while women gain a stronger sense of fairness and non-interference, even if that means hurting a person's feelings in order to maintain equality of treatment. The mature human being thus recognises the paradoxical challenges of justice and care, and combines both in his or her dealings with the world, as far as is achievable.

Kohlberg took Gilligan's critique seriously, and accepted in the mid-1980s that his method and model omitted a consideration of care for others and proactive moral behaviours (Levine, Kohlberg & Hewer, 1985). He stated at this point that his theory should be thought of specifically as a theory of conscious moral *reasoning and judgement*, while the issues of pro-social concern and care are valid moral domains that lie beyond its remit.

Gilligan's ideas have been developed further by the creation of the *Ethic of Care Interview* (Skoe & Gooden, 1993). This is an interview in which four dilemmas are discussed – one real-life dilemma, and three standardised dilemmas about (a) an unplanned pregnancy, (b) marital fidelity and (c) care for a parent. Women have been found score higher on this measure than men, supporting Gilligan's view on a basic gender difference in the development of care-based and prosocial morality (Skoe et al., 1996).

Jonathan Haidt and the Social Intuitionist Model

Jonathan Haidt is a proponent of the Social Intuitionist model of moral judgement, an approach views morality as a pragmatic product of evolution, rather than based a set of abstract, idealistic principles (Haidt & Joseph, 2004). Morality has evolved to bind communities together, to make communal life manageable, and to maintain personal reputation within a group. *All* moral communities are built on five foundations, which all have evolutionary origins:

1. *Harm/care*: A concern for the suffering of others, including virtues of caring and compassion. This stems from the evolutionary systems of attachment and social empathy.
2. *Fairness/reciprocity*: A concern for unfair treatment, cheating, and upholding abstract notions of justice and rights. This stems from the evolutionary process of reciprocal altruism (that is, 'you scratch my back and I'll scratch yours').
3. *In-group/loyalty*: A concern for maintaining group membership, group-based loyalty and self-sacrifice (that is, shown in patriotism). This originates the importance of being a member of a group to survive in humanity's hunter-gatherer past.
4. *Authority/respect*: A concern for social order and the obligations of hierarchical relationships, such as obedience, respect, and the fulfilment of role–based duties. This is shaped by our heritage of hierarchical social systems.
5. *Purity/sanctity*: A concern for avoiding physical and spiritual contagion, by way of virtues such as chastity, wholesomeness, and the control of desires. This is shaped by the emotions of disgust and fear of contamination.

Haidt & Kesebir (2010); Haidt & Graham (2007)

Haidt's research has found that liberals and conservatives tend to emphasise these foundations to differing degrees. Liberals, such as Kohlberg, tend to only emphasise the first two foundations of care and justice, while conservatives emphasise the third, fourth and fifth too, believing that in-group loyalty, respect for authority and sanctity/purity are as central to moral communities as are notions of justice and harm avoidance (Graham, Haidt & Nosek, 2009).

Kohlberg assumed that principled moral reasoning leads to ethical behaviour, whereas Haidt promotes an alternative view that moral judgements are made quickly and automatically, based on unconscious, emotionally-charged *social intuitions* of what is right or wrong (Haidt, 2007). In Haidt's research, it is frequently observed that such intuitions are hard to consciously articulate, and people can't describe their reasoning behind their moral opinion – they have a view, but they don't know why! (Haidt, 2001). Moral reasoning is said to kick in *after* a judgement has been made, to justify it, but it did not *cause* the moral opinion. Haidt has collected evidence from various domains that people rush intuitively to moral judgement, and rarely reason through a moral dilemma before coming to a judgement (Haidt, 2007). Reasoning is not however completely useless in his model, for it can over-ride the initial, intuitive moral response. However this rarely happens; most of the time moral reasoning is just a way of maintaining one's reputation and looking clever.

Emotion is central to the social intuition process, and therefore is at the heart of morality from Haidt's perspective. Psychopaths are an example of why moral emotions matter more than moral reasoning; psychopathic persons can reason through moral situations without difficulty, but lack empathy or compassion, and so have no concern for doing things that may harm others (Haidt, 2001). This may explain why research shows no relationship between moral reasoning and psychopathy when IQ is controlled for (Kane, Fawcett & Blackburn, 1996). In summary, moral development in Haidt's theory is not about reasoning, but about developing empathy and altruistic intuitions that make moral action an immediate response to distress in others and that promote harmonious social groups. Another theorist who has placed empathy at the heart of a moral development is Martin Hoffman, who we come to next.

Martin Hoffman and the theory of prosocial morality

Prosocial morality is the giving of help to others, or conversely the desire for reparation or apology if one causes harm to others. Prosocial dilemmas typically involve the question of whether and how one should provide *help*. Imagine, for example, that you are walking along the side of the river and you see someone thrashing around in the river, screaming for help, seemingly in trouble. Do you help, even though you know it will put you in danger and you don't know the person? Or alternatively you see two people who are in trouble in a river – one is an adult you know and care for, and the other is a child you don't know. Who do you help? Other dilemmas may be encountered when a prosocial desire to help someone may conflict with another moral principle. For example, a student asks for extra tuition to help pass their exam. The tutor will have to balance desire to help with the ethic of fairness – should one student get the advantage of extra help? What if all the other students come and ask for extra help too?

Box 8.3   Individual voices

When empathy is not helpful

The following are excerpts from individuals describing when they find empathy to be unhelpful, taken from Hoffman (2000):

> When it [death in the family] happened I was shocked and very upset. I took a week off from school to get myself together. And, afterwards, I just wanted to get my life back to where it was before the death. When people would call me all I could hear was sympathy and pity in their voices. But I didn't want to hear sadness and be sad. I wanted to go on with my life because I had accepted the death and was ready to move on. So I wanted to talk about other things and to laugh but I couldn't because others were still grieving around me – laughing just didn't seem right. (p. 78)

> Having spent last year battling advanced breast cancer, I have perhaps a different perspective of what I want in empathy. I greatly appreciate the outpouring of kindness of others, but I don't want pity; pity isn't constructive. During my ordeal, I valued people who, with underlying care and concern for my dire condition, could nevertheless remain cheerful and optimistic, who could encourage me to see the positive, beautiful, and wonderful – and, yes, the humorous ... Should we show our empathy by approaching each person with the knowledge of his certain mortality, or should we instead keep in mind another truth – that for now at least we are alive? (p. 78)

Martin Hoffman has spent decades studying what makes children and adults prosocial (Hoffman, 2000). In Hoffman's theory, prosocial morality is driven by three things; empathy, internalised prosocial norms and guilt. Empathy was discussed in Chapter 4 – it is the experience of feeling emotions that are appropriate to another person's situation, for example if a person is in trouble, you feel *their* distress. It can be observed in children as young as one when an infant responds to a distressed person by becoming distressed themselves. This egocentric empathy is replaced developmentally by empathy allied to the provision of help, such as when child sees a peer who is hurt and gives a comforting hug or gets help from an adult. This can be observed as early as age two. By adolescence, a person will be able to feel empathy for a person who is not directly perceived, based on an imagined model of a distressing situation. By adulthood, notions of empathy become more complex, and the realisation is made that the moral course of action sometimes involves *not* showing empathy. Hoffman (2000) gives several examples of when a victim prefers not to gain empathy from others, two of which are shown in Box 8.3.

In Hoffman's theory, after empathy the other key emotional capacity underlying prosocial morality is the emotion of *guilt*. Guilt is a painful feeling of self-disdain that results from appraising that one has caused distress in others or transgressed a personally held moral standard. Mature guilt should be in proportion to the extent of harm done and the extent of personal responsibility for that harm. It should be less if the harm was caused by accident, and more if the harm was intentional. A lack of guilt is a defining feature of psychopathy and antisocial tendencies (Hare, 1993).

In a nutshell, Hoffman's theory comes from a completely different direction to Kohlberg's theory. While Kohlberg's theory is based on acquiring an impartial, cognitive conception of justice, Hoffman's theory is based on the idea that moral behaviour is principally determined by emotion, in particular the capacity for mature guilt and mature empathy.

The pragmatic approach of Krebs and Denton

It is a credit to Kohlberg that the appetite for criticising his theory is undiminished. In 2005 Dennis Krebs and Kathy Denton produced a comprehensive critique of that Kohlberg's model and method, based on the key concern that it does not sufficiently deal with morality as it manifests in the *real* world. They pointed out that Kohlberg's method assesses how people reason abstractly about hypothetical scenarios involving fictional characters, when real-life dilemmas are different from hypothetical ones in the following important ways:

1. In a real-life moral dilemma, *you* are part of the dilemma yourself, and you may be motivated to maintain your reputation, to conform to pressures being exerted on you by others, and to protect your own interests. This doesn't happen in hypothetical dilemmas.
2. In real-life dilemmas, you may know other people who are part of the dilemma, and may feel a loyalty or obligation towards some and not others, or have an expectation of future involvement with some and not others that may bias your response to the situation.
3. Real-life moral dilemmas are full of emotion, frequently negative ones such as anger and anxiety, which may make detached reasoning difficult.

4. A common real-life moral dilemma is a conflict between an urge, desire or impulse to act in one way (for example, a sexual one), and a moral standard that leads to a different sense of what you *ought* to do (Staughan, 1985). This kind of problem cannot occur in hypothetical moral dilemmas, but is central to moral challenges in real life.

Krebs and Denton's research found that Kohlbergian reasoning level was lower when people are reasoning through a problem from their own life, than when they are reasoning about philosophical, abstract problems (Krebs & Denton, 2005). They have also found that individuals are more lenient towards themselves in moral dilemmas than they are towards fictional characters. Furthermore, they have found that *contexts* change moral reasoning – people do not consistently respond at one particular reasoning level, but adapt to the context they are in. For example people in bars and nightclubs and parties show moral reasoning at lower levels than in a university setting (Denton & Krebs, 1990). Does this relate to your own experience?

In contrast to the lack of real-life worldliness in Kohlberg's theory, Krebs and Denton (2005) suggest a 'pragmatic' framework. They suggest that morality is a system of co-operation designed to help self-interested individuals get along and live together, and in this sense are similar to Haidt's model that was mentioned earlier in the chapter. People need not over-complicate morality – they can use a moral concept that is as complicated as the situation requires – so in some instances, family loyalty, tit-for-tat reciprocation, or fair exchange, are satisfactory principles. In more complex situations, more complex moral judgements are necessary. People at all times evaluate moral situations pragmatically, by working out how their interests can be protected while the systems of social co-operation around them can be upheld. Thus moral judgements are a product not solely of developmental stage but also context and situational goals.

There isn't much scope for moral development at the individual level in this pragmatic theory, but there is scope for developing a more co-operative and harmonious society. Krebs and Denton suggest that improving morality should be done at a community level, through social policies that maximise the likelihood that people see their own interests as aligned with the system of co-operation. If people think behaving morally will suit them, then they probably will.

Crime in adulthood: When moral development fails

From a Kohlbergian perspective, criminal behaviour can be considered to be a reflection of a pre-conventional mentality of self-interest, disregard for others and opportunism. This hypothesis is supported by research showing that those with criminal records have lower moral development that matched control groups (Blasi, 1980). That criminality is a phenomenon relevant to adult development and ageing is reflected in its very pronounced relationship with age. In the UK, the National Statistics Office records the age and gender of criminal offenders, and so is a useful source of data on this issue. Figure 8.2 shows the age and gender distribution of offenders in England and Wales for the year 2006. It illustrates that the vast majority of offences are committed by males in late adolescence and emerging adulthood. In 2006, the peak age for convictions was 19 for males and 16 for females.[1] Just 4.6 per cent of all offences were committed by persons aged 35 or over. A very similar age pattern is shown in the USA (Moffitt, 1993). Such statistics make it clear that crime exists predominantly within the late adolescent and emerging adult life stages, which means it makes sense to study it as a developmental phenomenon (Patterson, Debaryshe & Ramsey, 1990). Terrie Moffit is one theorist who has done so, and it is to her model we turn now.

Moffit's developmental taxonomy of criminal activity

Moffitt (1993) proposes an influential *dual developmental taxonomy* of anti-social behaviour. The two developmental types that comprise the model are the *adolescence-limited* and *life-course-persistent* patterns of antisocial and criminal behaviour. The hallmark of the *life-course persistent* type is a continuous pattern of antisocial tendencies from early childhood to adolescence and into adulthood, as illustrated in Figure 8.3. This pattern typically starts with behaviours such as biting and hitting at age four, followed by shoplifting and truancy at age ten, then selling drugs and stealing cars at 16, robbery and rape by age 22 and later on fraud or violence.

Individuals with the life-course-persistent type of antisocial pattern are responsible for the most extreme crimes and also commit crimes with greatest frequency. Moffitt (1993) theorises that the life-course-persistent pattern stems from a biopsychosocial combination of neuropsychological impairment combined with social disadvantage and adverse environmental conditions in early life. The continuity of the pattern means that interventions with this group tend to lead to poor results, however the good news is that evidence suggests that criminality in this group tends to lessen over the age of 40 (Harpur & Hare, 1994).

---

[1] http://www.statistics.gov.uk/cci/nugget.asp?id=1661.

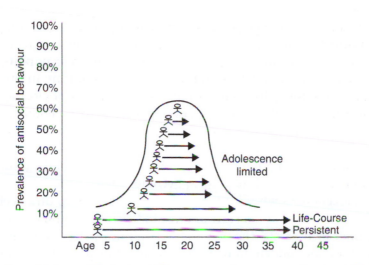

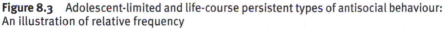

Figure 8.3 Adolescent-limited and life-course persistent types of antisocial behaviour: An illustration of relative frequency

Source: Moffit (1993, p. 677). Copyright © American Psychological Association. Reproduced with permission.

The *adolescent-limited* type only commits delinquent and antisocial acts during the teenage years and early twenties, and then desists during emerging adulthood. This is reflected in statistics – by the age of 28, 85 per cent of offenders have desisted from criminal activity (Farrington, 1992). Adolescent-limited delinquency/criminality is so common among males that it can be considered to be a non-pathological and normative occurrence, despite the social ills it causes. For example, in a longitudinal study of boys, at the age of 18, 93 per cent were found to be involved in at least one delinquent activity (Moffitt, 1993), but 75 per cent of them have desisted from such behaviours by their mid-twenties (Farrington, 1986). The majority of prisoners are young adult males, and interventions aimed to improve moral reasoning in this group are used in scores of prisons. An example is given in Box 8.4. Adult antisocial behaviour is strongly related to childhood antisocial behaviour, while this form adolescent delinquency is not (Loeber, 1982; Robins, 1978).

The adolescent-limited type of criminal behaviour accounts for the majority of crimes committed, but it is a relatively modern phenomenon – go back 100 years and the typical peak of adolescent criminal convictions was not so marked (Farrington, 1986). Moffitt (1993) proposes the root of modern problems with adolescent criminality is a 'maturity gap' that has developed between physical and social maturity. As society has advanced over the last few centuries, young people have typically married later and entered the work force later, while sexual maturity is reached younger than ever before, for reasons unknown. This means that there is a newly developed five–ten year gap between the onset of sexual maturity and social maturity. During this time, a person is at their physical and sexual peak, but is dependent on their parents, has little in the way of autonomy, and is not considered mature in the eyes of the law. Delinquent behaviours may become a way of closing that gap – they can lead to the acquisition of possessions, sexual relationships, autonomy from parents and freedom from social convention that young males crave and in the distant past were given in abundance. The life-course-persistent young male already has a fair bit of experience at this by the time adolescence hits, and so becomes the role model for those other adolescent boys who want to close the maturity gap and 'feel like an adult'. Once young men start to have independence and are able to acquire their own assets, the benefits of criminality decrease, and this would explain the sudden drop off in numbers of illegal activities by the mid-twenties.

Skardhamar (2009) presented a number of criticisms of Moffitt's theory. It is questioned whether the two developmental types, adolescent-limited and life-course persistent are really as separate as are described, or whether, for example, some individuals pick up criminal activity in adolescence but continue into adulthood. Furthermore, other taxono-mies of antisocial behaviour suggest that some persons may commence criminality in adulthood, but this fits into neither type (Skardhamar, 2009). There is also a lack of consideration of situational influences on antisocial behaviour in Moffitt's model. For example, at certain his-torical times and in certain places, antisocial behaviour is increased due to political or economic hardship. I am writing this in 2012, and the past year has seen violent revolutions across the Arab world and violent protests in Greece. These protests and revolutions are predomi-nantly manned by young men, but it would be grossly over-simplistic, or indeed plain wrong, to attribute this kind of antisocial action to either of Moffitt's types. Moffitt's dual taxonomy does have predictive value, but as with any theory of individual behaviour, one must remember to keep an eye on the social and cultural levels too.

Concluding comments

If you cast your mind back to Kohlberg's theory, you will recall that in his stage model the 'post-conventional' level is a developmentally advanced level that does not necessarily equate morality with legality – at this level, the illegal course of action may be seen to be the moral one, because guiding moral principles suggest that the law is unjust. Post-conventional morality can therefore justify crime in some situations, if it is motivated

---

Box 8.4   Real-world applications

Moral education with offenders

Gibbs (1996) has developed the EQUIP programme, which is a group-based moral education intervention to help adolescent and young adult males to develop mature moral judgement. Research shows it to be an effective way of developing responsible thought and behaviour (Devlin & Gibbs, 2010). As part of the programme, hypothetical situations are presented in which a person caused harm to another person, an example of which is as follows:

> Gary is in the kitchen with his girlfriend. Gary's girlfriend is angry at him for something he did to hurt her, so she yells at him and pushes him on the shoulder. Thoughts run through Gary's head, and he becomes furious. He swears at her. A sharp kitchen knife is lying on the kitchen surface nearby. He picks it up and stabs her, seriously wounding her.

The facilitator then asks the group: 'What thoughts do you think Gary had in that situation?' Among the most popular answers in young adult males with a history of delinquency is the following: 'Who does she think she *is*? Nobody touches *me*. I do what I want and nobody tells me what to do. How dare she touch *me*.' What does this kind of thinking suggest about the moral reasoning of adolescent/young adult male offenders?

---

by ideals of social justice or human rights, and if the law is upholding an unjust system.

Kohlberg was aware of this, and he was writing during the civil rights movement in America, when many individuals committed acts that at the time were deemed criminal, but were designed to further the cause of racial equality. A famous example was when Rosa Parks famously refused to give up her seat on a bus for a white person, and was arrested as a result. Martin Luther King was also arrested a number of times for his actions, as was Ghandi in his non-violent protest against British rule in India. History has shown us that moral right was on the side of the civil rights activists, even though the law was not.

However, while there are these instances of individuals who stretch the boundaries of morality in positive ways, there are many others who think they are post-conventional moral visionaries but are most certainly not. Hitler's book *Mein Kampf* shows that he believed he was trying to bring about a better world, which would promote the common good and protect the future of the human race. So bear in mind that if you are striving for justice that goes beyond conventional or legal views of what is right, you may be in the company of Martin Luther King, or you may be in the company of Hitler. Be careful where you tread in the world of post-conventional moral ideas.

Questions for you to reflect on

- Some people think you should have the right to end your own life if you are in chronic pain or terminally ill. Can you think of pre-conventional, conventional and post-conventional moral justifications for the right to die? (For some help with this, see Box 14.2 in Chapter 14.)
- Why is it that a person who shows highly advanced moral reasoning might end up making a poor moral choice in their personal life or sex life?
- At the age of 20 a person is typically more morally developed than they are at age 12, but they are much more likely to commit antisocial or delinquent acts. Based on what you have read in this chapter, why do you think that's the case?

Summary points

- Lawrence Kohlberg developed a theory of moral development based on Piaget's idea of stage development and a method called the Moral Judgement Interview.
- Kohlberg's model has three levels: Pre-conventional (morality is based on rewards and punishment), conventional (morality is based on social norms) and post-conventional (morality is based on abstract principles).
- The neo-Kohlbergian approach replaces the ideas of moral stages with moral schemas.
- Kohlberg's theory has been criticised as it does not relate to real-world moral dilemmas, which involve the control of impulses or emotions, and managing interpersonal interests.
- Carol Gilligan developed a theory of moral reasoning which balanced ethics based on justice and fairness, with ethics based on care and compassion. She believed that women were orientated towards the latter.
- Jonathan Haidt has developed a social intuitionist model of moral behaviour, which is premised on the idea that moral judgements generally stem from instinct and intuition, not complex reasoning.
- Martin Hoffman states that empathy is an emotional requirement for moral life, as it provides a motive for avoiding harm to others.
- Antisocial behaviour can be characterised into two developmental types: the adolescent-limited type and the life-course-persistent type. The former is a normal part of development for males in contemporary society,

while the latter is associated with childhood neglect and more extreme antisocial tendencies.

Recommended reading

Colby, A., Kohlberg, L., Gibbs, J., Lieberman, M., Fischer, K. & Saltzstein, H. D. (1983). A longitudinal study of moral judgment. *Monographs of the Society for Research in Child Development*, 48, 1–124.

Gilligan, C. (1982). *In a Different Voice: Psychological Theory and Women's Development*. Cambridge, MA: Harvard University Press.

Haidt, J. (2001). The emotional dog and its rational tail: A social intuitionist approach to moral judgment. *Psychological Review*, 108, 814–834.

Hoffman, M. L. (2000). *Empathy and Moral Development: Implications for Caring and Justice*. New York: Cambridge University Press.

Krebs, D. L. & Denton, K. (2005). Toward a more pragmatic approach to morality: A critical evaluation of Kohlberg's model. *Psychological Review*, 112, 629–649.

Moffitt, T. E. (1993). Adolescence-limited and life-course-persistent antisocial behavior: A developmental taxonomy. *Psychological Review*, 100, 674–701.

Recommended websites

For information on the DIT, including a sample dilemma and answer sheet, go to www.centerforthestudyofethicaldevelopment.net

For information on Haidt's theory and to have a go at his five foundations of morality test, go to http://www.yourmorals.org

9

Wisdom

The art of being wise is knowing what to overlook.

William James

'Do you think you have become wiser, as you have got older?' I asked Jane, aged 60. She responded that she was not sure, and described various ways in which she had changed as she had got older, which she thought may reflect what others may consider to be wisdom. Firstly she said that she was now more able to control her emotions than when she was young, and was more aware of her own emotional shortcomings. Secondly, when younger she was more focused on personal achievement and career success for its own sake, while now she was focused on employing her talents as a writer and speaker, to help others less fortunate than her, and to improve equality of opportunity in society more generally. Furthermore, having experienced some traumatic events as an adult, she felt she now had more perspective over the smaller ups and downs of life. All of these, she said, helped her to encounter the world in a wiser way than when she was a young adult.

Wisdom is an idea that has been around as long as recorded history. The wise sage is a revered, usually elderly, figure in traditions reaching back to ancient Greece, ancient China, and ancient Egypt (Assman, 1994). The wise man or woman has been traditionally portrayed as a calm, balanced and reflective character, purveying sound, pithy and truthful advice. Over the last 20 years, psychologists have attempted to turn these ancient folk ideas of wisdom into an empirically realisable and measurable construct. Spearheading this initiative has been the Max Planck Institute in Germany, whose 'Berlin Wisdom Paradigm' we turn to first. Then we will consider some alternative models and measures of wisdom, before reviewing the relationship between wisdom and age.

The Berlin Wisdom Paradigm

Paul Baltes, Ursula Staudinger and colleagues at the Max Planck Institute have been central in putting the study of wisdom onto the map of European psychology. The approach that they developed, the Berlin Wisdom Paradigm, views wisdom as a form of expertise in how best to handle and make judgements about important and difficult matters of personal and social significance, while giving sound advice on such issues (Baltes & Staudinger, 2000). Problems that wisdom helps to solve are inherently uncertain and complex – there are no predefined correct solutions. A wise solution is one that considers and embraces the irresolvable opposites that shape human life, such as certainty and doubt, dependence and independence, good and bad, or selfishness and altruism (Staudinger & Glück, 2011). Accordingly, wisdom requires at least five skills, which together comprise the five components of the Berlin model – these are described in Table 9.1.

Table 9.1   The five components of the Berlin model of wisdom

Component	Description
Factual knowledge of the pragmatics of life	Knowledge of mental life, ethics, interpersonal relations, social norms, life events, self-knowledge.
Strategic knowledge in the pragmatics of life	Strategies and rules-of-thumb for enhancing wellbeing in self and others, and strategies for providing useable guidance to others.
Lifespan Contextualism: Knowledge that considers *contexts* of life and change	When faced with life dilemmas, this is the capacity to take into account a person's age, development and the contexts of family, work, friends and community norms.
Knowledge of the *relativism* of values and life goals	Acknowledgement of the culturally-situated nature of one's own values and beliefs, while understanding the different values that other people and groups hold.
Knowledge that considers the *uncertainties* of life	Acceptance of the impossibility of perfect solutions to complex real-life situations, and acceptance of uncertainty in knowing all the outcomes of one's actions in these situations.

The Berlin paradigm includes a method for assessing wisdom-related expertise called the *Berlin Wisdom Interview*. It involves a series of six hypothetical real-life problem situations that are presented to the participant. The method employs the 'think aloud' method (see Chapter 2) in which participants voice their responses to the dilemmas out loud. These are then taped and transcribed. This protocol is similar to the method used by Sinnot (1991) to research postformal thought as well as the Moral Judgment Interview used by Kohlberg (Colby et al., 1983). Problems that are presented to participants in the Berlin Wisdom Interview include the following (Baltes & Staudinger, 2000; Ardelt, 2004):

- Someone receives a call from a good friend who says that he or she cannot go on anymore and wants to commit suicide. What should he/she do and consider?
- In reflecting over their lives, people sometimes realise that they have not achieved what they had once planned to achieve. What should they do and consider?
- A 15-year old wants to get married right away. What should she do and consider?

Trained raters then evaluate participants' responses to these dilemmas on five criteria that correspond to the five components of the model, giving a mark out of 7 for each criterion. If a response is scored 5 or more across all criteria, the response is considered a wise one. See Box 9.1 for examples of high and low scoring responses to the '15-year old marriage' problem.

Scores from the Berlin Wisdom Interview have been correlated with other psychological variables. In a sample of 125 adults, moderate positive correlations between wisdom and intelligence were found (fluid intelligence, $r = .29$, crystallised intelligence (vocabulary), $r = .34$) (Staudinger, Lopez & Baltes, 1997). This shows that wisdom has some relationship to intelligence but is far from identical to it. In fact, wisdom seems to be the result of a 'coalition' of multiple abilities and traits that each make a small predictive contribution. When intelligence, personality, creativity, cognitive style, social intelligence and life experiences are all deployed simultaneously in a regression model to predict wisdom, intelligence and personality contribute just 2 per cent unique variance each. Creativity, cognitive style and social intelligence together contribute 15 per cent unique variance, while life experiences contribute 15 per cent of the variance (Baltes & Staudinger, 2000). Moral reasoning has also been shown to relate to higher scoring in the Berlin Wisdom Interview ($r = 0.29$) (Pasupathi & Staudinger, 2001).

Box 9.1   Individual voices

Example low-score and high-score responses to the situation – a 15-year-old wants to get married right away. What should she do and consider?

Low score:

A 15-year-old girl wants to get married? No, no way. Marrying at age 15 would be utterly wrong. One has to tell the girl that marriage is not possible. [After further probing] It would be irresponsible to support such an idea. No, this is just a crazy idea. (p. 136)

High score:

Well, on the surface, this seems like an easy problem. On average, marriage for 15-year-old girls is not a good thing. I guess many girls might think about it when they fall in love for the first time. And, then, there are situations where the average case does not fit. Perhaps in this instance, special life circumstances are involved, such that the girl has a terminal illness. Or this girl may not be from this country. Perhaps she lives in another culture and historical period. Before I offer a final evaluation I would need more information.(p. 136)

Source: Baltes and Staudinger (2000, p. 136). Copyright © American Psychological Association. Reproduced with permission.

Kunzmann and Baltes (2003) looked at the relationship between wisdom, values, emotion and conflict resolution strategies. Wisdom was found to correlate with a value-orientation that focuses on others and personal growth, and negatively with values that promote hedonism, pleasure, wealth and personal happiness. This suggests that wisdom relates to the capacity to transcend one's own self-interest – we refer back to this later in the chapter when discussing 'transcendent wisdom'.

Wisdom has an unusual relationship to emotion, as it is negatively correlated with intensity of both negative *and* positive emotion (Kunzmann & Baltes, 2003). This suggests that being wise means experiencing less overall emotional fluctuation, an idea that mirrors the ancient Stoic definition of the wise sage, whose emotions are under control (Sihvola & Engberg-Pederson, 1998). This is not the end of the story however, as certain kinds of affective traits *are* related to wisdom, such as the tendency to be interested, alert, inspired and attentive (Kunzmann & Baltes, 2003).

Can wisdom be trained and increased? Participating in social dialogues seems to help; increases in wisdom performance on the Berlin Wisdom Interview are found if participants discuss the problem with a friend or a group first and then take part in the interview (Staudinger & Baltes, 1996). Secondly, being trained in a field that specialises in dealing with difficult life problems is related to higher wisdom scores, however a sample of clinical psychologists scored on average 3.8, which is still well below the cut-off point for wisdom (Baltes & Staudinger, 2000; Smith, Staudinger & Baltes, 1994). This supports the idea that wisdom is a kind of expertise and experts are by definition rare.

Criticisms of the Berlin model and method

Monika Ardelt (2004) wrote an extensive critique of the Berlin paradigm. The critique claimed that the model was excessively focused on wise *knowledge*, rather than wise action, conduct or emotion, and that the method was biased in favour of verbally articulate respondents. She emphasised that wisdom must involve an emotional component, for if a person does not have some mastery of their own emotions, as well as compassion for others, they have little hope of being wise. Yet there is no such component in the Berlin model. Also, there is little explicit focus on virtuous and compassionate action as part of wisdom. One of the five components is recognition of personal values in others, but it does not require or suggest that a wise person has to live in a virtuous way. Although Baltes & Staudinger (2000) admit that virtue is an *outcome* of wisdom, it is not an explicit part of the model, and is not a required element in the wisdom scoring process.

Furthermore, the think aloud method used in the Berlin Wisdom Interview requires skill to answer well, but this skill is heavily reliant on verbal articulacy – the method therefore benefits those who can 'talk a good talk'. Real-life wisdom however, is not necessarily manifested in articulate and complex reasoning, but more in humility, emotional balance and a prosocial orientation (Sternberg, 1998; Yang, 2008).

Finally, the Berlin Wisdom Interview is based on fictitious, hypothetical problems, rather than on problems and situations that a person has had to deal within in their own life. The interview at no point asks a person to reflect on themselves or their own life. This means that wisdom is assessed in a hypothetical and abstract way, outside of any relation to the self. Ardelt suggests that it is conceivable that a person may have apparently wise theoretical knowledge, while not acting wisely in her own life. Recently, Staudinger and Glück (2011) have drawn a line between these two kinds of wisdom – *personal wisdom* is that which is related on one's own life and *general wisdom* is that which applies more generally to the lives of others. One person may have one but not the other, for example being wise in matters of justice and politics but showing a lack of wisdom in private relationships – a split that was arguably evidenced by Martin Luther King (Sternberg, 2004b), who allegedly had a volatile romantic life and a string of extramarital affairs.

Sternberg's balance theory of wisdom

Robert Sternberg was instrumental in initiating the study of wisdom in psychology, by way of compiling and editing a pioneering multi-author book titled *Wisdom: Its Nature, Origins and Development* in 1990. He has been active in constructing strategies for educating wisdom in schools, and he has set out a provisional wisdom education curriculum (Sternberg, 2001). Sternberg's model of wisdom overlaps with the Berlin model but has some key differences. It emphasises finding optimal *balance* between competing interests and adaptive concerns, in order to maximise the *common good.* This involves the application of a person's intelligence and reserves of personal experiences. Wise solutions to real-life problems involve navigating competing options to find balance in three different areas:

Balancing competing interests:

  a) Intrapersonal interests – one's own interests and priorities
  b) Interpersonal interests – the interests of others involved in a situation
  c) Extrapersonal interests – those beyond the immediate situation, including the environment and the wider community

Balancing responses to the environment:

  a) Adaptation – changing yourself to fit the environment
  b) Shaping – changing the environment to fit in with you
  c) Selection – selecting different environments

Balancing change and stability:

  a) Intelligence – the capacity to solve problems and maintain stability
  b) Creativity – the capacity to think up new problems and so initiate change

Sternberg (2001; 1998; 2004a)

In order for the outcomes of this balancing act to be wise, it should be one that takes into account as implications for as many people as possible, and then aims for the 'common good' by way of finding a path forward that maximises respect for human life, honesty, sincerity, fairness, and enabling people to fulfil their potential. Because the interests of different people do not necessarily coincide, wisdom entails the capacity to handle contradictions and tensions. Its aim is therefore to act as virtuously as possible, given the inevitable constraints of any particular circumstance, while taking other people's perspectives and feelings into account. Sternberg's view of virtue as central to wisdom is echoed by cross-cultural folk descriptions of wise people, as illustrated by the excerpts from Taiwan in Box 9.2.

Box 9.2   Individual voices

What makes for a 'wise person'? Views from Taiwan

Yang (2008) asked a Taiwanese adult sample to describe a wise person that they know. The results show that some aspects of wisdom are common to East and West including cognitive ability, virtue, humility and interpersonal skill. Two examples are given here.

Most people taught by him have a high regard for him. He is a model of scholarly virtues. He makes people who interact with him feel as though they are 'bathing in a spring breeze' [a phrase used to describe Confucius by his disciples] – people feel comfortable, alive, and inspired whenever they are around him. He is very skilful in stimulating others to think, not only because he himself is a brilliant thinker and hence sets a good example, but also because he is humble and congenial. These are the qualities that strike me as remarkable. (p. 67)

He has a broad knowledge and profound discernment, which is demonstrated in his ability to solve difficult problems. He has the courage to speak out and the ability to present his ideas well without offending others. People are impressed by his logic, fairness and open-mindedness. By applying his skills at work, to both his supervisors and subordinates, he is able to create a harmonious working atmosphere in which a lot of good work is accomplished. In addition, he also takes good care of his family. Very few people could be considered equals. (pp. 67–8)

Source: Yang (2008, pp. 66–7). Copyright © Springer.

Practical and transcendent wisdom

Wink and Helson (1997) suggest that the difference between the Berlin model and Sternberg's model may be due to the existence of two different forms of wisdom. The first is *practical wisdom*, which is shown by wise action and guidance in day-to-day affairs (similar to the Berlin model), and secondly there is *transcendent wisdom*, which is the ability to transcend one's personal viewpoint and self-centredness (similar to Sternberg's model). Two assessment tools have been developed by Wink and Helson (1997) to assess these two forms of wisdom:

PWS (Practical Wisdom Scale) – This is scored using self-report ratings to 17 adjectives that are selected to be reflective of wisdom: *clearthinking, fair-minded, insightful, intelligent, interest wide, mature, realistic, reasonable, reflective, thoughtful, tolerant, understanding, wise, immature (contraindicative), intolerant (contraindicative), reckless (contraindicative)*. The practical wisdom score consists of the number of indicative items checked, minus the number of contraindicative items.

TWR (Transcendent Wisdom Responses) – Transcendent wisdom is assessed in an open-ended manner, by coding responses to the following question: 'Many people hope to become wiser as they grow older. Would you give an example of wisdom you have acquired and how you came by it?' Four trained judges then rate the responses from 1–5 to indicate level of transcendent wisdom shown. Scores mean the following: 5 = transcending the personal, insightful, integrative, deep. 4 = some of the key aspects of wisdom. 3 = some aspects covered but superficial. 2 = superficial, cynical, despairing. 1 = self-centred, bitter, unable to deal with question. Examples of responses rated at different levels are given in Box 9.3. The two measures of practical and transcendent wisdom do not correlate significantly ($r = 0.16$), supporting the notion of two separate kinds of wisdom.

As with the Berlin paradigm, high levels of transcendent wisdom seem to be rare. In a study of 138 participants, just 2 per cent received an average score of 5, while 21 per cent received a score of 4, 53 per cent received a score of 3, 22 per cent received a score of 2, and 2 per cent received a score of 1 (Wink & Helson, 1997). A longitudinal analysis in self-reported practical wisdom was conducted using the PWS. From age 27 to 52, it was found that both men and women increased in their self-reported ratings on the practical wisdom scale. It was also found that those who had been divorced scored higher in practical wisdom, suggesting a link between wisdom and life events (Wink & Helson, 1997). In a later study on middle-aged women, Helson and Srivastava (2002) used a combination of the Practical Wisdom Scale, the Transcendent Wisdom Response scale *and* one think-aloud dilemma from the Berlin Wisdom Interview. This composite wisdom index was related to longitudinal growth in openness and tolerance of ambiguity.

Box 9.3   Individual voices

Transcendent Wisdom Response Scale: Examples of differently rated responses to the question: *Many people hope to become wiser as they grow older. Would you give an example of a bit of wisdom you have acquired and how you came by it? (from Wink & Helson, 1997, p. 7)*

Response rated high (5):

My younger colleagues tend to be highly critical, questioning of policies established by a government, by a boss. That is the way it should be when you are younger; often such criticism is on the mark. But the older you get, the more you have to assume you can overcome the odds, be optimistic you can implement a change or a policy. Otherwise you are a leader with a self-fulfilling prophecy of doom and failure.

Responses rated high (4):

What seems to be in the way can become the way. I learned this by living with a physical disability, as well as through entering into many kinds of loss and constriction. No 'bits' of wisdom! An enlarged view of the world makes me more wise. I see long-term consequences and complex ramifications of actions. I also have a strong developmental perspective which puts things in place.

Responses given moderate ratings (3):

People think of one no more than what one thinks of oneself. I first learned this in my career when I presented myself mod-estly and was paid accordingly! Don't jump to conclusions about people. I have been wrong enough in the past to be much more patient now.

Box 9.3   Continued

Responses rated low (2):

In a no-win situation, don't do anything. You still won't win but there probably won't be too much of a mess. While in business I was appalled at the 'sue happy' attitude of employees and would not put myself in that vulnerable position again.

Response rated low (1):

Get what you can: nobody is going to give you anything.

Source: Wink and Helson (1997, p. 7). Copyright © Springer. Reproduced with permission.

Self-report questionnaires assessing wisdom

The Three Dimensional Wisdom Scale (3D-WS): This questionnaire is based on a model of wisdom that comprises self-reflective, cognitive and affective components (Ardelt, 2003). Cognitive wisdom is a desire to know the truth allied to the humility of accepting that ultimate truth can never be known, reflective wisdom is the awareness of one's limitations allied to the ability to look at things from different perspectives and affective wisdom is based around compassion for the plight of others (Ardelt, 2008). If all these occur together, a person will show wisdom. The questionnaire items are described in full in Ardelt (2003). Research with this instrument on adults over the age of 50 shows that it positively predicts life-satisfaction and wellbeing while being negatively related to mental health problems and fear of death (Ardelt, 1997; 2003).

The Self-Assessed Wisdom Scale (SAWS): Webster (2003) developed a questionnaire for assessing wisdom comprised of five components:

1. Personal experience of difficult and morally challenging life events
2. Sensitivity to emotions in oneself and others
3. The capacity to reflect and reminisce
4. Fourthly openness to new possibilities and opinions
5. The use of humour to manage difficult situations

Research with this instrument has found that it correlates with attributional complexity (a variable known to relate to reduced social prejudice), and a sense of personal coherence, and negatively with attachment anxiety and attachment avoidance (Webster, 2010).

A recent comparison of the SAWS and 3D-WS found that the correlation between the two was $r = 0.33$ (Taylor, Bates & Webster, 2011). This suggests that they tapping constructs that overlap but are not the same. Ardelt (2011) has argued the case that it is the 3D-WS that is measuring wisdom, while the SAWS is confounding wisdom with other traits, such as sense of humour and openness to experience, and with antecedents of wisdom such as challenging life events.

Wisdom and age

When people are asked to nominate someone who they think is wise, the wise nominee is invariably over 60, suggesting that in the minds of ordinary people, age is meaningfully related to wisdom (Orwoll & Perlmutter, 1990). But does research suggest that older people are really wiser? As it stands, research on the relationship of wisdom and age is limited to correlational, cross-sectional studies.

Cross-sectional data from the Berlin Wisdom Interview suggest that the period between late adolescence and early adulthood is the key time for developing wisdom (Baltes & Staudinger, 2000; Kunzmann & Baltes, 2003). This conclusion stems from a study in which 146 adolescents (ages 14–20) and 56 young adult (ages 21–37) were compared in their performance on the Berlin Wisdom Interview (Pasupathi, Staudinger & Baltes, 2001). Figure 9.1 shows the age-wisdom relation for the sample, including individual scores (shown as dots) and a regression line of best fit. The adolescent period showed a clear age-graded increase in wisdom performance, while no such age-related gradient was shown in adulthood. This suggests that wisdom-related performance in the Berlin paradigm is developed in adolescence and then levels off.

Staudinger & Pasupathi (2003) replicated the findings shown in Figure 9.1 in another sample of adolescents and adults, finding that wisdom correlated strongly with age in the adolescent sample ($r = .43$) but not at all in the adult sample ($r = -.06$). Wisdom was also more strongly associated with intelligence in the adolescent sample than in the adult sample. Wisdom in adolescents showed a correlation of $r = .35$ with fluid intelligence, and $r = .52$ with crystallised intelligence. In adults it was just $r = .09$ with fluid intelligence and $r = .25$ with crystallised intelligence. This suggests that wisdom performance is more dependent on intelligence in adolescence, but becomes more differentiated from intelligence in adulthood. Moral reasoning was correlated moderately with both wisdom in both age groups (.21 with adolescents, .25 with adults).

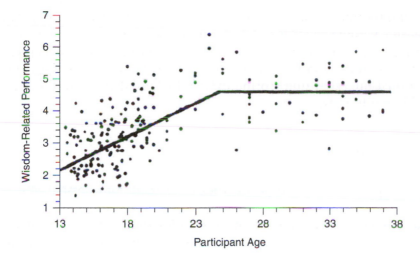

Figure 9.1 Age-wisdom performance profile in adolescents and young adults, including individual data points and regression line

Source: Pasupathi, Staudinger and Baltes (2001, p. 357). Copyright @ American Psychological Association. Reproduced with permission.

The lack of mean-level change in adulthood has been confirmed in a number of studies that have looked exclusively at an adult cross-sectional sample and have found non-significant correlations between wisdom and adult age in all (Staudinger, 1999). This further suggests that in the Berlin model, young adults and old adults are, on average, equally wise.

Other research contradicts these findings. Grossmann et al. (2010) criticise the Berlin paradigm research on adult age and wisdom for the use of non-representative well-educated samples, and criticise the use of very brief descriptions of problems for the think-aloud protocols. In their study, they gained socio-economically diverse adult samples from Michigan, and employed an adapted version of the Berlin Wisdom Interview, which employed more detailed and more contextualised dilemmas. They derived six rating criteria according to a content analysis (1 – search for compromise; 2 – uncertainty/recognition of limits of knowledge; 3 – rigid application of a rule vs. flexibility; 4 – taking other's perspective; 5 – recognition of change; 6 – search for a conflict resolution). Their findings contradict the Berlin findings quite dramatically. They find a clear positive age gradient across adulthood, in which the average of the top 20 per cent of performers is 65 and the average age of the bottom 80 per cent is 45.5. *All* of the top 5 per cent of performers were over 50.

Given these contradictory findings from cross-sectional data, at the moment it seems premature to conclude whether wisdom does or does not increase through adulthood. Only a systematic programme of longitudinal research, and continued refinement of techniques to measure wisdom will give conclusive answers either way. The Grossman et al. (2010) study fits more closely with the cross-culturally held opinion that wisdom grows with adult age, which may suggest that their modified interview and scoring protocol is an advance on the Berlin Wisdom Interview.

Concluding comments

This chapter has reviewed two alternative methods for assessing wisdom: (a) the think aloud method, in which a person responds to a problem and researchers rate the responses to index the wisdom embodied in the response, and (b) the self-report method, in which a person rates themselves on a series of questionnaire items that pertain to wisdom. It is a brave endeavour that researchers have embarked on here – to measure and quantify wisdom, and such pioneering research should be applauded. However, there are some nagging problems at the very heart of these two methods that should be considered in relation to wisdom assessment. Firstly, in the think aloud method, it is the researchers who decide how wise person's response to a dilemma is by rating the response. This of course assumes that the researchers *themselves* are sufficiently wise themselves to know wisdom when they see it. Can we be sure this is the case? Can we trust the trained raters of the Berlin Wisdom Paradigm to be the ultimate arbiters of what is and what is not the zenith of wisdom? It is possible that the raters may pass over a Yoda-like pithy response that contains reams of wisdom in a few words, in favour of something more clever and complex? In a nutshell, the method assumes that the trained wisdom raters are superior in their capacity to determine the presence of wisdom, and if we are to buy in to the method, we need to trust that they are getting it right. Given that there are lots of competing current models of what wisdom actually is, we may validly question whether they are rating wisdom according to one partial conception of the construct.

While the think aloud method places great trust in the researchers' capacity to find wisdom in verbal transcripts, the self-report method, on the other hand, places great trust in a person's own view of him/herself as a wise individual. Staudinger and Glück (2011) are critical of self-report wisdom scales, and even go so far as to claim that a high score on a self-report wisdom scale may in fact indicate low levels of wisdom! They suggest that a naïve person who has an elevated but inaccurate self-concept will score himself or herself higher than a person whose wisdom has led him or her to the humbling conclusion that wisdom is a goal that continually recedes into the distance, and that they own possession of it is, relative to their lofty ideals, meagre. This whole conundrum of self-rating wisdom is reminiscent of Shakespeare's famous quote from the play *As You Like It*: 'The fool doth think he is wise, but the wise man knows himself to be a fool.'

Sternberg also has problems with self-report wisdom scales, but for a different reason. He states that wisdom involves tacit knowledge as well as explicit knowledge. Tacit knowledge is unconscious knowledge about what the best course of action is, based on years of experience. Tacit knowledge is difficult to communicate when asked, and so any direct assessment tool that assesses wisdom through conscious self-reported response may miss the tacit component (Sternberg, 2001).

Questions for you to reflect on

- Can you think of any methods for collecting data on how wise people are, which have yet to be used by researchers? Have a look back at Chapter 2 to help stimulate your thinking on this question.
- Think of someone you know who you consider to be wise. What attributes and qualities do they possess that make them wise? Write down you answer to this question, and then see which model of wisdom it best fits with.
- What are the advantages and disadvantages of the think-aloud method (for example, Berlin Wisdom Interview) and the self-report method (for example, Three Dimensional Wisdom Scale) in assessing wisdom? Are the two methods in conflict?

Summary points

- Wisdom is valued in all cultures as an indication of psychological maturity and a valuable asset for society more generally.
- The Berlin Wisdom Paradigm conceptualises wisdom as a form of expertise in how to plan, manage and understand one's own life and the lives of others, in order to improve them and make the most of real-life situations.
- The Berlin Wisdom Interview involves responding to a series of difficult hypothetical challenges, and researchers then rate the responses for the wisdom it shows on five criteria: rich factual knowledge, rich procedural knowledge, lifespan contextualism, relative of values and priorities and recognition of uncertainty.
- Sternberg emphasises that wisdom is orientated towards promoting the common good, rather than just solving complex dilemmas. A wise person is focused on using his or her skills to maximise the benefits and positive outcomes to those involved.
- Several self-report wisdom questionnaires have been devised, such as the Three-Dimensional Wisdom Scale, which includes the importance

of affective wisdom – an issue that is arguably omitted from the Berlin Wisdom Paradigm. These questionnaires are open to the problems of a biased self-conception and intentional self-presentation. After all, who would not want to appear wise?

- Cross-sectional research on the relationship between wisdom and age has produced conflicting findings – the Berlin Wisdom Interview suggests that wisdom increases in adolescence but not in adulthood, while other research suggests that the top performers on wisdom scales are over 50. Longitudinal research is needed to offer more conclusive findings regarding the wisdom-age relation.

Recommended reading

Ardelt, M. (2003). Empirical assessment of a three-dimensional wisdom scale. *Research on Aging*, 25, 275–324.

Baltes, P. B. & Staudinger, U. M. (2000). Wisdom: A metaheuristic (pragmatic) to orchestrate mind and virtue toward excellence. *American Psychologist*, 55, 122–136.

Staudinger, U. M. (1999). Older and wiser? Integrating results on the relationship between age and wisdom-related performance. *International Journal of Behavioral Development*, 23, 641–664.

Staudinger, U. M. & Glück, J. (2011). Psychological wisdom research: Commonalities and differences in a growing field. *Annual Review of Psychology*, 62, 215–241.

Sternberg, R. J. (2001). Why schools should teach for wisdom: The balance theory of wisdom in educational settings. *Educational Psychologist*, 36, 227–245.

Recommended website

A website on Paul Baltes' wisdom research, including a bibliography of publications and various documents for download: http://www.baltes-paul.de/Wisdom.html.

10

Spirituality and Religiosity

Immature faith draws a circle that pencils some people out.
Mature faith draws a circle that pencils all people in.

George Vaillant (2008)

Evelyn was raised in a conservative Anglican family, and was a committed churchgoer up until the age of 20. In the first few years of her twenties, she married and became pregnant with her first child. The demands of family life increasingly meant that church and religion were sidelined. This was followed by a gradual loss of faith, and by the age of 30, religion was absent from Evelyn's life and belief system. In her late thirties, her marriage started to deteriorate, and by the age of 41 she was divorced. During this transition, she found herself reappraising spirituality and religion, but rather than returning to her Anglican roots, Evelyn started attending Quaker meetings, which involve no priests, no hierarchy and no central dogma. She found that the quiet, open and egalitarian practice gave her life a new sense of spiritual meaning. Over the ensuing decades, she became more involved in practising spirituality, and in learning about other religious traditions, and she linked this to a lessening interest in material possessions, and an increase in her desire to help others.

Spirituality and religiosity are central to the lives of the majority of human beings alive today, and are a key locus of both change and continuity through adulthood, as described in Evelyn's story previously. The study of spirituality and religion across the life course is a growth area in the field of adult development and ageing; since the 1990s a number of books have been published on the topic (for example, Atchley, 2009; Levin, 1994; Kimble et al., 1995; Thomas & Eisenhandler, 1994), as well as three special editions of the *Journal of Adult Development* on spiritual development (in 2000, 2001 and 2002), and substantive review chapters of the topic in mainstream developmental handbooks (for example, Day, 2011; Oser, Scarlett & Bucher, 2006; Levenson, Aldwin & D'Mello, 2005).

The terms 'spirituality' and 'religiosity' mean related but different things (Vaillant, 2008). *Religiosity* refers to three things: (1) the extent of involvement, attendance and interest in membership of a religious establishment, such as church, mosque, temple or synagogue; (2) the acceptance and adoption of the beliefs of that group, engagement with their practices, rituals and rules; and (3) the endeavour to use religious ideas to inform one's approach to life more generally. Religiosity is therefore a communal and social activity (Sinnott, 1998). The idea of faith is closely connected to religiosity – it refers to adopting religious beliefs based on a personal conviction that does not require external evidence.

Stating that one is a member of a particular religion seems to be categorically different from viewing oneself as a religious person, perhaps because membership of a religious group is a question of social identity, rather than of activity or interest. For example, a recent survey in the UK by YouGov (2011) found that when a question was asked of a nationally representative sample, 'What is your religion?' (a religious affiliation question), 61 per cent of people in England and Wales ticked a religious box (53 per cent Christian and 7 per cent other) while 39 per cent ticked 'No religion'. But, when the same sample was asked the question; 'Are you religious?' (a religiosity question), only 29 per cent of the same people said 'Yes' while 65 per cent said 'No', meaning over half of those who said they were members of a religious group said that they were not religious.[1]

Spirituality is a kind of personal enquiry defined by an active engagement with particular questions, experiences and practices, which together comprise a dynamic search for meaning, purpose, inner knowledge, deep connection, transcendence and 'ineffable' truths that cannot be encoded in words and numbers (Boyatzis, 2005; Day, 2011; Wink & Dillon, 2002; Wuthnow, 1998). Some refer to spirituality as mysticism and to spiritual experiences as mystical experiences (Atchley, 1997; Huxley, 2009). Spiritual enquiry often leads individuals to religious establishments in order to pursue their interest in spiritual practice and mystical texts, but not always; 20–30 per cent of individuals in America, and more in Europe, define themselves as 'spiritual but not religious' (Fuller, 2001; Saucier & Skrzypińska, 2006). Although spirituality may appear a more personalised affair than religiosity, it has in fact been found to be more

---

[1]http://www.humanism.org.uk/compaigns/religion-and-belief-survey-statistics

strongly correlated with generativity (that is, prosocial giving behaviour) than religiosity ($r = .30$ compared to $r = .20$) (Dillon, Wink & Fay, 2003).

A challenge for psychologists is operationalising both spirituality and religiosity in ways that can be used in empirical research. Religiosity can be measured by rating the extent of attendance and involvement with a religious group and place of worship, and the extent to which a person attempts to use religion to guide their life. Measures such as the *Duke University Religiosity Index* have been used widely for that purpose (Koenig & Büssing, 2010). Spirituality is harder to assess, as it is more subjectively and variously defined. Moberg (2002) highlights a number of difficulties with assessing spirituality, including the trade-off between focusing on universal features of spirituality, which may be relatively abstract and watered down, or particular aspects that are more specific to an individual's spiritual tradition and culture. Emmons (1999) assesses spirituality by way of personal goals that have spiritual content. For a review of various measures for assessing spirituality, read Hill (2005).

Spiritual/religious development: Differing empirical approaches

There are a number of ways that the development of spirituality or religiosity can be studied. These relate closely to the different definitions of development given in Chapter 1. The value-neutral definition of development construes it as an umbrella term for all the ways in which human beings change with age. This definition underpins the study of how religious involvement and spiritual interest change with age, and how such change relates to key life events. This approach does not require a value judgement about the developmental worth of religion or spirituality – it simply involves charting age-graded change.

The second approach to spiritual or religious development is the 'directional' perspective. Directional theories of development assume that there is an optimal path for changes across adulthood, and Chapter 1 of this book outlines five such directions – evolutionary, eudaimonic, orthogenetic, veridical and virtuous. When considered in relation to these five directions, religiosity and spirituality can be construed as optimal in the following ways:

- *Evolutionarily adaptive development:* If spirituality/religiosity enhance adaptive development, they should improve the prospects for reproduction and survival. Corresponding to this, research has found that religions sometimes promote reproduction strategies (for example, have lots of children or have few children) that are adaptive for the environment they are operating in (Reynolds & Tanner, 1983).

- *Eudaimonic development*: If spirituality and/or religiosity contribute to *eudaimonic* development, we would expect to see evidence that individuals engaging with spiritual or religious practices live a happier, fulfilled and healthy life than those that do not. This has empirical support; Day (2011) reviewed research that shows that both spirituality and religiosity are positively related to physical health, mental health and wellbeing.
- *Veridical development*: For spirituality to develop in a veridical direction, it should involve an increase in knowledge and understanding about truth and reality (Koenig, 1994; Wilber, 2006). To accept that spiritual/religious development is veridical requires a belief in the reality or truth that underpins them.
- *Virtuous development*: If religiosity or spirituality contribute to the virtuous developmental path, they should be related to morally developed cognition and to enhanced prosocial behaviour, and there is evidence to support this fact at the level of individual behaviour (Saroglou et al., 2005). However, on the flipside, it has also been argued that religiosity can lead to negative, destructive effects at the level of social group (Hitchens, 2007).
- *Orthogenetic development*: The orthogenetic direction of development is towards greater complexity. Corresponding to this view, research by Day (2008; 2010) has found evidence that religious development in characterised by increases in cognitive hierarchical complexity. This orthogenetic perspective also underpins Fowler's model of faith development, outlined later in the chapter.

The extent to which cultures view religion as a source of optimal development and therefore as a positive force in society is highly culturally variable. Box 10.1 reports the findings of a recent survey of 23 countries by IPSOS MORI on the question of whether religion is a force for good in the world.

Box 10.1   Cross-cultural perspectives

Is religion a force for good in the world? Views from 23 countries

In 2010, the polling organisation IPSOS MORI conducted a survey of views about religion, drawn from nationally representative adult samples in 23 countries (N = 18,192).[2] The results show substantial cross-cultural disparity in the extent of agreement with the following

---

[2] http://www.ipsos-na.com/news-polls/pressrelease.aspx?id=5058

Box 10.1   Continued

propositions: (a) religion is a requirement for an ethical society and (b) religion is an impediment to social development and source of division and intolerance. The percentages of respondents who agreed with these two propositions are presented for 17 of the countries in Table 10.1. The most positive towards religion was Saudi Arabia, and the least was Sweden. The United States is the sixth most positive towards religion in the list, while Great Britain is 13th. Clearly, the extent to which religion is perceived as a positive phenomenon in social development is strongly related to the norms of different national cultures.

Table 10.1   Percentage of sample from 17 countries agreeing with positive and negative propositions about the influence and role of religion

Country	Percentage who believe that religion provides the common values and ethical foundations that diverse societies need to thrive in the twenty-first century	Percentage who believe that religious beliefs promote intolerance, exacerbate ethnic divisions, and impede social progress
Saudi Arabia	92%	8%
India	69%	31%
Brazil	67%	33%
United States	65%	35%
Russia	59%	41%
Mexico	51%	49%
Italy	50%	50%
Argentina	44%	56%
Turkey	43%	57%
Poland	42%	58%
Canada	36%	64%
Germany	36%	64%
Great Britain	29%	71%
Japan	29%	71%
Spain	25%	75%
France	24%	76%
Sweden	19%	81%

Religiosity, spirituality and age

In cross-sectional and longitudinal samples, there is a consensus that at the mean level of the sample, religiosity tends to increase with adult age (Argue, Johnson & White, 1999; Sasaki & Suzuki (1987); Stolzenberg, Blair-Loy & Waite, 1995). Cross-sectional studies on age and religiosity are likely to be confounded by cohort effects, as younger individuals in any cohort tend to be less religious than older cohorts. So for evidence that religiosity changes as a result of age and life stage, longitudinal studies that track religiosity over adulthood are more reliable. However, there is a general lack of longitudinal studies, and almost all that exist are American. Given that America is a particularly religious nation relative to most other Western countries,[3] generalisation from such studies to the UK or any other culture might be unwarranted.

In one longitudinal study, Argue, Johnson and White (1999) followed a mixed-age sample of 1339 American adults for 12 years (1980–92) and found a positive relationship between religiosity and age, with the greatest increase occurring in early adulthood between 18 and 30. Early adult gains in religious participation were also found by Stolzenberg, air-Loy and Waite, (1995). They analysed data from over 11,000 individuals in the National Longitudinal Study of the High School Class of 1972 (NLS-72), taken in four phases between the ages of 18 and 32. Average-level increases in religious participation were found for both genders across this age range.

Average-level changes such as those found in the aforementioned studies may hide a variety of different age-linked trajectories in religiosity. McCullough et al. (2005) employed the statistical technique of growth mixture modelling to search for distinct types of developmental change in religiosity across adulthood. Their initial sample was 1110 Californians, who were interviewed in 1940, then in 1950, 1960, 1977, 1986 and 1991. Based on interview data, religiosity was rated at each time point by trained researchers on a five-point scale of 0–4.

Their analysis established a three-type growth curve model of religious change. The three patterns are shown in Figure 10.1. The first group is the *high/increasing* group, which comprised 19 per cent of the sample. This group are at all ages more religious than the other two groups and continue to increase up until their sixties. This group are less likely to be married than the other two groups, which suggests that a high commitment to religion in adult life may be associated with being

---

[3] Source: http://www.gallup.com/poll/114211/alabamians-iranians-common. aspx

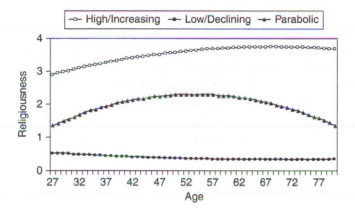

Figure 10.1   Mean growth curves for the trajectory classes resulting from the growth mixture model

Source: McCullough et al. (2005, p. 85). Copyright © American Psychological Association. Reprinted with permission.

single. The *parabolic* group comprises 40 per cent of the sample, and shows a religiosity peak in midlife, followed by a decline in old age. The *low/declining* group shows a lower level of religiosity which correspondingly declines gradually throughout adult life – this group comprises 41 per cent of the sample. This group are more likely to be male than the other two groups. As the diagram shows, these three trajectories do not overlap at any point –mean differences between them are significant and substantial at all ages. This reinforces the distinctiveness of the three types.

The problem with a growth-curve typology such as the one shown in Figure 10.1 is that it represents the general tendency of large subgroups, and so irons out individual changes in religiosity, which may be more discontinuous, for example if there is a sudden religious epiphany or loss of faith (James, 1983). Furthermore, a growth curve can only show quantitative change, but not qualitative change, such as conversion from one religion to another (Paloutzian, Richardson & Rambo, 1999).

As mentioned earlier, researchers tend to distinguish between religiosity and spirituality. Wink and Dillon (2002) investigated both spirituality and religiosity in a longitudinal study, in order to establish if they are indeed different and how spirituality is associated with age. 130 individuals from California, who were born in 1928/1929, were assessed in childhood and adolescence, and interviewed four times as adults in 1958, 1969, 1982 and 1997. One half of the sample was religiously affiliated, while the other half was not. Spirituality and religiosity were coded from interviews on a five-point scale. Spirituality was coded based on the person's concern with the sacred and use of spiritual practices. Religiosity was coded based on the stated importance of attendance at a religious place of worship and centrality of religious belief.

They found that spirituality and religiosity correlate with each other at $r = .30$ in early adulthood and at $r = .38$ in older adulthood. This suggests that the two constructs are related but are manifestly different too. Mean-level trajectories in spirituality showed a slight increase for both men and women between early and late middle adulthood, and then a more pronounced increase between late middle adulthood and older adulthood, leading the authors to conclude that there is a general tendency for individuals to become more concerned with issues of spirituality in older age.

Gerotranscendence theory

Why do religiosity and spirituality tend to become more prevalent as people age? One theory that puts forward a rationale for this finding is *gerotranscendence theory* (Tornstam, 1989; 2005; 2011). In a Danish sample of over-75s, the majority reported becoming more spiritual since the age of 50, and also reported an increased sense of communion and connection with the world, a greater capacity to be in the present moment rather than worrying about the future, a decreased fear of death, an increased affinity with past and future generations, and a lessening of materialistic concerns and self-centredness (Tornstam, 1994). These changes relate to changes in lifestyle that accompany retirement, higher levels of emotional maturity, and the gradual disengagement with the social world that occurs in later life. Ingersoll-Dayton, Krause and Morgan (2002) conducted interviews with elderly adults and found that a major reason given for increased religiosity and spirituality was having more time for personal reflection about the big questions of existence, and an increased interest in having a spiritual experience, in preference to having achievement-related or physically pleasurable experiences.

Life events and religiosity

The aforementioned research of McCullough et al. (2005) (illustrated in Figure 10.1) suggests that there are a variety of ways in which religiosity may change as individuals age. But what kind of events can send people down these different trajectories? One study employed a retrospective biographical method to investigate this question. Ingersoll-Dayton, Krause and Morgan (2002) interviewed 129 adults aged 65 or older about their religiosity across adulthood. Decreased religiosity was generally reported due to disillusionment with organised religion. On the other hand, increases in religiosity were reported following marriage and during child-rearing. One participant explained his increase in religious participation during child-rearing years by saying, 'Religion is an important part of children's upbringing ... [It's] more important to think about religion when children are involved. For the well-being of the children, they need a core set of values to live by' (Ingersoll-Dayton, Krause & Morgan, 2002, p. 74). Increased religious belief was also linked to adverse life events; close encounters with death were often described as being positive turning points in development of religious belief. For example, a man described being in two car crashes, which led him to a strong sense of being protected and looked out for by God (Ingersoll-Dayton, Krause & Morgan, 2002). Related to this, near-death experiences have been associated with increases in spiritual beliefs. For a brief summary of research on near-death experiences, see Box 10.2.

Box 10.2 Alternative perspectives

Near-death experiences and spirituality

Near death experiences (NDEs) are multi-sensory conscious experiences that occur after a person has had a heart attack or has been in an accident that led to clinical death for a period of time prior to resuscitation. NDEs occur in approximate a third of people who are resuscitated after having come close to death (Ring, 1984), and in 18 per cent of cardiac arrest patients (van Lommel et al., 2001). A variety of biological, psychological and socio-cultural theories have been advanced to account for the occurrence of NDEs, reviews of which can be found in Greyson (2006) and van Lommel (2006).

NDEs typically possess similar experiential features across different cultures and times. These experiences include: being out of one's body (typically above it, looking down), passing through a tunnel, meeting spiritual beings or deceased persons, encountering a 'being of light', and the feeling of being at peace. Although these same features occur in different persons and cultures, experiences also have unique features and are typically interpreted through a person's cultural and/or religious worldview (Greyson, 2006). Longitudinal and retrospective research has established that the occurrence of an NDE is not more likely in religious adults that those who profess atheistic or agnostic belief systems prior to the experience itself, so such experiences are not the product of a religious imagination (Greyson, 2006).

Although NDEs happen as frequently in non-religious people as religious people, undergoing such an experience is consistently associated with a subsequent increase in a person's interest in spirituality and religiosity. In some studies there is evidence of increased religious

Box 10.2   Continued

attendance (for example, McLaughlin and Malony, 1984) while in others no increase in formal religious participation is observed (Ring, 1980). Overall, evidence is more strongly in favour of post-NDE increases in spirituality rather than increases in formal religiosity. Musgrave (1997) surveyed 51 NDErs about their changes in attitudes, beliefs, and behaviour after the near-death event. Belief in God increased from 24 per cent before the NDE to 82 per cent after it; belief in an afterlife increased from 22 per cent to 92 per cent, and 88 per cent described a positive change in their sense of spirituality. In another study, Sutherland (1990) interviewed 50 individuals who had had an NDE and found evidence linking the experiences to spirituality but not to religion. 16 per cent of her sample described themselves as spiritual prior to their NDE, while 76 per cent did after the NDE. However there was a decrease in the number of people describing themselves as religious, from 24 per cent before the NDE to only 6 per cent afterwards. None of the participants described the NDE as a religious experience, but 70 per cent described it as a spiritual experience. When asked what the most significant change was that had resulted from the NDE, the single most common theme (31 per cent) was 'spiritual growth'. In another prospective study, van Lommell et al. (2001) found that effects of an NDE on increased belief in afterlife and interest in spirituality were still present 8 years after the event, and were significantly higher than a matched control group of cardiac arrest patients who did not have an NDE.

Bereavement is a life event that has been found to lead to temporarily enhanced religiosity. In a study of 103 widowed individuals, temporary increases in religiousness and church attendance were found after death of a spouse, which lasted several years (Brown et al., 2004). This increased religiosity was positively associated with effectively managing grief. Negative life events are not always a source of spiritual growth. Wink and Dillon (2002) found that negative life events were only related to enhanced spirituality if they occurred alongside the presence of a trait called 'cognitive commitment', which is a tendency to introspect and reflect on life events and experiences. So it may be that bad experiences can only be turned into fuel for development if a person has the capacity to reflect on how the event relates meaningfully to their life as whole. Furthermore, spiritual development related to experience of negative life events in the first half of life but not the second half, which suggests that as individuals grow older it becomes more difficult to transform experiences of adversity into sources of personal growth.

Having children seems to temporarily increase religious involvement. Stolzenberg, Blair-Loy and Waite (1995) found that adults with young children are more likely to increase religious participation than those who do not have children. This effect continues until the child is five, but then disappears once children become eight. The same study also noticed that marital disruption or divorce has different effects on men and women. For young adult men, marital disruption reduces religious participation, while for young adult women, it increases religious participation.

The directional perspective: Theories of religious or spiritual progress

Faith development theory

In 1981, a developmental psychologist named James Fowler put forward a theory of how religious faith should ideally develop, in a book called *Stages of Faith* (1981). Fowler had been a postgraduate student of Lawrence Kohlberg's, and so was steeped in Piagetian stage theory (see Chapter 8 for more on Kohlberg's theory). The theory postulated six stages of how a person's conception of 'faith' developed to be more complex, true and virtuous, over time.

The three childhood stages are as follows: Stage 1 is *Intuitive-projective faith*, which typifies children aged three–seven. It is a faith based on imagination and projection, and does not distinguish fantasy from reality. Stage 2 is *Mythic-literal faith*, which occurs typically in children aged seven–11. In this stage, beliefs and myths are literal and concrete, morals are absolute and deities are anthropomorphic. Stage 3 is *Synthetic-conventional faith*, which typifies adolescence. The perceived expectations of authorities and conventions shape this kind of faith, so a person is not yet autonomous in their religious orientation. A young person at this stage may be unaware of their own assumptions, and may find it difficult to see the spiritual viewpoints of others.

In adulthood, there are three further stages of faith development according to Fowler. These allow a person to increasingly transcend group affiliations, so that the common spiritual ground across different traditions can be perceived (Fowler, 1981). *The fourth stage of individual-reflective faith* begins in early adulthood, and is a stage during which a person turns away from external sources of authority, and instead focuses on a more internal source of faith. One could say it is a move from a religious to a more spiritual perspective. This turn away from authority and convention is not without its difficulties, and is often accompanied with tension and angst, as the young adult attempts to come to terms with a balance of subjective truth and objective fact, of aesthetic myth and adult critical thinking, and with the realisation that the stories that define the conventional level of faith may just be myths.

The fifth stage is *Conjunctive faith*. In this stage a person moves past the over-reliance on logic and rational thought that is sometimes typical of the individual-reflective stage, and opens up to deeper experiences that transcend thought and language. A more open attitude to other religious traditions continues to grow and the commonalities between different faiths are seen, while differences also accepted. The final and sixth stage is termed *Universalising faith*. This is a theoretical stage inferred from the lives and values of saints, mystics and great spiritual leaders, and was rarely scored in practice.

Most people never progress beyond individual-reflective faith, even in very old age (Fowler, 1981). Fowler (1981) found that the most common position for adults is in a transition place between Stage 3 – Synthetic-conventional faith, and Stage 4 – Individual-reflective faith, while less than 1 per cent of adults reach Stage 6. Longitudinal and cross-sectional research has shown that religious individuals tend to progress up Fowler's faith stages as they age. For example, Leak (2003) found that students at a Jesuit university, the majority of whom were practising Christians, over the course of their time at university moved up several points on the FDS.

The stages of Fowlers' model mirror the stages of Kohlberg's theory of moral development; in Kohlberg's moral development theory a person moves from egocentric to conventional to post-conventional morality, and in Fowler's theory a person moves in the same direction from egocentric faith to conventional faith to reflective post-conventional faith. The similarities between Fowler's approach and Kohlberg's approach are also found in the interview-based assessment tools they developed; Kohlberg developed the Moral Judgment Interview (MJI) to assess moral stage and Fowler developed the Faith Development Interview (FDI) to assess faith stage. Like Kohlberg's measure, it is very time-consuming and difficult to score, so has not been used much by researchers.

Several psychometric instruments have been devised to assess Fowler's faith development model. Leak, Loucks & Bowlin (1999) developed and validated an eight-item, forced-choice measure of faith development, the *Faith Development Scale* (FDS). There is also the *Faith Styles Scale* (FSS) (Barnes, Doyle & Johnson, 1989). For review of measures of faith development, see Parker (2006).

Critical evaluation of faith development theory

Faith development theory, being one of the most recognised theories in the field of religious/spiritual development, has come in for a lot of criticism. The theory makes universalising claims about what it means to have 'good faith' across all religious cultures and traditions. In its claim for universality, critics say Fowler's approach avoids the reality that religious/spiritual development through adulthood can take one of a number of paths, depending on a person's background, religious

Box 10.3   Cross-cultural perspectives

Conceptions of spiritual development in Sufism

Sufism is a mystical form of Islam that involves engaging in practices that lead to transcendence of one's individualised sense of self. Although it originated within Islam, it has also incorporated elements from neo-Platonic philosophy and Buddhism (Lewin, 2000). The ultimate goal of the Sufi is the experience of union with the Universal Self, to realise the Unity of Existence, and to realise the falsehood of being a separate, individual self. The developmental path towards this goal is realised by way of certain spiritual practices and engaging in helping others. Spiritual practices include *sama* (involving singing, music and poetry) and zikr (ceremonial recitation of prayers and spiritual words). The aim is to experience a higher, unitive state of consciousness, and gradually to develop to a sense of unity with all beings. Lewin (2000) analysed interviews with 13 Sufis about their perceptions of spiritual development. Next is an extract from one of Lewin's interviews, which describe one participant's view of what it means to develop spiritually:

> I no longer see any difference between my wishes and the wishes of others. When you feel unity with other people, you do not see any difference between 'mine' and 'theirs.' It seems that there is always a kind of self-satisfaction behind our altruistic deeds. Only those who have reached a stage of spiritual development where the individual self vanishes and transcends to *haag* [the Universal Self] have the capacity to serve others without looking for any self-satisfaction. They are 'self-less.' I refer to those whose hearts have become so pure that no kind of egoism can make their hearts dirty. Yet, such persons are few. (p. 141)

affiliation (or lack thereof), age, intelligence and life circumstances (Heywood, 2008). Research shows that this diversity of paths becomes particularly salient after midlife (Koenig, 1994).

Then there is the question of cultural diversity. Inevitably, Fowler's theory is shaped by his own monotheistic perspective (he was a Methodist minister as well as an academic) – for example, the final stage in the theory is one where a spiritual 'unity' is apprehended. This is arguably not appropriate to modelling development within polytheistic religions (Wulff, 1993). A more pluralistic approach to spiritual development suggests that it may branch off into various 'styles' rather than down a single linear direction (Streib, 2001). For example a Buddhist Lama may see a belief in, and worship of, God as a sign of spiritual immaturity, while a Christian bishop or Muslim Imam places such a belief as the defining feature of religious truth, and acceptance of God's existence as essential to spiritual maturity. Fowler's singular path is difficult to reconcile with these kinds of differences in conceptions of religious progress. For another cultural view of spiritual development, see Box 10.3 on Sufism (Levenson, Aldwin & D'Mello, 2005).

Finally, faith development theory fails to illuminate how individuals manage faith development during the later years of life when increasing complexity is unlikely despite the increased interest in spirituality that is associated with old age. Indeed the lack of older persons in studies on the theory has been criticised (McFadden, 1999). In summary, it may be that faith development theory defines religious development for monotheistic young adults, but not for others.

Transpersonal psychology and transpersonal development

In the late 1960s, a branch of psychology emerged that aimed specifically at studying the spiritual aspects of human experience and consciousness beyond the remit of religion, which was named *Transpersonal Psychology* (Sutich, 1968). Since the 1990s there has been an official Transpersonal Psychology section of the *British Psychological Society*, and their scope of interest is defined as 'the psychology of spirituality and of those areas of the human mind which search for higher meanings in life, and which move beyond the limited boundaries of the ego to access an enhanced capacity for wisdom, creativity, unconditional love and compassion' (http://tps.bps.org.uk). Transpersonal Psychology is not widely taught at undergraduate level, and it remains controversial because it goes beyond the orthodox materialist view of human beings a purely biological entities.

Theorists from Transpersonal Psychology have put forward models and concepts that pertain to optimal human development (for example,

Table 10.2   The three vectors of transpersonal development

	Ascending path	Descending path	Extending path
Key word	Enlightenment	Individuation	Participation
Key virtues	Wisdom, faith	Integration, wholeness	Compassion, charity, love
Realm of exploration	Higher mind; 'superconscious'	Unconscious	People, world
Goal of development	Union of self and divine	Union of conscious and unconscious	Union of self and other
Barrier to development	Lower nature	Psychic divisions	Self-centredness

Source: Based on Daniels (2009).

Wilber, 2000b). Daniels (2009) recently produced a concise synthesis of transpersonal development theories, by suggesting that all can be located on three 'vectors' of development, which when taken together equal optimal transpersonal development. These vectors are: the ascending path (towards spiritual truth), the descending path (towards self-understanding), and the extending path (towards love and compassion for others and the world). Features of these paths are summarised in Table 10.2.

Robert Atchley: Spiritual development through mystical experience

Robert Atchley's theory states that spiritual development is based on the refinement of consciousness through particular forms of practice, including praying, meditating, chanting, singing, dancing, or contemplating sacred texts or poetry (Atchley, 1997). All such practices aim at cultivating experiences beyond the limits of words and concepts (James, 1983). The aim of engaging in such spiritual practices is to have a *mystical experience*, during which a person experiences reality directly in ways that go beyond words and concepts. It is these mystical experiences that, according to Atchley, are the fuel for spiritual development. They are said to lead to qualitative leaps forward in development, by way of bringing about new conscious realisations. Unlike Fowler's model, there is no linear age-graded sequence of development stages on this mystical path, for it depends on commitment to practice and the occurrence of experiences that are by definition unpredictable. An individual description of a mystical experience is given in Box 10.4.

Box 10.4   Individual voices

Describing a mystical experience

Qualitative research on experiences of crisis in adults encountered descriptions given by participants of changes in spiritual or religious outlook (Robinson, 2008). One account was given by a man who in his late thirties encountered a difficult time of transition in which his wife initiated a divorce and he left his career as a banker (Robinson, 2008). He described becoming increasingly interested in spirituality through this difficult episode. As the emotional turmoil of his crisis was receding and he was starting to build a new life, he described a moment that fits the typical description of a mystical experience, and made a significant impression on him, as described next:

> One example was in Seattle, when I went out there for a study tour. I got to Seattle, it was late at night, and the rest of the group didn't turn up until about two or three hours later. So I walked into town to the local mall to get some presents to take home, and as I walked out what I realised was the Rocky mountains, and I just turned round and it was just an absolute sublime moment when I became one with them, so I stood on this pavement probably for about twenty minutes being one with mountains. And everyone was walking past me, looking at me and wondering what was going on, and it was just the most magical experience on earth. And I know that six months earlier, I would have gone, oh yeah mountains, and carried on walking ... For me it was a total experience that myself and the mountains were one and the same thing. We were connected, we were there, and every cell in my body had become aware of that. That's an experience I had never, ever experienced beforehand. My first true awakening.

The positive effects of meditation

According to Atchley's theory, spiritual practice promotes positive developmental outcomes. Corresponding to this, research has found that meditation improves health in all age groups. Meditation is a practice derived from spiritual traditions in the East and West, which involves concentrating on a particular sound, movement or stimulus in order to bring consciousness into focused and steady attention. It has been found that this practice has mental and physical benefits for all age groups, including the elderly. For some instructions on how to meditate using the 'mindfulness' approach, see Box 10.5.

Box 10.5   Real-world applications

Mindfulness meditation – How to do it

A popular form of meditation that has been adapted from Buddhist practice is mindfulness meditation. It involves cultivating a focus on the present moment through holding one's attention on the process of breathing. It has been shown to have positive effects on mental and physical health for all groups (Kabat-Zinn, 1994). Here is how to do it:

1. Find a quiet place and a comfortable chair with a straight back. Sit with your head, neck and back straight but relaxed.
2. Focus attention on the sensation of air moving in and out of your body as you breathe. Feel your belly rise and fall, the air enter your nostrils and leave your mouth. Keep paying attention to the way each breath moves in its own way.
3. If thoughts of the past and the future emerge, just acknowledge them and then come back to the present moment.
4. If emotions arise, such as fear, anxiety or excitement, just become aware of them, and come back focusing on your breathing.
5. If you get lost in a train of thought, when you become aware that you have lost focus, don't judge yourself negatively for it, just observe it and return to your breathing.
6. Initially try this for 15 minutes every day for one week, and observe if you notice any effects. If you feel motivated to continue, eventually increase the time you practice for to 30 minutes.

Source: Kabat-Zinn (1994).

A review by Lindberg (2005) summarised findings from studies on the health benefits of meditation, and found the following positive effects of interventions: improved immune functioning; lowered blood pressure; decreases in anxiety and depression; enhanced self-esteem, and increased restfulness and alertness. In dementia patients, meditation leads to a decrease in agitated behaviour, increased group participation, improved self-control and relaxation. Other studies have shown that meditation has cognitive and affective benefits, for example it has been found to lead to improved emotional self-regulation and behavioural flexibility (Brown & Ryan, 2003). Furthermore, brain imaging studies have found higher amounts of cortical grey-matter in brain areas associated with cognition and emotional regulation in regular meditators, when compared with matched controls (Lazar et al., 2005; Luders et al., 2009).

Studies have also shown that meditation is linked to a slowing of the ageing process and enhanced longevity in older persons (Alexander et al., 1989; Wallace et al., 1982). In one study, elderly persons in residential homes (mean age 81) were taught Transcendental Meditation (TM). After three years there was a significant difference in survival; all who had learnt the technique were alive, compared with just 75 per cent of persons in the non-treatment group.

Concluding comments

This chapter has explored changes in spiritual practice or religious belief over the course of the lifespan, but what about atheism? Psychologists who study spiritual development using a directional model such as Fowler's faith development theory must ask themselves how an atheist would perform on it. The answer is that they would likely be scored at the bottom, or not score at all. The atheist in turn would likely counter by saying that 'spiritual development' is a contradiction in terms, and that the acceptance of the reality of a Godless universe is a mark of psychological maturity, while those who adopt religion are in fact stuck in childish delusions based on supernatural beings, irrational superstition and invisible friends (Dawkins, 2007). Freud, for example, viewed religion as a form of infantile regression, and thus as antithetical to development (Freud, 1930). This is the conundrum at the heart of positive spiritual development as a topic of scientific study; what some see as progress others see as regress. But while the issue has debate woven into its very nature, value-neutral research that charts how religious belief and spiritual practices change with age and life events is something that atheists and religiously inclined researchers can engage in together, for it does not require any assumption that such change is a good thing or not.

Questions for you to reflect on

- Do you know people from different religious backgrounds? If so, ask them what religious development means to them. Do they respond in similar or different ways?
- More people are defining themselves as 'spiritual but not religious' than in the past. Why do you think this is?
- Certain life events such as having a child or bereavement lead to temporary increases in religiosity. Can you think of any reasons why that would be the case?

Summary points

- Spirituality and religiosity are related but different phenomena. Spirituality relates to a person's engagement in practices and enquiry about what it means to feel and be connected to something sacred, while developing ways of knowing that are not reliant on words or numbers. Religiosity is a person's engagement with a religious establishment and place of worship, and the adoption of a formal religious belief system.
- Spirituality and religiosity are an important locus of change and continuity for many, across the lifespan, and have typical trajectories across the lifespan. At the level of the average, there is an increase in spirituality and religiosity with age, but when broken down into subgroups, only a minority of individuals actually increase linearly in religiosity with age.
- Various life events temporarily increase religiosity and spirituality, including bereavement and having children. Negative events are only related to spiritual growth if a person has a tendency to reflect on the meaning of such events, and if a person is relatively young.
- Gerotranscendence theory states that as a person ages, he/she shifts in values and goals in ways that lead to more focus on spiritual questions and practices.
- Fowler's faith development theory states that as a person ages, he/she moves up through defined stages in an invariant, linear manner. These stages are *intuitive-projective faith, mythic-literal faith, synthetic-conventional faith, individual-reflective faith, conjunctive faith* and *universalising faith*. The typical stage for most adults is individual-reflective faith.
- Fowler's theory has been criticised as being only appropriate to monotheistic faith and to younger adults.
- Atchley suggests that mystical experiences are a key to spiritual development, and that a person must commit to engaging in spiritual practices to encounter such an experience.
- Meditation has proven positive effects on health and cognitive functioning, and evidence even suggests it enhances longevity in older adults.

Recommended reading

Alexander, C. N., Langer, E. J., Newman, R. I., Chandler, H. M. & Davies, J. L. (1989). Transcendental meditation, mindfulness, and longevity: An experimental study with the elderly. *Journal of Personality and Social Psychology*, 57, 950–964.

Daniels, M. (2009). Perspectives and vectors in transpersonal development. *Transpersonal Psychology Review*, 13, 87–99.

Fowler, J. W. (1981). *Stages of Faith: The Psychology of Human Development and the Quest for Meaning*. New York: Harper and Row.

Ingersoll-Dayton, B., Krause, N. & Morgan, D. (2002). Religious trajectories and transitions over the life course. *The International Journal of Aging and Human Development: A Journal of Psychosocial Gerontology*, 55, 51–70.

McCullough, M. E., Enders, C. K., Brion, S. L. & Jain, A. R. (2005). The varieties of religious development in adulthood: A longitudinal investigation of religion and rational choice. *Journal of Personality and Social Psychology*, 89, 78–89.

Oser, F. K., Scarlett, G. & Bucher, A. (2006). Religious and spiritual development throughout the life span. In W. Damon & R. M. Lerner (eds) *Handbook of Child Psychology: Theoretical Models of Human Development Vol. 1* (pp. 942–998). New York: John Wiley & Sons.

Tornstam, L. (1989). Gero-transcendence theory: A reformulation of the disengagement theory. *Aging*, 1, 55–63.

Recommended websites

Association for Transpersonal Psychology: www.atpweb.org

British Psychology Society – Transpersonal Psychology Section: http://tps.bps.org.uk.

Webpage listing publications on Gerotranscendence Theory: www.soc.uu.se/en/research/research-fields/the-social-gerontology-group/research/the-theory-of-gerotranscendence/.

11

Mental Disorder, Age and Adult Life Events

We do not have to visit a madhouse to find disordered minds; our planet is the mental institution of the universe.

Johann Wolfgang von Goethe

Loretta was diagnosed with depression when she was 26. At that time she was experiencing a highly stressful period of her life. Her work as a lawyer was extremely demanding and pressurised, and she had recently split from her long-term partner. By the time she received the diagnosis, her self-esteem and work motivation had plummeted, she was sleeping little, and her mood was very low. Over several years of therapy and occasional medication, she recovered. With the help of the therapist, she learnt how to put less pressure on herself at work, and to say 'no' to others who were asking more of her than she was able to manage or trying to control her. By the age of 30, she was feeling positive, balanced and optimistic about the future, and was in a happy and healthy relationship, with plans to get married.

Almost all recognised mental disorders have a peak period of risk in the lifespan, and are therefore causally linked to the course of human development. Early adulthood is a particularly vulnerable part of the lifespan; depression, panic disorder, schizophrenia and bipolar disorder are all most frequently diagnosed in this period of life. Late adulthood, in contrast, brings an elevated risk of degenerative disorders such as Alzheimer's disease, dementia and Parkinson's disease. Table 11.1 gives the approximate mean age of onset for a variety of recognised mental disorders, to give you a sense of how they are distributed across the lifespan.

This chapter will review research and theory on how and why eating disorders, anxiety and mood disorders, schizophrenia and degenerative disorders relate to adult age and life events. As well as referring to studies done by psychologists, it will refer to a number of research studies from the discipline of *psychiatric epidemiology*, which uses large-scale surveys of community and clinical populations to investigate how mental disorders are distributed across locations, occupations, ages and sexes. Prior to discussing research on particular disorders, the diathesis-stress approach to mental disorder is introduced, and the influential 'Bedford Method' for studying the relation between psychiatric disorder and adult life events is outlined.

Table 11.1   Approximate peak age of onset for various mental disorders

Peak age of onset	Disorder
2	Autism
6	Phobia
7	ADHD
15	Anorexia
21	Alcohol abuse
22	Agoraphobia
23	OCD and panic disorder
24	Bulimia
25	Bipolar
26	Schizophrenia
30	Depression
53	Frontotemporal Dementia
65	Alzheimer's Disease
75	Parkinson's Disease
80	Vascular Dementia

Diathesis-stress models

The paradigm upon which this textbook is based is the biopsychosocial approach to lifespan development, outlined in Chapter 1. Applying such an approach to mental illness requires a framework to conceive how social environments, life events, cognitive-affective tendencies and biological vulnerabilities interact over the course of a lifetime to cause mental disorders. One approach that integrates these levels of analysis is the *diathesis-stress* approach to mental disorder (Zuckerman, 1999), which is based on the premise that mental illness results from a combination of (a) an internal, long-term vulnerability to a disorder (termed a 'diathesis') *and* (b) exposure to stress-inducing events or trauma that triggers the vulnerability (Ingram & Luxton, 2005; Monroe & Simons, 1991).

There are different views on what leads to having a vulnerability to mental disorder. Some diathesis-stress models stated that the vulnerability is an inherited biological factor, such as Meehl's theory of *schizotaxic genes* as the key vulnerability for developing schizophrenia (Meehl, 1962). Research has also found that prenatal influences interact with genotype to create vulnerability – for example maternal smoking during pregnancy leads to an increased risk of Attention Deficit Hyperactivity Disorder in individuals with particular genotypes (Neuman et al., 2007). Recently, other models have suggested that early experiences of abuse, neglect or other stress-inducing events in childhood may also be responsible for creating a vulnerability to mental illness. In support of this last point, a large body of longitudinal and cross-sectional research now shows a robust link between early experiences such as child abuse, childhood trauma and major attachment disruptions, and adult mental illness (for example, Banyard, Williams & Siegel, 2001; Edwards et al., 2003; Heim & Nemeroff, 2001; Horwitz, Widom, McLaughlin & White, 2001).

The *traumagenic model* proposes why childhood trauma may create adult psychiatric vulnerability. It suggests that childhood trauma leads to a chronically elevated stress response in the central nervous system and endocrine system that persists into adulthood (Read et al., 2001). What this means is that the brain, having been exposed to extreme threat in its early developing state, is chronically over-sensitive to threat, which leads to imbalances in adulthood that make psychiatric disturbance more likely, such as excessive CRF (corticotropin-releasing factor), which is released under conditions of stress and leads to increased levels of cortisol and adrenalin (Heim & Nemeroff, 2001; Perry & Szalavitz, 2006). Major stressful life events or traumas in adulthood activate this sensitive stress response, which activates the diathesis.

Another reason why trauma can lead to disorder, is that individuals who have been traumatised may endeavour to self-medicate using drugs or alcohol, to suppress unwanted thoughts or memories of the trauma. This may lead to temporary relief, but can exacerbate psychological and relationship problems in the long-term and can lead to drug or alcohol dependence (Mueser et al., 2002).

In summary, the developmental pathway to adult psychopathology involves a complex interaction of genetic inheritance, adverse early experience, and later stressful events. In the rest of this chapter we focus on the stress side of the diathesis-stress equation, as that is the part that occurs within the domain of adult development. It should be borne in mind when reading the ensuing discussion of how life events relate to eating disorders, schizophrenia, bipolar disorder, depression and anxiety disorders, that within the diathesis-stress framework such events are *necessary but not sufficient* to initiate mental disorder – long-term vulnerabilities that stem from genes and/or adverse early experiences are also necessary. The question of how one actually measures stressful life events in relation to mental disorder is the question we come to next.

George W. Brown and the Bedford method of assessing life events

Research into the link between adult life events and the onset of mental disorder originated with the work of British psychologist George W. Brown. He was convinced that mental disorders were meaningfully linked to the ups and downs of life, and not purely the product of aberrant brain chemistry. Along with his colleague Tirril Harris and others at Bedford College in London, he spent four decades investigating whether life events relate to mental disorder. The method he devised for this purpose has come to be known as the 'Bedford College Method'. It involves the use of a structured interview called the *Life Events and Difficulties Schedule (LEDS)* (Brown & Harris, 1978). A LEDS interview elicits data on the timing, perceived importance and context of recent life events, and each event is coded into a particular event type, then rated for its *severity, difficulty, controllability*, and for experiences of *humiliation, entrapment, loss* and *danger* (Brown, Harris & Hepworth, 1998; Harris, 2001).

Typically, LEDS data is gathered from individuals with a mental disorder, about life events that occurred before and after the onset of their disorder. This data will then either be; (a) compared with another period of time in the lives of the same group of people, or (b) compared with a control group of healthy persons. The major weakness of the method is its retrospective nature, particularly given that many of the participants may have a current mental health problem that might limit their ability to recall the past accurately. Despite this, the LEDS has been shown to elicit reliable data that has been an important source of insight into the developmental course of mental disorder (Hlastala et al., 2000).

The remainder of the chapter outlines those disorders that are reliably associated with a developmental phase of adulthood, and reviews the research that links them to life events and other developmental risk factors. We start with disorders that are most likely to appear on the cusp of late adolescence and the transition to adulthood – eating disorders.

Disorders with typical onset in late adolescence/ emerging adulthood

Anorexia Nervosa and Bulimia Nervosa

Anorexia nervosa and bulimia nervosa are the two most frequently diagnosed eating disorders: 95 per cent of cases are diagnosed in women, and just 5 per cent in men (Woodside et al., 2001). Bulimia nervosa is characterised by episodes of binge eating followed by attempts to purge oneself of food through vomiting. It can lead to ill-health and decreased self-esteem (Vohs et al., 1999). Anorexia leads the sufferer to reduce their food intake so that they lose body weight, and in some cases to the point of starvation. It has the highest mortality rate of all psychiatric disorders (Attia, 2010). The risk of developing an eating disorder is influenced by individual, familial and socio-cultural factors, and for a comprehensive review of these, the reader is directed to Polivy and Herman (2002).

Epidemiological data from clinical samples in the UK, Finland and the USA show that anorexia diagnoses peak in late adolescence (Currin et al., 2005; Keski-Rahkonen et al., 2007). Halmi et al. (1979) found two peaks of highest frequency of anorexia diagnoses, first at age 14/15, and the second at age 18. The late-onset group showed greater severity and poorer outcomes. There is less cross-national agreement about the typical onset point of bulimia. In some studies, it peaks in the early twenties, in others it is in the teenage years (Currin et al., 2005; Keski-Rahkonen et al., 2007). Either way, both disorders appear to be definitively associated with the transition from adolescence to adulthood.

Using the *Life Events and Difficulties Schedule* (LEDS), Schmidt et al. (1997) found that out of 101 eating disorder patients, 77 per cent of anorexics and 76 per cent of bulimics report a major stressful event prior to the onset of their problems. This finding has been replicated in other studies (Horesh et al., 1995; Raffi et al., 2000). Furthermore, life events are more strongly related to the onset of combined bulimia and anorexia than to either one individually (Strober, 1984).

For both anorexia and bulimia, stressors that precede illness onset are most commonly *interpersonal stressors* – conflicts and difficulties concerning family and/or romantic partners (Horesh et al., 1995; Tozzi et al., 2003). For anorexia, stressful problems more often relate to sexuality than for bulimic patients or non-disordered controls (Schmidt et al., 1997). It is not just the nature of the events, but also how they are coped with, which relates to the onset of eating disorder. Troop and Treasure (1997) conducted a study with 32 females who had developed an eating disorder within the last four years, and compared them with 20 women who had no history of eating disorder. They gained data on life events and on coping strategies. In line with other research, they found that 58 per cent of the anorexia group and 77 per cent of the bulimia group experienced a severe stressful event or difficulty prior to the onset of the disorder, and discovered that the majority of these were to do with relationships. In terms of coping strategies, anorexic symptoms were related to cognitive avoidance (that is, ignoring or denying presence of stressful events), while bulimic symptoms were associated with cognitive rumination and worrying about the source of stress (that is, thinking about it obsessively). The authors point out the interesting similarity in cognitive coping and eating habits – anorexics tend towards both cognitive avoidance and avoidance of food, while bulimics tend to both over-think and over-eat. The study also found that the experience of *helplessness* was a defining feature of those with eating disorders; 0 per cent of the non-eating disordered control group reported helplessness in response to stress, while 73 per cent of the anorexia group and 40 per cent of the bulimia group did.

Disorders with typical onset in early adulthood

Depression

Depression is characterised by symptoms such as feeling sad, feeling hopeless, fatigue, unusual changes in appetite and sleep, low self-worth and losing interest or pleasure in activities. The DSM-IV-TR (the most widely used manual for diagnosing mental disorders) states that symptoms must be present for two weeks for a diagnosis to be made (APA, 2000). In both US and European epidemiological studies, the peak age of onset for general depression is in early adulthood, between the ages of 20 and 40. Ronald Kessler and colleagues (2005) analysed data from the US National Comorbidity Survey Replication to assess the prevalence and age-of-onset of various DSM-IV disorders. They established a typical age of onset for clinical depression of 32, with an interquartile range of ages 19 to 44.[1] In epidemiological studies in Europe and Australia, more depression has been found in young adults than in middle-aged or older adults, however prevalence continues to be high in midlife (Alonso et al., 2004; Henderson et al., 1998; Leach et al., 2008).

There is one subtype of depression that by definition can only occur after a particular event in the lifespan – postnatal depression (also called postpartum depression). This is an episode of clinical depression that occurs within four to six weeks of a woman giving birth to a child. Research from the USA estimates that 13–16 per cent of new mothers are affected by it (Robertson et al., 2004). A prior history of depression and depressive symptoms during pregnancy are the most well-established risk factors (Rich-Edwards et al., 2006; Robertson et al., 2004). Other risk factors include low income, young maternal age, single parent status and low levels of social support (Rich-Edwards et al., 2006). Box 11.1 provides excerpts from personal accounts of low-income mothers who received a diagnosis of postnatal depression.

Box 11.1   Individual voices

The experience of postnatal depression in low-income mothers

Excerpts are given next from an interview-based study Abrams and Curran (2009) with low-income mothers diagnosed with postnatal depression. The excerpts convey the profound challenges of depression during the early stages of motherhood.

Theme 1: Ambivalence about the pregnancy

I think ... a pregnancy is always good when you want to have it. When it's what you want and you'll do anything and everything that's possible to make it work. But if you're not deep down wanting it, you know, then it's like then every little thing bothers you. It's just me. Everything little thing just bothers me. (p. 356)

---

[1] The interquartile range is the portion of a distribution between the 25th and 75th percentiles of the data (that is, the middle 50 per cent of the distribution range).

Box 11.1   Continued

Theme 2: Caregiving overload

[Y]ou have to wake up, do the feedings, change the diapers, wash the clothes. You know, cook, and it becomes a lot. I think some-times I'm actually doing so much, and sometimes I couldn't explain how I manage to get through it all ... But I do have moments where after everything is done, I just go and I sit, and I think about it. 'Why? Why is it so hard? Can I really still do this?' 'Cause it's four of them now, 'can you really still do this?' I think on the hardest day, sometimes I almost say, 'just give em up, it's the right thing, somebody needs to take them from me.' 'Cause I can't do it any-more. (p. 356)

Theme 3: Mothering alone and lacking help

A down day for me, probably, probably like in these last few days. It's been harder because umm, his dad has been working a lot, a lot of overtime, so I don't even get his help or when I need him get the baby, or his bottle, or all that. (p. 358)

Theme 4: Financial worries

I guess it depends on the level of depression you have 'cause with me, my depression is, I think, totally different. That's from me not working, from not havin' a car, not havin' – you know, money just to go out and have a good time, go out to eat, shop ... You know, I'm poor. (p. 358)

Studies that have employed the *Life Events and Difficulties Schedule* have found wide-ranging evidence implicating life events in the onset and course of depression (Hlastala et al., 2000). Events that involve loss and humiliation are particularly predictive of depression (Brown, Harris & Hepworth, 1995) particularly when they occur within several months of onset of the condition (Livianos-Aldana et al., 1999; Jordanova et al., 2007; Kendler et al., 2003). Researchers have used twins to study the effects of both genes and life events on depression. In one study, Kendler, Karkowski and Prescott (1999) studied twins from the Virginia Twin Registry, and found that *both* genetic and environmental effects are involved in the aetiology of depression, which supports the diathesis-stress model that was discussed earlier in the chapter.

As with eating disorders, life events interact with coping strategies to predict depression. Bifulco and Brown (1996) studied the interaction of life events and cognitive coping responses in a sample of British mothers over a period of 12 months. They found that the occurrence of a severe life difficulty combined with a negative cognitive evaluation predicted depression, but neither factor alone did. Three ways of cognitively responding to stressful life events were particularly associated with depression: *denial* of the event, *blaming oneself* and *pessimistic predictions* about the future.

While an increase in stressful life events predicts the onset of depression, *a reduction* of such events also predicts recovery from depression (Brown, Adler & Bifulco, 1988). The occurrence of a 'fresh start' event or a 'positive life change' such as starting a new job, going back to education, establishing a new relationship, or clearing a long-term debt, is associated with recovery from chronic depression (Harris, 2001; Neeleman, Oldehinkel & Ormel, 2003).

Box 11.2   Cross-cultural perspectives

Suicide, gender and age in different countries

Suicidal thoughts and suicide are more common than you might think. The Adult Psychiatric Morbidity Survey 2007, a British epidemiological study, found that one in seven people have suicidal thoughts at some point in their life, and that one in 20 have attempted suicide (McManus & Bebbington, 2009). The World Health Organisation monitors annual suicide rates in countries across the globe, and their data show that suicide statistics vary widely by country.[2] The most common national age pattern is a gradual age-related increase in suicide rates across adult age groups, so that older persons are at highest risk. This pattern is shown by the USA, China, Germany, Brazil, Israel, Spain, Sweden and others. However another common pattern is where men in midlife are at greatest risk – this is the case in France, Australia, Iceland, Japan and Great Britain. Graphs showing World Health Organisation data from four example countries – Great Britain, Russia, the USA and Japan – are shown in Figure 11.1.

---

[2] World Health Organisation data on annual suicide rates is available for public access at http://www.who.int/mental_health/prevention/suicide/country_reports/en/index.html

Box 11.2   Continued

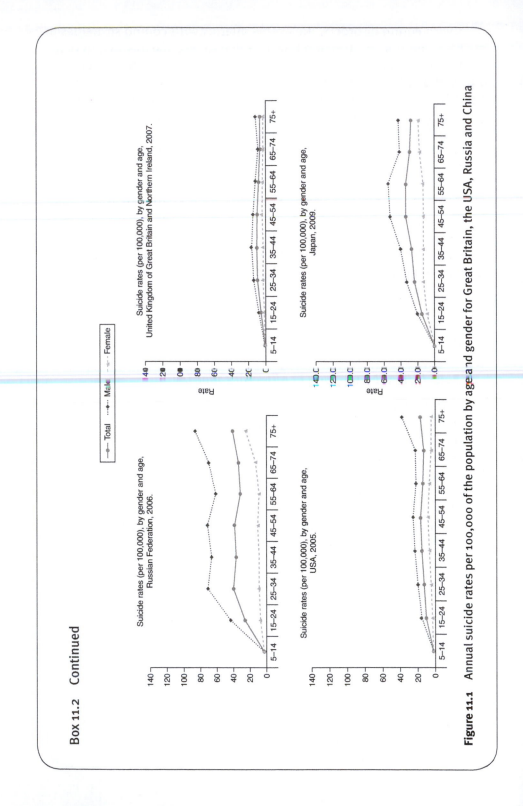

Figure 11.1   Annual suicide rates per 100,000 of the population by age and gender for Great Britain, the USA, Russia and China

Anxiety disorders

Anxiety disorders are characterised by an abnormal level of fear, anxiety and worry. They include obsessive compulsive disorder, panic disorder, post-traumatic stress disorder, phobias and generalised anxiety disorder (APA, 2000). Twice as many women are diagnosed with anxiety disorders than men (Regier, Narrow & Rae, 1990; Alonso et al., 2004).

Different anxiety disorders emerge at different points in the lifespan. Phobias of objects, animals or heights typically appear early, with the mean age-of-onset around six or seven; social phobias are most likely to appear in adolescence, and agoraphobia (a fear of being in open places or crowds) typically appears in early adulthood (Bienvenu et al., 2006). Panic disorder, post-traumatic stress disorder, obsessive compulsive disorder and generalised anxiety disorder all typically first appear in early adulthood too (Kessler et al., 2005).

Early adulthood is a key time for the onset of anxiety disorders and this tendency towards anxiety in young adults may be increasing. Research shows that young adults today may be more anxious than previous generations. Jean Twenge, in her article 'The Age of Anxiety', presented data showing that college-aged populations had significantly increased anxiety levels between the 1950s and 1990s (Twenge, 2000).

Research points towards a lesser tendency towards anxiety in older adults compared with young adults, which fits with the 'positivity effect' described in Chapter 4. Twelve-month prevalence rates for anxiety in a pan-European study show a decline in prevalence across adulthood; around 9.2 per cent of European adults between the ages of 18 and 24 have suffered from an anxiety disorder in the last 12 months, compared with 7.0 per cent of 25–34-year-olds, 6.5 per cent of 35–49-year-olds, 6.8 per cent of 50–64-year-olds and 3.6 per cent of over-65s (Alonso et al., 2004). In the British *Adult Psychiatric Morbidity Survey*, PTSD and OCD show the highest rates in early adulthood, while over 65s show the lowest rates (McManus & Bebbington, 2009).

Research has also looked into anxiety about death. When would you expect this to peak during adulthood? Perhaps towards the end of life, when a person is more abruptly faced with the inevitability of their mortality? In fact, cross-sectional research shows that death anxiety peaks in early adulthood; those in their twenties show more anxiety about death than adults of any other age (Russac et al., 2007).

Life events relate to depression and anxiety in different ways. Finlay-Jones and Brown (1981) elicited life events data from 164 young adult women diagnosed with depression, anxiety or mixed depression/anxiety, and a control group. It was found that events related to *loss* were most frequently found before the onset of depressive disorder, events presenting *threat and danger* were more commonly found prior to the onset of anxiety disorder, and reports of both were found mostly prior to a mixed anxiety/depression diagnosis. This suggests that the nature of stressful events predicts the type of subsequent mental illness, and this may be due to the kind of negative emotions that different stressful events typically elicit. Although most anxiety disorders seem to be related to life events, as the aforementioned research suggests, only one anxiety adult disorder actually *requires* the presence of recent trauma in order to be diagnosed – post-traumatic stress disorder. The symptoms of the disorder and treatments used to alleviate it are described in Box 11.3.

Box 11.3   Real-life applications

Treating post-traumatic stress disorder with TF-CBT

Post-traumatic stress disorder is a syndrome that appears following a traumatic event. The symptoms are involuntary recurrent memories of the traumatic event; flashbacks (a sense of reliving the event), nightmares, avoidance of stimuli associated with the trauma, sleep difficulties, anger and extreme sensitivity to threat (termed 'hypervigilance') (APA, 2000). The term was coined in 1980 to refer to the symptoms shown by soldiers who had been traumatised by their experiences when at war. Nowadays, it can be diagnosed in any case where a person shows the aforementioned symptoms following an event that induced a sense of fear, helplessness or horror.

There are a variety of treatments available, and one of the most effective is *Trauma-Focused Cognitive Behavioural Therapy (TF-CBT)* (Bisson & Andrew, 2007; Ponniah & Hollon, 2009). TF-CBT involves two key elements. The first is gradually and carefully engaging in a dialogue with the patient about the traumatic event, their feelings about it, other people involved, dreams they have had about the event and the effects that the trauma has had on them in terms of behaviour and emotions. This process is a form of 'exposure', which allows suppressed painful emotions to be voiced and processed. The second element is the provision of tools and techniques to improve coping with stress and its effects. Here are three example techniques:

> *Belly-breathing relaxation strategy* – Breathe in slowly and deeply, while counting to 5 in your head, as your belly and lungs fill up with air. As you breathe in, your belly should stick out. Then you

Box 11.3   Continued

let the air out, while counting to six, and watch your belly go back in as the air is slowly pushed out. Pay attention to the air as it moves in and out of your body as you count.

Strategy to stop recurrent thoughts – When recurrent negative thoughts or memories emerge, say forcefully to oneself 'stop!' and replace the thought or memory with an alternative positive one.

Strategy to replace negative thoughts – Notice a typical negative thought that you have about things that happened to you, which lead to negative feelings. Now think of an alternative positive thought that would make you feel better, and write it down on a piece of paper. Next time you find yourself thinking the negative thought, read the positive thought you have written down, until you really start to believe it.

Bipolar disorder

Bipolar disorder, also termed 'manic depressive' illness, is characterised by intermittent periods of depression and mania. During manic episodes a person will show elevated and unstable mood, grandiose or delusional ideas, a short attention span, a decreased need for sleep and impulsive spending or consumption behaviour. They may also become aggressive or prone to temper outbursts (APA, 2000). Kessler et al. (2005) found the modal age of onset for bipolar disorder is 25, and that prevalence declines in those over 30. Over-60s show bipolar prevalence at about 20 per cent the rate of those in early adulthood, suggesting a considerable amount of remission and recovery over the course of the adult life span.

Cross-sectional research using the *Life Event and Difficulty Schedule* (LEDS) has found that severe negative occurrences are more prevalent prior to the onset of bipolar depressive episodes than during comparison periods or compared with control groups (Ambelas, 1987; Kennedy et al., 1983; Malkoff-Schwartz et al., 1998). Manic episodes, on the other hand, can be triggered by positive events, such as the attainment of a major goal (Johnson, 2005). More recent research has suggested that the relation between stress and bipolar onset is stronger in younger adults than older adults (Hlastala et al., 2000). Relapse and recovery for bipolar patients also relate to life events – relapse is related to stressful life events

(Ellicott et al., 1990), while recovery is related to their absence (Johnson & Miller, 1997). For a comprehensive review of life event and developmental risk factors in bipolar disorder, the reader is directed to a review article by Alloy et al. (2005).

Schizophrenia

'Schizophrenia' is an umbrella term for a group of psychotic disorders (APA, 2000; Carpenter & Kirkpatrick, 1988). Subtypes of schizophrenia, including paranoid, disorganised and catatonic (APA, 2000), have little in common, but for epidemiological purposes, they are grouped together as a single category.[3] Symptoms that are indicative of schizophrenia include hallucinations (distorted or false perceptions such as hearing voices), delusions (distorted or false beliefs) and disorganised thinking (often manifested as incoherent speech). Box 11.4 describes an alternative therapeutic approach to dealing with hallucinatory voices.

Heinz Häfner and colleagues have researched the age of onset of schizophrenia in Germany and Denmark. They gathered data using semi-structured interviews with patients and relatives, and gained age-of-admission data from hospital records. They found that the mean age of onset of schizophrenic symptoms was 28, and the mean age of first admission to hospital was 30 (Häfner et al., 1993). However, when men and women were compared, a clear gender difference was apparent. The male peak age of onset is earlier than women, and women experience a second but less pronounced peak in the 45–9 age group. This gender difference in age of onset is shown in Figure 11.2 (Häfner et al., 1998).

Early onset schizophrenia, defined as symptoms appearing before the age of 21, is characterised by more severe symptoms compared with schizophrenia that occurs at a later age (Häfner et al., 1998). Late onset schizophrenia, occurring after the age of 40, is often related to the onset of physical illness, such as hearing loss and eye-related diseases (Harris & Jeste, 1988).

Schizophrenia is another disorder that has been found to relate to early trauma and adult stress (Read et al., 2001). The frequency of stressful life events has been found to be higher in the three weeks prior to a diagnosis of schizophrenia than in a control group, and tension in the home is a particularly predictive stressor in this period (Brown & Birley,

---

[3] At the time of writing, the DSM-V is proposing to remove all these subtypes of schizophrenia from diagnostic manuals, and thus to have just one single schizophrenia diagnosis (see www.dsm5.org).

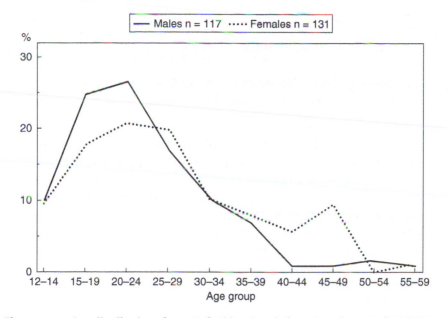

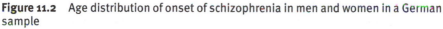

Figure 11.2   Age distribution of onset of schizophrenia in men and women in a German sample

Source: Häfner et al. (1998, p. 103). Reproduced with permission of Oxford University Press.

1968; Day et al., 1987). Norman & Malla (1993), in their review of the relation between life events and schizophrenia, caution that the link may be partially due to the increased sensitivity of patients to perceive events as stressful, compared with controls who are less sensitive. However this view seems to be at odds with the findings from Horan et al. (2005), who conducted a 12-month longitudinal study on schizophrenia patients. They found that it is only the frequency and intensity of stressful events reported *before* a diagnosis that predict it. Patients in fact report lower numbers of negative and positive life events in the period after diagnosis, relative to a control group.

Contrary to common assumptions, recovery from schizophrenia is a normal event, with 50–66 per cent of those who are hospitalised with a schizophrenia diagnosis showing either total recovery or improvement that is sufficient to lead an independent life (Ciompi, 1980; Harding et al., 1987). The course of schizophrenia does however often oscillate between periods of improvement and relapse for many sufferers (Thara, 2004). Malla et al. (1990) conducted a one-year longitudinal study with relapsing and non-relapsing patients, and found that relapsers reported significantly more major and minor stressful events than non-relapsers in the three months prior to relapse. Das, Kulhara & Verma (1997) compared life events over one year in 30 relapsing schizophrenics and

Box 11.4   Alternative perspectives

The Hearing Voices Movement and the Maastrict approach: A developmental approach to hallucinations

Taking a developmental perspective to therapy means exploring the possible ways that a person's problems and symptoms relate to the past experiences and events in their current life. It also involves providing clients with coping strategies and resources that are appropriate to their age and life stage. Such an approach requires that the clinician does not confine himself/herself to symptom checklists, but also aims to elicit information about the person's life story, which is akin to the formulation approach mentioned in Box 11.5.

A recent therapeutic movement takes just such an approach to treating hallucinations, particularly hearing voices. It is termed the *Maastrict Approach*, and is based on research and theory developed by the pioneering psychiatrist Marius Romme and his colleagues (Romme et al., 2009). The theory that underpins the approach states that the presence and content of hallucinatory voices link back to traumatic life events that a person has been through. A chronically hallucinated voice typically represents a significant individual involved in a past trauma (for example, has the same name, gender and voice as a past abuser or bully) or metaphorically represents emotions from the trauma that have not been consciously or properly processed. The Maastrict approach to therapy involves the following steps:

1. Provide reassurance, hope and a non-judgemental atmosphere.
2. Provide medication if necessary in the short-term to manage anxiety or depression.
3. Teach strategies to allow the voice-hearer to create 'space', for example, setting 'consulting time' to listen to the voices during the day and also allocating times for ignoring them.
4. Suggest creating a voice diary – this helps to explore how stress, emotions, times of day and interpersonal environments trigger the voices or make them louder or worse.
5. Practise expressing emotions, in assertiveness training or support groups, in order to minimise suppressive coping strategies.

Box 11.4   Continued

6. Exploring past trauma and associated anxiety and guilt in the process of therapy, to move towards acceptance and externalisation of those past experiences.

7. Engage in the process of 'voice dialogue': the therapist dialogues with a person's hallucinated voice, by getting the voice-hearer to speak it out loud, and then asking questions such as 'what is your task?' and 'what would happen if you left?'. The aim of this process is to understand the relationship of the voice to the person's past experiences, and also giving the voice-hearer an ability to build a bridge between their sense of self and the identity of the voice.

Support groups for voice-hearers have been set up around the world based on the Maastrict approach. The Hearing Voices Network runs 180 such groups across the UK. For more on these groups and this approach, please see the web addresses given at the end of the chapter, or read the book *Living with Voices* by Romme et al. (2009).

30 patients who were stable and functional. The group of relapsing schizophrenics showed a significantly greater number of life events and had a significantly higher stress score than the stable group.

Why is emerging adulthood/early adulthood associated with the onset of many mental disorders?

It is a paradox that early adulthood is the peak of the lifespan in terms of physical functioning, but also the peak point of the lifespan in terms of psychological vulnerability. Depression, anxiety disorders, bipolar disorder, schizophrenia and PTSD are most likely to be diagnosed in people who are in their twenties and early thirties. What is it about this point in the lifespan that increases the risk of being diagnosed with these disorders? There are a number of hypotheses, three of which are summarised next.

Hypothesis 1: Instability and Stress. As we have discussed in this chapter, stressful events are a common risk factor for the onset of depression, anxiety, bipolar disorder, eating disorders and schizophrenia. There is evidence that suggests that stress is particularly prevalent in the early years of adult life – recent cross-sectional studies of American adults have found that stress levels are particularly high in this age group, when compared with other adult age groups (Folkman et al., 1987; Stone et al., 2010).

Arnett (2010) points to various typical features of the stage of emerging adulthood that might help to explain the high amount of stress in this age group (see Chapter 6 for more on the theory of emerging adulthood). Emerging adulthood is the time of peak instability in relationships, jobs, goals and living arrangements, relative to childhood and later stages of adulthood, and this instability may precipitate stress, which in turn may trigger a latent mental disorder vulnerability. Furthermore, the heightened levels of stress in young adulthood might result from the excess of transitions that occur at this point in the life course (Gonzalez, 2011). These transitions include moving out of home, becoming sexually active, starting a career, marriage or finding a cohabiting partner, becoming a parent, getting a mortgage and other new financial responsibilities. These transition periods can be the trigger for high stress and even times of major crisis (Robinson & Smith, 2010a).

Hypothesis 2: Pre-existing problems and the challenge of independent living. During the transition to adulthood, young people typically move from living arrangements characterised by dependence on their parents or caregivers to ones which require independent, self-regulated functioning (Gonzalez, 2011; Robinson, 2011c). Any pre-existing vulnerabilities, eccentricities or abnormalities may suddenly become a more substantive problem when a person must manage their own affairs responsibly and effectively, and move out of the parental home. Thus diagnosis may occur in this age group because anxiety, depression, manic moods or hallucinations can for the first time bring about *social and occupational impairment*, which is a criterion for the diagnosis of most disorders.

Hypothesis 3: *Substance and alcohol abuse acting as trigger*. Emerging adulthood is the peak period of substance and alcohol abuse in the lifespan (McManus & Bebbington, 2009). This prevalent consumption of toxic substances may act as a trigger for turning latent mental health problems into a full-blown disorder (Henquet et al., 2005).

Disorders with typical onset in late adulthood

Disorders that have a typical age of onset in later life are the neurodegenerative disorders, such as dementia and Parkinson's.

Box 11.5   Alternative perspectives

Beyond diagnosis: Why some professionals prefer to work without labels

Diagnosis is the preserve of medical doctors and psychiatrists – it is the process of labelling a person's problems as a recognised medical disorder. It's very much an either–or system, as a person either gets the diagnosis or they don't, and there's no real in-between. There are four main problems with diagnosis. The first problem is that a person often qualifies for more than one diagnosis – this is called *co-morbidity*. The second problem is that diagnostic categories sometimes lack coherence – for example schizophrenia is a label that has been criticised because two individuals can receive a schizophrenia diagnosis but not have a single symptom in common (Bentall, 2003). The third problem is that diagnosis is based on a decision about whether someone is past a 'cut-off point' that distinguishes the healthy from the ill. Such cut-off points are essentially arbitrary. For example, a cut-off point for depression in the DSM-IV-TR is that a person must have experienced symptoms for more than two weeks (APA, 2000). This duration has no basis in science, but is purely a clinical guide. Horwitz and Wakefield (2007) in their book *The Loss of Sadness* suggest that depression may be over-diagnosed by as much as 20 per cent, as a result of ignoring the context of the feelings of sadness, and having inappropriate cut-off points for diagnosis. The fourth problem with diagnosis is that labels come with much stigma associated with them, and once someone has the diagnosis, it may be associated with them forever, even though they may fully recover.

Diagnosis is, however, not a necessity when it comes to mental ill health. A more individualised approach to assessing mental ill health is called *formulation*. A formulation is an *in-depth written summary* of a person's difficulties and distress, including symptoms, experiences, life events and sense of self (Johnstone, 2008). Such a formulation is devised by a therapist in conjunction with the patient, and is modified until it is considered accurate and comprehensive by both parties. A formulation includes any perceived links between life events, life changes and mental health problems, and thus is more intrinsically developmentally focused than diagnosis. Diagnosis and formulation are not mutually exclusive and can be conducted in conjunction.

Neurodegeneration is the decline in structure and function of the brain and nervous system, which leads to corresponding losses in cognitive, affective and behavioural capacities. Some degeneration in neural tissue is normal in persons in their later years, which is why individuals in very old age sometimes suffer from hearing or sight problems, or may have trouble remembering names or dealing with new problems (see Chapter 3). When decline occurs that is abnormally severe or abnormally early, then the person may be suffering from one of the disorders discussed further.

Alzheimer's disease

Alzheimer's disease is the most common form of dementia, accounting for over half of all cases (Di Carlo et al., 2002). The disorder was named after German psychiatrist Alois Alzheimer in 1906, after he clinically described the first case, but despite a century of research, scientists have yet to find a cure. The core symptom of Alzheimer's disease is an abnormal impairment in a person's memory, shown in a reduced ability to store new information and/or a diminished capacity to recall earlier memories (Baddeley et al., 1991; APA, 2000). In order for a diagnosis of Alzheimer's to be officially merited, memory impairment must occur alongside at least one other functional disturbance, either in language, motor activities, object recognition or goal setting/planning (these may well be a result of the memory disturbance).

A person who has Alzheimer's disease will show gradual but continuous decline in their memory and other cognitive abilities, and on average will live just six to seven years after diagnosis (Mölsä, Marttila & Rinne, 1995). Fewer than three per cent of individuals live more than 14 years after diagnosis and the disorder itself is the underlying cause of death in around two thirds of patients (Mölsä, Marttila & Rinne, 1986).

There are a number of 'neural markers' or brain-related changes that are indicative of having Alzheimer's disease. The most well-known of these at the cellular level are *amyloid plaques*, which are tangled masses of protein that are deposited between neurons, and *neurofibrillary tangles*, which are twisted fibres of protein found in brain cells (see Figure 11.3). The process by which proteins end up clustering into tangles and plaques is yet to be established (Wenk, 2003). A confounding finding is that some brains of deceased individuals have shown high levels of plaques and tangles, despite the person not exhibiting dementia or Alzheimer's whilst alive (Stern, 2006). Another neural marker is a decrease in the activity of 'cholinergic neurons' – cells in the hippocampus and cortex that employ acetylcholine as a neurotransmitter (Wenk, 2003). Brain imaging studies have also found markers of Alzheimer's disease at the level of the

Normal   Alzheimer's

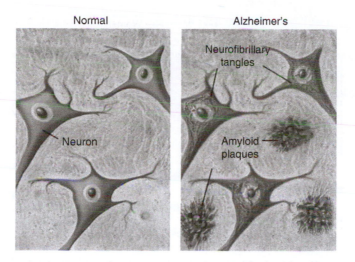

Figure 11.3   An illustration of neurofibrillary tangles and amyloid plaques in the brain of an Alzheimer's disease sufferer compared with a normal brain

Source: Illustration provided courtesy of Alzheimer's Disease Research, a programme of the American Health Assistance Foundation. Copyright © 2011, http://www.ahaf.org/alzheimers

whole brain; a recent meta-analysis of imaging studies concluded that progression from mild cognitive impairment to Alzheimer's is related to deterioration of activity in the hippocampus, amygdala, temporal lobe, and lower parietal lobe (Schroeter et al., 2009).

The risk of contracting Alzheimer's increases exponentially in old age. A person has a one per cent of contracting it when 60, and a 25 per cent risk when 85 (Ferri et al., 2006; Gao et al., 1998). The mean age of onset is approximately 65 (Huff et al., 1987). A robust prospective study that looked at Alzheimer's disease onset and age was conducted in the Netherlands as part of the 'Rotterdam Study' (Ruitenberg et al., 2001). Over the age of 55, 7000 persons in good health were followed over ten years, and out of those, 395 were diagnosed with dementia, of which 75 per cent were Alzheimer's disease diagnoses.

The incidence rates (per 1000 persons) by age group are shown in Figure 11.4. The incidence rate increases exponentially for both men and women up to the age of 85–98. But for those over the age of 90, the lines for men and women differ radically – while more women live into their 90s than men, their risk of getting Alzheimer's disease continues to increase, while for men it decreases. This same pattern has been observed in other studies (for example, Bermejo-Pareja et al., 2008; Ferri et al., 2006), and may be the result of a 'selective survival effect' – that is, men who are at risk of dementia are unlikely to survive into their nineties, so those that do, show a very low incidence (Ruitenberg et al., 2001). Women, on the other hand, live longer than men on average, and so

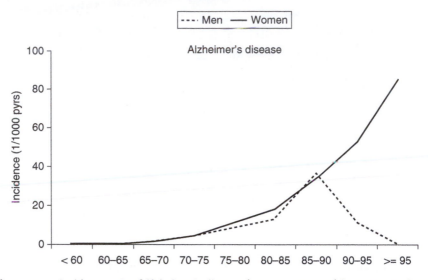

Figure 11.4 Incidence rate of Alzheimer's disease (per 1000 persons) in women and men
Source: Ruitenberg et al. (2001, p. 578). Copyright © 2001; reprinted with permission from Elsevier

those who have a vulnerability to dementia may live into their nineties and therefore show a continued increase of dementia incidence.

Biological, behavioural and environmental factors influence the likelihood of contracting Alzheimer's disease. Longitudinal research has found that people with raised systolic blood pressure or high cholesterol in midlife have a significantly higher risk of contracting Alzheimer's disease in later life than those with normal levels, even after controlling for age, body mass index, education, smoking and alcohol consumption (Kivipelto et al., 2001). Other research has found that the presence of high levels of a particular amino acid called *homocysteine* in blood plasma is a risk factor in contracting Alzheimer's and other forms of dementia (Seshadri et al., 2002). Homocysteine can be lowered by adhering to a diet that is high in folic acid.[4] Increasingly, diet is seen as a valid way of preventing the onset of Alzheimer's disease, as discussed in Box 11.6.

In terms of psychosocial factors, education seems to be protective of dementia in later life; a lower incidence of Alzheimer's and dementia in subjects with higher education has been observed in cohorts in France, Italy, Sweden, Finland, China and the USA (Di Carlo et al., 2002; Stern, 2006). Keeping mentally busy and active in old age has also been found to be beneficial – activities that have been found to be protective against dementia include travelling, knitting, gardening, socialising, intellectual

---

[4] For more information on homocysteine, go to: http://www.homocysteine.org.uk

activities such as reading or playing chess, and leisure activities such as dancing and playing musical instruments (Scarmeas et al., 2001; Wilson et al., 2002b; Zhang, Li & Zhang, 1999).

Box 11.6   Alternative perspectives

Is Vitamin B the answer to staving off Alzheimer's?

While writing this chapter, I went into the supermarket to buy a can of soup (there's not much time for cooking when you are writing a textbook), and the front page of a newspaper was dominated by the dramatic headline: *PILL TO BEAT ALZHEIMER'S*. I bought the paper to find out more. It went on to say that taking a Vitamin B pill each day could prevent 'millions' from contracting Alzheimer's or other forms of dementia. This media coverage, I later found out, was based on the results of a trial conducted at Oxford University in which 270 elderly persons with mild cognitive impairment took a pill with very high levels of vitamins B6, B9 and B12 (the B12 dose was 300 times higher than could be obtained by diet alone). This group was compared with a group of matched controls who either took a placebo or nothing, and it was found that the pill reduced brain shrinkage by up to 30 per cent, bolstered episodic memory, and made progression towards Alzheimer's less likely (de Jager et al., 2011). However, taking very high levels of vitamins is not without risk, and the authors of the study recommend that those considering the treatment should consult their doctor first.

Coping with the impact of Alzheimer's

Alzheimer's disease is a challenge for the patient and for the spouse or close family member who is caring for them. The experience of coping with Alzheimer's has been explored in qualitative research from the patient's and carer's perspective. Clare (2003) interviewed 12 individuals with early stage Alzheimer's disease. See Box 11.7 for example quotes from one participant in this study about the sources of stress that he experienced in the early stage of the disease. From an analysis of all the interviews, it was found that patients cope using two very different strategies: a *self-maintaining strategy* that attempts to normalise the situation and maintain continuity with the past, and a *self-adjusting strategy* that attempts to adapt oneself to the new difficulties associated with the progression of the disease. These two strategies relate to the primary and secondary control concepts discussed in Chapter 5.

A major qualitative cross-national study called EUROCARE has explored the experience of caregiving spouses for Alzheimer's sufferers in 14 countries in Europe. It found that the challenges and rewards of caring were described in similar terms across the countries (Murray et al., 1999). The three most commonly described difficulties were (1) the loss of companionship through the diminished quality of communication, (2) the loss of reciprocity as carers experience their partner's growing dependency and (3) the deterioration in the emotional state of their partner. These negatives were offset by continued mutual affection and a deep sense of moral obligation and fulfilling one's duty.

Box 11.7   Individual voices

The experience of early-stage Alzheimer's

Clare (2003) illustrated the sources of stress that people experience in early stage Alzheimer's. One participant, Iain, describes the following:

> Loss of authority and status

> Well, for years you see, when my boys were young, I've been an authority on something, you know, my status has gone ... you're no longer necessary. (p. 1024)

> Embarrassment

> Why I should find it so embarrassing I don't know ... I've always been fairly competent, useful in conversation, even sort of well thought of ... that is part of the contrast. (p. 1024)

> Suicidal ideation

> If I get really low sometimes ... I think well, you know, if you could snuff it, and I think, well I wouldn't mind actually, because I wouldn't have all this in front of me ... I think if I got to a stage where I was conscious enough, er, I would top myself ... I would like to think I was able to (a) recognise it and (b) have the courage to get off the earth. (p. 1024)

Vascular dementia

Vascular dementia is the second most common form of dementia after Alzheimer's disease. It is caused by chronically-reduced blood flow to the brain, often resulting from a stroke or series of strokes. Sometimes strokes are sufficiently small that each one is not noticed – these are called 'silent strokes'. Because vascular dementia can occur in different parts of the brain, it affects people in different ways but in all cases it leads to varying levels of cognitive impairment, as well as physical symptoms such as leg or arm weakness, tremors, balance problems, loss of bladder control and slurred speech. High blood pressure increases the risk of developing this form of dementia (Launer et al., 2000). The mean age of onset is later than that of the other dementias, at approximately 80 (Reitz et al., 2004).

Frontotemporal dementia

Frontotemporal dementia is a condition caused by degeneration of the frontal lobe of the brain, and in some cases the temporal lobe too. It typically appears earlier than Alzheimer's or vascular dementia, with an onset typically between the ages of 40 and 65, and a mean age of onset of approximately 53 (Ratnavalli et al., 2002). It is characterised by apathy, loss of inhibition and ritualistic behaviours. As it progresses, it gradually leads to immobility and loss of speech.

Parkinson's disease

In 1817, a London-based doctor called James Parkinson wrote 'An essay on the shaking palsy', in which he first described the clinical condition that was to later bear his name.[5] Parkinson's disease is a neurodegenerative disorder that is the second most common after Alzheimer's disease (de Lau & Breteler, 2006). It leads to progressive deterioration in the functioning of the central nervous system due to the loss of dopamine-producing neurons in the area just between the spinal cord and the brain called the midbrain. In addition to this, analysis of the midbrains of Parkinson's sufferers has found abnormal lumps of protein (similar to those found in Alzheimer's sufferers). In Parkinson's disease, these protein lumps are inside the nerve cell (unlike Alzheimer's, where the lumps are outside the cell) and are termed *Lewy bodies* (Gibb & Lees, 1988).

Parkinson's disease is principally characterised by symptoms of physical degeneration, in contrast to the dementias, which are characterised

---

[5] For a reprint of Parkinson's 1817 essay, see Parkinson (2002).

mainly by mental degeneration. The four principal clinical symptoms of Parkinson's can be grouped under the acronym TRAP (Jankovic, 2008):

- **T**remor at rest: tremors in the arms and hands, and also sometimes in legs, jaw, chin and lips.
- **R**igidity: increasing rigidity in the movement of limbs and joints, which may be associated with pain. A painful shoulder is often a common early sign of Parkinson's that may be mistaken for arthritis.
- **A**kinesia (also called bradykinesia): slowness of movement and performing activities, and difficulty with fine motor control (for example, buttoning, using utensils), freezing (a sudden inability to move) and a loss of facial expression.
- **P**ostural instability: unsteady standing or walking due to a decline in postural adjustment reflexes, which makes falling more likely.

Cognitive, emotional and behavioural problems are associated with advanced Parkinson's disease. As the disease progresses, sufferers are at an increased risk of contracting dementia, depression and obsessive-compulsive symptoms (Jankovic, 2008). Slowing of cognitive process and insomnia are also typical (Ondo et al., 2001; Sawamoto et al., 2007). There is currently no cure for Parkinson's disease, but medications can provide relief from some symptoms. The most widely used drug for treating the motor symptoms of Parkinson's is '*Levodopa*' or '*L-DOPA*', which increases the amount of dopamine in the brain, and temporarily improves the movement-related symptoms associated with the disease.

Age is the strongest predictor of Parkinson's onset. In a summary of the epidemiological evidence from a number of different countries, de Lau & Breteler (2006) conclude that Parkinson's is very rare before the age of 60 and that prevalence then increases with age, up to approximately 4 per cent prevalence in the highest age groups. See Figure 11.5 for a comparison of prevalence across age groups in different European countries – for all samples, risk increases exponentially after the age of 65. While the risk of contracting Parkinson's earlier in life is very low, it does occur in rare instances. The boxer Muhammad Ali famously started showing signs of Parkinson's from the age of 38, while the actor Michael J. Fox was diagnosed at the age of 30. Fox writes about his experience of early-onset Parkinson's in his memoir *Lucky Man* (Fox, 2003).

Risk factors and protective factors. It is common knowledge that coffee and cigarettes are not great for your health. Therefore you might be surprised to hear that smoking and caffeine consumption both *reduce* the risk of contracting Parkinson's (Costa, et al., 2010; de Lau & Breteler, 2006). Research suggests that the risk of contracting the disease is

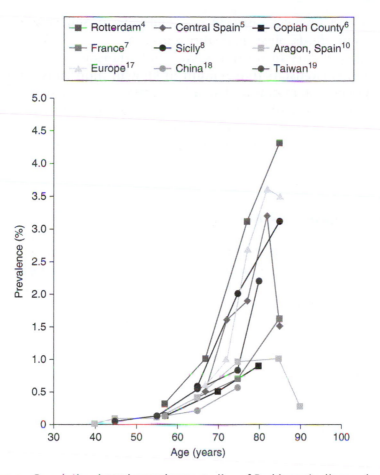

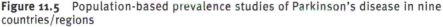

Figure 11.5 Population-based prevalence studies of Parkinson's disease in nine countries/regions

Source: de Lau and Breteler (2006, p. 526). Copyright © 2006; reprinted with permission from Elsevier.

30 per cent to 50 per cent less for smokers than non-smokers (Fratiglioni & Wang, 2000), and 50 per cent less when comparing coffee drinkers against non-coffee drinkers (Ross et al., 2006). It has been suggested that caffeine and nicotine may act as dopamine stimulants, and so counteract the decline in dopamine production evident in Parkinson's sufferers, but this is unproven as yet.

Dietary factors have also been explored in relation to the risk of contracting Parkinson's. In several major studies, a higher intake of polyunsaturated fatty acids (for example, Omega-3 and Omega-6) was associated with a significantly reduced risk of contracting the disease (Abbott et al., 2003; de Lau et al., 2005). Sources of Omega-3 include fish, seafood, soybean, rapeseed, eggs and walnuts. Sources of Omega-6 include nuts, seeds, olive oil, poultry and eggs.

Another dietary factor that relates to Parkinson's disease is dairy products. For reasons that remain unknown, high consumption of dairy products in midlife and later life increases the risk of contracting Parkinson's, particularly in men (H. Chen et al., 2002; 2007; Park et al., 2005). It has been speculated that this may be due to modern dairy products in industrialised countries being contaminated with neurotoxic chemicals (H. Chen et al., 2007).

Concluding comments

This chapter has collated evidence that suggests that the onset and prognosis of mental disorders are intricately related to adult development and life experiences. The onset of disorder occurs when personal vulnerabilities and life stressors overcome the resilience of a person's body and mind; that is the central premise of the diathesis-stress model. But what is it that makes some people more vulnerable than others, and others more tolerant and resilient? What is it that makes some people able to bounce back from adversity, while others crumble? Does maturity lessen diathesis? There are lots of questions that remain unanswered, but the current status of research points towards the view that adult development is an important contributing field to a comprehensive understanding of mental ill health.

Questions for you to reflect on

- Do you know anyone who has developed a mental disorder? The likelihood is that you do, as they are very common. Do you know what age the disorder first appeared, and whether it was related to stressful events in the person's life at the time?
- What are the pros and cons of using the Life Events and Difficulties Schedule to assess how life events relate to the onset of mental disorder?
- What are the difficulties associated with the diagnosis of mental disorder, and what are the alternatives?
- Why is it that some disorders tend to hit in early adulthood, and others tend to hit in late adulthood?

Summary points

- Developmental researchers are interested in how the onset and recovery from mental disorders relates to stressful and positive life events. The Bedford method for assessing life events and difficulties, innovated by

George Brown and Tirril Harris, has been the main method used for researching this.

- Mental disorders are diagnosed by psychiatrists and doctors, if a patient fits the criteria given in standardised diagnostic handbooks such as the DSM-IV and ICD-10. These handbooks are sometimes criticised for diagnosing mental disorder in too many individuals and therefore medicalising normal human experience.
- Anorexia nervosa and bulimia nervosa are the two most common eating disorders. They are both mainly diagnosed in women who are teenagers or young adults, and frequently occur as a result of relationship stress or family conflict. The experience of helplessness in the face of stress is strongly associated with the onset of anorexia.
- Postnatal depression is one of the few mental disorders that by definition occurs after a specified developmental life event – the birth of a child. It is a common phenomenon, with estimates suggesting that approximately one in six women will experience it to some degree.
- The onset of depression and anxiety relates to the occurrence of stressful life events, and recovery from these disorders is assisted by positive events.
- Bipolar disorder tends to be diagnosed in young adults, and its course is related to life events. Depressed episodes tend to be preceded by negative events, while manic episodes tend to be preceded by positive events.
- The course of schizophrenia is varied, and recovery from a schizophrenic life episode is normal and common. The onset of a schizophrenic episode is often preceded by stress, and recovery is most likely in conditions of low stress, minimal conflict and maximised relaxation.
- Neurodegenerative disorders tend to appear in later life, and their onset and prognosis is predicted by a variety of biological, behavioural and social factors.
- Alzheimer's disease is characterised by abnormal impairment of memory and by the presence of amyloid plaques in the brain. The risk for developing Alzheimer's increases exponentially after the age of 65.
- Vascular dementia is caused by strokes and other events that disrupt blood flow to the brain.
- Parkinson's disease is characterised principally by physical impairments such as tremor, rigidity in movement, slowness of movement and postural instability. It occurs as a result of neurodegeneration in the midbrain. Smoking and caffeine intake are protective factors.

Recommended reading

Brown, G. W. & Harris, T. O. (1978). *Social Origins of Depression: A Study of Psychiatric Disorder in Women*. London: Tavistock.

De Lau, L. M. & Breteler, M. M. B. (2006). Epidemiology of Parkinson's disease. *The Lancet Neurology*, 5, 525–535.

Finlay-Jones, R. & Brown, G. W. (1981). Types of stressful life event and the onset of anxiety and depressive disorders. *Psychological Medicine*, 11, 803–815.

Kessler, R. C., Berglund, P., Demler, O., Jin, R., Merikangas, K. R., Walters, E. E. (2005). Lifetime prevalence and age-of-onset distributions of DSM-IV disorders in the National Comorbidity Survey Replication. *Archives of General Psychiatry, 62,* 593–602.

Read, J., Perry, B. D., Moskowitz, A. & Connolly, J. (2001). The contribution of early traumatic events to schizophrenia in some patients: A traumagenic neurodevelopmental model. *Psychiatry, 64,* 319–345.

Ruitenberg, A., Ott, A., van Swieten, J. C., Hofman, A. & Breteler, M. M. B. (2001). Incidence of dementia: Does gender make a difference? *Neurobiology of Aging, 22,* 575–580.

Zuckerman, M. (1999). *Vulnerability to Psychopathology: A Biosocial Approach.* Washington, DC: American Psychological Association.

Recommended websites

Helpguide.org provides excellent summaries of the key features of most mental disorders. To find the information page for a particular disorder, go to the website and input the name of the disorder that you are looking for into the search box: www.helpguide.org

The Alzheimer's Society – provides information, support and training on Alzheimer's Disease: www.alzheimers.org.uk

Hearing Voices Network: www.hearing-voices.org

Maastrict approach to hearing voices: www.hearingvoicesmaastricht.eu/page10.php

12

Social Developments in Adulthood

One of the oldest human needs is having someone to wonder where you are when you don't come home at night.

Margaret Mead

Ethel had always been a sociable person. During her adult life she had maintained a happy marriage, organised regular lunches with close friends and had cared for her grandchildren for a day every week. These opportunities for social interaction had been a source of enjoyment, intimacy and support for many decades. But in her early seventies, her husband died of cancer and her son and his family moved to a distant part of the country for work. She wanted to continue seeing her friends, but this was becoming increasingly difficult because her health problems made driving or walking any distance difficult. As the months went by, she found herself increasingly socially isolated and reliant on her neighbours for help with shopping and basic tasks at home. When her son came to visit, they talked about her moving to a residential home or community. The more she thought about it, the more she thought it was the right way forward, as she hoped that it might bring back the regular social contact that she had enjoyed so much in the past but had lost over the last few years.

A person's developmental path through adulthood is defined by various key social developments, in addition to the biological and psychological changes covered in this book so far. These social changes include entering into romantic partnership, marriage or cohabitation, parenthood, changes in friend networks, grandparenthood and social disengagement later in life. This chapter covers all of these changes, which together comprise developments in the 'microsystem' and 'mesosystem' of human development (Bronfenbrenner, 1979). See Chapter 1 for more on these social systems.

Romantic attachment in adulthood

Attachment is a phenomenon that first appears in infancy, and is evidenced by the baby's efforts to maintain proximity to the mother/caregiver, distress upon separation from the mother/caregiver, and the tendency to use his or her caregiver as a place of refuge or 'safe haven' under experience of stress or emotional upset (Bretherton, 1992). Following this formative early relationship, attachment behaviours are shown in other close relationships across the lifespan (Ainsworth, 1985), for example with romantic partners in adulthood (Fraley & Shaver, 2000).

Romantic love relationships are attachment bonds that share many similarities with the infant-caregiver relationship, such as the desire to maintain proximity, distress at separation or the ending of a relationship, and using the partner as a 'secure base' in times of stress (Hazan & Shaver, 1987). The presence of 'baby talk' between romantic partners in adulthood has been said to be a sign of activating this attachment system that harks back to infancy (Bombar & Littig, 1996).

Research by Fraley and Shaver (2000) found that the development of clear-cut romantic attachment is a slow process – on average it takes two years to turn a close romantic relationship into a full-blown attachment. Once that attachment is formed, typical attachment behaviours will be observed, such as proximity maintenance, separation distress, safe haven and secure base behaviour (Fraley & Shaver, 2000). Eleanor Maccoby (1995) suggests that young childless couples show a peculiarly intense tendency towards proximity maintenance, compared with adult couples at other life stages.

Attachment security to caregivers in childhood has been found to relate to the quality of romantic attachments in adulthood (Grossman, Grossman & Waters, 2005; Waters et al., 2000). Bowlby (1973) explained this long-term link by recourse to the idea of internal working models – mental representations of how close relationships should function, which are forged during the infant–caregiver relationship, and continue to shape relationship expectations in adulthood. A positive working model derives from the presence of an available, responsive and reliable attachment figure in infancy and childhood (Bowlby, 1980).

Internal working models involve two parts; self and other (Bowlby, 1973). The *self* part consists of expectations as to whether 'I' am worthy of love and support, and am the sort of person whom other people would want to be close to and respond to. The *other* part is a set of expectations about whether attachment figures and romantic partners are to be relied upon, trusted and opened-up to. Working models operate mainly outside of conscious awareness, and are therefore difficult to consciously change (Bowlby, 1973). They are emotionally charged, so activating a working model leads to the experience of associated emotion that has its origins in childhood (Pietromonaco & Feldman-Barrett, 2000).

Although internal working models are stable over many decades, they can change as a response to some adult life events. For example, there is evidence that people, on average, show positive changes in attachment security during the early years of marriage (Davila, Karney & Bradbury, 1999), while events such as bereavement or divorce can lead to negative change (Waters et al., 2000).

Brennan, Clark and Shaver (1998) found that romantic attachment insecurity in adults can be organised on two dimensions. The first of these, *attachment anxiety*, is shown when a person is insecure about being rejected or abandoned by their partner. The second, *attachment avoidance*, is manifest when a person is uncomfortable with physical and emotional closeness, and so avoids romantic relationships in adult life (Chopik, Edelstein and Fraley, 2012). These two dimensions are assessed using the *Experiences in Close Relationship Scale* (Brennan, Clark & Shaver, 1998). Cross-sectional research shows that the tendency towards attachment anxiety declines with age, while the tendency towards attachment avoidance increases with age (Chopik, Edelstein & Fraley, 2012). See Figure 12.1 for a visual representation of these age differences, based on data gained from a sample of over 22,000 participants. These cross-sectional trends suggest that romantic relationships generally become less anxiety-provoking with age, but also typically become progressively less intimate (Chopik, Edelstein & Fraley, 2012).

One model of adult romantic attachment states that there are four adult attachment styles, based on positive and negative working models of self and others (Bartholomew & Horowitz, 1991). If a person has a positive working model of the self *and a positive working model of the other*, this provides a cognitive basis for **secure** romantic attachment. If a person has a positive model of the self, but a negative model of others, this leads to a **dismissive** style in which an adult will remain independent and thus protect themselves against disappointment. If, on the other hand, the model of self is negative but the model of others is positive, then a person becomes **preoccupied** with proving themselves to others and with gaining their acceptance. If both self and other models are negative, then a **fearful** style emerges where a person avoids and fears romantic commitment and intimacy.

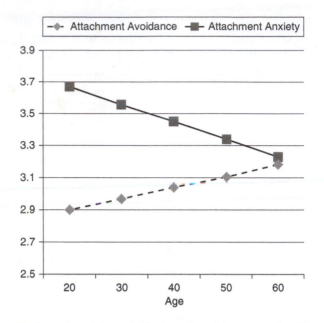

Figure 12.1 Attachment anxiety and attachment avoidance as a function of age

Note: Values for each age group are derived from a regression model.

Source: Data taken from Experience in Close Relationship Scale norms, http://internal.psychology. illinois.edu/~rcfraley/measures/ecrr.htm. Reproduced with permission from Chris Fraley.

Attachment to parents in adulthood

The Adult Attachment Interview (AAI) is a semi-structured interview devised by George, Kaplan and Main (1996) to study how adults describe their relationship with their parents. Interviews are rated for *coherence, clarity, feelings, acceptance,* and *recall* of a person's account of their relationship with their parents. Participants are then categorised into one of three adult-parent attachment types, described in Table 12.1. If a person has also experienced an unresolved trauma in relation to parental attachment, they are given an additional label of 'unresolved'.

AAI types have been shown to relate to a person's eventual attachment to their own children, suggesting that attachment quality across generations is related (Benoit & Parker, 1994; van Ijzendoorn, 1995). There is also evidence that AAI attachment types relate to mental health; the 'insecure-preoccupied' category (see Table 12.1) shows higher scores on a range of psychiatric symptom indices than the other two groups (Pianta, Egeland & Adam, 1996). A limitation with both the Adult Attachment Interview and the Experiences in Close Relationships Scale is that they are measuring self-reports of attachment, rather than inferring attachment based on observing behaviour with partner or parents, and so are really assessing a

Table 12.1   Adult attachment of parents: Three types

Adult-parent attachment style	Description of childhood attachment-related experiences
1. Secure-autonomous	• A coherent, consistent, clear and reasonable account of relationships with parents
	• Reasonable and succinct evaluations of parental care
	• Acceptance of both positive and negative aspects of childhood
2. Insecure-dismissing	• Excessively brief verbal accounts of child-parent relationships
	• Mixture of very positive statements and contradicting negative statements
	• Apparent problems with recall of parents in childhood
3. Insecure-preoccupied	• Confusion and anger shown in interview
	• Excessively long and embellished accounts belying an unhealthy and unresolved preoccupation with parental relationships

person's cognitive constructs of attachment, rather than attachment itself. This contrasts with attachment assessments with infants that are based on observing behaviour, such as the Strange Situation Experiment.

Box 12.1   Cross-cultural perspectives

Close relationships in America and Japan

A recent study compared a cross-section of children and adults in America and Japan to explore relationships at different points in the lifespan (Antonucci, Akiyama & Takahashi, 2004). Participants were asked to nominate 'close' or 'very close' relationships. There was a difference found in adolescence – Japanese adolescent females nominate five people in the close relationship category, but American adolescent females name just two. In adulthood there is much similarity in Japan and America – adults in both countries classify parents, children and spouse as 'very close' relationships while friends and siblings are typically rated as 'close'. In late adulthood, relationships to grandchildren are typically described as very close in both countries. The study suggests that in terms of close family and friend relationships, the similarities between America and Japan outweigh differences and the network of close relationships is similar in content and size across cultures.

Love

Attachment is a similar concept to love, but is different in important respects. According to Robert Sternberg (2000), love has three parts to it: *intimacy, passion* and *commitment*. Intimacy refers to *feelings* of closeness and connectedness, commitment is the *cognitive* decision and *behavioural* tendency to maintain proximity and a loving relationship, and passion refers to *physical* attraction, sexual desire and sexual activity. It is the passion part of love that distinguishes it from attachment, as an attachment system need not include passion.

In Sternberg's theory, these three components of love are represented as three parts of a triangle. The components can be combined in different ways to create seven kinds of love, as represented in Figure 12.2. If just intimacy is present, then a *liking* relationship results. If commitment is added to intimacy, but passion is still absent, this is *companionate love*. If just passion is present without commitment or intimacy, this is referred to as *infatuated love*, and if commitment is added to that, Sternberg refers to this as *fatuous love*. If commitment is present without any other element, this is called *empty love*, and if intimacy and passion together are present, but

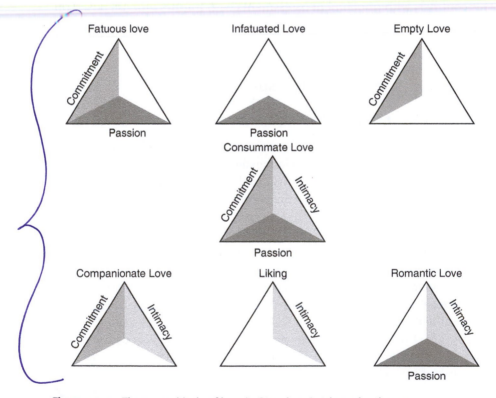

Figure 12.2   The seven kinds of love in Sternberg's triangular theory

without commitment the result is *romantic love*. Finally, if all three elements are present in a relationship, the ideal of *consummate love* is realised.

The perceived importance of each of the three different components of love depends on the duration of any relationship. Passion is rated as the most important of the components in short-term romantic relationships, but is less important than the other two in long-term ones (Sternberg, 2000). Commitment is the strongest predictor of long-term relationship satisfaction (Acker & Davis, 1992), and is the only one of the three to increase with age (Ahmetoglu, Swami & Chamorro-Premuzic, 2010). However, some theorists think that commitment is not one construct but two, as described in Box 12.2.

Box 12.2 Alternative perspectives

Is commitment one thing or two?

Sternberg includes *commitment* in his model of love but he doesn't differentiate between kinds of commitment. In contrast, Stanley and Markman (1992) distinguish two forms of commitment that keep relationships together over time; *personal dedication commitment*, and *constraint commitment*.

Personal dedication commitment is the intrinsic desire to maintain a relationship. According to Stanley and Markman's research, it emerges from the following:

a. A general trait-like tendency for commitment.
b. An explicit long-term plan for keeping the relationship together despite the inevitable ups and down of adult life.
c. A shared sense of identity as a couple.
d. Giving priority to the relationship relative to work and leisure.
e. An acceptance of the personal sacrifice involved in committed relationships.

Constraint commitment is the result of external pressures that make terminating a relationship a difficult or impossible prospect. These include the following:

a. The prospect of loss of money, possessions and resources.
b. Perceived social pressures to remain in a relationship, for example due to beliefs that preclude divorce or marital separation.

Box 12.2 Continued

c. Consideration of others who may suffer in the instance of a break-up, such as children.
d. A perceived lack of alternative available partners.

Constraint commitment is only perceived as negative by those in a relationship *if* personal dedication is lacking (Stanley & Markman, 1992). To put it another way, feeling obliged to remain in a relationship is no bad thing, as long as you *want* to remain in it too.

Marriage and cohabitation

In the UK, a person must be of age 16 or over to marry. Currently in the UK, the word 'marriage' may only be used to refer to a legally recognised union between a man and a woman, but in some European countries and in South Africa, same-sex marriage is now legal, as will be discussed later in the chapter. In the past, and still in traditional societies or religious subcultures, marriage is a moral or even legal requirement for sex and procreation. Nowadays, pre-marital sex is widely accepted (Harding & Jencks, 2003), but attitudes are still very variable across cultures, as discussed in Box 12.3.

Box 12.3 Cross-cultural perspectives

Attitudes to non-marital sex in 24 countries

In 1994, a study was conducted in 24 countries on attitudes to (a) sex before marriage, and (b) sex with other partners during marriage (Widimer, Treas & Newcomb, 1998). The most permissive countries with regards to sex before marriage were Germany, Sweden, Slovenia, Austria and the Czech Republic. In all of these countries, 5 per cent of individuals or fewer rated pre-marital sex as always wrong. This is in stark contrast with the Philippines, in which 60 per cent rated pre-marital sex as always wrong. Ireland was the second least permissive, with 35 per cent rating pre-marital sex as always wrong.

Box 12.3   Continued

Sex with other partners during marriage was more widely disapproved of, but again the frequencies vary substantially between countries. Bulgaria showed the most tolerance of extra-marital sex, with only 51 per cent rating it as always wrong. This was followed by West Germany, where 55 per cent rated extra-marital sex as always wrong. The Philippines was again the least permissive, with 88 per cent rating extra-marital sex is always wrong, followed by Ireland and the USA, both of which were at 80 per cent. Given how fast attitudes to marriage and sex are changing across the world, there is a question mark over the extent to which this data would be replicated if it was run again now, but it is an important cross-cultural snapshot nonetheless.

The popularity of marriage has been in steep decline for 40 years. Prior to the mid 1970s, marriage rates in the UK increased in line with population, but since then, despite a 10 per cent growth in the British population, annual marriage rates have declined by almost 50 per cent, as illustrated in Figure 12.3. Corresponding to the decline in marriage rates since the 1970s, the percentage of children born to unmarried couples increased from 12 per cent in 1980 to 47 per cent in 2009, according to the Office of National Statistics.[1]

Despite this decline, marriage still seems to be an aspiration for the majority of young people. A recent survey of 1200 girls between the ages of 11 and 21 in the UK showed differing views towards marriage. 77 per cent of girls stated an intention to get married in the future, but when asked if marriage is the 'best kind of relationship', only 42 per cent agreed. Just 29 per cent agreed that married couples make better parents than unmarried couples.[2] So while marriage remains the aspiration for the majority of young girls, there is a substantial proportion for whom marriage is not an active aspiration and for whom the benefits of marriage to family life are unclear.

Couples who are unmarried but live together are classified as *cohabiting*. In the 1960s and 1970s, cohabitation had a negative stigma attached to it, and was widely viewed as immoral (Haskey, 2001). But such attitudes

---

[1] http://www.ons.gov.uk/ons/rel/vsob1/birth-summary-tables–england-and-wales/2010/index.html

[2] Data taken from: http://girlsattitudes.girlguiding.org.uk

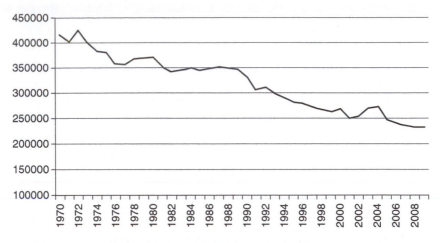

Figure 12.3   Annual number of marriages in England and Wales from 1970 to 2009
Source: Office of National Statistics, www.ons.gov.uk

have all but disappeared over the intervening decades – cohabitation prior
to marriage has changed from being a rare and unconventional option, to
being the choice of the majority. The statistics support this; less than 10 per
cent of couples cohabited prior to marriage in the 1970s, but 80 per cent
did in the year 2000 (Haskey, 2001). Cohabitation is projected to continue
increasing in prevalence given the decline in the popularity of marriage.

What makes for a good marriage or cohabiting relationship?

Research into what makes for a satisfying, enjoyable, successful marriage
has found that marital satisfaction depends on a variety of factors.
Similarity in values between partners is one predictor (Gaunt, 2006;
Rosen-Grandon, Myers & Hattie, 2004), and a strong sense of attachment
helps (Hirschberger et al., 2009). Once in a marriage, it's really all about
communication. If partners are honest and open about their feelings
(Hendrick, 1981), able to engage in constructive dialogue about problems in the relationship (Litzinger & Gordon, 2005) and able to control
any feelings of anger (Gottman & Krokoff, 1989), then they are likely
to remain satisfied. Sexual satisfaction can act to compensate for poor
communication (Litzinger & Gordon, 2005), but does not predict marital
satisfaction on its own. Perceived equality of input by spouses into the
marriage is also a key to success (Rusbult & Buunk, 1993).

These are just a few of the many robust quantitative predictors of a
good marriage. Another way of researching what promotes a successful
marriage is to ask those in long-term harmonious marriages their thoughts
on why their own marriage has lasted so long and been a positive relationship. Excerpts from such a qualitative study are given in Box 12.4.

Box 12.4   Individual voices

Happy, long-term marriages

Bachand and Caron (2001) interviewed 15 heterosexual couples who had been married for 38 years or more. Participants were asked, 'Why do you think that you have been married as long as you have?' and the most common response themes were: friendship, love, similar backgrounds/interests, commitment and freedom within the relationship to pursue own goals. Example responses from one male and one female participant are given next:

> When I got married I was absolutely sure that X was the person that I wanted to spend the rest of my life with. We had dated for several years, and although I knew when I met her that she was the one I would love forever, I wanted to be sure that we were compatible to spend the rest of our lives together. We were careful to get to know one another very well. Time is important. It's not everything, but for us it was important. We are best friends and lovers. We don't agree on many topics, but are willing to hear the other's point of view. Man, married 41 years (p. 112)

> We have a lot of respect for one another. We are best friends. We grew up together and have always been close. I always knew that I would marry X. He is careful of my feelings and I am of his. We have our own space and do not always have to see eye to eye. I enjoy our heated disputes on all sorts of topics. We truly love one another and that has kept us very happy. Woman, married 51 years (p. 113)

Parenthood and the family life-cycle

In the 1960s, the sociologist Evelyn M. Duvall set forth a developmental model of the family life-cycle. Based on her research with families and married couples, she postulated eight normative stages to family life in adulthood, which are described briefly in Table 12.2. For more on the transition to first-time parenthood (the shift from Stage 1 to 2 in the model), see Chapter 6.

The family life-cycle model is a useful framework for conceiving qualitative changes within the childrearing and family process. However, many families do not progress through these stages in an orderly or linear

Table 12.2   The family life-cycle model

No.	Stage name	Approximate time frame	Developmental Task	Key challenges for couple
1	Pairing/ Beginning family	Cohabiting without children	Developing a sustainable relationship	Challenges to commitment and maintenance of passion
2	Childbearing families	Oldest child 0–30 months	Managing the transition to parenthood	Navigating new role conflicts (for example, wife, mother, worker)
3	Families with preschool children	Oldest child 2.5–5 years old	Nurturing children who are living at home	Finding a balance between control of, and acceptance of, children
4	Families with school-age children	Oldest child 6–13 years old	Moving beyond parent role	Partial disengagement from primary caregiver role and exploration of alternative roles
5	Families with teenagers	Oldest child 13–20 years old	Managing children engaged in boundary-testing and peer-group focus	Control versus freedom Power struggle Social and sexual exploration
6	Families as 'launching ground'	First child gone to last child leaving home	Letting go of children, and providing a solid launching ground for independence	Managing loss of children in family home and daily structure surrounding that
7	Middle family years	Empty nest to retirement	Rediscovering the marital relationships	Radical change in home environment from childrearing years
8	Ageing family	Retirement to death of both spouses	Adapting to spending much more time together and coping with loss	Achieving serenity Bereavement Isolation/ dependency

Source: Based on Duvall (1970) and Neighbour (1985).

manner. The model is premised on the evolution of a two-parent family where parents remain together, but such a family is not as common as it used to be. Statistics show that half of all children will reside at some point in single parent households (as a result of both divorce and births outside of marriage), while one in seven children live with a parent and a step-parent (Amato, 2000). In sum, there has been a social shift away from lifelong marriage to 'one of serial marriage punctuated by periods of being single' (Amato, 2000, p. 1269). This means that for many, the family life-cycle is experienced in a more fragmentary manner. However, despite these changes in family life over recent decades, certain basic transitions that characterise phase shifts in the model have not changed – the birth of the first child, the child's first day at school, the child's shift into pubertal adolescence and children leaving the family home. All of these are still important qualitative changes in family life, whatever the residential or marital status of the parents.

Research has investigated the relationship between the course of family life and satisfaction with marriage and life. Belsky and Kelly (1995), followed 250 couples for four years over the transition to first-time parenthood, and found that 51 per cent reported decline in their marriage, 30 per cent reported no change and 19 per cent improved. These authors suggest that the prevalence of marital decline after the birth of the first child relates to a number of challenges that parenthood presents. Firstly, there is typically diminished interest in sex after childbirth that is compounded by fatigue and sleep deprivation. This decline only partially recovers at one year post-birth (Condon, Boyce & Corkindale, 2004). Secondly, the mutual activities that created a bond between partners before parenthood may be sidelined by the new baby, which may in turn lead to a loss of conversation topics and common interests. Thirdly, the baby may interrupt moments that may otherwise have provided a source of intimacy between a couple, leading to a growing sense of emotional distance and lost affection. Fourthly, there may be resentment felt if a partner is perceived to be not doing their fair share of childcare tasks (Ockenden, 2002). Given these potential points of conflict or difficulty in the months following the commencement of parenthood, couples are encouraged to discuss the topics listed in Box 12.5 *before* the birth of the child.

Box 12.5   Real-world applications

Key discussion areas for couples prior to the transition to parenthood

Based on a review of research and interventions on couples during the transition to parenthood, Brotherson (2007) lists key topics that couples should discuss *prior* to the birth of their first child, so that they have some provisional agreement on how they will address them:

1. Dividing housework and childcare
   a. Make a list of child care and housework tasks
   b. Identify and discuss expectations of who does what task

Box 12.5   Continued

2. Worries about money
    a. Discuss attitudes to managing money
    b. Take classes on budgeting and money management
3. Relationships difficulties
    a. Identify what changes will result from having the child
    b. Set aside at least 15–20 minutes every day to talk to each other
4. Balancing career and work issues
    a. Discuss and plan for family's future, in terms of who will work and how much
    b. Create shared family goals
5. Social activities
    a. Seek to give each other opportunities to 'get out'
    b. Plan for who might be able to help out with babysitting

In 1970, Rollins and Feldman gathered quantitative data on family satisfaction and marital satisfaction from 852 middle-class couples who represented all eight stages of the family life-cycle described in Table 12.2. Figure 12.4 shows several key findings from the study; the graph on the left shows a curvilinear relationship between satisfaction with family life and family life-cycle stage – the dip bottoms out in stage six, which is when children leave home. By Stage 8 (retirement), mean satisfaction levels for family and marriage return to the same level shown in Stages one and two. The right hand graph shows a similar curvilinear U-shaped relationship between family stage and marital satisfaction. Both men and women show a mean-level dip around stage four (the school-aged children stage), with women showing an initially higher level of satisfaction than men, but then men showing higher levels than women in later stages.

Rollins and Feldman's study was cross-sectional, therefore the pattern in Figure 12.4 may have been partially a product of cohort differences between the different age groups. For example, the higher satisfaction rates in later stages compared with the middle stages could be partially due to the fact that dissatisfied couples tend to divorce in midlife and so mean scores from older age groups reflect only those long-term marriages that are based on enduring satisfaction.

Longitudinal research on the relation between marital satisfaction and family life stage generally supports the findings of Rollins and Feldman

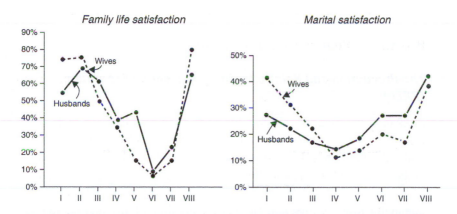

Figure 12.4   Family life satisfaction and marital satisfaction across the eight family life-cycle stages

Note: Family life satisfaction: Percentage of individuals at each stage of family cycle reporting that the present stage of family life is 'very satisfying'. Marital satisfaction: Percentage of individuals at each stage of family cycle reporting that their marriage was going well 'all the time'.

Source: Rollins and Feldman (1970, pp. 25–6). Copyright © Wiley-Blackwell Ltd. Reproduced with permission.

(1970). A mean-level longitudinal decline in marital satisfaction occurs at the onset of parenthood and continues into the phase of having adolescent children (Hirschberger et al., 2009; Lawrence et al., 2008). By the time the first child is 15, marital satisfaction has on average decreased by one standard deviation from initial pre-child levels (Hirschberger et al., 2009). This decline is then followed by a mean-level rise in marital satisfaction during the Phase 6 'launching ground' period when children leave home (Gorchoff, John & Helson, 2008; White & Edwards, 1990). This rise is maintained if regular contact is kept with non-resident children (White & Edwards, 1990). The increase in marital satisfaction in the 'empty nest' phase may be due to the lessening role conflicts that partners experience as parents, and the extra time and energy that is present to invest into the marriage and personal interests (Gorchoff, John & Helson, 2008).

While mean-level in marital satisfaction declines are observed through the most involved parenthood years of marriage, many individuals do maintain or increase marital satisfaction in this part of the family life-cycle (Vaillant & Vaillant, 1993). It is important to remember that a mean does not represent everybody, as discussed in Chapter 1. However, given that the maintenance of satisfaction in a marriage or civil partnership is a major challenge for many couples, intervention programmes have been designed to help improve marital satisfaction. See Box 12.6 for more on one such programme.

Box 12.6   Real-world application

The Prevention and Relationship Enhancement Programme (PREP)

PREP is a group-based relationship-enhancement intervention that has been used for over 30 years to enhance relationship satisfaction and reduce relationship-related conflict in couples. Typically, three to eight couples will attend five three-hour long sessions and be required to engage in homework between sessions. Topics covered include communication, conflict management, commitment, friendship, sensuality, problem-solving, and emotional supportiveness. Research has shown that the programme has beneficial effects that last at least five years (Markman et al., 1993). Example tasks from the programme include:

> *Friendship talk.* Spouses set aside a block of time outside PREP sessions to 'talk like friends'. During this talk, discussion of problems is prohibited, and partners are encouraged to talk about things that have nothing to do with their life as a couple, much as they would do with other friends.
> *The 'fun deck'.* The couple brainstorms a list of fun activities. Each partner then picks their three favourites from the list. The partners then exchange their favourite activities, and commit to doing at least one of each other's top activities in the following week.
>
> Clements et al. (1997)

Divorce

Divorce is the end point of an 'uncoupling' process in marriage, during which the spouses become more and more emotionally and physically estranged – this may lead to sleeping in separate beds and spending less time together (Amato, 2000; Kayser, 1993). There is often overt conflict during this phase of growing estrangement, which affects both adults and children in negative ways. In most cases, one spouse wants a divorce more than the other, and the one who initiates the divorce process will experience the process differently to the spouse who is less motivated to divorce. For example it has been found that the initiating spouse tends to experience relief after the marriage is legally terminated, while the non-initiating spouse will feel grief and distress (Amato, 2000).

To start divorce proceedings, according to UK law the spouse who wants the divorce or decides to initiate it must draft a *petition for divorce* (usually with the help of a divorce lawyer), which will then be sent to a divorce court. The Petition must state the grounds for divorce, by proving one of the following facts:

1. Adultery – the spouse has committed adultery.
2. Unreasonable behaviour – the spouse has behaved antisocially or neglectfully.
3. Desertion – the spouse has deserted the marriage for two years or more.
4. Two years' separation and consent – the spouses have lived apart for more than two years and both consent to the divorce.
5. Five years' separation – the spouses have lived separately for five years or more.

If there is a child in the marriage, then a Statement of Arrangement must be filed as part of the divorce application, which must state childcare arrangements and maintenance payments.[3]

Prior to the 1970s, marriages that ended in divorce were rare in the UK compared with now. Before 1970 fewer than 40,000 married couples a year divorced. In the 1970s, this number started rising dramatically, and rose to over 150,000 a year by the mid-1980s, and stayed around that rate until 2005. Since then, divorce numbers have been on a downward trend across the UK. This may be due to the increasing popularity of cohabitation in recent years, meaning that dysfunctional relationships are likely to be terminated before marriage, so avoiding legal divorce.

In England and Wales, there is clear relation between how long a marriage has lasted and divorce prevalence, as shown in Figure 12.5. The number of divorces rises sharply in the first five years of marriage, and peaks around six to seven years. The number of divorces then decreases for every year after the seventh year of marriage, showing that the longer a marriage lasts after the seventh year, the less likely it is to be terminated. In 2009, the mean age of divorce in the UK was 44 for men, and 41 for women. Remarriage after divorce is common, but second marriages have an even greater likelihood of ending in divorce than first marriages. Therefore, about one in six adults go through two or more divorces (Cherlin, 1992).

---

[3] For up-to-date information on UK divorce processes and law, go to http://www.direct.gov.uk/en/Governmentcitizensandrights/index.htm

Figure 12.5 Divorce numbers by duration of marriage in England and Wales in 2002
Source: Office of National Statistics, UK, www.ons.gov.uk

Effects of divorce on adults and children

The divorce process has been shown to impart stress and strain on the partners involved. Post-divorce stressors including losing contact with children (for the noncustodial parent), sole responsibility for childcare (for the custodial parent), conflict over child support, loss of emotional support, loss of financial support and moving into smaller or temporary accommodation (Amato, 2000). Cross-sectional research shows that compared with married individuals, divorced individuals have more health problems and a greater risk of mortality (Hemstrom, 1996; Zick & Smith, 1991). Longitudinal research has found that the transition from marriage to divorce is associated with an increase in symptoms of depression and increase in alcohol use (Aseltine & Kessler, 1993; Power, Rodgers & Hope, 1999).

Levels of stress vary over the course of the divorce process: for the initiating spouse, the highest level of stress in the divorce process occurs *before* the decision to divorce, and the lowest level is directly after the final separation (Kitson, 1992). For the non-initiating spouse, it is directly *after* the divorce that is the hardest, and the post-divorce adjustment period takes longer (Kitson, 1992). The negative effects of divorce tend to last on average 2 to 3 years (Booth & Amato, 1991; Lorenz et al., 1997). However the outcomes of divorce are not all bad – several studies show that some divorced individuals report increased levels of autonomy, control and personal growth (Kitson, 1992; Marks, 1996). Also, a qualitative study found that women report more self-confidence following divorce than before it (Riessmann, 1990). So divorce may, in some specific circumstances, be an opportunity for growth, particularly when the previous marriage was conflictual or abusive.

There are certainly very variable outcomes after divorce – For Kitson (1992) found that half of divorcees improved and recovered from a divorce in a matter of several years – much like any other developmental crisis (see Chapter 6) – while a quarter described a decline in wellbeing over time without a clear sense of recovery.

Just over half of divorces occur in couples who have children under the age of 18 (Amato, 2000). For children, divorce presents a variety of stressors, including exposure to parental conflict, confusion and uncertainty over the future, decline in contact with the noncustodial parent, feelings of blame in some instances, and changes in residence and school. Amato and Keith (1991) conducted a meta-analysis of 92 studies that compared the wellbeing of children of divorced parents and married parents. It was found that the children of divorced parents were rated lower on academic achievement, conduct, self-concept and self-confidence. However, the effect sizes of the differences between the groups were small. Other studies have found that the effect of divorce depends on the quality of the preceding marriage. Hanson (1999) and Jekielek (1998) found that offspring were better off after divorce if the preceding marriage was characterised by a high level of conflict.

Same-sex couples

Over the past 40 years, there has been a substantial change in the attitude of many societies towards acceptance and legal recognition of same-sex relationships and homosexuality. Lawrence Kurdek has conducted a series of studies on the nature and outcomes of cohabiting same-sex relationships, compared with heterosexual married couples (Kurdek, 1998; 2004; 2005). His findings show that there are similarities and differences. One similarity is in relationship satisfaction – the mean level for same-sex cohabiting couples and married heterosexual couples is the same, and it tends to decline over time for both kinds of couple.

In terms of household chores and tasks, gay and lesbian couples are more likely than heterosexual couples to engage equally in household tasks. Observational studies of conflict resolution suggest that same-sex couples use less dominant-submissive conflict resolution strategies, and engage in 'effective arguing' more. However what couples argue about is very similar in heterosexual and homosexual couples; finances, affection, sex, criticism, driving style and household tasks are the pre-eminent points of contention and conflict in both relationship types (Kurdek, 2005).

Civil partnerships

Since the 1990s, a number of countries have instituted legal recognition for same-sex couples. In some countries, such as Sweden, Norway, Iceland, Canada, Argentina, South Africa and Belgium, this is termed same-sex marriage. In other countries, such as the United Kingdom, France and Germany, same-sex couples are able to gain the status of civil partnership or civil union, which brings all the rights and responsibilities of marriage but does not legally permit the union to be called a marriage. In the UK, civil partnerships have been available since 2005. However, the world remains a deeply divided place on the acceptability of homosexuality, and in some countries such as Saudi Arabia, Sudan and Iran it is still punishable by life imprisonment or death.

Andersson et al. (2006) collated registry office data from Norway and Sweden, in order to analyse same-sex partnerships. Same-sex partnership data was gathered for 1993–2001 in Norway, and for 1995–2002 in Sweden. Over that time, across the two countries 2819 partnerships were commenced, compared with 470,000 heterosexual marriages. In both countries, the number of male partnerships was 60 per cent higher than that of female partnerships. It was found that substantial age differences in couples are more common in male partnerships. Around 35 per cent of all male partnerships involve an age difference or ten years or more, compared with 15 per cent of female partnerships and 9 per cent of heterosexual marriages. One quarter of lesbian relationships involve at least one partner who has been previously married to a man. Compared with heterosexual couples, those in homosexual partnerships have a higher educational attainment. Approximately 60 per cent have a degree, compared with 44 per cent of heterosexual marriages.

The same research showed that same-sex marriages shows that lesbian partnerships are 77 per cent more likely to lead to divorce than male gay partnerships. Both forms of homosexual partnership are more likely to lead to dissolution than heterosexual marriage, and are comparable with dissolution rates of heterosexual cohabitants (Andersson et al. 2006; Kurdek, 2005).

Friendship in adulthood

Adult friendship is a voluntary relationship that involves enjoyable social contact but usually no romantic physical intimacy (Goldman et al., 1981). A recognised factor behind friendship formation in adults is the tendency to make friends with people who are similar to you in some way, which is called homophily. This has been found to underpin friendship formation at all stages of life (Blieszner & Roberto, 2004; McPherson, Smith-Lovin & Cook, 2001). It can refer to similarity in demographic factors such as gender and socio-economic status, or psychological factors such as interests, beliefs and values. *Homophily* results from a variety of factors. Firstly, people who are in close proximity at home and at work are likely to have a similar income and social background, and more likely to become friends. Secondly, people become more similar to their friends over time as a result of emulating their habits or electing to engage in the same activities. This is referred to as *mutual socialisation* (Hartup & Stevens, 1997). While homophily predicts friendship, it is by no means an exclusive principle. In fact, compared with adolescents there is a greater tendency in adults to make friends with individuals of different ages and ethnicities (Galupo, 2009), and this tendency towards friendship diversity is positively correlated with post-formal thinking capacities (Galupo, Cartwright & Savage, 2010).

The function of friendship is the provision of trust, reciprocity, equality, exchange and support, for both men and women (Hartup & Stevens, 1997). The visible features of friendship vary by gender; women generally engage in gift-giving more than men, and disclose more intimate information to friends than men do. Men, on the other hand, place more value on instrumental help and the exchange of material or financial resources than women do (Adams, Blieszner & de Vries, 2000). If expectations of a friendship are violated by one party, a friendship is likely to be weakened or eventually ended (Giddens, 1991; Blieszner & Roberto, 2004).

In adulthood, individuals spend considerably less time with their friends than adolescents do. While adolescents spend around 30 per cent of their time with friends, adults spend on average only 10 per cent of their time (Larson & Bradney, 1988). However the structure of friendship becomes more elaborate in adulthood and includes more forms of exchange, such as letters, gifts, doing favours and helping out when ill or injured (Hartup & Stevens, 1997).

In early adulthood, new opportunities for friendship creation are presented as a result of commencing a career and changes in residence, but at the same time in the majority there is a clear shift *away* from friends *towards* partner and children (Antonucci, Akiyama & Takahashi,

2004). Friendship is appraised as more valuable by adults who do not have a partner or spouse, than by those that do (Carbery & Buhrmester, 1998; Hartup & Stevens, 1997). At the beginning of life as a married or cohabiting couple, a new kind of friendship emerges in the form of *couple friends*. These are friends with whom social exchanges are always at the level of the couple rather than one-to-one. This new kind of friendship provides opportunities for cross-sex friendships, when one-to-one cross-sex relationships can be problematic in a marriage (Bendtschneider & Duck, 1993).

As young adults move into midlife, there is less time available for friends, due to the competing demands of work and family. Figure 12.6 shows the relation between close friend numbers and family life-stage – it is apparent from the graphs that numbers decrease slightly in later stages of family life, but actually increase slightly in the case of divorce. Midlife is the peak era of occupational and civic responsibilities for most people, and friendship network size decreases by over a third compared with young adults (Adams & Blieszner, 1996; Lowenthal, Thurnher & Chiriboga, 1975). After retirement, social networks tend to increase in size relative to middle adulthood, as individuals have renewed time for socialising (Lowenthal, Thurnher & Chiriboga, 1975). Indeed friendship is arguably as important to retirement as it is to adolescence – retirees without friends have far lower life satisfaction than those that do (Robinson, Demetre & Corney, 2010).

As a person makes the transition from retirement (the Third Age of life) to age-related dependency (the Fourth Age of life),[4] network size declines again as individuals reduce contact frequency with casual friends (Hatch & Bulcroft, 1992). There are several theories that predict reduced social network size in older persons. One of these, socio-emotional selectivity theory, was discussed in Chapter 4, and the other, disengagement theory, is discussed towards the end of this chapter. Close friends play an essential role in the final decades of life, particularly when a spouse or partner is widowed or lacks immediate family help, and is not living in assisted accommodation (Adams & Blieszner, 1995; Ferraro, Mutran & Barresi, 1984; Litwak, 1985). Indeed, there is evidence to suggest that the typical number of very close friendships changes little across the whole life span (Dickens & Perlman, 1981; Fung, Carstensen & Lang, 2001; Lang & Carstensen, 1994).

Friendlessness is the phenomenon of having no friendship network at all – this is prevalent in persons with mental health problems or who are vulnerable due to disability, and is also prevalent in older age groups

---

[4] See Chapter 6 for more on these psychosocial life stages.

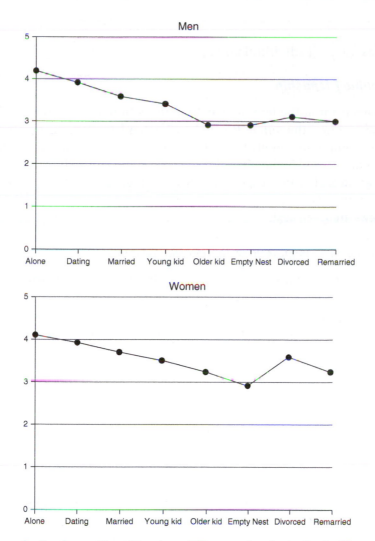

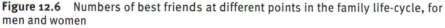

Figure 12.6   Numbers of best friends at different points in the family life-cycle, for men and women

Source: Kalmijn (2003, p. 242). Copyright © 2003; reprinted with permission from Elsevier.

(Hartup & Stevens, 1999). American research shows that individuals over the age of 65 are over twice as likely as younger adults to report having 'no friends' (Fischer & Phillips, 1982); while severe loneliness is reported by approximately 7 per cent of persons over the age of 65 in the UK (Victor et al., 2005). Being widowed and being in a marriage which lacks intimacy both predict higher levels of loneliness in old age (Victor et al., 2005).

Box 12.7   Individual voices

Online friendship

The advent of the Internet has brought with it a new category of friendship – the *online friendship*. Such a friendship is created and maintained purely through computer-mediated interactions. Henderson and Gilding (2004) conducted interviews with 17 Internet users to explore their experiences of online friendships and submitted them to a qualitative analysis. Themes and extracts from the interviews are given next.

Enhanced authentic self-expression and risk-taking

> Online it's different, I don't care about what people think of what I say, because I can just turn off the computer. I find myself taking more risks online, saying things I might not normally say in real life ... Don't get me wrong, I don't play at being someone that I'm not. It's just, online, I'm *me* in a much more pronounced way. (p. 499)

A special source of support

> The people I am close to online understand me in a way that my friends in real life don't. We share something very special. We talk about our experiences, and support each other. I knew there had to be other people out there that felt the way I do. Through various chatrooms on the Internet, I've not only found some great people, but I'm learning to trust them as well. (p. 498)

A different kind of trust

> I don't know if anyone can build that deep, no-holds-barred trust online. How am I going to spill my guts to the Dragon Master or the Elf King? Those people are not there because they care about what's going on in my 'real world' life. They are there because they want to escape that sort of life for a few hours. At the same time, I *would say* I trust them, in a different way perhaps. It's still trust to me when I know I can log off and no one is going to make moves to blow up my castle. (p. 500)

Box 12.7 Continued

Intimacy through words and screens

Text is the only medium you have online, and typing to each other, and revealing information about yourself, is about the only way you can get close to someone. In real life, you *can* just hang out with the person, and not say a word. Spending time together, and sharing experiences in real life brings you closer. Online, you share words. (emphasis in original; p. 500)

Grandparenthood

Becoming a grandparent is a transition that people adapt to in varying ways. Some enjoy spending regular time with their grandchildren, while others remain formal and distant, only being seen at family gatherings (Neugarten & Weinstein, 1964). An analysis of the 1998 British Social Attitudes survey found that 30 per cent of grandparents see their grandchildren every week, while at the other end of the spectrum, 32 per cent said they saw their grandchildren less than once a month (Dench & Ogg, 2002). What is it that determines the level of grandparent involvement? You might think it is about personality, but its more to do with geography; of grandparents who live within 15 minutes of a grandchild, 74 per cent reported weekly contact, for those who live between 15 minutes and an hour away, 37 per cent have weekly contact, and of those who live more than an hour away, none have weekly contact (Dench & Ogg, 2002). Grandparents and grandchildren also tend to have more frequent contact if the quality of the parent-grandparent relationship is good (Barnett & Hyde, 2001; Mueller & Elder, 2003; Oppelaar & Dykstra, 2004).

The grandparent 'career'

Despite the variability of the grandparent role, there is a normative sequence that it tends to take. Due to increases in life expectancy, grandparenting now evolves over longer timeframes than ever before – most people will be a grandparent for about a third of their lifespan (Silverstein & Marenco, 2001; Smith, 2005). Over this time the role will change as both grandparents and grandchildren get older, and the resulting *grandparent career* can be described as a sequence of three phases (Oppelaar & Dykstra, 2004):

Phase 1 runs from birth of the grandchild up to adolescence. It is the period of greatest grandparent involvement, and provision of childcare and/or financial assistance may often be a feature (Clarke & Roberts, 2003; Gray, 2005). This phase is typically the most rewarding period of grandparenthood for the majority (Silverstein & Marenco, 2001).

Phase 2 commences when an adolescent grandchild starts to distance themselves from family more generally. There is a gradual decline in contact frequency with grandparents over the course of this phase (Silverstein & Marenco, 2001). *If* a close relationship is maintained through these years, it is ideally characterised by reciprocity; grandchildren help out with chores and computers, while grandparents help with homework and hobbies. Adolescents who maintain a good relationship with grandparents at this time are generally more pro-social and have fewer emotional problems than those who do not (Glaser et al., 2010).

Phase 3 starts when grandchildren become adults and start families themselves. By this phase, contact between grandparents and grandchildren is generally limited to holidays, family celebrations and birthdays. Research in the Netherlands has found that face-to-face contact between young adults and grandparents is fairly low, approximately 5 to 10 times a year on average (Geurts et al., 2009).

Sources of satisfaction and stress in the grandparent role

Being a grandparent is a source of satisfaction, purpose, meaning and happiness for the majority who have grandchildren (Jendrek, 1993; Neugarten & Weinstein, 1964). 90 per cent of British grandparents agree or strongly agree with the statement that 'grandparenting is a very rewarding aspect of my life' (Dench & Ogg, 2002), while Clarke and Roberts (2003) found that 55 per cent of grandparents said that it contributed 'enormously' to their quality of life; 31 per cent said it contributed 'a lot'; and only 4 per cent 'not at all'. Although satisfaction levels with grandparenting are generally high, enjoyment of the grandparent role does depend on a person's age; those who become grandparents in midlife find it less rewarding than those who become grandparents after midlife (Burton & Bengtson, 1985).

Kivnick (1982; 1983) investigated the sources of meaning that grandparenthood brings using interviews and a structured questionnaire. Five sources of meaning were found. The first is *centrality*, which refers to the desire to see grandchildren and their central place in a grandparent's priorities – this motivation provides meaning for the present and the future. This relates to the second theme of *indulgence*; the sense of delight gained from spoiling grandchildren that in turn reinforces a personal sense of generosity and lenience. The third source of meaning is feeling like a *valued elder*; the sense of being a grandchild's connection to history and valued advice. The fourth is a sense of *immortality*, which is a sensed continuity of existence through the family line that grandchildren provide. The fifth and final one is *reinvolvement with the personal past*, which relates to the way that grandchildren lead to positive reflections of grandparents' own childhood, thus helping them to review and make sense of the past (see Chapter 7 for more on the 'life review'). All of these five features of the grandchild–grandparent relationship impart a sense of meaning to the grandparent's life. Box 12.8 shows excerpts of individual grandparents and grandchildren's responses from a more recent qualitative study on this topic (Kemp, 2005).

Box 12.8   Individual voices

The grandparent-grandchild relation: a link across time and history

Kemp (2005) interviewed 18 grandparents over the age of 65 as well as 19 young adult grandchildren, in order to explore the personal meanings of the relationship. A salient theme found across the interviews was 'linkages through time'. This referred to the fact that for grandparents, grandchildren symbolically represent the future, while for grandchildren, their grandparents represent the past. By maintaining the grandparent-grandchild relationship, a bond across time and history is forged, creating continuity between generations. Example quotes illustrating this theme are given next.

> Adult grandchildren and great-grandchildren are a form of eternal life ... it certainly gives me a feeling of continuity ... I think it's through the sense of your own part of history. Grandfather, 88 (p. 167)

> They keep you young with their coming and telling what they've been doing ... It gives you an ongoing view of something, instead of 'Oh well, I'm getting near the end of my life and what is there to show for it?' Grandmother, 78 (p. 168)

> **Box 12.8   Continued**
>
> I would say that there is something special about the grandparent–adult grandchild relationship. It is very important for knowing your roots and for family history and for knowing where you came from. I think that's one of the most important things, because that's what I have found. It's like a key. Grandson, 29 (p. 168)
>
> You get a sense of history. It's who you are. You really do. And then, as you learn more about their parents, where they came from, you can appreciate maybe why they are stubborn about some of the things they are, or where they get some of their ideas from, that sort of thing. Granddaughter, 32 (p. 168)

Research suggests there is widespread desire among grandparents to spend more time with their grandchildren; a nationwide UK study found that 40 per cent of grandparents would like more interaction, while only 1 per cent wanted less contact (Clarke & Roberts, 2003). Spending time with grandchildren is made more difficult when individuals reach very old age – health problems and mobility difficulties may mean that they are less able to participate in activities with the grandchildren than they would like (Smith, 2005).

While grandparenting can bring a sense of meaning and satisfaction, there are also possible sources of distress in the role. If grandparents experience a permanent loss of contact with grandchildren due to parental divorce or if the parents move to another country, this may be experienced as a traumatic loss, with similar symptoms to bereavement (Drew & Smith, 2002). Drew and Silverstein (2007) followed 442 grandparents longitudinally for 15 years and found that those who had lost contact with their grandchildren showed greater levels of depression than other grandparents, before returning to normal after three years.

Grandparents as a source of support and childcare

Over the past 40 years, the increase of women in the workforce, of part-time work, and of single-parent families has led to a greater need for flexible and reliable childcare. Filling this growing need, grandparents are playing an increasingly prominent role (Glaser et al., 2010; Gray, 2005). In the UK, approximately 25 per cent of children now receive regular weekly care from grandparents (Gray, 2005), while 50 per cent provide occasional care (Hank & Buber, 2008). This number is greater in families where the mother is working part-time or full-time (Smith,

2005). Extent of grandparental involvement in childcare also varies across different countries, as discussed in Box 12.9. In all countries it is the grandmother who is most involved in the care role, and the grandfather's participation is generally conditional on the grandmothers' involvement. Grandparents on the mother's side are typically involved more than those on the father's side (Dench & Ogg, 2002).

Box 12.9   Cross-cultural perspectives

Differences across European countries in prevalence of grandparent childcare

Hank & Buber (2008) analysed data from the 2004 Survey of Health, Ageing, and Retirement in Europe (SHARE). This was gathered from 22,000 individuals aged 50 or older across Austria, Denmark, France, Greece, Germany, Italy, the Netherlands, Sweden, Switzerland, and Spain. In all countries, grandmothers were more involved in childcare than grandfathers, but other than that, grandparental involvement differs widely across these ten countries.

Perceived norms relating to grandparent and grandchildren are highly cross-culturally variable. For example, in Greece approximately 90 per cent of grandparents see it as their duty to help parents with childcare, while in the Netherlands and Denmark, only 40 per cent agree that they have a duty to help. Corresponding to these different norms, frequency of actual childcare differs. The countries that showed the highest frequency of *weekly* grandparent childcare were Italy and Greece, with over 40 per cent of grandmothers providing weekly childcare, and over 35 per cent of grandfathers. Spain, Austria, Switzerland and Germany were similar; between 30 per cent and 35 per cent of grandmothers provided weekly childcare. Sweden and Denmark showed the lowest prevalence of grandparent childcare; just 18–22 per cent of grandparents provided weekly childcare.

However, when respondents were asked if they had provided any childcare to their grandchildren over the last year or so, the national pattern is to a large degree reversed, with Denmark and the Netherlands showing highest prevalence rates (65–75 per cent of grandmothers), and Spain and Italy showing lowest prevalence (just over 50 per cent). Therefore in some countries such as Italy, grandparents are either very involved or not at all, while in other countries such as Denmark, most grandparents are involved in sporadic, infrequent care.

When exposed to a parental divorce, children are likely to experience high levels of disruption and stress. Grandparents can be an important source of support during this time; they can provide stability, support, and financial assistance through the transition (Dench & Ogg, 2002). Correspondingly, British research shows that maternal grandparents spend more time with grandchildren if the parents are divorced than if they are still together (Dench & Ogg, 2002). In a five-year longitudinal study of separated families, closeness to maternal grandparents predicted grandchild adjustment through the divorce, for the mother typically has custody of the children so her parents can provide all kinds of help (Bridges et al., 2007). On the other hand, grandparents of the non-custodial parent experience a marked decrease in contact after divorce (Glaser et al., 2010).

Eventually, the provision of care may reverse direction in the grandparent–grandchild relationship. As grandparents move into their eighties or beyond, it becomes increasingly likely that they themselves will need to be recipients of care (Spitze & Logan, 1992). However it is still rare that the grandchildren provide such care; in a 2004 survey of 10 European nations, it was found that just 1 per cent of older Europeans receive financial support from grandchildren, and 4 per cent receive personal care or practical help from them (Attias-Donfut, Ogg & Wolff, 2005).

Box 12.10   Alternative perspectives

Custodial grandparents

In rare cases, grandparents act as surrogate parents with primary childcare responsibility – they are referred to as *custodial grandparents*, and a household that contains just grandparents and grandchildren is termed a *skipped-generation household*. Research shows that such arrangements are becoming more prevalent, and that the most common reasons for custodial grandparents are a parents' drug or alcohol abuse or mental health problems (Hayslip Jr. & Kaminski, 2005). Custodial grandparenting is a very different role from standard grandparenting, and Jendrek (1993) reported that custodial grandparents report a lack of privacy, decreased contact with friends and less time for leisure and their own personal needs. As a result they have lower average satisfaction ratings than non-custodial grandparents (Hayslip et al., 1998). In a study of 129 skipped-generation families in America, higher levels of stress were particularly associated with young grandparent age, grandchildren with physical and psychological problems and the presence of low family cohesion (Sands & Goldberg-Glen, 2000).

Disengagement theory and social relationships in old age

Disengagement theory was developed by Elaine Cumming and William Henry in the early 1960s (Cumming & Henry, 1961). The theory proposes that as individuals enter old age and their energy and mobility decreases, the size of their social networks shrink, frequency of contact with friends decreases, and they gradually withdraw from active participation in social institutions. The theory is supported by cross-sectional data that shows that over the age of 60, increasing age is related to fewer daily interactions with others and taking on fewer roles relative to younger groups (Cumming et al., 1960; van Tilburg, 1998). However, critics have pointed out that approximately 20–30 per cent of older individuals do not disengage from social life but rather continue to have extensive social interaction in their seventies and eighties (Hochschild, 1975). While these people may be in the minority, they show that disengagement is not inevitable.

Wenger (1997) has researched social networks in old age, and has found that individual differences are more salient than any general tendency towards disengagement. Five distinguishable kinds of social support networks emerged from her analysis:

1. *Locally integrated support network*: This is the most common and most robust support network. Help is provided by friends, community groups, local family and neighbours.
2. *Wider-community focused support network*: This is principally based on help from friends, community groups and neighbours, without much family support.
3. *Local family-dependent support network*: The person with this network is heavily reliant on local family and there is some contact with neighbours. There is a low level of community group involvement and friendship networking.
4. *Local self-contained support network*: This person is primarily reliant on neighbours, due to a private and self-contained life-style that involves little in the way of social commitments.
5. *Private restricted support network*: There is an absence of local family, no local informal support and little contact with friends. Occasional contact from family who live at a distance.

The quality of life in the period of elderly dependency substantially depends on which of these social networks are present. Types 4 and 5 are most likely to lead to social isolation and loneliness, and research shows that people in these two social environments are more likely to be admitted to residential care in the absence of dementia or other mental illness than those older adults who have more comprehensive social networks (Wenger,

1997). Is there anything that can be done to lessen the chance of loneliness in older adults? The Internet may be one solution; a study has found that providing older adults with access to and training in Internet and e-mail reported reduced loneliness (White et al., 1999). Residential communities are another popular strategy for enhancing social contact and creating new friendships in later life, and are discussed in Chapter 6.

Concluding comments

It is important that you realise that you are living through a time of social revolution. The revolution to which I am referring started in the early 1970s and has led to changes in almost all cultural norms and practices in Western countries surrounding relationships, sex, marriage, gender roles and family. Conventions that endured for centuries if not millennia have been summarily questioned and overthrown in 40 years. The outcome of the revolution has been far less marriage, more divorce, greater acceptance of and rights for same-sex couples, more cohabitation before marriage, more single parents and more children born to unmarried couples. In the next chapter we will continue discussing the revolution in terms of gender balance and equality in the workplace. The course of adulthood has been re-sculpted by these dramatic cultural changes, which is a stark reminder of the profound social influences on the course of individual development.

Questions for you to reflect on

- If you reflect on the romantic relationships that you have had in the past, can you match each relationship to the love types described in Figure 12.2? You may well have experienced more than one kind.
- What are the key differences between an attachment and a friendship?
- What do you think are the relative advantages and disadvantages of cohabitation and marriage?

Summary points

- Friends, romantic partners, spouses, children, parents and grandparents constitute the 'mesosystem' of development.
- Friendship is a voluntary relationship based on mutual support and exchange without physical intimacy. It is often initiated based on the principle of homophily – becoming friends with people who are psychologically and demographically similar to you.
- Adolescents spend more time with friends than do adults, often in the context of 'cliques' – small groups of friends based around similar interests

and activities. Single adults spend more time with friends than do those who are married or in long-term cohabiting relationships.

- Couple friends are formed and maintained at the level of the married or cohabiting dyad.
- Adults show attachment behaviours towards romantic partners to differing degrees. Normatively, attachment anxiety decreases with age, while attachment avoidance increases slightly.
- The Adult Attachment Interview categorises adult relationship to parents into three types: *secure-autonomous*, *insecure-dismissing*, and *insecure-preoccupied*.
- Love is ideally comprised of commitment, emotional intimacy and physical passion, according to the triangular theory of love depicted in Figure 12.2. Commitment is the strongest predictor of long-term successful relationships.
- Marriage is a cultural institution which creates a legally binding contract between two persons, the dissolution of which is a legal matter and is referred to as divorce. It has declined in popularity considerably over the past 40 years. At the same time cohabitation of unmarried couples has increased in popularity.
- Same-sex couples may get married in some countries (for example, Norway). In the UK, same-sex couples are entitled to civil partnership, which has the same rights as married couples.
- The family life-cycle posits eight stages through which a childbearing couple pass as they and their children develop. The stages move from childless, to the onset of parenthood, to the onset of schooling, to the onset of the child's adolescence, to children leaving home and the couple regaining an identity as a couple, rather than as a family.
- Divorce has proven to have negative stress-related effects on both adults and children involved, although in marriages defined by high levels of conflict, divorce can bring psychological benefits.
- When grandchildren are young, grandparents are often involved in childcare. This is seen as a social norm in some countries but not others. In the UK, grandparent care is becoming more popular and more common.
- Disengagement theory states that as a person reaches old age, a reduction in the size of their social network occurs as a result of disengaging from social roles and peripheral friendships.

Recommended reading

Amato, P. R. (2000). The consequences of divorce for adults and children. *Journal of Marriage and Family*, 62, 1269–1287.

Cumming, E., Dean, L. R., Newell, D. S. & McCaffrey, I. (1960). Disengagement – A tentative theory of aging. *Sociometry*, 23, 23–35.

Fraley, R. C. & Shaver, P. R. (2000). Adult romantic attachment: Theoretical developments, emerging controversies, and unanswered questions. *Review of General Psychology*, 4, 132–154.

Hartup, W. W. & Stevens, N. (1997). Friendships and adaptation in the life course. *Psychological Bulletin*, 121, 355–370.

Markman, H. J., Renick, M. J., Floyd, F. J., Stanley, S. M. & Clements, M. (1993). Preventing marital distress through communication and conflict management training: A 4-and 5-year follow-up. *Journal of Consulting and Clinical Psychology*, 61, 70–77.

Oppelaar, J. & Dykstra, P. A. (2004). Contacts between grandparents and grandchildren. *Netherlands' Journal of Social Sciences*, 40, 91–113.

Rollins, B. C. & Feldman, H. (1970). Marital satisfaction over the family life cycle. *Journal of Marriage and the Family*, 32, 20–28.

Sternberg, R. J. (2000). *Cupid's Arrow: The Course of Love through Time*. New York: Cambridge University Press.

Recommended website

Publications on grandparenting: http://www.grandparentsplus.org.uk/reports-and-publications

13

Career Development and Retirement

In the best instances the person and his job fit together and belong together perfectly, like a key and a lock.

Abraham Maslow (1974, p. 47)

Richard recalled a moment in his mid-thirties when he was looking down across the lights of London one evening from his office on the 15th floor of an office block, and he thought to himself, 'This is it ... I've made it!' He was a high-flying marketing executive, with all the trappings of success, and had worked hard to get there. However, soon after that moment, a nagging sensation that something was absent in his career started to grow and would not go away. After taking a month off work, he realised what was missing – his work did not reflect his own values and interests and it was purely a means to an end. After a time of personal reflection, he started to train as a counsellor, but soon realised that that was not for him either and pulled out of the training programme. After a year or so of freelance work and further thinking, he found a job in a charity, helping run their marketing and communications. He still wasn't certain that this was what he wanted for the rest of his career, but it gave him a strong sense of satisfaction and allowed him to use his skills in a setting that reflected his personal values.

A career is about a lot more than making money. It is about identity, finding a place in the adult world, independence, maturity and personal growth (Warr, 1987). The idea of a career stretches beyond the workplace, and for some a career is principally forged within the home as parent or carer (Super, 1980). Although the work of a stay-at-home mother or father receives less social recognition than paid work, it is increasingly appreciated as a career path. All careers eventually come to an end, but retirement is only the conclusion of a career in some ways, while in other ways a career continues beyond retirement in unpaid roles or grandparental care duties (Davis, 2003). This chapter is an overview of the key elements of the career journey, starting with the process of deciding upon which career to pursue, then moving on to career change, unemployment, balancing work and home life and finally the nature and challenges of retirement.

Career decision-making

Selecting a career to devote one's adult life to from the thousands available is a beguiling prospect, and in reality is full of compromises, trial-and-error and false starts. Andreas Hirschi and Damian Lage (2007) reviewed the various theories of the career decision-making process and concluded that there are six agreed stages to the process. These are:

1. *Becoming concerned*: Developing a long-term concern for, and interest in, the nature of one's career.
2. *Generating and exploring alternatives*: Entertaining possible alternatives for career by way of reflecting on one's interests, skills and values, or by searching and trying out available options.
3. *Short-listing*: Reducing alternative careers to a manageable number for further exploration through work experience or placements.
4. *Deciding*: Provisionally picking a career from among alternatives.
5. *Confirmation*: Confirming that one's choice is the right one and gradually building a long-term commitment to it.
6. *Commitment*: Being firmly decided upon and committed to a career direction.

Phase 1, the becoming concerned phase, typically appears in adolescence and grows in intensity as the transition to adulthood becomes closer. During this time, an adolescent may conclude that they have already 'chosen' their career; for example, in a study of Swiss secondary school children, Hirschi and Lage (2007) found that 40 per cent of adolescents described themselves as having decided upon their career. This reflects the fact that adolescents will envisage an ideal career, unburdened by the practicalities of actually attaining this career (Lent, Brown & Hackett, 1994). In reality, ideal career and attained career may be quite different (Vroom, 1964).

Phase 2 of the career decision-making process is the exploration of alternatives, and engaging in it is associated with positive eventual outcomes such as vocational maturity, occupational satisfaction and attainment (Taveira & Moreno, 2003). The career exploration process involves (a) introspective consideration of one's own interests, motives and talents, and (b) work experience, apprenticeships, short-term contracts or part-time work (Super, 1980). The *social cognitive theory of career choice* states that appraisals of self-efficacy and anticipated outcomes of success or failure both play an important role in shaping career exploration and career choice; for example career interests at this stage are stronger in those who have higher self-efficacy (Lent, Brown & Hackett, 1994). Exploration is also positively related to having supportive family and peer relationships (Felsman & Blustein, 1999).

To move from Phase 2 to Phase 3 of the career selection process, a person must stop exploring and start eliminating alternatives. This process is termed *career circumscription* by Linda Gottfredson (1981). Circumscription of socially unacceptable careers may occur as a result of perceived fit with gender, social class or ethnicity (Gottfredson, 2005). For example, certain careers are strongly linked to gender stereotypes – in the USA, 98 per cent of all secretaries, 93 per cent of all nurses and 84 per cent of primary school teachers are female, while similar proportions are observed in the opposite direction for the construction industry (Walsh, 2001). Gender opportunities in professions are more equal now than at any time in the past, but there are still stereotypes about what men and women should do or can do that influence young people's career exploration and elimination (Anker, 1997).

In Phase 4, a person must come to a provisional decision about their career direction. This is a time of *compromise*, for a person can no longer simply dream, they have to be realistic and pragmatic about what is available to them and what they can actually achieve (Gottfredson, 2005). Those with generally low self-efficacy will be more likely to compromise at lower levels (Lent, Brown & Hackett, 1994). During Phase 4, a young person must apply for posts and go through job selection processes. If they are repeatedly unsuccessful, this may negatively affect confidence and lead to further compromise of ideals.

Having made a decision and gained a job in the intended area, Phase 5 involves personal *confirmation* that the career decision is the right one. A person will monitor his/her performance and interest in the job, and if performance and/or interest is particularly low then they may consider an early career change (Lent, Brown & Hackett, 1994). Research suggests that 25 per cent of people in their twenties may undergo a career change after trying one career for a period of time (Holland, 1996). Quarterlife crisis, discussed in Chapter 6, often involves this kind of career shift in early adulthood, following a realisation that one's current career path is unsustainable or no longer desired. In summary, career selection is a long-winded process that often takes place over many years. Interventions have been devised to help smooth this process along. Box 13.1 describes one such intervention, exploring entrepreneurial career interests in adolescents.

Box 13.1   Real-world applications

Intervention to explore entrepreneurial career interests in German adolescents

Society needs entrepreneurs – people who are willing to take on the risks involved in setting up a new company, initiative or enterprise. They are a key engine of economic growth and innovation. To help young people decide if such a direction is for them, Schroder and Schmitt-Rodermund (2006) put 321 adolescents through a group-based intervention called 'Who wants to become an entrepreneur?' The aim was to help participants define their career interests and aid them in career exploration. The prediction was that after the programme, those who had gone through it would have more polarised views on pursuing an entrepreneurial career – that is, they would be clearer as to whether they *did* or *did not* want to consider it as an option for the future.

The programme involved group-based participative exercises exploring key features of entrepreneurial life: the role of the leader; how to use creative ideas to start a business; how to calculate risk and understand the kinds of risks entrepreneurs face; how to formulate convincing arguments for selling an idea; what abilities are necessary for entrepreneurship; and facts about what governmental and financial help there is for start-up businesses.

Before and after the programme, interest in entrepreneurship was measured. As predicted, those who had been through the programme showed significant increases *and* decreases in interest in entrepreneurship. This showed that the course had helped to crystallise participants' decisions either way, which is what it was designed to do. Those who benefitted most from the programme were those who had entrepreneurial personality traits (that is, achievement-focused, not risk-averse, socially confident and possessing an internal locus of control) but were not from entrepreneurial families. The researchers concluded that the intervention had 'awakened dormant potential' in this group (Schroder & Schmitt-Rodermund, 2006, p. 505).

John Holland's theory of career selection

John L. Holland entered the military in the 1940s as an interviewer and psychological test administrator. In 1947 he left the army and moved into applied psychology, working in a counselling centre and then a psychological testing centre until 1970. During this time he developed and published his theory of vocational choice, which has been one of the most enduring and popular career selection theories ever devised (Holland, 1959; 1996). Based on his decades of working in psychological testing and counselling, Holland put forward a typology of six basic career interest types: Realistic (R), Investigative (I), Artistic (A), Social (S), Enterprising (E) or Conventional (C). The key features of these types are shown in Table 13.1. The theory stated that career selection should be based on trying to maximise the *fit* between a person's interests in these six domains and his/her career.

The six types can by graphically portrayed around the periphery of a hexagon, as shown in Figure 13.1, in order to illustrate how they relate to one another. In this hexagon, adjacent types are most similar, while those that are opposite one another on the hexagon are most different.

Table 13.1   The key features of Holland's six occupational personalities

	Occupational interests	Values	Avoids
Realistic (R)	Manipulation of machines, tools and things	Material rewards for tangible accomplishments	Interaction with people
Investigative (I)	Exploration, understanding and prediction of natural or social phenomena	Development or acquisition of knowledge	Persuasion or sales activities
Artistic (A)	Literary, musical or artistic activities	Creative expression of ideas, emotions or sentiments	Routines and conformity to established rules
Social (S)	Helping, teaching, treating, counselling, working with groups	Fostering the welfare of others, social service	Mechanical and technical activity
Enterprising (E)	Persuading, manipulating or directing others	Material accomplishments and social status	Scientific or abstruse topics
Conventional (C)	Establishing or maintaining orderly routines, application of standards	Material or financial accomplishments and power	Ambiguous or unstructured undertakings

Source: Based on descriptions in Holland (1996).

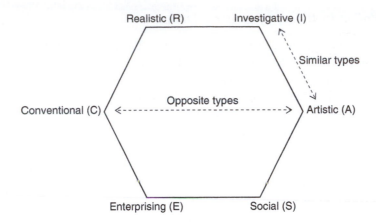

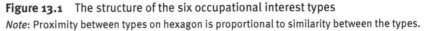

Figure 13.1   The structure of the six occupational interest types

Note: Proximity between types on hexagon is proportional to similarity between the types.

This similarity/difference structure has been replicated in the USA, Italy, Iceland and the Netherlands (Spokane & Cruza-Guet, 2005).

Holland's principle objective for the theory was to help young people match their interests to appropriate careers. To this end, Holland devised an assessment tool called *Self-Directed Search* (SDS). This inventory firstly requires a person to rate their match with the six types. The person is then given a code that denotes their interests in the six types, from highest to lowest. For example, if someone's scored highest for Investigative, followed by Realistic, Conventional, Artistic, Enterprising then Social, their dominant code would be I, their summary code (first three types in order) would be IRC, and their total code would be IRCAES. At the end of the assessment, a computer algorithm selects those occupations that fit the person's type based on an exhaustive list of professions called the Dictionary of Holland Occupational Codes. A website is given at the end of the chapter if you fancy having a go at the SDS yourself for a $5 charge (it's an American site).

In the theory, the degree of fit between a person's occupational interests and their work environment is referred to as *congruence*. There are two aspects of congruence – *motivational congruence* is the fit between goals/interests and job, while *ability congruence* is the fit between abilities and job (Tinsley, 2000). Both need to be maximised for an ideal person-job fit. The search for congruence is part of the career decision-making process; people who are exploring options for a career tend to search for environments that have a high level of congruence with their personality (Holland, 1996). Research using experimental, correlational, longitudinal and qualitative methods shows that congruence predicts eventual job satisfaction, tenure and performance across a variety of occupational settings (Spokane, Meir & Catalano, 2000). However, correlations are not large – typically in the 0.3 range (Tinsley, 2000).

There is a question mark over the cross-cultural validity of the Holland Model of career selection. Firstly, the structure of the interest types does not seem to be universal; for example Artistic and Realistic types were not found in a sample from Singapore (Soh & Leong, 2001). Also, the importance of congruence may not be cross-culturally valid – for example in an Indian study, congruence only had only a small positive correlation with job satisfaction (Leong et al., 1998). It may be that congruence between one's interests and one's career is a concern in environments where incomes are generally good and basic needs are easily met. If incomes are low and jobs are scarce, as they typically are in countries such as India (average daily income is £1.50), then financial needs rather than aspirations of congruence are likely to dominate career choices. This fits with Maslow's hierarchy of needs (see Chapter 5), as the search for person-career congruence relates conceptually to the search for self-actualisation (see Chapter 7 for more on self-actualisation).

Box 13.2   Real-world application

Strategies for optimising the career search and career decision-making process

Gottfredson (2005) lists a number of straightforward strategies that people can employ to optimise the career decision-making process. These are as follows:

1. Try to learn as much as possible about different career paths, even if some of those paths initially appear unappealing or socially unacceptable.

2. Use career services and guidance centres if you have access to them, and study job advertisements in the area of work that in which you are interested. The broader your horizons, the more likely it is you will find the path for you.

3. Remember that finding a career and a job involves a lot of compromise – don't just think about what you *want* to do, but also think about what is available and what you *can* do. If you have one career path you strongly desire, make contingency plans in case that doesn't work out.

Box 13.2   Continued

4. List your goals and write down what you really want out of life, including your goals for family or relationships. Consider your career in relation to other commitments you intend to make and think about how to make your career goals fit with your other life goals.

5. Learn about the nuts and bolts of applying for jobs, such as CV writing, application procedures, what employers in a particular field look for in an employee. Your career choice will only be made a reality if you know how to make a good impression in the job application process.

6. Don't be afraid to change your mind, even after you have started a job or career.

Career change

Career change occurs when a person decides to change from one profession or occupation to a different one. It usually requires training in the new profession or occupation, so going back to education for a time is often integral to the career change process. Career change is more likely to occur in early adulthood than in later life, therefore career stability gets progressively greater with age (Gottfredson, 1977). Given that career change is a major disruption to adult life, why do people do it? Research suggests that it is initiated only if one's current career is dissatisfying and incongruent with one's personality (Smart & Peterson, 1997). The kinds of job dissatisfaction that precede career change include the following (Rhodes & Doering, 1983):

- Perceived unfairness in pay and rewards
- Interpersonal conflict with superiors and/or co-workers
- A lack of autonomy and sense of being controlled
- Lack of a sense of fit between career and personal interests/abilities
- Lack of career growth opportunities
- Poor work–home balance
- Perceived higher levels of satisfaction in alternative careers

The process of career change proceeds in a phased manner (Rhodes & Doering, 1983; Smart & Peterson, 1997). Initially, a person must compare the benefits and disadvantages of their current career with an alternative one, and then work out the probability of attaining the alternative career, including the chance of completing the training required for the alternative career. If the benefits of embarking on the alternative career are perceived to outweigh the costs, then a withdrawal process is initiated. Withdrawal starts with a *search* phase, during which a person searches for alternative careers and the means to reach those alternatives. This is then followed by the *preparation* phase, during which preparatory activities are taken alongside current career, such as taking courses and/or putting aside money for social support (Rhodes & Doering, 1983). The search and preparation phases may, or may not, lead to the *actual change* process. Actual change starts with leaving one's old job and is completed when the new career has begun. Career changes tend to be in the direction of moving to a career that is a better fit with abilities and interests than one's previous job, supporting Holland's theory of person-job congruence (Donohue, 2006).

Career changes are often not isolated decisions, but instead are part of larger life changes or crises (Robinson, 2008). A new career can be a way of integrating emerging and/or previously excluded aspects of personality into daily life, or expressing previously hidden or recently acquired values (Young & Rodgers, 1997). The outcome of an intentional career change is generally positive – those who have completed one have a higher mean level of job satisfaction than those who are contemplating, searching, preparing or implementing a change, and also have a higher satisfaction level than those who have no intention to change career (Smart & Peterson, 1997). This suggests that career change has the power to invigorate job satisfaction to levels that are typically higher than individuals who have a stable career, but the process itself is fraught with potential stress, and there is a chance that the person will revert back to their original career when they realise the difficulty of forging a new career direction, a new reputation and the loss of status associated with re-starting a career from the bottom rung of the ladder (Robinson, 2008).

Unemployment and job loss

Having a career and being in active employment provides an opportunity for income, independence, use of skills, variety, social contact, social status and a sense of purpose (Warr, 1987). Unemployment, conversely, means the loss of all these opportunities. Box 13.3 provides excerpts of accounts describing the challenges and stressors of unemployment in recent recession-hit Ireland.

Box 13.3   Individual voices

The social effects of unemployment in recession-hit Ireland

Delaney, Egan and O'Connell (2011) conducted 13 focus groups with individuals who were unemployed in 2010, following a job loss. Participants were recruited through job centres in Ireland. The findings illustrated the many ways that unemployment and the associated loss of income affects life adversely. A selection of illustrative quotes is given next.

Challenges to relationships

We're still together and we're still doing our thing together, but there is a vibe and there always will be because even if I think everything is alright I'm still sitting with this guilt feeling, you know, I've always been the breadwinner, bringing in quite a bit of money … and that just all disappeared. And it has caused a big rift in the house. (p. 21)

When poverty comes in, love flies out the window … you might be madly in love with your partner but when you've no money, you can't do anything … the worst comes out … that ruins relationships and families. (p. 21)

Losing social contact and confidence

Because the job is not only gone but all the people you were with every day, they're all gone different ways as well. So you lose more than just a job and money. You lose a lot of relationships. (p. 34)

You are used to working with people, and you are not meeting them anymore and that makes a big difference. You lose a lot of self-confidence as a result. (p. 34)

Damage to social identity and status

I got hand outs from family. When you come to my age, like I'm 46, so you can't be at an age that you can't be asking your parents. When you're independent, you're independent. (p. 33)

You feel, you're not yourself, the person you used to be, 'the cook' or whatever, you're just, 'on the Dole' and you don't want to be that. You've spent 30 plus years being somebody with a title, regardless of what level it was at and all of a sudden, it's all gone. (p. 32)

Box 13.3   Continued

Worries about future

I recently had a birthday and I'm on the slippery slope to 40 now. So if I want to settle down with my partner, have children and do all that kind of thing, I really have to start thinking about doing that now ... I don't want a situation where there is hardship within a family, that causes real strain within relationships, when there are children involved, I just think that's irresponsible for me, but I have to get a job, for my own sanity, for my own life, to move forward. (p. 37)

There is robust evidence that unemployment increases the risk of mental health problems. McKee-Ryan and colleagues (2005) conducted a meta-analysis of 104 studies that looked at the relationship between unemployment and mental health/wellbeing, including cross-sectional and longitudinal studies. Cross-sectional studies found that unemployed adults have significantly lower mental health, life satisfaction, marital or family satisfaction and subjective physical health than matched groups of working adults, while longitudinal findings showed a reduction in mental health following job loss, and an increase in mental health and life satisfaction following re-employment. This shows that, at the average level, unemployment is bad for wellbeing. Duration of unemployment makes a difference – the longer it goes on, the more it negatively affects a person's sense of wellbeing (McKee-Ryan et al., 2005). Also, unemployment has a different effect depending on when it occurs in adulthood. It has a worse effect on wellbeing in young adults than older adults, particularly those who have just left university or school (McKee-Ryan et al., 2005).

The meta-analysis also explored which personal and social variables make wellbeing decline more or less likely in unemployment. Those individuals who identify strongly with their job suffer more when unemployed, as do those who think that losing their job is their fault, while self-efficacy and self-esteem protect against mental health problems in the unemployed. In terms of family, being married is associated with better mental health in unemployment, but having dependent children during an unemployed period is associated with lower mental health (McKee-Ryan et al., 2005). Engaging in job search activities when unemployed is mixed blessing – it is in fact linked to *more* anxiety and depression, which reflects the fact that job search involves inevitable rejection and anxiety. However, the act of searching for a job makes reemployment more likely, and thus decreases unemployment duration. It seems that active job search during unemployment is a classic case of enduring short-term pain for long-term gain (McKee-Ryan et al., 2005).

Gender and the changing challenges of work–family balance

During the World War II, millions of men left their jobs to join the military. When this happened, women entered the civilian workforce in previously unheard of numbers to fill the vacancies that resulted from the military draft. During the war, 39 per cent of the civilian workforce was female, and a million more women were in the workforce at the end of the war than at the beginning (Walsh, 2001). When the war ended, many women left the workforce, but many stayed. Following this, between 1950 and 1990 the numbers of working women in the UK rose steadily from 7 million to 23 million (Walsh, 2001). Nowadays, half the workforce is female, compared with under ten per cent before World War II (Barnett & Hyde, 2001). The biggest employment growth area of all has been middle-aged women and mothers (Gilbert, 1994; Walsh, 2001).

This rise in female participation in the workforce has coincided with an increase in prevalence of part-time jobs. Part-time work has become more common over the past half-century, as a result of employers increasingly valuing a flexible labour supply that can be boosted or reduced depending on demand and economic climate. About one quarter of the workforce is now part-time (Walsh, 2001). Women comprise the majority of the part-time workforce, and in the UK that proportion is particularly high – between 80 per cent and 90 per cent (compared with approximately 68 per cent in the USA) (Walsh, 2001). So part-time work is strongly associated with female work – in 2008, 40 per cent of women in the UK worked part-time, compared with 11 per cent of men (Office for National Statistics, 2008). Mothers who take a substantial career break to look after children and then return to the workforce are referred to 're-entry mothers'. Over 50 per cent of them return as part-timers or in flexible work schemes (Walsh, 2001).

Catherine Hakim, in her book *Social Change and Innovations in the Labour Market* (1998), suggests that the reason for the close association between part-time working and women is that women are still predominantly responsible for family life, and therefore prefer jobs that offer flexibility of hours to work around children and household tasks. Furthermore, she suggests that the majority of women still regard themselves as secondary earners who supplement their partner's source of income. At the same time, male participation in parenting has increased; Cabrera et al. (2000) reported on a study conducted in the late 1990s that fathers who live with their children spend double the amount of time with their children than those in the 1970s. They suggest that this reflects the changing role of father over this period from 'breadwinner' to 'co-parent'.

In an analysis of the *British Household Panel Survey* (Thomas, Benzeval & Stansfeld, 2005), employment transitions were recorded over a period of nine years (1991–9) for 5092 people. Of recorded transitions from employment into full-time childcare, 97 per cent were taken by women and just 3 per cent by men, showing that in the 1990s only a small minority of men were taking time off work for children. During the survey period, five times as many men took a break from work to study than took a break to take care of children. The likelihood of men and women taking a career break for children is partially influenced by governmental policy, and such policies differ widely from country to country; see Box 13.4 for policies on maternity/paternity leave in different countries. The duration of this break from work is highly variable. Leonard (1993, cited in Nelson, 2003) found that all mothers who returned to work within three months of giving birth regretted it and felt that they had done so too soon, but in many single-parent families there is no choice – the mother will need to return to work to provide for her child, even though she may not want to.

Fathers who choose to take the role of primary caregiver to children are a small minority, but are increasing in prevalence. They are referred to as 'stay-at-home fathers'. In the UK, the Office of National Statistics cites a rise in the number of stay-at-home fathers from being not statistically registered in the 1970s, to 118,000 in 1993, and then to 192,000 in 2009 (Grigg, 2009). For many families, the decision for the father to be primary caregiver may be influenced by the wife being the primary earner; in a recent UK survey, women were found to earn more than men in 21 per cent of households (Women and Equality Unit, 2006).

Rochlen et al. (2008) conducted a qualitative study with 14 stay-at-home fathers, all of whom were college educated, to explore their experiences of this role. They interviewed each participant, and after conducting a grounded theory analysis, explored the reasons for becoming a stay-at-home father. Reasons were typically based on (a) the belief that one parent should stay at home, (b) the assessment that their personality was more suited to the task of parenting than their wife and/or (c) their wives having higher incomes. One participant said:

> I always knew I would make a better parent than my wife. Just because of the way that she handled things and reacted versus how I did. I think

it has worked out well. As much as our society would want to make it, not every woman makes a good parent. (Rochlen et al., 2008, p. 198)

All 14 participants defined masculinity in personal and flexible terms, and reported feeling uninfluenced by masculine stereotypes and social norms. Ten of the 14 reported significant changes in their personality since becoming a stay-at-home father, including exhibiting more traditional female characteristics, such as being more affectionate, more aware of their feelings and more nurturing. There are few studies on the psychology of stay-at-home fathers, and this small exploratory study suggests that larger studies would be warranted, particularly given that policies that encourage fathers being involved with family duties vary substantially across different countries (see Box 13.4).

Box 13.4   Cross-cultural perspectives

Maternity and paternity leave in different countries

The way that couples manage childcare after the birth of a child is substantially shaped by the benefits available to them in their country of residence (Gilbert, 1994). The majority of countries have a legal statutory requirement specifying the amount of time employers must allow staff for maternity and/or paternity leave, the cost of which is sometimes paid by the state, sometimes by the employer or sometimes a mixture of both. Legal requirements for parental leave are given next for China, Iran, Sweden, the UK and the USA, to illustrate the cross-cultural diversity of such policies:

China: Women are entitled to 3 months paid maternity leave at 100 per cent of salary. There is no law pertaining to paternity leave.

Iran: Women are entitled to 6 months paid maternity leave at 100 per cent of salary. There is no law pertaining to paternity leave.

Sweden: All working parents are entitled to 16 months leave per child at 80 per cent pay, the cost being shared between employer and the state. To encourage greater paternal involvement in child-rearing, a minimum of 2 months out of the 16 is to be used by the father. Iceland, Norway and Denmark also have a required quota of a certain amount of leave to be used by the father. This is referred to colloquially as the 'daddy quota'.

Box 13.4   Continued

UK: Employed women are legally permitted 52 weeks' maternity leave, 26 of which is paid. Fathers have two weeks' paid paternity leave. There is also a state-funded allowance for mothers not in full-time employment. Fathers can also claim an additional 26 weeks of paid leave (between 5 months and 1 year after birth of child) *if* their wife has returned to work.

USA: There is no policy on paid maternity leave. USA law requires employers to grant 12 weeks' unpaid maternity leave and 12 weeks unpaid paternity leave, and only 42 per cent of mothers in America access some form of paid maternity cover through their employer. This lack of policy on paid maternity leave is rare; only three other countries in the world have no law on paid maternity leave: Liberia, Swaziland, and Papua New Guinea (Heymann, Earle & Hayes, 2007).

Dual-career families

The term 'dual-career family' was coined by Rapoport and Rapoport (1969). In a dual-career family, both woman and man pursue long-term career paths, and childcare is partially managed by paid carers or nannies. In such families, 18 per cent of fathers provide the primary childcare role, a far higher proportion than in single-earner families (Gilbert, 1994). Life satisfaction in dual career families is highest if partners feel comfortable sharing the parenting role and are satisfied with the childcare personnel they employ (Gilbert, 1994). Life satisfaction also depends on the fit between the couples' expectations of gender roles and how they run the family. If there is a good fit, then satisfaction is enhanced (Gilbert, 1994). Three distinct patterns of dual-career family balance have been established by research (Gilbert, 1994):

1. **Conventional** – Both partners have careers but responsibility for housework and parenting is retained by the woman. This results in a 'second shift' of family-related tasks for women in the evenings (Hochschild & Machung, 1990). Men are typically more professionally ambitious than women in these families and help out as long as it doesn't interfere with their career pursuits.

2. **Modern** – Parenting is shared by spouses, with the wife taking more responsibility for household work. Men are motivated to be active fathers, but not to achieve total role equality.

3. **Role-sharing** – This is a more egalitarian pattern. Both partners involve themselves in household work and family life as well as careers. Approximately one third of heterosexual dual-career families fit this variation.

Although you might expect that in dual-career families parents spend less time with children, studies show that the combined time that fathers and mothers spend in direct interaction with their children is about the same on average as single-earner families. This is achieved by allocating more time to children on weekends and evenings, and so compensating for weekday absences (Gilbert, 1994).

The **multiple roles hypothesis** states that if an adult has *both* work and family roles, as is typical in dual-career families, their psychological health is likely to be better than if their life is devoted exclusively to work or children. In support of this, a three year longitudinal study of women showed that those who changed from being a full-time mother, to combining their domestic role with part-time work, showed fewer symptoms of depression (Wethington & Kessler, 1989). Similarly, men who engage in childcare report lower psychological distress than those who do not (Ozer et al., 1998).

Barnett and Hyde (2001) propose a number of factors that contribute to the beneficial effect of combining work and family roles. The first is that if one role is causing stress, the other can potentially act to offset it by providing continued satisfaction and opportunities for success. Secondly, the added income that occurs if both partners work can help to prevent financial stress. Thirdly, having work and home roles increases the opportunities for social support and friendship formation. Finally, if both women and men work and engage in childcare, there is more common ground in their relationship, which may facilitate communication and relationship satisfaction.

There is still research to be done on the effects of dual-career families. For example, research does not yet point clearly towards whether flexible work, part-time work or full-time work is the most conducive to wellbeing in dual-career families, or whether that depends on personalities and number of children. This is an important issue, as overload in family or work roles has been found to negate the benefits of combining them (Barnett & Hyde, 2001).

Retirement

Historically speaking, retirement is a relatively recent idea. Germany was the first to recognise that people could be generally expected to stop working at some point in their life, and in 1883 introduced the first state pension for over-65s. Britain was the next country to bring about a state pension in 1908 for all individuals over the age of 70. In Britain and Germany at this time, average life expectancy was between 40 and 50 (Kinsella, 1992), so retirement was for the lucky few who made it to retirement age – the majority died before they got there.

It was after the World War II that retirement became something that most people could look forward to. The pension age in the UK was brought down to 65 for men, and to 60 for women, while companies increasingly started to provide their own pension schemes. Life expectancy rose to over 70 after the war (Kinsella, 1992), so for the first time in human history, retirement was something that most people could look forward to, at least for a few years.

Nowadays, life expectancy for both sexes is over 80, so a British person can expect to spend up to a quarter of their life in retirement, which is a remarkable change from 100 years ago, when the majority didn't even make it to retirement age. This new landscape of extended retirement means that providing pensions is becoming increasingly expensive. The UK government has correspondingly decided to raise the age at which a state pension can be taken to 66 by 2020, and to 68 by 2046, and other governments are responding similarly. Meanwhile, employers in the private sector and public sector are reforming their pension policies to make them affordable in the long term. At the time of writing, the government is wrangling with unions about how public-sector pensions should be reformed, and protests over the issue are frequent.

Why do people retire?

Retirement can be initiated for all sorts of reasons. Robert Weiss, in his book *The Experience of Retirement* (2005), collated qualitative descriptions of the retirement process from 89 American professionals, and categorised the reasons for becoming retired into nine types, which are summarised in Table 13.2. Only one of these nine reasons is the actual desire to retire, while the other eight are situational factors such as being pressured to retire, feeling too old for the job or personal health problems. Research supports that a third of individuals approaching retirement are in fact not looking forward to it and have no ambition to do so (Atton, 1985).

The extent to which the retirement decision is experienced as voluntary, rather than forced or coerced, is one of the key determinants of how well people adjust to retirement and how satisfying they find it (Calvo, Haverstick & Sass, 2009). A voluntary retirement allows a person

Table 13.2 A taxonomy of reasons to retire, derived from interviews with retirees

	Theme	Description of theme
1	Wanting the freedom to do something new	Retirement is initiated voluntarily to pursue a hobby, do more travelling, or take more time to see children and grandchildren, or even to start a new business or career.
2	Family obligations	A partner has retired and the person feels obliged to do the same, or a partner or family member is ill and requires care.
3	Feeling too old for the job	Retirement is initiated because they feel that their age is a problem at work, either because they have lost the energy required to work, or because new technology has been introduced that they don't know how to use.
4	Illness or physical disability	Health problems, such as cancer, heart attack or mental illness enforce retirement from work.
5	Disliking an aspect of the job	Retirement is initiated to escape from a job that has become stressful, dissatisfying and frustrating.
6	Resolving conflict by retiring	Retirement is initiated to escape a conflict in their work life, usually with a superior.
7	Being bought out	Firms sometimes offer special incentives to prompt older employees to retire, such as enhanced benefits, a bonus year of salary or an increased pension, which may be very hard to refuse.
8	Being nudged out or pushed out	Firms can subtly force people to retire by either making a job unpleasant, or threatening with dismissal.
9	Retirement as an alternative to unemployment	If a person has been unemployed for some time, when they hit retirement age, or is made unemployed late in their career, they may assume the label of 'retired' as preferable to 'unemployed'.

Source: Weiss (2005).

to follow their own schedule into this new phase of life, and gives them the opportunity to prepare and plan for the changes in lifestyle that lie ahead. Furthermore, a voluntary retirement has the benefit of permitting a person to coincide their own retirement with that of their partner, should that be a concern for them (Ho & Raymo, 2009). In addition to this, a voluntary retirement gives a person the sense of being in control, which is important to wellbeing no matter what stage of life you are in (Spector et al., 2002).

Postretirement income is a key factor in facilitating a voluntary decision to retire (Szinovacz & Deviney, 2000). It derives from a combination of pension plans, state pension (or equivalent government scheme), personal assets and continued income from part-time work. Retirement will only be voluntarily undertaken if a person evaluates that their postretirement income is sufficient for their needs. If a retiree is married or cohabiting, their spouse or partner's postretirement income will also be part of the retirement calculation (Clark, Johnson & McDermed, 1980; Szinovacz & Deviney, 2000). Due to continuing sex discrimination in wages, and the greater female tendency for career breaks during childrearing years, women are currently more reliant on men for postretirement income than vice versa (Slevin & Wingrove, 1995).

Abrupt, gradual and ambiguous retirement transitions

Your mental image of retirement may well be something like this – a person has a salaried, full-time career in a particular industry, then hits 65, has a farewell party, and never works in paid employment again. This is an example of what is called *abrupt* retirement, which does exist, but it's increasingly rare – nowadays the retirement transition can also take *gradual* or *ambiguous* paths, as illustrated in Figure 13.2 (Calvo, Haverstick & Sass, 2009). The *gradual* retirement path involves spending some years in part-time work after leaving full-time work, a phenomenon known as *partial retirement* or *bridge employment* (Davis, 2003; Honig & Hanoch, 1985). In the early 1990s, 40–50 per cent of retirees were found to engage in bridge employment (Ruhm, 1994), and that proportion is likely to be larger now. Some people who are in bridge jobs consider themselves to be retired, while others don't, which illustrates the in-between nature of partial retirement (Hodkinson et al., 2008).

A qualitative study of American retirees who had taken bridge employment found a variety of reasons for people doing it (in addition to the provision of continued income) – they said it gave their life meaning, filled their time, maintained their sense of status, and kept them connected to their career social worlds (Ulrich & Brott, 2005). Within two months of retiring 70 per cent started the new part-time role, while 20 per cent started within a year of retirement, and 10 per cent within four years. This illustrates the possibility of taking an abrupt retirement, then being out of the workforce for a while before coming back into bridge employment, as illustrated by the arrow from full retirement to bridge employment in Figure 13.2.

The *ambiguous path* into retirement shown in Figure 13.2 is taken by individuals who have had a freelance career or who have worked part-time while raising a family. For example, a freelance writer in his late sixties was interviewed as part of a study on the experience of retirement (Robinson, Demetre & Corney, 2011). The writer said he had

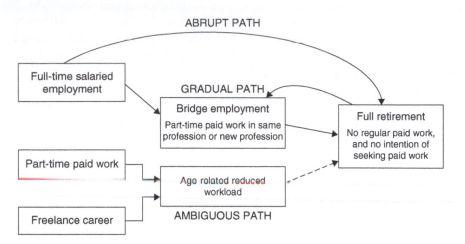

Figure 13.2 Abrupt, gradual and ambiguous paths to retirement

reduced the amount of writing he did due to having less energy than he had when he was younger, but he said that he intended to write at least one more book in the future, and so was unsure if the word retirement applied in any meaningful sense to his life. The idea of retirement is also ambiguous for mothers who combine being a stay-at-home mother with a part-time job. For both part-time workers and freelance workers, the moment of retirement is far less clear cut, hence the dashed line in Figure 13.2 from reduced workload to full retirement.

Retirement and couples

For those who are married, retirement is a challenge for both partners. For single-earner couples, retirement for the working partner is a potentially difficult experience for the stay-at-home partner to adjust to. One study of non-working spouses of retirees actually found that retirees find the retirement process easier to adapt to than their spouses (Guerriero Austrom et al., 2003). Box 13.5 provides excerpts from an interview with the wife of a retired man in which she discusses his reaction to retirement and how they manage this new situation of both being in the house together all the time.

spouse finds it more difficult

Box 13.5 Individual voices

Adapting to life as a couple after retirement: A wife's perspective

Mark was a successful literary agent during his career. He chose to take an abrupt retirement, at which point he had to adapt to spending more

Box 13.5   Continued

time in the house with his wife than ever before. In an interview, his wife Elisa described the challenges of this new situation, and talked of Mark's efforts to become more domesticated. Selected excerpts from the interview are shown next (Robinson, Demetre & Corney, 2011).

> He had terrible temper tantrums. He was a bit volatile really at that time [directly after retirement]. And I think it was adjusting to his loss of status. In the office you're somebody and then here you are at home, and you're a nobody: you're mucking in, really. (p. 9)
>
> I became very independent really in running the house and everything at home when Mark was working ... you get into the way of leading rather separate lives, really. Mark actually hides away in his study for hours on end. And it is very like the old days of him hiding himself away to read manuscripts, actually. So he's not there; he's not hanging around the kitchen, having a chat and that sort of thing. And so he doesn't get in my way – some women might say, 'My husband gets in the way.' And then I have my corners of the house where I go to do certain things, yes. And that's nice – to have our own space. We're lucky to have a big house, actually. (p. 17)
>
> He was living in a different context after retirement and wasn't quite sure where he fitted in. Perhaps I should have given him more guidance. 'Here ...' hand him the drying-up towel. No, but ... He's good at doing that sort of thing. He does do a few things automatically round the house, like drying up. He irons his own shirts. Now he actually *empties* the washing machine – doesn't load it but he empties it. He knows what to do with the wet washing. (p. 17)

You may notice how Elisa refers to her husband – a man who has retired after having reached the top of his career – in a slightly childish way. Why do you think this might be?

In dual-career couples, men tend to retire earlier than women, as the normative pattern in couples is for men to be older than women and thus reach retirement age before their partner. This can be a challenge to the marriage, for the man may find himself taking on new domestic roles while his wife is breadwinner. This temporary reversal of traditional gender roles can be a challenge to a man's sense of status and identity (Szinovacz & Deviney, 2000). A 'joint retirement' is when dual-career couples retire at the same moment – this is a choice that is increasing in popularity, but it requires sufficient funds for both partners to leave work simultaneously (Ho & Raymo, 2009; O'Rand, Henretta & Krecker, 1992). If one partner reaches retirement but postretirement funds are yet not sufficient, the other partner may have to remain in work to maintain a source of income (Szinovacz & Deviney, 2000).

Once both partners are retired, a couple will experience a situation that they may have never encountered before in their lives together – spending every day in each other's company (Weiss, 2005). For the preceding decades, most couples will have been separated from each other from Monday to Friday, and suddenly they are living in constant, close proximity. This tends to make good marriages better and make fragile marriages worse (Dorfman, 2002; Weiss, 2005). A study in the UK found that approximately 70 per cent of retired individuals reflected that retirement had a positive effect on their relationship, while approximately 30 per cent reported a negative effect (Robinson, Demetre & Corney, 2010).

Retirement and wellbeing

Eudaimonic development, mentioned in Chapter 1, is long-term change over time in the direction of enhanced happiness, wellbeing and quality of life. A number of studies has explored the effects of retirement on eudaimonic development. When cross-sectional and longitudinal quantitative research has endeavoured to establish a mean-level effect of retirement on eudaimonic variables across a population, the findings have been ambiguous – in some studies retirement has a slight positive effect on wellbeing at the mean level (Mein, et al., 2003; Midanik et al., 1995), while in others it has a negative effect (Butterworth et al., 2006; Gill et al., 2006). When genders have been compared in retirement adjustment, findings have been equally ambiguous, with some findings suggesting that women experience more problems than men (Neuhs, 1990), and others suggesting women experience less difficulty in retirement (Quick & Moen, 1998).

These ambiguous findings are due to diverse individual experiences that cancel each other at the mean level or at the level of gender. For example, in a study of doctors, 43 per cent were more satisfied with their life following retirement, 50 per cent did not experience a marked change in satisfaction, while 7 per cent felt less satisfied after retirement (Guerriero Austrom et al., 2003). New studies have been conducted that analyse subgroups of retirees separately, to capture and analyse the variability in the retirement transition experience. The findings from these show that the effect of retirement on wellbeing is individually diverse, with some people finding it a liberating release and others finding it tediously boring (Kloep & Hendry, 2006; Robinson, Demetre & Corney, 2011).

A recent study by Wang (2007) analysed archival longitudinal data from the Health and Retirement Survey, gathered over an eight-year period, to explore different wellbeing trajectories in retirement. Three growth curve patterns of psychological wellbeing were identified using a technique called Growth Mixture Modelling. These types were termed *Maintaining, U-Shaped and Recovering*. The Maintaining type (a pattern of continued high wellbeing across the retirement transition) was shown by 70 per cent of retirees. The U-shaped pattern (negative changes in psychological wellbeing directly after retirement followed by improvements) was manifested by 25 per cent of retirees. 5 per cent of retirees showed a Recovering pattern (significant positive changes in psychological wellbeing, having started with a lower level than the other two groups). These findings were replicated on a nationally representative sample in Germany by Pinquart and Schindler (2007), with 75 per cent as Maintaining, 9 per cent as U-shaped and 15 per cent as Recovering.

A qualitative study by myself and colleagues supported the different types that Wang found, but added another group that, being a minority, may not have been picked up in these large-sample studies (Robinson, Demetre & Corney, 2011). We found a group for whom retirement is principally described in terms of 'restriction, regret and decline'. The main themes in this group were that retirement was not their choice, that they would like to go back into full-time work but can't get a job, and that retirement itself is a waste of their abilities and a time of reduced opportunities. Another recent qualitative study conducted in Norway found a similar group of participants who were defined predominantly by the sense that there is 'not much to live for' in retirement (Kloep & Hendry, 2006), while a study from Israel found both positive and negative experiences in retirement (Nuttman-Schwartz, 2004). See Box 13.6 for individual extracts from this study.

Box 13.6   Individual voices

Perceptions of retirement in Israeli men – hopes, fears and the reality

Orit Nuttman-Shwartz (2004) interviewed 56 Israeli men about retirement, both in their final year of work prior to retirement at 65, and directly after. The study shows variety in the experience of retirement.

Box 13.6   Continued

Prior to retirement, some participants described fears, others described positive expectations, while after retirement some reported entirely positive evaluations and others highly negative ones.

Pre-retirement fears – loss of status

> After I leave, who will remember me? It's not only that I'm retiring. It's also that my best friends are all leaving ... The new management, the young workers ... they won't remember who built the factory. (p. 232)

Pre-retirement hopes – being free

> Retirement is a bursting out into light. To retire is to walk in the light in the air in the sunshine. To see green and brown—such beautiful colours. I'll start to look for pleasures ... Today I can be freer. To go to the beach. I want freedom to find the golden mean. I reached a point in life where I can be free. I can make decisions on my own do what's good for me and not be tied to work in an office in the dark. (p. 233)

Post-retirement – positive evaluation

> Before retirement I didn't think it was possible not to work. I was sure that I would look for work ... Today I'm busy all day. I'm a member of a sports club. I'm active in its administrative committee. I'm responsible for some of its activities ... I might volunteer as I'd thought before retirement ... But it doesn't look like I'll go back to work. Things are good and I'm pleased. (p. 234)

Post-retirement – loss of meaning

> I haven't managed to find a meaningful framework for myself. Though the pressure has declined, I still feel frustration. (p. 234)

> The gleam in my eyes has dulled. Retirement is routine. Another movie. Another café. You get used to the long vacation. (p. 234)

> Life really has ended ... I know that the sand is flowing out of the hour glass. (p. 234)

Box 13.7   Real-world application

What makes for a happy, satisfying and well-adjusted retirement?

There is an ever-growing body of research on what makes for a good retirement. Recent studies have endeavoured to synthesise findings into integrative models (Wang, Henkens & van Solinge, 2011; Wong & Earl, 2009), while others have summarised them into a set of structured recommendations for retirees (Weiss, 2005). The following are agreed key factors that help with making retirement a positive and stress-free transition:

- Plan financially for retirement – Before you reach retirement age, carefully think through your postretirement income and your needs, and plan your savings accordingly.
- Plan with your partner – If you are married or have a partner, talk to each other about your expectations for retirement, and try to retire at the same time as each other if possible.
- Maintain a life beyond work – Try and maintain social contacts and hobbies beyond your career, to avoid feeling too bereft or isolated when retirement arrives.
- Don't be afraid to put retirement off – If you don't feel motivated to retire, make plans to postpone it or find alternative employment options or a bridge job. Retirement is not for everybody.
- Keep control over when you retire, if you possibly can – By communicating to others at work that you have an intended age of retirement, they may work with you to facilitate that, rather than feeling like they have to forcibly push you out. Retiring on good terms will help leave you with happy memories of your working life prior to retirement.
- Bridge employment is a good idea for many people – Retirement is one of life's biggest social transitions, and bridge employment can give you time to adapt to the changes, while bringing in additional income for some years. Voluntary work also enhances retirement satisfaction, so try to find something that draws on your skills and expertise.
- Sharing retirement with someone – Retirement is experienced more positively by people who are part of a couple. If you are retired and single, don't be afraid to approach the many dating agencies that exist for people over the age of 50 or 60 – these are designed for you and are becoming very popular.

Box 13.7   Continued

- Make efforts to see your friends regularly – Being part of social groups who meet regularly can make all the difference to the quality of your retirement, particularly if those groups meet to engage in an activity that you personally enjoy.
- Keep a healthy diet and exercise regime– Robust health makes for good retirement, and there is evidence that exercise in this age group can lead to cognitive gains and emotional benefits.
- Try and see the glass as half full, not half empty – Optimism predicts a good retirement. Make a list of all the good things that retirement has brought or will bring, and focus on maximising those. There is inevitable loss that occurs at retirement, but there are many gains to enjoy too.

Concluding comments

Once upon a time, a career was for life. A person would enter a profession, advance in it as far as they could and eventually retire. Career change was rare, and if someone wanted to retrain in a new profession they would be hard pushed to know where to go, for there was barely any adult education around until the 1970s. Since then, part-time jobs and freelance work have become more popular, while job security in most professions has significantly decreased. Furthermore there are now opportunities for adults to learn new trades and professions, as the adult education sector has expanded considerably.

Research into career development and retirement must continue to explore non-traditional career paths, and you should take them into account too when planning your own career. Rather than relying on a single career path, you might want to consider building up a portfolio of skills that are of use to different organisations and professions (Templer & Causey, 1999). This is a new way of thinking – its means changing one's thought processes from 'this is what I want to do, and these are the qualifications I need to get there' to 'these are my skills, and these are all the work environments that might value them'. There's a strong chance if you are reading this that you are hoping to be a psychologist, so instead of making this an exclusive career aim you might want to consider instead how to build up skills and experience that would make you employable in related professions too. Also, you might want to consider registering as self-employed in the future, so that you can do freelance work instead of, or as well as, your main job. In today's tough job market, the old adage of 'don't put all your eggs in one basket' has never been more apt.

Questions for you to reflect on

- Why do you think that Gottfredson emphasises that career choice is all about compromise? Why can't people just follow their dreams?
- List the various ways that having children affects a woman's career and the challenges for work–home balance that it leads to. How would you personally deal with these challenges, either as a woman or a male partner?
- Do you know anyone who has retired from full-time work? If so, ask them about it – for example find out whether they retired abruptly or gradually, and ask them why. You will find out that people's motivations to retire are complex and often relate to their home life situation.

Summary points

- Career decision-making involves six fundamental processes; becoming concerned about one's career, exploring alternatives, short-listing a set of possible careers, making a decision, confirming that decision and committing to it.
- Compromise is central to career selection. A chosen career may not be the ideal or dreamt-of career, as factors such as accessibility, availability and success/failure in job selection processes are very influential in shaping a career.
- Holland's RIASEC model of career selection involves a person comparing their career interests with possible jobs, and searching for a fit between them. The six domains of career interest are: Realistic, Investigative, Conventional, Enterprising, Social and Artistic. If a person finds a career where they can express the relevant interest types, this is termed *career congruence*.
- Career change is initiated if, during a career, a person feels that the costs of staying in their current career outweigh the costs of retraining and embarking on a different career. This is more likely to occur in early adulthood than later on in adult life.
- Unemployment can lead to the loss of income, independence, skills use, variety, social contact, social status and a sense of purpose. Correspondingly, it is associated with depression.
- Women have joined the workforce in increasing numbers over the last 60 years, and they constitute the majority of the part-time workforce. The majority of career breaks taken for childcare are by women.

- Stay-at-home fathers are increasing in prevalence, as more and more women become primary income generators in families.
- Dual-career families are those where both parents have full-time careers. The multiple roles hypothesis states that individuals who have both family and work roles are more mentally healthy on average than those who have one role and not the other.
- Retirement as a life stage is a recent development – only since the 1950s have the majority of people lived longer than the retirement age, and only for several decades have they people typically lived beyond retirement age for more than a decade.
- Retirement is taken for many reasons, a number of which are not under a person's control, such as being forced out at work, retiring due to illness or being fired when approaching retirement age.
- An abrupt retirement occurs when a person leaves the workforce suddenly, a gradual retirement occurs when a person goes into part-time work for some time prior to full retirement, while an ambiguous retirement is when a person has a freelance or part-time career anyway, and so may not retire in any clear-cut sense. There is evidence that bridge employment, that is, part-time work after retirement, is associated with better adjustment.
- Some find retirement to bring a sense of liberation and to be a positive step in life, while others describe it as a time of limited opportunities and boredom. Planning for retirement financially, socially and psychologically helps to prevent the latter.

Recommended reading

Gilbert, L. A. (1994). Current perspectives on dual-career families. *Current Directions in Psychological Science*, 3, 101–105.

Gottfredson, L. S. (1981). Circumscription and compromise: A developmental theory of occupational aspirations. *Journal of Counseling Psychology*, 28, 545–579.

Hirschi, A. & Lage, D. (2007). The relation of secondary students' career-choice readiness to a six-phase model of career decision making. *Journal of Career Development*, 34, 164–191.

Hochschild, A. R. & Machung, A. (1990). *The Second Shift: Working Parents and the Revolution at Home*. London: Piatkus London.

Holland, J. L. (1959). A theory of vocational choice. *Journal of Counseling Psychology*, 6, 34–45.

Holland, J. L. (1996). Exploring careers with a typology: What we have learned and some new directions. *American Psychologist*, 51, 397–406.

McKee-Ryan, F., Song, Z., Wanberg, C. R. & Kinicki, A. J. (2005). Psychological and physical well-being during unemployment: A meta-analytic study. *The Journal of Applied Psychology*, 90, 53–76.

Robinson, O. C., Demetre, J. D. & Corney, R. H. (2011). The variable experiences of becoming retired and seeking retirement guidance: A qualitative thematic analysis. *British Journal of Guidance & Counselling*, 39, 239–258.

Thomas, C., Benzeval, M. & Stansfeld, S. A. (2005). Employment transitions and mental health: An analysis from the British household panel survey. *Journal of Epidemiology and Community Health*, 59, 243–249.

Wang, M. (2007). Profiling retirees in the retirement transition and adjustment process: Examining the longitudinal change patterns of retirees' psychological well-being. *The Journal of Applied Psychology, 92*, 455–474.

Wang, M., Henkens, K. & van Solinge, H. (2011). Retirement adjustment: A review of theoretical and empirical advancements. *American Psychologist, 66*, 204–213.

Warr, P. (1987). *Work, Unemployment and Mental Health.* Oxford: Oxford University Press.

Weiss, R. (2005). *The Experience of Retirement.* New York: Cornell University Press.

Recommended website

Holland's self-directed search tool, which is a psychometric instrument based on his RIASEC model, can be completed online for $5 here: http://www.self-directed-search.com/paymentinfo.aspx

14

Dying and Bereavement

Happy endings depend entirely on stopping the story before it's over.

Orson Welles

David's wife Sally was diagnosed with terminal cancer a year before she died. She spent the last six months of her life in a hospice before passing away on the day before her 65th birthday. Although David had known the death was coming, he was consumed with grief after it for many months, and was also profoundly anxious about how he would cope without Sally, for he didn't know how to cook or even use the washing machine, and all his plans for retirement revolved around activities that he and his wife would do together. What was he going to do now? He was faced with confusion, doubt and uncertainty. Many times in the months following Sally's death, he found himself talking to her as though she was there, and felt her presence in the house. Five months after the loss, David started attending group-based counselling for bereaved spouses and found consolation in being able to talk about his feelings with others. He found out that it was quite normal to feel the continued presence of a deceased partner, and also to have deep pangs of grief for a year or more. Slowly, his sense of loss abated and, with the help of his children, he learnt how to live on his own.

For the majority of human history, people typically died at a younger age than they do today. Homo sapiens has been around for 200,000 years, but until just 100 years ago, only the minority made it past 50 (Hicks & Allen, 1999). Death was traditionally very likely to occur in the *first* year of life: for example, during famine years in the Middle Ages infant mortality was as high as 50 per cent (Scott, Duncan & Duncan, 1995), and even by 1900 there was still around a 14 per cent chance that a child born in the UK would die before his/her first birthday (Hicks & Allen, 1999). Infant mortality steadily declined in prevalence over the course of the twentieth century, so that it is now less than 1 per cent (see Figure 14.1). Over the same period, there has been a dramatic increase in average life expectancy from around 50 to 80, as was illustrated in Figure 6.2 in Chapter 6.

The context of death has changed over the course of history too. In the nineteenth century, over 95 per cent of people who died of natural causes died in the family home (Rosenblatt, 1981), whereas nowadays death mostly commonly occurs in a hospital, hospice or nursing home. This 'institutionalisation' of death means that fewer people witness death than in the past, which may relate to a growing tendency in society to avoid discussing it (O'Gorman, 1998).

This chapter first covers research on the process of dying from terminal illness, and how the patient and their loved ones come to terms with this. Secondly the literature on bereavement is reviewed, including studies that look at the nature of grief and how people cope with losing a partner or a child. Research shows that paying attention to death can lead to a greater appreciation of life, as illustrated in Box 14.1, and so hopefully you'll find reading a chapter about death and dying to be a life-affirming experience rather than an uncomfortable one.

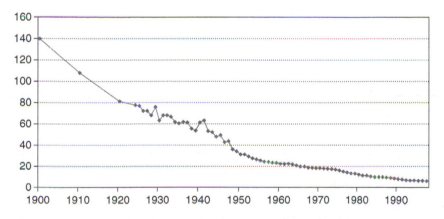

Figure 14.1   Infant mortality per 1000 births in the United Kingdom from 1900 to 2000

Note: Data collected in 1900, 1910, 1920 and then annually from 1924 onwards.

Source: Hicks and Allen (1999). Reproduced with permission.

Box 14.1 Cross-cultural perspectives

Funeral therapy in South Korea

Death is a topic that is rarely discussed in contemporary Western society – we prefer a collective hush about its inevitability (Kübler-Ross, 1969). In other cultures, there is less of a taboo over the topic. For example, in South Korea an organisation called *The Coffin Academy* provides a service for healthy adults to experience their own mock funeral. During a session, a group of participants will be asked to write their own will, write a letter to their loved ones and say a goodbye speech to the assembled group. They are then led into a candlelit room where a photo of them is placed next to a wooden coffin. They lie down in the coffin, the lid is put on and a hammer is banged on the top to symbolise nails being driven in. The coffin remains shut for ten minutes while the participants lie in claustrophobic darkness. At the end of the ten minutes there is a 'rebirth' ceremony, during which the person emerges from their coffin and is pronounced reborn.

Reports of clients who have undergone this 'funeral therapy' suggest that it has a powerful positive transformational effect on them; the confrontation with death that they experience leads to a clearer perspective on what they value about their own life and what they want to do with it. The transformational nature of the Coffin Academy reflects research on the effects of near-death experiences (Noyes, 1980; van Lommel et al., 2001). See Box 10.2 in Chapter 10 for more on near-death experiences.

To watch a news report that shows the process that clients undergo at the Coffin Academy, visit the web link given at the end of this chapter.

The process of dying: Coping with terminal illness

Elisabeth Kübler-Ross was a controversial and pioneering researcher in the study of how people come to terms with being diagnosed with terminal illness. Her book *On Death and Dying* (1969) was first published on this topic in the sixties, when academic discussion of how patients cope with terminal illness was minimal. It was written in an accessible style and promptly became a bestseller. The book presents a five-phase theory of coping with terminal illness, derived from 200 interviews that were conducted as part of a weekly educational seminar with terminally ill patients. The five phases are not meant as strict sequential stages, but more like five waves that peak at different times between being informed of the terminal nature of one's illness and death.

Stage one of the model is *Denial* of the diagnosis and its full implications. This is said to be a normal and healthy first step in dealing with shocking news, for it acts as a *temporary buffer* and defence against being overwhelmed by the trauma. When a person receives a terminal diagnosis, some denial or avoidance allows him or her to regain cognitive composure and gradually assimilate the implications of the news. It is only after a person has come out of shock and has fully processed what they have been told that they can come out of denial, sit down and talk about their situation. Kübler-Ross found about one per cent of her sample never got past the denial stage and became stuck in a fantasy that they would recover; so denial in very rare cases becomes a permanent fixture.

Stages two, three and four are *Anger, Bargaining* and *Depression.* These three stages overlap to a great extent. They are all ways of coping with and coming to terms with the deterioration and loss of independence associated with advancing illness, and the grief they feel at the loss of health and the prospect of their death. *Anger* is often projected outwards at doctors, nurses and family, and the patient may find himself thinking 'why me?', as described in the following extract:

> I suppose ... anybody in my position would look at somebody else and say, 'Well, why couldn't it have been him?' and this has crossed my mind several times ... An old man whom I have known ever since I was a little kid came down the street. He was eighty-two years old, and he is of no earthly use as far as we mortals can tell. He's rheumatic, he's a cripple, he's dirty, just not the type of a person you would like to be. And the thought hit me strongly, now why couldn't it have been old George instead of me? Male interviewee (pp. 63–4)

Bargaining is a process that has a strongly spiritual emphasis. It has been found that terminally ill patients have a greater interest in spiritual matters compared with other adults (Reed, 1987), and the bargaining process involves praying for a postponement or avoidance of death, in return for committing life to a morally positive cause, or in return for making up for past unfulfilled promises or harm done.

Depression is emphasised by Kübler-Ross to be an important and normal experience for coming to terms with dying and relates it to the combined operation of two kinds of grief: *reactive grief* due to facing the losses that one has already experienced, and *preparatory* or *anticipatory grief* in anticipation of one's own death. An extract from the diary of a woman dying from cancer, written several months before her death, illustrates this sense of grief:

> There is a sadness growing within me. I do not want it so, but I know I cry with bitterness filling me. It does not hurt the way it did yesterday. There is only room for just so much sorrow. What will I put in its place tomorrow? (Kübler-Ross, 1978, p. 40)

Stage five is *Acceptance*. This is not necessarily a happy stage, but the feelings of despair and fear that typically define earlier stages do diminish. The struggle to live is over and a person is therefore calmer than before. At this stage, interest in other people and the outside world diminishes and the patient may eat less. The detachment from loved ones in this stage makes the final moments easier, but it can appear to them as a kind of rejection. It is important for partners and relatives to accept this gradual detachment and also reach their own point of acceptance (Kübler-Ross, 1969).

A less discussed aspect of Kübler-Ross's theory is her emphasis on the importance of *hope* throughout the whole terminal illness process. She writes that hope is typically reported by the patient right up until stage five. However there are rare instances in which a terminally ill person shows hopelessness and a wish to end their life on their own terms, particularly if their prognosis is for a long period of painful deterioration. The arguments surrounding this issue of 'voluntary euthanasia' for terminally ill patients are briefly summarised in Box 14.2.

Criticisms and developments of Kübler-Ross's model

The phase model of Kübler-Ross has been highly influential, but has also been widely criticised. Her methodology had severe limitations – the details of the sample (for example, gender, illnesses, duration of terminal illness) were not given and the process of analysing the interviews was not specified (Copp, 1998). Based on the interview excerpts in the book, it has been suggested that intuition was the primary vehicle for extrapolating the phase model from the data (Schulz & Aderman, 1974).

Another criticism levelled at the model is that the phases are not actually found in sequential form in longitudinal research. Research has in fact found that while denial, depression, fear, hope and anger *are* often present in terminally ill patients, they show no particular chronology or stages (Schulz & Aderman, 1974; Shneidman, 1973).

Further criticism of the theory is that it takes no account of differences in personality, maturity or age in relation to the dying process, when research

Box 14.2   Alternative perspectives

Should the terminally ill have the right to choose when their life ends?

In cases of terminal illness, some patients may desire to end their life before they have reached the stage at which pain is unbearable, or disability so advanced that they are unable to move or talk. Whether or not they should be allowed to choose the allotted time of their death is referred to as *voluntary euthanasia*, or *assisted dying*. Currently, it is illegal in certain countries and states but not others. In the USA, it is legal in the states of Oregon, Montana and Washington, and in Europe both Switzerland and the Netherlands permit it. In Britain, assisted dying is illegal, but individuals can travel to Switzerland to end their life through an assisted dying service there. The competing ethical arguments for and against assisted dying are summarised next (Harris, Richard & Khanna, 2006).

Arguments for assisted dying:

- The majority of doctors and the general public in the UK support it (Braithwaite, 2005; Sommerville, 2005). Recent surveys suggest that over 50 per cent of doctors and over 80 per cent of the general public favour assisted dying (Harris, Richard & Khanna, 2006).
- Confidential reports from doctors in the UK and across Europe suggest that assisted dying is already widely practiced by doctors, for example by withdrawing treatment if the patient requests, but it is just not admitted to (van der Heide et al., 2003).
- Certain terminal illnesses can lead to loss of dignity, incontinence, loss of capacity to eat or drink, and constant pain for many years. If a person can voluntarily choose to avoid that suffering and gradual loss of function, and so depart when they are still able to 'say goodbye', they should be allowed to.
- Comprehensive legislation can ensure that only terminally ill patients with extreme suffering and pain can access an assisted dying service.
- Respecting an adult patient's autonomy and personal choice is central to all other laws – it is central to a society based on liberty that an adult may choose to live their life in any way they like as long as it does not harm others, and so they should be able to choose to end their life in a way that they choose.

Box 14.2   Continued

Arguments against assisted dying:

- Assisted dying could end up being seen as a cheaper alternative to investing in palliative care and hospice care, leading to a decline in hospice provision.
- A terminally ill person may well go through depression, during which they may lose the will to live. However, research shows that such depression is temporary and that they normally come out of this phase. Assisted dying services may be used by those who are depressed, before they have a chance to recover and reach the stage of acceptance that Kübler-Ross describes.
- If assisted dying is legal, then vulnerable patients could be forced or persuaded by relatives or professionals to take the option. Thus the decision may on the surface seem like the person is exercising free choice, but they may in fact be pressurised by others into it.
- The terminal nature of an illness is sometimes diagnosed by mistake, and people may make an unexpected recovery. It may therefore occur that someone would choose assisted dying when they are not in fact suffering a terminal illness and would not have died.
- Assisted dying legislation may help to promote an unhelpful and dangerous attitude in society that suffering should not be part of life, and/or that disability means that life is not worth living.
- Assisted dying may be the first step down a 'slippery slope' of euthanasia, which could evolve over time into agreeing the involuntary euthanasia of terminally ill patients without their consent, to 'put them out of their suffering'.

has shown that there are differences in how the process is coped with that depend on age and personality (Shneidman, 1973). Kastenbaum and Costa Jr. (1977) express concern that the stages of the model isolate the emotions of the dying person from the context of a person's life, and could in principle encourage staff or family to observe a dying person's anger or depression and dismiss it as 'going through the anger stage' or 'going through the depression stage', when in fact it may be based on shortcomings in the provision and quality of care or to some personal unresolved issue.

Buckman (1998) and Pattison (1977) distinguish phases of the whole terminal illness process in a different way to Kübler-Ross, and in many ways present a development of her model. They describe three psychosocial stages – *initial crisis*, *chronic illness* and the *terminal phase*. Being informed of the terminal nature of the illness precipitates the *initial crisis* phase, in which fear, anxiety, shock, disbelief, anger, denial, guilt and bargaining are prominent. Buckman (1998), distinguishes between adaptive and maladaptive variants of the coping responses that are typical in this stage, which Kübler-Ross does not. For example, hope can be both adaptive and maladaptive. Gum and Snyder (2002) found that hope need not be shaped by a false hope of recovery but can be found through the pursuit of achievable goals such as the hope of better pain and symptom management, the hope of resolving part conflicts or arguments, the hope of gaining more independence (for example, being moved out of hospital) and the hope of finding spiritual fulfilment (Gum & Snyder, 2002).

The crisis stage is followed by a *chronic illness* stage, during which there is a lessening in intensity of emotions and arousal, meaning that individuals can function and interact with others in a more stable manner. Depression is common at this stage, and is treatable with psychotherapy and medication (Brugha, 1993). The third and final stage in this model is the *terminal stage*, during which the patient will need constant care or hospitalisation, and will endeavour to accept the prospect of their death. Acceptance at this terminal stage is appropriate, but if adopted too soon it may be a maladaptive form of passive resignation than a dignified relinquishing of the struggle to survive.

Family, friends and professionals: Coping with terminal illness and dying

The process of coping with a terminal illness is a major challenge not only for the patient, but also for those who care for them. Coping strategies observed in the family of a dying person include a cognitive appraisal of the death as being 'far off' in the future, even when it is not; a constant hope for an improvement or the arrival of a new cure; an attempt to live in the present and 'take each day as it comes' and drawing on others for support (Benkel, Wijk & Molander, 2010). After the death, a search for meaning may occur in the events surrounding the death, which may account for the coincidence experiences described in Box 14.3.

Doctors, nurses and paramedics who work with terminally ill patients also devise ways of coping with death and dying. Schulman-Green (2003) conducted 20 interviews with doctors who routinely care for dying patients, and found that they use various ways to create a *distance* between themselves and the patient. *Medicalisation* is one such process – it involves only using medical terminology to refer to the patient, for example only referring to them as a 'case' with 'outcomes'. *Euphemisms* are used instead of words such as dying or death, for example paramedics refer to a dead body as a 'Signal 27' (Palmer, 1983). *Emotional distancing* is also used to guard against developing attachments to patients. One doctor was quoted as saying:

> I feel sad for them and sad for the families, but I don't engage because if I engage with every patient that got sick or died, then I would be an emotional wreck and then I wouldn't be able to do my job properly … So, I am able to distance myself from those feelings and have a professional approach. It doesn't mean I can't feel sad, it doesn't mean I can't acknowledge the sadness. GP7, male, age 56, in Schulman-Green (2003)

Box 14.3   Alternative perspectives

Deathbed coincidences

Partners and relatives frequently report experiences around the moment of death that neuropsychiatrist Peter Fenwick refers to as *deathbed coincidences* (Fenwick & Fenwick, 2008). These may be part of the coping process itself; the endeavour to find meaning in the final throes of a life and in the loss of a loved one. Deathbed coincidences involve dreams, apparitions or intuitions of the death around the very time that the person dies. Fenwick and Fenwick (2008) recount a number of individual examples of these experiences, including the following:

> On the night of his death he was at his own home in Darlington. I was with my own family at my home in a neighbouring village. At some time in the night I was woken up by my father calling my name. As he was calling, I could see what I can only assume to be his spirit rising into the night sky. Before picking up our telephone, which rang earlier than usual on the following morning, I was able to tell my wife that it was my mother ringing to tell me that my father had died. (p. 68)

Bereavement and grief

Bereavement that induces grief typically involves the death of a romantic partner or spouse, the loss of a child or the loss of a parent. Over 80 per cent of those who lose a spouse are female (Maciejewski et al., 2007) – this is because wives are typically younger than their husbands and women live on average longer than men. After the death of a spouse, men tend to become more depressed than women (Bonanno & Kaltman, 1999), while after the death of a child, mothers experience more intense and prolonged grief than fathers (Rando, 1983). Parental grief at losing a child leads to deeper and more enduring grief than other losses (Middleton et al., 1998; Sanders, 1979), and can endure for three years or more (Rando, 1983).

Grief includes biological, emotional, cognitive and behavioural features. Biological symptoms of grief include lowered immune functioning, heightened autonomic arousal, insomnia and increased risk of mortality (Parkes, 1996). For example, a person is 21 times as likely to have a heart attack in the 24 hours following bereavement than at other times (Mostofsky et al., 2012). Behavioural features of grief include disruption in work performance and the avoidance of intimate relationships. The defining emotional core of grief is a *yearning* or *pining* for the lost person, which stems from an intense but thwarted desire for continued attachment (Maciejewski et al., 2007; Parkes, 1996). Cognitive features include confusion and difficulty accepting the reality of loss; for example one study found that 70 per cent of the bereaved find it hard to believe that their spouses had died, up to two months after a spousal loss (Schucter & Zisook, 1993). Preoccupation with memories and thoughts of the deceased is also a key cognitive feature (Bonanno & Kaltman, 2001). Finally, a person's sense of self is typically disturbed by bereavement – 87 per cent of bereaved spouses agree with the statement 'a piece of me is missing' (Bonanno & Kaltman, 2001).

The phases and process of grief

At about the same time that Kübler-Ross was developing a stage model of coping with terminal illness, John Bowlby was developing a stage model of mourning and grief (Bowlby, 1961). Bowlby's model proposed that a normal grief reaction involves a phase of shock, followed by pangs of yearning and searching, then a disorganised spell during which a person may become depressed, followed by eventual reorganisation, all within six months to a year (Bowlby, 1980). Jacobs (1993) updated this four-stage model and synthesised it with a similar model developed by Parkes and Weiss (1983). Jacob's four phases of the bereavement process are:

1. Numbness-disbelief
2. Separation distress (yearning-anger-anxiety)
3. Depression and mourning
4. Recovery and readjustment

A recent quantitative longitudinal study put this four-phase theory to the test (Maciejewski et al., 2007). 233 participants were interviewed three times after the bereavement of a spouse due to chronic illness, at approximately six months, one year and 20 months after the loss. Disbelief, yearning, depression, anger and acceptance were measured at each time point. Findings showed that when trajectories of these five variables were compared, peak values were ordered in the sequence predicted by the phase model: disbelief peaked first, followed by yearning, anger, depression and finally acceptance. However, *yearning* was found to be the dominant negative experience at *all* time points, – anger, disbelief and depression peaked at different times but were always significantly lower than yearning. Also, a general acceptance of death was shown at all time points, which may relate to the fact that (a) no measurements were taken directly after the bereavement (that is, within a matter of days), and (b) all participants had lost their spouse after a chronic illness, rather than in unexpected circumstances, and had thus had a chance to mentally prepare for the event and avoid post-loss shock and disbelief.

Recovery from grief can lead to a perceived level of functioning that is experienced as superior than before the bereavement (Znoj, 2005). This is referred to as post-traumatic growth, and it has been known to result from a variety of life crises (Tedeschi & Calhoun, 2004). Calhoun and Tedeschi (1989) interviewed 52 adults about an experience of bereavement, and found that the majority described themselves as stronger, more mature, more independent and better able to face other crises, as a result of going through the bereavement. Clearly, reactions to bereavement vary substantially, and sometimes seeds of growth and positive change are sown in the seemingly infertile soil of loss.

Grief and attachment

Attachment theory has been used to explain the grief reaction. Attachment, as discussed in Chapter 12, is a bond between two persons that makes both parties desire proximity and find separation difficult. Grief over the death of an attachment figure can be conceived as an intense form of separation anxiety, for grief is typically proportional to the strength of attachment the bereaved had to the deceased (Parkes, 1996).

The **continuing bonds hypothesis** states that grief and mourning serves the functioning of maintaining an attachment bond with the deceased person, until such time as a person is ready to let go of the attachment they have with the deceased (Bowlby, 1980). This may help to gradually facilitate the dismantling of all the learnt attachment behaviours that typify a healthy marriage and ease the transition to full recovery (Klas, Silverman & Nickman, 1996). The continuing bonds hypothesis is supported by the finding that 80 per cent of widows and widowers have a strong sense of a continued emotional bond to their partner six months after their death (Bonanno & Kaltman, 1999). Schucter and Zisook (1993) found that 71 per cent of widows and widowers at two months after bereavement felt that deceased spouses were with them and 61 per cent felt that they were 'watching out for them'. 39 per cent reported that they actually talked to their deceased spouse regularly. Kübler-Ross (1978) quotes a parent who lost her daughter to cancer, describing this sense of a continuing bond:

> I miss Jamie so much, but out of the pain has come much growth and learning. I no longer fear death, for as I held Jamie in my arms as she died, I saw nothing to fear. I no longer believe that death is an end. Even as I drove off from the cemetery, I had no feeling of having left my child there. She was with me as she has been many times since her death. (p. 75)

Different kinds of bereavement: Deaths from natural causes, unexpected deaths, suicides and stillbirths

The majority of deaths result from natural causes – 94 per cent of deaths recorded in the US census are due to illness or old age (Maciejewski et al., 2007). In such instances, a person has time to become accustomed to the prospect of losing their loved one and can work through some of their grief before the event of death. If the illness lasts longer than six months, there is typically a greater acceptance of the death when it comes (Maciejewski et al., 2007).

There are other forms of bereavement that are unanticipated and unexpected, and these show more negative effects than bereavement from chronic illness. Lundin (1984) compared the outcome of sudden bereavement and bereavement from illness, eight years after the death of spouse. Even after eight years it was found that the majority of those who had lost their spouse unexpectedly had higher levels of grief, anger and a greater sense of yearning than those who had lost their spouse to chronic illness. Zisook, Chentsova-Dutton and Shuchter (1998) found that 36 per cent of bereaved spouses whose partner had died from accident or suicide showed all the symptoms of Post-Traumatic Stress Disorder (PTSD), whereas of those whose partners had died of natural causes, only 10 per cent showed those symptoms (see Chapter 11 for more on PTSD).

Deaths caused by traffic accidents involve additional stressors on top of the sense of loss, as a result of anger and blame directed at the person thought to be responsible for the accident, and also stress from any resulting trial or lawsuit (Weinberg, 1994). Those who feel a desire for revenge against the person who is perceived to have been the cause of the death show worse health outcomes than those who do not wish revenge (Weinberg, 1994). Alternatively, if a person blames himself for the death of a loved one in a traffic accident, this can lead to a burden of guilt (Weinberg, 1994). A fictional portrayal of self-blame in bereavement is shown in the 2008 film *Seven Pounds* featuring Will Smith. The story recounts the emotional pain and coping strategies of a character who blames himself for causing a car crash that leads to multiple fatalities, including his own girlfriend.

Bereavement from suicide has been shown to produce an intense form of grief reaction. One study compared college students who were bereaved as a result of homicide, suicide, accidental death, natural anticipated death and natural unanticipated death. The suicide bereavement group reported more intense grief than all the other types of bereavements (Silverman, Range & Overholser, 1994). In a study of parents whose child had committed suicide, 92 per cent described feeling guilty about the death – a far higher proportion than parents who were bereaved due to accident or disease (Miles & Demi, 1991). Furthermore, the study showed that for suicide-bereaved parents, guilt is the most distressing aspect of their grief. The challenges of coping with bereavement due to suicide are such that in the UK there is a nationwide charity called *Survivors of Bereavement Suicide* that is devoted to providing support groups and services to those who are bereaved from suicide. Their web address is provided at the end of this chapter.

Unexpected death can occur at the beginning of life too, as a result of stillbirth (baby dying in utero), perinatal death (death within seven days of birth) or Sudden Infant Death Syndrome (SIDS – an infant dying suddenly of unknown causes). All these forms of bereavement are traumatic and extremely distressing for parents (Dyregrov & Dyregrov, 1999). Stillbirth occurs when a baby dies of natural causes before it is born, or during the birth process. This is typically sudden and unexpected, and is made harder by being less often recognised as bereavement by other people (Lewis & Liston, 1981). After a stillbirth, parents must make several important decisions. Firstly, they will be asked whether to see and hold their baby or not. Secondly they will be asked if they want to have the baby buried, or bury him/her themselves. These decisions are often made in the midst of shock and grief, and research shows that while many parents choose not to hold the baby or bury it, many later deeply regret not doing so (Lewis & Liston, 1981). Personal testimonies of how parents have coped with the experience of stillbirth are available to view on the website of the *Stillbirth and Neonatal Death Charity* – the web address is provided at the end of the chapter. They are deeply moving and affecting to read and convey the immense emotional impact when the expectation of a new life is turned suddenly into a traumatic loss of life.

Box 14.4   Individual voices

Joan Didion – The Year of Magical Thinking

Much of what is discussed in the abstract about bereavement in this chapter is articulately described in personal detail within Joan Didion's autobiographical account of the loss of her husband to a sudden heart attack (Didion, 2005). In the book, called *The Year of Magical Thinking*, she describes the shock, numbness and denial that she initially experienced after he suddenly passed away, the pangs of anxious grief that periodically flooded her, the irrational thoughts she had that he might return, and the secondary stressors related to the death, such as the job of informing her friends and family that he had passed away. Here is her vivid description of the grief she felt at the time:

> Grief, when it comes, is nothing we expect it to be. It was not what I felt when my parents died: my father died a few days short of his eighty-fifth birthday and my mother a month short of her ninety-first, both after some years of increasing debility. What I felt in each instance was sadness, loneliness (the loneliness of the abandoned child of whatever age), regret for time gone by, for things unsaid ... Grief is different. Grief has no distance. Grief comes in waves, paroxysms, sudden apprehensions that weaken the knees and blind the eyes and obliterate the dailiness of life ... Tightness in the throat. Choking, need for sighing. Such waves began for me on the morning of December 31, 2003, seven or eight hours after the fact, when I woke alone in the apartment. (p. 28)

Coping with bereavement of a partner: The dual process model

Losing a spouse or partner is not only a source of grief and stress, it also leads to secondary stressors such as lacking important household skills that the partner took care of, dealing with post-bereavement arrangements such as selling the house, looking for a source of additional income, and accepting the identity of 'widow' or 'widower' (Stroebe & Schut, 1999; Stroebe & Schut, 2010).

According to the dual process model of bereavement coping, effectively managing both the grief of bereavement and these secondary stressors requires two different kinds of coping: *loss-oriented* and *restoration-oriented* (Stroebe, Schut & Stroebe, 2005). These are summarised visually in Figure 14.2. Loss-oriented coping strategies involve ways of managing the grief and depression of loss. For example, when a bereaved person tries to assuage their grief by looking through old photos or reminiscing about good times together, they are engaging in loss-oriented coping. This kind of coping predominates in the months directly after bereavement.

Restoration-oriented coping includes all attempts made to manage and reduce secondary stressors that result from the bereavement. It involves activities such as making arrangements for a funeral, thinking about how to master new skills that the deceased partner had undertaken in the house, learning about the legal issues surrounding bereavement such as wills and inheritance, and making new plans for the future. One qualitative study investigated the nature and use of loss-oriented and restoration-oriented coping in Chinese widowers – excerpts from this study are shown in Box 14.5.

Both loss-oriented and restoration-oriented coping are important for healthy recovery from the grief of conjugal bereavement but are not engaged in all the time. Ideally, as time progresses after the bereavement, a person will *oscillate* between loss-oriented coping and

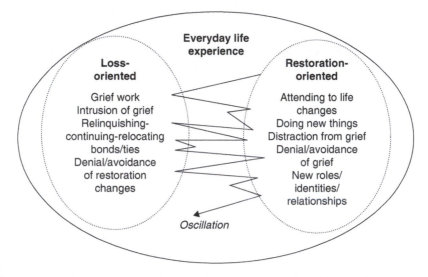

Figure 14.2   The key features of the dual process model of coping with bereavement

Source: Stroebe, Schut and Stroebe (2005, p. 51). Copyright © American Psychological Association. Reproduced with permission.

restoration-oriented coping (Stroebe, Schut & Stroebe, 2005). This back-and-forth transitioning allows for some balance between mourning and making plans. Eventually, restoration-oriented coping becomes the dominant concern as grief recedes. Interventions that use support groups to help improve both loss-oriented and restoration-oriented coping have proven to be effective ways of helping bereaved partners. Box 14.6 outlines the content of one such intervention (Lund et al., 2010).

Box 14.5   Individual voices

Loss-oriented and restoration-oriented coping in Chinese widowers

Loss-oriented coping – a 48-year old man describes suicidal thoughts after losing his wife and using social support to move past those thoughts:

> I felt really down after she passed away. I had thoughts of suicide. Then I thought to myself, 'my son is grown-up and has a stable job. He is able to support himself. As for my daughter, I can leave her an inheritance of one to two million Hong Kong dollars that can see her through her studies and pay for her daily living expenses while she is completing her studies. I also have siblings who can care for them in my absence. If I were to follow my wife, I would have no regrets.' When I shared my thoughts with my friends, they asked me, 'Would you want your daughter to lose you and gain two million Hong Kong dollars?' I gave further thought to my friends' question and the suicidal ideation vanished. (Woo et al., 2008, p. 284)

Restoration-oriented coping – A 37-year old man describes using a new hobby to help forge plans for the future:

> When I was preparing the funeral for my wife, I was wondering what I could do afterwards. So, on my way to the funeral home, I had some time and decided to drop in to the public library. I looked through some magazines and decided to get a diving magazine. After reading it, I became fascinated with the world under the sea. So, I decided to go on a diving trip to Thailand, and I made that decision before the funeral ... Since then, I have been addicted to diving. (Woo et al., 2008, p. 291)

There appears to be a normative gender difference in bereavement coping (Stroebe, Schut & Stroebe, 2005). Women tend to focus on loss-oriented coping more than men, while men focus more on restoration-oriented coping. As a result, bereaved men benefit more from counselling that focuses on the emotional aspect of grief and loss-orientation, while bereaved women gain more from restoration-orientation counselling that focuses on how to manage secondary stressors (Stroebe, Schut & Stroebe, 2005).

Box 14.6   Real-world applications

Helping the bereaved partner: Applying the dual-process model

Lund et al. (2010) designed and conducted a 14-session series of support-groups for widows based on the dual-process model of bereavement. Participants were persons over 50 whose spouse or partner had died within the previous two to six months. The evaluative data suggests that the intervention was effective in helping these participants to adjust to life without their partner. Sessions oscillated between loss-oriented and restoration- oriented topics.

Loss-oriented topics included:

- Discussion about the feelings and thoughts that grief brings.
- Discussion of the circumstances surrounding one's partner's death.
- Discussion about how grief and the sense of loss affects daily functioning.
- Exercises aimed at helping participants to express grief-related feelings.
- Exercises for dealing with loneliness and feelings of isolation.
- How to cope with the stress of birthdays and holidays.
- Open discussion of what one misses and does not miss about one's partner.

Restoration-oriented topics included:

- Self-care and health care: Exploring what the partner did in the way of health-related needs and how to manage that.
- Wills and trusts: Filing legal documents, understanding statements, developing and managing a household budget, making

Box 14.6   Continued

decisions about property issues, recognising and avoiding
scams aimed at widows.

- Household and vehicle responsibilities: Breaking household
duties into small, manageable steps, following regular maintenance schedules for home and car, identifying and remedying
household hazards.
- Nutrition for one: Shopping for one and understanding labels,
preparing one, or two-step meals, freezing portions for later use,
sharing recipes, finding nutritional assistance in the community.
- Ways of remaining socially connected: Discussing inexpensive
and accessible entertainment or leisure activities, comparing
and sharing new socialisation experiences, finding voluntary
work.

Pathological grief

Grieving in response to the death of a loved one is painful but not
pathological. It reflects the very real difficulty of coming to terms with
an all-consuming loss. However, in some instances, grief takes forms that
are abnormal. The most commonly described abnormal grief reaction
is *chronic grief*, which is characteristically lasts for several years or more
following the death (Parkes, 1996), and is found in approximately
15 per cent of widowed persons (Bonanno & Kaltman, 2001). Other
abnormal forms include grief that is seemingly *absent* or *suppressed*
despite an attachment to the deceased, or grief that is *distorted* or *conflicted* by guilt or anger (Rando, 1992). *Delayed* grief occurs when a person
experiences grief at some duration after the loss (Parkes, 1996). Lewis and
Liston (1981) state that a delayed grief reaction is common in the case of
stillbirth, and the following extract from a woman, nine years after the
stillbirth of twins, clearly describes this phenomenon:

At the time of my babies' death I put my thoughts and feelings away
as I put clothes and equipment away in the room that had been ready
for them. Without taking time to mourn and think about the deaths,
I set about having the family I had always wanted. Now, nine years
and four children later, I find myself thinking about them. With time
on my hands because the youngest is at school, thoughts about my
dead twins creep in unbidden and unwanted. I am in tears as I stand
in the larder trying to work out what to do during the day. (p. 154)

Depression and bereavement

Around half those who lose a spouse experience an episode of clinical depression in the months following the bereavement (for example, Zisook et al., 1997). In 2002, a quantitative longitudinal study on this topic was published that was groundbreaking in a number of respects (Bonanno et al., 2002). It was the first study to successfully measure depressive symptoms *before* and *after* the death of a spouse in older adults. It was also the first to use longitudinal data to calculate *different trajectories* of depressive symptoms across the course of a bereavement transition. Additional data was gathered on the pre-bereavement quality of marriage, pre-bereavement attachment to spouse, and presence of pre-death illness in the deceased spouse.

Participants were all married couples from the city of Detroit in which the husband was aged 65 or over. The first assessment of depressive symptoms was taken from 1532 individuals. Researchers then monitored the sample over the ensuing two years, and for the 205 individuals whose spouse died, they would be assessed for depression at six months and 18 months after the death. Change in depression scores for individuals was calculated by comparing pre- and post-measures. If a person increased *or* decreased by more than one standard deviation in their depressive symptoms from before to after the bereavement, this was labelled a significant change. From this, various *trajectories of depression* were established, the five most common of which were:

1. *Common grief*: Low depression pre-loss, increase at six months post-loss, and then decrease by 18 months after
2. *Resilient*: Low depression at all three time points
3. *Chronic grief*: Low depression pre-loss, increase at six months and also at 18 months
4. *Chronic depression*: High depression at all time points
5. *Depressed-improved*: High depression pre-loss, decrease at six months and also at 18 months

The mean depression scores for these five depression trajectory groups are illustrated in Figure 14.3. The most common pattern was the resilient pattern (46 per cent of the sample), suggesting that for many people bereavement does not lead to depression. Chronic grief (16 per cent of the sample) was more common than common grief (11 per cent of the sample), suggesting that common grief (that is, depression lasting under a year) is not in fact so common after all.

The depressed-improved group constituted 10 per cent of the sample – they were those persons for whom mental health actively *improved* over the

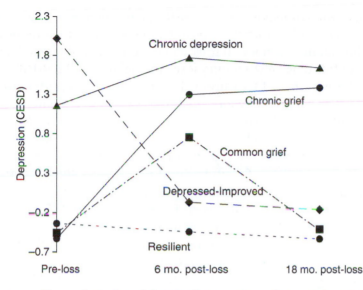

Figure 14.3   Five trajectories of depressive symptoms from pre-bereavement to 18 months post-loss

Note: Depressive symptoms measured using Center for Epidemiological Studies Depression (CESD) inventory.

Source: Bonanno et al. (2002, p. 1157). Copyright © American Psychological Association. Reproduced with permission.

course of a conjugal bereavement. It was found that they had (a) the most negative evaluations of their marriage, (b) the most ambivalent attachment to their spouse, and usually (c) a spouse that was ill prior to bereavement. This suggests that if a marriage lacks an emotional attachment and/or a spouse is chronically ill, bereavement may in fact be experienced as a positive transition. That said, *all* groups were assessed for grief as well as depression, and all described experiencing grief at six months and 18 months.

While this longitudinal study was an important contribution to the bereavement literature, it should be borne in mind that the sample had a mean age of over 70, and it may be that adults in midlife or early adulthood would react quite differently to losing a spouse. For example, the high proportion of resilience may relate to the fact that older adults may, due to their age, expect bereavement more and be more prepared for it than adults in younger age groups.

Concluding comments

The literature on dying and bereavement is substantial and varied, but there are some areas that still lack research. How individuals who are diagnosed with terminal illness cope with the prospect of their own death is widely researched, but what people actually *do* during their months following the diagnosis is not well researched. Longitudinal research on the structure of this time between diagnosis and death is still needed.

In the bereavement literature, it is common that reports based on research with widows and widowers make sweeping statements about the effects of losing a loved one, however losing a parent or child leads to different challenges and emotions than losing a partner, but there is less research on these. There is also little literature on how people cope with the death of siblings. For understandable reasons, there is very little research on the effects of becoming bereaved due to murder – although discussion of this issue is not absent from the literature (for example, Staudacher, 1987), it lacks a wide research basis.

Finally, grief from bereavement is assumed in much of the medical literature to be characterised emotionally by depression; for example there is a 'bereavement exclusion' in the Diagnostic and Statistical Manual of Mental Disorders (DSM) for depression, which states that a person should not be diagnosed with clinical depression if they have just experienced a close bereavement (APA, 2000). The rationale for this exclusion is that sadness and grief is a normal reaction to bereavement, and so should not be medicalised. However, research suggests that anxious 'yearning' rather than depression is the most characteristic emotional reaction to loss; thus there should arguably be a bereavement exclusion in the DSM for anxiety too (Maciejewski et al., 2007).

Questions for you to reflect on

- Funeral therapy, mentioned in Box 14.1, is popular in South Korea. How do you think you would feel if you went through this?
- Is it possible to grieve for someone without being attached to them? Why do you think so many people grieved when Princess Diana died? Had they all developed an attachment to her?
- Try and think of the various possible difficulties that crop up in someone's life when their spouse dies, and write them down. Divide them into primary stressors and secondary stressors (see dual process model of coping for a reminder about these).

Summary points

- Kübler-Ross developed a model of how a person comes to terms with terminal illness, which involves moving through a sequence of phases: (1) Denial, (2) Anger, (3) Bargaining, (4) Depression and (5) Acceptance.

- The model has been criticised as longitudinal research and has showed that these aspects of the dying process are not inevitable, and not sequenced in this particular order.
- Research suggests that doctors cope with having to frequently encounter death and dying by using ways of depersonalising dying patients and creating emotional distance between themselves and dying patients.
- Bereavement leads to grief in instances where a surviving person was attached to the deceased and laments their passing. Grief involves biological features, such as compromised immune system, affective features such as anxiety and yearning, cognitive features such as confusion and irrational thinking, and behavioural factors such as social withdrawal and difficulties with work.
- Unexpected deaths are harder to cope with than those that occur after a chronic illness. Suicide can lead to a painful mixture of guilt as well as grief in a surviving partner, and deaths that result from vehicle accidents can lead to anger at the person at fault combined with grief at the loss.
- Coping with bereavement involves coming to terms with the loss and restoring life to build a new future. These two challenges are the key components of the dual process model of bereavement coping. Loss-oriented coping predominates directly after a death, and over time this oscillates with restoration-oriented coping, until restoration becomes the dominant focus.
- Pathological grief can manifest itself either in an absence of symptoms despite being attached to the deceased, or prolonged symptoms that become chronic and last years without showing improvement. In such cases, a person may require specialist help to recover.
- A proportion of individuals show depression in the run up to a bereavement that disappears after the event. This suggests that bereavement for some is a release and a relief, and reflects the fact that as with all major life transitions, bereavement is beguilingly complex and can lead to reactions ranging from chronic mental illness in some persons, to a sense of improved wellbeing and personal growth in others.

Recommended reading

Bonanno, G. A. & Kaltman, S. (1999). Toward an integrative perspective on bereavement. *Psychological Bulletin*, 125, 760–776.

Harris, D., Richard, B. & Khanna, P. (2006). Assisted dying: The ongoing debate. *Postgraduate Medical Journal*, 82, 479–82.

Kübler-Ross, E. (1969). *On Death and Dying: What the Dying Have to Teach Doctors, Nurses, Clergy and Their Own Families*. London: Simon & Schuster.

Maciejewski, P. K., Zhang, B., Block, S. D. & Prigerson, H. G. (2007). An empirical examination of the stage theory of grief. *JAMA: The Journal of the American Medical Association*, 297, 716–23.

Parkes, C. M. (1996). *Bereavement: Studies of Grief in Adult Life*, 3rd edn. London: Routledge.

Recommended websites

BBC page on coping with bereavement: www.bbc.co.uk/health/emotional_health/bereavement.

Report on the Coffin Academy in South Korea: www.youtube.com/watch?v=bVX3-hHnttU.

Survivors of Bereavement Suicide (UK support organisation): www.uk-sobs.org.uk/.

Stillbirth and Neonatal Death Charity – personal accounts of coping with stillbirth: www.uk-sands.org/Support/Personal-experiences.html.

Glossary

Accelerated longitudinal study A longitudinal research design that involves studying persons of varying ages for a period of time (for example, a year), and then combining the year-long change profiles found in different age groups into one single growth curve for the whole age range of the sample.

Adult Attachment Interview (AAI) A structured interview used for assessing the quality of attachment between an adult and his/her parents. It leads to categorising a person into one of three types: secure-autonomous, insecure-dismissing or insecure-preoccupied.

Affect A collective term for all aspects of subjective experience that have a 'valence' (a sense of being pleasant or unpleasant), such as emotional feelings and other subjectively felt drives such as hunger or sex drive.

Affect complexity The variety, breadth and depth of a person's consciously experienced affective feelings.

Age effect A measured difference in a variable that is attributable to ageing (for example, hair going grey). In research, age effects are often mixed up with cohort effects and time-of-measurement effects (see entries for these).

Age of majority The age at which a person is legally recognised as an adult in a particular culture. The most common age of majority is 18.

Agoraphobia A fear of open or public spaces, often combined with the fear of having a panic attack in such a place.

Alzheimer's disease The most common form of dementia, principally characterised by an abnormal decline in memory capacity, and also in later stages by physical degeneration.

Amygdala An almond-shaped group of nuclei located within the temporal lobe of the brain, known to be involved in processing emotions such as fear and pleasure.

Amyloid plaques Tangled masses of proteins that are deposited between neurons in individuals who suffer from Alzheimer's disease.

Andropause   (also called male menopause) A speculative male equivalent of the female menopause, characterised by decreasing sexual function and sex drive in midlife.

Angiogenesis   The capacity of blood vessels in the brain to increase in number during both childhood and adulthood, leading to greater brain oxygenation.

Anorexia Nervosa   A disorder characterised by an extreme chronic decline in food intake, leading to dangerous weight loss. It is more prevalent in females than males and typically first appears in adolescence.

Anorexia of ageing   A phrase used to describe the decline in appetite and eating shown by older persons, seemingly due to a reduction in the hunger drive.

Antioxidants   A group of substances such as Vitamin A, C and E, which are known to protect cells by breaking down free radicals (molecules that are highly reactive and can damage cells).

Adolescent-limited vs. life-course-persistent antisocial behaviour
A typology of two antisocial behaviour patterns. 'Adolescent-limited' occurs within adolescence as a normative part of development, particularly in males. Life-course-persistent is a chronic pattern that has its roots in adverse neurological and environmental conditions early in life, and continues throughout childhood, adolescence and adulthood.

Anxiety disorders   A group of mental illnesses characterised by abnormal levels of worry and fear, such as phobia, post-traumatic stress disorder, obsessive-compulsive disorder and generalised anxiety disorder.

Archival records   Any data that are collected prior to the beginning of a research study. These may be public datasets from large research studies, or data gathered for non-research purposes such as medical records, credit histories or governmental census data.

Assimilation/accommodation   Two processes that Jean Piaget postulated as underlying cognitive development. Assimilation involves the integration of new information into existing schemas, while accommodation involves changing existing schemas to fit new, discrepant information.

Attachment anxiety (in adults)   The tendency to find close relationships anxiety-provoking and/or jealousy-provoking.

Attachment avoidance (in adults)   The tendency to avoid getting into close romantic relationships.

Attention Deficit Hyperactivity Disorder (ADHD)   A behavioural disorder, diagnosed mainly in pre-adolescent boys, defined by a mixture of low attention span, impulsivity and hyperactivity.

Attentional deficit theory   A theory that cognitive ageing is associated with a reduction in the amount of attentional capacity, which is in turn linked to a reduced frontal lobe efficiency.

Attrition effect   The tendency for some people to drop out of longitudinal research studies, leading to smaller sample numbers at later points in the study.

Authenticity   The expression of one's inner feelings, goals, values and preferences in behaviour and roles, allied to the self-knowledge required to have a clear sense of what one's 'inner feelings, goals, values and preferences' actually are.

Autism   A spectrum of developmental disorders, characterised by communication difficulties, language delay and repetitive behaviour. These disorders first appear in infancy and range from mild to severe.

Autobiographical memory   (also called episodic memory)   A person's memory for events, people and occurrences in his/her own life, which together help to define his/her personal history and identity.

Behavioural genetics   A form of research that employs twin studies and adoption studies to establish the relative contribution of genes and environment to the shaping of traits and abilities.

Berlin Wisdom Interview   A structured interview that assesses wisdom, during which participants must voice aloud their responses to six hypothetical real-life problem situations. Responses are coded by trained researchers to assess the presence of the five components of the Berlin Wisdom Model (*see entry*).

Berlin Wisdom Model   A model that conceives of wisdom as expertise in dealing with complex interpersonal situations, through the use of five components: (1) factual knowledge of real life, (2) strategic knowledge in the pragmatics of life, (3) lifespan contextualism, (4) understanding the relativism of values and (5) knowledge of the uncertainties of life.

Biographical studies   Research designs that gain retrospective data from participants about their past, usually by way of interviews or written narratives.

Biopsychosocial paradigm   A scientific approach to development that emphasises the importance of studying development at biological, psychological and social levels, and understanding how these levels interact.

Bipolar disorder   A mental disorder (also called manic depression) characterised by oscillation between periods of elevated mood and periods of depression or agitation.

Bulimia Nervosa   A behavioural disorder characterised by cycles of binge eating followed by purging through vomiting. It typically appears first in adolescence and is more common in girls than boys.

Civil partnership   A term for the legal union of two same-sex individuals, used in countries where such a union is legally recognised but not given the term marriage.

Co-action   The term coined by Gilbert Gottlieb to describe a reciprocal influence between two levels of development – for example, where biological development affects social development, and social development then in turn affects the biological level.

Cognitive Reserve Hypothesis   The hypothesis that those who have more enriched socio-economic environments during childhood and early adulthood have more resilient cognitive and/or neurobiological architectures that protect against age-related cognitive deficits later in adulthood.

Cohort effect   Differences found between persons of different ages in a cross-sectional study that are due to historical differences between them (for example, growing up in different social eras), rather than due to ageing or adult development.

Content analysis   A process of analysing qualitative data (*see entry*), by way of allocating segments of the data to pre-decided content categories.

Continuing bonds hypothesis   The hypothesis that a person who is bereaved continues to feel attachment to the deceased person for a time after their death, and may continue to search for the person or feel their presence even though they know that such an action or feeling is irrational.

Continuous change   Quantitative change that occurs gradually, leading to a continuous line of change in a graph that is not broken by any sudden shifts up or down.

Couple friends   Friendships that are formed and maintained at the level of couple-to-couple, rather than at the level of individual-to-individual.

Crisis   An episode of a person's life during which he/she experiences a major stressful transition in a core area of life such as work or relationship that leads to changes in lifestyle and identity.

Cross-sectional design   A research design in which individuals of different ages are studied and compared. Differences between age groups may be used as evidence of adult development or ageing.

Crystallised intelligence   Cognitive ability in the domain of knowledge storage and memorisation, shown by tests such as vocabulary tests or general knowledge tests.

Defence mechanisms   Processes such as suppression, humour, altruism, projection, dissociation and fantasy, which are used to help cope with stress, conflict and painful memories.

Deferred empathy   Empathy for another person that is experienced after a delay of months or years, due to a new realisation gained about the other person's emotional or cognitive state that was not achieved at the time of interacting with them.

Defining Issues Test (DIT)   A pencil-and-paper test of moral reasoning, designed by James Rest, which categorises a person's predominant moral schema as *personal interest, maintaining norms* or *principled.*

Dialectical thinking   An adult thinking ability defined by understanding that two points can be opposed to each other and yet both be true or valid: for instance, that two opposed approaches to a moral dilemma can both be valid in different ways – for example, arguments about the right to die (see Chapter 14).

Diathesis stress model   A model of mental disorder aetiology, which states that personal vulnerability and ongoing stress must combine to cause the onset of mental illness.

Diffusion Tensor Imaging (DTI)   A form of magnetic resonance imaging (MRI) that can be used to image white matter in the brain, and thus assess its structural integrity.

Dilemma of the aggregate   Quantitative research often presents data at the level of the group average or group aggregate; however, average-level change may not reflect individual change. This presents a dilemma in how or whether to apply quantitative aggregate findings to individual people.

Direction of development   Positive adult development must change in a particular direction, in order to distinguish it from negative development. There are a number of directions for positive development, including evolutionary (increasing reproductive success), eudaimonic (increasing wellbeing), orthogenetic (becoming more complex), veridical (perceiving reality more accurately and ridding oneself of personal biases) and virtuous (becoming more ethical or prosocial).

Discontinuous change   Quantitative change in a variable, found over a period of time, which is sudden and abrupt and shows a clear discontinuity with change gradients before and after.

Disengagement theory   A theory stating that elderly adults gradually disengage from social and productive roles, in order to cope with decreasing physical energy, and changing social expectations after active parenting and retirement.

Dual-career families   Families in which both parents are in paid work.

Dual-process model of coping with bereavement   A model proposed to describe the process of coping with bereavement of one's partner. It specifies that a person must cope in two ways: firstly with the feelings of grief, and secondly with the challenges of building a new life as a widow or widower. Oscillation between these two coping challenges is considered to be appropriate and beneficial to health.

Dynamic Integration Theory   A theory that states that human beings aim at increasing both their emotional wellbeing (affect optimisation) and emotional complexity (affect complexity). Mature emotional regulation is said to involve an integration of both.

Early adult crisis   Crisis that occurs in the first decade of adult life (also called quarterlife crisis), characterised by an emotionally distressing termination of a recently undertaken major life role – for example, a relationship or job – followed by a period of moratorium and rebuilding a new life structure.

Eden Alternative   A movement that is orientated towards providing humane, vibrant and meaningful environments to elderly adults in care.

Efficient cause explanation   An explanation of a behaviour that works by recourse to a causal process or set of antecedent phases. This type of explanation is contrasted with final, formal and material explanations (see entries).

Ego development theory   A school of theories, including those of Jane Loevinger and Robert Kegan, postulating a series of discrete stages that individuals pass through on the way to developing a mature ego. Ego here is defined as the integrating process/structure of personality.

Emerging adulthood theory   A theory proposed by Jeffrey Arnett that postulates a phase of life through which young adults pass after adolescence, which runs approximately from age 18 to 25. It is defined by an ambiguous adult status, frequent changes in relationships and residence, and high levels of stress.

Emotional intelligence   The measureable capacity to perceive, understand and manage emotions in oneself and others.

Emotional regulation   The process of maintaining one's negative emotions within normal and healthy levels, and increasing the experience of positive emotions.

Empathy   The inference of another person's emotional state from their behaviour, body language or speech, in some cases leading to the generation of that same emotion in oneself.

Enriched environment   The term used to describe a laboratory environment created for rats or another laboratory animal, which is enriched with sensory stimulation, social interaction and opportunities for physical activity.

Epigenetics   The processes by which experience and environments affect the behaviour of genes, either within the context of the lifespan (developmental epigenetics), or over subsequent generations (inheritance epigenetics).

Epistemic cognition   The process of thinking about abstract concerns pertaining to knowledge, such as the nature of right and wrong, truth and falsity, and the basis of authority.

EQUIP programme   A group-based moral education intervention to help adolescent and young adult males develop more mature moral judgement and prosocial choices.

Ethic of Care Interview   A structured interview developed to measure the extent to which adults care for others and have a prosocial attitude to others.

Experience sampling   The method of gathering self-report data in 'real-time' by getting participants to respond to a pager or phone signal at points during the day to rate or describe their feelings at that exact moment.

Faith Development Theory   A theory developed by James Fowler to describe a sequence of stages that the development of mature religious faith moves through, from *Intuitive-Projective faith* to *Mythic-Literal faith* to *Synthetic-Conventional faith* to *Individual-Reflective faith* to *Conjunctive faith* and finally to *Universalizing faith.*

Family life cycle theory   A theory that proposes a normative series of stages through which adults pass when they start a family, which are *pairing/ beginning family, childbearing families, families with preschool children, families with school-age children, families with teenagers, families as 'launching ground', middle family years* and *post-active-parenting/retirement.*

Final cause explanation   An explanation of a behaviour that is based on inferring the goal towards which it is aimed or the function that it serves. This type of explanation is contrasted with efficient, formal and material explanations (see entries).

Five Factor Model (The Big Five)   A trait model of personality that stipulates five basic traits as the source of interpersonal variability: Openness to Experience, Conscientiousness, Extraversion, Agreeableness and Neuroticism.

Fluid intelligence   Cognitive ability in the domain of novel problem-solving.

Flynn Effect   The fact, found by James Flynn, that average performance on IQ tests has continuously increased in industrialised countries over the past 100 years.

Formal cause explanation   Explaining a psychological phenomenon by recourse to an abstract formal theory or law. This type of explanation is contrasted with efficient, final and material explanations (see entries).

Formal operational thinking   A form of thinking that emerges first in adolescence, and is characterised by an understanding of theory, causality, hypotheses and abstract systems of thought such as law, metaphor and algebra.

Formulation (in assessment of mental disorder) An approach to assessing a person in distress, which aims at producing a coherent formulated summary of a person's total pattern of symptoms, current life circumstances and potential aetiological factors. It is contrasted with the process of mental illness diagnosis, which aims at giving a person a singular and static label.

Four Component Model of morality A model that conceptualises moral functioning as the integrated outcome of (1) ethical sensitivity – the ability to attend to and identify moral issues, (2) moral judgement – the ability to reason and justify moral courses of action, (3) moral motivation – prioritising morally correct choices against other drives and goals, and (4) moral character – the trait-like tendency to be prosocial.

Four quadrant model Ken Wilber's four-quadrant theory that views development as occurring concurrently in four domains: inner-singular (psychology), inner-collective (society), outer-singular (biology) and outer-collective (ecology).

Fourth Age The psychosocial life stage encountered in old age, characterised by a reduction in personal independence and the corresponding need for living arrangements that offer help and support, such as living with grown-up children, in a residential home for the elderly or in a nursing home.

Frontal lobe An area of the brain located at the front of each cerebral hemisphere, separated from the parietal lobe by a gap called the central sulcus, and from the temporal lobe by a fold called the lateral (Sylvian) sulcus. Frontal lobes are functionally implicated in complex reasoning, executing functioning (for example, decision-making and goal-setting) and emotional control.

Fronto-amygdalar Age-related Differences in Emotion (FADE) A term that describes the finding that, compared with younger adults, older adults show a different use of the amygdala and greater use of the frontal cortex in emotion-processing.

Frontotemporal dementia A condition caused by degeneration of the frontal lobe of the brain, characterised by apathy, loss of inhibition and ritualistic behaviours.

Functionalist theory of emotions The theory that emotions have a functional role in adaptation and development, and are linked to particular action tendencies.

Generativity The motive to create something positive or give to others, in ways that benefit future generations or younger people.

Gero-transcendence theory   The theory that older adults become increasingly spiritual and focused on concerns that transcend the self, while becoming less concerned with material gain and achievement.

Grandparenthood career   The changes involved in being an active grandparent, resulting from the changing age of the grandchild – from infant to child to adolescent to adult. Typically the grandparent is most involved when the grandchild is pre-adolescent.

Grey matter   A major component of the brain and nervous system composed mainly of neural cell bodies, glial cells and capillaries. It appears grey to the eye.

Grief   Behavioural, cognitive and affective reactions to the experience of loss. It is typically proportionate to the strength of an attachment to the bereaved person or lost object/role. When grief occurs following bereavement, it involves continued thoughts about the deceased person, depressive and anxious feelings.

Grounded theory   A qualitative analytic methodology focused on developing theory inductively from open-ended verbal data or text.

Guided autobiography   A group-based technique in which individuals explore their personal life story and resolve past conflicts, by way of sharing stories from their past over a series of group sessions. It is used mostly with elderly persons.

Harvard Grant Study of Adult Development   A long-term longitudinal adult development study conducted by George Vaillant and colleagues at Harvard, which has focused mainly on health and personality.

Hearing Voices Movement   A self-help movement for individuals who suffer from auditory hallucinations, which employs user-led discussion groups (for example, those run by the Hearing Voices Network) and promotes open disclosure of voice-hearing experiences in safe, non-judgemental environments. It is affiliated to the Maastricht approach to hearing voices (*see entry*).

HEXACO model of personality   A trait model of personality that specifies six basic traits of personality, five of which are the same as the five factor model of personality (*see entry*), and the sixth being *honesty/humility*.

Hierarchy of needs   A part of Abraham Maslow's theory of development, which stipulates that higher-order needs emerge only after once lower needs are met, starting with physical needs such as food, thirst, safety and security, followed by psychological needs such as belonging, self-esteem and knowledge. The pinnacle of the hierarchy is *self-actualisation* (*see entry*).

Hippocampus   A horseshoe-shaped structure that is part of the limbic system in the brain. There are two in each brain: one in the left hemisphere one in the right hemisphere. They are involved in the formation, organisation and storage of memory.

Homophily, principle of   The empirically supported principle that people tend to seek friends and partners who are similar to them in interests, traits and socio-economic criteria.

Identity statuses, theory of   Marcia's theory of identity statuses describes four forms of identity status in adolescence: *diffuse, foreclosed, moratorium* and *achieved*. Achieved identity is found through a combination of identity exploration and commitment, and is associated with positive developmental outcomes.

Inhibition deficit theory   A theory that locates the source of age-related cognitive decline in the failure to inhibit irrelevant information from being processed in working memory.

Inspection time   A way of assessing visual processing speed. Two lines are flashed on a screen for under a second, and the person being assessed must say which line was longest. The presentation time then gradually decreases, to find the lowest threshold at which a person can see the difference between the lines.

Internal working model   A cognitive representation of close attachment relationships that is developed in early childhood, and continues to act as a set of expectations for relationships in adulthood.

Interpretative phenomenological analysis (IPA)   A qualitative analytical method that employs intensive thematic analysis of interviews or focus groups, in order to gain an empathic representation of the personal, subjective experience of individuals, and the common experiential themes across persons.

Intra-individual variability   Variability in how a single person behaves, thinks or feels over time, contrasted with inter-individual variability, with is differences *between* people in how they behave, feel or think.

Intrinsic motivation   Engagement in an activity because that activity is enjoyable, interesting or satisfying. It is contrasted with extrinsic motivation, which is engagement in an activity for the purposes of later gain or outcome.

Ipsative trait change   Change over time in the overall quantitative profile that a person shows across multiple personality traits.

Kohlberg's stage theory of moral development   A theory that postulates a series of sequential stages that a person passes through as they develop the capacity for moral judgement. These stages are *preconventional* (based on self-interest and tit-for-tat exchange), *conventional* (based on social norms and relationships) and *post-conventional* (based on principles and concepts of justice).

Latent-growth-curve analysis (latent growth modelling)   A form of statistical analysis based on structural equation modelling, used for analysing longitudinal data to estimate quantitative change over time.

Lexical Abstraction Assessment System (LAAS)   A computerised system for assessing the hierarchical complexity of thought, evidenced within a person's oral and written textual output.

Life Events and Difficulties Schedule (LEDS)   A structured interview designed to elicit information on recent stressful life events and difficulties, employed in research on the relationship between life events and mental illness.

Life review   The process of intensively reviewing one's autobiographical memories in order to find coherence in one's own life story, and to make peace with past conflicts or regrets. It is purported to occur frequently in older adults and terminally ill adults.

Life story   A life story is an aggregation of episodes from a person's past that together make a single first-person narrative about 'who I am and how I came to be here', which is first achieved in adolescence and continues to develop through adulthood. There may be public and private versions of a life story in adulthood, and there are various systematic interview-based and group-based methods for eliciting life story data.

Life structure   A working integration of inner traits, values, beliefs and goals, and external commitments, roles and residence. This is a developmental achievement in adulthood, which when successful leads to a manageable lifestyle and sense of identity. When a life structure is out of balance, a person is likely to experience a time of transition prior to a balanced life structure being refound.

Longitudinal designs   Research designs that involve repeated assessment of the same group of individuals over time. Such designs can be *dynamic* (aimed at tracking trajectories of change over time) or *predictive* (aimed at establishing whether a variable measured earlier in life predicts a different variable later in life – for example, whether smoking at age 40 predicts cancer at age 60).

Maastrict Approach to hearing voices   A theoretical and practical approach to understanding hallucinatory voice-hearing, pioneered by Dutch psychiatrist Marius Romme. It involves examining the meaning, character and content of the voice that a person hears, and relating them to past traumas and life experiences, and using that as the basis of therapy and intervention.

Male menopause   (see andropause).

Material cause explanation   An explanation of a behaviour that is made by recourse to the biological substrate that underpins it. This type of explanation is contrasted with efficient, final and formal explanations (see entries).

Maternity leave/paternity leave   Time taken off work by a mother or father before and/or after the birth of a child, the duration of which is affected by corporate and national policy on statutory maternity and paternity leave.

Meaning in life   A combined sense of significance, excitement, value and ultimate purpose that makes life worth living. Meaning in life is sought and possessed in differing degrees, depending on the individual.

Meditation   A collective term for practices that involve focusing concentration on a stimulus such as breathing or walking, which help to still the mind and create emotional balance. These practices can be used for health purposes, for relaxation or as a form of spiritual practice.

Menopause   The period of a woman's life, typically occurring around the late forties or early fifties, during which menstruation permanently ceases and the fertile period of a woman's life ends. This is often linked to other challenges associated with late midlife, such as the increasing signs of ageing and lowering sex drive.

Metacognition   The capacity to reflect on and monitor one's own thoughts.

Midlife   The period of adult life running approximately between the ages of 40 and 60.

Midlife crisis   An episode of crisis (*see entry*) that occurs within the midlife period, and may be related to the concerns about ageing that are common in this age group.

Mindfulness meditation   A form of meditation that involves being physically still and focusing attention on the passing of the present moment and any thoughts that arise, in a non-judgemental way.

Model of Hierarchical Complexity   A model of adult cognitive development that stipulates a number of stages of increased cognitive complexity that emerges over the course of development. Adult stages in the model include systematic, meta-systematic, paradigmatic and cross-paradigmatic stages.

Moral Judgement Interview   A structured interview designed to elicit a person's open-ended responses to a series of moral dilemmas. Responses are scored and categorised into Kohlberg's stage scheme of moral development.

Multilevel modelling   A form of statistical analysis based on regression, which can be used to examine predictors of change at multiple 'nested' levels – for example, wellbeing change over time as a function of neighbourhood, city, region and country.

Mystical experience   A first-person experience that is felt to be spiritual or ecstatic in nature and brings a strong sense of connection, awe or oneness.

Such experiences are often said to transcend the capacity of words to describe them.

Narrative analysis   A method for analysing qualitative data that focuses on the use of narrative and plot to relay autobiographical events and past experiences.

Near-death experience (NDE)   A multi-sensory conscious experience that appears to occur following a life-threatening event such as a car accident or heart attack that led to clinical death for a period of time prior to resuscitation.

Negativity bias   The tendency of adult humans to focus more on negative or threatening stimuli than positive stimuli.

Neo-Piagetian paradigm   An approach to studying cognitive development across the lifespan based on the basic assumptions and theory of Jean Piaget's child development theory: for example, stages of development, holistic structures and the search for equilibrium.

Neurodegeneration   Deterioration of cell structure and function in the brain and nervous system, occurring as a result of ageing or disease.

Neurofibrillary tangles   Twisted fibres of protein found in the brain cells of Alzheimer's disease sufferers.

Neuroplasticity   The capacity of the brain to change its structure and function in response to experiences, environment or damage.

Obsessive Compulsive Disorder   A mental disorder characterised by high levels of anxiety, obsessive unwanted thoughts and repetitive behaviours (for example, hand washing or counting).

Online friendship   A friendship formed and maintained through the medium of the Internet.

Parkinson's disease   A neurodegenerative disease characterised by physical symptoms, including tremor, limb rigidity, slowness of movement and postural instability. It can be treated with drugs aimed at increasing dopamine levels in the brain.

Perceptual speed   A cognitive measure of the rate and accuracy at which an individual is able to compare similarities and differences among sets of letters, numbers, objects, pictures, or patterns, or react to a visual/auditory stimulus.

Person–job congruence   The extent to which a person feels that the requirements of a job are a good 'fit' with their own abilities, motivations and traits. This has been shown to predict health, satisfaction and job performance.

Phobia   An anxiety disorder characterised by intense fear of a particular place or object, leading to chronic avoidance of that place or object.

Positivity effect   The finding that, compared with younger adults, older adults on average experience fewer negative emotions, more positive emotions and greater life satisfaction.

Postformal thinking stages   Cognitive developmental stages that emerge after the 'formal operational period', that is, the stage typically reached at the beginning of adolescence, according to Piaget.

Postnatal Depression (also called Postpartum Depression)   An episode of clinical depression that occurs within four to six weeks of a woman giving birth to a child.

Post-traumatic growth   The experience of personal growth and positive change following an experience of trauma.

Post-Traumatic Stress Disorder (PTSD)   An anxiety disorder that occurs after a traumatic event and is defined by nightmares, flashbacks, avoidance of things that remind a person of the trauma, and by ongoing anxiety.

Practical wisdom   Wisdom inferred through self-reported responses to the following adjectives: clear-thinking, fair-minded, insightful, intelligent, interest wide, mature, realistic, reasonable, reflective, thoughtful, tolerant, understanding, wise, immature (contraindicative), intolerant (contraindicative), reckless (contraindicative).

Prefrontal cortex   The anterior part of the frontal lobes of the brain (*see entry* for frontal lobes), positioned in front of the motor and premotor areas of the lobes.

Prevention and Relationship Enhancement Programme (PREP)   A group-based relationship-enhancement intervention that is used to enhance relationship satisfaction and reduce relationship-related conflict in couples.

Primary drive   An unlearnt, instinctual urge to satisfy a biological need, such as sex drive, hunger, thirst and the drive to sleep.

Primary Mental Abilities Test (PMA)   A form of cognitive ability test, developed by L. L. Thurstone, which measures the following abilities: inductive reasoning, spatial orientation, number skills, verbal ability (meaning and fluency), perceptual speed and memory.

Probabilistic epigenesis   A theory proposed by Gottlieb that postulates that genes interact with the body and outer environment in complex reciprocal ways, meaning that developmental outcomes can only be specified probabilistically.

Processing speed   The speed of information processing in neurons and synapses. It is thought to typically decrease with age.

Prosocial morality   The form of morality shown in a desire to care for others and actively help others.

Psychiatric epidemiology   A discipline that aims at establishing the prevalence and demographic distribution of mental illnesses in the population.

Psychometric paradigm of cognitive ageing   An approach to studying cognitive ageing that employs IQ tests and other cognitive tests, and uses this data to model quantitative cognitive change.

Purpose   A long-term goal towards which a person aims and which imparts meaning and significance to life.

Qualitative change   A change in kind rather than a change in amount: for example, a switch from one career to another.

Qualitative data   Open-ended written data, either transcribed from spoken data, written as field notes, taken second-hand from a textual source such as the Internet or an autobiography, or written as responses to open-ended questions.

Qualitative research paradigm   A research movement that combines the deployment of qualitative data, qualitative analysis and philosophies that emphasise the interpretive role of the researcher and the socially embedded nature of scientific knowledge.

Quarterlife crisis   (see early adult crisis).

Rank-order trait change/stability   Change over time in the rank order of a group of persons on a particular trait, shown statistically using test-rest correlation. Higher test-rests correlations show higher rank-order stability.

Reaction time   The time it takes to respond to a visual or auditory stimulus. Tests can measure either *simple reaction time* (the time it takes to respond to a single stimulus), or *choice reaction time* (the time it takes to respond to an indicated stimulus from an array of different ones).

Real-world problem-solving   The process of dealing with 'ill-defined' problems that occur in everyday life. These invariably involve interpersonal issues and a large number of possible solutions.

Redemptive episode   An episode within a person's life story in which negative events or experiences are described as being turned around so that they have a positive effect on development.

Reflective Judgement Interview (RJI)   A structured interview during which four problems representing science, social science, religion and history are presented to participants, and responses are coded into one of the stages of the Reflective Judgement Model (*see entry*).

Reflective Judgement Model   A model of cognitive development that postulates a series of seven phases in three higher-order stages. The higher-order stages are termed *pre-reflective reasoning, quasi-reflective reasoning* and *reflective reasoning*. The Reflective Judgement Interview is used to assess individuals' stage of reflective judgement.

Relational analysis   A form of qualitative analysis that involves exploring relationships between themes or content categories, in order to help combine them into a meaningful whole, pattern or model.

Reliable Change Index (RCI)   A statistic used to calculate whether a change in an individual's score over time is statistically significant or not. It is calculated by dividing the change in a person's score by the 'standard error of the difference' for the test(s) being used, which takes into account the standard deviation of scores in a sample and the reliability of the test.

Religiosity   The extent to which a person (a) believes in a set of religious beliefs, (b) engages in the rites, rituals and practices of a religion, and (c) applies their religious beliefs to their life more generally.

Reminiscence   The process of consciously reflecting on autobiographical memories, which can be conducted in ways that can be both adaptive and maladaptive, depending on the context and extent of reminiscence.

RIASEC model of career choice   John Holland's model of career choice, which emphasises the importance of *fit* between a person's career interests and their actual career path. There are six domains of career interest in the model: *Realistic, Investigative, Artistic, Social, Enterprising* and *Conventional* (which gives rise to the acronym RIASEC).

Schizophrenia   A recognised psychotic disorder (or cluster of disorders), characterised by hallucinations such as hearing voices, delusions, disorganised thinking and a tendency to withdraw from social interaction. It typically first appears in early adulthood and has a very variable prognosis, ranging from total recovery to chronic deterioration.

Selection, optimisation and compensation (SOC) theory   The theory that older adults can strategically maintain or improve their performance at tasks by (a) being more *selective* about what to focus on, (b) *optimising* their performance through practice, and (c) *compensating* for age-related losses by finding new ways of doing a task.

Self-actualisation   This is the peak motivation in Maslow's hierarchy of needs (*see entry*), characterised by focusing action on trying to maximise one's own potential and improving oneself for the good of others.

Self-efficacy   A person's cognitive appraisal of the degree to which he/she is an effective and able person. If this is made in relation to a particular task or task area it is *domain-specific* self-efficacy, or if it is a more general evaluation, it is referred to as *global* self-efficacy.

Self-esteem   A person's cognitive positive or negative evaluation of their own worth. Positive self-esteem leads to positive beliefs about the self such as 'I am a good person' or 'I am worthy of other people's affection', which in turn lead to positive feelings about the self.

Sensory deficit theory   A theory of cognitive ageing that suggests decline in sensory functioning, particularly sight and hearing, may causally lead to cognitive decline.

Skipped generation household   A household in which grandparents live with their grandchildren, without parents being present.

Social Intuitionist Model of morality   This model states that morality is mainly a matter of immediate intuitions or 'gut feelings' that human beings learn evolutionarily from living in social groups, rather than being a matter of cognitive reasoning.

Social Paradigm Belief Inventory (SPBI) A psychometric test that measures the presence of absolutist, relativistic and dialectical thinking.

Socioanalytic Model of Maturity   A model of personality maturity that states that a mature person is respected, socially effective, and able to engage in productive work and loving relationships. The model is critical of individualist or idealistic models of maturity.

Socio-Emotional Selectivity Theory   The theory that if a person perceives the remaining time they have in life as limited or constrained (for example, if terminally ill), he/she will be focused more on cultivating positive feelings and emotions, and less on acquisition or achievement.

Spirituality   A form of personal enquiry defined by an active engagement with particular questions, experiences and practices, which together comprise a dynamic search for meaning, purpose, inner knowledge, deep connection, transcendence and 'ineffable' truths that cannot be encoded in words and numbers.

Stay-at-home father   A father who chooses to forego a paid career to stay at home with his child/children, while his partner/wife acts as primary source of income.

Sternberg's balance theory of wisdom   A theory that wisdom is the ability to balance intrapersonal interests, interpersonal interests, extrapersonal interests, while also balancing the inevitable requirements for change and stability in life.

Stillbirth   A stillborn baby is a baby who is born dead after at least 24 completed weeks of pregnancy. If the baby dies before 24 completed weeks, it is known as a late miscarriage.

Subject–Object Interview   A structured interview designed by Robert Kegan to measure developmental level within his stage-based developmental scheme.

Terminal illness   A disease that cannot be cured or adequately treated, and is expected to result in the death of the patient within a short period of time. The majority of such diagnoses are given for cancer.

The Seattle Longitudinal Study (SLS)   A long-term longitudinal and cross-sectional study of cognitive abilities conducted in Seattle by K. Warner Schaie and colleagues, which has been conducted for over 50 years.

Third Age   The period of life that is defined by a person being retired from full-time work and no longer living with children, but still being independent and physically healthy.

Three Dimensional Wisdom Scale (3D-WS)   A self-report questionnaire that assesses reflective, cognitive and affective aspects of wisdom.

Time-of-measurement effect   A measured change (found in a longitudinal study) that is due to the effects of an environmental event, such as a natural disaster, rather than ageing or development.

Time-sequential design   A research design in which a series of cross-sectional studies are conducted at different times and then compared.

Transcendent wisdom   Wisdom that is assessed by responses to the question, 'Many people hope to become wiser as they grow older. Would you give an example of wisdom you have acquired and how you came by it?' It is contrasted with practical wisdom (*see entry*).

Transition   A period of life during which major qualitative changes are experienced in one key domain of life or more, leading to both internal and external changes in a person's life.

Transition to adulthood   The period of life following adolescence during which a young person lessens adolescent behaviour and identity, while trying out adult roles and commitments.

Transpersonal Psychology   A branch of psychology that is dedicated to studying spirituality and spiritual experience from a non-religious, non-denominational perspective.

Trauma-focused Cognitive Behavioural Therapy (TF-CBT)   A form of therapy that is designed for individuals who suffer from Post-Traumatic Stress Disorder. It involves (a) dialogue with the patient about the traumatic event, to allow suppressed painful emotions to be voiced and processed, and (b) the provision of cognitive and behavioural techniques to improve coping with stress and its effects.

Traumagenic model   The theory that childhood trauma leads to a chronically elevated stress response in the central nervous system and endocrine system, which persists into adulthood. This in turn leads to higher risk of mental disorders such as schizophrenia.

Triangular theory of love   Sternberg's triangular theory of love stipulates that *passion*, *intimacy* and *commitment* are required to converge for the experience of consummate love. Different combinations of two or one of these elements lead to six kinds of partial love (fatuous, infatuated, empty, companionate, liking, romantic). Consummate love predicts positive relationship outcomes.

Vascular dementia   A form of dementia caused by chronically reduced blood flow to the brain, often resulting from a stroke or series of strokes. It leads to cognitive impairment, leg or arm weakness, tremors, balance problems, loss of bladder control and slurred speech.

Voluntary euthanasia (assisted dying)   The practice of allowing a person (for example, someone with pain-inducing, degenerative terminal illness) to choose the time of their death and be assisted in the process. This is currently legal in some countries such as Switzerland.

Volunteering   Unpaid work or unpaid structured activity, often undertaken for charitable reasons.

Washington Sentence Completion Test   A test used for assessing ego development in Loevinger's model, in which participants must finish off a series of incomplete sentences, and their responses are coded according to ego development level.

Wellbeing   The 'hedonic' definition of wellbeing (also referred to as subjective wellbeing) comprises positive affect, a lack of negative affect and being satisfied with life. The 'eudaimonic' definition includes a number of other components such as personal growth, purpose, mastery, autonomy, positive relationships and self-acceptance.

White matter   The part of the brain that appears white due to the dominant presence of myelinated axons (that is, axons surrounded by a fatty, white myelin sheath).

Wisdom   A particular form of virtuous maturity that is considered to be a form of expertise in handling complex interpersonal problems (see Berlin Wisdom Model and Sternberg's Balance Theory) and balancing competing interests (see Sternberg's balance model).

Work–family balance   The extent of balance between the time a person spends at home with their partner and/or children, and the time they spend at work. This is a trade-off, as more time at work means less time with family and vice versa.

References

American Psychiatric Association (2000). *Diagnostic and Statistical Manual of Mental Disorders*, 4th edn, text rev. Washington, DC: American Psychiatric Association.

Abbott, R. D., Ross, G. W., White, L. R., Sanderson, W. T., Burchfiel, C. M., Kashon, M., Sharp, D. S., Masaki, K. H., Curb, J. D. & Petrovitch, H. (2003). Environmental, life-style, and physical precursors of clinical Parkinson's disease: Recent findings from the Honolulu-Asia Aging Study. *Journal of Neurology*, 250(Suppl. 3), 30–39.

Abendroth, M. & Flannery, J. (2006). Predicting the risk of compassion fatigue: A study of hospice nurses. *Journal of Hospice and Palliative Nursing*, 8, 346–356.

Abrams, L. S. & Curran, L. (2009). 'And you're telling me not to stress?' A grounded theory study of postpartum depression symptoms among low-income mothers. *Psychology of Women Quarterly*, 33, 351–362.

Acker, M. & Davis, M. H. (1992). Intimacy, passion and romantic commitment in adult romantic relationships: A test of the triangular theory of love. *Journal of Social and Personal Relationships*, 9, 21–50.

Adams, R. G. & Blieszner, R. (1995). Aging well with friends and family. *American Behavioural Scientist*, 39, 209–224.

Adams, R. G. & Blieszner, R. (1996). Midlife friendship patterns. In N. Vanzetti & S. Duck (eds), *A Lifetime of Relationships* (pp. 336–363). Pacific Grove, CA: Brooks/Cole.

Adams, R. G., Blieszner, R. & de Vries, B. (2000). Definitions of friendship in the Third Age: Age, gender, and study location effects. *Journal of Aging Studies*, 14, 117–133.

Affleck, G. & Tennen, H. (1996). Construing benefits from adversity: Adaptational significance and dispositional underpinnings. *Journal of Personality: Special Issue on Personality and Coping*, 64, 899–922.

Agren, M. (1998). Life at 85 and 92: A qualitative longitudinal study of how the oldest old experience and adjust to the increasing uncertainty of existence. *International Journal of Aging & Human Development*, 47, 105–117.

Ahmetoglu, G., Swami, V. & Chamorro-Premuzic, T. (2010). The relationship between dimensions of love, personality, and relationship length. *Archives of Sexual Behavior*, 39, 1181–1190.

Ainsworth, M. D. S. (1985). Attachments across the life span. *Bulletin of the New York Academy of Medicine*, 61, 792–812.

Alexander, C. N., Langer, E. J., Newman, R. I., Chandler, H. M. & Davies, J. L. (1989). Transcendental meditation, mindfulness, and longevity: An experimental study with the elderly. *Journal of Personality and Social Psychology*, 57, 950–964.

Allemand, M., Gomez, V. & Jackson, J. J. (2010). Personality trait development in midlife: Exploring the impact of psychological turning points. *European Journal of Ageing*, 7, 147–155.

Alloy, L. B., Abramson, L. Y., Urosevic, S., Walshaw, P. D., Nusslock, R. & Neeren, A. M. (2005). The psychosocial context of bipolar disorder: Environmental, cognitive, and developmental risk factors. *Clinical Psychology Review*, 25, 1043–1075.

Allport, G. W. (1961) *Pattern and Growth in Personality*. London: Holt, Rinehart and Winston.

Allport, G. W. (1979). *The Nature of Prejudice*. Reading, MA: Addison-Wesley Pub. Co.

Allport, G. W. & Odbert, H. S. (1936). Trait names: A psycho-lexical study. *Psychological Monographs*, 47(1), 1–171.

Alonso, J., Angermeyer, M. C., Bernert, S., Bruffaerts, R., Brugha, T. S., Bryson, H., de Girolamo, G., de Graaf, R., Demyttenaere, K., Gasquet, I., Haro, J. M., Katz, S. J., Kessler, R. C., Kovess, V., Lepine, J. P., Ormel, J., Polidori, G., Russo, L. J., Vilagut, G. (2004). Prevalence of mental disorders in Europe: Results from the European Study of the Epidemiology of Mental Disorders (ESEMeD) project. *Acta Psychiatrica Scandinavica. Supplementum*, 109(420), 21–7.

Amato, P. R. (2000). The consequences of divorce for adults and children. *Journal of Marriage and Family*, 62, 1269–1287.

Amato, P. R. & Keith, B. (1991). Parental divorce and the well-being of children: A meta-analysis. *Psychological Bulletin*, 110(1), 26–46.

Ambelas, A. (1987). Life events and mania: A special relationship? *British Journal of Psychiatry*, 150, 235–240.

Amore, M., Di Donato, P., Papalini, A., Berti, A., Palareti, A., Ferrari, G., Chirico, C., De Aloysio, D. (2004). Psychological status at the menopausal transition: An Italian epidemiological study. *Maturitas*, 48, 115–124.

Andersson, G., Noack, T., Seierstad, A. & Weedon-Fekjaer, H. (2006). The demographics of same-sex marriages in Norway and Sweden. *Demography*, 43, 79–98.

Angera, J. J. & Long, E. C. J. (2006). Qualitative and quantitative evaluations of an empathy training program for couples in marriage and romantic relationships. *Journal of Couple and Relationship Therapy*, 5, 1–26.

Anker, R. (1997). Theories of occupational segregation by sex: An overview. *International Labour Review*, 136, 315–339.

Antonucci, T. C., Akiyama, H. & Takahashi, K. (2004). Attachment and close relationships across the life span. *Attachment & Human Development*, 6, 353–370.

Ardelt, M. (1997). Wisdom and life satisfaction in old age. *The Journals of Gerontology Series B: Psychological Sciences and Social Sciences*, 52, 15–27.

Ardelt, M. (2003). Empirical assessment of a three-dimensional wisdom scale. *Research on Aging*, 25, 275–324.

Ardelt, M. (2004). Wisdom as expert knowledge system: A critical review of a contemporary operationalization of an ancient concept. *Human Development*, 47, 257–285.

Ardelt, M. (2008). Self-development through selflessness: The paradoxical process of growing wiser. In H. A. Wayment & J. J. Bauer (eds), *Transcending Self-interest: Psychological Explorations of the Quiet Ego* (pp. 221–233). Washington, DC: American Psychological Association.

Ardelt, M. (2011). The measurement of wisdom: A commentary on Taylor, Bates, and Webster's comparison of the SAWS and 3D-WS. *Experimental Aging Research*, 37, 241–255.

Argue, A., Johnson, D. R. & White, L. K. (1999). Age and religiosity: Evidence from a three-wave panel analysis. *Journal for the Scientific Study of Religion*, 38, 423–435.

Armon, C. & Dawson, T. L. (1997). Developmental trajectories in moral reasoning across the life span. *Journal of Moral Education*, 26, 433–453.

Arnett, J. J. (1998). Learning to stand alone: The contemporary American transition to adulthood in cultural and historical context. *Human Development*, 41, 295–315.

Arnett, J. J. (2000). Emerging adulthood: A theory of development from the late teens through the twenties. *American Psychologist*, 55, 469–480.

Arnett, J. J. (2001). Conceptions of the transition to adulthood: Perspectives from adolescence through midlife. *Journal of Adult Development*, 8, 133–143.

Arnett, J. J. (2006). *Adolescence and Emerging Adulthood: A Cultural Approach*. London: Pearson Education.

Arnett, J. J. (2007a). Emerging adulthood: What is it, and what is it good for? *Child Development Perspectives*, 1, 68–73.

Arnett, J. J. (2007b). Emerging adulthood, a 21st century theory: A rejoinder to Hendry and Kloep. *Child Development Perspectives*, 1, 80–82.

Arnett, J.J. (2010). Emerging adulthood: The perils and promise of a new life stage. *Yellowbrick Journal of Emerging Adulthood,* 3, 4–5.

Arnett, J. J. & Galambos, N. L. (2003). Culture and conceptions of adulthood. *New Directions for Child and Adolescent Development*, 100, 91–98.

Aseltine, R. H. & Kessler, R. C. (1993). Marital disruption and depression in a community sample. *Journal of Health and Social Behavior*, 34, 237–251.

Assink, M. & Schroots, J. J. F. (2010). *The Dynamics of Autobiographical Memory Using the LIM/Lifeline Interview Method*. Cambridge, MA: Hogrefe Publishing.

Assman, A. (1994). Wholesome knowledge: Concepts of wisdom in a historical and cross-cultural perspective, Vol. 12. In D. L. Featherman, R. M. Lemer & M. Perlmutter (eds), *Life-span Development and Behavior* (pp. 187–224). Hillsdale, NJ: Erlbaum.

Atchley, R. (2009). *Spirituality and Aging*. Baltimore: The Johns Hopkins University Press.

Atchley, R. C. (1997). Everyday mysticism: Spiritual development in later adulthood. *Journal of Adult Development*, 4, 123–134.

Attia, E. (2010). Anorexia nervosa: Current status and future directions. *Annual Review of Medicine*, 61, 425–435.

Attias-Donfut, C., Ogg, J. & Wolff, F. C. (2005). European patterns of intergenerational financial and time transfers. *European Journal of Ageing*, 2, 161–173.

Atton, H. (1985). The psychology of retirement. *British Journal of Occupational Therapy*, 48, 375–378.

Aubin, E. de S. & McAdams, D. P. (1995). The relations of generative concern and generative action to personality traits, satisfaction/happiness with life, ego and development. *Journal of Adult Development*, 2, 99–112.

Bachand, L. L. & Caron, S. L. (2001). Ties that bind: A qualitative study of happy long-term marriages. *Contemporary Family Therapy*, 23, 105–121.

Baddeley, A. D., Bressi, S., Della Sala, S., Logie, R. & Spinnler, H. (1991). The decline of working memory in Alzheimer's disease. *Brain*, 114, 2521–2542.

Bakan, D. (1971). Adolescence in America: From idea to social fact. *Daedelus*, 100, 979–995.

Baltes, P. B. (1987). Theoretical propositions of life-span developmental psychology: On the dynamics between growth and decline. *Developmental Psychology*, 23, 611–626.

Baltes, P. B. (1997). On the incomplete architecture of human ontogeny. Selection, optimization, and compensation as foundation of developmental theory. *The American Psychologist*, 52, 366–380.

Baltes, P. B. (2003). Extending longevity: Dignity gain – or dignity drain? *Aging Research*, 3, 15–19.

Baltes, P. B. & Lindenberger, U. (1997). Emergence of a powerful connection between sensory and cognitive functions across the adult life span: A new window to the study of cognitive aging? *Psychology and Aging*, 12, 12–21.

Baltes, P. B. & Nesselroade, J. R. (1979). History and rationale of longitudinal research. In J. R. Nesselroade & P. B. Baltes (eds), *Longitudinal Research in the Study of Behavior and Development* (pp. 1–39). New York: Academic Press.

Baltes, P. B., Reese, H. W. & Lipsitt, L. P. (1980). Life-span developmental psychology. *Annual Review of Psychology*, 31, 65–110.

Baltes, P. B. & Smith, J. (2003). New frontiers in the future of aging: From successful aging of the young old to the dilemmas of the fourth age. *Gerontology*, 49, 123–35.

Baltes, P. B. & Staudinger, U. M. (2000). Wisdom: A metaheuristic (pragmatic) to orchestrate mind and virtue toward excellence. *American Psychologist*, 55, 122–136.

Baltes, P. B. & Willis, S. L. (1977). Toward psychological theories of aging and development. In J. E. Birren & K. W. Schaie (eds), *Handbook of the Psychology of Aging* (pp. 128–154). New York: Van Nostrand Reinhold Company.

Bandura, A. (1977). Self-efficacy: Towards a unifying theory of behavioral change. *Psychological Review*, 84, 191–215.

Bannister, D. & Fransella, F. (1986). *Inquiring Man: The Psychology of Personal Constructs*, 3rd edn. London: Routledge.

Banyard, V. L., Williams, L. M. & Siegel, J. A. (2001). The Long-Term Mental Health Consequences of Child Sexual Abuse: An Exploratory Study of the Impact of Multiple Traumas in a Sample of Women. *Journal of Traumatic Stress*, 14, 697–716.

Bar-On, R. (1997). *The Bar-On Emotional Quotient Inventory (EQ-i): A Test of Emotional Intelligence*. Toronto: Multi-Health Systems.

Barlow, D. H. & Hersen, M. (1984). *Single Case Experimental Designs: Strategies for Studying Behavior Change*, 2nd edn. New York: Allyn and Bacon.

Barnes, M., Doyle, D. & Johnson, B. (1989). The formulation of a Fowler scale: An empirical assessment among Catholics. *Review of Religious Research*, 30, 412–420.

Barnett, R. C. & Hyde, J. S. (2001). Women, men, work, and family: An expansionist theory. *American Psychologist*, 56, 781–796.

Baron-Cohen, S. & Wheelwright, S. (2004). The empathy quotient: An investigation of adults with Asperger syndrome or high functioning autism, and normal sex differences. *Journal of Autism and Developmental Disorders*, 34, 163–175.

Barr, D. (2004). *Get it Together: A Guide to Surviving your Quarterlife Crisis*. London: Hodder & Stoughton Ltd.

Bartholomew, K. & Horowitz, L. M. (1991) Attachment styles among young adults: A test of a four-category model. *Journal of Personality and Social Psychology*, 61, 226–244.

Basseches, M. (1980). Dialectical schemata: A framework for the empirical study of the development of dialectical thinking. *Human Development*, 23, 400–421.

Basseches, M. (2003). Adult Development and the Practice of Psychotherapy. In J. Demick and C. Andreoletti (Eds.) *The Handbook of Adult Development* (pp. 533–564). New York: Plenum Press.

Batson, C. D. (2009). These things called empathy: Eight related but distinct phenomena. In J. Decety & W. Ickes (eds), *The Social Neuroscience of Empathy* (pp. 3–15). Cambridge: MIT Press.

Bauer, J. J., McAdams, D. P. & Sakaeda, A. R. (2005). Interpreting the good life: Growth memories in the lives of mature, happy people. *Journal of Personality and Social Psychology*, 88, 203–217.

Bear, G. G. & Richards, H. C. (1981). Moral reasoning and conduct problems in the classroom. *Journal of Educational Psychology*, 73, 664–670.

Bebeau, M. J. (2002). The defining issues test and the four component model: Contributions to professional education. *Journal of Moral Education*, 31, 271–295.

Belsky, J. & Kelly, J. (1994). *The Transition to Parenthood: How a First Child Changes a Marriage–Why Some Couples Grow Closer and Others Apart*. New York: Delacorte.

Belsky, J. (1995). Expanding the ecology of human development: An evolutionary perspective. In P. Moen, G. H. Elder & K. Luscher (eds), *Examining Lives In Context: Perspectives on the Ecology of Human Development* (pp. 19–60). Washington, DC: American Psychological Association.

Belsky, J. & Kelly, J. (1995). *The Transition to Parenthood*. New York: Dell.

Bendtschneider, L. & Duck, S. (1993). What's yours is mine and what's mine is yours: Couple friends. In P. J. Kalbfleisch (ed.) *Interpersonal Communication: Evolving Interpersonal Relationships* (pp. 169–186). Oxford: Psychology Press.

Benkel, I., Wijk, H. & Molander, U. (2010). Using coping strategies is not denial: Helping loved ones adjust to living with a patient with a palliative diagnosis. *Journal of Palliative Medicine*, 13, 1119–1123.

Benoit, D. & Parker, K. (1994). Stability and transmission of attachment across three generations. *Child Development*, 65, 1444–1456.

Bentall, R. (2003). *Madness Explained: Psychosis and Human Nature*. London: Penguin Books.

Bermejo-Pareja, F., Benito-León, J., Vega, S., Medrano, M. J. & Román, G. C. (2008). Incidence and subtypes of dementia in three elderly populations of central Spain. *Journal of the Neurological Sciences*, 264, 63–72.

Berterö, C. (2003). What do women think about menopause? A qualitative study of women's expectations, apprehensions and knowledge about the climacteric period. *International Nursing Review*, 50, 109–118.

Beutel, M. E., Stöbel-Richter, Y. & Brähler, E. (2007). Sexual desire and sexual activity of men and women across their lifespans: Results from a representative German community survey. *British Journal of Urology International*, 101, 76–82.

Bienvenu, O. J., Onyike, C. U., Stein, M. B., Chen, L-S., Samuels, J., Nestadt, G. & Eaton, W. W. (2006). Agoraphobia in adults: Incidence and longitudinal relationship with panic. *British Journal of Psychiatry*, 188, 432–438.

Bifulco, A. & Brown, G. W. (1996). Coping with severe events and onset of depression. Social *Psychiatry and Psychiatric Epidemiology*, 31, 163–172.

Birren, J. E. & Cochran, K. N. (2001). *Telling the Stories of Life through Guided Autobiography Groups.* Baltimore: The Johns Hopkins University Press.

Birren, J. E. & Fisher, L. M. (1995). Aging and speed of behavior: Possible consequences for psychological functioning. *Annual Review of Psychology,* 46, 329–353.

Bisson, J. & Andrew, M. (2007). Psychological treatment of post-traumatic stress disorder (PTSD). *Cochrane Database of Systematic Reviews (Online),* 18, CD003388.

Bittman, E. L., Tubbiola, M. L., Foltz, G. & Hegarty, C. M. (1999). Effects of photoperiod and androgen on proopiomelanocortin gene expression in the arcuate nucleus of golden hamsters. *Endocrinology,* 140, 197–206.

Black, J. E., Isaacs, K. R., Anderson, B. J., Alcantara, A. A. & Greenough, W. T. (1990). Learning causes synaptogenesis, whereas motor activity causes angiogenesis, in cerebellar cortex of adult rats. *Proceedings of the National Academy of Science,* 14, 5568–5572.

Black, J. E., Zelazny, A. M. & Greenough, W. T. (1991). Capillary and mitochondrial support of neural plasticity in adult rats visual cortex. *Experimental Neurology,* 111, 204–209.

Blanchard, J. A. (2006). Hospital volunteers: A qualitative study of motivation. *The International Journal of Volunteer Administration,* 24, 31–40.

Blanchard-Fields, F., Jahnke, H. C. & Camp, C. (1995). Age differences in problem-solving style: The role of emotional salience. *Psychology and Aging,* 10, 173–180.

Blasi, A. (1976). Concept of development in personality theory. In J. Loevinger (ed.) *Ego Development* (pp. 29–53). San Francisco, CA: Jossey-Bass.

Blasi, A. (1980). Bridging moral cognition and moral action: A critical review of the literature. *Psychological Bulletin,* 88, 1–45.

Blieszner, R. & Roberto, K. A. (2004). Friendship across the life span: Reciprocity in individual and relationship development. In F. R. Lang & K. L. Fingerman (eds), *Growing together: Personal Relationships across the Life Span* (pp. 159–182). Cambridge University Press.

Block, J. (1971). *Lives through Time.* Berkeley, CA: Bancroft Books.

Bohlmeijer, E., Smit, F. & Cuijpers, P. (2003), Effects of reminiscence and life review on late-life depression: A meta-analysis. *International Journal of Geriatric Psychiatry,* 18, 1088–1094.

Bombar, M. L. & Littig, L. W. (1996). Babytalk as a communication of intimate attachment: An initial study in adult romances and friendships. *Personal Relationships,* 3, 137–158.

Bonanno, G. A. & Kaltman, S. (1999). Toward an integrative perspective on bereavement. *Psychological Bulletin,* 125, 760–776.

Bonanno, G. A. & Kaltman, S. (2001). The varieties of grief experience. *Clinical Psychology Review,* 21, 705–734.

Bonanno, G. A., Wortman, C. B., Lehman, D. R., Tweed, R. G., Haring, M., Sonnega, J., Carr, D., Ness, R. M. (2002). Resilience to loss and chronic grief: A prospective study from preloss to 18-months postloss. *Journal of Personality and Social Psychology,* 83, 1150–1164.

Booth, A. & Amato, P. R. (1991). Divorce and psychological stress. *Journal of Health and Social Behavior,* 32, 396–407.

Bowlby, J. (1961). Processes of mourning. *International Journal of Psychoanalysis,* 42, 317–339.

Bowlby, J. (1973). *Attachment and loss, Vol. 2: Separation*. New York: Basic Books.

Bowlby, J. (1980). *Attachment and Loss: Vol. 3, Loss: Sadness and Depression*. New York: Basic Books.

Boyatzis, C. J. (2005). Religious and spiritual development in childhood. In R. F. Paloutzian & C. L. Park (eds), *Handbook of the Psychology of Religion and Spirituality* (pp. 123–143). New York: Guilford Press.

Braithwaite, M. A. (2005). Taking the final step: Changing the law on euthanasia and physician assisted suicide. *British Medical Journal*, 331, 681–683.

Branchi, I., D'Andrea, I., Fiore, M., Di Fausto, V., Aloe, L. & Alleva, E. (2006). Early social enrichment shapes social behavior and nerve growth factor and brain-derived neurotrophic factor levels in the adult mouse brain. *Biological Psychiatry*, 60, 690–696.

Brandtstädter, J. & Renner, G. (1990). Tenacious goal pursuit and flexible goal adjustment: Explication and age-related analysis of assimilative and accommodative strategies of coping. *Psychology and Aging*, 5, 58–67.

Brandtstädter, J. & Rothermund, K. (2002). The life-course dynamics of goal pursuit and goal adjustment: A two-process framework. *Developmental Review*, 22, 117–150.

Bremner, J. D. (1999). Does stress damage the brain? *Biological Psychiatry*, 45(7), 797–805.

Brennan, K. A., Clark, C. L. & Shaver, P. R. (1998). Self-report measurement of adult attachment: An integrative overview. In J. Simpson & W. Rholes (eds.) *Attachment Theory and Close Relationships* (pp. 46–76). New York: Guilford Press.

Bretherton, I. (1992). The origins of attachment theory: John Bowlby and Mary Ainsworth. *Developmental Psychology*, 28, 759–775.

Bretherton, I. & Beeghly, M. (1982). Talking about internal states: The acquisition of an explicit theory of mind. *Developmental Psychology*, 18, 906–921.

Bretherton, I., Fritz, J., Zahn-Waxler, C. & Ridgeway, D. (1986). Learning to talk about emotion: A functionalist perspective. *Child Development*, 57, 529–548.

Bridges, K. M. B. (1932). Emotional development in early infancy. *Child Development*, 3, 324–341.

Bridges, L. J., Roe, A. E. C., Dunn, J. & O'Connor, T. G. (2007). Children's perspectives on their relationships with grandparents following parental separation: A longitudinal study. *Social Development*, 16, 539–554.

Brim, O. G. (1992). *Ambition*. New York: Basic Books.

Bronfenbrenner, U. (1979). *The Ecology of Human Development*. Boston, MA: Harvard University Press.

Bronfenbrenner, U. (1994). Ecological models of human development. *International Encyclopedia of Education*, 3, 37–43.

Bronner, L. L., Kanter, D. S. & Manson, J. E. (1995). Primary prevention of stroke. *New England Journal of Medicine*, 333, 1392–1400.

Brotherson, S. E. (2007). From partners to parents: Couples and the transition to parenthood. *International Journal of Childbirth Education*, 22, 7–12.

Brown, G. W., Adler, Z. & Bifulco, A. (1988). Life events difficulties and recovery from chronic depression. *British Journal of Psychiatry*, 152, 487–498.

Brown, G. W. & Birley, J. L. (1968). Crises and life changes and the onset of schizophrenia. *Journal of Health and Social Behavior*, 9, 203–214.

Brown, G. W. & Harris, T. O. (1978). *Social Origins of Depression: A Study of Psychiatric Disorder in Women*. London: Tavistock.

Brown, G. W., Harris, T. O. & Hepworth, C. (1995). Loss, humiliation and entrapment among women developing depression: A patient and non-patient comparison. *Psychological Medicine*, 25, 7–21.

Brown, G. W., Harris, T. O. & Hepworth, C. (1998). Loss, humiliation, and entrapment among women developing depression. In J. Jenkins, K. Oatley & N. Stein (eds) *Human Emotion: A Reader* (pp. 337–351). Malden, MA: Blackwell Publishers.

Brown, J. W., Chen, S., Mefford, L., Brown, A., Callen, B. & McArthur, P. (2011). Becoming an older volunteer: A grounded theory study. *Nursing Research and Practice*, 2011, 1–8.

Brown, K. W. & Ryan, R. M. (2003). The benefits of being present: Mindfulness and its role in psychological well-being. *Journal of Personality and Social Psychology*, 84, 822–848.

Brown, S. L., Nesse, R. M., House, J. S. & Utz, R. L. (2004). Religion and emotional compensation: Results from a prospective study of widowhood. *Personality & Social Psychology Bulletin*, 30, 1165–1174.

Brugha, T. S. (1993). Depression in the terminally ill. *British Journal of Hospital Medicine*, 50, 175–81.

Bryk, A. S. & Raudenbush, S. W. (1987). Application of hierarchical linear models to assessing change. *Psychological Bulletin*, 101, 147–158.

Buckman, R. (1998). Communication in palliative care: A practical guide. In D. Doyle, G. W. C. Hanks & N. MacDonald (eds) *Oxford Textbook of Palliative Medicine*, 2nd edn (pp. 141–158). Oxford: Oxford University Press.

Burton, L. M. & Bengtson, V. L. (1985). Black grandmothers: Issues of timing and continuity of roles. In V. L. Bengtson & J. F. Robertson (eds) *Grandparenthood* (pp. 61–77). Beverley Hills, CA: Sage Publications.

Butler, R. N. (1963). The life review: An interpretation of reminiscence in the aged. *Psychiatry*, 26, 65–76.

Butler, R. N. (1980). The life review: An unrecognized bonanza. *The International Journal of Aging and Human Development*, 12, 35–38.

Butt, D. S. & Beiser, M. (1987). Successful aging: A theme for international psychology. *Psychology and Aging*, 2, 87–94.

Butterworth, P., Gill, S. C., Rodgers, B., Anstey, K. J., Villamil, E. & Melzer, D. (2006). Retirement and mental health: Analysis of the Australian national survey of mental health and well-being. *Social science & medicine*, 62, 1179–1191.

Bühler, C. (1935). *From Birth To Maturity*. London: Kegan Paul, Trench & Trubner.

Bühler, C. (1951). Maturation and motivation. *Personality*, 1, 184–211.

Bühler, C. (1959). Theoretical observations about life's basic tendencies. *American Journal of Psychotherapy*, 13, 501–581.

Bühler, C. (1964). The human course of life in its goal aspects. *Journal of Humanistic Psychology*, 4, 1–18.

Bühler, C. (1967). Human life goals in the humanistic perspective. *Journal of Humanistic Psychology*, 7, 36–52.

Bühler, C. (1968). Fulfillment and failure of life. In C. Bühler & F. Massarik (eds) *The Course of Human Life: A Study of Goals in the Humanistic Perspective* (pp. 400–403). New York: Springer Publishing Company.

Cabeza, R., Daselaar, S. M., Dolcos, F., Prince, S. E., Budde, M. & Nyberg, L. (2004). Task independent and task-specific age effects on brain activity during working memory, visual attention and episodic retrieval. *Cerebral Cortex*, 14, 364–375.

Cabrera, N. J., Tamis-LeMonda, C. S., Bradley, R. H., Hoffert, S. & Lamb, M. E. (2000). Fatherhood in the twenty-first century. *Child Development*, 71, 127–136.

Calhoun, L. G. & Tedeschi, R. G. (1989). Positive aspects of critical life problems: Recollections of grief. *OMEGA Journal of Death and Dying*, 20, 265–272.

Calvo, E., Haverstick, K. & Sass, S. A. (2009). Gradual retirement, sense of control, and retirees' happiness. *Research on Aging*, 31, 112–135.

Cameron, P. & Biber, H. (1973). Sexual thought throughout the lifespan. *The Gerontologist*, 13, 144–147.

Campbell, A., Converse, P. E. & Rodgers, W. L. (1976). *The Quality of American Life*. New York: Russell Sage Foundation.

Caplan, G. (1964). *Principles of Preventive Psychiatry*. New York: Basic Books Inc.

Cappeliez, P. & O'Rourke, N. (2002). Personality traits and existential concerns as predictors of the functions of reminiscence in older adults. *Journal of Gerontology B; Psychological Sciences and Social Sciences*, 57, 116–123.

Caprara, G. V. & Cervone, D. (2000). *Personality: Development, Dynamics and Potentials*. New York: Cambridge University Press.

Carbery, J. & Buhrmester, D. (1998). Friendship and need fulfillment during three phases of young adulthood. *Journal of Social and Personal Relationships*, 15, 393–409.

Carpenter, W. T. & Kirkpatrick, B. (1988). The heterogeneity of the long-term course of schizophrenia. *Schizophrenia Bulletin*, 14, 645–652.

Carroll, J. B. (1993). *Human Cognitive Abilities*. Cambridge: Cambridge University Press.

Carstensen, L. L. & Mikels, J. A. (2005). At the intersection of emotion and cognition: Aging and the positivity effect. *Current Directions in Psychological Science*, 14, 117–121.

Carstensen, L. L., Gottman, J. M. & Levenson, R. W. (1995). Emotional behavior in long-term marriage. *Psychology and Aging*, 10, 140–149.

Carstensen, L. L., Isaacowitz, D. M. & Charles, S. T. (1999). Taking time seriously. A theory of socioemotional selectivity. *The American Psychologist*, 54, 165–181.

Carstensen, L. L., Pasupathi, M., Mayr, U. & Nesselroade, J. R. (2000). Emotional experience in everyday life across the adult life span. *Journal of Personality and Social Psychology*, 79, 644–655.

Carstensen, L. L., Turan, B., Scheibe, S., Ram, N., Ersner-Hershfield, H., Samanez-Larkin, G. R., Brooks, K. P. & Nesselroade, J. R. (2011). Emotional experience improves with age: Evidence based on over 10 years of experience sampling. *Psychology and Aging*, 26, 21–33.

Caspi, A., Roberts, B. W. & Shiner, R. L. (2005). Personality development: Stability and change. *Annual Review of Psychology*, 56, 453–484.

Cattell, R. B. (1943). The description of personality: Basic traits resolved into clusters. *Journal of Abnormal and Social Psychology*, 38, 476–506.

Cattell, R. B. (1945). The principle trait clusters for describing personality. *Psychological Bulletin*, 42, 129–161.

Cattell, R. B. (1971). *Abilities: Their Structure, Growth, and Action*. New York: Hougton Mifflin.

Cavanaugh, J. C. & Blanchard-Fields, F. (2006). *Adult Development and Aging*, 6th edn. New York: Wadsworth.

Chapman, C. R., Nakamura, Y. & Flores, L. Y. (1999). Chronic pain and consciousness: A constructivist perspective. In R. J. Gatchel & D. C. Turk (eds) *Psychosocial Factors in Pain: Evolutions and Revolutions* (pp. 35–55). New York: Guilford Press.

Charles, S. T. & Almeida, D. M. (2007). Genetic and environmental effects on daily life stressors: More evidence for greater variation in later life. *Psychology and Aging*, 22, 331–340.

Charles, S. T. & Carstensen, L. L. (2008). Unpleasant situations elicit different emotional responses in younger and older adults. *Psychology and Aging*, 23, 495–504.

Charles, S. T. & Carstensen, L. L. (2010). Social and emotional aging. *Annual Review of Psychology*, 61, 383–409.

Charles, S. T., Mather, M. & Carstensen, L. L. (2003). Aging and emotional memory: The forgettable nature of negative images for older adults. *Journal of Experimental Psychology: General*, 132, 310–324.

Charles, S. T., Reynolds, C. A. & Gatz, M. (2001). Age-related differences and change in positive and negative affect over 23 years. *Journal of Personality and Social Psychology*, 80, 136–151.

Charlesworth, W. R. & Kreutzer, M. A. (1973). Facial expression of infants and children. In P. Ekman (eds) *Darwin and Facial Expressions* (pp. 91–162). New York: Academic Press.

Chen, D., Lew, R., Hershman, W. & Orlander, J. (2007). A cross-sectional measurement of medical student empathy. *Journal of General Internal Medicine*, 22, 1434–1438.

Chen, H., O'Reilly, E., McCullough, M. L., Rodriguez, C., Schwarzschild, M. A., Calle, E. E., Thun, M. J. & Ascherio, A. (2007). Consumption of dairy products and risk of Parkinson's disease. *American Journal of Epidemiology*, 165, 998–1006.

Chen, H., Zhang, S. M., Hernán, M. A., Willett, W. C. & Ascherio, A. (2002). Diet and Parkinson's disease: A potential role of dairy products in men. *Annals of Neurology*, 52, 793–801.

Cherlin, A. J. (1992). *Marriage, Divorce, Remarriage. Social Trends in the United States*. Cambridge, MA: Harvard University Press.

Chopik, W. J., Edelstein, R. S. & Fraley, R. C. (2012). From the cradle to the grave: Adult attachment across the lifespan. *Journal of Personality*. DOI: 10.1111/j.1467-6494.2012.00793.x.

Christensen, H., Mackinnon, A. J., Korten, A. E., Jorm, A. F., Henderson, A. S., Jacomb, P. & Rodgers, B. (1999). An analysis of diversity in the cognitive performance of elderly community dwellers: Individual differences in change scores as a function of age. *Psychology and Aging*, 14, 365–379.

Cifcili, S. Y., Akman, M., Demirkol, A., Unalan, P. C. & Vermeire, E. (2009). 'I should live and finish it': A qualitative inquiry into Turkish women's menopause experience. *BMC Family Practice*, 10, 1–9.

Ciompi, L. (1980). Catamnestic long-term study on the course of life and aging of schizophrenics. *Schizophrenia Bulletin*, 6, 606–618.

Cirulli, F., Berry, A. & Alleva, E. (2003). Early disruption of the mother–infant relationship: Effects on brain plasticity and implications for psychopathology. *Neuroscience & Biobehavioral Reviews*, 27, 73–82.

Claassen, G. (2004). *Male Menopause and Decision-Making: A Qualitative Study*. Rand Afrikaans University.

Clare, L. (2003). Managing threats to self: Awareness in early stage Alzheimer's disease. *Social Science & Medicine, 57,* 1017–1029.

Clark, R. L., Johnson, T. & McDermed, A. A. (1980). Allocation of time and resources by married couples approaching retirement. *Social Security Bulletin,* 43, 3–13.

Clarke, L. & Roberts, C. (2003). *Grandparenthood: Its Meaning and its Contribution to Older Peoples' Lives.* Sheffield: University of Sheffield ESRC Growing Older Programme.

Clary, E. G., Snyder, M., Ridge, R. D., Copeland, J., Stukas, A. A., Haugen, J. & Miene, P. (1998). Understanding and assessing the motivation of volunteers: A functional approach. *Journal of Personality and Social Psychology,* 74, 1516–1530.

Clausen, J. A. (1995). Gender, contexts, and turning points in adults' lives. In P. Moen, G. H. Elder Jr. & K. Lüscher (eds) *Examining Lives in Context: Perspectives on the Ecology of Human Development* (pp. 365–392). Washington, DC: American Psychological Association.

Clements, M. L., Cordova, A. D., Markman, H. J. & Laurenceau, J. P. (1997). The erosion of marital satisfaction over time and how to prevent it. In R. Sternberg & M. Hojjat (eds) *Satisfaction in Close Relationships* (pp. 335–355). New York: Guilford Press.

Cnaan, R. A., Handy, F. & Wadsworth, M. (1996). Defining who is a volunteer: Conceptual and empirical considerations. *Nonprofit and Voluntary Sector Quarterly,* 25, 364–383.

Coan, J. A. & Allen, J. J. B. (2007). Introduction: Organizing the tools and methods of affective science. In J. A. Coan & J. J. B. Allen (eds) *Handbook of Emotion Elicitation and Assessment* (pp. 3–8). New York: Oxford University Press.

Colby, A., Kohlberg, L., Gibbs, J., Lieberman, M., Fischer, K. & Saltzstein, H. D. (1983). A longitudinal study of moral judgment. *Monographs of the Society for Research in Child Development,* 48, 1–124.

Colcombe, S. J., Erickson, K. I., Scalf, P. E., Kim, J. S., Prakash, R., McAuley, E., Elavsky, S., Marquez, D. X., Hu, L., Kramer, A. F. (2006). Aerobic exercise training increases brain volume in aging humans. *The Journals of Gerontology Series A: Biological Sciences and Medical Sciences,* 61, 1166–1170.

Colcombe, S. & Kramer, A. F. (2003). Fitness effects on the cognitive function of older adults: A meta-analytic study. *Psychological Science: A Journal of the American Psychological Society/APS,* 14, 125–130.

Coleman, P. G. (1974). Measuring reminiscence characteristics from conversation as adaptive features of old age. *The International Journal of Aging and Human Development,* 5, 281–294.

Coleman, P. G. & O'Hanlon, A. (2004). *Ageing and Human Development.* London: Arnold Publishers.

Commons, M. L. (2002). Introduction: Attaining a new stage. *Journal of Adult Development,* 9, 155–157.

Commons, M. L. (2008). Introduction to the model of hierarchical complexity and its relationship to postformal action. *World Futures,* 64, 305–320.

Commons, M. L. & Ross, S. N. (2008). What postformal thought is, and why it matters. *World Futures,* 64, 321–329.

Commons, M. L., Richards, F. A. & Kuhn, D. (1982). Systematic and metasystematic reasoning: A case for levels of reasoning beyond Piaget's stage of formal operations. *Child Development*, 53, 1058–1069.

Condon, J. T., Boyce, P. & Corkindale, C. J. (2004). The first-time fathers study: A prospective study of the mental health and wellbeing of men during the transition to parenthood. *Australian and New Zealand Journal of Psychiatry*, 38, 56–64.

Conner, T. S., Tennen, H., Fleeson, W. & Barrett, L. F. (2009). Experience sampling methods: A modern idiographic approach to personality research. *Social and Personality Psychology Compass*, 3, 292–313.

Copp, G. (1998). A review of current theories of death and dying. *Journal of Advanced Nursing*, 28, 382–390.

Costa, J., Lunet, N., Santos, C., Santos, J. & Vaz-Carneiro, A. (2010). Caffeine exposure and the risk of Parkinson's disease: A systematic review and meta-analysis of observational studies. *Journal of Alzheimer's Disease*, 20, 221–238.

Cotman, C. W., Berchtold, N. C. & Christie, L. A. (2007). Exercise builds brain health: Key roles of growth factor cascades and inflammation. *Trends in Neurosciences*, 30, 464–472.

Crabb, W. T., Moracco, J. C. & Bender, R. C. (1983). A comparative study of empathy training with programmed instruction for lay helpers. *Journal of Counseling Psychology*, 30, 221–226.

Craik, F. I. M. (1986). A functional account of age differences in memory. In F. Lix & H. Hagendorf (eds) *Human Memory and Cognitive Capabilities, Mechanisms, and Performances* (pp. 499–422). North-Holland: Elsevier.

Crain, W. (2005). *Theories of Development: Concepts and Applications*, 5th edn. London: Pearson Education.

Crain, W. (2010). *Theories of Development: Concepts and Applications*, 6th edn. London: Pearson Education.

Creswell, J. W. & Plano Clark, V. L. (2007). *Designing and Conducting Mixed-methods Research*. London: Sage Publications.

Cumming, E. & Henry, W. E. (1961). *Growing Old*. New York: Basic Books.

Cumming, E., Dean, L. R., Newell, D. S. & McCaffrey, I. (1960). Disengagement – A tentative theory of aging. *Sociometry*, 23, 23–35.

Cummings, R., Dyas, L., Maddux, C. D. & Kochman, A. (2001). Principled moral reasoning and behavior of preservice teacher education students. *American Educational Research Journal*, 38, 143–158.

Currin, L., Schmidt, U., Treasure, J. & Hershel, J. (2005). Time trends in eating disorder incidence. *British Journal of Psychiatry*, 186, 132–135.

Côté, J. (2000). *Arrested Adulthood: The Changing Nature of Maturity and Identity in the Late Modern World*. New York: New York University Press.

Daniels, M. (2009). Perspectives and vectors in transpersonal development. *Transpersonal Psychology Review*, 13, 87–99.

Das, M. K., Kulhara, P. L. & Verma, S. K. (1997). Life events preceding relapse of schizophrenia. *International Journal of Social Psychiatry*, 43, 56–63.

Davila, J., Karney, B. R. & Bradbury, T. N. (1999). Attachment change processes in the early years of marriage. *Journal of Personality and Social Psychology*, 76, 783–802.

Davis, M. A. (2003). Factors related to bridge employment participation among private sector early retirees. *Journal of Vocational Behavior*, 63, 55–71.

Davis, M. H. (1983). Measuring individual differences in empathy: Evidence for a multidimensional approach. *Journal of Personality and Social Psychology*, 44, 113–126.

Dawkins, R. (2007). *The God Delusion*. London: Black Swan.

Dawson, T. (2004). Assessing intellectual development: Three approaches, one sequence. *Journal of Adult Development*, 11, 71–85.

Dawson-Tunik, T. L., Commons, M., Wilson, M. & Fischer, K. W. (2005). The shape of development. *European Journal of Developmental Psychology*, 2, 163–195.

Day, J. M. (2008). Human development and the model of hierarchical complexity: Learning from research in the psychology of moral and religious development. *World Futures*, 64, 452–467.

Day, J. M. (2010). Religion, spirituality and positive psychology in adulthood: A development view. *Journal of Adult Development*, 17, 215–229.

Day, J. M. (2011). Religious, spiritual, and moral development and learning in the adult years: Classical and contemporary questions, cognitive-developmental and complementary paradigms, and prospects for future research. In C. Hoare (ed.) *Oxford Handbook of Reciprocal Adult Development & Learning*, 2nd edn (pp. 318–346). Oxford: Oxford University Press.

Day, R., Nielsen, J., Korten, A., Ernberg, G., Dube, K., Gebhart, J., Jablensky, A., Leon, C., Marsella, A. & Olatawura, M. (1987). Stressful life events preceding the acute onset of schizophrenia: A cross-national study from the World Health Organization. *Culture, Medicine and Psychiatry*, 11, 123–205.

De Jager, C. A., Oulhaj, A., Jacoby, R., Refsum, H. & Smith, A. D. (2011). Cognitive and clinical outcomes of homocysteine-lowering B-vitamin treatment in mild cognitive impairment: A randomized controlled trial. *International Journal of Geriatric Psychiatry*, 27, 592–600.

De Lau, L. M. & Breteler, M. M. B. (2006). Epidemiology of Parkinson's disease. *The Lancet Neurology*, 5, 525–535.

De Lau, L. M., Bornebroek, M., Witteman, J. C., Hofman, A., Koudstaal, P. J. & Breteler, M. M. (2005). Dietary fatty acids and the risk of Parkinson disease: The Rotterdam study. *Neurology*, 64, 2040–2045.

De Robertis, E. M. (2006). Charlotte Bühler's existential–humanistic contributions to child and adolescent psychology. *Journal of Humanistic Psychology*, 46, 48–76.

De Vries, B., Birren, J. E. & Deutchman, D. E. (1990). Adult development through guided autobiography: The family context. *Family Relations*, 39, 3–7.

DeNeve, K. M. & Cooper, H. (1998). The happy personality: A meta-analysis of 137 personality traits and subjective well-being. *Psychological Bulletin*, 124, 197–229.

Deary, I. J. & Der, G. (2005). Reaction time, age, and cognitive ability: Longitudinal findings from age 16 to 63 years in representative population samples. *Aging, Neuropsychology, and Cognition*, 12, 187–215.

Deary, I. J., Johnson, W. & Starr, J. M. (2010). Are processing speed tasks biomarkers of cognitive aging? *Psychology and Aging*, 25, 219–228.

Deci, E. L. & Ryan, R. M. (1985). *Intrinsic Motivation and Self-determination in Human Behavior*. New York: Plenum.

Delaney, L., Egan, M. & O'Connell, N. (2011). The experience of unemployment in Ireland: A thematic analysis. *Working Papers*, 2011.

Dench, G. & Ogg, J. (2002). *Grandparenting in Britain*. London: Institute of Community Studies.

Denne, J. M. & Thompson, N. L. (1991). The experience of transition to meaning and purpose in life. *Journal of Phenomenological Psychology*, 22, 109–133.

Dennis, N. A. & Cabeza, R. (2008). Neuroimaging of healthy cognitive aging. In F. I. M. Craik & T. A. Salthouse (eds) *The Handbook of Aging and Cognition*, 3rd edn (pp. 1–54). Mahwah, NJ: Erlbaum.

Denton, K. & Krebs, D. L. (1990). From the scene to the crime: The effect of alcohol and social context on moral judgment. *Journal of Personality and Social Psychology*, 59, 242–248.

Der, G. & Deary, I. J. (2006). Age and sex differences in reaction time in adulthood: Results from the United Kingdom health and lifestyle survey. *Psychology and Aging*, 21, 62–73.

Deutsch, F. M., Ruble, D. N., Fleming, A., Brooks-Gunn, J. & Stangor, C. (1988). Information-seeking and the self-definitional processes accompanying the transition to motherhood. *Journal of Personality and Social Psychology*, 55, 420–431.

Devlin, R. E. & Gibbs, J. C. (2010). Responsible adult culture (RAC): Cognitive and behavioral changes at a community-based correctional facility. *Journal of Research in Character Education*, 8, 1–20.

Di Carlo, A., Baldereschi, M., Amaducci, L., Lepore, V., Bracco, L., Maggi, S., Bonaiuto, S., Perissinotto, E., Scarlato, G., Farchi, G. & Inzitari D. (2002). Incidence of dementia, Alzheimer's disease, and vascular dementia in Italy. The ILSA Study. *Journal of the American Geriatrics Society*, 50, 41–48.

Diamond, L. M. & Aspinwall, L. G. (2003). Emotion regulation across the life span: An integrative perspective emphasizing self-regulation, positive affect, and dyadic processes. *Motivation and Emotion*, 27, 125–156.

Dickens, W. J. & Perlman, D. (1981). Friendship over the life cycle. In S. Duck & R. Gilmour (eds) *Personal Relationships. Vol. 2: Developing Personal Relationships* (pp. 91–122). London: Academic Press.

Didion, J. (2005). *The Year of Magical Thinking*. London: Harper Perennial.

Diehl, M., Coyle, N. & Labouvie-Vief, G. (1996). Age and sex differences in strategies of coping and defense across the life span. *Psychology and Aging*, 11, 127–139.

Diener, E. & Suh, M. E. (1997). Subjective wellbeing: An international analysis. In K. W. Schaie & M. Powell Lawton (eds) *Annual Review of Gerontology and Geriatrics, Volume 17*. New York: Springer Publishing Co.

Diener, E., Suh, E. M., Lucas, R. E. & Smith, H. L. (1999). Subjective well-being: Three decades of progress. *Psychological Bulletin*, 125, 276–302.

Dijk, D. J., Groeger, J. A., Stanley, N. & Deacon, S. (2010). Age-related reduction in daytime sleep propensity and nocturnal slow wave sleep. *Sleep*, 33, 211–223.

Dillon, M., Wink, P. & Fay, K. (2003). Is spirituality detrimental to generativity? *Journal for the Scientific Study of Religion*, 42, 427–442.

Dobson, K. & Franche, R. L. (1989). A conceptual and empirical review of the depressive realism hypothesis. *Canadian Journal of Behavioural Science*, 21, 419–433.

Doidge, N. (2008). *The Brain that Changes Itself: Stories of Personal Triumph from the Frontiers of Brain Science*. London: Penguin.

Donnellan, M. B. & Lucas, R. E. (2008). Age differences in the big five across the life span: Evidence from two national samples. *Psychology and Aging*, 23, 558–566.

Donnellan, M. B., Conger, R. D. & Burzette, R. G. (2007). Personality development from late adolescence to young adulthood: Differential stability, normative maturity, and evidence for the maturity-stability hypothesis. *Journal of Personality*, 75, 237–263.

Donohue, R. (2006). Person-environment congruence in relation to career change and career persistence. *Journal of Vocational Behavior*, 68, 504–515.

Dorfman, L. T. (2002). Retirement and family relationships: An opportunity in later life. *Generations*, 26, 74–79.

Doyle, D. & Forehand, M. J. (1984). Life satisfaction and old age: A re-examination. *Research on Aging*, 6, 432–448.

Drew, L. M. & Silverstein, M. (2007). Grandparents' psychological well-being after loss of contact with their grandchildren. *Journal of Family Psychology*, 21, 372–379.

Drew, L. & Smith, P. K. (2002). Implications for grandparents when they lose contact with their grandchildren: Divorce, family feud and geographical separation. *Journal of Mental Health and Aging*, 8, 95–119.

Duvall, E. M. (1970). *Family Development*. Philadelphia: Lippincott.

Dyregrov, A. & Dyregrov, K. (1999). Long-term impact of sudden infant death: A 12- to 15-year follow-up. *Death Studies*, 23, 635–661.

Ebner, N. C., Freund, A. M. & Baltes, P. B. (2006). Developmental changes in personal goal orientation from young to late adulthood: From striving for gains to maintenance and prevention of losses. *Psychology and Aging*, 21, 664–678.

Edison, T. (1968). *Diary and Sundry Observations of Thomas Alva Edison*. Westport, CT: Greenwood Publishing Group.

Edwards, V. J., Holden, G. W., Felitti, V. J. & Anda, R. F. (2003). Relationship Between Multiple Forms of Childhood Maltreatment and Adult Mental Health in Community Respondents: Results From the Adverse Childhood Experiences Study. *American Journal of Psychiatry*, 160, 1453–1460.

Elder Jr., G. H. (1994). Time, human agency, and social change: Perspectives on the life course. *Social Psychology Quarterly*, 57, 4–15.

Elder Jr., G. H. (1998). The life course as developmental theory. *Child development*, 69, 1–12.

Ellicott, A., Hammen, C., Gitlin, M., Brown, G. & Jamison, K. (1990). Life events and the course of bipolar disorder. *American Journal of Psychiatry*, 147, 1194–1198.

Elliott, R., Fischer, C. T. & Rennie, D. L. (1999). Evolving guidelines for publication of qualitative research studies in psychology and related fields. *The British Journal of Clinical Psychology/The British Psychological Society*, 38, 215–29.

Emmons, R. (1999). *The Psychology of Ultimate Concerns: Motivation and Spirituality in Personality*. New York: Guilford Press.

Erera, P. (1997). Empathy training for helping professionals: Model and evaluation. *Journal of Social Work Education*, 33, 245–260.

Erickson, K. & Kramer, A. F. (2009). Aerobic exercise effects on cognitive and neural plasticity in older adults. *British Journal of Sports Medicine*, 43, 22–24.

Ericsson, K. A. & Simon, H. A. (1993). *Protocol Analysis: Verbal Reports as Data*. Cambridge, MA: MIT Press.

Erikson, E. H. (1950). *Childhood and Society*. New York: Norton.

Erikson, E. H. (1968a). *Identity, Youth and Crisis*. New York: Norton.

Erikson, E. H. (1968b). Generativity and Ego Integrity. In B. L. Neugarten (ed.) *Middle Age and Aging* (pp. 85–87). London: The University of Chicago Press.

Erikson, E. H. (1980). *Identity and the Life Cycle*. London: W. W. Norton & Co.

Eriksson, P. S., Perfilieva, E., Björk-Eriksson, T., Alborn, A. M., Nordborg, C., Peterson, D. A. & Gage, F. H. (1998). Neurogenesis in the adult human hippocampus. *Nature Medicine*, 4, 1313–1317.

Extremera, N., Fernández-Berrocal, P. & Salovey, P. (2006). Spanish version of the Mayer-Salovey-Caruso emotional intelligence test (MSCEIT). Version 2.0: Reliabilities, age and gender differences. *Psicothema*, 18, 42–48.

Eysenck, H. J. (1952). *The Scientific Study of Personality*. London: Routledge & Kegan Paul.

Eysenck, S. B. G., Pearson, P. R., Easting, G. & Allsopp, J. F. (1985). Age norms of impulsiveness, venturesomeness and empathy in adults. *Personality and Individual Differences*, 6, 613–619.

Farrell, M. J., Zamarripa, F., Shade, R., Phillips, P. A., McKinley, M., Fox, P. T., Blair-West, J., Denton, D. A. & Egan, G. F. (2008). Effect of aging on regional cerebral blood flow responses associated with osmotic thirst and its satiation by water drinking: A PET study. *Proceedings of the National Academy of Sciences of the United States of America*, 105, 382–387.

Farrington, D. P. (1986). Age and crime. In M. Tonry & N. Morris (eds) *Crime and Justice: An Annual Review of Research, Volume 7* (pp. 189–250). Chicago: University of Chicago Press.

Farrington, D. P. (1991). Longitudinal research strategies: Advantages, problems, and prospects. *Journal of the American Academy of Child & Adolescent Psychiatry*, 30, 369–374.

Farrington, D. P. (1992). Criminal career research in the United Kingdom. *British Journal of Criminology*, 32, 521–536.

Fasick, F. A. (1994). On the 'invention' of adolescence. *The Journal of Early Adolescence*, 14, 6–23.

Feldman, D. H. & Fowler, R. C. (1997). The nature(s) of developmental change: Piaget, Vygotsky, and the transition process. *New Ideas in Psychology*, 15, 195–210.

Felsman, D. E. & Blustein, D. L. (1999). The role of peer relatedness in late adolescent career development. *Journal of Vocational Behavior*, 54, 279–295.

Fenell, D. (1993). Characteristics of long-term first marriages. *Journal of Mental Health Counseling*, 15, 446–460.

Fenwick, P. & Fenwick, E. (2008). *The Art of Dying*. London: Continuum Publishing.

Ferraro, K. F., Mutran, E. & Barresi, C. M. (1984). Widowhood, health, and friendship support in later life. *Journal of Health and Social Behavior*, 25, 246–259.

Ferri, C. P., Prince, M., Brayne, C., Brodaty, H., Fratiglioni, L., Ganguli, M., Kathleen Hall, Kazuo Hasegawa, Hugh Hendrie, Yueqin Huang, Anthony Jorm, Colin Mathers, Paulo R Menezes, Elizabeth Rimmer, Marcia Scazufca, and Alzheimer's Disease International (2006). Global prevalence of dementia: A Delphi consensus study. *The Lancet*, 366, 2112–2117.

Finlay-Jones, R. & Brown, G. W. (1981). Types of stressful life event and the onset of anxiety and depressive disorders. *Psychological Medicine*, 11, 803–815.

Fischer, C. S. & Phillips, S. L. (1982). Who is alone? Social characteristics of people with small networks. In L. A. Peplau & D. Perlman (eds) *Loneliness: A Sourcebook of Current Theory, Research, and Therapy* (pp. 21–39). New York: Wiley.

Fischer, K. & Yan, Z. (2002). The development of dynamic skill theory. In R. Lickliter & D. Lewkowicz (eds) *Conceptions of Development: Lessons from the Laboratory* (pp. 279–312). Hove: Psychology Press.

Fisher, T. D., Moore, Z. T. & Pittenger, M. J. (2012). Sex on the brain? An examination of frequency of sexual cognitions as a function of gender, erotophilia, and social desirability. *Journal of Sex Research*, 49, 69–77.

Flavell, J. H. (1963). *The Developmental Psychology of Jean Piaget*. Princeton, NJ: Van Nostrand Co.

Flavell, J. H. (1996). Piaget's legacy. *Psychological Science*, 7, 200–203.

Flynn, J. R. (1999). Searching for justice: The discovery of IQ gains over time. *American Psychologist*, 54, 5–20.

Folkman, S., Lazarus, R. S., Pimley, S. & Novacek, J. (1987). Age differences in stress and coping processes. *Psychology and Aging*, 2, 171–184.

Follett, K. J. & Hess, T. M. (2002). Aging, cognitive complexity, and the fundamental attribution error. *Journal of Gerontology: Psychological Sciences*, 57, 312–323.

Fowler, C. D., Liu, Y., Ouimet, C. & Wang, Z. (2002). The effects of social environment on adult neurogenesis in the female prairie vole. *Journal of Neurobiology*, 51, 115–128.

Fowler, J. W. (1981). *Stages of Faith: The Psychology of Human Development and the Quest for Meaning*. New York: Harper and Row.

Fox, M. J. (2003). *Lucky Man: A Memoir*. London: Ebury Press.

Fozard, J. L., Vercruyssen, M., Reynolds, S. L., Hancock, P. A. & Quilter, E. R. (1994). Age differences and changes in reaction time: The Baltimore longitudinal study of aging. *Journal of Gerontology: Psychological Sciences*, 49, 179–189.

Fraley, R. C. & Shaver, P. R. (2000). Adult romantic attachment: Theoretical developments, emerging controversies, and unanswered questions. *Review of General Psychology*, 4, 132–154.

Frankl, V. (1984). *Man's Search for Meaning* (Rev. ed.). London: Hodder & Stoughton.

Fratiglioni, L. & Wang, H. (2000). Smoking and Parkinson's and Alzheimer's disease: Review of the epidemiological studies. *Behavioural Brain Research*, 113, 117–120.

Fredrickson, B. L. & Carstensen, L. L. (1990). Choosing social partners: How old age and anticipated endings make people more selective. *Psychology and Aging*, 5, 335–347.

Freud, S. (1930). *Civilisation and its Discontents*. London: Hogarth Press.

Freund, A. M. & Baltes, P. B. (1998). Selection, optimization, and compensation as strategies of life management: Correlations with subjective indicators of successful aging. *Psychology and Aging*, 13, 531–543.

Freund, A. M. & Ritter, J. O. (2009). Midlife crisis: A debate. *Gerontology*, 55, 582–91.

Fuller, R. C. (2001). *Spiritual, but not Religious: Understanding Unchurched America*. Oxford: Oxford University Press.

Fung, H. H., Carstensen, L. L. & Lang, F. R. (2001). Age-related patterns in social networks among European Americans and African Americans: Implications for socioemotional selectivity across the life span. *International Journal of Aging & Human Development*, 52, 185–206.

Galupo, M. P. (2009). Cross-category friendship patterns: Comparison of heterosexual and sexual minority adults. *Journal of Social and Personal Relationships*, 26, 811–831.

Galupo, M. P., Cartwright, K. B. & Savage, L. S. (2010). Cross-category friendships and postformal thought among college students. *Journal of Adult Development*, 17, 208–214.

Galli, R. L., Shukitt-Hale, B., Youdim, K. A. & Joseph, J. A. (2002). Fruit polyphenolics and brain aging: Nutritional interventions targeting age-related neuronal and behavioral deficits. *Annals of the New York Academy of Sciences*, 959, 128–132.

Gao, S., Hendrie, H. C., Hall, K. S. & Hui, S. (1998). The relationships between age, sex, and the incidence of dementia and Alzheimer disease: A meta-analysis. *Archives of General Psychiatry*, 55, 809–815.

Gaunt, R. (2006). Couple similarity and marital satisfaction: Are similar spouses happier? *Journal of Personality*, 74, 1401–1420.

Gecas, V. (1989). The social psychology of self-efficacy. *Annual Review of Sociology*, 15, 291–316.

George, C., Kaplan, N. & Main, M. (1996). *The Adult Attachment Interview*. University of California at Berkeley: Unpublished manuscript.

Geurts, T., Poortman, A-R., van Tilburg, T. & Dykstra, P. A. (2009). Contact between grandchildren and their grandparents in early adulthood. *Journal of Family Issues*, 30, 1698–1713.

Gibb, W. R. G. & Lees, A. J. (1988). The relevance of the Lewy body to the pathogenesis of idiopathic Parkinson's disease. *Journal of Neurology, Neurosurgery, and Psychiatry*, 51, 745–752.

Gibbs, J. C. (1996). Socio-moral group treatment for young offenders. In C. R. Hollin & K. Howells (eds) *Clinical Approaches to Working with Young Offenders* (pp. 129–149). New York: Wiley.

Giddens, A. (1991). *Modernity and the Self: Self and Society in the Late Modern Age*. Stanford, CA: Stanford University Press.

Gilbert, L. A. (1994). Current perspectives on dual-career families. *Current Directions in Psychological Science*, 3, 101–105.

Gill, S. C., Butterworth, P., Rodgers, B., Anstey, K. J., Villamil, E. & Melzer, D. (2006). Mental health and the timing of men's retirement. *Social Psychiatry and Psychiatric Epidemiology*, 41, 515–522.

Gillath, O., Sesko, A. K., Shaver, P. R. & Chun, D. S. (2010). Attachment, authenticity, and honesty: Dispositional and experimentally induced security can reduce self- and other-deception. *Journal of Personality and Social Psychology*, 98, 841–855.

Gilligan, C. (1982). *In a Different Voice: Psychological Theory and Women's Development*. Cambridge, MA: Harvard University Press.

Gilligan, C. & Murphy, J. M. (1979). Development from adolescence to adulthood: The philosopher and the dilemma of the fact. *New Directions for Child and Adolescent Development*, 5, 85–99.

Glaser, R., Kennedy, S., Lafuse, W. P., Bonneau, R. H., Speicher, C., Hillhouse, J. & Kiecolt-Glaser, J. K. (1990). Psychological stress-induced modulation of interleukin 2 receptor gene expression and interleukin 2 production in peripheral blood leukocytes. *Archives of General Psychiatry*, 47, 707–712.

Glaser, K., Ribé, E., Montserrat, U. W., Waginger, U., Price, D., Stuchbury, R. & Tinker, A. (2010). *Grandparenting in Europe*. London: Grandparents Plus. Retrieved on 30 January 2012 from http://www.grandparentsplus.org.uk/wp-content/uploads/2011/03/Grandparenting-in-Europe-executive-summary.pdf.

Gluckman, P. D., Hanson, M. A., Buklijas, T., Low, F. M. & Beedle, A. S. (2009). Epigenetic mechanisms that underpin metabolic and cardiovascular diseases. *Nature Reviews. Endocrinology*, 5, 401–408.

Goble, F. (1970). *The Third Force: The Psychology of Abraham Maslow*. New York: Grossman.

Goldberg, L. R. (1993). The structure of phenotypic personality traits. *American Psychologist*, 48, 26–34.

Goldman, J. A., Cooper, P. E., Ahern, K. & Corsini, D. A. (1981). Continuities and discontinuities in the friendship descriptions of women at six stages in the life-cycle. *Genetic Psychology Monographs*, 103, 153–167.

Gonzalez, R.G. (2011). Learning to be illegal: Undocumented youth and shifting legal contexts in the transition to adulthood. *American Sociological Review*, 76, 602–619.

Gorchoff, S. M., John, O. P. & Helson, R. (2008). Contextualizing change in marital satisfaction during middle age: An 18-year longitudinal study. *Psychological Science*, 19, 1194–1200.

Gottfredson, G. D. (1977). Career stability and redirection in adulthood. *Journal of Applied Psychology*, 62, 436–445.

Gottfredson, L. S. (1981). Circumscription and compromise: A developmental theory of occupational aspirations. *Journal of Counseling Psychology*, 28, 545–579.

Gottfredson, L. S. (2005). Applying Gottfredson's theory of circumscription and compromise in career guidance and counseling. In S. D. Brown & R. L. Lent (eds) *Career Development and Counseling: Putting Theory and Research to Work* (pp. 71–100). Hoboken, NJ: John Wiley & Sons Inc.

Gottlieb, G. (1991). Experiential canalization of behavioral development: Theory. *Developmental Psychology*, 27, 4–13.

Gottlieb, G. (1998). Normally occurring environmental and behavioral influences on gene activity: From central dogma to probabilistic epigenesis. *Psychological Review*, 105, 792–802.

Gottman, J. M. & Krokoff, L. J. (1989). Marital interaction and satisfaction: A longitudinal view. *Journal of Consulting and Clinical Psychology*, 57, 47–52.

Gottschalk, L. A. & Gleser, G. C. (1979). *The Measurement of Psychological States Through the Content Analysis of Verbel Behavior Edition*. Berkeley, CA: University of California Press.

Gould, R. (1978). *Transformations: Growth and Change in Adult Life*. New York: Simon and Schuster.

Graham, J., Haidt, J. & Nosek, B. A. (2009). Liberals and conservatives rely on different sets of moral foundations. *Journal of Personality and Social Psychology*, 96, 1029–1046.

Gray, A. (2005). The changing availability of grandparents as carers and its implications for childcare policy in the UK. *Journal of Social Policy*, 34, 557–577.

Greendale, G. A., Lee, N. P. & Arriola, E. R. (1999). The menopause. *Lancet*, 353, 571–580.

Greyson, B. (2006). Near-death experiences and spirituality. *Zygon*, 41, 393–414.

Grigg, C. (2009). House husbands: Are you man enough? *The Telegraph*. Retrieved on 30 January 2012 from http://www.telegraph.co.uk/family/4600556/House-husbands-Are-you-man-enough.html.

Gross, J. J., Carstensen, L. L., Pasupathi, M., Tsai, J., Skorpen, C. G. & Hsu, A. Y. (1997). Emotion and aging: Experience, expression, and control. *Psychology and Aging*, 12, 590–599.

Grossmann, I., Na, J., Varnum, M. E. W., Park, D. C., Kitayama, S. & Nisbett, R. E. (2010). Reasoning about social conflicts improves into old age. *Proceedings of the National Academy of Sciences of the United States of America*, 107, 7246–7250.

Grossmann, K. E., Grossmann, K. & Waters, E. (2005). *Attachment from Infancy to Adulthood: The Major Longitudinal Studies*. New York: Guilford Publications.

Grühn, D., Rebucal, K., Diehl, M., Lumley, M. & Labouvie-Vief, G. (2008). Empathy across the adult lifespan: Longitudinal and experience-sampling findings. *Emotion*, 8, 753–765.

Guerriero Austrom, M., Perkins, A. J., Damush, T. M. & Hendrie, H. C. (2003). Predictors of life satisfaction in retired physicians and spouses. *Social Psychiatry and Psychiatric Epidemiology*, 38, 134–141.

Gum, A. & Snyder, C. R. (2002). Coping with terminal illness: The role of hopeful thinking. *Journal of Palliative Medicine*, 5, 883–894.

Gunther, M. (2008). Deferred empathy: A construct with implications for the mental health of older adults. *Issues in Mental Health Nursing*, 29, 1029–1040.

Gurin, P. & Brim, O. G. (1984). Change in self in adulthood: The example of sense of control. In P. B. Baltes & O. G. Brim (eds) *Life-Span Development and Behavior*, Vol. 6 (pp. 281–334). New York: Academic Press.

Habermas, T. & Bluck, S. (2000). Getting a life: The emergence of the life story in adolescence. *Psychological Bulletin*, 126, 748–769.

Haag, M. (2003). Essential fatty acids and the brain. *Canadian Journal of Psychiatry*, 48, 195–203.

Häfner, H., Maurer, K., Loffler, W. & Riecher-Rossler, A. (1993). The influence of age and sex on the onset and early course of schizophrenia. *The British Journal of Psychiatry*, 162, 80–86.

Häfner, H., an der Heiden, W., Behrens, S., Gattaz, W. F., Hambrecht, M., Löffler, W., Kurt Maurer, Povl Munk-Jorgensen, Birgit Nowotny, Anita Riecher-Rossler & Astrid Stein (1998). Causes and consequences of the gender difference in age at onset of schizophrenia. *Schizophrenia Bulletin*, 24, 99–113.

Haggbloom, S. J., Warnick, R., Warnick, J. E., Jones, V. K., Yarbrough, G. L., Russell, T. M., Chris M. Borecky, McGahhey, R., John L. Powell III, Beavers, J. & Monte, E. (2002). The 100 most eminent psychologists of the 20th century. *Review of General Psychology*, 6, 139–152.

Haidt, J. (2001). The emotional dog and its rational tail: A social intuitionist approach to moral judgment. *Psychological Review*, 108, 814–834.

Haidt, J. (2007). The new synthesis in moral psychology. *Science*, 316, 998–1002.

Haidt, J. & Graham, J. (2007). When morality opposes justice: Conservatives have moral intuitions that liberals may not recognize. *Social Justice Research*, 20, 98–116.

Haidt, J. & Joseph, C. (2004). Intuitive ethics: How innately prepared intuitions generate culturally variable virtues. *Daedalus: Special Issue on Human Nature*, 133, 55–66.

Haidt, J. & Kesebir, S. (2010). Morality. In S. Fiske, D. Gilbert & G. Lindzey (eds) *Handbook of Social Psychology*, 5th edn (pp. 797–832). Hobeken: Wiley.

Haight, B.K. (1988). The therapeutic role of a structured life review process in homebound elderly subjects. *Journals of Gerontology: Psychological Sciences*, 43, 40–44.

Hall, L., Callister, L. C., Berry, J. A. & Matsumura, G. (2007). Meanings of menopause: Cultural influences on perception and management of menopause. *Journal of Holistic Nursing*, 25, 106–118.

Halmi, K. A., Casper, R. C., Eckert, E. D., Goldberg, S. C. & Davis, J. M. (1979). Unique features associated with age of onset of anorexia nervosa. *Psychiatry Research*, 1, 209–215.

Hakim, C. (1998). *Social Change and Innovation in the Labour Market: Evidence from the Census SARs on Occupational Segregation and Labour Mobility, Part-Time Work and Students' Jobs, Homework and Self-Employment*. Oxford: Oxford University Press.

Hank, K. & Buber, I. (2008). Grandparents caring for their grandchildren: Findings from the 2004 survey of health, ageing, and retirement in Europe. *Journal of Family Issues*, 30, 53–73.

Hanson, T. L. (1999). Does parental conflict explain why divorce is negatively associated with child welfare? *Social Forces*, 77, 1283–1316.

Harbison, J. (2002). Sleep disorders in older people. *Age and Ageing*, 31-S2, 6–9.

Harding, C., Brooks, G., Ashikaga, T., Strauss, J. & Breier, A. (1987). The Vermont longitudinal study of persons with severe mental illness, II: Long-term outcome of subjects who retrospectively met DSM-III criteria for schizophrenia. *The American Journal of Psychiatry*, 144, 727–735.

Harding, D. J. & Jencks, C. (2003). Changing attitudes toward premarital sex: Cohort, period, and aging effects. *The Public Opinion Quarterly*, 67, 211–226.

Hare, R. D. (1993). *Without Conscience: The Disturbing World of the Psychopaths among us*. New York: Guilford Press.

Harpur, D. J. & Hare, R. D. (1994). Assessment of psychopathy as a function of age. *Journal of Abnormal Psychology*, 103, 604–609.

Harris, D., Richard, B. & Khanna, P. (2006). Assisted dying: The ongoing debate. *Postgraduate Medical Journal*, 82, 479–82.

Harris, M. J. & Jeste, D. V. (1988). Late-onset schizophrenia: An overview. *Schizophrenia Bulletin*, 14, 39–55.

Harris, T. (2001). Recent developments in understanding the psychosocial aspects of depression. *British Medical Bulletin*, 57, 17–32.

Harré, R. (1998). *The Singular Self: An Introduction to the Psychology of Personhood*. London: Sage Publications.

Harter, S., Waters, P. L. & Whitesell, N. R. (1997). Lack of voice as a manifestation of false-self behavior among adolescents: The school setting as a stage upon which the drama of authenticity is enacted. *Educational Psychologist*, 32, 153–173.

Hartup, W. W. & Stevens, N. (1997). Friendships and adaptation in the life course. *Psychological Bulletin*, 121, 355–370.

Hartup, W. W. & Stevens, N. (1999). Friendships and adaptation across the life span. *Current Directions in Psychological Science*, 8, 76–79.

Hasher, L. & Zacks, R. T. (1988). Working memory, comprehension and aging: A review. In Bower, G. (ed.) *The Psychology of Learning and Motivation* (pp. 193–225). New York: Academic Press.

Haskey, J. (2001). Cohabitation in Great Britain: past, present and future trends – and attitudes. *Population Trends*, 103, 4–25.

Hatch, L. R. & Bulcroft, K. (1992). Contact with friends in later life: Disentangling the effects of gender and marital status. *Journal of Marriage and the Family*, 54, 222–232.

Hauser, S. T. (1976). Loevinger's model and measure of ego development: A critical review. *Psychological Bulletin*, 33, 928–955.

Hauser, S. T. (1993). Loevinger's model and measure of ego development: A critical review II. *Psychological Inquiry*, 4, 23–30.

Hays, N. P. & Roberts, S. B. (2006). The anorexia of aging in humans. *Physiology and Behaviour*, 88, 257–266.

Hayslip Jr., B. & Kaminski, P. L. (2005). Grandparents raising their grandchildren: A review of the literature and suggestions for practice. *The Gerontologist*, 45, 262–269.

Hayslip, B., Shore, R., Henderson, C. & Lambert, P. (1998). Custodial grandparenting and the impact of grandchildren with problems on role satisfaction and role meaning. *Journals of Gerontology Series B-Psychological Sciences and Social Sciences*, 53, S164–S173.

Hazan, C. & Shaver, P. (1987). Romantic love conceptualized as an attachment process. *Journal of Personality and Social Psychology*, 52, 511–524.

Heckhausen, J. (2000). Developmental regulation across the life span: An action-phase model of engagement and disengagement with developmental goals. In Heckhausen, J. (ed.) *Motivational Psychology of Human Development: Developing Motivation and Motivating Development* (pp. 213–231). Oxford, UK: Elsevier Science.

Heckhausen, J., Wrosch, C. & Schulz, R. (2010). A motivational theory of life-span development. *Psychological Review*, 117, 32–60.

Heinz, W. R. (2002). Self-socialization and post-traditional society. In R. A. Settersten & T. J. Owens (eds) *Advances in Life Course Research: New Frontiers in Socialization*, Vol. 7 (pp. 41–64). New York: JAI Press.

Heim, C. & Nemeroff, C. B. (2001). The Role of Childhood Trauma in the Neurobiology of Mood and Anxiety Disorders: Preclinical and Clinical Studies. *Biological Psychiatry*, 49, 1023–1039.

Helson, R. & Picano, J. (1990). Is the traditional role bad for women? *Journal of Personality and Social Psychology*, 59, 311–320.

Helson, R. & Srivastava, S. (2002). Creative and wise people: Similarities, differences, and how they develop. *Personality and Social Psychology Bulletin*, 28, 1430–1440.

Helson, R., Jones, C. & Kwan, V. S. Y. (2002). Personality change over 40 years of adulthood: Hierarchical linear modeling analyses of two longitudinal samples. *Journal of Personality and Social Psychology*, 83, 752–766.

Hemstrom, O. (1996). Is marriage dissolution linked to differences in mortality risks for men and women? *Journal of Marriage and the Family*, 58, 366–378.

Henderson, A. S., Jorm, A. F., Korten, A. E., Jacomb, P., Christensen, H. & Rodgers, B. (1998). Symptoms of depression and anxiety during adult life: Evidence for a decline in prevalence with age. *Psychological Medicine*, 28, 1321–1328.

Henderson, S. & Gilding, M. (2004). 'I've never clicked this much with anyone in my life': Trust and hyperpersonal communication in online friendships. *New Media Society*, 6, 487–506.

Hendrick, S. S. (1981). Self-disclosure and marital satisfaction. *Journal of Personality and Social Psychology*, 40, 1150–1159.

Hendry, L. B. & Kloep, M. (2007). Conceptualizing emerging adulthood: Inspecting the emperor's new clothes? *Child Development Perspectives*, 1, 74–79.

Henquet, C., Krabbendam, L., Spauwen, J., Kaplan, C., Lieb, R., Wittchen, H. U. & van Os, J. (2005). Prospective cohort study of cannabis use, predisposition for psychosis, and psychotic symptoms in young people. *British Medical Journal (Clinical research ed.)*, 330, 1–5.

Herzog, A. R., Rogers, W. & Woodworth, J. (1982). *Subjective Wellbeing among Different Age Groups*. Ann Arbor, MI: Institute for Social Research.

Heywood, D. (2008). Faith development theory: A case for paradigm change. *Journal of Beliefs & Values*, 29, 263–272.

Hicks, J. & Allen, G. (1999). A century of change: Trends in UK statistics since 1900. *House of Commons Research Paper*. Retrieved on 29 January 2012 from www.parliament.uk/documents/commons/lib/research/rp99/rp99-111.pdf.

Hill, P. C. (2005). Measurement in the psychology of religion and spirituality. In R. F. Paloutzian & C. L. Park (eds) *Handbook of the Psychology of Religion and Spirituality* (pp. 43–61). New York: Guilford Press.

Hirschberger, G., Srivastava, S., Marsh, P., Cowan, C. P. & Cowan, P. A. (2009). Attachment, marital satisfaction, and divorce during the first fifteen years of parenthood. *Personal Relationships*, 16, 401–420.

Hirschi, A. & Lage, D. (2007). The relation of secondary students' career-choice readiness to a six-phase model of career decision making. *Journal of Career Development*, 34, 164–191.

Hitchens, C. (2007). *God is Not Great: How Religion Poisons Everything*. London: Atlantic Books.

Hlastala, S. A., Frank, E., Kowalski, J., Sherrill, J. T., Tu, X. M., Anderson, B. & Kupfer, D. J. (2000). Stressful life events, bipolar disorder, and the 'kindling model'. *Journal of Abnormal Psychology*, 109, 777–786.

Ho, J. H. & Raymo, J. M. (2009). Expectations and realization of joint retirement among dual-worker couples. *Research on Aging*, 31, 153–179.

Hochschild, A. R. (1975). Disengagement theory: A critique and proposal. *American Sociological Review*, 40, 553–569.

Hochschild, A. R. & Machung, A. (1990). *The Second Shift: Working Parents and the Revolution at Home*. London: Piatkus London.

Hodkinson, P., Ford, G., Hodkinson, H. & Hawthorn, R. (2008). Retirement as a learning process. *Educational Gerontology*, 34, 167–184.

Hoffman, M. L. (2000). *Empathy and Moral Development: Implications for Caring and Justice*. New York: Cambridge University Press.

Hogan, R. & Roberts, B. W. (2004). A socioanalytic model of maturity. *Journal of Career Assessment*, 12, 207–217.

Hojat, M., Gonnella, J. S., Mangione, S., Nasca, T. J., Veloski, J. J. & Erdmann, J. B., Callahan, C. A., Magee, M. (2002). Empathy in medical students as related to academic performance, clinical competence and gender. *Medical Education*, 36, 522–527.

Hojat, M., Mangione, S., Nasca, T. J., Rattner, S., Erdmann, J. B., Gonnella, J. & Magee, M. (2004). An empirical study of decline in empathy in medical school. *Medical Education*, 38, 934–41.

Hojat, M., Vergare, M. J., Maxwell, K., Brainard, G., Herrine, S. K. Isenberg, G. A., Veloski, J. & Gonnella, J. S. (2009). The devil is in the third year: A longitudinal study of erosion of empathy in medical school. *Academic Medicine*, 84, 1182–1191.

Holaday, M., Smith, D. A. & Sherry, A. (2000). Sentence completion tests: A review of the literature and results of a survey of members of the Society for Personality Assessment. *Journal of Personality Assessment*, 74, 371–383.

Holland, J. L. (1959). A theory of vocational choice. *Journal of Counseling Psychology*, 6, 34–45.

Holland, J. L. (1996). Exploring careers with a typology: What we have learned and some new directions. *American Psychologist*, 51, 397–406.

Hollis, J. (1993). *The Middle Passage: From Misery to Meaning in Midlife*. Toronto: Inter City Books.

Holstein, C. B. (1976). Irreversible, stepwise sequence in the development of moral judgment: A longitudinal study of males and females. *Child Development*, 47, 51–61.

Honig, M. & Hanoch, G. (1985). Partial retirement as a separate mode of retirement behavior. *Journal of Human Resources*, 20, 21–46.

Hooker, K. & McAdams, D. P. (2003). Personality reconsidered: A new agenda for aging research. *The Journals of Gerontology. Series B, Psychological Sciences and Social Sciences*, 58, 296–304.

Hopkins, D. R., Murrah, B., Hoeger, W. W. K. & Rhodes, R. C. (1990). Effect of low-impact aerobic dance on the functional fitness of elderly women. *The Gerontologist*, 30, 189–192.

Hopson, B. & Adams, J. (1976). Dynamics, towards an understanding of transition: Defining some boundaries of transition. In J. D. Adams, J. Hayes & B. Hopson (eds) *Transition: Understanding & Managing Personal Change* (pp. 3–25). London: Martin Robertson.

Horan, W. P., Ventura, J., Nuechterlein, K. H., Subotnik, K. L., Hwang, S. S. & Mintz, J. (2005). Stressful life events in recent-onset schizophrenia: Reduced frequencies and altered subjective appraisals. *Schizophrenia Research*, 75, 363–374.

Horesh, N. N., Apter, A., Lepkifker, E. E. & Ratzoni, G. G. (1995). Life events and severe anorexia nervosa in adolescence. *Acta Psychiatrica Scandinavica*, 91, 5–9.

Horn, J. L. & Cattell, R. M. (1967). Age differences in fluid and crystallized intelligence. *Acta Psychologica Scandinavica*, 26, 107–129.

Horton, S. L. (2002). Conceptualizing transition: The role of metaphor in describing the experience of change at midlife. *Journal of Adult Development*, 9, 277–290.

Horwitz, A. V., Widom, C. S., Mclaughlin, J., White, H. R., Horwitz, A. V. & Mclaughlin, J. (2001). The Impact of Childhood Abuse and Neglect on Adult Mental Health: A Prospective Study. *Journal of Health and Social Behavior*, 42, 184–201.

Horwitz, A. V. & Wakefield, J. C. (2007). *The Loss of Sadness: How Psychiatry Transformed Normal Sorrow Into Depressive Disorder*. Oxford: Oxford University Press.

Howitt, D. (2010). *Introduction to Qualitative Methods in Psychology*. London: Prentice Hall.

Hsieh, H.-F. & Shannon, S. E. (2005). Three approaches to qualitative content analysis. *Qualitative Health Research*, 15, 1277–1288.

Huff, F. J., Growdon, J. H., Corkin, S. & Rosen, T. J. (1987). Age at onset and rate of progression of Alzheimer's disease. *Journal of the American Geriatrics Society*, 35, 27–30.

Hull, C. (1943). *Principles of Behavior*. New York: Appleton-Century-Crofts.

Huxley, A. (2009). *The Perennial Philosophy*. London: Harper Perennial.

Hvas, L. (2001). Positive aspects of menopause: A qualitative study. *Maturitas*, 39, 11–17.

Impett, E., English, T. & John, O.P. (2010). Women's emotions during interactions with their grown children in later adulthood: The moderating role of attachment avoidance. *Social Psychological and Personality Science*, 2, 43–50.

Ingersoll-Dayton, B., Krause, N. & Morgan, D. (2002). Religious trajectories and transitions over the life course. *The International Journal of Aging and Human Development: A Journal of Psychosocial Gerontology*, 55, 51–70.

Ingram, R. E. & Luxton, D. D. (2005). Vulnerability-stress models. In B. L. Hankin & J. R. Z. Abela (Eds.) *Development of Psychopathology: A Vulnerability-Stress Perspective* (pp. 32–46). London: Sage.

Inhelder, B. & Piaget, J. (1958). *The Growth of Logical Thinking from Childhood to Adolescence*. New York: Basic Books Inc.

Izard, C. E. (1978). Emotions as motivations: An evolutionary–developmental perspective. In S. S. Tomkins & R. A. Dienstbier (eds) *Nebraska Symposium on Motivation* (pp. 163–200). Lincoln: University of Nebraska Press.

Izard, C. E. (1993). Four systems for emotion activation: Cognitive and noncognitive processes. *Psychological Review*, 100, 68–90.

Izard, C. E. (2009). Emotion theory and research: Highlights, unanswered questions, and emerging issues. *Annual Review of Psychology*, 60, 1–25.

Izard, C. E. & Ackerman, B. P. (2000). Motivational, organizational, and regulatory functions of emotions. In M. Lewis & J. M. Haviland-Jones (eds) *Handbook of Emotions*, 2nd edn (pp. 253–264). New York: Guilford Press.

Jacobs, S. (1993). *Pathologic Grief: Maladaptation to Loss*. Washington, DC: American Psychiatric Press.

James, W. (1983). *The Varieties of Religious Experience*. London: Penguin Books Ltd.

Jankovic, J. (2008). Parkinson's disease: Clinical features and diagnosis. *Journal of Neurology, Neurosurgery, and Psychiatry*, 79, 368–376.

Jekielek, S. M. (1998). Parental conflict, marital disruption and children's emotional well-being. *Social Forces*, 76, 905–935.

Jendrek, M. P. (1993). Grandparents who parent their grandchildren: Effects on lifestyle. *Journal of Marriage and the Family*, 4, 609–621.

Jin, K., Wang, X., Xie, L., Mao, X. O., Zhu, W., Wang, Y., Shen, J., Mao, Y., Banwait, S. & Greenberg, D. A. (2006). Evidence for stroke-induced neurogenesis in the human brain. *Proceedings of the National Academy of Sciences of the United States of America*, 103, 13198–13202.

John, O. P., Caspi, A., Robins, R. W., Moffitt, T. E. & Stouthamer-Loeber, M. (1994). The 'little five': Exploring the nomological network of the five-factor model of personality in adolescent boys. *Child Development*, 65, 160–178.

Johnson, S. L. (2005). Life events in bipolar disorder: Towards more specific models. *Clinical Psychology Review*, 25, 1008–1027.

Johnson, S. L. & Miller, I. (1997). Negative life events and time to recovery from episodes of bipolar disorder. *Journal of Abnormal Psychology*, 106, 449–457.

Johnstone, L. (2008). *Psychiatric Diagnosis: Critical Issues in Mental Health* (pp. 5–22). London: Palgrave Macmillan.

Jordanova, V., Stewart, R., Goldberg, D., Bebbington, P. E., Brugha, T., Singleton, N., Lindesay, J. E. B., Jenkins, R., Prince, M. & Meltzer, H. (2007). Age variation in life events and their relationship with common mental disorders in a national survey population. *Social Psychiatry and Psychiatric Epidemiology*, 42, 611–616.

Joseph, J. A., Shukitt-Hale, B., Denisova, N. A., Bielinski, D., Martin, A., McEwen, J. J. & Bickford, P. C. (1999). Reversals of Age-Related Declines in Neuronal Signal Transduction, Cognitive, and Motor Behavioral Deficits with Blueberry, Spinach, or Strawberry Dietary Supplementation. *The Journal of Neuroscience*, 19, 8114–8121.

Jourard, S. (1971). *The Transparent Self*. New York: Van Nostrand Reinhold.

Jung, C. G. (1966). *The Collected Works of C. G. Jung – Two Essays on Analytical Psychology*. London: Routledge.

Kabat-Zinn, J. (1994). *Wherever You Go There You Are: Mindfulness Meditation in Everyday Life*. New York: Hyperion.

Kallio, E. (2011). Integrative thinking is the key: An evaluation of current research into the development of adult thinking. *Theory and Psychology*, 21, 785–801.

Kalmijn, M. (2003). Shared friendship networks and the life course: An analysis of survey data on married and cohabiting couples. *Social Networks*, 25, 231–249.

Kane, A. O., Fawcett, D. & Blackburn, R. (1996). Psychopathy and moral reasoning: Comparison of two classifications. *Personality and Individual Differences*, 20, 505–514.

Kang, J. H. & Ascherio, A. (2005). Fruit and vegetable consumption and cognitive decline in aging women. *Annals of Neurology*, 57, 713–720.

Kastenbaum, R. & Costa Jr., P. T. (1977). Psychological perspectives on death. *Annual Review of Psychology*, 28, 225–249.

Kayser, K. (1993). *When Love Dies: The Process of Marital Disaffection*. New York: Guilford Press.

Kegan, R. (1982). *The Evolving Self*. Cambridge, MA: Harvard University Press.

Kegan, R. (1994). *In Over Our Heads: The Mental Demands of Modern Life*. Cambridge, MA: Harvard University Press.

Kegan, R. & Lahey, L. (2009). *Immunity to Change: How to Overcome it and Unlock the Potential in Yourself and Your Organization*. Cambridge, MA: Harvard Business School Press.

Kemp, C. L. (2005). Dimensions of grandparent–adult grandchild relationships: From family ties to intergenerational friendships. *Canadian Journal on Aging*, 24, 161–178.

Kendler, K. S., Hettema, J. M., Butera, F., Gardner, C. O. & Prescott, C. A. (2003). Life event dimensions of loss, humiliation, entrapment, and danger in the prediction of onsets of major depression and generalized anxiety. *Archives of General Psychiatry*, 60, 789–796.

Kendler, K. S., Karkowski, L. M. & Prescott, C. A. (1999). Causal relationship between stressful life events and the onset of major depression. *American Journal of Psychiatry*, 156, 837–841.

Kennedy, K. M. & Raz, N. (2009). Aging white matter and cognition: Differential effects of regional variations in diffusion properties on memory, executive functions, and speed. *Neuropsychologia*, 47, 916–927.

Kennedy, Q., Mather, M. & Carstensen, L. L. (2004). The role of motivation in the age-related positivity effect in autobiographical memory. *Psychological Science*, 15, 208–214.

Kennedy, S., Thompson, R., Stancer, H., Roy, A. & Persad, E. (1983). Life events precipitating mania. *British Journal of Psychiatry*, 142, 398–403.

Kenney, W. L. & Chiu, P. (2001). Influence of age on thirst and fluid intake. *Medicine & Science in Sports & Exercise*, 33, 1524–1532.

Kenrick, D. T., Griskevicius, V., Neuberg, S. L. & Schaller, M. (2010). Renovating the pyramid of needs: Contemporary extensions built upon ancient foundations. *Perspectives on Psychological Science*, 5, 292–314.

Kernis, M. & Goldman, B. (2006). A multicomponent conceptualization of authenticity: Theory and research. *Advances in Experimental Social Psychology*, 38, 283–357.

Keski-Rahkonen, A., Hoek, H. W., Susser, E. S., Linna, M. S., Sihvola, E., Raevuori, A., Bulik, C. M., Kaprio, J. & Rissanen, A. (2007). Epidemiology and course of anorexia nervosa in the community. *The American Journal of Psychiatry*, 164, 1259–1265.

Kessler, R. C., Berglund, P., Demler, O., Jin, R., Merikangas, K. R., Walters, E. E. (2005). Lifetime prevalence and age-of-onset distributions of DSM-IV disorders in the National Comorbidity Survey Replication. *Archives of General Psychiatry*, 62, 593–602.

Ketterer, M. W., Denollet, J., Chapp, J., Thayer, B., Keteyian, S., Clark, V., Keteyian, S., Chapp, J., Thayer, B. & Deveshwar, S. (2004). Men deny and women cry, but who dies? Do the wages of 'denial' include early ischemic coronary heart disease? *Journal of Psychosomatic Research*, 56, 119–123.

Keyes, C. L. M. & Ryff, C. D. (1998). Generativity in adult lives: Social structural contours and quality of life consequences. In D. P. McAdams & E. de St Aubin (eds) *Generativity and Adult Development* (pp. 227–264). Washington, DC: American Psychological Association.

Killeen, P. R. (2001). The four causes of behaviour. *Current Directions in Psychological Science*, 10, 136–140.

Kim, J. E. & Moen, P. (2001). Moving into retirement: Preparation and transitions in late midlife. In M. E. Lachman (ed.) *Handbook of Midlife Development* (pp. 487–527). New York: Wiley.

Kimble, M., McFadden, S. H., Ellor, J. W. & Seeber, J. J. (1995). *Aging, Spirituality, and Religion: A Handbook*. Minneapolis: Augsburg Fortress Publishers.

King, L. A. (2001). The hard road to the good life: The happy, mature person. *Journal of Humanistic Psychology*, 41, 51–72.

King, L. A. & Hicks, J. A. (2006). Narrating the self in the past and the future: Implications for maturity. *Research in Human Development*, 3, 121–138.

King, L. A. & Hicks, J. A. (2007). Whatever happened to 'What might have been'? Regrets, happiness, and maturity. *The American Psychologist*, 62, 625–636.

King, P. & Mayhew, M. (2002). Moral judgement development in higher education: Insights from the defining issues test. *Journal of Moral Education*, 31, 247–270.

King, P. M. & Kitchener, K. S. (1994). *Developing Reflective Judgment: Understanding and Promoting Intellectual Growth and Critical Thinking in Adolescents and Adults*. San Francisco, CA: Jossey-Bass.

King, P. M. & Kitchener, K. S. (2002). The reflective judgment model: Twenty years of research on epistemic cognition. In B. K. Hofer & P. R. Pintrich (eds)

Personal Epistemology: The Psychology of Beliefs about Knowledge and Knowing (pp. 37–61). Mahway, NJ: Lawrence Erlbaum.

Kinsella, K. G. (1992). Changes in life expectancy 1900–1990. *The American Journal of Clinical Nutrition*, 55, 1196S–1202S.

Kitchener, K. & King, P. M. (1981). Reflective judgment: Concepts of justification and their relationship to age and education. *Journal of Applied Developmental Psychology*, 2, 89–116.

Kitchener, K. S., King, P. M., Wood, P. K. & Davison, M. L. (1989). Sequentiality and consistency in the development of reflective judgment: A six-year longitudinal study. *Journal of Applied Developmental Psychology*, 10, 73–95.

Kitson, G. C. (1992). *Portrait of Divorce: Adjustment to Marital Breakdown*. New York: Guilford Press.

Kivipelto, M., Helkala, E. L., Laakso, M. P., Hänninen, T., Hallikainen, M., Alhainen, K., Soininen, H., Tuomilehto, J. & Nissinen, A. (2001). Midlife vascular risk factors and Alzheimer's disease in later life: Longitudinal, population based study. *British Medical Journal*, 322, 1447–1451.

Kivnick, H. Q. (1982). Grandparenthood: An overview of meaning and mental health. *The Gerontologist*, 22, 59–66.

Kivnick, H. Q. (1983). Dimensions of grandparenthood meaning: Deductive conceptualization and empirical derivation. *Journal of Personality and Social Psychology*, 44, 1056–1068.

Klas, D., Silverman, P. R. & Nickman, S. L. (1996). *Continuing Bonds: New Understandings of Grief*. Washington, DC: Taylor & Francis.

Kloep, M. & Hendry, L. B. (2006). Pathways into retirement: Entry or exit? *Journal of Occupational and Organizational Psychology*, 79, 569–593.

Kneip, R. C., Delameter, A. M., Ismond, T., Milford, C., Salvia, L. & Schwartz, D. (1993). Self- and spouse-ratings of anger and hostility as predictors of coronary heart disease. *Health Psychology*, 12, 301–307.

Koenig, H. G. (1994). *Aging and God: Spiritual Pathways to Mental Health in Midlife and Later Years*. Binghamton, NY: Haworth Press.

Koenig, H. G. & Büssing, A. (2010). The Duke University Religion Index (DUREL): A five-item measure for use in epidemiological studies. *Religions*, 1, 78–85.

Kohlberg, L. (1970). Education for justice: A modern statement of the platonic view. In N. F. Sizer and T. R. Sizer (eds.) *Moral Education: Five Lectures* (pp. 57–83). Cambridge, MA: Harvard University Press.

Kopp, C. B. (1982). Antecedents of self-regulation: A developmental perspective. *Developmental Psychology*, 18, 199–214.

Kotre, J. (1995). *White Gloves: How We Create Ourselves Through Memory*. New York: The Free Press.

Kramer, D. A. (1989). A developmental framework for understanding conflict resolution processes. In J. D. Sinnott (ed.) *Everyday Problem-Solving in Adulthood* (pp. 133–152). New York: Praeger.

Kramer, D. A., Kahlbaugh, P. E. & Goldston, R. B. (1992). A measure of paradigm beliefs about the social world. *Journal of Gerontology: Psychological Sciences*, 47, 180–189.

Krebs, D. L. & Denton, K. (2005). Toward a more pragmatic approach to morality: A critical evaluation of Kohlberg's model. *Psychological Review*, 112, 629–649.

Kübler-Ross, E. (1969). *On Death and Dying: What the Dying Have to Teach Doctors, Nurses, Clergy and Their Own Families*. London: Simon & Schuster.

Kübler-Ross, E. (1978). *To Live Until We Say Goodbye*. Englewood Cliffs, NJ: Prentice Hall.

Kunzmann, U. & Baltes, P. B. (2003). Wisdom-related knowledge: Affective, motivational, and interpersonal correlates. *Personality & Social Psychology Bulletin*, 29, 1104–1119.

Kunzmann, U., Little, T. D. & Smith, J. (2000). Is age-related stability of subjective well-being a paradox? Cross-sectional and longitudinal evidence from the Berlin Aging Study. *Psychology and Aging*, 15, 511–526.

Kuper, H. & Marmot, M. (2003). Intimations of mortality: perceived age of leaving middle age as a predictor of future health outcomes within the Whitehall II study. *Age and Ageing*, 32, 178–184.

Kurdek, L. A. (1998). Relationship outcomes and their predictors: Longitudinal evidence from heterosexual married, gay cohabiting, and lesbian cohabiting couples. *Journal of Marriage and Family*, 60, 553–568.

Kurdek, L. A. (2004). Are gay and lesbian cohabiting couples really different from heterosexual married couples? *Journal of Marriage and Family*, 66, 880–900.

Kurdek, L. A. (2005). What do we know about gay and lesbian couples? *Current Directions in Psychological Science*, 14, 251–255.

Labouvie-Vief, G. & Medler, M. (2002). Affect optimization and affect complexity: Modes and styles of regulation in adulthood. *Psychology and Aging*, 17, 571–588.

Labouvie-Vief, G., DeVoe, M. & Bulka, D. (1989). Speaking about feelings: Conceptions of emotion across the life span. *Psychology and Aging*, 4, 425–37.

Labouvie-Vief, G., Grühn, D. & Studer, J. (2010). Dynamic integration of emotion and cognition: Equilibrium regulation in development and aging. In R. M. Lerner, M. E. Lamb & A. M. Freund (eds) *The Handbook of Life-Span Development, Social and Emotional Development*, Vol. 2 (pp. 79–115). Hoboken, NJ: Wiley.

Lachman, M. E. (1986). Locus of control in aging research: A case for multidimensional and domain-specific assessment. *Journal of Psychology and Aging*, 1, 34–40.

Lachman, M. E. (2004). Development in midlife. *Annual Review of Psychology*, 55, 305–331.

Lachman, M. E., Lewkowicz, C., Marcus, A. & Peng, Y. (1994). Images of midlife development among young, middle-aged, and older adults. *Journal of Adult Development*, 1, 201–211.

Laing, R. D. (1969). *The Divided Self*. London: Penguin Books.

Lang, F. R. & Carstensen, L. L. (1994). Close emotional relationships in late life: Further support for proactive aging in the social domain. *Psychology and Aging*, 9, 315–324.

Lanz, M. & Tagliabue, S. (2007). Do I really need someone in order to become an adult? Romantic relationships during emerging adulthood in Italy. *Journal of Adolescent Research*, 22, 531–549.

Larson, R. (1978). Thirty years of research on the subjective well-being of older Americans. *Journal of Gerontology*, 33, 109–125.

Larson, R. W. & Bradney, N. (1988). Precious moments with family members and friends. In R. M. Milardo (ed.) *Families and Social Networks* (pp. 107–126). Newbury Park, CA: Sage Publications.

Laslett, P. (1989). *A Fresh Map of Life: The Emergence of the Third Age*. London: George Weidenfeld & Nicolson Limited.

Launer, L. J., Ross, G. W., Petrovitch, H., Masaki, K., Foley, D., White, L. R. & Havlik, R. J. (2000). Midlife blood pressure and dementia: The Honolulu-Asia aging study. *Neurobiology of Aging*, 21, 49–55.

Lawrence, E., Rothman, A. D., Cobb, R. J., Rothman, M. T. & Bradbury, T. N. (2008). Marital satisfaction across the transition to parenthood. *Journal of Family Psychology*, 22, 41–50.

Lawton, M. P., Kleban, M. H., Rajagopal, D. & Dean, J. (1992). Dimensions of affective experience in three age groups. *Psychology and Aging*, 7, 171–184.

Lazar, S. W., Kerr, C. E., Wasserman, R. H., Gray, J. R., Greve, D. N., Treadway, M. T., McGarvey, M., Quinn, B. T., Dusek, J. A., Benson H., Rauch, S. L., Moore, C. I. & Bruce Fischl (2005). Meditation experience is associated with increased cortical thickness. *Ageing*, 16, 1893–1897.

Leach, L. S., Christensen, H., Mackinnon, A. J., Windsor, T. D. & Butterworth, P. (2008). Gender differences in depression and anxiety across the adult lifespan: The role of psychosocial mediators. *Social Psychiatry and Psychiatric Epidemiology*, 43, 983–998.

Leak, G., Loucks, A. & Bowlin, P. (1999). Development and initial validation of an objective measure of faith development. *International Journal for the Psychology of Religion*, 9, 105–124.

Leak, G. K. (2003). Validation of the faith development scale using longitudinal and cross-sectional designs. *Social Behavior and Personality*, 31, 637–642.

Lee, K. & Ashton, M. C. (2008). The HEXACO personality factors in the indigenous personality lexicons of English and 11 other languages. *Journal of Personality*, 76, 1001–1053.

Lemme, B. H. (2005). *Development in Adulthood*, 4th edn. Boston: Allyn and Bacon.

Lent, R. W., Brown, S. D. & Hackett, G. (1994). Toward a unifying social cognitive theory of career and academic interest, choice, and performance. *Journal of Vocational Behavior*, 45, 79–122.

Leong, F. T., Austin, J. T., Sekaran, U. & Komarraju, M. (1998). An evaluation of the crosscultural validity of Holland's theory: Career choices of workers in India. *Journal of Vocational Behavior*, 52, 441–455.

Lerner, R. M. (2001b). *Adolescence: Development, Diversity, Context, and Application.* New Jersey: Prentice Hall.

Lerner, R. M. & Kauffman, M. B. (1985). The concept of development in contextualism. *Developmental Review*, 5, 309–333.

Lerner, R. M., Lerner, J. V., von Eye, A., Ostrom, C. W., Nitz, K. Talwar-Soni, R., & Tubman, J. G. (1996). Continuity and discontinuity across the transition of early adolescence: A developmental contextual perspective. In Graber, J. A., Brooks-Gunn, J., Petersen, A. C. (eds.) *Transitions through Adolescence: Interpersonal Domain and Context* (pp. 1–10). Mahwah: Lawrence Erlbaum Associates.

Lerner, R. M., Schwartz, S. J. & Phelps, E. (2009). Problematics of time and timing in the longitudinal study of human development: Theoretical and methodological issues. *Human Development*, 52, 44–68.

Levenson, M. R., Aldwin, C. M. & D'Mello, M. (2005). Religious development from adolescence to middle adulthood. In R.F. Paloutzian & C. L. Park (eds) *Handbook of the Psychology of Religion and Spirituality* (pp. 144–161). New York: The Guilford Press.

Levin, J. (ed.) (1994). *Religion in Aging and Health: Theoretical Foundations and Methodological Frontiers.* London: Sage Publications.

Levine, C., Kohlberg, L. & Hewer, A. (1985). The current formulation of Kohlberg's theory and a response to critics. *Human Development*, 28, 94–100.

Levinson, D. J. (1978). *The Seasons of a Man's Life*. New York: Ballantine Books.

Levinson, D. J. (1986). A conception of adult development. *American Psychologist*, 41, 3–13.

Levinson, D. J. (1996). *The Seasons of a Woman's Life*. New York: Ballantine Books.

Lewin, F. A. (2000). Development towards wisdom and maturity: Sufi conception of self. *Aging and Identity*, 5, 137–149.

Lewis, H. & Liston, J. (1981). Stillbirth: Reaction and effect. In P. F. Pegg & E. Metze (eds) *Death and Dying: A Quality of Life* (pp. 147–156). Bath: Pitman.

Lewis, M. (1990). The development of intentionality and the role of consciousness. *Psychological Inquiry*, 1, 231–247.

Lidz, T. (1976). *The Person: His and Her Development throughout the Life Cycle*. New York: Basic Books Inc.

Lieberman, M. A. & Falk, J. M. (1971). The remembered past as a source of data for research on the life cycle. *Human Development*, 14, 132–141.

Lindberg, D. A. (2005). Integrative review of research related to meditation, spirituality, and the elderly. *Geriatric Nursing*, 26, 372–377.

Lindh-Astrand, L., Hoffmann, M., Hammar, M. & Kjellgren, K. I. (2007). Women's conception of the menopausal transition – a qualitative study. *Journal of Clinical Nursing*, 16, 509–17.

Lishman, W. A. (1990). Alcohol and the brain. *British Journal of Psychiatry*, 156, 635–644.

Litwak, E. (1985). *Helping the Elderly*. New York: Guilford Press.

Litzinger, S. & Gordon, K. C. (2005). Exploring relationships among communication, sexual satisfaction, and marital satisfaction. *Journal of Sex & Marital Therapy*, 31, 409–424.

Livianos-Aldana, L., Rojo-Moreno, L., Cervera-Martinez, G. & Dominguez-Carabantes, J. A. (1999). Temporal evolution of stress in the year prior to the onset of depressive disorders. *Journal of Affective Disorders*, 53, 253–262.

Lledo, P-M., Alonso, M. & Grubb, M. S. (2006). Adult neurogenesis and functional plasticity in neuronal circuits. *Nature Reviews Neuroscience*, 7, 179–193.

Lockenhoff, C. E., Terracciano, A., Patriciu, N. S., Eaton, W. W. & Costa Jr., P. T. (2009). Self-reported extremely adverse life events and longitudinal changes in five-factor model personality traits in an urban sample. *Journal of Traumatic Stress*, 22, 53–59.

Loeber, R. (1982). The stability of antisocial and delinquent child behavior: A review. *Child Development*, 53, 1431–1446.

Loeber, R. & Farrington, D. P. (1994). Problems and solutions in longitudinal and experimental treatment studies of child psychopathology and delinquency. *Journal of Consulting and Clinical Psychology*, 62, 887–900.

Loevinger, J. (1976). *Ego Development*. San Francisco, CA: Jossey-Bass.

Loevinger, J. (1985). Revision of the sentence completion test for ego development. *Journal of Personality and Social Psychology*, 48, 420–427.

Loevinger, J. (1998). *Technical Foundations for Measuring Ego Development: The Washington University Sentence Completion Test. The Washington University Sentence Completion Test*. Mahwah: Lawrence Erlbaum Associates, Inc.

Loevinger, J. & Knoll, E. (1983). Personality: Stages, traits and the self. *Annual Review of Psychology*, 34, 199–222.

Logroscino, G., Marder, K., Cote, L., Tang, M. X., Shea, S., Mayeux, R. (1996). Dietary lipids and antioxidants in Parkinson's disease: a population-based, case-control study. *Annals of Neurology*, 39, 89–94.

Long, E. C. J., Angera, J. J., Carter, S. J., Nakamoto, M. & Kalso, M. (1999). The one you love: Understanding a longitudinal assessment of an empathy training program for couples in romantic relationships. *Family Relations*, 48, 235–242.

Lopez, D., Chervinko, S., Strom, T., Kinney, J. & Bradley, M. (2005). What does it mean to be an adult? A qualitative study of college students' perceptions and coping processes. *Journal of College and Character*, 6, 1–31.

Lopez, F. G. & Rice, K. G. (2006). Preliminary development and validation of a measure of relationship authenticity. *Journal of Counseling Psychology*, 53, 362–371.

Lorenz, F. O., Simons, R. L., Conger, R. D., Elder, G. H., Johnson, C. & Chao, W. (1997). Married and recently divorced mothers' stressful events and distress: Tracing change over time. *Journal of Marriage and the Family*, 59, 219–232.

Lowenthal, M. F., Thurnher, M. & Chiriboga, D. (1975). *Four Stages of Life: A Comparative Study of Women and Men Facing Transitions*. San Francisco, CA: Jossey-Bass Publishers.

Lucas, R. E. & Donnellan, M. B. (2009). Age differences in personality: Evidence from a nationally representative Australian sample. *Developmental Psychology*, 45, 1353–1363.

Luchsinger, J. A., Tang, M. X., Shea, S., Mayeux, R. (2002). Caloric intake and the risk of Alzheimer disease. *Archives of Neurology*, 59, 1258–1263.

Luders, E., Toga, A. W., Lepore, N. & Gaser, C. (2009). The underlying anatomical correlates of long-term meditation: Larger hippocampal and frontal volumes of gray matter. *Neuroimage*, 45, 672–678.

Lund, D., Caserta, M., Utz, R. & de Vries, B. (2010). Experiences and early coping of bereaved spouses/partners in an intervention based on the Dual Process Model (DPM). *OMEGA Journal of Death and Dying*, 61, 291–313.

Lundin, T. (1984). Long-term outcome of bereavement. *The British Journal of Psychiatry*, 145, 424–428.

Lupien, S. J., de Leon, M., de Santi, S., Convit, A., Tarshish, C., Nair, N. P. V., Thakur, M., et al. (1998). Cortisol levels during human aging predict hippocampal atrophy and memory deficits. *Nature Neuroscience*, 1, 69–73.

Lyubomirsky, S. (2008). *The How of Happiness: A Scientific Approach to Getting the Life You Want*. New York: Penguin Books.

Maccoby, E. E. (1995). The two sexes and their social systems. In P. Moen, G. H. Elder Jr & K. Lüscher (eds) *Examining Lives in Context: Perspectives on The Ecology of Human Development* (pp. 347–364). Washington, DC: American Psychological Association.

Maciejewski, P. K., Zhang, B., Block, S. D. & Prigerson, H. G. (2007). An empirical examination of the stage theory of grief. *JAMA: The Journal of the American Medical Association*, 297, 716–23.

Mackavey, W. R., Malley, J. E. & Stewart, A. J. (1991). Remembering autobiographically consequential experiences: Content analysis of psychologists' accounts of their lives. *Psychology and Aging*, 6, 50–59.

MacLean, K. A., Johnson, M. W. & Griffiths, R. R. (2011). Mystical experiences occasioned by the hallucinogen Psilocybin lead to increases in the personality domain of openness. *Journal of Psychopharmacology*, 25, 1453–1461.

Madden, D. J. (2001). Speed and timing of behavioural processes. In J. E. Birren & K. W. Schaie (eds) *Handbook of the Psychology of Aging*, 5th edn (pp. 288–312). San Diego, CA: Academic Press.

Madden, D. J., Whiting, W. L., Huettel, S. A., White, L. E., MacFall, J. R. & Provenzale, J. M. (2004). Diffusion tensor imaging of adult age differences in cerebral white matter: Relation to response time. *NeuroImage*, 21, 1174–1181.

Magnusson, D. (1995). Individual development: A holistic, integrated, model. In P. Moen, G. H., Jr Elder & K. Lüscher (eds) *Examining Lives in Context: Perspectives on the Ecology of Human Development* (pp. 19–60). Washington, DC: American Psychological Association.

Malamuth, N. M. & Spinner, B. (1980). A longitudinal content analysis of sexual violence in the bestselling erotic magazines. *The Journal of Sex Research*, 16, 226–237.

Malinowski, C. I. & Smith, C. P. (1985) Moral reasoning and moral conduct: an investigation prompted by Kohlberg's theory. *Journal of Personality & Social Psychology*, 49, 1016–1027.

Malkoff-Schwartz, S., Frank, E., Anderson, B., Sherrill, J. T., Siegel, L., Patterson, D. & Kupfer, D. J. (1998). Stressful life events and social rhythm disruption in the onset of manic and depressive bipolar episodes: A preliminary investigation. *Archives of General Psychiatry*, 55, 702–707.

Malla, A. K., Cortese, L., Shaw, T. S. & Ginsberg, B. (1990). Life events and the relapse in schizophrenia. *Social Psychiatry and Psychiatric Epidemiology*, 24, 221–224.

Manca, D. P. & Bass, M. J. (1991). Women's experience of miscarriage: A qualitative study. *Canadian Family Physician*, 37, 1871–1877.

Manners, J., Durkin, K. & Nesdale, A. (2004). Promoting advanced ego development among adults. *Journal of Adult Development*, 11, 19–27.

Marcia, J. E. (1966). Development and validation of ego identity status. *Journal of Personality and Social Psychology*, 3, 551–558.

Marcia, J. E. (1993). The ego identity status approach to ego identity. In J. E. Marcia, A. S. Waterman, D. R. Matteson, S. L. Archer & J. L. Orlofsky (eds) *Ego Identity: A Handbook for Psychosocial Research* (pp. 3–21). London: Springer Verlag.

Markman, H. J., Renick, M. J., Floyd, F. J., Stanley, S. M. & Clements, M. (1993). Preventing marital distress through communication and conflict management training: A 4-and 5-year follow-up. *Journal of Consulting and Clinical Psychology*, 61, 70–77.

Marks, N. F. (1996). Flying solo at midlife: Gender, marital status, and psychological well-being. *Journal of Marriage and the Family*, 58, 917–932.

Maslow, A. H. (1950). Self-actualizing people: A study of psychological health. *Personality*, 1, 11–34.

Maslow, A. H. (1966). *The Psychology of Science: A Reconnaissance*. New York: Harper & Row.

Maslow, A. H. (1968). *Toward a Psychology of Being*, 2nd edn. New York: D Van Nostrand Company.

Maslow, A. H. (1971). *The Farther Reaches of Human Nature*. New York: Penguin Arkana.

Maslow, A. H. (1974). The good life of the self-actualizing person. In T. Covin (ed.) *Readings in Human Development: A Humanistic Approach* (pp. 46–53). New York: MSS Information Corp.

Maslow, A. H. (1987). *Motivation and Personality*. London: HarperCollins.

Maslow, A. H. (1998). Some basic propositions of a growth and self-actualization psychology. In C. L. Cooper & L. Pervin (eds) *Personality: Critical Concepts in Psychology* (pp. 189–202). London: Routledge.

Mather, M. & Carstensen, L. L. (2003). Aging and attentional biases for emotional faces. *Psychological Science*, 14, 409–415.

Mather, M. & Carstensen, L. L. (2005). Aging and motivated cognition: The positivity effect in attention and memory. *Trends in Cognitive Sciences*, 9, 496–502.

Mattson, M. P., Chan, S. L. & Duan, W. (2002). Modification of brain aging and neurodegenerative disorders by genes, diet, and behavior. *Physiological Reviews*, 82, 637–672.

May, R. M., Sugihara, G. & Levin, S. A. (2008). Ecology for bankers. *Nature*, 451, 893–895.

Mayer, J. D., Caruso, D. R. & Salovey, P. (2000). Emotional intelligence meets traditional standards for an intelligence. *Intelligence*, 27, 267–298.

Mayer, J. D., DiPaolo, M. T. & Salovey, P. (1990). Perceiving affective content in ambiguous visual stimuli: A component of emotional intelligence. *Journal of Personality Assessment*, 54, 772–781.

Mayer, J. D., Salovey, P. & Caruso, D. R. (2004). Emotional intelligence: Theory, findings and implications. *Psychological Inquiry*, 15, 197–215.

McAdams, D. P. (1985). *Power, Intimacy and the Life Story: Personological Inquiries into Identity*. New York: Guilford Press.

McAdams, D. P. (1992). The Five-Factor Model in personality: A critical appraisal. *Journal of Personality*, 60, 329–361.

McAdams, D. P. (1993). *The Stories We Live By: Personal Myths and The Making of the Self*. New York: Guilford Press.

McAdams, D. P. (2001). The psychology of life stories. *Review of General Psychology*, 5, 100–122.

McAdams, D. P. (2006). *The Redemptive Self: Stories Americans Live By*. New York: Oxford University Press.

McAdams, D. P., Hart, H. M. & Maruna, S. (1998). The anatomy of generativity. In D. P. McAdams & E. de S. Aubin (eds) *Generativity and Adult Development* (pp. 7–44). Washington, DC: American Psychological Association.

McArdle, J. J., Ferrer-Caja, E., Hamagami, F. & Woodcock, R. W. (2002). Comparative longitudinal structural analyses of the growth and decline of multiple intellectual abilities over the life span. *Developmental Psychology*, 38, 115–142.

McConatha, J. T. & Huba, H. M. (1999). Primary, secondary, and emotional control across adulthood. *Current Psychology*, 18, 164–170.

McCullough, M. E., Enders, C. K., Brion, S. L. & Jain, A. R. (2005). The varieties of religious development in adulthood: A longitudinal investigation of religion and rational choice. *Journal of Personality and Social Psychology*, 89, 78–89.

McDowd, J. M. & Shaw, R. J. (2000). Attention and aging: A functional perspective. *The Handbook of Aging and Cognition*, 2nd edn (pp. 221–292). Mahwah, NJ: Lawrence Erlbaum Associates.

McEvoy, G. M. & Cascio, W. F. (1989). Cumulative evidence of the relationship between employee age and job performance. *Journal of Applied Psychology*, 74, 11–17.

McEwen, B. S. (1999). Allostasis and allostatic load: Implications for Neuropsychopharmacology. *Neuropsychopharmacology*, 22, 108–124.

McEwen, B. S. (2000). Effects of adverse experiences for brain structure and function. *Biological Psychiatry*, 48, 721–731.

McFadden, S. H. (1999). Religion, personality, and aging: A life span perspective. *Journal of Personality*, 67, 1081–1104.

McGrew, K. S. (1997). Analysis of the major intelligence batteries according to a proposed comprehensive Gf-Gc framework. Contemporary intellectual assessment: Theories, tests, and issues. In D. P. Flanagan, J. L. Genshaft & P. L. Harrison (eds) *Contemporary Intellectual Assessment: Theories, Tests, and Issues* (pp. 151–119). New York: Guilford Press.

McGrew, K. S. (2009). CHC theory and the human cognitive abilities project: Standing on the shoulders of the giants of psychometric intelligence research. *Intelligence*, 37, 1–10.

McGue, M., Bacon, S. & Lykken, D. T. (1993). Personality stability and change in early adulthood: A behavioral genetic analysis. *Developmental Psychology*, 29, 96–109.

McKee-Ryan, F., Song, Z., Wanberg, C. R. & Kinicki, A. J. (2005). Psychological and physical well-being during unemployment: A meta-analytic study. *The Journal of Applied Psychology*, 90, 53–76.

McLaughlin, S. A., and Malony, H. (1984). Near-death experiences and religion: A further investigation. *Journal of Religion and Health*, 23, 149–59.

McManus, S. & Bebbington, P. (2009). *Adult Psychiatric Morbidity in England, 2007: Results of a Household Survey. Health (San Francisco)*. Leicester: National Centre for Social Research.

McPherson, M., Smith-Lovin, L. & Cook, J. M. (2001). Birds of a feather: Homophily in social networks. *Annual Review of Sociology*, 27, 415–444.

Meehl, P. E. (1962). Schizotaxia, schizotypy, schizophrenia. *American Psychologist*, 17, 827–838.

Mein, G., Martikainen, P., Hemingway, H., Stansfeld, S. & Marmo, M. (2003). Is retirement good or bad for mental and physical health functioning? Whitehall II longitudinal study of civil servants. *Journal of Epidemiological Community Health*, 57, 46–49.

Mercer, R. T. (2004). Becoming a mother versus maternal role attainment. *Journal of Nursing Scholarship*, 36, 226–232.

Mezulis, A. H., Abramson, L. Y., Hyde, J. S. & Hankin, B. L. (2004). Is there a universal positivity bias in attributions? A meta-analytic review of individual, developmental and cultural differences in the self-serving bias. *Psychological Bulletin*, 130, 711–747.

Midanik, L. T., Soghikian, K., Ransom, L. J. & Tekawa, I. S. (1995). The effect of retirement on mental health and health behaviors: The Kaiser Permanente Retirement Study. *Journals of Gerontology Series B: Psychological Sciences and Social Sciences*, 50, 59–61.

Middleton, W., Raphael, B., Burnett, P. & Martinek, N. (1998). A longitudinal study comparing bereavement phenomena in recently bereaved spouses, adult children and parents. *Australian and New Zealand Journal of Psychiatry*, 32, 235–241.

Miles, M. B. & Huberman, A. M. (1994). *Qualitative Data Analysis: An Expanded Sourcebook*. London: Sage Publications.

Miles, M. S. & Demi, A. S. (1991). A comparison of guilt in bereaved parents whose children died by suicide, accident, or chronic disease. *OMEGA Journal of Death and Dying*, 24, 203–215.

Miller, P. & Eisenberg, N. (1988). The relation of empathy to aggressive and externalizing/antisocial behavior. *Psychological Bulletin*, 103, 324–344.

Miller, P. A., Eisenberg, N., Fabes, R. A. & Shell, R. (1996). Relations of moral reasoning and vicarious emotion to young children's prosocial behavior toward peers and adults. *Developmental Psychology*, 32, 210–219.

Moberg, D. O. (2002). Assessing and measuring spirituality: Confronting dilemmas of universal and particular evaluative criteria. *Journal of Adult Development*, 9, 47–60.

Moffitt, T. E. (1993). Adolescence-limited and life-course-persistent antisocial behavior: A developmental taxonomy. *Psychological Review*, 100, 674–701.

Molenaar, P. C. M., Sinclair, K. O., Rovine, M. J., Ram, N. & Corneal, S. E. (2009). Analyzing developmental processes on an individual level using nonstationary time series modeling. *Developmental Psychology*, 45, 260–71.

Mölsä, P. K., Marttila, R. J. & Rinne, U. K. (1986). Survival and cause of death in Alzheimer's disease and multi-infarct dementia. *Acta Neurologica Scandinavica*, 74, 103–107.

Mölsä, P. K., Marttila, R. J. & Rinne, U. K. (1995). Long-term survival and predictors of mortality in Alzheimer's disease and multi-infarct dementia. *Acta Neurologica Scandinavica*, 91, 159–164.

Molteni, R., Barnard, R. J., Ying, Z., Roberts, C. K., & Gómez-Pinilla, F. (2002). A high-fat, refined sugar diet reduces hippocampal brain-derived neurotrophic factor, neuronal plasticity, and learning. *Neuroscience*, 112, 803–814.

Molteni, R. (2004). Exercise reverses the harmful effects of consumption of a high-fat diet on synaptic and behavioral plasticity associated to the action of brain-derived neurotrophic factor. *Neuroscience, 123*, 429–440.

Monroe, S. M. & Simons, A. D. (1991). Diathesis—stress theories in the context of life stress research implications for the depressive disorders. *Psychological Bulletin*, 110, 406–425.

Morley, J. E. (1997). Anorexia of aging: Physiologic and pathologic. *American Journal of Clinical Nutrition*, 66, 760–773.

Morgan, J. & Robinson, O. C. (2012). Intrinsic aspirations and personal meaning across adulthood: Conceptual inter-relations and age/sex differences. *Developmental Psychology*. DOI: 10.1037/a0029237.

Morrison, J. H. & Hof, P. R. (1997). Life and death of neurons in the aging brain. *Science*, 278, 412–419.

Morse, C. A., Buist, A. & Durkin, S. (2000) First-time parenthood: influences on pre- and postnatal adjustment in fathers and mothers. *Journal of Psychosomatic Obstetrics and Gynaecology*, 21, 109–120.

Mostofsky, E., Maclure, M., Sherwood, J. B., Tofler, G. H., Muller, J. E. & Mittleman, M. A. (2012). Risk of acute myocardial infarction after death of a significant person in one's life: The determinants of Myocardial Infarction onset study. *Journal of the American Heart Association*, 125, 491–496.

Mroczek, D. K. & Kolarz, C. M. (1998). The effect of age on positive and negative affect: A developmental perspective on happiness. *Journal of Personality and Social Psychology*, 75, 1333–1349.

Mueller, M. & Elder, G. H. (2003). Grandparent–grandchild relationships in holistic perspective. *Journal of Marriage and Family*, 65, 404–417.

Mueser, K. T., Rosenberg, S. D., Goodman, L. A. and Trumbetta, S. L. (2002). Trauma, PTSD, and the course of severe mental illness: An interactive model. *Schizophrenia Research*, 53, 123–143.

Murray, J., Schneider, J., Banerjee, S. & Mann, A. (1999). EUROCARE: A cross-national study of co-resident spouse carers for people with Alzheimer's disease: II – A qualitative analysis of the experience of caregiving. *International Journal of Geriatric Psychiatry*, 14, 662–667.

Muthén, L. K. & Muthén, B. O. (1998). *Mplus User's Guide. Sixth Edition. Acta Psychiatrica Scandinavica*, Vol. 123. Los Angeles, CA: Muthén & Muthén.

Musgrave, C. (1997). The near-death experience: A study of spiritual transformation. *Journal of Near-Death Studies*, 15, 187–201.

Neale, M. C., Boker, S. M., Xie, G. & Maes, H. H. (2006). *Mx: Statistical Modeling. Matrix*, 7th edn. VCU Box 900126, Richmond, VA 23298: Department of Psychiatry.

Neeleman, J., Oldehinkel, A. & Ormel, J. (2003). Positive life change and remission of non-psychotic mental illness: A competing outcomes approach. *Journal of Affective Disorders*, 76, 69–78.

Neighbour, R. H. (1985). The family life-cycle. *Journal of the Royal Society of Medicine*, 78, 11–15.

Nelson, A. M. (2003). Transition to motherhood. *Journal of Obstetric, Gynecologic, & Neonatal Nursing*, 32, 465–477.

Nesselroade, J. & Ram, N. (2004). Studying intraindividual variability: What we have learned that will help us understand lives in context. *Research in Human Development*, 1, 9–29.

Neugarten, B. L. (1996). Continuities and discontinuities of psychological Issues into adult life. In D. A. Neugarten (ed.) *The Meanings of Age: Selected Papers of Neugarten, B. L.* (pp. 88–95). London: University of Chicago Press.

Neugarten, B. L. & Datan, N. (1996). Sociological perspectives on the life cycle. In D. A. Neugarten (ed.) *The Meanings of Age: Selected Papers of Bernice L. Neugarten* (pp. 96–113). London: University of Chicago Press.

Neugarten, B. L., Moore, J. & Lowe, J. (1968). Age, norms, age constraints, and adult socialization. In B. L. Neugarten (ed.) *Middle Age and Aging* (pp. 22–28). London: The University of Chicago Press.

Neugarten, B. L. & Weinstein, K. K. (1964). The changing American grandparent. *Journal of Marriage and the Family*, 26, 199–204.

Neuhs, H. P. (1990). Predictors of adjustment in retirement of women. In J. D. Hayes (ed.) *Preretirement Planning for Women: Program Design and Research* (pp. 133–149). New York: Springer.

Neuman, R. J., Lobos, E., Reich, W., Henderson, C. A., Sun, L. W. & Todd, R. D. (2007). Prenatal smoking exposure and dopaminergic genotypes interact to cause a severe ADHD subtype. *Biological Psychiatry*, 61, 1320–1328.

Nielsen, L., Knutson, B. & Carstensen, L. L. (2008). Affect dynamics, affective forecasting, and aging. *Emotion*, 8, 318–30.

Norman, R. M. & Malla, A. K. (1993). Stressful life events and schizophrenia. I: A review of the research. *The British Journal of Psychiatry*, 162, 161–166.

Norman, W. T. (1963). Toward an adequate taxonomy of personality attributes: Replicated factor structure in peer nomination personality ratings. *Journal of Abnormal and Social Psychology*, 66, 574–583.

Noyes, R. (1980). Attitude change following near-death experiences. *Psychiatry: Journal for the Study of Interpersonal Processes*, 43, 234–241.

Nuttman-Shwartz, O. (2004). Like a high wave: Adjustment to retirement. *The Gerontologist*, 44, 229–236.

Ockenden, J. (2002). Antenatal education for parenting. In M. L. Nolan (ed.) *Education and Support for Parenting: A Guide for Health Professionals* (pp. 89–110). Edinburgh: Baillière Tindall.

O'Connor, D. J. & Wolfe, D. M. (1987). On managing midlife transitions in career and family. *Human Relations*, 40, 799–816.

Office for National Statistics. (2008). *Labour Market Statistics December 2008*. Newport: National Statistics.

O'Gorman, S. M. (1998). Death and dying in contemporary society: An evaluation of current attitudes and the rituals associated with death and dying and their relevance to recent understandings of health and healing. *Journal of Advanced Nursing*, 27, 1127–1135.

Ohab, J. J., Fleming, S., Blesch, A. & Carmichael, S. T. (2006). A neurovascular niche for neurogenesis after stroke. *The Journal of Neuroscience*, 26, 13007–13016.

Okun, M. A., Barr, A. & Herzog, A. (1998). Motivation to volunteer by older adults: A test of competing measurement models. *Psychology and Aging*, 13, 608.

Okun, M. A. & Schultz, A. (2003). Age and motives for volunteering: Testing hypotheses derived from socioemotional selectivity theory. *Psychology and Aging*, 18, 231–239.

Ondo, W. G., Dat Vuong, K., Khan, H., Atassi, F., Kwak, C. & Jankovic, J. (2001). Daytime sleepiness and other sleep disorders in Parkinson's disease. *Neurology*, 57, 1392–1396.

Oppelaar, J. & Dykstra, P. A. (2004). Contacts between grandparents and grandchildren. *Netherlands' Journal of Social Sciences*, 40, 91–113.

O'Rand, A. M., Henretta, J. C. & Krecker, M. L. (1992). Family pathways to retirement. In M. Szinovacz, D. J. Ekerdt & B. H. Vinick (eds) *Families and Retirement* (pp. 81–98). Newbury Park, CA: Sage Publications.

Orwoll, L. & Perlmutter, M. (1990). The study of wise persons: Integrating a personality perspective. In Sternberg, R. J. (ed.) *Wisdom: Its Nature, Origins, and Development* (pp. 160–180). Cambridge: Cambridge University Press.

Oser, F. K., Scarlett, G. & Bucher, A. (2006). Religious and spiritual development throughout the life span. In W. Damon & R. M. Lerner (eds) *Handbook of Child Psychology: Theoretical Models of Human Development Vol. 1* (pp. 942–998). New York: John Wiley & Sons.

Ozer, E. M., Barnett, R. C., Brennan, R. T. & Sperling, J. (1998). Does child care involvement increase or decrease distress among dual-earner couples? *Women's Health*, 4, 285–311.

Palkovitz, R. (2007). Transitions to fatherhood. In S. E. Brotherson & J. M. White (eds) *Why Fathers Count* (pp. 25–41). Harriman, TN: Men's Studies Press.

Palkovitz, R., Christiansen, S. & Dunn, C. (1998). Provisional balances: Fathers' perceptions of the politics and dynamics of involvement in family and career development. *Michigan Family Review*, 3. Retrieved on 25 April 2012 from http://hdl.handle.net/2027/spo.4919087.0003.105.

Palmer, B. R., Gignac, G., Manocha, R. & Stough, C. (2005). A psychometric evaluation of the Mayer–Salovey–Caruso emotional intelligence test version 2.0. *Intelligence*, 33, 285–305.

Palmer, C. E. (1983). A note about paramedics' strategies for dealing with death and dying. *Journal of Occupational Psychology*, 56, 83–86.

Paloutzian, R. F., Richardson, J. T. & Rambo, L. R. (1999). Religious conversion and personality change. *Journal of Personality*, 67, 1047–1079.

Park, M., Ross, G. W., Petrovitch, H., White, L. R., Masaki, K. H., Nelson, J. S., Tanner, C. M., Curb, J. D., Blanchette, P. L. & Abbott, R. D. (2005). Consumption of milk and calcium in midlife and the future risk of Parkinson disease. *Neurology*, 64, 1047–1051.

Parker, S. (2006). Measuring faith development. *Journal of Psychology and Theology*, 34, 337–348.

Parkes, C. M. (1996). *Bereavement: Studies of Grief in Adult Life*, 3rd edn. London: Routledge.

Parkes, C. M. & Weiss, R. S. (1983). *Recovery from Bereavement*. New York: Basic Books.

Parkinson, J. (2002). An essay on the shaking palsy. *Journal of Neuropsychiatry and Clinical Neuroscience*, 14, 223–236.

Parry, G. (1990). *Coping with Crises*. Chichester: Wiley-Blackwell.

Pasupathi, M. (2001). The social construction of the personal past and its implications for adult development. *Psychological Bulletin*, 127, 651–672.

Pasupathi, M. & Staudinger, U. M. (2001). Do advanced moral reasoners also show wisdom? Linking moral reasoning and wisdom-related knowledge and judgement. *International Journal of Behavioral Development*, 25, 401–415.

Pasupathi, M., Staudinger, U. M. & Baltes, P. B. (2001). Seeds of wisdom: Adolescents' knowledge and judgment about difficult life problems. *Developmental Psychology*, 37, 351–361.

Patterson, G., Debaryshe, B. & Ramsey, E. (1990). A developmental perspective on antisocial behaviour. *American Psychologist*, 44, 329–335.

Pattison, E. M. (1977). *The Experience of Dying*. New York: Simon and Schuster.

Peabody, D. & De Raad, B. (2002). The substantive nature of psycholexical personality factors: A comparison across languages. *Journal of Personality and Social Psychology*, 83, 983–997.

Pembrey, M. E., Bygren, L. O., Kaati, G., Edvinsson, S., Northstone, K., Sjöström, M. & Golding, J. (2006). Sex-specific, male-line transgenerational responses in humans. *European Journal of Human Genetics*, 14, 159–66.

Pennebaker, J. W. & Stone, L. D. (2003). Words of wisdom: Language use over the life span. *Journal of Personality and Social Psychology*, 85, 291–301.

Perry, B. D. & Szalavitz, M. (2006). *The Boy who was Raised as a Dog, and Other Stories from a Child Psychiatrist's Notebook*. New York: Basic Books.

Perry, W. (1970). *Forms of Intellectual and Ethical Development in the College Years: A Scheme*. New York: Holt, Rinehart and Winston, Inc.

Peteet, J. (1994). Male gender and rituals of resistance in Palestinian intifada: a cultural politics of violence. *American Ethnologist*, 21, 31–49.

Pfefferbaum, A., Sullivan, E. V., Mathalon, D. H. & Lim, K. O. (1997). Frontal lobe volume loss observed with magnetic resonance imaging in older chronic alcoholics. *Alcoholism: Clinical and Experimental Research*, 21, 521–529.

Phillips, L. H., Henry, J. D., Hosie, J. A. & Milne, A. B. (2006). Age, anger regulation and well-being. *Aging & Mental Health*, 10, 250–256.

Piaget, J. (1972). Intellectual evolution from adolescence to adulthood. *Human Development*, 15, 1–12.

Piaget, J. (1981). *Intelligence and Affectivity: Their Relationship during Child Development*. Palo Alto, CA: Academic Review Inc.

Piaget, J. (1994). *Six Psychological Studies*. London: Vintage Books.

Pianta, R. C., Egeland, B. & Adam, E. K. (1996). Adult attachment classification and self-reported psychiatric symptomatology as assessed by the Minnesota Multiphasic Personality Inventory – 2. *Journal of Consulting and Clinical Psychology*, 64, 273–281.

Pietromonaco, P. R. & Barrett, L. F. (2000). The internal working models concept: What do we really know about the self in relation to others? *Review of General Psychology*, 4, 155–175.

Pinquart, M. & Schindler, I. (2007). Changes of life satisfaction in the transition to retirement: A latent-class approach. *Psychology and Aging*, 22, 442–455.

Plomin, R. & Nesselroade, J. R. (1990). Behavioral genetics and personality change. *Journal of Personality*, 58, 191–220.

Polivy, J. & Herman, C. P. (2002). Causes of eating disorders. *Annual Review of Psychology*, 53, 187–213.

Ponniah, K. & Hollon, S. D. (2009). Empirically supported psychological treatments for adult acute stress disorder and posttraumatic stress disorder: A review. *Depression and Anxiety*, 26, 1086–109.

Power, C., Rodgers, B. & Hope, S. (1999). Heavy alcohol consumption and marital status: Disentangling the relationship in a national study of young adults. *Addiction*, 94, 1477–1497.

Preston, S. D. & de Waal, F. B. M. (2002). Empathy: Its ultimate and proximate bases. *Behavioral and Brain Sciences*, 25, 1–72.

Pulkkinen, L., Nurmi, J. E. & Kokko, K. (2002). Individual differences in personal goals in mid-thirties. In L. Pulkkinen & A. Caspi (eds) *Paths to Successful Development: Personality in the Life Course* (pp. 331–352). Cambridge: Cambridge University Press.

Querstret, D. & Robinson, O. C. (in press). Person, persona and personality modification: A sequential mixed-methods study. *Qualitative Research in Psychology*.

Quick, H. E. & Moen, P. (1998). Gender, employment and retirement quality: A life course approach to the differential experiences of men and women. *Journal of Occupational Health Psychology*, 3, 44–64.

Raffi, A. R., Rondini, M., Grandi, S. & Fava, G. A. (2000). Life events and prodromal symptoms in bulimia nervosa. *Psychological Medicine*, 30, 727–731.

Rando, T. A. (1983). An investigation of grief and adaptation in parents whose children have died from cancer. *Journal of Pediatric Psychology*, 8, 3–20.

Rando, T. A. (1992). The increasing prevalence of complicated mourning: The onslaught is just beginning. *OMEGA Journal of Death and Dying*, 26, 43–59.

Rapkin, B. R. & Fischer, K. (1992). Framing the construct of life satisfaction in terms of older adults' personal goals. *Psychology and Aging*, 7, 138–149.

Rapoport, R. & Rapoport, R. N. (1969). The dual-career family: A variant pattern and social change. *Human Relations*, 22, 3–30.

Ratnavalli, E., Brayne, C., Dawson, K. & Hodges, J. R. (2002). The prevalence of frontotemporal dementia. *Neurology*, 58, 1615–1621.

Rawls, J. (1971). *A Theory of Justice*. Cambridge, MA: Belknap Press.

Read, J., Perry, B. D., Moskowitz, A. & Connolly, J. (2001). The contribution of early traumatic events to schizophrenia in some patients: A traumagenic neurodevelopmental model. *Psychiatry*, 64, 319–345.

Reed, P. G. (1987). Spirituality and well-being in terminally ill hospitalized adults. *Research in Nursing and Health*, 10, 335–344.

Regier, D. A., Narrow, W. E. & Rae, D. S. (1990). The epidemiology of anxiety disorders: The Epidemiologic Catchment Area (ECA) experience. *Journal of Psychiatric Research*, 24, 3–14.

Rehberg, W. (2005). Altruistic individualists: Motivations for international volunteering among young adults in Switzerland. *Voluntas: International Journal of Voluntary and Nonprofit Organizations*, 16, 109–122.

Reicher, S. & Haslam, S.A. (2006). Rethinking the psychology of tyranny: The BBC prison study. *British Journal of Social Psychology*, 45, 1–40.

Reisenzein, R. (1994). Pleasure-arousal theory and the intensity of emotions. *Journal of Personality and Social Psychology*, 67, 525–539.

Reitz, C., Tang, M. X., Luchsinger, J. & Mayeux, R. (2004). Relation of plasma lipids to Alzheimer disease and vascular dementia. *Archives of Neurology*, 61, 705–714.

Reker, G. (2005). Meaning in life of young, middle-aged, and older adults: Factorial validity, age, and gender invariance of the Personal Meaning Index (PMI). *Personality and Individual Differences*, 38, 71–85.

Reker, G. T., Peacock, E. J. & Wong, P. T. P. (1987). Meaning and purpose in life and well-being: A life-span perspective. *Journal of Gerontology*, 42, 44–49.

Rest, J. R., Cooper, D., Coder, R., Masanz, J. & Anderson, D. (1974). Judging the important issues in moral dilemmas – an objective test of development. *Developmental Psychology*, 10, 491–501.

Rest, J., Narvaez, D., Bebeau, M. & Thoma, S. (1999). A neo-Kohlbergian approach: The DIT and schema theory. *Educational Psychology Review*, 11, 291–324.

Rest, J., Narvaez, D., Thoma, S. & Bebeau, M. (2000). A neo-Kohlbergian approach to morality research. *Journal of Moral Education*, 29, 381–396.

Reynolds, V. & Tanner, R. E. S. (1983). *The Biology of Religion*. London: Addison-Wesley Educational Publishers Inc.

Rhodes, S. R. & Doering, M. (1983). An integrated model of career change. *The Academy of Management Review*, 8, 631–639.

Rich-Edwards, J. W., Kleinman, K., Abrams, A., Harlow, B. L., McLaughlin, T. J. & Joffe, H. (2006). Sociodemographic predictors of antenatal and postpartum depressive symptoms among women in a medical group practice. *Journal of Epidemiology and Community Health*, 60, 221–227.

Riegel, K. (1973). Dialectical operations: The final period of cognitive development. *Human Development*, 16, 346–370.

Riessmann, C. K. (1990). *Divorce Talk: Women and Men Make Sense of Personal Relationships*. New Brunswick, NJ: Rutgers University Press.

Ring, K. (1980). *Life at Death: A Scientific Investigation of the Near-Death Experience*. New York: Coward, McCann and Geoghegan.

Ring, K. (1984). *Heading toward Omega: In Search of the Meaning of the Near-Death Experience*. New York: Morrow.

Robbins, A. & Wilner, A. (2001). *Quarter-life Crisis*. London: Bloomsbury.

Roberts, B. W. (1997). Plaster or plasticity: Are adult work experiences associated with personality change in women? *Journal of Personality*, 65, 205–232.

Roberts, B. W., Caspi, A. & Moffitt, T. E. (2001). The kids are alright: Growth and stability in personality development from adolescence to adulthood. *Journal of Personality and Social Psychology*, 81, 670–683.

Roberts, B. W. & DelVecchio, W. F. (2000). The rank-order consistency of personality traits from childhood to old age: A quantitative review of longitudinal studies. *Psychological Bulletin*, 126, 3–25.

Roberts, B. W. & Mroczek, D. (2008). Personality trait change in adulthood. *Current Directions in Psychological Science*, 17, 31–35.

Roberts, B. W., Walton, K. E. & Viechtbauer, W. (2006). Patterns of mean-level change in personality traits across the life course: A meta-analysis of longitudinal studies. *Psychological Bulletin*, 132, 1–25.

Roberts, W. & Strayer, J. (1996). Empathy, emotional expressiveness, and prosocial behavior. *Child Development*, 67, 449–470.

Robertson, E., Grace, S., Wallington, T. & Stewart, D. E. (2004). Antenatal risk factors for postpartum depression: A synthesis of recent literature. *General Hospital Psychiatry*, 26, 289–295.

Robins, L. N. (1978). Sturdy childhood predictors of adult antisocial behaviour: Replications from longitudinal studies. *Psychological Medicine*, 8, 611–622.

Robinson, O. C. (2008). *Developmental Crisis in Early Adulthood: A Composite Qualitative Analysis*. Dissertation: Birkbeck College, University of London.

Robinson, O. C. (2009). On the social malleability of traits: Variability and consistency in Big 5 trait expression across three interpersonal contexts. *Journal of Individual Differences*, 30, 201–208.

Robinson, O. C. (2011a). Relational analysis: An add-on technique for aiding data integration in qualitative research. *Qualitative Research in Psychology*, 8, 197–209.

Robinson, O. C. (2011b). *Quarterlife Crises and Why They Can Be Good For You*. Presented at British Psychological Society Annual Conference.

Robinson, O. C. (2011c). Quarterlife crisis: A developmental concept with clinical implications. *London Deanery Annual Psychiatry Conference*.

Robinson, O. C. (2012). *Values and Age in Western Europe: A Time Sequential Analysis*. Unpublished manuscript.

Robinson, O. C., Demetre, J. D. & Corney, R. (2010). Personality and retirement: Exploring the links between the Big Five personality traits, reasons for retirement and the experience of being retired. *Personality and Individual Differences*, 48, 792–797.

Robinson, O. C., Demetre, J. D. & Corney, R. H. (2011). The variable experiences of becoming retired and seeking retirement guidance: A qualitative thematic analysis. *British Journal of Guidance & Counselling*, 39, 239–258.

Robinson, O. C. & Smith, J. A. (2010a). Investigating the form and dynamics of crisis episodes in early adulthood: The application of a composite qualitative method. *Qualitative Research in Psychology*, 7, 170–191.

Robinson, O. C. & Smith, J. A. (2010b). The stormy search for self in early adulthood: Developmental crisis and the dissolution of dysfunctional personae. *The Humanistic Psychologist*, 38, 120–145.

Robinson, O. C., Smith, J. A. & Wright, G. (2012). *The Multilevel Phase Model of Early Adult 'Quarterlife' Crisis*. Unpublished manuscript.

Rochlen, A. B., Suizzo, M. A., McKelley, R. A. & Scaringi, V. (2008). 'I'm just providing for my family': A qualitative study of stay-at-home fathers. *Psychology of Men & Masculinity*, 9, 193–206.

Roff, M. & Ricks, D. F. (eds) (1970). *Life History Research in Psychopathology*. Minneapolis: University of Minnesota Press.

Rogers, C. (1961). *On Becoming a Person – A Therapist's View of Psychotherapy*. London: Constable.

Rollins, B. C. & Feldman, H. (1970). Marital satisfaction over the family life cycle. *Journal of Marriage and the Family*, 32, 20–28.

Rolls, B. J. & Phillips, P. A. (1990). Aging and disturbances of thirst and fluid balance. *Nutrition Reviews*, 48, 137–144.

Romme, M., Escher, S., Dillon, J., Corstens, D. & Morris, M. (2009). *Living with Voices: 50 Stories of Recovery*. London: PCCS Books.

Ronnlund, M. & Nilsson, L. (2006). Adult life-span patterns in WAIS-R Block Design performance: Cross-sectional versus longitudinal age gradients and relations to demographic factors. *Intelligence*, 34, 63–78.

Rosenblatt, P. C. (1981). Grief in cross-cultural and historical perspective. In P. F. Pegg & E. Metze (eds) *Death and Dying: A Quality of Life* (pp. 11–18). Bath: Pitman.

Rosen-Grandon, J., Myers, J. E. & Hattie, J. (2004). The relationship between marital characteristics, marital interaction processes, and marital satisfaction. *Journal of Counseling and Development*, 82, 58–68.

Rösler, A., Ulrich, C., Billino, J., Sterzer, P., Weidauer, S., Bernhardt, T., Steinmetz, H., Frölich, L. & Kleinschmidt, A. (2005). Effects of arousing emotional scenes on the distribution of visuospatial attention: Changes with aging and early subcortical vascular dementia. *Journal of the Neurological Sciences*, 229–230, 109–16.

Ross, G. W., Abbott, R. D., Petrovitch, H., Morens, D. M., Grandinetti, A., Tung, K. H., Tanner, C. M., Masaki, K. H., Blanchette, P. L., Curb, J. D., Popper, J. S. & White, L. R. (2006). Association of coffee and caffeine intake with the risk of Parkinson disease. *JAMA: The Journal of the American Medical Association*, 283, 2674–2979.

Rossouw, J., Anderson, G., Prentice, R., Lacroiz, A., Kooperberg, C. & Stefanick, M. (2002). Risks and benefits of estrogen plus progestin in healthy postmenopausal women: Principal results from the women's health initiative randomized controlled trial. *Journal of the American Medical Association*, 288, 321–333.

Rotkirch, A. & Janhunen, K. (2009). Maternal guilt. *Evolutionary Psychology*, 8, 90–206.

Rozin, P. & Royzman, E. B. (2001). Negativity bias, negativity dominance, and contagion. *Personality and Social Psychology Review*, 5, 296–320.

Rubin, R. (1984) *Maternal Identity and Maternal Experience*. New York: Springer.

Ruhm, C. J. (1994). Bridge employment and job stopping: Evidence from the Harris/Commonwealth Fund Survey. *Journal of Aging and Social Policy*, 6, 73–99.

Ruitenberg, A., Ott, A., van Swieten, J. C., Hofman, A. & Breteler, M. M. B. (2001). Incidence of dementia: Does gender make a difference? *Neurobiology of Aging*, 22, 575–580.

Rusbult, C. E. & Buunk, B. P. (1993). Commitment processes in close relationships: An interdependence analysis. *Journal of Social and Personal Relationships*, 10, 175–204.

Ruspini, E. (2002). *Introduction to Longitudinal Research*. New York: Routledge.

Russac, R. J., Gatliff, C., Reece, M. & Spottswood, D. (2007). Death anxiety across the adult years: An examination of age and gender effects. *Death Studies*, 31, 549–561.

Russell, B. (1928). *Sceptical Essays*. London: George Allen & Unwin.

Ryan, R. M. & Deci, E. L. (2000). Self-determination theory and the facilitation of intrinsic motivation, social development, and well-being. *American Psychologist*, 55, 68–78.

Ryan, R. M, Laguardia, J. G. & Rawsthome, L. J. (2005). Self-complexity and the authenticity of self-aspects: Effects on well-being and resilience to stressful events. *North American Journal of Psychology*, 7, 431–448.

Ryff, C. D. (1989a). In the eye of the beholder: View of psychological well-being among middle-aged and older adults. *Psychology and Aging*, 2, 195–210.

Ryff, C. D. (1989b). Happiness is everything, or is it? Explorations on the meaning of psychological well-being. *Journal of Personality and Social Psychology*, 57, 1069–1081.

Ryff, C. D. (1995). Psychological well-being in adult life. *Current Directions in Psychological Science*, 4, 99–104.

Saetermoe, C. L., Beneli, I. & Busch, R. M. (1999). Perceptions of adulthood among Anglo and Latino parents. *Current Psychology*, 18, 171–184.

Salthouse, T. A. (1984). Effects of age and skill in typing. *Journal of Experimental Psychology: General*, 113, 345–371.

Salthouse, T. A. (1996). The processing-speed theory of adult age differences in cognition. *Psychological Review*, 103, 403–428.

Salthouse, T. A. (2004). What and when of cognitive aging. *Current Directions in Psychological Science*, 13, 140–144.

Salthouse, T. A. (2012). Consequences of age-related cognitive declines. *Annual Review of Psychology*, 63, 201–226.

Sameroff, A. (2010). A unified theory of development: A dialectic integration of nature and nurture. *Child development*, 81, 6–22.

Sampsell, B. G. (2003). The promise, practice and problems of the Eden Alternative. *Long-Term Living Magazine*, 1, December.

Sanders, C. M. (1979). A comparison of adult bereavement in the death of a spouse, child, and parent. *OMEGA Journal of Death and Dying*, 10, 303–322.

Sands, R. G. & Goldberg-Glen, R. S. (2000). Factors associated with stress among grandparents raising their grandchildren. *Family Relations*, 49, 97–105.

Sapolsky, R. M. (1999). Glutocorticoids, stress and their adverse neurological effects: relevance to aging. *Experimental Gerontology*, 34, 721–732.

Saroglou, V., Pichon, I., Trompette, L., Verschueren, M. & Dernelle, R. (2005). Prosocial behavior and religion: New evidence based on projective measures and peer ratings. *Journal for the Scientific Study of Religion*, 44, 323–348.

Sasaki, M. & Suzuki, T. (1987). Changes in Religious Commitment in the United States, Holland, and Japan. *American Journal of Sociology*, 92, 1055–1076.

Saucier, G. & Skrzypioska, K. (2006). Spiritual but not religious? Evidence for two independent dispositions. *Journal of Personality*, 74, 1257–1292.

Sawamoto, N., Honda, M., Hanakawa, T., Aso, T., Inoue, M., Toyoda, H., Ishizu, K., Fukuyama, H. & Shibasaki, H. (2007). Cognitive slowing in Parkinson disease is accompanied by hypofunctioning of the striatum. *Neurology*, 68, 1062–1068.

Scarmeas, N., Levy, G., Tang, M. X., Manly, J. & Stern, Y. (2001). Influence of leisure activity on the incidence of Alzheimer's disease. *Neurology*, 57, 2236–2242.

Schaie, K. W. (1965). A general model for the study of developmental problems. *Psychological Bulletin*, 64, 92–107.

Schaie, K. W. (1988). Internal validity threats in studies of adult cognitive development. In M. L. Howe & C. J. Brainerd (eds) *Cognitive Development in Adulthood: Progress in Cognitive Development Research* (p. 241). New York: Springer Verlag, 241–272.

Schaie, K. W. (1994). The course of adult intellectual development. *American Psychologist*, 49, 304–313.

Schaie, K. W. (1996). *Intellectual Development in Adulthood: The Seattle Longitudinal Study*. New York: Cambridge University Press.

Schaie, K. W. & Baltes, P. B. (1975). On sequential strategies in developmental research. *Human Development*, 18, 384–390.

Schaie, K. W. & Willis, S. L. (2002). *Adult Development and Aging*, 5th edn. New York: Prentice Hall.

Scharfe, E. & Bartholomew, K. (1994). Reliability and stability of adult attachment patterns. *Personal Relationships*, 1, 23–43.

Schieman, S. (1999). Age and anger. *Journal of Health and Social Behavior*, 40, 273–289.

Schlegel, R. J., Hicks, J. A., Arndt, J. & King, L. A. (2009). Thine own self: True self-concept accessibility and meaning in life. *Journal of Personality and Social Psychology*, 96, 473–90.

Schlossberg, N. K. (1981). A model for analyzing human adaptation to transition. *The Counseling Psychologist*, 9, 2–18.

Schmidt, U. H., Tiller, J. M., Andrews, B., Blanchard, M. & Treasure, J. (1997). Is there a specific trauma precipitating anorexia nervosa? *Psychological Medicine*, 27, 523–530.

Schneider, Z. (2002). An Australian study of women's experiences of their first pregnancy. *Midwifery*, 18, 238–249.

Schroder, E. & Schmitt-Rodermund, E. (2006). Crystallizing enterprising interests among adolescents through a career development program: The role of personality and family background. *Journal of Vocational Behavior*, 69, 494–509.

Schroeter, M. L., Stein, T., Maslowski, N. & Neumann, J. (2009). Neural correlates of Alzheimer's disease and mild cognitive impairment: A systematic and quantitative meta-analysis involving 1351 patients. *Neuroimage*, 47, 1196–1206.

Schroots, J. J. F. & van Dijkum, C. (2004). Autobiographical memory bump: A dynamic lifespan model. *Dynamical Psychology*, 1–13.

Schucter, S. R. & Zisook, S. (1993). The course of normal grief. In M. Stroebe, W. Stroebe & R. O. Hansson (eds) *Handbook of Bereavement: Theory, Research and Practice* (pp. 23–43). Cambridge: Cambridge University Press.

Schulman-Green, D. (2003). Coping mechanisms of physicians who routinely work with dying patients. *OMEGA Journal of Death and Dying*, 47, 253–264.

Schulz, R. & Aderman, D. (1974). Clinical research and the stages of dying. *OMEGA Journal of Death and Dying*, 5, 137–143.

Schulz, R & Heckhausen, J. (1996). A life span model of successful aging. *American Psychologist*, 51, 702–714.

Schunk, D. H. (1991). Self-efficacy and academic motivation. *Educational Psychologist*, 26, 207–231.

Schwartz, S. (2001). The evolution of Eriksonian and Neo-Eriksonian Identity theory and research: A review and integration. *Identity*, 1, 7–58.

Scott, S., Duncan, S. R. & Duncan, C. J. (1995). Infant mortality and famine: A study in historical epidemiology in northern England. *Journal of Epidemiology and Community Health*, 49, 245–252.

Seligman, M. E. P. (2011). *Flourish: A New Understanding of Happiness and Well-Being – and How to Achieve Them*. Boston, MA: Nicholas Brealey Publishing.

Selman, R. L. (1981). What children understand of the intrapsychic processes: The child as budding personality theorist. In E. K. Shapiro & E. Weber (eds) *Cognitive and Affective Growth* (pp. 187–215). Hillsdale, NJ: Erlbaum.

Seshadri, S., Beiser, A., Selhub, J., Jacques, P. F., Rosenberg, I. H., D'Agostino, R. B., Wilson, P. W. F. & Wolf, P. A. (2002). Plasma homocysteine as a risk factor for dementia and Alzheimer's disease. *The New England Journal of Medicine*, 346, 476–483.

Sheehy, G. (1976). *Passages: Predictable Crises of Adult Life*. New York: Bantam Books.

Sheldon, K. M. & Kasser, T. (2001). Getting older, getting better? Personal strivings and psychological maturity across the life span. *Developmental Psychology*, 37, 491–501.

Sheldon, K., Houser-Marko, L. & Kasser, T. (2006). Does autonomy increase with age? Comparing the goal motivations of college students and their parents. *Journal of Research in Personality*, 40, 168–178.

Sherman, J. J. & Cramer, A. (2005). Measurement of changes in empathy during dental school. *Journal of Dental Education*, 69, 338–345.

Shneidman, E. S. (1973). *Deaths of Man*. Baltimore: Penguin Books.

Sihvola, J. & Engberg-Pederson, T. (1998). *The Emotions in Hellenistic Philosophy*. Dordrecht: Kluwer Academic Publishers.

Silverman, E., Range, L. & Overholser, J. (1994). Bereavement from suicide as compared to other forms of bereavement. *OMEGA Journal of Death and Dying*, 30, 41–51.

Silverstein, M. & Marenco, A. (2001). How Americans enact the grandparent role across the family life course. *Journal of Family Issues*, 22, 493–522.

Simmons, R. K., Singh, G., Maconochie, N., Doyle, P. & Green, J. (2006). Experience of miscarriage in the UK: Qualitative findings from the National Women's Health Study. *Social Science & Medicine*, 63, 1934–1946.

Singer, J. D. & Willett, J. B. (2003). *Applied Longitudinal Data Analysis: Modelling Change and Event Occurrence*. New York: Oxford University Press.

Sinnott, J. D. (1991). Limits to problem solving: Emotion, intention, goal clarity, health and other factors in postformal thought. In J. D. Sinnott & J. C. Cavanaugh (eds) *Bridging Paradigms: Positive Development in Adulthood and Cognitive Aging* (pp. 169–203). New York: Praeger.

Sinnott, J. D. (1998). *The Development of Logic in Adulthood: Postformal Thought and its Applications*. New York: Springer Publishing Co.

Sinnott, J. D. & Johnson, L. (1997). Brief report: Complex postformal thought in skilled research administrators. *Journal of Adult Development*, 4, 45–53.

Skardhamar, T. (2009). Reconsidering the theory of adolescent-limited and life-course persistent anti-social behaviour. *British Journal of Criminology*, 49, 863–878.

Skoe, E. E. & Gooden, A. (1993). Ethic of care and real-life moral dilemma content in male and female early adolescents. *The Journal of Early Adolescence*, 13, 154–167.

Skoe, E. E., Pratt, M. W., Matthews, M. & Curror, S. E. (1996). The ethic of care: Stability over time, gender differences, and correlates in mid-to late adulthood. *Psychology and Aging*, 11, 280–292.

Slaikeu, K. A. (1990). *Crisis Intervention – A Handbook for Practice and Research*, 2nd edn. Boston: Allyn and Bacon.

Slevin, K. F. & Wingrove, C. R. (1995). Women in retirement – A review and critique of empirical research since 1976. *Sociological Inquiry*, 65, 1–20.

Smart, R. & Peterson, C. (1997). Super's career stages and the decision to change careers. *Journal of Vocational Behavior*, 374, 358–374.

Smith, J. (2002). The fourth age: A period of psychological mortality? *Max Planck Forum*, 4, 75–88.

Smith, J., Staudinger, U. M. & Baltes, P. B. (1994). Occupational settings facilitating wisdom-related knowledge: The sample case of clinical psychologists. *Journal of Consulting and Clinical Psychology*, 62, 989–999.

Smith, J. A., Flowers, P. & Larkin, M. (2009). *Interpretative Phenomenological Analysis*. London: Sage Publications.

Smith, L. F., Frost, J., Levitas, R., Bradley, H. & Garcia, J. (2006). Women's experiences of three early miscarriage management options a qualitative study. *The British Journal of General Practice*, 56, 198–205.

Smith, P. (2005). Grandparents & grandchildren. *The Psychologist*, 18, 684–687.

Smith, T. R. (2009). *Child 44*. London: Pocket Books.

Smith, T. W., Uchino, B. N., Berg, C. A., Florsheim, P., Pearce, G., Hawkins, M., Henry, N., Beverage, R., Skinner, M., Hopkins, P. N. & Yoon, H.-C. (2008). Associations of self-reports versus spouse ratings of negative affectivity, dominance and affiliation with coronary artery disease: Where should we look and who should we ask when studying personality and health? *Health Psychology*, 27, 676–684.

Soh, S. & Leong, F. T. (2001). Cross-cultural validation of Holland's theory in Singapore: Beyond structural validity of RIASEC. *Journal of Career Assessment*, 9, 115–133.

Soldz, S. & Vaillant, G. E. (1999). The big five personality traits and the life course: A 45-year longitudinal study. *Journal of Research in Personality*, 33, 208–232.

Solfrizzi, V., Panza, F. & Capurso, A. (2003). The role of diet in cognitive decline. *Journal of Neural Transmission*, 110, 95–110.

Sommerville, A. (2005). Changes in BMA policy on assisted dying. *British Medical Journal*, 331, 686–688.

Spataro, J., Mullen, P. E., Burgess, P. M., Wells, D. L. & Moss, S. A. (2004). Impact of child sexual abuse on mental health: Prospective study in males and females. *The British Journal of Psychiatry*, 184, 416–21.

Spector, P. E., Cooper, C. L., Sanchez, J. I., O'Driscoll, M. & Sparks, K. (2002). Locus of control and well-being at work: How generalizable are Western findings? *Academy of Management Journal*, 45, 453–466.

Speizer, F. E., Colditz, G. A., Hunter, D. J., Rosner, B. & Hennekens, C. (1999). Prospective study of smoking, antioxidant intake, and lung cancer in middle-aged women (USA). *Cancer Causes and Control*, 10, 475–482.

Spitze, G. & Logan, J. (1992). Helping as a component of parent–adult child relations. *Research on Aging*, 14, 291–312.

Spokane, A. R. & Cruza-Guet, M. C. (2005). Holland's theory of vocational personalities in work environments. In S. D. Brown & R. W. Lent (eds) *Career Development and Counseling: Putting Theory and Research to Work* (pp. 24–41). Hoboken, NJ: John Wiley & Sons, Inc.

Spokane, A. R., Meir, E. L. & Catalano, M. (2000). Person–environment congruence and Holland's theory: A review and reconsideration. *Journal of Vocational Behavior*, 57, 137–187.

Srivastava, S., John, O. P., Gosling, S. D. & Potter, J. (2003). Development of personality in early and middle adulthood: Set like plaster or persistent change? *Journal of Personality and Social Psychology*, 84, 1041–1053.

Sroufe, L. A. (1997). *Emotional Development: The Organization of Emotional Life in the Early Years*. New York: Cambridge University Press.

St. Jacques, P. L., Bessette-Symons, B. & Cabeza, R. (2009). Functional neuroimaging studies of aging and emotion: Fronto-amygdalar differences during emotional perception and episodic memory. *Journal of the International Neuropsychological Society*, 15, 819–825.

Stanley, S. M. & Markman, H. (1992). Assessing commitment in personal relationships. *Journal of Marriage and the Family*, 54, 595–608.

Staudacher, C. (1987). *Beyond Grief: A Guide for Recovering from the Death of a Loved One*. London: Souvenir Press.

Staudinger, U. (2001). Life reflection: A social-cognitive analysis of life review. *Review of General Psychology*, 5, 148–160.

Staudinger, U. M. (1999). Older and wiser? Integrating results on the relationship between age and wisdom-related performance. *International Journal of Behavioral Development*, 23, 641–664.

Staudinger, U. M. & Baltes, P. B. (1996). Interactive minds: A facilitative setting for wisdom-related performance? *Journal of Personality and Social Psychology*, 71, 746–762.

Staudinger, U. M. & Glück, J. (2011). Psychological wisdom research: Commonalities and differences in a growing field. *Annual Review of Psychology*, 62, 215–241.

Staudinger, U. M., Lopez, D. F. & Baltes, P. B. (1997). The psychometric location of wisdom-related performance: Intelligence, personality, and more? *Personality and Social Psychology Bulletin*, 23, 1200–1214.

Staudinger, U. M. & Pasupathi, M. (2003). Correlates of wisdom-related performance in adolescence and adulthood: Age-graded differences in 'paths' toward desirable development. *Journal of Research on Adolescence*, 13, 239–268.

Staughan, R. (1985). Why act on Kohlberg's moral judgments? (or how to reach stage 6 and remain a bastard). In S. Modgil & C. Modgil (eds) *Consensus and Controversy* (pp. 149–157). Hants: The Falmer Press.

Stepien, K. & Baernstein, A. (2006). Educating for empathy. A review. *Journal of General Internal Medicine*, 21, 524–530.

Stern, Y. (2006). Cognitive reserve and Alzheimer disease. *Alzheimer Disease and Associated Disorders*, 20, 69–74.

Stern, Y. (2009). Cognitive reserve. *Neuropsychologia*, 47, 2015–2028.

Sternberg, R. J. (1998). A balance theory of wisdom. *Review of General Psychology*, 2, 347–365.

Sternberg, R. J. (2000). *Cupid's Arrow: The Course of Love through Time*. New York: Cambridge University Press.

Sternberg, R. J. (2001). Why schools should teach for wisdom: The balance theory of wisdom in educational settings. *Educational Psychologist*, 36, 227–245.

Sternberg, R. J. (2004a). Words to the wise about wisdom? *Human Development*, 47, 286–289.

Sternberg, R. J. (2004b). What is wisdom and how can we develop it? *The Annals of the American Academy of Political and Social Science*, 591, 164–174.

Stevens, R. (2008). *Erik Erikson*. Basingstoke: Palgrave Macmillan.

Stevens-Long, J. & Michaud, G. (2002). Theory in adult development: The new paradigm and the problem of direction. In J. Demick & C. Andreoletti (eds) *Handbook of Adult Development* (pp. 3–22). New York: Plenum Press.

Stolzenberg, R. M., Blair-Loy, M. & Waite, L. J. (1995). Religious participation in early adulthood: Age and family life cycle effects on church membership. *American Sociological Review*, 60, 84–103.

Stone, A. A., Schwartz, J. E., Broderick, J. E. & Deaton, A. (2010). A snapshot of the age distribution of psychological well-being in the United States. *Proceedings of the National Academy of Sciences of the United States of America*, 107, 9985–9990.

Stotland, N. L. (2002). Menopause: Social expectations, women's realities. *Archives of Women's Mental Health*, 5, 5–8.

Stranahan, A. M., Khalil, D. & Gould, E. (2006). Social isolation delays the positive effects of running on adult neurogenesis. *Nature Neuroscience*, 9, 526–533.

Strauss, A. & Corbin, J. M. (1998). *Basics of Qualitative Research: Techniques and Procedures for Developing Grounded Theory*. Thousand Oaks, CA: Sage Publications.

Strayer, J. (1993). Children's concordant emotions and cognitions in response to observed emotions. *Child Development*, 64, 188–201.

Streib, H. (2001). Faith development theory revisited: The religious styles perspective. *International Journal for the Psychology of Religion*, 11, 143–158.

Strober, M. (1984). Stressful life events associated with Bulimia in Anorexia Nervosa: Empirical findings and theoretical speculations. *International Journal of Eating Disorders*, 3, 3–16.

Stroebe, M. & Schut, H. (1999). The dual process model of coping with bereavement: Rationale and description. *Death Studies*, 23, 197–224.

Stroebe, M. & Schut, H. (2010). The dual process model of coping with bereavement: A decade on. *OMEGA Journal of Death and Dying*, 61, 273–289.

Stroebe, M., Schut, H. & Stroebe, W. (2005). Attachment in coping with bereavement: A theoretical integration. *Review of General Psychology*, 9, 48–66.

Strough, J., Berg, C. A. & Sansone, C. (1996). Goals for solving everyday problems across the life span: Age and gender differences in the salience of interpersonal concerns. *Developmental Psychology*, 32, 1106–1115.

Suarez-Orozco, C. Yoshikawa, H. Teranishi, R. T. & Suarez-Orozco, M. M. (2011). Growing up in the shadows: The developmental implications of unauthorized status. *Harvard Educational Review*, 81, 438–472.

Sullivan, E. V., Rosenbloom, M. J., Lim, K. O. & Pfefferbaum, A. (2000). Longitudinal changes in cognitive, gait, and balance in abstinent and relapsed alcoholic men: Relationships to changes in brain structure. *Neuropsychology*, 2, 178–188.

Sullivan, S., Ruffman, T. & Hutton, S. B. (2007). Age differences in emotion recognition skills and the visual scanning of emotion faces. *Journals of Gerontology*, 62, 53–60.

Super, D. E. (1980). A life-span, life-space approach to career development. *Journal of Vocational Behavior*, 16, 282–298.

Sutherland, C. (1990). Changes in religious beliefs, attitudes, and practices following near-death experiences: An Australian study. *Journal of Near-Death Studies*, 9, 21–31.

Sutich, A. J. (1968). Transpersonal psychology: An emerging force. *Journal of Humanistic Psychology*, 8, 77–78.

Szinovacz, M. E. & Deviney, S. (2000). Marital characteristics and retirement decisions. *Research on Aging*, 22, 470–498.

Taveira, M. D. C. & Moreno, M. L. R. (2003). Guidance theory and practice: The status of career exploration. *British Journal of Guidance & Counselling*, 31, 189–208.

Taylor, S. (1989). *Positive Illusions: Creative Self-Deception and the Healthy Mind*. New York: Basic Books Inc.

Taylor, M., Bates, G. & Webster, J. D. (2011). Comparing the psychometric properties of two measures of wisdom: Predicting forgiveness and psychological well-being with the Self-Assessed Wisdom Scale (SAWS) and the Three-Dimensional Wisdom Scale (3D-WS). *Experimental Aging Research*, 37, 129–41.

Tedeschi, R. G. & Calhoun, L. G. (1995). *Trauma and Transformation: Growing in the Aftermath of Suffering*. London: Sage Publications.

Tedeschi, Richard G. & Calhoun, L. G. (2004). Posttraumatic growth: Conceptual foundations and empirical evidence. *Psychological Inquiry*, 15, 1–18.

Templer, A. J. & Causey, T. F. (1999). Rethinking career development in an era of portfolio careers. *Career Development International*, 4, 70–76.

Thara, R. (2004). Twenty-year course of schizophrenia: The Madras longitudinal study. *Canadian Journal of Psychiatry*, 49, 564–569.

Thoma, S. (2002). An overview of the Minnesota approach to research in moral development. *Journal of Moral Education*, 31, 225–245.

Thomas, C., Benzeval, M. & Stansfeld, S. A. (2005). Employment transitions and mental health: An analysis from the British household panel survey. *Journal of Epidemiology and Community Health*, 59, 243–249.

Thomas, L. E. & Eisenhandler, S. A. (eds) (1994). *Aging and the Religious Dimension*. Westport, CT: Greenwood Publishing Company.

Thomas, W. H. (1992). *The Eden Alternative*. Columbia, MO: University of Missouri Press.

Thomas, W. H. (1996). *Life Worth Living: How Someone You Love Can Still Enjoy Life in a Nursing Home; The Eden Alternative in Action*. St Louis, MO: Vanderwyk & Burnham.

Thompson, S. C., Thomas, C., Rickabaugh, C. A., Tantamjarik, P., Otsuki, T., Pan, D., Garcia, B. F. & Sinar, E. (1998). Primary and secondary control over age-related changes in physical appearance. *Journal of Personality*, 66, 583–605.

Thompson, P. M., Hayashi, K. M., Simon, S. L., Geaga, J. a, Hong, M. S., Sui, Y., Lee, J. Y., et al. (2004). Structural abnormalities in the brains of human subjects who use methamphetamine. *The Journal of Neuroscience*, 24, 6028-36.

Thurstone, L. L. (1943). *Chicago Tests of Primary Abilities*. Oxford: Science Research Associates.

Tinsley, H. E. A. (2000). The congruence myth: An analysis of the efficacy of the person–environment fit model. *Journal of Vocational Behavior*, 56, 147–179.

Tornstam, L. (1989). Gero-transcendence theory: A reformulation of the disengagement theory. *Aging*, 1, 55–63.

Tornstam, L. (2005). *Gerotranscendence: A Developmental Theory of Positive Aging*. London: Springer Publishing Company.

Tornstam, L. (2011). Maturing into gerotranscendence. *Journal of Transpersonal Psychology*, 43, 166–180.

Tozzi, F., Sullivan, P. F., Fear, J. L., McKenzie, J. & Bulik, C. M. (2003). Causes and recovery in anorexia nervosa: The patient's perspective. *The International Journal of Eating Disorders*, 33, 143–154.

Troop, N. A & Treasure, J. L. (1997). Psychosocial factors in the onset of eating disorders: Responses to life-events and difficulties. *The British Journal of Medical Psychology, 70*, 373–385.

Tsai, J. L., Levenson, R. W. & Carstensen, L. L. (2000). Autonomic, subjective, and expressive responses to emotional films in older and younger Chinese Americans and European Americans. *Psychology and Aging, 15*, 684–693.

Tucker Drob, E. & Salthouse, T. A. (2011). Individual differences in cognitive aging. In T. S. Chamorro-Premuzic, V. Stumm & A. Furnham (eds) *The Wiley-Blackwell Handbook of Individual Differences* (pp. 242–267). London: Wiley-Blackwell.

Twenge, J. M. (2000). The age of anxiety? Birth cohort change in anxiety and neuroticism, 1952–1993. *Journal of Personality and Social Psychology, 79*, 1007–1021.

Ulrich, L. B. & Brott, P. E. (2005). Older workers and bridge employment: Redefining retirement. *Journal of Employment Counseling, 42*, 159–170.

Uno, H., Tarara, R., Else, J. G., Suleman, M. A. & Sapolksy, R. M. (1989). Hippocampal damage associated with prolonged and fatal stress in primates. *The Journal of Neuroscience, 9*, 1705–1711.

Uttal, D. H. & Perlmutter, M. (1989). Toward a broader conceptualization of development: The role of gains and losses across the life span. *Developmental Review, 9*, 101–132.

Vaillant, C. & Vaillant, G. E. (1993). Is the U-curve of marital satisfaction an illusion? A 40-year study of marriage. *Journal of Marriage and the Family, 55*, 230–239.

Vaillant, G. E. (1976). Natural history of male psychological health: The relation of choice of ego mechanisms of defense to adult adjustment. *Archives of General Psychiatry, 33*, 535–545.

Vaillant, G. E. (1977). *Adaptation to Life*. Boston: Little, Brown and Company.

Vaillant, G. E. (2002). *Aging Well*. London: Little, Brown and Company.

Vaillant, G. (2008). *Spiritual Evolution: A Scientific Defense of Faith*. New York: Broadway Books.

Valsiner, J. (2000). *Culture and Human Development*. London: Sage Publications.

Valsiner, J. (2005). Transformations and flexible forms: Where qualitative psychology begins. *Qualitative Research in Psychology, 4*, 39–57.

Van der Heide, A., Deliens, L., Faisst, K., Nilstun, T., Norup, M., Paci, E., van der Wal, G. & van der Maas, P. J. (2003). End-of-life decision-making in six European countries: Descriptive study. *Lancet, 362*, 345–350.

Van Gennep, A. (1960). *The Rites of Passage*. London: Routledge and Kegan Paul.

Van Hiel, A. & Vansteenkiste, M. (2009). Ambitions fulfilled? The effects of intrinsic and extrinsic goal attainment on older adults' ego-integrity and death attitudes. *The International Journal of Aging and Human Development, 68*, 27–51.

Van Ijzendoorn, M. H. (1995). Adult attachment representations, parental responsiveness, and infant attachment: A meta-analysis on the predictive validity of the Adult Attachment Interview. *Psychological Bulletin, 117*, 387–403.

Van Lommel, P., van Wees, R., Meyers, V. & Elfferich, I. (2001). Near-death experience in survivors of cardiac arrest: A prospective study in the Netherlands. *Lancet, 358*, 2039–45.

van Lommel, P. (2006). Near-death experience, consciousness, and the brain: A new concept about the continuity of our consciousness based on recent scientific research on near-death experience in survivors of cardiac arrest. *World Futures*, 62, 134–151.

Van Praag, H., Kempermann, G. & Gage, F. H. (1999). Running increases cell proliferation and neurogenesis in the adult mouse dentate gyrus. *Nature Neuroscience*, 2, 266–270.

Van Tilburg, T. (1998). Losing and gaining in old age: Changes in personal network size and social support in a four-year longitudinal study. *Journal of Gerontology*, 53B, 313–323.

Van Rooy, D. L., Alonso, A. & Viswesvaran, C. (2005). Group differences in emotional intelligence scores: Theoretical and practical implications. *Personality and Individual Differences*, 38, 689–700.

Vandewater, E. A. & Stewart, A. J. (1998). Making commitments, creating lives: Linking women's roles and personality at midlife. *Psychology of Women Quarterly*, 22, 717–738.

Vercruyssen, M. (1993). Slowing of behavior with age. In R. Kastenbaum (ed.) *Encyclopedia of Adult Development* (pp. 457–467). Arizona: The Oryx Press.

Vermeulen, A. (1993). Environment, human reproduction, menopause, and andropause. *Environmental Health Perspectives*, 101, 91–100.

Vermeulen, A. (2000). Andropause. *Maturitas*, 34, 5–15.

Victor, C. R., Scambler, S. J., Bowling, A. & Bond, J. (2005). The prevalence of, and risk factors for, loneliness in later life: A survey of older people in Great Britain. *Ageing and Society*, 25, 357–375.

Vohs, K. D., Bardone, A. M., Joiner, T. E., Abramson, L. Y. & Heatherton, T. F. (1999). Perfectionism, perceived weight status, and self-esteem interact to predict bulimic symptoms: A model of bulimic symptom development. *Journal of Abnormal Psychology*, 108, 695–700.

Vroom, V. H. (1964). *Work and Motivation*. New York: Wiley.

Wadsworth, B. J. (1996). *Piaget's Theory of Cognitive and Affective Development*. White Plains, NY: Longman.

Wainwright, P. E. (2002). Dietary essential fatty acids and brain function: a developmental perspective on mechanisms. *Proceedings of the Nutrition Society*, 61, 61–69.

Wallace, R. K., Dillbeck, M. C., Jacobe, E. & Harrington, B. (1982). Effects of the transcendental meditation and TM-Sidhi program on the aging process. *International Journal of Neuroscience*, 16, 53–58.

Walsh, M. (2001). Womanpower: The transformation of the labour force in the UK and the USA since 1945. *ReFresh*, 30, 1–4. Retrieved on 29 January 2012 from http://www.ehs.org.uk/othercontent/Walsh30a.pdf.

Wang, M. (2007). Profiling retirees in the retirement transition and adjustment process: Examining the longitudinal change patterns of retirees' psychological well-being. *The Journal of Applied Psychology*, 92, 455–474.

Wang, M., Henkens, K. & van Solinge, H. (2011). Retirement adjustment: A review of theoretical and empirical advancements. *American Psychologist*, 66, 204–213.

Wapner, S. & Demick, J. (2002). Adult development: The holistic, developmental, systems-oriented perspective. In J. Demick & C. Andreoletti (eds) *Handbook of Adult Development* (pp. 63–84). New York: Plenum Press.

Warr, P. (1987). *Work, Unemployment and Mental Health*. Oxford: Oxford University Press.

Waterman, A. S. (1993). Developmental Perspectives on Identity Formation. In J. E. Marcia, A. S. Waterman, D. R. Matteson, S. L. Archer & J. L. Orlofsky (eds) *Ego Identity: A Handbook for Psychosocial Research* (pp. 42–68). London: Springer Verlag.

Waters, E., Merrick, S., Treboux, D., Crowell, J. & Albersheim, L. (2000). Attachment security in infancy and early adulthood: A twenty-year longitudinal study. *Child Development*, 71, 684–689.

Webster, J. D. (2003). An exploratory analysis of a self-assessed wisdom scale 1. *Journal of Adult Development*, 10, 13–22.

Webster, J. D. (2010). Wisdom and positive psychosocial values in young adulthood. *Journal of Adult Development*, 17, 70–80.

Weinberg, N. (1994). Self-blame, other blame, and desire for revenge: Factors in recovery from bereavement. *Death Studies*, 18, 583–593.

Weiss, R. (2005). *The Experience of Retirement*. New York: Cornell University Press.

Wenger, G. C. (1997). Social networks and the prediction of elderly people at risk. *Aging & Mental Health*, 1, 311–320.

Wenk, G. L. (2003). Neuropathologic changes in Alzheimer's disease. *Journal of Clinical Psychiatry*, 64, 7–10.

Werner, H. (1940). *Comparative Psychology of Mental Development*. New York: International Universities Press, Inc.

Wethington, E. (2000). Expecting stress: Americans and the 'midlife crisis'. *Motivation and Emotion*, 24, 85–103.

Wethington, E. & Kessler, R. C. (1989). Employment, parental responsibility and psychological distress. *Journal of Family Issues*, 10, 527–546.

Wethington, E., Kessler, R. C. & Pixley, J. E. (2004). Turning points in adulthood. In O. G. Brim, C. D. Ryff & R. C. Kessler (eds) *How Healthy Are We? A National Study of Well-Being at Midlife* (pp. 586–613). London: The University of Chicago Press.

Winson, N. (2009) Transition to motherhood. In C. Squire (ed.) *Social Context of Birth* (pp.145–160). Oxon: Radcliffe Publishing Ltd.

White, H., McConnell, E., Clipp, E., Bynum, L., Teague, C., Navas, L., Craven, S. & Halbrecht, H. (1999). Surfing the net in later life: A review of the literature and pilot study of computer use and quality of life. *Journal of Applied Gerontology*, 18, 358–378.

White, L. & Edwards, J. N. (1990). Emptying the nest and parental well-being: An analysis of national panel data. *American Sociological Review*, 55, 235–242.

White, R. W. (1975). *Lives in Progress*. London: Holt, Rinehart & Winstone Inc.

Wibbels, T., Bull, J. J. & Crews, D. (1991). Chronology and morphology of temperature dependent sex determination. *The Journal of Experimental Zoology*, 260, 371–381.

Widimer, E. D., Treas, J. & Newcomb, R. (1998). Attitudes towards nonmarital sex in 24 countries. *The Journal of Sex Research*, 35, 349–358.

Wiggins, B. J. (2011). Confronting the dilemma of mixed methods. *Journal of Theoretical and Philosophical Psychology*, 31, 44–60.

Wilber, K. (1997). An integral theory of consciousness. *Journal of Consciousness Studies*, 4, 71–92.

Wilber, K. (2000a). Waves, streams, states, and self: Further considerations for an integral theory of consciousness. *Journal of Consciousness Studies*, 7, 145–76.

Wilber, K. (2000b). *Integral Psychology: Consciousness, Spirit, Psychology, Therapy*. Boulder, CO: Shambhala Publications Inc.

Wilber, K. (2006). *Integral Spirituality: A Startling New Role for Religion in the Modern and Postmodern World.* Boulder, CO: Shambhala Publications Inc.

Willis, S. L., Tennstedt, S. L., Marsiske, M., Ball, K., Elias, J., Koepke, K. M., Morris, J. N., Rebok, G. W., Unverzagt, F. W., Stoddard, A. M. & Wright, E. (2006). Long-term effects of cognitive training on everyday functional outcomes in older adults. *Journal of the American Medical Association, 296,* 2805–2814.

Wilson, R. S., Beckett, L. A., Barnes, L. L., Schneider, J. A., Bach, J., Evans, D. A. & Bennett, D. A. (2002a). Individual differences in rates of change in cognitive abilities of older persons. *Psychology and Aging, 17,* 179–193.

Wilson, R. S., Mendes De Leon, C. F., Barnes, L. L., Schneider, J. A., Bienias, J. L., Evans, D. A. & Bennett, D. A. (2002b). Participation in cognitively stimulating activities and risk of incident Alzheimer disease. *Journal of the American Medical Association, 287,* 742–748.

Wilson, W. (1967). Correlates of avowed happiness. *Psychological Bulletin, 67,* 294–306.

Wilt, J., Cox, K. S. & McAdams, D. P. (2010). The Eriksonian life story: Developmental scripts and psychosocial adaptation. *Journal of Adult Development, 17,* 156–161.

Wink, P. & Dillon, M. (2002). Spiritual development across the adult life course: Findings from a longitudinal study. *Journal of Adult Development, 9,* 79–94.

Wink, P. & Helson, R. (1997). Practical and transcendent wisdom: Their nature and some longitudinal findings. *Journal of Adult Development, 4,* 1–15.

Wink, P. & Schiff, B. (2002). To review or not to review? The role of personality and life events in life review and adaptation to older age. In J. D. Webster & B. K. Haight (eds) *Critical Advances in Reminiscence Work: From Theory to Applications* (44–60). New York: Springer.

Women and Equality Unit. (2006). *Individual Incomes of Men and Women 1996/97 –2004/05.* London: WEU.

Wong, C., Wong, P. & Law, K. S. (2005). The interaction effect of emotional intelligence and emotional labour on job satisfaction: A test of Holland's classification of occupations. In C. E. J. Hartel, W. J. Zerbe & N. M. Ashkanasy (eds) *Emotions in Organizational Behavior* (pp. 235–250). Mahwah, NJ: Lawrence Erlbaum Associates.

Wong, C. S., Foo, M. D., Wang, C. W. & Wong, P. M. (2007). The feasibility of training and development of EI: An exploratory study in Singapore, Hong Kong and Taiwan. *Intelligence, 35,* 141–150.

Wong, J. Y. & Earl, J. K. (2009). Towards an integrated model of individual, psychosocial, and organizational predictors of retirement adjustment. *Journal of Vocational Behavior, 75,* 1–13.

Wong, M. K. Y., Crawford, T. J., Gask, L. & Grinyer, A. (2003). A qualitative investigation into women's experiences after a miscarriage: Implications for the primary healthcare team. *The British Journal of General Practice, 53,* 697–702.

Wong, P. T. P. & Watt, L. M. (1991). What type of reminiscence are associated with successful aging? *Psychology and Aging, 6,* 272–279.

Woo, I. M. H., Chan, C. L. W., Chow, A. Y. M. & Ho, R. T. H. (2008). Management of challenges of conjugal loss among Chinese widowers: An exploratory study. *OMEGA Journal of Death and Dying, 58,* 275–297.

Wood, A. M., Linley, P. A., Maltby, J., Baliousis, M. & Joseph, S. (2008). The authentic personality: A theoretical and empirical conceptualization and the development of the Authenticity Scale. *Journal of Counseling Psychology*, 55, 385–399.

Woodside, D. B., Garfinkel, P. E., Lin, E., Goering, P., Kaplan, A. S., Goldbloom, D. S. & Kennedy, S. H. (2001). Comparisons of men with full or partial eating disorders, men without eating disorders, and women with eating disorders in the community. *The American Journal of Psychiatry*, 158, 570–574.

Woodward, N. J. & Wallston, B. S. (1987). Age and health care beliefs: Self-efficacy as a mediator of low desire for control. *Psychology and Aging*, 2, 3–8.

Wulff, D. M. (1993). On the origins and goals of religious development. *International Journal for the Psychology of Religion*, 3, 131–186.

Wuthnow, R. (1998). *After Heaven: Spirituality in America since the 1950s*. Berkeley, CA: University of California Press.

Yang, C. C., Wan, C. S. & Chiou, W. B. (2010). Dialectical thinking and creativity among young adults: A postformal operations perspective. *Psychological Reports*, 106, 1–14.

Yang, S. Y. (2008). A process view of wisdom. *Journal of Adult Development*, 15, 62–75.

Yardley, L. (2000). Dilemmas in qualitative health research. *Psychology and Health*, 15, 215–228.

Young, J. B. & Rodgers, R. F. (1997). A model of radical career change in the context of psychosocial development. *Journal of Career Assessment*, 5, 167–182.

Zacks, R. T., Hasher, L. & Li, K. Z. H. (2000). Human memory. In F. I. M. Craik & T. Salthouse (eds) *The Handbook of Aging and Cognition*, 2nd edn (pp. 293–357). Mahwah, NJ: Lawrence Erlbaum Associates, Inc.

Zhang, X., Li, C. & Zhang, M. (1999). Psychosocial risk factors of Alzheimer's disease. *Zhonghua Yi Xue Za Zhi*, 79, 335–338.

Zhao, C., Deng, W. & Gage, F. H. (2008). Mechanisms and functional implications of adult neurogenesis. *Cell*, 132, 645–660.

Zick, C. D. & Smith, K. R. (1991). Marital transitions, poverty, and gender differences in mortality. *Journal of Marriage and the Family*, 53, 327–336.

Zisook, S., Paulus, M., Shuchter, S. R. & Judd, L. J. (1997). The many faces of depression following spousal bereavement. *Journal of Affective Disorders*, 45, 85–95.

Zisook, S., Chentsova-Dutton, Y. & Shuchter, S. R. (1998). PTSD following bereavement. *Annals of Clinical Psychiatry*, 10, 157–163.

Znoj, H. (2005). Bereavement and posttraumatic growth. In L. G. Calhoun & R. G. Tedeschi (eds) *Handbook of Posttraumatic Growth: Research and Practice* (pp. 176–196). Mahwah, NJ: Lawrence Erlbaum Associates.

Zuckerman, M. (1999). *Vulnerability to Psychopathology: A Biosocial Approach*. Washington, DC: American Psychological Association.

Index